COMPUTER-AIDED PROJECT MANAGEMENT

GEORGE SUHANIC

New York Oxford
OXFORD UNIVERSITY PRESS
2001

Oxford University Press

Oxford New York
Athens Auckland Bangkok Bogotá Buenos Aires Calcutta
Cape Town Chennai Dar es Salaam Delhi Florence Hong Kong Istanbul
Karachi Kuala Lumpur Madrid Melbourne Mexico City Mumbai
Nairobi Paris São Paulo Singapore Taipei Tokyo Toronto Warsaw

and associated companies in
Berlin Ibadan

Published by Oxford University Press, Inc.
198 Madison Avenue, New York, New York 10016
http://www.oup-usa.org

Library of Congress Cataloging-in-Publication Data

Suhanic, George.
Computer-aided project management / George Suhanic.
p. cm.
Includes bibliographical references and index.
ISBN 0-19-511591-0 (cloth)
1. Industrial project management—Data processing. I. Title.
T56.8. S79 2000
658.4′04′0285—dc21 00-020032

Printing (last digit): 9 8 7 6 5 4 3 2 1

Printed in the United States of America
on acid-free paper

This book is dedicated to the memory of
my father, George Suhanic Sr.,
a great concrete construction man
whose motto was
"You've got to produce."

CONTENTS

PART 4: PROJECT MANAGEMENT SUPPORT SYSTEMS

PREFACE

This textbook arises out of my belief that there is nothing like it out there. This is partly due to the fact that Part 3 provides case histories based on actual project experience, namely, the preparation of proposals by the author and his associates to obtain work in the highly competitive North American project industry, as well as extensive exercises to illustrate computer-aided project management.

Why is this important? Because most textbooks, and most software packages, are based on overly simplistic models. As pointed out by a reviewer, he liked the cases since the "inconsistencies, redundancies, and omissions are all perfectly acceptable, even desirable in case studies because they are so much a reflection of the setting in which real work must typically be done." The reviewer concluded that "the case studies in this text are very good."

One case describes the development of an engineering cost control system and a project expenditure and cost control system. This is highlighted because it discusses how the computerized system can work as a tool for project people as well as providing control information for top management and other corporate functions.

This textbook looks at project management from a systems perspective, including extensive project coding, which is essential for project database management. Some might say that coding is only for project "administration." Not so. Cost engineers in Europe and North America developed the basis for project cost coding as a means to track the project scope from the time the project is known only by a ballpark estimate to when it becomes a definitive estimate, which forms the basis for project cost control.

Cost engineering coding, developed for the same process industries that invented the critical path method (CPM), is similar to the program evaluation and review technique (PERT) developed work breakdown (WBS) and organizational breakdown (OBS) structures, the main purpose of which is project control through coding. In this text the cost code has been promoted to be the project code. It is the language and glue that integrates all project parameters for quality, cost, and schedule, not only for delivering the project, but also for all other corporate purposes.

The book presents postmodern project management systems. Modern systems were born with computerized CPM and PERT. The postmodern era started with the revolutionary invasion of the project management office by the PC. Today PC project management and CAD software packages draw and calculate CPM/PERT charts, bar and Gantt charts, WBSs, and OBSs in a GUI setting. The pride of PC project management applications is WYSIWYG systems.

What does this means to you? Do you need to know how to calculate a CPM network manually to obtain the critical path? If you have a PC project management package, it will do it for you. Your aim may be more in line with developing a capability to write a better PC project management application for your own needs. Indeed, what with network computers, the Internet, three-dimensional CAD systems, and audiovisual packages, it may well be that we are entering a new-age era in project management.

If the computer does it all, what is the purpose of this textbook? You will see how to define a project in language the customer can understand and the project team can use to deliver the finished job. You will see the differences between "hard" system activities, developed through phases, and bad activities. You will see what makes for good and bad characteristics in WBSs. The OBS is defined by code and as cost source. Progressive cost estimates are seen to be developed from the earliest conceptual numbers to approved budgets against which commitments and expenditures are measured.

Most important, the reader will be able to visualize how the project management systems are integrated for scope, quality, cost, and schedule control, and how the project code ties in with the corporate code to serve the project as well as with corporate functions with a need to know.

The exercises in the text were processed by different computers. A number of software packages are discussed. The interesting feature of PCs is that they are becoming very powerful and made to work in client/server networks, and thus, in a sense, are emulating earlier big computers. As the 1990s saw an explosion of new-age, PC-based information technology for all kinds of enterprise productivity systems, including project management, the way project management will be practiced in the 21st century will be different from the way it was practiced in 1990, as it was different from the 1980s.

This condition is reflected in this textbook in the development of exercises and problems. The intent is that your answers will be based on new-age technology downloaded as educational or commercial software from the Internet. Although the computer technology is new-age, the difficulties and attitudes that bedevil projects are age-old. This book looks to build the bridge between the two.

There are some topics not discussed at great length. Some attention is payed in this text to the topic of resource leveling. Although it has a very high profile in PC project management systems marketing, project resources allocation and leveling is intensely complex because of the difficulty in defining the project scope and estimating its human resources component. This is discussed in every chapter and in a number of cases.

Another reason why human resources and leveling is not dwelt upon in this textbook is that most corporations do not employ large numbers of project employees. "Make" or "buy" is hardly ever debated in postmodern project settings. "Buy" wins out most often for just-in-time delivery. And it is up to vendors and contractors to staff their jobs to meet their customers' schedules. But the activities based on the systems presented in this work are essential for cost control, and when developed for project control purposes, human resources scheduling and leveling is a natural system outcome.

CPM/PERT networks are referenced and discussed extensively, but manual calculations are not covered. The new-age processing of CPM /PERT networks is intricately tied to the computer. It is not thought reasonable that a project manager will have to calculate a network manually. But it is essential that project planning be done by CPM /PERT logic networks, as will be discussed at length.

The earned value or performance measurement system, based on C/SCSC, is widely referenced, but as its use is aimed mostly at government megaprojects, it is not covered in depth. Value engineering is considered a normal routine in project definition, design, and engineering and is not covered as a separate topic. Risk analysis and Monte Carlo simulations are the purview of cost engineers and project management scientists, and are not covered herein. But they are useful tools for some projects. A prudent project manager would enlist specialists in these topics in the early planning stages of a project.

Trending is seen by PC project management software designers and by management scientists as an important graphic. But an accurate trend line depends on accurate project cost and schedule information, which is the main thrust of computer aided project management. Most high-end PC project management packages can create all kinds of graphic illustrations based on the input of information.

Some corporate functions that affect project outcomes are often not under the purview of the project manager. Two such functions are purchasing and materials management. Both are discussed in a separate part with extensive references to the systems of project management. Corporate functions such as accounting, accounts payable, corporate administration, corporate finance, operations, and especially the idea of a corporate department as "customer" are included throughout.

The intended audiences for this textbook are senior students majoring in construction, engineering, or project management as well as postgraduate students in these subjects. The language used in the text assumes some familiarity with corporate and construction terminology in the broadest sense, including aspects such as accounting, contracting, financing, procurement, and scheduling. Computer literacy is a prerequisite. Another audience is the working administrator or manager who wishes to acquire additional insight into computer-aided project management.

Others are computer analysts and programmers who may benefit by becoming more conversant with the use of this project management terminology. Computer analysts and advanced students may wish to create improved PC project management programs based on the systems, case histories, and problems and exercises presented herein.

ACKNOWLEDGMENTS

The design of this textbook is based on a project management systems course that I presented at the University of Toronto, Faculty of Applied Science and Engineering, Continuing Engineering Education.

Software used to run the cases was provided to the University by Primavera Systems Inc. and by HMS Software, marketers of Open Plan. CA-SuperProject and Microsoft Project were purchased by me at educational prices.

As a project manager my interest in and work with computerized project management goes back to the days when only mainframes were available. My computer resource then, and later in working with the Artemis Prestige PC system, was Jack Way.

As a project management systems engineer I coordinated the needs of the users and top management, and wrote the performance criteria for the engineering cost control system and the project expenditure and cost control system. The computer systems analysis and the programming were carried out by David Mayhew. The diagrams are based on his work.

One of my most important professional associations is my membership in the American Association of Cost Engineers. Members of AACE International invented cost engineering, eventually including scheduling and project management as a discipline. I learned from other skilled and dedicated engineers and presented my own concepts of project management at many conferences.

The concepts that I presented to AACE and my professional project management work are the basis for this textbook.

Bill Zobrist first saw the potential in my work, *The Systems of Project Management,* as a book project, and Peter C. Gordon, Senior Editor, Oxford University Press, brought this effort into production.

I thank you all.

PROJECT MANAGEMENT AS PARADIGM

Project management is nothing if not graphic. Its earliest manifestation was an open rectangle, or bar, on a grid depicting time. Attributed to Henry Gantt in the early 20th century, the bar or Gantt chart depicts a time plan for an activity. As progress is made, the open bar is filled in to show progress.

In the mid-20th century, modern project management planning and scheduling was depicted by networks of logical lines, circles, arrows, rectangles, dummies, lags, leads, early and late start and finish dates, total floats, free floats, and something called the longest irreducible sequence of events, or critical path. Named critical path method (CPM) and program evaluation and review technique (PERT), its complexity required computer calculations. Although logically elegant but difficult to make, the network was a visual nightmare and an almost impossible communication tool.

It was thus ultimately seen by some as a more accurate way to make bar charts. That is why some people do not plan projects with networks, and only use computer-generated bar charts to schedule work. But bar charts are not logic tools, and schedules are not plans.

The postmodern age of project management came with the invasion of the business office by the PC programmed to create, calculate, and display CPM, PERT, Gantt charts, and more. The 1990s saw an explosion of new-age Internet and WWW-based information technology and sysetms for project management purposes.

This textbook is all about project lines, arrows, circles, bars, and graphs, now invariably made by computers, wherever located, which aim to help manage projects. This approach to understanding is timeless and universal, as may be seen in a quotation attributed to Galileo Galilei (1564–1642):

> Philosophy is written in this grand book—I mean the universe—which stands continually open to our gaze, but it cannot be understood unless one first learns to comprehend the language and interpret the characters in which it is written. It is written in the language of mathematics, and its characters are triangles, circles, and other geometrical figures, without which it is humanly impossible to understand a single word of it; without these, one is wandering about in a dark labyrinth.
>
> *Il Saggiatore [1623]*

ABBREVIATIONS, ACRONYMS, AND DEFINITIONS

Activity An activity has a scope, a code, a cost, and a duration. In this text it represents a piece of the project work that can only be completed, changed, or deleted as a scope change. A group of activities may comprise a package, which may become an assignment, a purchase order, or a contract.

Area Division of a project or subproject, which will perform a specific role in the completed project. A project comprises a number of areas.

Code A combination of (1) the first address of a project deliverable as defined by the PDS, (2) the second address of an activity as developed by a WBS, and (3) the final address of a cost source as defined by an OBS.

Cost Source A company or corporate department which has a contract, purchase order, or authorization to deliver a package of activities or an activity and invoice or bill for the work to the code account.

CPM Critical path method of scheduling activities by networks of activities on arrows (AOA) or activities on nodes (AON). AON is commonly referred to as precedence diagramming method. In this text networks are meant to be prepared and calculated by computer packages.

Definition Defining a project based on the completed project as seen and used by the customer, but using project management language.

ECCO Engineering cost control system, which aims to budget planning, design, and engineering "skill" activities, drawings, and specifications, and to capture resulting actual time and expense charges for cost control purposes. The planned skills and activities are based on management and engineering disciplines required to work on the project.

Element Building block in a system. A physical entity like a building comprises groups of like elements, as well as individual elements. Element is a breakdown of a function and is coded within the PDS code.

Function Division of an area, which performs a specific role in the subject area. A number of functions comprise the area. A function is coded as a significant part of the area code.

GUI Graphical user interface, which is the process of responding to computer menus and dialog boxes in the creation of project management graphics and data.

Hard Activity Billable activity or part of an activity assigned to a project supplier or vendor by contract or purchase order, and invoiced to the project as progress is made. (Also defined as activity.)

Level Vertical position of an area, function, element, etc., in a hierarchical PDS, WBS, OBS, with level 1 representing the top of the hierarchy, or the project objective.

OBS Organizational breakdown structure, which is the technique to structure and code the project's human resources made up of companies, consultants, contractors, and individuals. In this text it must lead to a code system and act as part of the project cost accounts. OBS was at one time also referred to as organizational analysis table (OAT).

PC PM Personal computer project management application or software program running project management routines, including the preparation and calculation of networks, bar charts, and reports depicting scheduling data such as start and finish dates and cost control information.

PDM Precedence diagramming method, which is the networking technique most commonly used for postmodern planning and scheduling of all kinds of projects. The basis for PDM is said by some project management scientists to be CPM. Current usage by PC project management applications seems to attribute it more to PERT.

PDS Project definition structure, although similar to a WBS, aims to define and code the scope and quality of the functions and permanent elements comprising the completed project, as seen by the project customer, in project management language.

PERT Program evaluation and review technique, which is the modern system of planning and scheduling projects. Originally meant for government megaprojects, it is widely used in postmodern PC PM applications to plan and schedule all kinds of projects by bar chart convertible to PERT networks, or PERT networks convertible to bar charts.

Phase Key word in the development of the WBS. Projects have life cycles made up of phases. Each phase acts as input to and a baseline for the succeeding phase. Synonymous with stage. Usage depends on local preferences.

Postmodern In this text postmodern project management refers to the introduction of the personal computer, programmed with project management language, to the business office in 1983. (Modern project management occurred with the development of computerized CPM and PERT, c. 1950s.)

Quality Meant to qualify scope in defining a project. In itself it is definable in project definition by words and terms that define function, usage, and performance criteria. Quality establishes project cost.

Scope Quantity and quality of a completed project from the perspective of the customer, but written and coded in project management language. It may be classified by the accuracy of its estimates. The less we know about the scope, the less accurate the estimate.

Stage Definitive step in the development of a WBS. The project life cycle comprises a number of stages, each one a more detailed expression of the project, from a conceptual stage to the ultimate obsolescence and decommissioning stage. Synonymous with phase. Usage is a local preference.

Subfunction Process or physical unit in a function of the PDS.

WBS Work breakdown structure, which is a multilevel hierarchical structure, intended to develop coded project activities based on phases or stages. The top of the structure is level 1. Level 1 of a WBS may be a project, a subproject, an area, a function, a subfunction, an element group, or an element.

WYSIWYG Graphic interface of postmodern PC project management systems, which aims to provide what you see is what you get screen graphics. This means that the screen graphic matches as closely as possible the hard-copy printout.

PART 1

INTRODUCTION TO PROJECT MANAGEMENT

1 INTRODUCTION

Modern project management is considered to have started with the invention of the critical path method (CPM) and the program evaluation and review technique (PERT). For many years, project management systems were largely limited to major construction projects for the defense industries and nuclear power generating stations. During that period, the age of mainframes, computers were very expensive and unavailable except to the largest corporations. The proponents of computerization started winning the argument as mainframes gave way to minicomputers and eventually to today's portable microcomputers. Faster and cheaper computerization expedited the application of these systems to all kinds of projects.

Postmodern project management systems arrived on the scene with the advent of personal computers (PCs). The revolution came in 1983, when PCs started being widely used in the business office. Almost immediately vendors of mainframe project control systems and software vendors saw a market for PC-based project management programs.

As introduced in this text, postmodern project management means that the routines of creating definition structures, work breakdowns, organizational structures, project codes, cost codes, networks and their schedule calculations, bar charts, databases, reports of all kinds, graphics of all kinds, and indeed drawings and specifications are all computerized. This does not mean that work is done manually and then computerized. It means that the computer is the tool that project people use to create, manage, control, and deliver the project.

Project management means different things to different people, meaning that it is sometimes cloudy, sometimes obscure, and maybe sometimes even unintelligible. Anything that one undertakes may be considered a project. Life is a project. Most of us prefer not to admit that we do not manage our projects.

Most human activities, according to the proponents of project management, can be done better, more accurately, and quicker with project management, or one of the techniques that gave rise to the concept of project management.

As project management computerization went from mainframes to PCs, many more project organizations could afford PCs. This gave rise to the development of PC-based project management software by dozens of vendors. Not all of this software was based on project management principles. There was software that was originally run on mainframes, which was progressively modified for minicomputers and, eventually, for PCs. These programs are considered to be high-end experienced packages.

Some PC software developed around this time did not necessarily adopt the fundamentals of good project management. This software was largely based on the way work was done. This allowed the users of the software to continue to work in the same way that they had always worked, except that now some of the work, such as scheduling, was computerized. The systems of project management, however, aim to put in place an approach and fundamentals that drive the project for all the project participants, not only the schedulers.

This text builds a bridge from the genesis of project management principles to today's software. It shows what project management principles are, what they do, and how they work in the software environment. Computerization is always in the forefront of these systems. The book shows progressive applications of the systems of project management from early examples processed on mainframes to the use of current PC project management software.

What should become evident to the reader is that although computers may change and improve, tough project management problems remain to be solved.

This text demonstrates a great variety of computer-aided project management. For obvious reasons, software vendors and their engineers and systems developers base their PC project management application examples on fairly simple routines, or hypothetical activities. The cases in this book and the examples cited are varied across a number of different industries and business sectors, and across the many project stages and phases that make up a project life cycle, from its identification as an opportunity or a problem to its obsolescence and recycling.

1.1 What Is a Project?

A project is any capital undertaking leading to the delivery of a work, whether it is a facility or building, new software, or a computerized project control system.

The project is considered to have been successfully completed if it is capable of delivering the goods, products, or services that it was intended to provide. If the undertaking is completed for the budget amount set for it, it may be said to have been completed on budget. If the time for its completion is important (and it usually is) and a schedule was established, and the project was completed within that time, one may say that the work was completed on schedule.

Perhaps most important, if the undertaking is of good quality, does not cause operational problems, and produces the intended product, or a space that, say, does not leak if it is an accommodation building, it may be said that the completed project is of good quality.

The definition of a capital project in this context includes all of its phases or stages, or the steps required in its delivery, that is, from the identification of the problem or opportunity to the final decommissioning and recycling. These systems will provide techniques and methods to incorporate the initial planning for the feasibility study, estimating, the design stages from concept to completion, procurement and bidding in all of their manifestations, construction, and the eventual startup and operation.

At times capital projects are achieved in steps or stages with periods of time between the stages. This type of condition may arise because of cash-flow problems or differing priorities. These situations should not detract from the usefulness of the system proposed. On the contrary, the system could be more necessary than ever to preserve and keep the project scope valid and intact over a longer period of time.

Examples of capital projects are transportation systems, environmental facilities, urban infrastructures, bridges, tunnels, plants, industrial, commercial, and institutional buildings of all kinds, software and hardware undertakings, banking systems, and medical delivery systems.

The banking sector and many other service industries, including the insurance sector and commercial, manufacturing, and retail firms, have taken to using project management concepts to control and manage the installation of large computer systems or to launch new products. The term project manager is used extensively in many business sectors. The computer-aided project management systems encouraged in this text act as the tool for the project managers.

1.2 Projects as Horror Stories

One school of thought says that a project will cost what it will cost. Another school considers that it does not matter what the cost is, since the market will bail out the project. Still others, highly placed project influencers and approvers consider that if a project's true cost is known, the project will never be approved in advance. So these people attempt to "lowball" its cost estimates and schedules in order to get it going, to dig that hole.

There are very real dangers that many successful corporations will be buried by their projects. Let us consider a few world-class cases of projects that may have run out of control, or were never in control.

Eurotunnel

The English Channel tunnel between England and France was approved at about $9 billion in 1986. In 1992 Reuters News Agency reported that "the financial basis of the project was dealt a blow when its building consortium Transmanche Link put in a claim for $2.6 billion in cost overruns." In 1993 the project was expected to cost on the order of $18 billion. The impact of the cost overruns (at the time) remained to be seen, but it has been reported that crossing prices through the tunnel may not be competitive. On October 3, 1996, Bloomberg and Reuters reported that the "Eurotunnel narrowly avoided bankruptcy yesterday with a preliminary agreement to restructure its debt of $18.45 billion." At the time of the restructuring, Eurotunnel had not paid interest since 1995. The project was reported to have 225 lenders and 750,000 shareholders.

Would those lenders and shareholders have been happy with the project cost overrun? After the restructuring, the shareholders' equity was reduced to 54.5%. The lenders took a 45.5% stake in lieu of debt, and in the process the lenders also wiped out $2.2 billion of the project's debt.

In January 1998 it was reported that Eurotunnel's future had been put on a firmer footing with the signing of a new $15 billion financial restructuring agreement to free the Channel tunnel operator of the debt mountain left by extra costs associated with the biggest construction project of its kind in the world.

Skydome

In 1984 the construction budget for the Skydome sports stadium in Toronto, home of the repeat World Series champions, the Toronto Blue Jays, was $150 million. When completed, the price tag was $578 million and counting. The direct result of the approximately 400% overrun is that the debt cannot be carried by the revenues from operations.

When considering these kinds of projects, people mistakenly claim that overruns only happen on government projects. Overruns happen on private projects as often, and with similar dire results. Since private-sector companies cannot turn to taxpayers to bail them out, they may suffer very severe consequences, including near bankruptcy, loss of competitive edge, loss of market, massive borrowing, and the ultimate price: going out of business.

The systems of project management and computer-aided project management do not claim to solve the world's project problems, but they are meant to aim you, the project manager, toward success.

Denver International Airport Project

When Denver International Airport opened on February 28, 1995, it was the first entirely new airport to be built in the United States in the past 21 years, according to the March 13, 1995, issue of *Engineering News-Record.* The article was reprinted in *Cost Engineering,* vol. 37, December 1995. These comments are based on the reprint.

The article reported that the airport's final cost was around $4.7 billion, which was $3.0 billion over its original budget of $1.7 billion. The article said that the original $1.7 billion "was widely promoted, but was merely the project construction cost." Not included were land costs, interest, or "about $675 million in facilities built by airlines, cargo companies, rental car firms, and the Federal Aviation Administration." (There is no comment as to the final cost of construction originally promoted at $1.7 billion.)

When the airport opened, the $193 million automated baggage system was not fully operational and was awaiting final testing. Problems with the high-technology automated baggage-handling system led to the addition of a $53 million "traditional tug-and-cart baggage system" by the airport owner. Some informed sources claim that the tug-and-cart system was unnecessary. The article said that it is true that "politics, turf wars, and school yard challenges on site hurt the airport more than anything else."

Information Technology Projects

A recent business newspaper headline read: "Technology project costly and often flops, study finds; budget overruns common; project management often 'amateurish'."

The headlines introduced a study by the accounting firm KPMG International of The Netherlands that "there's an astonishing waste of money" because of mismanagement of projects to develop technology systems. A partner of KPMG was quoted as saying that "the management of projects is still treated in a very amateurish way."

The 100 failed information technology projects analyzed in the study had a cumulative budget of about $240 million. Their final cost was $360 million. The study declared a project a failure if it was canceled or deferred because it was not delivering its planned benefits or if it had a budget or schedule overrun of more than 30%. Of the projects that failed, 87% went more than 50% over budget.

The study concluded that among projects in the $500,000 to $3 million range 92% went over schedule. Among projects planned to take more than a year, 86% went over schedule.

A 1995 study showed that 31% of software projects will be canceled. Of those completed, 53% will cost 189% of their original estimates.

The study found three primary reasons for project failures: poor planning, a weak business case for the project, and lack of involvement from top management.

1.3 Project Management Is Difficult

That projects are difficult is seen from the horror stories. Adding to the difficulty with project management is that no two projects are the same. Many projects are not successful in that they finish behind schedule and over budget. Many suffer poor management. Many are victimized by faulty design and poor drawings. Some were victimized by inflation. Some were saved by inflation. Labor productivity is sometimes a problem. Often the owners are their own worst enemy in that they approve project budgets on unbelievably skimpy information. Then they make numerous changes, largely because the initial scope of work was inadequately defined. They set unrealistic schedules and will not or do not know how to produce adequate and accurate drawings and specifications. When the project slips because of these owner-induced problems, they often authorize massive and costly overtime and shift work to meet a time commitment that was set inaccurately in the first place. And then they complain bitterly that the project industry is ineffective and nonproductive.

Systems of project management, including new concepts of organization, new methodologies, new tools such as computers, and combinations of all three, aim to reverse these trends and provide solutions to solve the inherently tough project problems.

The objective of this book is to show how to create a management system to control an entire project from concept to operation. What a project needs for success is to be glued together; scoped and defined; coordinated and controlled; scheduled and monitored; costed and accounted for; and managed as a single entity for successful completion. You will see in this book a comprehensive method to bring the project together. Look for real techniques to scope, size, and define the project. Look for a discussion of what project quality is. Look for how to be able to identify what project codes are, what cost and quality trade-offs mean, what a schedule comprises, what a breakdown is as compared to a definition, how procurement ties in, and finally how to determine the place of project startup and operation in the life of the project management system.

Projects are becoming more complicated and more difficult to deliver, given increasing concern for environmental impact, energy conservation, public interest involvement, regulations, the cost of money, and the need to prove project feasibility through modeling for lenders. Given the foregoing, can any project owner in the future afford not to apply professional project management methods to a tough, expensive undertaking?

To understand what these systems are and why they evolved, it is useful to look at the way things were done previously. The traditional approach to deliver projects was based on owner need, architect and engineer design, and contractor bid and build. From a systems perspective, this approach may be referred to as totally decentralized. Total decentralization in large corporations starts within the organization itself. Large corporate or public bodies invariably comprise function-driven departments, with each group, such as, corporate engineering, purchasing, finance, accounting, and operations, being responsible for its own domain. A project would thus go from group to group to group. Each group has its own language and coding system, and as the project progresses, it would be cast into these different modes. Eventually, sometimes years later, the project would be delivered. But the process was not friendly to the success of the project. Here are some of the causes of difficulties:

- There is loss of control through lack of systematic analysis of information gathered on a common base.
- There is no system to integrate the needs of time, cost, scope, and quality.
- Carried to extremes, some managers create project organizations within the corporate organization which may lead to duplication, overlapping, and an expensive management structure.

The classic example of a totally decentralized project environment is any large construction project carried out under the traditional owner/consultant/contractor arrangement as introduced in the preceding section. The principal project mover, the owner's own organization, is decentralized vis-à-vis the project. The consultant organizations are similarly fragmented in that the various disciplines operate using different systems in relation to each other and the owner. Contractors and subcontractors have their own inherently adversarial systems vis-à-vis the consultants and the owner. To complicate project matters even more, governmental agencies and various approval bodies operate to their own bureaucratic goals.

Thus project complexity, organizational confusion, lengthy schedules, duplication of services, costly overruns, poor productivity, unacceptable quality, lack of teamwork, and a myriad of related problems eventually had to lead to new ways to deliver projects.

One way was the invention of fast tracking of construction projects. This is an organizational approach, to be discussed later in this book, which involves the management of overlapping design and construction packages largely through better scheduling. Regardless of the way human resources are organized, there is still a need to develop and implement modern project management systems, the key subject of this book. The need for modern management systems to improve productivity and reduce time in project work was the driving force that led to the invention of CPM and PERT and their current state of computerization. The Construction Industry Cost Effectiveness Project of the New York–based Business Roundtable, in its report "More Construction for the Money" concluded that construction dollars are not being used effectively. No one party is to blame. The industry needs to employ more modern systems of project management, including CPM and computerization.

To resolve the project delivery difficulties, it is important to understand where the problems lie. Understanding the root sources of project difficulties requires experience in and an appreciation of the life cycle process by which projects are conceptualized and eventually started up. The answers to solving project difficulties lie in the five principal project management systems introduced in this book.

1.4 The Systems of Project Management

Figure 1.1 aims to depict project complexity as a living tree with roots and branches. Roots are things like market needs and various approvals required to grow the project tree. The branches produce project progress, including budgets, drawings, and so on, which result from the systems of project management acting as the project nutrient. The systems are the following.

1. *Project Definition Structure.* The project definition structure (PDS) is a systematic means to establish project scope and quality parameters of elements as deliverables. In project work, scope and quality are synonymous terms. PDS is the basis for the project code system. The earliest cost estimates and budgets are tied to it.

2. *Project Work Breakdown Structure.* The work breakdown structure (WBS) identifies project activities or tasks that create the PDS deliverables. The words "tasks" and "activities" are considered by many as interchangeable. WBS activities take on code numbers based on the structure, and become the code of accounts for estimates and budgets. The WBS budget is compared to the PDS as the first measure of project cost control.

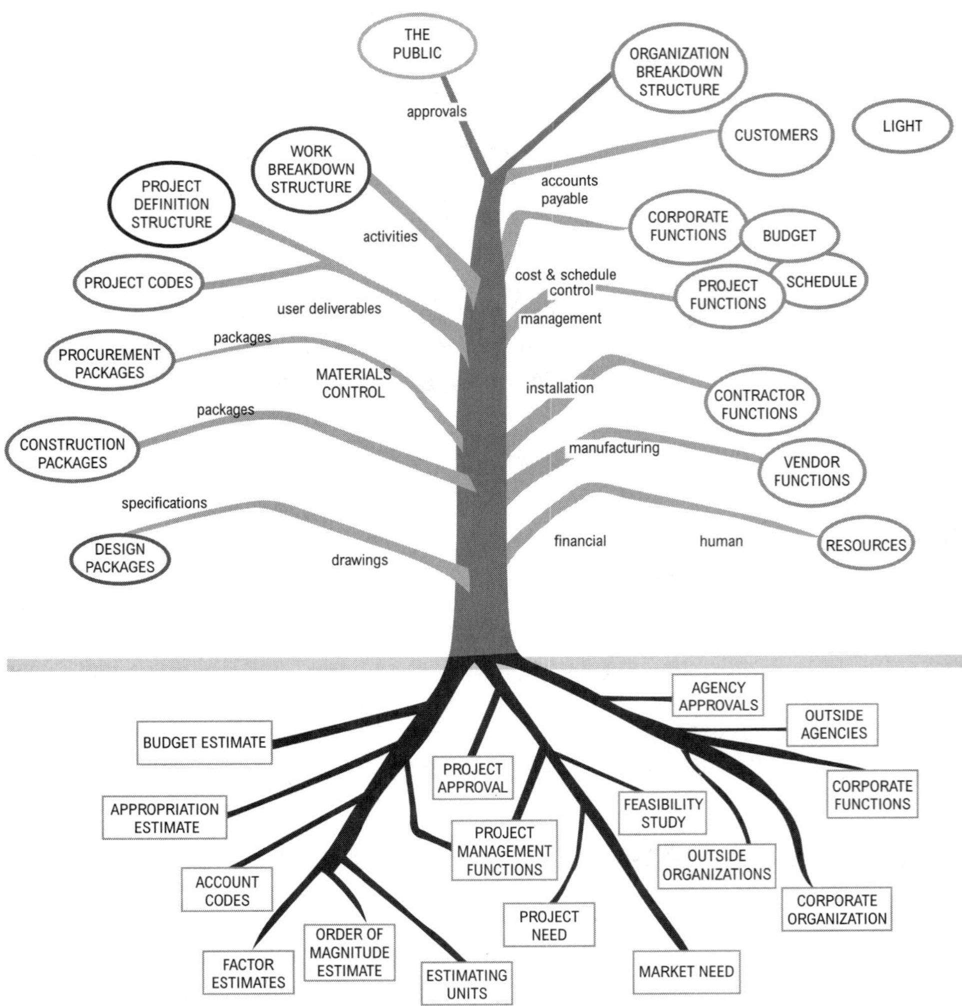

FIGURE 1.1 PROJECT TREE. Projects are conceptualized in hostile environments and are subjected to conflicting inputs and changes. The systems of project management aim to make sense out of the conflict and nurture the tree until a successful project is produced.

3. *Organizational Breakdown Structure.* The organizational breakdown structure (OBS) aims to define and code the organizations and their project human resources wherever they are located, who will carry out the tasks and activities assigned to them by fiat, by contract, by purchase order, or for which they are responsible by law. Every element of project work ultimately has three code numbers, one for each of PDS, WBS, and OBS. Sometimes, depending on project circumstances, the codes are merged, with one code number fulfilling all of these roles.

4. *Project Budget and Cost Control.* Project budgets are based on estimates. Estimates are derived from scope and quality information set by progressive developments in the PDS, WBS, and OBS exercises. Each exercise develops more precise information about the project, leading to more accurate cost information. Through the use of codes, the final cost for an element may be referred to the initial budget for the same element. Constant comparisons of cost to budget provide the means for cost control.

5. *Project Schedule and Progress Control.* Time is of the essence in project work. CPM and PERT were invented to better plan and schedule the project activities. Computer programs were written to process the results of CPM/PERT networks and convert the information to schedules. As planning networks are poor communication tools, computers were programmed to convert the information to bar charts. Bar charts, sometimes called Gantt charts after their inventor Henry Gantt, show activities against calendars as timelines. Progress control is achieved by ensuring that activities are carried out within the timeline.

The five systems aim to integrate project information into a common database to facilitate project control. The systems identify who does what, when, and for how much without the imposition of a rigid, hierarchical organization structure.

Each system has a distinct purpose or project function to perform. Each in its own right may exist on a project as a stand-alone system or as an individual exercise in some form or other. A system may be as simple as it needs to be to suit the project needs and the needs of the project manager. The systems are not an end in themselves. They are meant as tools to facilitate the work of doing a project successfully.

They are intended to complement each other and to integrate the yardsticks of measurement, namely, cost, quality, scope, and time. These systems are aimed to be understood by all project participants. They are not to be created in a vacuum. Because computers are powerful tools and have the capability to play an important role in project work, the systems are compatible with computerization. The fundamentals, however, stand on their own merit. The systems are listed in order of preference or priority. This is simply an orderly way to think of a new project undertaking. Project definition should always come first. That it often does not is a principal source of project grief. The systems are meant to work together from one end of the project to the other.

Using the systems of project management described herein, the project manager and the project manager's boss's boss are able to see and to know where the project is going in terms of quality, scope, cost, and schedule. They will know where they have been and have a record of how they arrived at their present location and the successful project finish.

Computerized project management is driven by structures and code systems. Code systems are the language of databases, and databases are roots for project information and control. Although project structures are commonly drawn as pyramids, or "Christmas trees," the cost control tree seen in Fig. 1.1 illustrates the idea of postmodern project management thought that the whole is greater than the sum of the parts.

1.5 Computer-Aided Project Management

Ultimately, project management is a combination of systems tools and organizational processes. As organizations exist for reasons that often have nothing to do with the delivery of projects, this introduction does not intend to dwell on the why and how of reengineering and restructuring of human resources. Although organizations may not be designed for project delivery, they are nevertheless often made responsible for large and small projects. When this happens, it is unlikely that the organization will restructure itself as a project manager. What usually happens is that the organization will start on the road to deliver the project and at the same time look toward the identification and possible purchase of computer tools to aid it in the delivery process.

In general, a firm's computer usage concerns such tasks as human resources management, payroll processing, corporate finance, accounting, capital cost maintenance, sales, and similar information. Unless an organization is geared to project delivery, it is unlikely to have project-specific databases.

When large projects are undertaken, the enterprise may look to hire a project manager or a project management firm. This new hire is expected to bring in project management attitudes and skills as well as computing tools.

Unless the enterprise, or the selected project manager, owns a proprietary computer system, or they decide to develop a dedicated system, they will turn to the commercial project management software market. The market has a complete range of applications from very expensive to low-priced packages operating on a variety of platforms.

The most widely known computer tools for project management are based on computer processing of CPM and PERT networks for project scheduling. Some current software products that will be discussed in this textbook are Artemis, Open Plan, Primavera, and SuperProject. These planning- and scheduling-based programs are now compatible with PC desktops, client/server systems, local-area networks, intranets, and the Internet. These software products with graphic user interfaces (GUIs) which run on Windows and other operating systems, are suitable for large, complex multiple-project environments.

Systems such as Open Plan Professional and Primavera Project Planner are designed to process schedule activities based on processing CPM and PERT networks. Current PC-based project management software generally is geared to a time-scaled Gantt chart of project activities. If the user wishes, the software can convert the schedule to a network. The problem with this "what you see is what you get" (WYSIWYG) approach is that it tends to bypass four of the five systems of project management. It encourages computer bar chart scheduling as a means of project management.

Computerized bar chart building does not mean project management. To succeed in project management, it is essential to develop the project parameters of scope, quality, cost, and organizational responsibility for each activity, as defined in the systems of project management.

Project management software does not usually stand alone in a corporate environment. When a project comes along, there is competition for its management from many departments, including corporate finance, accounting, and engineering, or enterprise-wide software.

Enterprise management software products aim to capture, create, coordinate, and deliver to management all kinds of information, including the financial aspects of cash flow, cost control, engineering change management, what-if analysis, and document and drawings control. Other features of the enterprise information systems could be earned value analysis, profit analysis forecasts, as well as a wide range of project reports. Corporate information technology invariably also has capability for intranet as well as Internet communication.

The intention of this discussion is to make clear that a "core business" project management system may not be the same system as the enterprise-wide software solution. Although it is seen from current marketing activity that high-end commercial project management software applications have been expanding their sphere of influence to incorporate all aspects of the business information needed by the corporation, it may also be concluded that the postmodern enterprise needs what may be termed the "business of the enterprise" system plus dedicated core business tools, which in our case create and run PDSs, WBSs, OBSs, estimating and cost control products and reports, and planning, scheduling, and progress control systems, which are all needed in project work. For example, if the enterprise is a bank, the "business of the enterprise system" would be concerned with the management of deposits, withdrawals, loan payments, automated teller machines, facilities, and employee management. When the bank decides on a new headquarters project, the enterprise banking system should not be expected also to handle the business of project management. But the two systems will need to be integrated at some point.

Both enterprise software providers and project management software vendors have indeed recognized that the respective systems need to be cooperative and compatible, and there are efforts to achieve this goal by many vendors of software aimed both at niche professional and technical markets and at the businesses of the enterprises.

As it is necessary for people and teams from different departments and companies to cooperate and work together to achieve project aims and individual corporate objectives, it is only reasonable to assume that the various software systems that people use as tools and as information gatherers and providers need to cooperate and communicate with each other. The integration and incorporation of systems project management for the core business of project management as presented in this textbook with an enterprise-wide business information system, as marketed worldwide by major vendors, is illustrated in Fig. 1.2. The intent of Fig. 1.2 is to show the re-

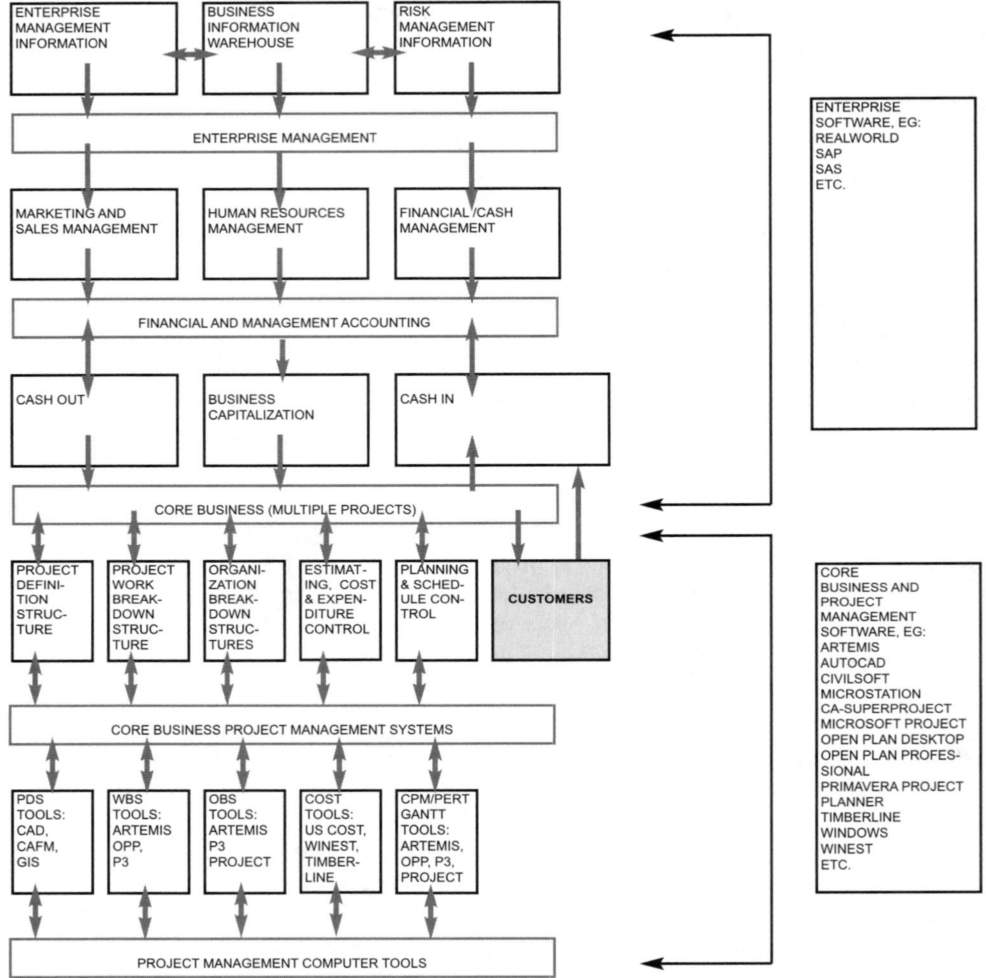

FIGURE 1.2 SOFTWARE INTEGRATION. All enterprises have business software which needs to tie in with projects. Projects require dedicated project management software to run the systems of project management, which enterprise software is not necessarily designed to handle.

lationship between the business of the enterprise software and the very specific, dedicated project management software.

1.6 Computer Tools and Projects

Computer applications are playing an ever-increasing role in the delivery of projects. Software programs are involved in just about every facet of project work, from the discovery of the problem or an opportunity to the commissioning and startup of the completed facility. There are problems where some of the parties to the project are highly computerized and others are less so. The worst of these cases leads to disputes. As one of the aims of systems project management is to reduce disputes in the delivery of projects, we look at how computer tools add to the potential for disputes while aiding the industry in terms of better productivity, lower costs, and faster project turnarounds.

A widely used computer tool in the planning, design, and drawing of a project is ArchiCAD, which is able to communicate with other computer-aided design (CAD) programs as well as spreadsheets, databases, and word processors. Programs such as ArchiCAD may be customized for specific industry applications.

The questions that arise in connection with ArchiCAD type programs include the quality of their output as drawings and details, and their capability to preclude disputes caused by coordination. Coordination and fit are most difficult in the project design and drawing phase.

Microsoft Windows programs, including digitizers, takeoffs, and estimator systems such as WinEst Pro Plus, Takeoff For Windows, and GTCO 3036 Roll Up Digitizer with Stylus, are widely marketed for the project industry. A mature estimating program, including takeoff and digitizing, Precision Estimating, is marketed by Timberline Software.

There are questions: How are applications such as ArchiCAD and Precision Estimating integrated? by whom? What is their impact on project delivery? How often are computerized estimates inaccurate, not necessarily on account of the software, and what kind of effect does that have on the project ? These questions and issues invariably become the project manager's problems.

Postmodern project management techniques have generated a great deal of new-age project management software. A recent addition is AutoPROJECT, based on AutoCAD. Other popular project management software packages are Primavera Project Planner, CA-SuperProject , and Microsoft Project. How widely used are these computer management tools by the project delivery industry? Are they used as top-down systems to control the entire project life cycle, or are they used from the bottom up as work tools by architects, engineers, and builders? Are they used by consultants? Are they used by contractors? Or are they used by owner/consultant teams to build cases against contractors? Experience shows that they often play the latter role.

Computer tools are here now. Their availability and usage on projects is growing. How are they integrated? How are they used? Does current construction contract language reflect the reality of the usage of computer tools today? This book encourages their use as a tool by all parties to a project.

1.6.1 Computer Design Tools

The marketing of architectural, engineering, and construction (A/E/C) software is very impressive, exemplified by colors, three-dimensional drawings, animation, and audiovisual effects. Reality of usage is somewhat different. The first lesson is that the demo included in the software is simplistic and inadequate. The second lesson is that much more dedicated software will be needed, and that the length of the learning curve is long indeed. But the software is here to be applied. Powerful clients want it. New graduate architects and engineers must have it. And government may not award work without it.

A professional package such as ArchiCAD aims to do architectural design and construction documentation, including drafting, plotting, printing, and bills of material. The design module models and draws plans, sections, and elevations. The most widely marketed aspect of advanced CAD applications is their capability to produce better presentations and communications.

Less spectacular than CAD's design and drawing capability is its facility to prepare quantity calculations and bills of material. A CAD bill of material is usually not a construction document, unless it is specifically made so. During preliminary design and drawing, a bill of material can be priced by the CAD system, so that element type alternatives may be compared during the design process.

Softdesk produces Coordinate Geometry (COGO) for civil engineering and surveying, Digital Terrain Modeling (DTM), Hydrology Tools for piped and surface water management, Landscape, Architectural Base, Auto-Architect, Piping, HVAC, Plumbing, Electric, Plans & Elevations for structures, Steel Detailer, Details, and a comprehensive DataBase/Query.

Softdesk also has an estimating feature which produces takeoffs and simple quantity counts. The estimating module works in conjunction with Softdesk's Auto-Architect, HVAC, Electric, Plumbing, Piping, and Landscape.

Softdesk also works in conjunction with AutoFM from Decision Graphics. This is a computer-aided facilities management (CAFM) program which has a number of modules, including Space and Asset Manager, Strategic Planner, and Property Manager. Another program from IntelliCAD called Powerpak works with Autodesk's AutoCAD Data Extension (ADE) to design and manage water, gas, electric, facilities management, and base mapping.

Research Engineers Inc. markets CivilSoft, comprising AutoCivil and Advanced Designer Series (ADS), including Survey, Roads, Contours, DTM, Earthwork, Sewer, Storm, Hydraulics and Hydrology, plus Architectural CadPlus-3D and Structural.

In the "big" CAFM picture, as seen by large public-sector and corporate owners, the CAD systems that produce designs and drawings, as well as those used for takeoffs and estimating and in the management of the construction process, are small cogs. For example, in the Archibus/FM application range of modules, Design Management is only one of seven packages.

Archibus/FM is not a prime CAD design system, but a system that takes over after the project is completed and goes into its intended use and operation.

A designer need not utilize commercial CAD applications, but can go directly to the source language, AutoCAD, or an alternative such as MicroStation, to create new and unique applications.

How do these computer design tools impact the A/E/C project? One would expect that they would reduce the time required to do the project. Since the owner and consultant resources required to do the project are fewer and more productive because of the new computer tools, less time is required for the delivery of the concept, design, drawings, and procurement stages. Similarly, because of the new features such as takeoffs, quantities, and bills of materials, and the pricing capabilities contained in the CAD systems and the associated databases, the results of the design and drawing effort from the owners and their designers would be more accurate and closer to the functional needs and budgets established for the projects.

Most projects are being designed, drawn, plotted, and produced on CAD systems. There is no chance that this trend will reverse itself. So how do computer tools contribute to the potential for project difficulties and disputes at this time and into the next century?

A big problem is that experienced designers may not be computer literate and must delegate the operation of the computer applications to new operators who may know the systems but not know design. Hence it is possible to create scenarios that may look realistic but are not. Only a professional architect or planner will be able to analyze and judge the output correctly and ultimately select the right specific solution.

1.6.2 Cost Estimating

The traditional project delivery system consists of owner need, architect/engineer design, and construction contractor build. That process has given us the A/E/C computer tools of which software applications based on AutoCAD and MicroStation are at the forefront. When we speak of computer tools, we are generally looking at systems to reduce or eliminate labor. We wish to do this for a number of reasons, the main ones being (1) the elimination of repetitive and tedious tasks, and (2) to cut cost through the reduction of human resources input.

When we transfer a knowledge-based job such as quantity surveying and cost estimating from a skilled individual to a computer tool, what happens is that first of all there is a loss of the skill of the individual and, second, the digitization of the process may be initially at least less than dependable.

Given time and resources, the programming is eventually improved and starts emulating the reliability of the quantity surveyor and cost estimator functions. Ultimately the target of the CAFM/CAD systems purchasers is to eliminate people from the design, drawing, quantity takeoff, and estimating process and have the system do it all. Where are we in the process as it pertains to estimating and cost control?

Although some design packages have the capability to generate quantities and cost comparisons, they are not yet used to prepare project budgets. If CAD systems are based on the selection of components and items from menus, it is possible that as selections are made, the selected components will be quantified and priced from a database of prices. There are vendors of price databases such as R.S. Means. They provide construction costs for software applications. Spreadsheets produced by Lotus, QuattroPro, and Excel will tie into the Means data. Estimating software that utilizes Means data includes products from CONAC Group, Timberline Software, SoftCOST, and WinEstimator.

The Means database is large. Means' Square Foot Cost alone contains 6000 different configurations in its manual. There are 6500 unit in-place costs. Means' Assemblies Cost Data lists costs for 14,500 assemblies. For plumbing there are over 12,000 plumbing and fire protection units. Hanscomb's Yardsticks for Costing contains over 65,000 unit prices, composite rates, and gross building costs in its manual. Another estimating database is General Construction Estimating Standards maintained by Richardson Engineering Services Inc.

CAD packages such as ArchiCAD and Softdesk first of all develop a capability to design, draw, and output drawings. Second they incorporate many details and standards so that a user can simply point and click to produce drawings. As the system becomes more sophisticated in a specific discipline, the elements can be counted as they are picked, and they can be priced from a database. In theory one system can do all of it, from the design concept to a budget estimate. In practice, because of the complexity of combining design and drawing skills with quantity surveying, takeoff, estimating, and pricing skills, it does not happen. There are development efforts now toward computer-integrated construction (CIC). The concept is that CIC applications will recast the information for each function or discipline that uses it.

Where are the pitfalls? From experience it is known that there are huge differences in the way we design a project, cost estimate and budget it, and schedule and manage it. Construction drawings comprise landscape, architectural, structural, mechanical, electrical, and user-specific general arrangements, plans, elevations, sections, details, schedules, and specifications. As a rule, in today's construction marketplace a job could not be costed from CAD drawings alone. A typical database may contain over 40,000 trade items. Design drawings are not necessarily trade specific, nor are they all that is required to estimate a job. Thus it is unlikely that a project budget could be prepared solely from CAD output.

Second, in early project stages, estimates are not based on itemized details but on project functional costs, that is, costs per square meter of space for the intended use. These are generally composite costs based on a database of experiential cost information and widely used for budgeting purposes. These composite cost databases are maintained as commercial, civil, and facilities units, and may be entered as computer databases.

Design and cost can be and are being integrated. There is no doubt that they are different disciplines and skill sets. It is unlikely that estimators will become AutoCAD designers, nor is it automatic that designers will be able to point and click to estimates. That does not mean that the creators of computer tools will stop the integration process, nor should they. Based on the current state of the CIC development, there is a wide gap between an AutoCAD application package claiming that it can do an estimate, and what is a reliable project estimate. It would not be remiss at this stage of integration of the design and drawing modules with the digitizing and estimating modules to write disclaimers to the effect that it may look like an estimate, but it may not be one.

It should be seen that the computer linking of the design, quantifying the design elements, and their costing is strictly the bare bones of an estimate that may become a budget. There are many computer tools aimed at making estimates and budgets and managing the project to ensure its delivery to the magic formula of "high quality/on budget/on time." Some of the cost-side computer tools, developed for cost purposes and not as an add-on to a drawing package, are the Decision Sciences Range Estimating Program (REP/PC) to analyze risks and to establish contingencies; FMC Engineering Service's ICARUS Cost Estimating System, and the ICARUS Process Evaluator (IPE). The ICARUS IPE links process changes with corresponding cost and time impacts.

1.6.3 Project Scheduling and Management

A long-time concern of the A/E/C industry has been the concept of project scheduling by CPM. For many in the industry, CPM was seen as a system that somebody else should use. Of all modern A/E/C tools, CPM was one of the very first to be computerized.

CPM was initially aimed to improve construction labor productivity. Eventually other aspects such as procurement and management decisions were included in the CPM planning networks and schedules. Today there are many CPM-based computer tools for scheduling and project management.

A widely used package, created for the A/E/C industry, is Primavera Project Planner (P3). Now written for Windows as a GUI package, P3 offers to organize, analyze, communicate, and accelerate projects. The main planning graphic in P3, as in most other GUI packages, is the Gantt bar depicting a task applied onto a calendar.

Where at one time most schedules showed only construction activities, current usage includes a full range of project phases and tasks, including predesign services, site analysis activities, schematic design services, design development services, and so on. P3 offers to manage not only the project time, but cost and the use of resources. This is done by estimating activities in terms of their time, their resource requirements, and their cost.

Although the initial concept of CPM was to plan activities using networks of logical relationships and then creating Gantt or bar charts to communicate the information, the current marketing approach is to plan the work on screen using bar charts, connecting the bars for logic if needed, and then automatically converting the plan to a CPM/PERT network in precedence diagram format.

Another planning, scheduling, project management package suitable for the A/E/C industry is Artemis for Windows. Artemis utilizes a GUI in a client/server architecture or as a stand-alone PC.

The rationale driving project management systems such as P3 and Artemis is to make them easy to use, and at the same time to obtain the planning power endemic in the CPM or PERT concept. They were made easier to use with the advent of Windows and the introduction of the GUI method of working. The result is that a user can point and click to create bar charts. When connected by predecessor/successor links, the bar charts become PERT charts.

A bar chart initially shows time. As a task is assigned a code of accounts and priced, and as resources are applied to the task, the system is made capable of producing not only time reports, but cost reports as well. This is achieved through the integration of systems such as Artemis with industry standard databases such as Oracle and SQLBase. P3, on the other hand, supports databases such as Lotus 1-2-3 and dBASE. Both systems are enhanced with report writers and graphics systems. Both P3 and Artemis may be considered to be professional, high-end project management software packages.

A high-end package is capable of handling a wide range of hierarchical and coded information for planning, scheduling, cost and resources control purposes, and the generation of custom schedule and cost control reports and graphics.

A possible negative may be the apparent degradation of the CPM/PERT network planning procedure in favor of the easy to use GUI-produced bar chart. Are screen-produced bar charts as effective as logic diagrams which may not necessarily lend themselves to screen production? This text will answer that question.

Another project management software package created specifically for the A/E/C industry is Open Plan Professional. Open Plan works with database packages such as Microsoft's FoxPro or the Borland dBASE IV.

A recent addition to the ranks of project management software is AutoPROJECT, written in AutoCAD. An important feature of AutoPROJECT may be its capability to exchange data with project management software such as Microsoft Project, Open Plan, and Primavera, as well as with database managers such as dBASE.

Project management software not specifically written for the A/E/C industry includes Microsoft Project and Computer Associates SuperProject. Microsoft Project is seen by some as a lower cost, individual scheduling tool suitable as a feeder to more comprehensive project management software for large projects, such as Artemis, Open Plan, and Primavera.

Some lower priced applications are Timeline, SureTrak from Primavera, and Open Plan Desk Top. SureTrak and Timeline are simple, computerized bar chart drawing tools.

1.6.4 Computer Tools and Construction Documents

The North American A/E/C industry comprises mostly small, independent firms and individuals who come together as creators of big and small projects, sometimes working for themselves as entrepreneurs, but usually under the aegis of large and powerful bureaucracies and corporations. The use of computer tools has come about, not solely because of the wish of the A/E/C practitioners, but on account of the desire of the big buyers of these services to improve productivity, cut costs, and shorten project time.

Architects and engineers are now obliged to use CAD, or they are not eligible for work from most large buyers of their services. At the same time they want to use CAD because it makes them better designers. It reduces their payroll, and it shortens the delivery time. As CAD progress is made, a designer may be able to do the entire project. To carry this to an absurd length, as the CAD system is advanced and becomes expert, not even the designer will be required. Evidence of this trend may be extrapolated from packages such as Archibus/FM.

Within the construction sector computer systems are used primarily for managing the business, that is, accounting. As for the architects, engineers, and constructors, they are being forced into computer tools by large public and corporate buyers of their services.

The systems that A/E/C firms select may be dictated by their clients. If a firm's client base is big government, does it not follow that the firm will employ the systems used by big government? Is it realistic to believe that a system selected by the corporate owner for facility management will be suitable for the creative design work and drawing production that is the role of the architect and the engineer? By the same token, are architectural and engineering design and drawing systems suitable for the estimating and construction management systems used by constructors? Chances are that the answers to both questions are no, or at least, not yet.

Currently architects may share their computer drawings with engineers, but may not share their disks with constructors. There is evidence that owners do not wish to pay for electronic information. And this leads into a whole new discussion area as to how different aspects of the A/E/C industry work with, contract for, and use and divulge CAD-produced construction information. As this text aims to include issues pertaining to design, contract documentation, and construction disputes, a first question that might be asked is: what role do computer-produced documents play in the bidding and construction process? The answer is no role, as such. It does not matter how the documents are produced.

Many standard construction contracts are generally silent on the means and methods of producing designs, drawings, and specifications. As far as most construction contracts are concerned, we could be back in the days of blue prints. Computer-produced drawings are not mentioned and therefore do not exist, as far as the language of the contract is concerned.

Presumably if the parties to the construction agreement wished to, they could list pertinent computer products in the articles on definitions. In currently used standard contract forms there are no definitions for computer products or computer-produced documents. It is almost as if the computer had not yet been invented.

For example, considering a current standard construction contract prepared and approved by the A/E/C industry–based Canadian Construction Documents Committee CCDC2-1994, it becomes evident that this document is written for a former time and a different way to do projects. It certainly has no resemblance to the way people are meant to work with computer tools. For example, GC 1.1.2 of the General Conditions states that "nothing contained in the Contract Documents shall create any contractual relationship between:

> GC 1.1.2.1 the Owner and a Subcontractor, a Supplier, . . . , and
> GC 1.1.2.2 the Consultant and the Contractor, a Subcontractor, a Supplier, ..."

These clauses, and others like them, would preclude the cooperative use of CAD disks, designs, drawings, and databases such as computerized bills of materials, unit prices, and estimates. It is simply not enough for any party to the A/E/C process to say that this provision can easily be added through supplementary conditions. Supplementary conditions are at best subjective. Only an industry-wide statement would have a chance of being acceptable to all the parties to the contract.

Another source of dispute based on contract language would be:

> GC 1.1.7 The drawings are the graphic and pictorial portions of the Contract Documents, wherever located and whenever issued, showing the design, location, and dimensions of the Work, generally including plans, elevations, sections, details, schedules, and diagrams.

This is the kind of contract statement that influences negatively the present use of computer tools for design, drawings, details, bills of material, takeoffs, and estimates, as well as the products' integration and usage for shop drawings and progress billings. In other words, in the "old days," hand-drafted drawings were just that: drawings and nothing more. In today's world of CAD-designed and -drawn and laser-produced documents and three-dimensional views, the drawings are only one of many looks at CAD-produced project information. And standard industry-wide modern contract language, written for use now and into the 21st century, must start to reflect this reality.

The ultimate source of disputes based on standard contract language must be:

> GC 1.1.9 If there is a conflict within Contract Documents:
> 1 the order of priority of documents from highest to lowest, shall be
> - The agreement between the owner and the contractor,
> - The definitions,
> - Supplementary conditions,
> - The general conditions,
> - Division 1 of the specifications,
> - Divisions 2 through 16 of the specifications,
> - Material and finishing schedules,
> - Drawings.

This condition has to be a serious detriment to the full, integrated use of modern computer tools in the A/E/C industry. The reality is that seven sets of words take precedence over the drawings. How can drawings be in last place when the depictions of projects by computer-produced views, drawings, and pictures gets only better and better, and there is no end to the extent and variety of A/E/C information that the computer tool can produce.

With A/E/C computer tools, and with the integration of design, drawings, takeoffs, bills of material, unit prices, estimates, budgets, and schedules, the drawings must be moved up in the priority list, and the words downgraded until the concept of contract control clauses as seen in the above list disappears from the A/E/C lexicon.

1.6.5 Change Orders

A major concern for everybody in the project industry is the subject of change orders, however caused. Changes in project work are big business. Computer tools, if anything, should make changes easier and faster to implement. There should be less delay in getting the new information from the owner to the architects and engineers, and to the contractor, subcontractors, and vendors. On the other hand, because changes are now easier, will the bidding documents be less complete, and therefore create an atmosphere for more changes?

Shop drawings get a lot of attention whenever construction disputes are discussed. As we make progress with computer tools in the A/E/C process, does it not follow that shop drawings will become another product of the CAD system. As more manufacturers and vendors get into CAD, it should become possible to integrate the vendors' drawings and bills of material right into the architectural and engineering drawings and specifications.

Another problem area is the sometimes "no-man's" land between drawings and specifications. As CAD becomes more generally used, and more information appears on the drawings, there should be less dependence on the dense verbiage of the specifications. It is known that bidding drawings and specifications are not construction drawings. The information, after bidding, must be converted for construction through the vendors' and manufacturers' drawings. With CAD this has to become a more seamless process.

As to the computers tools for cost and schedule control, the impetus first came from the vendors of CPM/PERT scheduling software. More recently the AutoCAD system takeoffs and lists of materials have been tied in with cost databases for estimating and budgeting purposes.

But the way a project is designed is different from the way it is constructed, meaning that the budget from CAD will need a system to convert it to the cost control system in CPM/PERT. Resources leveling is geared to the CPM/PERT systems.

Computer tools for the A/E/C industry need more recognition in standard contract forms before the full benefits flow to the entire industry, and not only to some of its members.

In discussing the subject of CIC, one industry professional suggested that the matter might be better discussed under the heading "roadblocks to computer-integrated construction." This may be true in the sense that the road to CIC is not easy, and like the Internet, it is not owned by anyone. This is perhaps in the true tradition of the entrepreneurial spirit of the firms and professionals comprising the North American construction, engineering, and architecture industries.

1.6.6 Expert Systems

When will computer-aided project management become computerized project management through expert systems?

None of the computer tools discussed in this chapter are deemed expert systems. They work as menu-driven graphical point and click systems, as two-dimensional and three-dimensional views, item or text copy and paste applications, or in some cases as object linking and embedding (OLE) applications. The expert systems that are being put in place emulate administration procedures.

To design and draw a project requires a very large library of elements that are specific for that project. The way the project is drawn is not the way it is estimated and budgeted, and it is not the way in which it will be assembled, constructed, and delivered. For instance, the cost database for plumbing alone has over 12,000 cost estimating units. But estimating units are not necessarily relatable to material management units nor to purchasing procedures. These points are made to reflect the kind and quality of human skills and resources that are required for the delivery of a project, that would have to be emulated by expert systems.

A growing area in computing technologies is the development of automation capabilities to link and embed objects and data across programs and applications running on different platforms. Some project management applications can now be used with industry standard programming tools to integrate planning and scheduling activities from engineering, construction, architecture, utilities, and manufacturing with other corporate systems. The aim is to make corporate systems communicate with project management systems. This process may be viewed as the precursor to expert systems.

In terms of where the future of expert technologies will be in the 21st century, it is not enough to consider only the systems that relate to project management and to the business of the enterprise. Projects are the result of entrepreneurial and creative thought and action, which need to be captured digitally and rendered as concepts, sketches, drawings, two-dimensional views, three-dimensional views, and audiovisual animations.

This creative process is captured by many different computer systems among other creative, business, and manufactured products, created and managed by other computer systems. The problem is that they all speak different computer languages.

CAD professionals are finding it increasingly necessary to exchange digital drawings with design team members, outside contractors, project managers, and customers. Not only are AutoCAD systems required to communicate with project management and enterprise business systems, they need to communicate with other systems such as MicroStation. The creation of expert systems will require computers to communicate one on one, without loss of data, as a seamless process.

Systems like CAFM and computer-integrated facilities management (CIFM) are driven by and linked to information databases or data warehouses created and maintained by all kinds of software. Postmodern software developments eventually all aim for enterprise-wide control. Some, like SAP, may be seen as top-down business systems, which after successful implementation for such services as cash-flow control delve deeper into the core business, for example, engineering and construction, and are linked to discipline systems, such as project estimating, human resources scheduling, and ultimately CAD design and drawings.

This is seen to work in reverse bottom up, where a discipline system such as Primavera designed to process CPM planning and scheduling grows to encompass and become the basis for the enterprise-wide system through a computing technology such as RA Primavera Automation Engine.

If SAP is seen as an accounting-based software system (cash flow) and Primavera as a management system (schedule), systems based on AutoCAD, MicroStation, and Graphisoft must be considered to be creative software languages (design and drawings). They would need to be seen to be the ultimate bottom-up technology, because nothing is created without a concept, a line, a sketch, a drawing, a two-dimensional drawing, a three-dimensional view, an audiovisual animation, a virtual model. The answer is seen to be that software systems need to be designed to communicate and deliver information and processes in the same way that human resources hand off and deliver their project contributions to each other. Software packages only deliver discrete packages. The packages are coordinated and connected by human skills to create projects. Many packages can receive copies from other packages as pasteups.

More and more packages are now communicating. As more progress is made, the result will be more than the sum of those parts. It may very well be called the process.

1.7 Summary

A project may be any undertaking, large, small, or megasized. That project cost overruns can cause long-lasting financial havoc to their sponsors is demonstrated by selected horror stories. Project difficulties are depicted and the five systems of project management are introduced as the means to solving problems and controlling projects. Computer systems are shown to have a role in all aspects of an enterprise, including projects. The question then is which system is to play what role, and how do systems communicate to be effective management tools. Computer tools are shown to play various enterprise and project roles. Although each has a specific job, all aim to broaden their influence, clamoring to become the prime system. A key role for the project manager is to coordinate these systems. Expert systems are not here yet. There are developments aiming to be the systems of the future, taking over the coordinating and management roles now performed by managers.

REFERENCES

Antill, J. M., and R. W. Woodhead, *Critical Path Methods in Construction Practice,* 4th ed. (Wiley, New York, 1990).

Bartlett, J., *Bartlett's Familiar Quotations* (Little Brown, Boston, 1980).

Blough, R. M., "More Construction for the Money," Summary Report of the Construction Industry Cost Effectiveness Project (The Business Roundtable, New York, 1983).

Clough, R. H., and G. A. Sears, *Construction Project Management,* 3rd ed. (Wiley, New York, 1991).

Hendrickson, C., and T. Au, *Project Management for Construction* (Prentice-Hall, Englewood Cliffs, NJ, 1989).

Johnson, L., *Project Management,* audiocassette (CareerTrack, Boulder, CO, 1981).

Kerzner, H., *Project Management, a Systems Approach to Planning, Scheduling, and Controlling,* 3rd ed. (Van Nostrand Reinhold, New York, 1989).

Kliem, R. L., and I. Ludin, *The Noah Project* (Gower Press, Farnborough, UK, 1993).

Levine, H. A., *Project Management Using Microcomputers* (Osborne McGraw-Hill, Berkeley, CA, 1986).

Lock, D., *Project Management,* 2nd ed. (Gower Press, Farnborough, UK, 1981).

Peart, A. T., *Design of Project Management Systems and Records* (Gower Press, Farnborough, UK, 1971).

Weiss, J. W., and R. K. Wysocki, *5-Phase Project Management* (Addison-Wesley, Reading, MA, 1992).

Software Vendors

ArchiCAD, Grapisoft USA, 400 Oyster Point Blvd., South San Francisco, CA
AutoDesk, 2320 Marinship Way, Sausalito, CA
AutoProject, Research Engineers, Inc., 22700 Savi Ranch, Yorba Linda, CA
Civil Soft, AutoCivil, Research Engineers, Inc., 22700 Savi Ranch, Yorba Linda, CA
Hanscomb's Yardsticks for Costing, Southam, 1450 Don Mills Road, Toronto, ON, Canada
Icarus Corp., One Central Plaza, 11300 Rockville Pike, Rockville, MD
Primavera Systems, Inc., Two Bala Plaza, Bala Cynwyd, PA
R. S. Means, 100 Construction Plaza, Kingston, MA
Softdesk 7, Softdesk, Inc., 7 Liberty Hill Rd., Henniker, NH
The Archibus/FM, Archibus, Inc., 177 Milk Street, Boston, MA
Timberline Software, 9600 S.W. Nimbus, Beaverton, OR

Software Vendor Sites on the WWW

Archibus: www.archibus.com
Artemis: www.artemispm.com
Autodesk: www.autodesk.com
Bentley: www.bentley.com
CA-SuperProject: www.cai.com
Graphisoft: www.graphisoft.com
Open Plan: www.wst.com
Primavera: www.primavera.com
RealWorld: www.pass-port.com
SAP: www.sap.com
SAS Institute: www.sas.com
WST: www.wst.com

PART 2

SYSTEMS OF PROJECT MANAGEMENT

PROJECT DEFINITION STRUCTURE 2

Project definition aims to describe the scope and quality of a project from the perspective of the users of the finished project. Project participants often resist definition to the point where some claim that a project is not defined until after completion, and that it will cost what it costs. The intent of project definition is to overcome this inertia and resistance to making scope and quality decisions by project participants, especially from the perspective of the project customers and ultimate users of the completed project. Top management is often reluctant to participate in progressive decision making. The discussion will show how to respond to top management questions.

Project definition as a system is placed in relation to the other systems of project management. It is seen how they are all equally important, how they interface, and how each has a role resulting in a specific deliverable.

Two streams of modern project management thought are explored, developed, and set as the basis for the concept of project definition. The principal driver for the theory is the concept of work breakdown and project code that derives from the program evaluation review technique (PERT). Equally important, but not as highly profiled, are cost codes that flow from cost engineering theory. Both of these streams merge into the idea of a project code based on a project definition structure (PDS).

The theoretical discussion aims to present project definition as a concept that may be applicable in all kinds of projects, in all kinds of businesses and enterprises. Two examples are developed along different lines, for different projects. Both illustrate project definition.

2.1 What Is Project Definition?

It is important for project participants to understand the roles to be played by the various corporate groups in the definition of a project. The operating group is the customer for the finished facility and will operate it. Their input is essential for establishing the scope and quality, but they may or may not be cooperative in the essential, early front-end work, or may not have the time. Sometimes they want to act in a project management capacity, even though they may not have the skills.

The project manager, the project engineer, and the discipline engineers have the required project skills. But they are not building for their own account; they will not be operating the finished facility, hardware, or software system. If they are experienced, the wisest decision that they can make is to recognize and treat the users of the finished project as their clients, their valuable customers. Similarly, the smart users must sooner or later recognize that project management is immensely complex, and that their cooperation and timely decision making will only lead to a better, earlier project.

Then within the project team itself there are the differences between the project engineers, the discipline engineers, the designers, the support groups such as cost engineers, cost accountants, purchasing, corporate finance, and asset management, and finally corporate executive management itself. These diverse and talented groups need to work together to define the project.

A project is defined when its scope and quality are known. What is project scope? The dictionary definition of scope does not help the project manager in that it is general and speaks of application, outlook, or range of view. In project management the word scope takes its definition from cost engineering usage to mean the size or magnitude of an undertaking in terms of its cost, volume or output of product, process equipment requirements, or other measurables that make up a project.

Clark and Lorenzoni state in *Applied Cost Engineering* that the scope definition evolves during a very short period of constant change at the project's beginning. However, due to the difficulty in establishing the project scope initially, the final scope may not be set until the project is completed. Professional project managers know that changes in project work cause great difficulty in controlling project scope, cost, and quality.

Hackney, in *Control and Management of Capital Projects,* describes project definition for a capital project as a "practical plan" for the project which includes plant capacity, raw material sources, and quality, product types and quality, marketing and distribution methods, flow sheets, layouts, equipment lists, and specifications. Quality is thus tied to scope for true project definition.

How does one define project quality? Hackney stresses quality as it relates to both raw materials as input and the finished product as output. These same attributes must then be applied to the project elements.

In this text, project scope and quality are inextricably linked, and are to be considered an integral part of project definition. The terms "scope" and "quality" are sometimes treated as synonyms.

While project managers and engineers may have the responsibility to define the scope of the project, they may not have the authority. To define the project, the project manager needs to have sufficient authority. This is the ideal environment that project management people strive for. It generally does not happen. And that is another reason why project definition is difficult. Operations won't let go, but they do not have the time to devote to the project. Project management, on the other hand, cannot on its own make the necessary decisions.

If a system of project definition was to be put in place, it did not necessarily follow that the lines of communication, responsibility, and authority which may have been the cause of the problem of definition in the first place were being resolved. The process of project definition was to be a vehicle to facilitate and structure definition, not to resolve organizational problems. In project work, however, project definition is the first of a number of project difficulties. In solving the problem of definition it is necessary to resolve the other problems, as will be seen in this text.

For these reasons, the need for a system of project management was seen as the way to break the gridlock.

The development and implementation of management systems invariably point out deficiencies in the way things are being done. This is true in the case of the systems of project management, and is applicable when considering the system of project definition. One of the first issues to face the system developers is the impact that the system would have on the project participants, particularly on project leadership. Project leadership is sooner or later vested in project engineers and project management, so that the first impact of any system development and implementation would be felt by the professional project participants including project engineers, who are normally the first line of attack in setting up a project.

In the case on which this discussion is based, there were many questions that needed to be answered in the development of the project definition process. The answers became the basis for describing what the system would be. These were some of the comments, concerns, questions, and answers:

- Project leadership is invariably vested in the project engineer. Project engineers by virtue of the heavy burden of responsibility that they carry tend to be conservative and suspicious of new approaches, including new systems. As a result, they may be the most reticent to consider a system that the system proponents say will help them.
- Project technical expertise is vested in discipline engineers (civil, structural, mechanical, electrical, etc.). As they deal in life safety systems, they too tend to be conservative and suspicious of new systems of management. Their usual problem is having to wait for project definition.
- Project engineers take a proprietary interest in the project; it is theirs. It is almost as if they fear loss of control if they use a system and are able to define a project faster, better, and more accurately. It is as if the project would no longer be theirs; it would belong to everybody.
- But this is exactly what everybody else wanted, and what corporate management was after—a project definition that was understandable to all corporate functions that need to know.
- On the one hand there are the discipline engineers, administrators, corporate accountants, controllers, and corporate management who need the project definition as soon as possible. But the project engineers are reticent and hold back, not wishing to make the commitment leading to a hard project definition.

Any attempt at introducing systems of project management to project work will usually lead to resistance, as was the case in the introduction of the system of project definition just discussed. Specific reasons for resistance to change in this case included the following:

- There is fear that systematic definition could lead to too rigid an approach. The system could stifle freedom.
- There is concern that the integration concept inherent in systems would take away control from the responsible engineer and vest it in the system operators.
- In a corporate environment, which projects would be incorporated in the systems? The thinking is that some jobs are more easily defined than others, so that only complicated projects would be scoped within the system.
- Project engineers say that they never have enough time to define the scope of the project before having to get on with it. If a new, perhaps complex system is introduced to help define the project, its first impact would be to add to the time needed to define the work. But the time available was not enough to begin with.
- Project participants need leadership. Technical leadership within the project management umbrella is best provided by the project engineer. The project engineer would take on the stewardship of the project definition.
- A system by definition looks for uniformity in project terminology. The introduction of a project definition system will identify inconsistencies in terms that are often based on personal experiences. When project engineers come from different backgrounds, they bring with them differences in project language. As these words define project deliverables, an early problem is to resolve the differences. This effort improves project communications through the use of more standard project language.
- Experienced project engineers say that the single most difficult aspect of project work is controlling its scope.
- Projects are just not planned enough, particularly in the early stages, say project engineers.

In the case history on which the preceding examples are based, there were three main conclusions reached.

1. Project engineers will resist the introduction of the system of project definition.
2. Corporate management, discipline engineers, and the project support groups want the project definition system.
3. Not enough time had ever been spent on project definition before having to get on with the project.

That project definition is a source of concern, and a long-standing difficulty in the delivery of projects, may be seen from the work of others in the field.

Wysocki, Beck, and Crane state in *Effective Project Management* that a definition of project work represents an agreement between top management and the project manager. This text develops the scope and quality features comprising the project definition. Projects not adequately scoped initially may be subject to serious, ongoing scope changes, termed "scope creep" by Wysocki et al.

In *The Implementation of Project Management*, Stuckenbruck discusses defining the project objectives (scope and quality) as an integral part of the project manager's charter.

The scope of work sometimes is referred to as a statement of work, as discussed in Cleland, *Project Management, Strategic Design and Implementation.* A statement of work is a derivative of the work breakdown structure (WBS), as is project definition. In this text PDS will be seen to be more focused and precise in terms of scope and quality.

Stewart defines in *Cost Estimating* the elements needed for an estimating phase. The estimating phase follows a WBS, which follows preliminary design, as well as inputs from major equipment vendors. These estimating elements are seen to contain components of the project scope definition.

Based on the development of modern project management systems, including the WBS, cost engineering methodology, and estimating processes, it is concluded that scope and quality are difficult to define, but essential for project success.

2.2 Management's View of Project Definition

What does the chief executive officer want out of all this talk of project definition?

Management has a problem that it wishes to solve or an opportunity to take advantage of with a project that must finish "soonest." Management may need to market a new product, provide a service, or fulfill a commitment which requires a capital cost project. It wishes to do this quickly and for as little outlay as possible. It needs to know with all haste how much the project will cost and how long it will take to deliver. As a rule, management does not want to spend a great deal of money and time to obtain answers to two fundamental project questions: How much will it cost? How long will it take? Management wants to get on with it, or drop it.

That is the kind of environment in which the project team finds itself. That is the cause of the frustrations described earlier in attempting to define project work in definitive engineering terms before having to get on with it. Just how will management's unreasonable questions be answered? How can project managers survive in this kind of an atmosphere?

In the case on which this discussion is based, top management saw the need for a computerized system of project control. In developing the project control system, it became immediately evident that the biggest problem area was that of project definition.

A project definition system would go a long way to resolve many of the problems and concerns raised. Addressed would be issues such as lines of communications, responsibility, and project authority. There would be better and more precise usage of terminology to describe front-end deliverables, and a recognition that early cost and schedule numbers are guesstimates and therefore imprecise.

In those situations where corporate management or the client department needs "snap" answers, there has to be in place a terminology and a system of responses which knowledgeable management and clients understand and can live with. The system of responses is geared to cost and schedule mostly. The answers are short on detail and long on assumptions, and are a mirror image of the lack of detail in the project front end. Since these early broad scope definitions lead to later detailed scope and cost measurements, these two most important measures of a project definition are integrated by using professional cost engineering terminology. (Cost estimating is covered at length in Chapter 5 on cost control, including extensive references.)

When top management decides on the need for a project, it wants to know its cost and its completion date immediately. Project management wants to define the scope so as to estimate it and set the completion date. This condition requires that all aspects of the project process go into effect, including definition, breakdown, organization, cost, and schedule. The immediate answers that must flow to top management, however, are invariably tied to cost. Thus the first answers relating to project scope are identified by cost engineering terminology.

2.2.1 Ballpark Project Definition

Because of the importance of cost in project risk analysis and in the corporate management approval process, project definitions are named in these introductory pages after cost estimates. Thus a ballpark type project definition is named after a ballpark estimate, which is based on very sketchy project information. If engineering design is used to establish project scope and quality, the ballpark estimate is based on design being about 3% completed.

The accuracy of a project ballpark estimate is on the order of −30% to +50%. A ballpark estimate is sometimes called an order-of-magnitude estimate.

The earliest definition may be structured by comparing the proposed project to a completed similar project and making allowances for differences in volume, product output, site conditions, soft costs such as inflation, and the cost of money. The definition exercise may consist of considering a number of levels of project breakdown and comparing the new project elements to those of a completed project. For repetitive projects there may be fairly accurate databases in place, which would make scoping new projects easier. But ballpark estimates are often just guesstimates and highly unreliable.

This is where project managers may run into their first serious problem. You can tell the chief executive officer that this estimate is a ballpark figure. (In your mind, you are sure that it will never be the minus number, because experience shows that projects never cost less.) And top management will usually agree that this is only a ballpark number, and more design and scope definition are needed to produce a reliable, better accuracy estimate.

If top management really want this project, they will say, look, here's the money; forget the plus/minus stuff; do it for the amount, and don't ask for another dollar. And you will be so happy to do the project that you will agree, and all your discipline engineers will agree, and the operating group will not say a word, because the project is for them; and the next thing you know, there is a sod turning ceremony with your picture in the papers.

And you will have been taken in. There is no full bore project definition. The operating people did not say a thing before the project was given the green light, and now they have found out that millions of dollars worth of equipment and computers were forgotten. And the approved amount is not enough, and the time frame is much too short, and in a year you are looking for another job.

2.2.2 Budget Project Definition

A budget estimate is in the −15% to +30% accuracy range.

The scope and quality definition exercises define, design, and specify subprojects, functional areas, important subfunctions, and major elements, so that cost engineers are able to prepare budgets that are more reliable than a ballpark estimate. In engineering design terms, the average design is on the order of about 10%.

2.2.3 Appropriation-Grade Project Definition

This type of definition is expected by cost engineers to be accurate to within −5% and +15% accuracy. The average design completion is required to be 40%.

There is indeed a great deal of quantifiable information backing this class of definition. Scope is measured in terms of user major areas, functions, subfunctions, element types, and elements. The quality of systems such as heating, lighting, instrumentation, and finishes is stated on concept drawings and in written specifications.

Some corporations may refer to the design, detailing, and engineering effort required for an appropriation grade estimate as the final budget approval phase and control budget preparation. The result is expected to be a ±5% to 10% accuracy estimate.

Experience on complex industrial research projects shows that the project definition, including conceptual drawings and outline specifications for a ±10% accuracy estimate, will cost about 15% of the project design budget. The estimate itself would cost about 0.50% of the design budget. The design budget in this case was 8.5% of the project construction budget. The construction budget was on the order of $15 million.

An appropriation-grade definition, requiring time and cost to prepare, will ensure to the project owner that there is a high probability that the project will be delivered for the funds approved. As a general rule, in knowledgeable repeat project corporate environments, a project that comes in within ±10% of the approved, definitive budget is considered a success.

The chief executive officer wants the project. The project manager wants to deliver the project that the chief executive officer wants. The progressive creation of project scope and its identification in cost terms ensures that both are speaking the same language. Each earlier definition or price acts as a launching pad for the next level of definition until the project manager is able to back up the price with an appropriation-grade budget estimate.

2.3 The Place of Project Definition

Project definition, in this text, is seen as the most important of all the systems of project management on the grounds that:

- The project scope and quality need to be defined before the project can be designed, engineered, procured, contracted, constructed, commissioned, and started up so that it meets the stated and necessary requirements of scope and quality.
- There are levels of definition, based on the amount and kind of design and engineering completed, identified by the accuracy of the estimate that accompanies the definition.
- The completed project must meet the needs of the people who will occupy it and use it to meet their objectives.
- In addition, for the project to be successful it must be completed within budget and on time.

To reiterate, the systems of project management are designed as a tool to help the project manager achieve the stated objectives of quality, cost, and time.

As project management is a group of systems, project definition is positioned in the systems of project management, as seen in Fig. 2.1.

Project definition, as the number one system, is shown at the top of the hierarchy. Listing definition at the top is not to downgrade the others, nor is it intended that they be listed in any order of priority.

From a systems perspective, and because of usage in project management, the system of project definition may be considered by some practitioners to be synonymous with the system of WBS. Breakdown will be discussed in the next chapter. In this text, definition is given the very specific project role of defining and developing a project coding system which first aims to identify and incorporate the needs of the users of the completed project, incorporating in the process language and code for the professional management of the project.

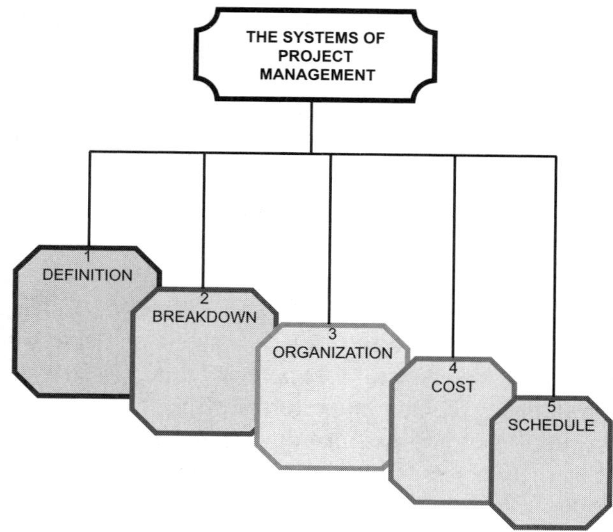

FIGURE 2.1 THE PLACE OF PROJECT DEFINITION. Project definition is the first of the five systems of project management if the project is so managed. This does not always happen. A project may be anywhere in its life, at any time, and it will not be stopped so that it may continue in an orderly fashion, as listed here. Indeed, all systems are always under way to some extent.

The places of the systems of organization, cost, and schedule, to be discussed in later chapters, are interchangeable, depending on specific project objectives. The main thrust is to make the systems relate to each other, to integrate their databases. Each impacts on the others and influences them at every step of the process. There is to be nothing done in a vacuum.

2.3.1 Genesis of Project Definition

As much of the work on which the systems of project management are based was done for the industrial sector in general, and in particular for the process industry, the first examples will be based on those experiences. It is intended that fundamentals to be seen in these examples will be useful in extrapolating the concepts for other business sectors and many different types of projects.

The aim of the project definition system is to control that which is to be delivered, in the project language that will be developed in these pages. Before an undertaking can be constructed (the word "constructed" is to be taken in the broadest sense) it needs to be identified, classified, arranged, measured, sketched, and so on, in terms that apply to it or express its value so that it may be progressed as a project undertaking.

Hackney originally illustrated the basis for a dual-decimal system of cost coding for the management of corporate chemical, petrochemical, and process plant projects. The code described by Hackney is seen in this text as the obvious result of project definition structuring exercises. The terms "project definition" and "work breakdown" do not appear in Hackney's sample code, but that is what was being developed in the process of cost coding.

In this light, Hackney's work in the process industry is seen as precedent to the concept of PDS and WBS, which took hold with the introduction of PERT/Cost. As a reference for cost coding, Hackney cited the American Society of Civil Engineers' manual, *Classification of Cost Accounts,* Section IV, "Construction Cost Control."

As Hackney aimed to identify deliverables, namely, the plant, the function, the subfunction, the piping, the type of piping, and so on, before identifying their tasks, I consider it to be the development of a PDS, as opposed to a WBS.

In *Process Plant Capital Cost Estimating,* Miller discussed a system of project definition and project coding for process plant projects. Miller's approach depicts a process plant project as comprising four discrete areas: (1) battery limits, (2) storage and handling, (3) utilities, and (4) services. Each area performs a specific function. The objective of the delineation of a project into its functional areas, that is, definition breakdown, is the development of a modern construction cost code.

Miller's hypothesis was not said to be dependent on a definition structure, nor was Hackney's. But clearly the approach is a form of hierarchical definition breakdown similar to the accepted definition of a modern WBS. This is made more readily apparent as the derived code numbers are significant digits, that is, the location of a numeric digit indicates its level in a code hierarchy.

Hackney depicted the areas of a process project as project components. The project components as seen here comprise five main areas. Some subareas are also shown.

- 10 Process units
  - 1010 Process unit 1
  - 1020 Process unit 2
  - 1030 Process unit 3
- 30 Utilities
- 40 Services
  - 4010 Tankage
  - 4020 Receiving and shipping
  - 4030 Service buildings and systems
  - 4040 Site and site development
- 50 Indirect costs
- 90 Contingencies

It can be argued that Hackney and Miller, and other cost engineers based on their process plant work, were developing project definitions and breakdown structures leading to cost code systems without the benefit of formal WBSs.

Essentially, the development of project code systems was cost driven in the process industries. In NASA megaproject work, the development of PERT was initially time driven until the advent of PERT/Cost and formal WBSs and code systems.

This text aims to combine both streams of development into a project management systems concept based on definition, breakdown, organization, cost, and schedule. The glue that keeps the systems integrated is the language of the project code system, which starts with the project definition.

2.3.2 Application of Project Definition

For example, the project may be a fertilizer plant, a pet food factory, or a soup canning facility. The project manager would use the system of project definition to establish the project parameters in specific terms, which could be similar to those from the process industry already introduced, called battery limits, utilities requirements, storage and handling facilities, site services, warehousing areas, offices, and so on.

In project definition language these elements have evolved as areas. Areas have specific area functions, as seen by plant operations or the users of the finished project. Areas are defined in terms such as quantity of product, gross square meters of space, specific equipment requirements, energy needs, or resources consumption. The language of area definitions becomes more specific as the project progresses from feasibility studies through to preliminary design.

In project work it is not enough to define only the project hardware, or the facility left in place upon completion. Projects can only be achieved through the consumption of both material and creative effort, as well as that resource without which nothing is possible—money. The plant areas are therefore matched with project resources such as areas of money for reserves and contingencies, special costs, provision for inflation, and the project soft costs such as the cost of money, the cost of management, administration, design, and engineering, and the costs of construction, such as temporary roads, generally referred to as construction indirect costs.

Therefore a description of only the physical areas of a project would not be adequate for project management purposes. A definition also makes provision for the indirect and soft costs.

Considering again the process plant referred to earlier, Fig. 2.2 illustrates how a definition structure depicts areas, in a hierarchical structure at level 2, assuming that the project objective is at level 1. To apply the definition as a systems concept and start a database, the project areas in Fig. 2.2 have been assigned single alpha characters as their codes. It is seen that A through E code the hard functional areas, and F through K represent the project soft and indirect costs.

The areas listed as project soft costs are worthy of note as they are applicable for all projects. For example area F, Reserves & Contingencies, is most important because of its potential impact on a project cost and quality. Reserves are useful to allow for currency fluctuations, risks, or opportunities. Contingencies occur in a number of shapes and sizes. The three most common are design, market conditions (bidding), and construction.

The definition example in Fig. 2.2 is a simple functional breakdown of a small project. The single alpha character code to identify each area may appear overly sim-

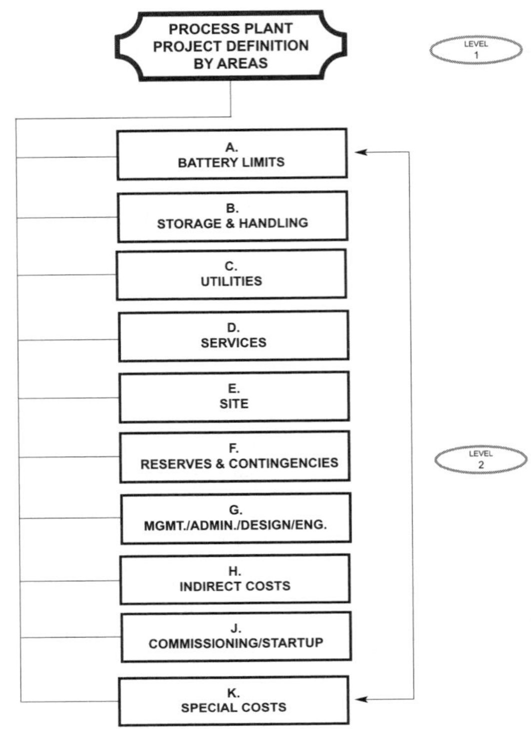

FIGURE 2.2 PROCESS PLANT PROJECT DEFINITION, LEVEL 2, AREAS. The project definition structure is coded and encompasses all aspects of a project, first from the perspective of the user of the finished facility, and also to inlude all costs that will be consumed by the project.

plistic and commonplace. The newness is in the treatment and identification of hard functional areas, as completed, and combining them with soft costs to create a coded project picture for project coordination and eventual cost control purposes. The new concept is the idea of an open, purposeful project framework that will be filled with detailed information, but only to the extent needed for project management purposes. Each coded area needs definition statements in terms of its quality, quantity, and eventually an estimated cost. The project budget is the total of the area budgets. Area definitions are not necessarily mysterious unless, as happens frequently, the project owners or users, in other words the customers, keep changing their minds or do not know what it is that they want or need.

The project is represented as a top-down structured development to identify, code, scope and quantify the completed facility at the functional level. The development leads to identifying and classifying the areas into their specific functional groups and providing more detail in a systematic way. It provides for an extension of the code system; a relationship is built in; continuity is provided.

The development of the definition structure using area E, Site, is demonstrated in Fig. 2.3.

The area codes are set as alpha characters at level 2. At level 3 the function codes are numeric. As part of the code, a special character "." is imbedded simply for il-

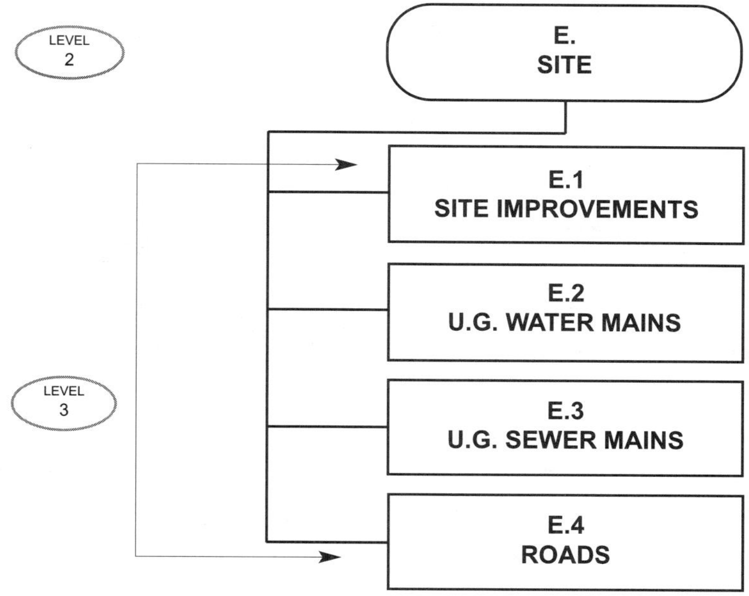

FIGURE 2.3 PROCESS PLANT PROJ-ECT DEFINITION, LEVEL 3, FUNCTIONS. Project areas are defined into their functions at level 3 of the definition structure and coded numerically.

lustrative purposes in this exercise. In computerized project management systems, the use of characters as a part of database codes is an important consideration. In real life the project management system designer should pay close attention to the selection of codes to ensure that they are meaningful and useful for all project purposes, as seen by the project owners, eventual users, designers, and the project managers. At best the code system chosen should be simple and flexible. In a multiproject environment it should be able to accommodate both large and small projects. For small projects it should not be necessary to carry large arrays of alphanumeric characters to identify small components. Conversely, for large projects the system needs to fit without major tinkering.

The system designers also need to consider that the code must be understandable to the project's users; that it be such that it becomes a part of the permanent facility's operational identification. Not only that, but it should also be suitable for other corporate purposes and, above all, computerization, not after the fact, but as part of the way things are done, records created, and information is communicated. If the project is one of many, or is similar to other undertakings, it is useful that there be consistency and continuity in the code systems.

To provide another example of definition at the project function level, Fig. 2.4 is a breakdown of area F, Reserves & Contingencies. In this example the definition of area F, Reserves and Contingencies, at level 2 is taken to the function level 3. F.1, Currency Exchange; F.2, Contingencies; and F.3, Reserves, at level 3. F.1 is taken to the subfunction level 4, coded F.1.1, Current Account, and F.1.2, Hedge Fund. F.2,

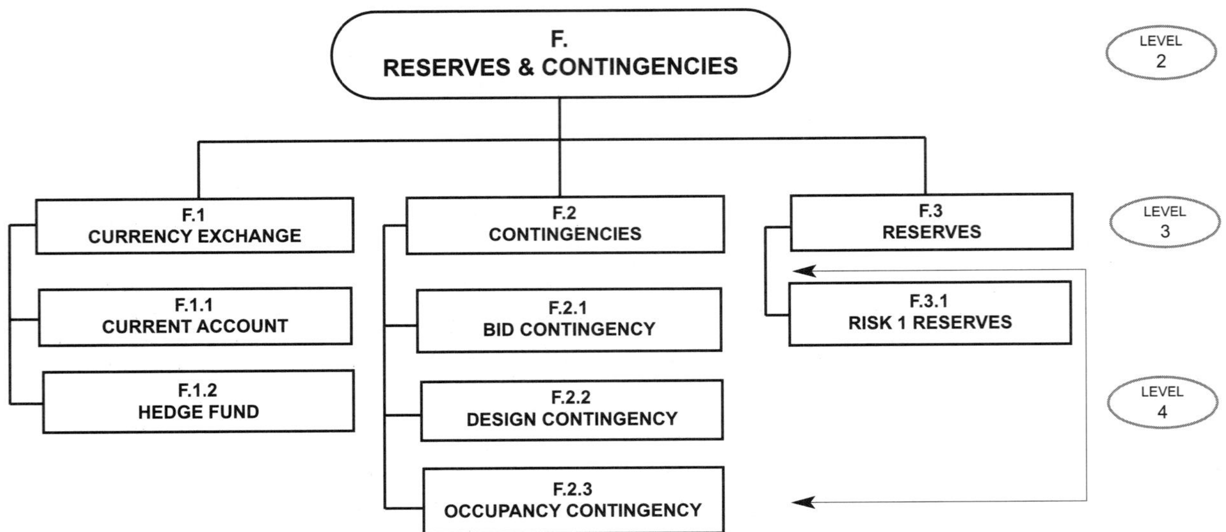

FIGURE 2.4 PROCESS PLANT PROJECT DEFINITION, LEVELS 3 AND 4, FUNCTIONS AND SUBFUNCTIONS. The definition structure and its code system are extended to level 4.

Contingencies is taken to the subfunction level 4 as subfunctions F.2.1, Bid Contingency; F.2.2, Design Contingency; and F.2.3, Occupancy Contingency. F.3, Reserves, shows an area called F.3.1, Risk 1 Reserves. The intent here is to show as simply as possible the definition of areas into functions and subfunctions through a related code structure. The degree and amount of area breakdown needed for a project is something for the project manager and the client to establish. This is generally a tougher call than may be thought. Systems methodologies are expensive. They cannot be done casually. They are no good in a vacuum. They don't come off a shelf. They are not cheap. And their impact is sometimes similar to what a bowling ball does to the ten pins at the end of the alley.

The foregoing examples define the project into user areas and area functions, and the functions are divided into subfunctions. The definitions are along the lines of the facility makeup as far as the hardware is concerned. As we are dealing with hardware and software, the soft costs that the project consumes are coded into the system along the same lines as the facility itself. The soft cost comprises money, design, engineering, management, and so on. The definition of hard, or direct, cost is self-explanatory, that is, it is whatever the "nuts and bolts" are aimed to do.

If the project happens to be a capital facility, such as a building, its definition as nuts and bolts, bricks and mortar, starts at the next lower level, level 5. At this level the project is changed from how the project users see it to how the project management team will deliver it. The delivery components comprise drawings, specifications, equipment, material, life support systems, instrumentation, and finishes, all incorporating human resources input (labor).

To demonstrate this aspect of the definition process, the exercise will be based on the process plant introduced before. Fig. 2.5 illustrates one vertical breakdown based on area B, Storage & Handling. It shows the definition breakdown of the storage and handling facility at level 2 down the vertical structure to level 7, Windows, for one building. To relate project terminology to Fig. 2.5, the following usage applies:

Level 1: Project—Process Plant

Level 2: Area—Storage & Handling

Level 3: Function—Raw Material Warehouse

Level 4: Subfunction—Raw Material Liquid Storage Area

Level 5: SubsubFunction—Storage Building

Level 6: Element Group—Building Exterior Envelope

Level 7: Element—Windows

Between Figs. 2.4 and 2.5 three additional levels of information have been introduced, seen as levels 5 through 7 and coded as a continuation of the adopted code system. The terminology for components at levels 2 through 5 is strictly user-specific, that is, fully geared to the project in question. Levels 6 and 7 in this example represent building element groups and elements, which will be discussed later.

The graphics and codes are demonstrated as simple connected parts and expanded alphanumerically in single vertical chains. The big picture, however, is a large pyra-

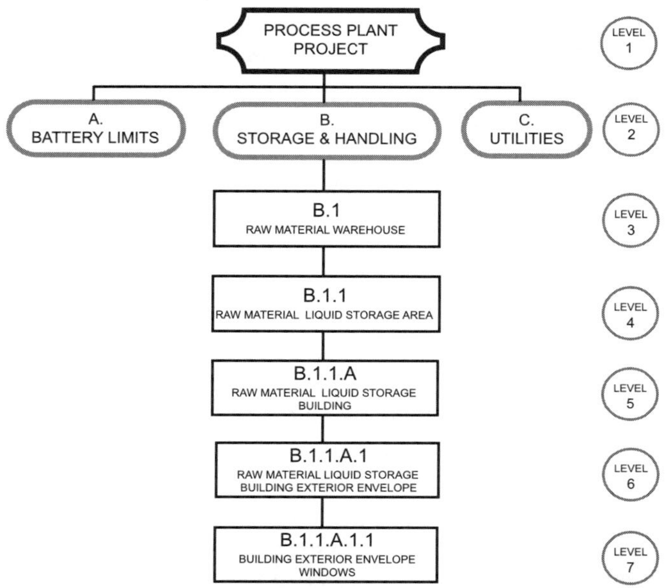

FIGURE 2.5 PROCESS PLANT PROJECT DEFINITION, AREA B, STORGAGE AND HANDLING, CODED TO LEVEL 7. The concept is to create a project definition of the scope and quality of all the deliverables that create the finished area, B, from construction elements, as illustrated by the element Windows.

midal structure of a project made up of seven levels of connected, coded soft costs and hard parts. There is some other very important information that needs to be highlighted:

- The definition structure comprises deliverables only. Although the definition comprises hard permanent elements and soft cost services, both are project deliverables.
- The definition structure is not a list of tasks, but a list of the results of tasks. A definition structure is not a journey. It is the result of a journey; but only if the journey is successful.

2.4 Theory of Project Definition

This theory of PDS combines two distinct, diverse streams of project management thought and practice.

The first stream is based on practice by cost engineers in the chemical, petrochemical, and process industries in North America. In Europe Peart described in *Design of Project Management Systems and Records* coding systems which incorporated typical subjective cost codes, human resources codes, and multiproject codes. Cost engineers generally did not refer to PDSs nor to WBSs.

The second stream of project management theory is the development of the WBS.

The theory of project definition presented in these pages is based on both concepts. The difference is that both the cost engineering cost code and the WBS and code are made into the project code.

The process plant and related code examples presented earlier may seem simplistic to some and overly complex to others. The intent of the exercise is to point to the visualization of a theory of project definition, which identifies and structures project deliverables for any kind of undertaking.

For nonspecific projects the theory may be demonstrated by Fig. 2.6. The terminology in the PDS in Fig. 2.6 is based on a typical building project. Different projects will have different terms, as will be seen in other examples. But the project manager should not reinvent the wheel in the design of the project code system. This is particularly true in corporate environments that have a history of project work. One cannot just introduce any definition breakdown and expect it to be useful and fulfill project management expectations.

An aspect of project management design that receives much attention is the concept of multiproject control. This concept can be visualized through the content of Fig. 2.7, which illustrates the PDS to the function level. The levels below functions would be the same as those in Fig. 2.6. Project managers need to be able to visualize a very large pyramidal definition structure with this kind of an approach.

Corporate capital work is sometimes called a program. A program could comprise a number of projects. Naming them programs, multiprojects, projects, or subprojects is a matter of corporate decision making. It stands to reason that the simpler

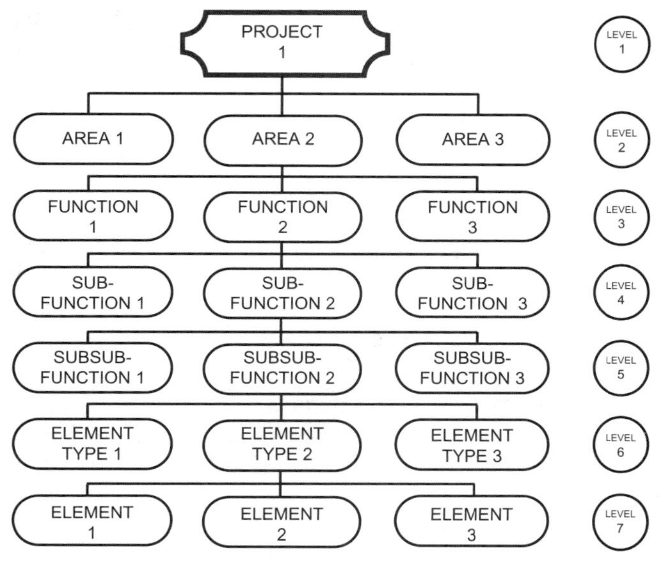

Figure 2.6 Generic Project Definition Structure. This concept and the related code system are applicable to any kind of project definition.

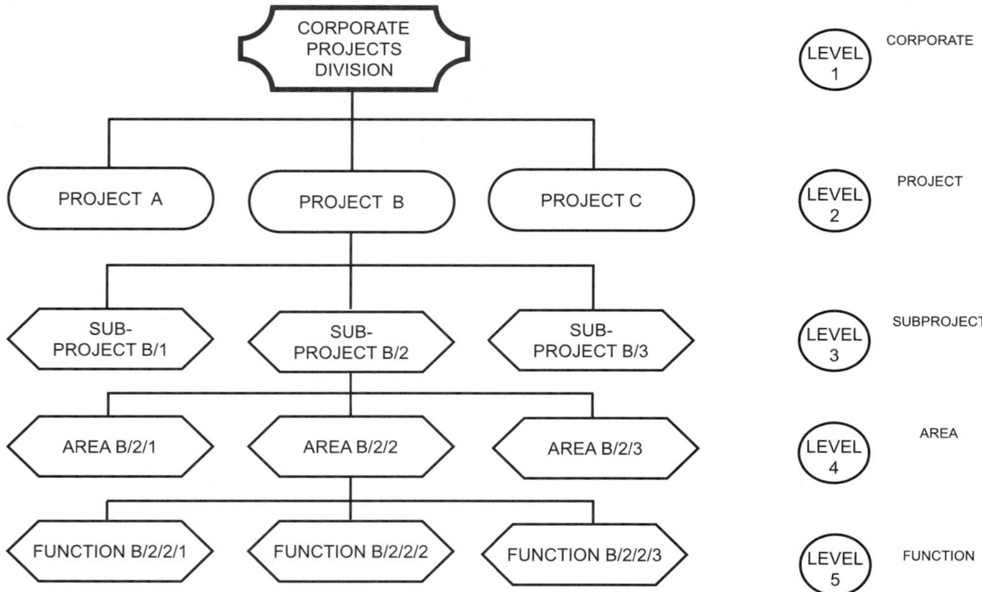

Figure 2.7 Generic Multiproject Definition Structure to Level 5, Functions. If corporate projects are considered as parts of a program, or if the project control system treats them as members of a multiproject system, both the structure and the code system need to reflect that.

the code system, the easier it is to process and manage information. A management system that can be served by a simple code structure is preferable to one that requires large, complicated codes.

Is it necessary to tie together elements from project to project, or does the manager of projects have enough information for control purposes at higher or summary levels?

In drawing PDSs, as seen in Figs. 2.6 and 2.7, the intent is to generate code systems that will identify and label project elements for the measurement of project parameters such as scope, quality, cost, and schedule.

Figure 2.6 shows a single project code. Level 1 represents the project; level 3 shows functions; level 5 shows subsubfunctions; and so on. This is representative of a single PDS.

To show a multiple-project environment, Fig. 2.7 depicts the corporate projects division at level 1 of the PDS. The projects division would have a number of projects underway at any given time. A project function in this case occurs at level 5; subsubfunctions would occur at level 7; and so on. As the basis for a project control system, this is obviously a deeper, more complex code than that shown in Fig. 2.6. It is the basis for a multiproject code system.

To illustrate, a code that would emanate from Fig. 2.7 might be similar to the concept seen in Fig. 2.8. The × designators could be alpha characters, alphanumerics, or numerics. The / character could be any other, such as ., :, or ', or it may be eliminated altogether.

That project coding in multiproject environments is important for project cost control can be demonstrated by a number of references.

Hackney assigned four digits to a project in a multiproject code system, followed by three digits to depict the function, subfunction, and a unit number, followed by two digits to show material class and specific type, followed by a single digit to depict labor, material, or subcontract.

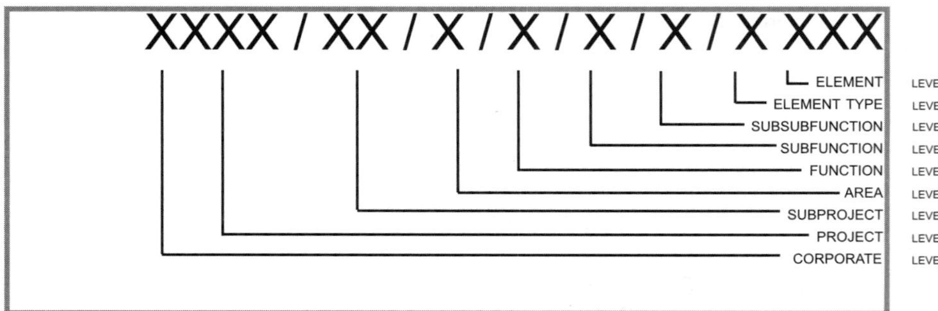

FIGURE 2.8 GENERIC MULTIPROJECT DEFINITION STRUCTURE CODE SYSTEM TO LEVEL 9, ELEMENTS. This is a multiple-project code system that derives from a definition structure such as that seen in Fig. 2.7.

The digits are in significant positions in the array separated by special characters, as depicted in the array of ×s that follows, for a total of thirteen characters, including the special characters:

××××.×××-××.×

Peart used the first digit to depict an export or a domestic project, the second digit depicts a fixed price or cost-plus contract, the third digit a product group, and the last two digits a sequential number in the group, for a total of five digits with no separators:

×××××

Clark and Lorenzoni depicted the individual project make up as area (two digits), main cost source, that is, labor, material, or subcontract (two digits), a subsource, that is, element (one digit), and a detail element (three digits), with dividers as follows:

××-×-×-×××

Miller presented a cost coding system in which the first two digits identify a component of the plant; the next two digits identify the function and its subfunction; the next three digits identify the construction element; and the final digit identifies a detail of the construction element, for a total of eight digits, with significant fields separated by spaces:

×× ×× ××× ×

The four code system concepts depicted here are not meant as stand-alone systems. They are invariably combined with a human resources code, a material code, or a subcontract code. If the projects being coded are part of a multiproject control system, they would be preceded by a corporate projects code number system, as discussed and illustrated in Fig. 2.8.

In this multiproject code diagram the project itself is considered to be at level 2 of the definition structure. The lowest level, level 9, defines an element. If there is no need for a subproject, one level is eliminated, thus simplifying the code. This is true also if the subsubfunction is eliminated. If both subsubfunction and subproject are eliminated, or are not required, the code structure is further simplified, and there are that much fewer data to be processed.

In the design of the project definition code system, the corporate managers and the project manager must establish the degree of detail that will be applied to the lowest level of information. For example, is it necessary for the element at level 9 of a project to be labeled with the entire project code array consisting of the 20 characters seen in Fig. 2.8, or is it enough to label it only within that level, and the next level within that level, and so on, up the structure until a point is reached where it

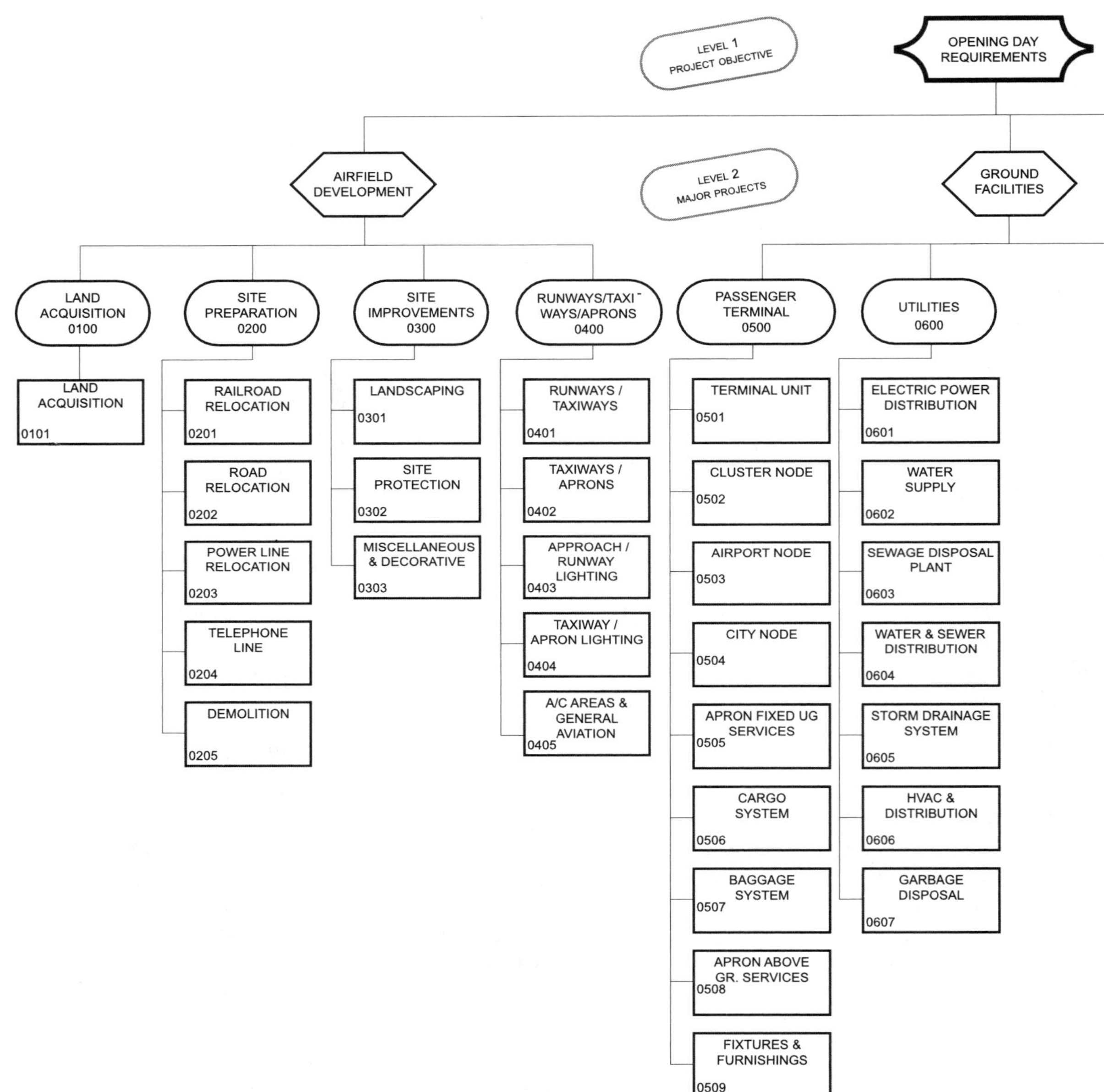

FIGURE 2.9 AIRPORT PROJECT DEFINITION STRUCTURE AND CODE CONCEPT. The structure shows the defining deliverables of an airport project based on the theory of project definition, which requires that the projet soft costs, to be consumed, also be shown.

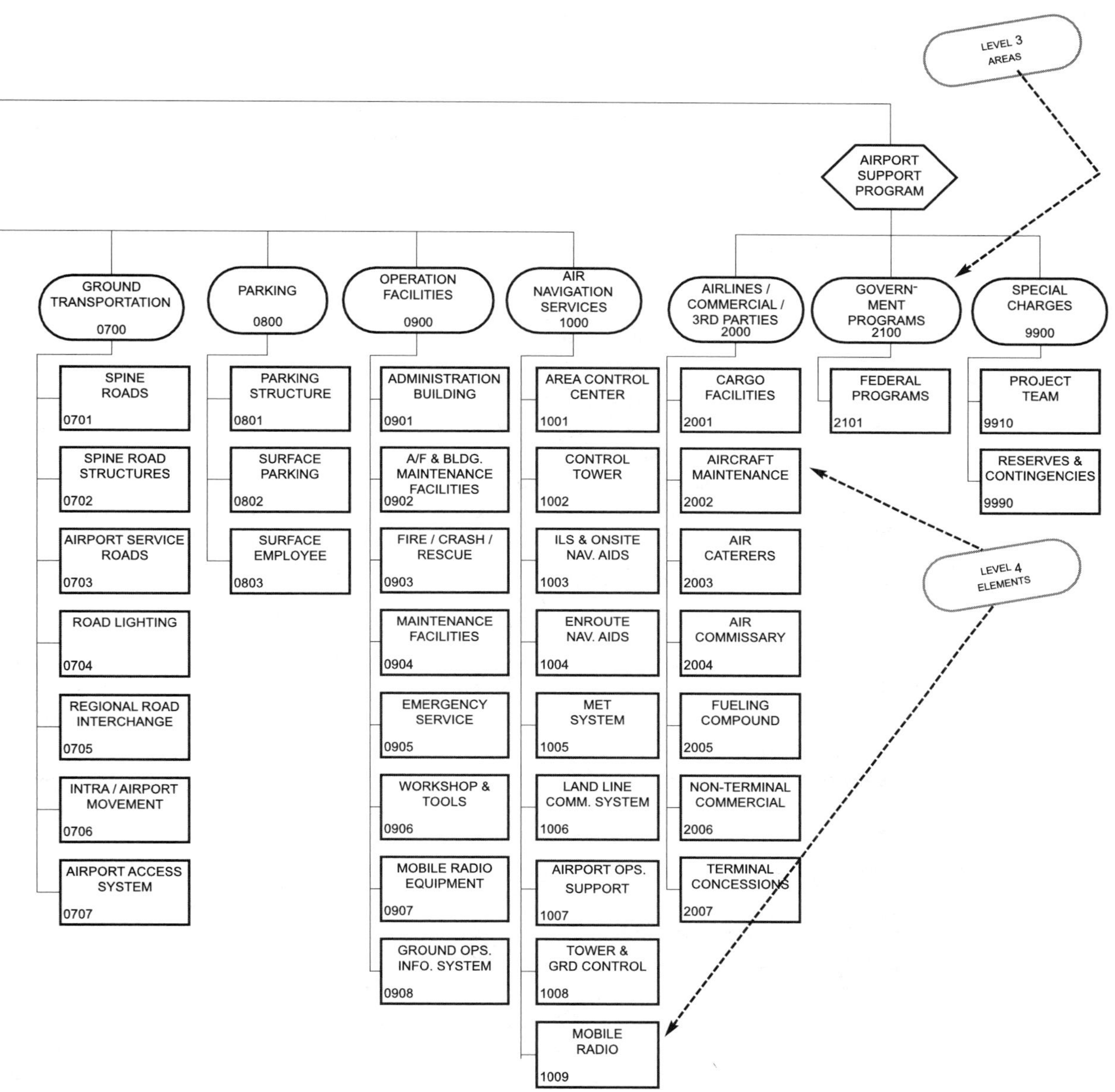

FIGURE 2.9 (CONTINUED).

becomes necessary to code that level with the full project code for comparisons to like levels in other projects at that particular level.

2.5 Airport PDS Example

The concept of project definition and the related project code system are based both on facility function codes developed by cost engineers for process plant projects and on the hierarchical breakdown, known as the WBS. This example is based on WBS.

The first example is of an international airport project. An airport project perhaps is as far removed from a process plant as one can get in terms of technology and facility usage. A process facility converts crude oil or natural gas into polyethylene, jet fuel, or some other useful derivatives. An airport is meant to handle planes, people, and cargo. When is an airport like a process plant? Only when they are both projects; when they are being scoped, conceptualized, designed, and delivered; when they are consuming capital and employing human resources in the delivery process, and before any payback has started.

In conceptualizing an airport, the project designers are confronted with the problem of what to tackle first: the runways? the terminals? airside? landside? all of them? The right answer is, all of them. A first question is how much, and what quality of each area of the airport project is needed for a viable facility. And this is where a system of project definition starts to come into play.

The airport project needs enough of each facility to open to serve the people and planes it is meant for. Anything more than just enough is a frill, and anything less may be a reduction in the quality of the service to be provided by the finished facility. The principle of just enough (and just on time) is highly recommended for all project definition work. If followed successfully, it works well in keeping cost down and projects on schedule. The big problem that the project manager faces at the start of a project is ascertaining the operating managers' requirements, and convincing them that bigger everything is not necessarily better.

The airport project scope is stated as Opening Day Requirements. Identifying minimum requirements, and coordinating and controlling the scope and quality as the project goes from feasibility through to the opening day is a nightmare of complexity, regardless of the cost and schedule considerations. Figure 2.9 depicts the airport definition exercise to level 4 of the structure.

Level 1 is the project objective. Level 2 of the structure shows three major projects, Airfield Development, Ground Facilities, and Airport Support Program. The three major projects are broken down into thirteen areas at level 3. The areas are broken down into elements at level 4. Neither level 1, Opening Day Requirements, nor major projects at level 2 are coded in this case, but they could have been. Areas at level 3 and elements at level 4 are coded with significant digits.

The next step lists the level 4 elements in tabular form, with provision made for additional coding below the element level, as seen in the two sets of zeros appended to each array, as illustrated in Fig. 2.10.

Code	Description
01010000	Land Acquisition
02000000	Site Preparation
02010000	Railroad Relocation
02020000	Road Relocation
02030000	Power Line Relocation
02040000	Telephone Line
02050000	Demolition
03000000	Site Improvements
03010000	Landscaping
03020000	Site Protection
03030000	Miscellaneous & Decorative
04000000	Runways/ Taxiways/Aprons
04010000	Runways / Taxiways
04020000	Taxiways / Aprons
04030000	Approach / Runway Lighting
04040000	Taxiway / Apron Lighting
04050000	A/C Areas & General Aviation
05000000	Passenger Terminal
05010000	Terminal Unit
05020000	Cluster Node
05030000	Airport Node
05040000	City Node
05050000	Apron Fixed UG Services
05060000	Cargo System
05070000	Baggage System
05080000	Apron Above GR. Services
05090000	Fixtures & Furnishings
06000000	Utilities
06010000	Electric Power Distribution
06020000	Water Supply
06030000	Sewage Disposal Plant
06040000	Water & Sewer Distribution
06050000	Storm Drainage System
06060000	HVAC & Distribution
06070000	Garbage Disposal
07000000	Ground Transportation
07010000	Spine Roads
07020000	Spine Road Structures
07030000	Airport Service Roads
07040000	Road Lighting
07050000	Regional Road Interchange
07060000	Intra / Airport Movement
07070000	Airport Access System

Code	Description
08000000	Parking
08010000	Parking Structure
08020000	Surface Parking
08030000	Surface Employee
09000000	Operation Facilities
09010000	Administration Building
09020000	A/F & Bldg. Maintenance
09030000	Fire/Crash/Rescue
09040000	Maintenance Facilities
09050000	Emergency Service
09060000	Workshop & Tools
09070000	Mobile Radio Equipment
09080000	Ground Ops. Info. System
10000000	Air Navigation Services
10010000	Area Control Center
10020000	Control Tower
10030000	ILS & Onsite Nav. Aids
10040000	Enroute Nav. Aids
10050000	Met System
10060000	Land Line Comm. System
10070000	Airport Ops. Support
10080000	Tower & Grd Control
10090000	Mobile Radio
20000000	Airlines/Commercial/3rd Parties
20010000	Cargo Facilities
20020000	Aircraft Maintenance
20030000	Air Caterers
20040000	Air Commissary
20050000	Fueling Compound
20060000	Non-Terminal Commercial
20070000	Terminal Concessions
21000000	Government Programs
21010000	Federal Programs
99000000	Special Charges
99100000	Project Team
99900000	Reserves & Contingencies

FIGURE 2.10 AIRPORT PROJECT DEFINITION STRUCTURE CODE SYSTEM. The purpose of the definition structure is to define and code the deliverables for all project management purposes. Each element has a relatable position in the project, identifiable by its structural code.

Although maybe not evident from the two simplified illustrations, the airport PDS would generate a large amount of coded information as project areas, functions, subfunctions, subsubfunctions, element groups, and elements.

If the entire PDS were drawn, it would resemble a pyramid or a giant Christmas tree. The code system would be expanded accordingly. Figure 2.11 demonstrates the idea of pyramid and code, tied to language which names the descending levels of the database of project information.

Figures 2.8 through 2.11 depict project definition structuring. The idea of a breakdown is to set up a code system to control project scope and quality, and its cost and schedule.

A definition breakdown aims to define deliverables. These are not tasks, but the results of tasks.

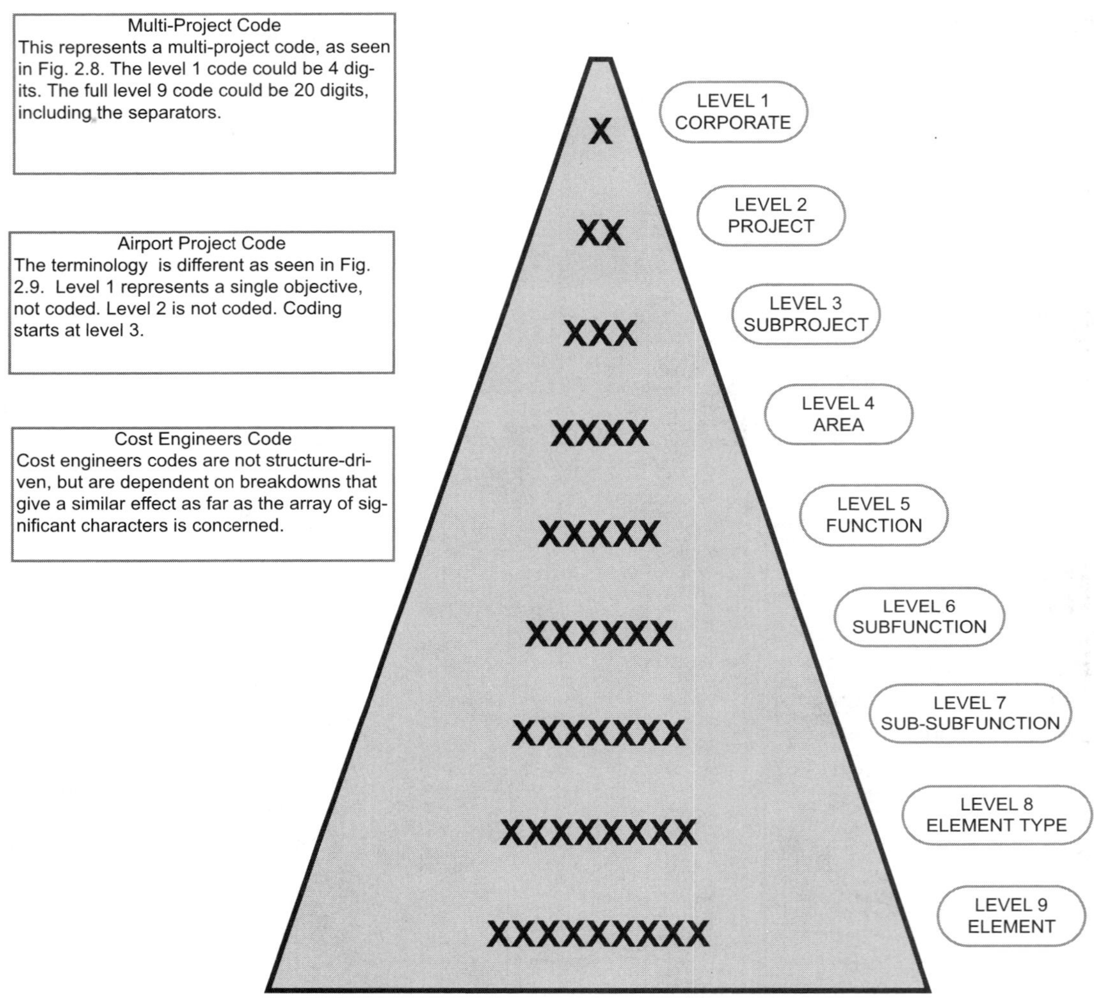

Multi-Project Code
This represents a multi-project code, as seen in Fig. 2.8. The level 1 code could be 4 digits. The full level 9 code could be 20 digits, including the separators.
Airport Project Code
The terminology is different as seen in Fig. 2.9. Level 1 represents a single objective, not coded. Level 2 is not coded. Coding starts at level 3.
Cost Engineers Code
Cost engineers codes are not structure-driven, but are dependent on breakdowns that give a similar effect as far as the array of significant characters is concerned.
X
XX
XXX
XXXX
XXXXX
XXXXXX
XXXXXXX
XXXXXXXX
XXXXXXXXX
LEVEL 1 CORPORATE
LEVEL 2 PROJECT
LEVEL 3 SUBPROJECT
LEVEL 4 AREA
LEVEL 5 FUNCTION
LEVEL 6 SUBFUNCTION
LEVEL 7 SUB-SUBFUNCTION
LEVEL 8 ELEMENT TYPE
LEVEL 9 ELEMENT

FIGURE 2.11 GENERIC PROJECT DEFINITION STRUCTURE AND CODE SYSTEM. The intent is that any project may be structured, but along meaningful, user-specific lines with functional relationships, and coded to create project memories so that what is delivered is comparable to what was intended, in terms of scope, quality, and cost. This leads to project control.

In these four graphic illustrations only the hard deliverables are shown (except for code 9900 in Fig. 2.9). Soft costs such as contingencies, design, engineering, management, and administration must be included in any PDS. They are a part of every project. Their presence is the difference between project work and a laundry list of a facility.

The airport project is an example of the concept of project definition applied to a large complex civil undertaking. The concept could be used to define residential, commercial, and public works.

The idea is to see the theory as a principal developer of project scope and quality. More than that, it will be seen that the system is the genesis of a management and project control methodology.

2.6 Research Center PDS Example

This example is based on the cost engineering approach of defining project functions. It could be drawn as a WBS.

A modern high-technology research center comprising chemistry, physics, and material engineering laboratories and their support services, all requiring a wide assortment of power and piped services, is representative of a most challenging and complex project. The challenge in this case was to deliver a new and expanded research facility to a corporate owner whose main focus was the marketing of high-technology products. The corporation was a sophisticated, technology-driven, repeat multiproject plant builder. The new unit was for a research group consisting of highly skilled and experienced managers, Ph.D. scientists, engineers, technicians, and administrative personnel, a demanding client user group indeed.

The project manager's role was to deliver a research facility that will meet corporate guidelines and the scientists' needs. Consider the potential pitfalls that may exist in such an environment. Tough, demanding, savvy corporate managers on the one hand, scientific specialists on the other. How are you going to keep them all satisfied and happy. The corporate managers will do almost anything to save, or not spend, corporate funds, including not seeing the project go ahead. And the scientists? Well, it can never be big enough or advanced enough to do things which even they may not yet understand, but hope to solve and be in line for a promotion, a visiting postdoctoral fellowship, or, indeed, a Nobel prize in chemistry or physics.

That was approximately the scene for the project manager to come in and start applying the systems of project management, starting with project definition. It should be understood that a project manager in this kind of an environment is a servant to both the corporate managers, whose role is to enforce corporate standards and guard the corporate treasury, and the corporate and lab-located scientists in research and development, whose job it is to improve existing products or develop new ones for which corporate marketing have identified a niche.

The project definition list seen in Fig. 2.12 is the result of an intensive, time-limited exercise of understanding corporate standards and project expectations, of determining the corporate research objectives, and finally of establishing and recording the research center user needs and preferences. In architect circles this kind of exercise may be referred to as facility programming and developing space schematics and flow diagrams. In the systems of project management it is known as defining the project, which resulted in a facility project program, the main feature of which is the list in Fig. 2.12.

The project definition seen in Fig. 2.12 is not easy to create. Input from hard-pressed scientists and users provides bits and pieces of individual requirements and

RESEARCH CENTER
PROJECT FUNCTIONAL AREAS

CODE	DESCRIPTION
A	PHYSICS & ENGINEERING
C	MATERIALS & EXPLORATORY RESEARCH
E	COLLOIDS & INTERFACE
G	MATERIALS & CONTROL ENGINEERING
H	POLYMERIZATION
I	COMMON RESEARCH
J	FUTURE RESEARCH
K	ADMINISTRATION & TECHNICAL SERVICES
M	SHIPPING/RECEIVING/STORAGE
N	MAINTENANCE (BUILDING)
O	MECHANICAL & ELECTRICAL SERVICES
P	OUTSIDE SERVICES
Q	PROJECT MANAGEMENT
R	DESIGN/DRAWINGS/SPECS/CONTRACT DOCS.
T	MOVING & OCCUPANCY
Z	RESERVES & CONTINGENCIES

FIGURE 2.12 RESEARCH CENTER PROJECT DEFINITION LIST, FUNCTIONAL AREAS. This represents a project definition structure in the form of a table of functions as seen from the perspective of the users of the finished project, written in project management terms, if only because areas Q to Z are included. In project management terms these areas are considered at level 2 of a single project structure, and become the basis for the first project codes for all scope, quality, and cost references.

expensive wish lists, which they themselves may know are unrealistic. Corporate managers on the other hand could be impatient, highly structured, and wanting hard financial answers to definition questions that are in the process of being established. This coded project definition list evolved through the actions of the project manager working closely with the manager of administration, the research center director, and corporate project management. It is a team task from day one.

The project functional areas in Fig. 2.12 are seen to be identified and coded with a single alpha character. The alpha code is the basis for what could be an extensive scope, quality, and, eventually, cost system. The code defines and glues together the various aspects of the project. As is seen, the area names in this case describe a function. In some cases, area descriptions may be synonymous with user department organization titles. And provision must always be made for project soft costs, as seen in codes Q through Z.

The next level of definition consists of the functional breakdown of each area. The parameters were identified as:

Building Spaces
Research Equipment
Fixtures & Furnishings
People.

As the project is primarily a facility, the size and quality of the space itself was of prime consideration and was looked at first. Facility space was seen as:

Labs
Offices
Other Spaces

The definition exercise up to this point has generated orderly project information, which in project definition parlance defines and codes areas, their functions, and their subfunctions. Coded, the information would look like:

A User Functional Area
S Building Space
L Lab Space
M Other Space
O Office Space

This rather simplistic exercise would generate a code system, as seen next, and which would be used to control the project scope development exercise. For example, in the Physics and Engineering Department the coded spaces might have the following labels or definition codes:

ASL Lab Space
ASM Other Space
ASO Office Space.

The next level of definition was at the subfunction of each of the lab functions, offices, and other spaces. In the case of area A, Lab Space, specific-use labs were identified and coded. For example, one lab was:

ASL1.2-8. Laminar Flow Room

This specific room is in area A, Physics and Engineering. S is the space indicator, L stands for lab space. The numeric 1 indicates the first functional grouping in the Physics and Engineering area, and 2 is to represent the Imaging Application Group. The numeric 8 is assigned for Vacuum Coating.

After discounting the simplistic breakdown process, the important consideration is that the definition structure and code system are driven not by architectural, engineering, or construction considerations, but by a system oriented to the way in which users will see their finished facility. At the same time the project manager is developing a systems base for the scope and cost control measures, which are always some of the key responsibilities of the project manager. It should also become evident that the definition so far has very little relationship to a construction project. This will come in time, and there will be seen a very strong link between the construction project and the user-oriented functional definition.

2.6.1 Scoping the Research Center Project

Having the basis for a coded PDS, the project manager is in position to coordinate and, in the process, exercise project control. In this case, as in most instances, the project owners, users, and the project manager had an idea as to what would be the size and scope of the new facility. But the numbers would be ballpark or order-of-magnitude numbers, that is, on the order of −30% to about +50%.

Sometimes project owners will make it known exactly how much they wish to spend on a project. In those cases the project manager will need to tailor the project to suit the stated budget. In the present case, although the project team had a ballpark figure in mind, the exercise was to establish the project size, scope, quality, and cost measures of the facility needed to house and equip the complex research operation. This could only be achieved by working with the research managers, who knew their research mandate, and within corporate guidelines as set by corporate managers, and through this process scope and size the project as labs, offices, and other spaces. The initial process was to work with net usable spaces and facilities needs. In this way the restrictions of architectural and engineering design are not being introduced until after the user space needs and relationships have been set. The final building would incorporate the architectural and engineering considerations. Essential features such as life safety measures would be incorporated into the facility design.

RESEARCH CENTER
PROJECT DEFINITION
FUNCTIONAL SPACE QUESTIONNAIRE

No.	Item		Description
1	Function Name		______________
2	Function Code		______________
3	Specifications & Requirements		
	3.1	Size	______________
	3.2	Environment & Services	
	3.2.1	Heating	______________
	3.2.2	Ventilating	______________
	3.2.3	Airconditioning	______________
	3.2.4	Exhaust	______________
	3.2.6	Lighting	______________
	3.2.7	Outlets	______________
	3.2.8	Telephone	______________
	3.2.9	Special	______________
	3.3	Finishes	
	3.3.1	Floors	______________
	3.3.2	Walls	______________
	3.3.3	Ceilings	______________
4	Space Relationships		______________
5	Other		______________
6	Diagrams		______________

Figure 2.13 Research Center Project Definition, Space Specifications and Requirements. This is to define the kind and quality of finishes of a functional area from the perspective of the occupant or user of the finished space.

Facility space is only one measure of project scope. Scope is also a function of facility performance and servicing. As the functional area spaces are identified, their quality is specified. In this case each space was tested against the questions listed in Fig. 2.13. Those questions may be suitable for general-purpose facilities, but for a research center, more demanding individual services are needed, as listed in Fig. 2.14.

RESEARCH CENTER PROJECT DEFINITION
FUNCTIONAL SPACE SPECIAL SERVICES QUESTIONNAIRE

No.	Item		Description
1	Function Name		____________
2	Function Code		____________
3	Space Services		____________
	3.1	Mechanical	____________
	3.1.1	Cold Water	____________
	3.1.2	Hot Water	____________
	3.1.3	Process Water	____________
	3.1.4	Deionized Water	____________
	3.1.5	Drain	____________
	3.1.6	Sink	____________
	3.1.7	Drinking Fountain	____________
	3.1.8	Compressed Air	____________
	3.1.9	Instrument Air	____________
	3.1.10	Natural Gas	____________
	3.1.11	Steam	____________
	3.1.12	Vacuum	____________
	3.1.13	Liquid Nitrogen	____________
	3.1.14	Fume Hood	____________
	3.1.15	Exhaust	____________
	3.2	Electrical Services	____________
	3.2.1	480 V	____________
	3.2.2	208 V	____________
	3.2.3	120 V	____________
	3.2.4	Bus Duct	____________
	3.3	Communication	
	3.3.1	Telephone	____________
	3.3.2	LAN Ethernet	____________
	3.3.3	A/V	____________
	3.4	Safety & Security	
	3.4.1	Safety Showers	____________
	3.4.2	Eye Wash Fountains	____________
	3.4.3	Sprinklers	____________
	3.4.4	Fire Hose	____________
	3.4.5	Extinguishers	____________
	3.4.6	Air Packs	____________
	3.4.7	Fire Blankets	____________

FIGURE 2.14 RESEARCH CENTER PROJECT DEFINITION, SPECIAL SPACE SERVICE REQUIREMENTS. In addition to typical service requirements, labs have special service needs, as scoped and defined by this sheet.

2.6.2 Advancing the Scope of the Research Center Project

In a research facility, as in most projects, there are standards based on safe practice and effective usage. There are norms based on experience to be followed. The project users and the project manager decide how much and to what extent the standards are to be modified, that is, improved for the project.

Examples of corporate facility standards are office sizes, furnishings, finishes, and facility specifications concerning safety and security. Then there are regulations imposed by local, state, and federal agencies. For example, government regulations require that a chemistry research lab have a secondary emergency exit. Similarly each single-bay lab must have a fume hood. The fume hood exhaust air velocity, and therefore the room air changes, is set as a corporate guideline, once local laws are met.

The corporate guidelines, safety measures, statutory regulations, and, most importantly, the users' own needs and preferences all affect the area and lab functions and therefore set the quality standards for the project. These measures are usually described by sketches and diagrams necessitating an expansion of the language of definition to include a structure, a code system, a book of words or a program, and drawings.

Figure 2.15 shows the type of sketch that may be used to expand the scope description of a unit in a research facility. Another, more complicated lab space with more functions and equipment is illustrated in Fig. 2.16. These kinds of sketches and diagrams are strictly functional representations of needs and requirements, which are

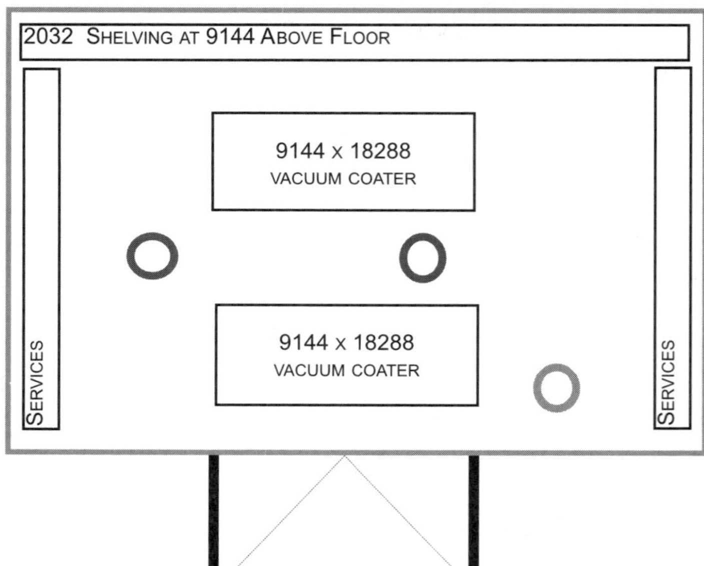

Figure 2.15 Research Center Project Definition, Sketch SK-ASL 1.2-8 (nts), Imaging Applications, Vacuum Coating Lab. This sketch is prepared from the lab user's input to establish the functionality of the space, to aid scope development, and to serve as an instruction to the architects and engineers.

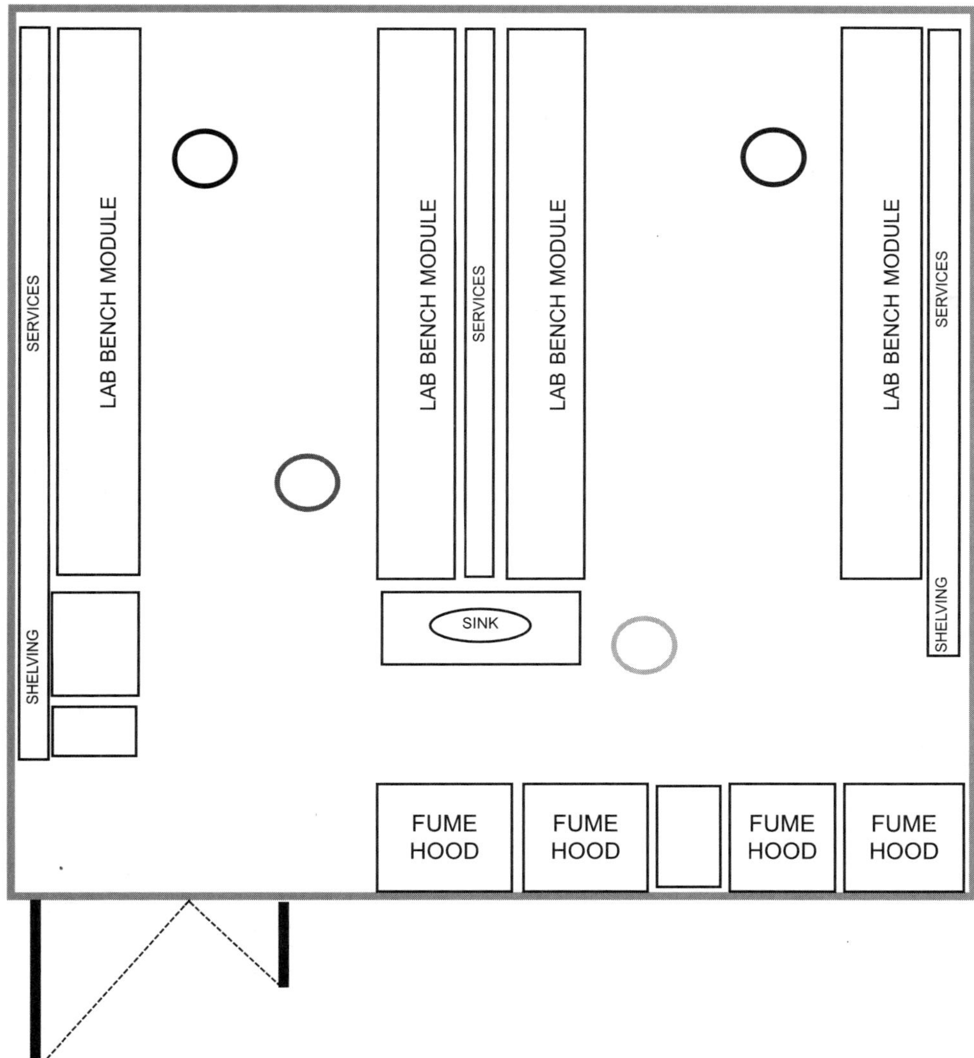

FIGURE 2.16 RESEARCH CENTER PROJECT DEFINITION, SKETCH SK-ASL 1.3-4 (NTS). This sketch aims to define the lab functions based on user needs, to develop project scope and quality, and to act as an instruction to the architects and engineers.

meant to augment words and numbers. They are not architectural or engineering drawings. Indeed, they are based on communications gathered from researchers by the project manager, long before the architects and engineers are on board. This is useful at this stage in that the users are not being influenced by design-driven professionals. What is being developed are user instructions for the design process. But the process is based on need, function, scope, and quality control as opposed to image and perhaps ego building.

To expand on the information in the sketch in Fig. 2.16 (which for the purpose of this book is simplified) and to make the scope and quality information complete for the designers, the sketch would be accompanied by space specification information. For complex lab areas the information would be augmented by space services sheets, as seen in Figs. 2.17 and 2.18.

2.6.3 Project Scope as A/E Concept Drawings and Specifications

To put the preceding steps of scoping and sizing the research center project into as broad a perspective as possible, and at the same time relate them to industry terminology, which is by no means standard, it is pointed out that the process of definition goes by many names. In an architectural and engineering environment the pro-

RESEARCH CENTER
SPACE SPECIFICATIONS SHEET

FUNCTION NAME: Paper Science, 2 Bay Chemistry Lab

FUNCTION CODE: ASL1.3-4

SPECIFICATIONS & REQUIREMENTS

SIZE	52 m^2
ENVIRONMENT	
Heating	Yes
Ventilating	Yes
A/C	Yes
Exhaust	Yes (See Space Services)
Electric Power	ditto
Lighting	ditto
Outlets	ditto
Telephone	ditto
Specials	ditto
FINISHES:	
Floors	V.T.
Walls	Painted
Ceilings	Open, Painted
SPACE RELATIONSHIPS	
OTHER	
DIAGRAMS	See SK-ASL 1.3-4

FIGURE 2.17 RESEARCH CENTER PROJECT DEFINITION, LAB ASL 1.3-4, SPACE SPECIFICATIONS. The listing of these finishes establishes the scope and quality of the space, as part of its definition, and serves to instruct the designers.

RESEARCH CENTER
SPACE SERVICES SHEET

FUNCTION NAME: Paper Science, 2 Bay Chemistry Lab

FUNCTION CODE: ASL1.3-4

SPACE SERVICES

MECHANICAL

Cold Water	Comp.Air (Plant)	Fume Hood
Hot Water	Comp Air (Inst.)	
Process Water	Natural Gas	
Deionized Water	Steam	F.H. Exhaust
Drain	Vacuum (Central)	
Sink	Vacuum (Special)	Drink Fountain

ELECTRICAL SERVICES

480 V	Lighting Intensity	Special
208V		
120V		
Bus Duct		
NEMA		

COMMUNICATION

Tel./FAX	Paging	A/V
LAN	WAN	Ethernet

SAFETY & SECURITY

Safety Shower	Fire Hose
Eye Wash	Extinguishers
Sprinklers	Scott Air Pack

FIGURE 2.18 RESEARCH CENTER PROJECT DEFINITION, LAB ASL 1.3-4, SPACE SERVICES. The listing of these special services establishes the scope and quality of the space, as part of its definition, and serves to instruct the designers.

cedure may be called programming. Programming is the process, by an analyst or architect, of interviewing the client to establish the client's systems or facility needs. If the project involves a process other than just space requirements, the programming might be led by a project engineer who would be supported by a group of analysts and designers.

The difference between definition as discussed here and traditional programming is that definition goes much further in that the result becomes the basis for a total concept of project control. This means that in addition to the establishment of the functional program, the procedure sets up a database concept and the basis for total scope and cost control. The result of programming in the traditional sense establishes a project program only.

The project program is sometimes called a "project brief." In certain corporate environments a project program may be called a "memo to accompany the appropriation request." Another term for project definition is the term "work breakdown structure (WBS)." If it is agreed that a PDS is a systems term, with all that it implies, a list of "near" synonyms, based on traditional usage, might be:

Project Definition Structure (PDS)

Project Program

Project Brief

Memo to Accompany Appropriation Request

Work Breakdown Structure (WBS)

In other words, they all might mean the same thing.

Keeping in mind what might be called the project management systems' "prime directive" that you first work with what is there, none of the terms is incorrect. In the case of the WBS the project management systems use that approach for the sole purpose of establishing tasks, as will be discussed at length in the next chapter, as compared to the PDS, which states the project in its functional terms as seen by the project users.

Project work is different from other work in that a project is different every day of its life if progress is being made. Thus the project manager, the users, and corporate management will eventually complete the process of definition to the extent that its scope, quality, and functions have been defined as much as it can be in words and sketch diagrams. The form of definition at this stage is probably a word-processed hard copy, some flow diagrams, not to scale sketches, and most likely contained in a three ring binder of anywhere from about a dozen to 200 pages, depending on the size and scope of the project.

During the project definition period, which itself may be in two or three stages, as will be discussed later, the architectural and engineering designers and other project specialists are selected. The project definition, or project brief, is handed to them as the project terms of reference, and the project enters a new stage in its life cycle, but still in the process of being defined. The architect or systems analyst as the design leader will develop a number of design concepts in response to the functional needs set by the users in the definition. Spaces and systems will be programmed and related. Provisions will be made to accommodate regulations. If the project is a building space, functional areas will be "grossed up" to incorporate corridors, stairs, washrooms, emergency exits, and mechanical and electrical spaces. It is expected that functional areas will be labeled in keeping with the project code system, not only to ensure that none are missed but as a means of scope and cost control from the definition program to the design concept. Building and systems performance specifications covering energy considerations, materials, finishes, and so on, will be prepared to the extent needed to establish concepts and enable the estimates leading to the funding approval.

If a project involves a building, the other design disciplines in addition to the architect are structural, mechanical, and electrical engineering. Because of the closeness of the architectural design to the structural frame, both architecture and structural engineering may be done in the same design shop. The structural engineering concepts consist of selection of the framing system, spans, materials of construction, and the development of enough engineering information to ensure that the architectural design will work and is constructable. As the project scope involves both quality and cost, the design has to be advanced enough to ensure that an accurate cost estimate can be made.

In a complex research center the mechanical systems are quite extensive. They can account for up to 50% of the overall construction cost. Conceptual mechanical engineering consists of flow diagrams, riser diagrams, HVAC air volumes, and loads for heating and cooling. The mechanical equipment rooms must be laid out and sized in cooperation with the functional needs, architecture, and structural considerations. Enough engineering needs to be done to relate mechanical systems to the building systems. Units such as heaters, pumps, thermostats, air mixing boxes, reheat coils, air diffusers, duct runs, pipe routes, vertical risers, and all similar components must be considered, included, and costed. This kind of information is shown on schematic drawings, based on architectural outlines, single-line diagrams, equipment tables, and outline performance specifications. But the information is intentionally limited to only what is needed to express the project definition and facilitate an appropriation-grade estimate.

The quality of electrical engineering information is similar to that for mechanical engineering. Electrical engineers will often wait for architectural, structural, and mechanical designs to be firmed up before they will make a move. This approach is better discouraged by the project manager as it preempts innovation. It will be a better project if all systems designers provide their best input before concepts are frozen, rather than some holding back and having decisions made by others. Electrical engineering in the concept definition stage consists of the design of the lighting systems, services such as communications and power distribution, control schematics, power loads, transformation requirements, and schematic layouts based on the architectural and mechanical engineering layouts. Again, the amount and quality of electrical engineering information needs to be enough to confirm an appropriation-grade estimate.

The objective of the definition exercise is to prove the project at each stage of the project life leading up to the appropriation of funds. The project information becomes progressively harder and more accurate as the project goes from the identification of the problem, or opportunity, to the conceptual drawings and outline specifications, which can be cost estimated by professional estimators to the required accuracy. A corporate owner, client, or agency can have confidence in this kind of an approach if there are measures in place to ensure that the process is being followed. That means that the project management team will deliver that which has been conceptualized and costed, and which has been "crunched" into the financial return-on-investment numbers, and is otherwise fully acceptable to management.

2.7 Summary

This chapter has presented a concept to define a project scope of work in terms of its size and quality from the point of view of the customers and users of the finished work. The definition is based on structuring a project using proven cost engineering principles in combination with the WBS. A PDS provides the basis for a project code, not only for cost control but for the management and control of all project parameters of quality, cost, and schedule. It is concluded through examples provided that project definition ends with concept drawings and specifications, which can be priced as an appropriation-grade estimate.

REFERENCES

Blok, F. G., "Contingency: Classification, Definition and Probability," *Trans. 7th Int. Cost Engineering Cong.* (London, UK, 1982), p. B3-1.

Blough, R. M., "More Construction for the Money," Summary Report of the Construction Industry Cost Effectiveness Project (The Business Roundtable, New York, 1983).

Clark, F. D., and A. B. Lorenzoni, *Applied Cost Engineering* (Marcel Dekker, New York, 1978).

Cleland, D. I., *Project Management, Strategic Design and Implementation,* 2nd ed., (McGraw-Hill, New York, 1994).

Hackney, J. W., *Control and Management of Capital Projects* (Wiley, New York, 1965).

Haviland, D. S., Ed., *Project Delivery Approaches, An AIA Guide* (American Institute of Architects, Washington, DC, 1976).

Hendrickson, C., and T. Au, *Project Management for Construction* (Prentice-Hall, Englewood Cliffs, NJ, 1989).

Miller, C. A., "Process Plant Capital Cost Estimating, a Science Rather than an Art, in *Cost Engineers Notebook* (Am. Assoc. of Cost Engineers, Morgantown, WV, 1992).

Peart, A. T., *Design of Project Management Systems and Records* (Gower Press, Farnborough, UK, 1971).

Schoemann, F. H., and M. J. Bachynsky, "Shortcut Capital Cost Estimating for Low-Volume Batch-Operated Plants," *Trans. Am. Assoc. of Cost Engineers* (Washington, DC, 1980, p. B.8.1).

Stewart, R. D., *Cost Estimating,* 2nd ed. (Wiley, New York, 1991).

Stuckenbruck, L. C., Ed., *The Implementation of Project Management, The Professional's Handbook,* Project Management Institute (Addison-Wesley, Reading, MA, 1981).

Stukhart, G., "Cost Management Report: The Business Roundtable Project," *Trans. Am. Assoc. of Cost Engineers* (*Proc. 8th Int. Cost Egineering Cong.,* Montreal, PQ, 1984), p. C.1.1.

Wysocki, R. K., R. Beck, Jr., and D. B. Crane, *Effective Project Management* (Wiley, New York, 1995).

QUESTIONS AND EXERCISES

2.1 What is the principal purpose of the project definition structure (PDS)?

2.2 Both cost engineering principles and PERT techniques gave rise to the concept of project definition. What is the main purpose of the cost engineering exercises? By comparison, what is the main purpose of the definition structuring associated with PERT?

2.3 Using the principles presented in this chapter, prepare a definition structure to level 3 based on the following expressions:

> Living room, Washrooms, Landscaping, Bedrooms, Garage, Soft costs, Contingencies, Living spaces, Grounds, Dining room, Move into new house, Kitchen, Financing and mortgage, Plumbing and drainage, Service areas, Heating and ventilating, Family room, Electric power and lighting, Paving, Landscaping, Utilities, Laundry room, Design, drawings and specifications

2.4 Based on the theories and examples presented in this chapter, prepare a coded PDS to the lowest level possible, based on the following array of expressions:

> Windows, Doors, Exterior cladding, Roofing, New house, Interior finishes, Excavation, Foundations, Substructure, Structure, Interior partitions and doors, Services, Windows, Brickwork, Electrical, Plumbing and drains, Heating, ventilating, and air-conditioning, Site development, Seeding and sodding, Slab, Steel frame, Exterior doors, Partitions, Driveway and sidewalks, Soft costs, Contingencies

2.5 Describe the main difference between the preceding two definition structures, using words such as scope, quality, customer, function, subfunction, element group, element.

3 WORK BREAKDOWN STRUCTURE

The work breakdown structure (WBS) creates tasks and activities to deliver the project. The project definition structure (PDS) discussed in the previous chapter defines completed project elements, as delivered to the customer, as a project, in project management language. Some see both structures as one and the same. They started out as one structure. It is very important to understand the differences, and where they intersect and hand off to each other.

This text shows that at least three breakdown structures are needed for effective project control. This is done by going back to the invention of breakdown structures and showing their evolution into current usage.

The use of PDS and WBS codes as "project glue" or "project language" is explained.

Not all structures are useful for project management purposes. "Good" and "bad" breakdowns are discussed. Descriptions of various work breakdowns, their validity and usage are discussed.

References are made to levels in breakdown structures.

Definitive terms such as project stages and phases and the resulting activities and tasks are defined.

Examples of the usage of WBSs are given.

The Cost/Schedule Control System Criteria (C/SCSC), which became a performance measurement system, are reviewed.

3.1 Purpose of the Work Breakdown Structure

A project cannot be controlled unless it is broken down into its tasks and coded for computer processing. The purpose of the WBS is to create the tasks.

As projects are unique, and project teams are formed specifically for individual projects, a common language or project "glue" is needed which keeps them together for key project objectives, such as scope, quality, budget, cost, and schedule control. That is why structures, including PDS, discussed previously, WBS, discussed in this chapter, and organizational breakdown structure (OBS) to be discussed in Chapter 4 are essential for project control.

Structures create coding systems, not only for project control purposes and computer processing, but also to provide information to corporate functions such as accounting, accounts payable, finance, banking, human resources management, operations, marketing, and information technologies. If the project does not have a dedicated project information system, including its coding system, someone other than the project manager may impose a system that may or may not meet the needs of project management objectives.

3.2 Evolution of Work Breakdown Structures and Codes

An early description of a WBS stated that the WBS is a method to establish tasks needed to be done to complete a capital project.

This is a simple definition with room for broad interpretation. At the beginning of the application of the concept, work breakdown was used to cover all aspects of project definition, including functions, stages of project work, work packages, corporate structures, and the various departments having a role in the project. Although this approach may be used, the aim is to move into the project management sysetms concept, which directs a project into at least three distinct but essentially inter-related vertical streams. The first of these is definition, the second is WBS, and the third is the functional organization.

Another early description of a WBS said that the WBS is a readily understandable method to systematically identify relatable packages of work or tasks which, when completed, create a project.

It is perhaps axiomatic that a task that consumes resources and time becomes its own product. If the task is defined, it should follow that the result of that task, the product or system, is defined.

In project work, however, the result of the work or tasks, the facility or a computer program takes on an identity that is totally different from the task itself, that is, it is the sum of all the tasks or activities. And that is why the definition of the project is along one set of parameters and values, and the work breakdown and identification of the tasks and activities follow another chain. Eventually the third or subsequent chains define the functional organizations that will deliver the tasks. Another description of a WBS is a means of fragmenting a complex project into its component parts and inversely summarizing the parts into the project. The WBS fulfills these key requirements:

1. WBS defines the work to be accomplished in manageable terms and establishes the relationship between the project and the end objectives.
2. WBS establishes the framework for summarizing costs for progressively higher levels of management.
3. WBS develops the units of work, which become the activities on a network for time planning, scheduling, and progress reporting.

4. WBS serves to integrate time, cost, and performance through one work classification and code system.

Although the preceding descriptions are not literally incorrect, they could be interpreted to mean that one breakdown is suitable for all project control purposes. That may be workable and desirable in some project environments, but it is not in keeping with the intent of the project management systems approach.

3.3 Earliest Work Breakdown Structures

The earliest project WBSs were single, multipurpose pyramids that combined area functions (deliverables) with tasks (activities). An example of such a structure based on an original WBS depicting a weapons system is illustrated in Fig. 3.1.

Figure 3.1 depicts a six-level structure, with the sixth level listing what could be tasks, or the deliverables from the tasks, that is, drawings and specifications. This kind of structure shows both end items and the tasks that contribute to their delivery. In the project management systems approach, the deliverables are defined by the PDS, which has an area for soft costs, and the activities are developed through the WBS. Thus there are two structures serving two distinct but integrated goals. Other systems recognized the need for this distinction, and most systems programs now have this recognition built in.

Another project management approach turned the tables on the approach to project management seen in Fig. 3.1 by first depicting the organization and then assigning work to it, as may be seen in Fig. 3.2.

The project management structure in Fig. 3.1 aims to break down a project by starting at the principal deliverable, the program or project, or the objective at level 1. The objective is then broken down through a connected pyramid until at about level 6 or level 7 and below, tasks being carried out by people are identified and coded. The idea is one structure for all project control purposes. What would happen with this approach is that the project code would need to be applied and used by all organizations working on the project. At the same time many contractors, subcontractors, and vendors would need to run their own in-house systems for their own corporate use. The pyramidal system could be very large and complex, and for that reason was subsequently modified.

The system seen in Fig. 3.2 was conceptualized to do the same thing. Except in this case the pyramid started with the organization at level 1, corporate divisions at the second level, projects at the third level, hard deliverables at the next levels, and finally tasks and components at the lowest levels. Referred to as the organizational analysis table (OAT), the concept produced massive, complicated codes for very large programs which were being undertaken by big corporations for even bigger clients, such as NASA and the Department of Defense.

These kinds of breakdowns, although on much smaller scales, are still being seen. Although not technically incorrect, they may not be suitable for the management of

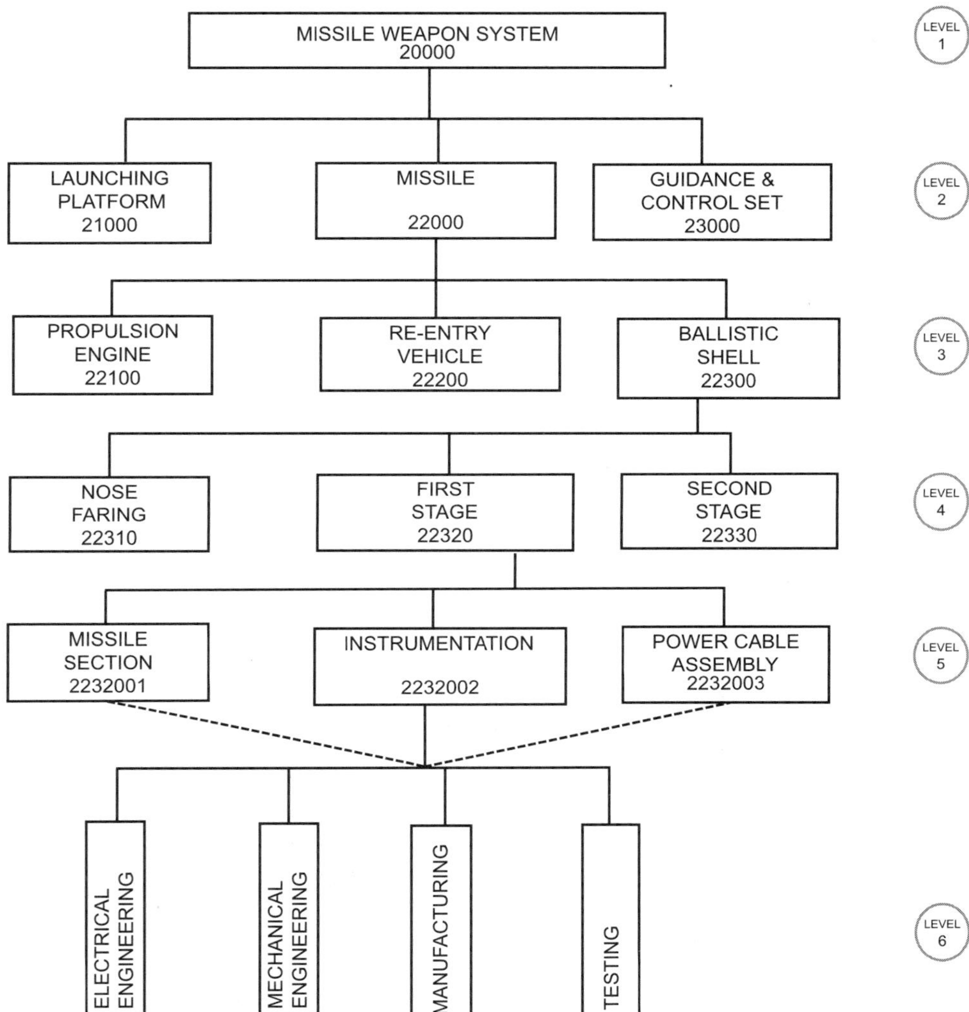

FIGURE 3.1 EARLIEST WORK BREAKDOWN STRUCTURE, MISSILE SYSTEM. This figure depicts the earliest work breakdown structure showing hard deliverables at the top of the structure, packages at level 5, and schedule activities at the lowest level of the breakdown, in this case level 6. The level 5 packages connected by dashed lines to level 6 would also be processed as activities.

multidisciplinary projects in the private sector and in public works organizations. Indeed, their imposition on some projects may be harmful in that they may deliver much less project management power than they promise.

Having looked at the genesis of the systems, their current equivalents are designed to be much simpler and decentralized, and deconstructed into a definition structure, a breakdown, and a functional organization structure. Their implementation re-

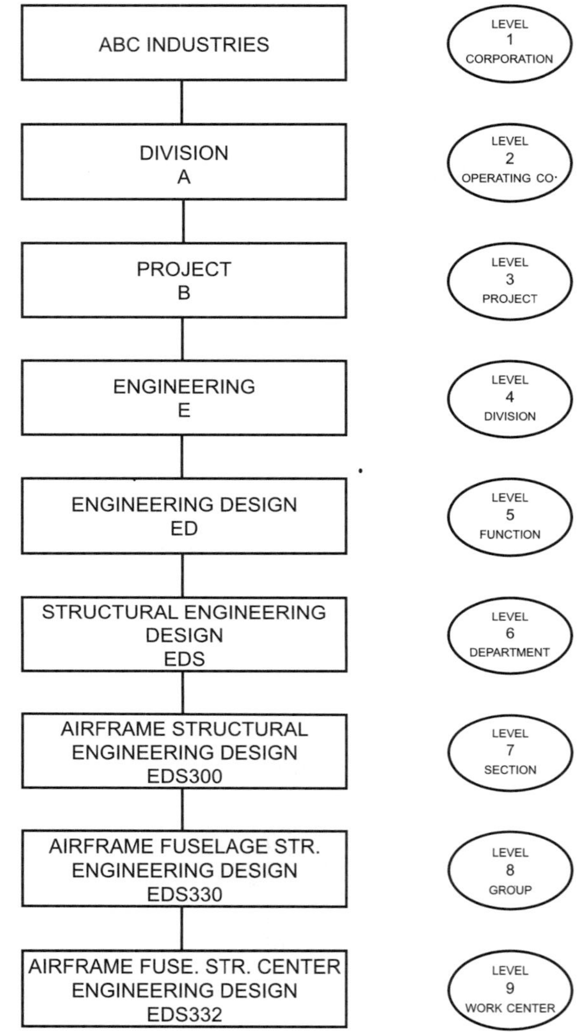

FIGURE 3.2 EARLIEST WORK BREAKDOWN STRUCTURE, ORGANIZATIONAL ANALYSIS TABLE. This breakdown method depicts the top-down structure of an organization, with the corporate divisions taking on projects for assignment to departments of human resources at the middle of the structure, e.g., engineering, and the packages and activities at the lower levels. If this structure is applied to the missile weapon system in Fig. 3.1, any of the elements at levels 1 through 5 could be the project at level 3 of the above structure.

quires that a system's prime directive be followed, namely, apply what is there, use what is known, and do not reinvent the wheel.

Although the earliest WBSs aimed project management in a new, modern direction, the process has evolved in the direction described in this text. But there are still many "bad," old-style breakdowns. The aim of this book is to see how to make a good breakdown, and to learn how to differentiate between a project definition and a work breakdown. These differences lead to the delivery of excellent project management services.

3.4 Performance Measurement Structures

Of the two WBSs depicted earlier, Fig. 3.1 includes descriptions of the elements along with the associated code numbers. The location of the number is significant in that it relates an element to its level in the project structure. The code numbers stop at level 5 of the structure. This is in keeping with PERT/Cost rules, which provide for cost codes at all levels of the WBS down to the lowest level, called packages of work. The activities for scheduling that flow from the packages were not coded for cost control purposes. The reason given then was that there would be a large quantity of detail generated, which would be difficult to manage and not necessarily helpful to the control of the project. With postmodern computers this is no longer the case.

Figure 3.2 depicts the OAT, which later became known generally as the OBS, the name by which it is most commonly referred to today. In this figure the associated code is shown as alphanumeric characters.

In Fig. 3.1 the structure starts by depicting five levels of hardware components, the deliverables or "things." Level 6 consists of activities or tasks, such as engineering, manufacturing, and testing.

In Fig. 3.2 level 1 of the structure is a corporation, that is, a "person" in the eyes of the law, a company of people. The "thing," in this case the project, occurs at level 3, and tasks and people activities occur at subsequent, lower levels.

That a single huge project structure was too complicated to manage became evident to customers of the WBS/OBS concept. In megaproject work, carried out by NASA type organizations, the idea of more than one structure, or a combination of structures, led to the evolution of the WBS/OBS-based performance measurement system. The U.S. Air Force added the "value earned for work accomplished" concept, which became C/SCSC. Figure 3.3 depicts an early WBS/OBS C/SCSC structure.

This concept is driven by two structures, a vertical WBS for the product (things) coding and a horizontal OBS for the people (tasks). The intersection of the two lines forms an account code, or cost account.

This concept, which comprises two or more structures of elements and tasks, continues to be the basis for most computer-aided project management systems.

3.5 The Less Traveled Project Cost Code Road

The use of WBSs, OATs, and OBSs and related PERT systems, designed for large-scale military and industrial projects, was encouraged as a new project management tool for the highly competitive, entrepreneurial private-sector construction industry. As the applications had to be simplified for the much more individualistic, fragmented private sector, and because of its cost and wide implications, the concept was never widely accepted.

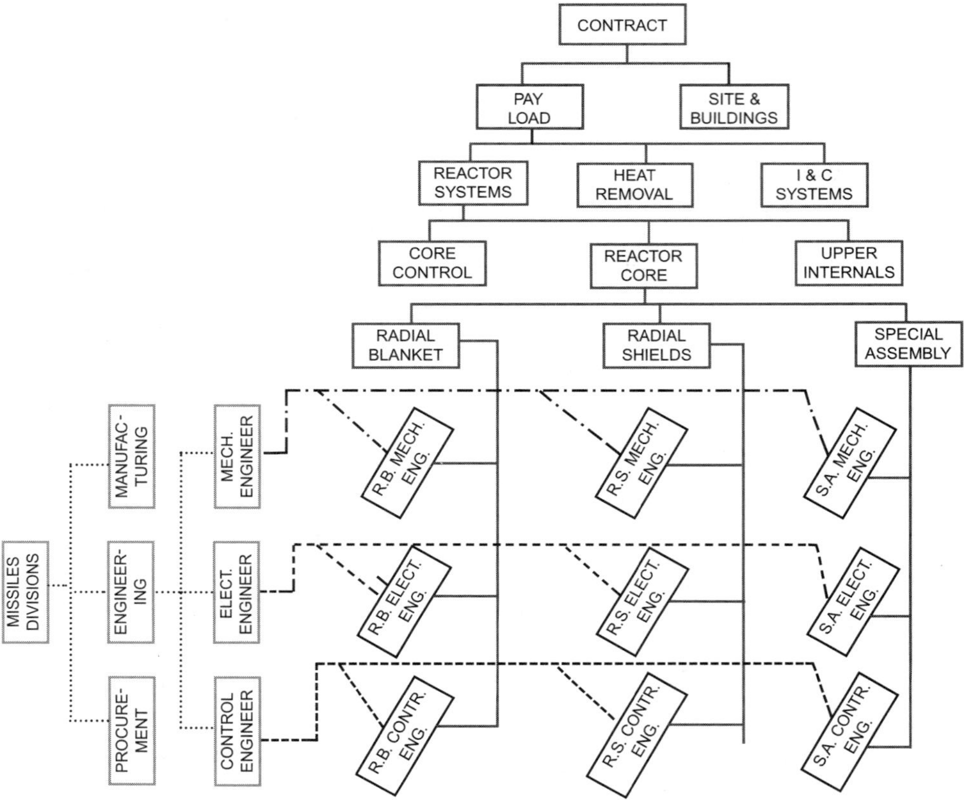

FIGURE 3.3 PERFORMANCE MEASUREMENT SYSTEM, C/SCSC WBS/OBS STRUCTURE. Project breakdown structuring evolved from a single WBS or OAT approach into the above "double-barreled" structure to reflect project deliverables and organizational tasks with the intent of creating project codes.

The private sector, particularly the multiproject process industry, was in the process of creating its own systems of project management, including cost code systems.

One such code system described by Hackney in *Control and Management of Capital Projects* is depicted in Fig. 3.4. In the terminology of this text, the cost code is seen as a derivative of project definition; its use is similar to that of a WBS-based code structure.

In *Applied Cost Engineering* Clark and Lorenzoni discussed the importance of coding in the preparation of accurate and reliable estimates, and designed the cost code illustrated here in Fig. 3.5.

The Fig. 3.4 code provides for the identification of the resources to be used (labor or material) in the last significant position of the 13 characters depicted. The labor and material may be classified further as required.

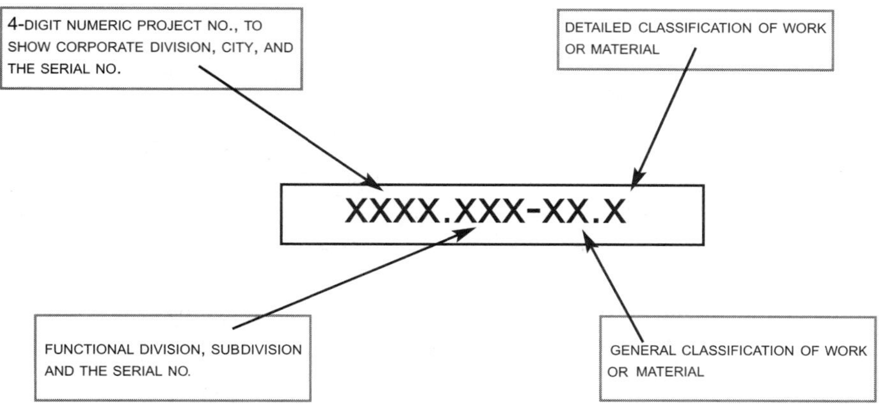

FIGURE 3.4 PROCESS INDUSTRY PROJECT COST CODE, BASED ON HACKNEY. This code system was developed at the same time as the WBS/OBS code systems for defense megaprojects. Although not based on definition and breakdown structures, the resulting codes are similar, and their use is to control project cost.

The Fig. 3.5 code makes provision to code resources in the third significant position of a 10-character field. Resources can be labor, materials (usually a purchase order), or a subcontractor (usually a contract or subcontract).

Although neither of these codes depicts a PDS, WBS, or OBS, it is seen from the code structure that the project is being broken down for control purposes. The importance of the construction code of accounts as the sole mechanism to link the scope of the project and its budget estimate with the actual cost cannot be overstressed. The code is in effect the dictionary for the language being used for all the scope cost records. It is essential for cost forecasting and cost reporting, the two main elements of project cost control.

The single structures seen in Figs. 3.1 and 3.2 are unsuitable for project control systems. The double-barreled structure in Fig. 3.3 is more suitable. But the codes in Figs. 3.4 and 3.5 show that scope and cost control need to identify three project issues:

- Scope defined as deliverables at various levels
- People activities and tasks
- Organizations that carry out the tasks and activities

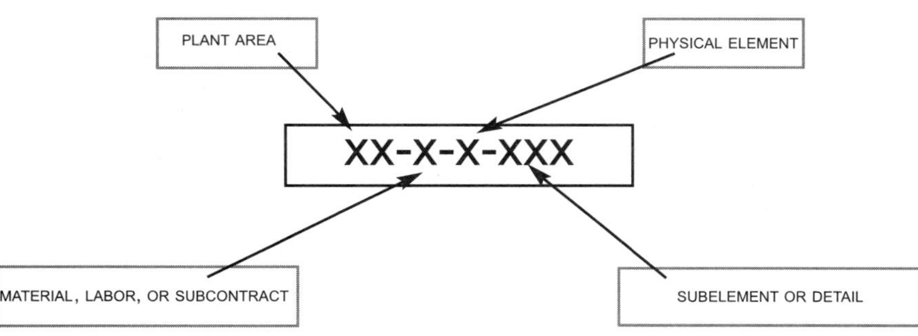

FIGURE 3.5 PROCESS INDUSTRY PROJECT COST CODE, BASED ON CLARK AND LORENZONI. This code system was developed at the same time as the WBS/OBS code systems for defense megaprojects. Although not based on definition and breakdown structures, the resulting codes are similar, and their use is to control project cost.

In this text the features of PDS, WBS, and OBS (to be discussed in the next chapter) will be combined with the concepts of project code systems, as practiced by cost engineers to create the systems of project management.

To illustrate the thrust of these systems further, Fig. 3.6 depicts an early application of a simplified PDS/WBS structure to develop a code system for an international airport project. The concept introduces the idea of two structures, one to define the deliverables, as seen in Chapter 2, and the other the tasks and their packages, and eventually the organizations responsible for the packages. The basis for the code system that resulted is seen in Fig. 3.6.

The project management systems approach used on the airport project is discussed extensively in this book, both to present project management fundamentals for definition, breakdown, and organization, and as a case history exercise.

Sometimes it is not clear in project work whether we are depicting a definition structure or a breakdown structure. Using the breakdown concept discussion from Chapter 2 and keeping in mind the basis for and the intent of the earliest breakdowns, as depicted in Figs. 3.1 and 3.2, as well as the concepts of code promulgated by the cost engineers, the idea of code as a function of a breakdown may be advanced as seen in Fig. 3.6.

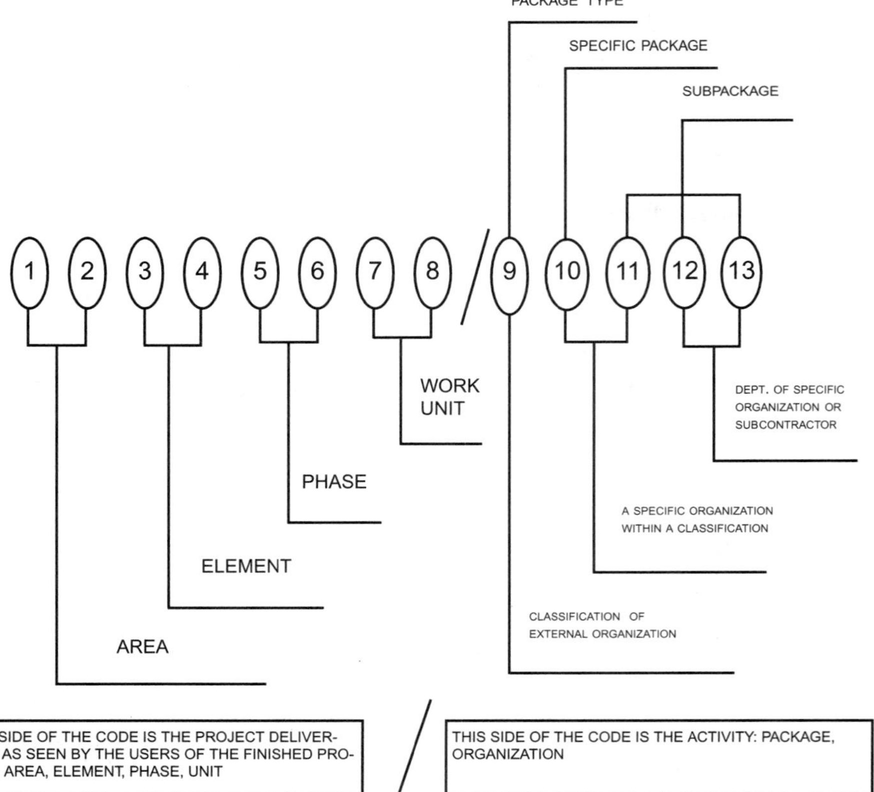

FIGURE 3.6 PROJECT CODE BASED ON CONCEPT OF PROJECT DEFINITION AND WORK BREAKDOWN STRUCTURES. The reason to break down a project is to define its components and create activities that will lead to its delivery. Both components and packages as well as their subcomponents and activities must be coded for control of all project parameters, including quality, cost, and schedule.

It is obvious that the code system in Fig. 3.6 looks nothing like the codes discussed and demonstrated in Chapter 2. The message to look for is that the earliest WBSs intended the kind of project code depicted in Fig. 3.6. Whether the approach was from the elemental objective at level 1, as seen in Fig. 3.1, or the corporation at level 1, as seen in Fig. 3.2, the intent was and is to identify and code project deliverables, project activities and packages, and the project organization.

3.6 Characteristics of Work Breakdown Structures

Work is action. WBSs define actions. That is the difference between work breakdown and project definition. PDS defines the deliverables. The WBS codes the activities and packages.

The PDS in Chapter 2 looks like a WBS. It is, and it is not. The intent of a definition structure is to relate the completed project to the owners or users of the completed facility. The users, as the project customers, not being project professionals may not know or not have the time to follow what is happening in the development of the project, so that it is up to the project manager to scope the project, set the quality standards, and provide the cost estimate.

This is best done in a language that is understandable to the users, if only because the facility is being delivered for their use. The language also needs to be designed as the control system for project management purposes. The PDS, the resulting code system, and the inclusion of the project soft costs in the definition do all this.

What then is the WBS? We have seen three work breakdown concepts and a code concept resulting from a structure comprising definition and breakdown. The code concept identifies the basis for project management: the deliverable element, the activity and package, and the organization. Single, large structures are not capable of easily achieving the desired code systems, and as a result the project management systems approach recommends at least three structures. The second of the three is the breakdown structure, or WBS.

On first impression all breakdown structures look the same. They are not. To be effective they should reflect the way in which the work is to be carried out. It is simple enough to generate a tree like structure that purports to represent a project work breakdown suitable for coding and project control purposes. The reality is different. The problem is that many structures have little or no relationship to the way in which the work is being done.

3.6.1 Bad Work Breakdown Structures

The following is a list of some of the characteristics that may be seen in what are considered "bad" (meaning not suitable for project control) WBSs.

- A structure is time oriented. It has no permanency in the scheme of the project.
- The WBS may have little or no relevance to the way in which the organization carries out its work.
- The resulting code system is not relevant to project needs nor to corporate needs.
- The WBS mixes elements and tasks, that is, it reverts back to a single structure.
- Instead of incorporating standard elemental breakdowns, new ones are invented, which may be known only to the designer of the breakdown.

Of the many misconceptions about the purpose and use of the WBS the principal problem is with the single-project structure: the idea that one structure does it all. From experience this is not the case. Second, the complexity of project breakdowns is more often than not underestimated. Not just any structure will do.

Structures do not by themselves solve project problems. If a structure has little or no relation to the way in which a company is organized and the way in which elements are delivered and work flows, it is of little value as a project management tool.

The WBS will be seen to evolve as a distinct breakdown system, which establishes the tasks that have to be carried out by the project functional organization (to be identified later as the OBS) to achieve the project scope and quality set by the PDS.

3.6.2 Good Work Breakdown Structures

The main purpose of the WBS is to identify tasks and activities which are carried out individually or in packages. Project work normally follows a pattern from the project's conceptualization to its putting into operation through to the decommissioning and taking out of service of the completed facility. The pattern may be a stable, stepwise procedure or, as is more likely the case, there is an overall project direction, with the details being carried out in various degrees of chaos and disorder.

A classic approach to project work breakdown needs to follow the stages depicted in Fig. 3.7. Shown are nine typical project stages. Stage 1 is the project definition stage. The project definition stage is in itself an extensive exercise to define the project as it will be delivered to the owners or users. Although difficult to grasp by beginning project managers and by most project owners, the final scope of a project often is not defined until the work is completed.

In this instance the stage 1 definition depends on the results of activities and actions shown in the succeeding stages 2 through 9. If a project is broken down as shown in Fig. 3.7, it needs to be made clear that the breakdown is a progressive exercise, with the degree of detail for any element at any stage sufficient only to progress the project to the next stage of the decision-making process. In this particular con-

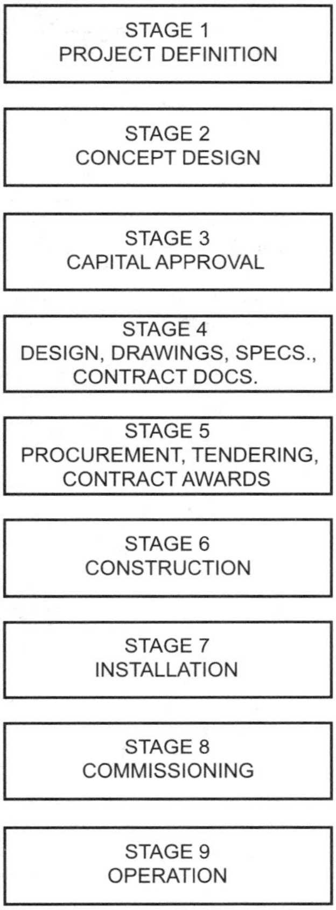

STAGE 1
PROJECT DEFINITION

STAGE 2
CONCEPT DESIGN

STAGE 3
CAPITAL APPROVAL

STAGE 4
DESIGN, DRAWINGS, SPECS., CONTRACT DOCS.

STAGE 5
PROCUREMENT, TENDERING, CONTRACT AWARDS

STAGE 6
CONSTRUCTION

STAGE 7
INSTALLATION

STAGE 8
COMMISSIONING

STAGE 9
OPERATION

FIGURE 3.7 PROJECT WORK BREAKDOWN STRUCTURE, CONCEPT 1. This is the ultimate work breakdown structure in that it incorporates the definition as well if the breakdown applies to the whole project. This is a specific breakdown, leading to approval of project funding.

cept of breakdown, stages 1, 2, and 3 are aimed at developing enough project detail to obtain approval of the capital funding from the owner's board of directors. In this case stage 3 represents a decision. If the stage 3 answer is no, the project ends there or goes back to the drawings boards, but the buck stops there. There would be little or no expenditures in connection with stages 4 through 9.

A WBS as seen in Fig. 3.7 would be suitable for a project handled in the manner indicated, that is, where approval takes place as a stage 3 action. The details of stages 1 and 2 would be geared exclusively to enable stage 3 to occur. For this to happen, the future stages 4 through 9 would need to be addressed and conceptualized on paper to the degree necessary to ensure accuracy.

Project terminology, including terms used in WBSs, varies widely from industry to industry. In Fig. 3.7 the word "stage" was used to depict the progress of project activities. It was seen also that stage 3 may be considered a very important stage in that the project ground to a full stop pending approval of capital funds. Not all projects are handled in this way, and not all projects are "staged." Figure 3.8 illustrates a different approach in the delivery of a project through phasing.

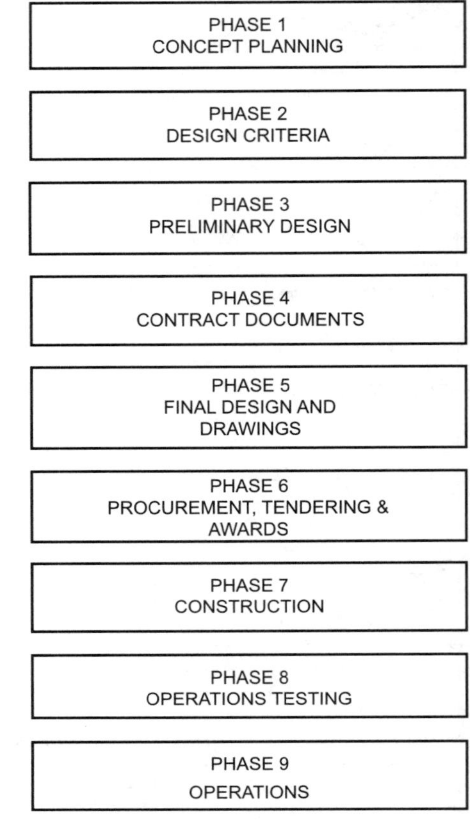

Figure 3.8 Project Work Breakdown Structure, Concept 2, Phases. This is a more conventional breakdown structure in which a project is handled as part of a program, or one of many projects in a multiproject environment, where the financial approvals may be handled separately.

The WBS concept in Fig. 3.8 depicts a project starting at ground zero, that is, it starts with a concept. There is nothing there except a problem, or an opportunity that has been identified, and a project is being visualized as a solution to grasp the opportunity or to solve the problem. The structure is depicted as phases of project work, with each phase dependent on the successful completion of some or all of the activities in the previous phase. The words used to describe each phase comprise typical project engineering or problem solving language, applicable to a wide usage.

The concept in Fig. 3.8 makes no provision for an approval phase wherein the project stops while the capital (or lease) funds are approved by the board of directors. It may be assumed that the organization is handling this aspect separately. The funds may have been approved already. This is often the case where a project is part of a large program. Omission of this particular step could detract from the effectiveness of the project control system that is expected to be the natural result of the work breakdown concept.

Another example of a WBS concept is seen in Fig. 3.9. In this case the work breakdown activities are labeled within stages. A number of points may be highlighted in the concept in Fig. 3.9. First there is no separate or stand-alone stage for the ap-

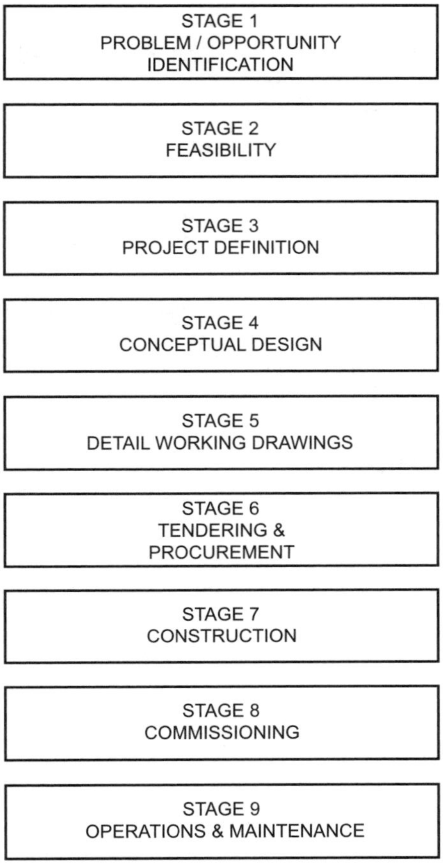

STAGE 1
PROBLEM / OPPORTUNITY
IDENTIFICATION

STAGE 2
FEASIBILITY

STAGE 3
PROJECT DEFINITION

STAGE 4
CONCEPTUAL DESIGN

STAGE 5
DETAIL WORKING DRAWINGS

STAGE 6
TENDERING &
PROCUREMENT

STAGE 7
CONSTRUCTION

STAGE 8
COMMISSIONING

STAGE 9
OPERATIONS & MAINTENANCE

FIGURE 3.9 PROJECT WORK BREAKDOWN STRUCTURE, CONCEPT 3, OPTIMUM. This breakdown structure depicts the way all projects should be done. The concept is that real feasibility studies with real concepts are carried out before the project is defined as a stage 3 occurrence.

proval of the project funding.The cost control function in this concept, as in the concept in Fig. 3.8, would be exercised as part of the work in each stage. This breakdown approach, with no separate funding approval stage, is used in many business environments, including large corporations and bureaucracies. The funding approval in these cases is outside of the project management scope of influence. It may generate project outlooks that deny the reliability of all cost control measures. The thinking could well be that since the project team was not responsible for the budget, how could they be held accountable.

It should be a given that any project definition exercise includes the identification of the problem to be resolved, or an opportunity to be grasped by a project as part of the process. Experience shows that this does not always happen, which has led to the concept of work breakdown incorporating a separate stage for each of problem/opportunity (stage 1) and feasibility (stage 2) followed by project definition (stage 3) as seen in Fig. 3.9. The intention is to formalize the first part of the front-end process incorporating stages 1 and 2 and make it more controllable in a large business environment.

Figure 3.7 shows stage 1 as the project definition stage, which would imply that the problem/opportunity and the feasibility exercises have been carried out as steps in stage 1. The project definition is followed by stage 2, concept design, which then leads to stage 3, capital approval. The Fig. 3.7 concept is most suitable for an accountable, cost-driven business environment, not one where the current thinking might be that the project will cost what it will cost.

The intent of any breakdown system being to provide management with a means to control the project, the extent and degree of breakdown must be a function of what management needs to accomplish its objectives. The project manager must recognize the control needs and be able to develop and implement the control system that will do the job at hand. Whether the result is more breakdown, or less detail, or fewer stages or phases is not a result of the system structures, but of project management need.

3.7 Examples of Work Breakdown Structures

Any breakdown may be called a WBS. In the project management systems approach as presented in this text, a WBS aims to develop and define activities and packages based on distinct project stages or phases. A WBS not following this rule may be considered to be a "bad" breakdown in that although it may look like a WBS, its inherent qualities may represent something else. A "good" breakdown on the other hand follows the rules of a staged breakdown, which have been set up to reflect the way in which the project owners will deliver the project.

It is also not difficult to confuse a PDS, with a WBS. The PDS in the systems of project management defines the deliverables as seen by the owners or users of the completed project, with the added dimension of an area for the project soft costs, sometimes called the front end. As the PDS sets the project scope and quality, its approved estimate forms the basis for the project budget, and therefore the firm target for cost control. If the PDS defines the finished good in measurable terms, the WBS defines the acts of getting there.

Finally, there is the third aspect of project management, the assignment of activities and their packages to the project functional organization through the approach known as the OBS. Although there are three distinct breakdowns named, each with its own management objective, they work together and are meant to deliver and measure the project progressively.

Early in its life cycle a project becomes chaotic and disjointed. Some parts of the work quickly become more advanced than others. An activity may be considered complete when a succeeding activity is started, but the predecessor has been completed only just enough to allow its successors to start. The reality is that the definition structure functions are in various stages of completion; the breakdown activities in the project stages are similarly in disarray, many started, many partly completed, with the activities and packages being delivered by individuals and various organizational groups.

The project management system aims to keep together all of this seemingly disjointed action through a systematic triple-thread coding system based on structures. Sometimes it may be difficult or seemingly redundant to try to differentiate between a definition structure and a breakdown structure. If this is the case and there are no apparent differences, and the resulting code from the single-purpose structure is suitable for project management purposes, it is reasonable to go with the single structure.

Although the systems of project management are composed of distinct, individual operations, they are generally interdependent. To be useful for project control, to help deliver successful projects, the systems are meant to be supportive of each other. They are not subservient to each other. They represent the different looks that a project takes on through its meteoric life cycle.

3.7.1 Airport Project WBS Example

In Chapter 2 the examples include a PDS of an airport project as Fig. 2.9. This section expands the look of the project through work breakdown structuring, as seen in Fig. 3.10, a WBS of the airport project. The graphic depicts eight phases as the project structure, from concept planning to operations testing and startup.

The phase 1 through 4 boxes contain short descriptions of the results expected from the phase actions. Phase 5 through 8 descriptions are self-explanatory as to the phase results.

Although the graphic is based on an airport project, it may be seen as the basis for a generic WBS. The eight phases are obviously suitable for many different types of projects, whether they be a capital project like an airport or a software system or, for that matter, an engineering project. If we establish the project scope and cost through its PDS and by estimating, it must then be processed through each of the phases shown in the breakdown.

As each phase is responsible for its own deliverables, it may be that the breakdown in reality leads to eight WBSs, one for each phase. And that is just one of the reasons why the concept of one breakdown, as sometimes proposed, or even of two, as seen in the C/SCSC approach, may be unworkable for project management purposes.

The airport project WBS in Fig. 3.10 is similar to the WBS concept presented in Fig. 3.8. The phase names, their order, and the resulting deliverables may be more or less consistent from project to project. These kinds of breakdowns may be considered to be generic, suitable for many different applications. But they should only be applied as a systems solution in an environment where the results of the breakdown have significance in the scope, cost, and schedule control of the project work. As breakdown exercises are demanding, with possibly severe consequences for organizations, their application must be considered and consensual. There is more likelihood of successful applications if the structures follow known paths. Generic structures will help in this respect.

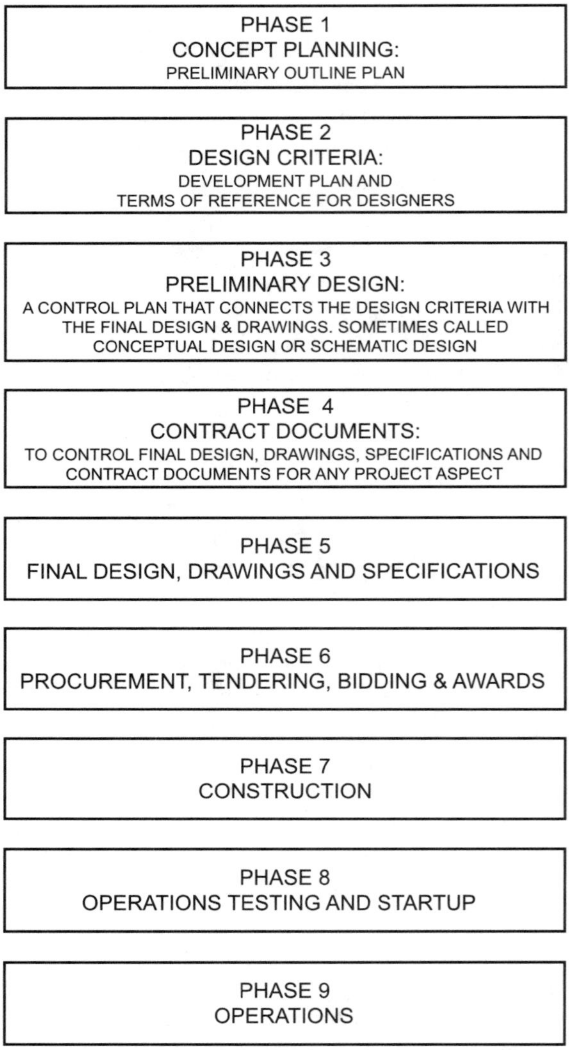

PHASE 1
CONCEPT PLANNING:
PRELIMINARY OUTLINE PLAN

PHASE 2
DESIGN CRITERIA:
DEVELOPMENT PLAN AND
TERMS OF REFERENCE FOR DESIGNERS

PHASE 3
PRELIMINARY DESIGN:
A CONTROL PLAN THAT CONNECTS THE DESIGN CRITERIA WITH THE FINAL DESIGN & DRAWINGS. SOMETIMES CALLED CONCEPTUAL DESIGN OR SCHEMATIC DESIGN

PHASE 4
CONTRACT DOCUMENTS:
TO CONTROL FINAL DESIGN, DRAWINGS, SPECIFICATIONS AND CONTRACT DOCUMENTS FOR ANY PROJECT ASPECT

PHASE 5
FINAL DESIGN, DRAWINGS AND SPECIFICATIONS

PHASE 6
PROCUREMENT, TENDERING, BIDDING & AWARDS

PHASE 7
CONSTRUCTION

PHASE 8
OPERATIONS TESTING AND STARTUP

PHASE 9
OPERATIONS

FIGURE 3.10 AIRPORT PROJECT WORK BREAKDOWN STRUCTURE. The WBS creates and codes the activities and tasks in each phase of the project elements defined and coded by the companion airport PDS. The activities lead to the delivery of the elements.

3.7.2 Power Generating Project WBS

A hydroelectric power generating station comprises areas such as river diversions, dam structures, generators, and related infrastructure works. The project management terminology for this type of undertaking may be similar to the language of the airport project, but there are differences, and it is these differences that are explored. Differences exist between projects, and that is why it is necessary to tailor generic systems to specific projects.

Figure 3.11 depicts a WBS for a major civil engineering hydro project. As a hydro project or a nuclear power plant could be a very large undertaking, engineering

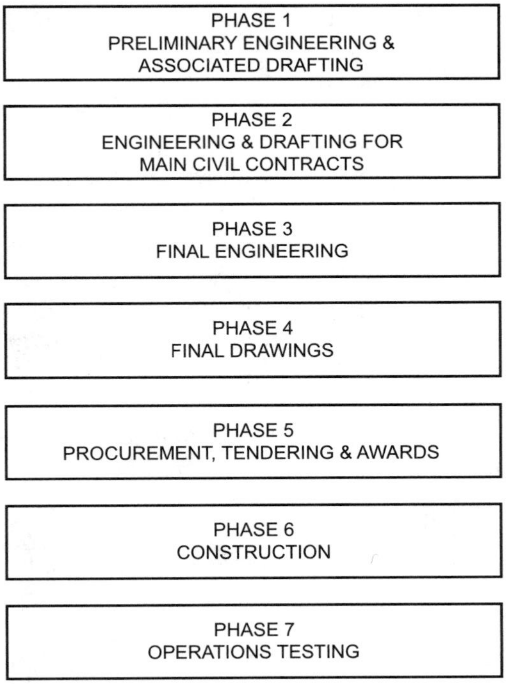

PHASE 1 PRELIMINARY ENGINEERING & ASSOCIATED DRAFTING
PHASE 2 ENGINEERING & DRAFTING FOR MAIN CIVIL CONTRACTS
PHASE 3 FINAL ENGINEERING
PHASE 4 FINAL DRAWINGS
PHASE 5 PROCUREMENT, TENDERING & AWARDS
PHASE 6 CONSTRUCTION
PHASE 7 OPERATIONS TESTING

FIGURE 3.11 POWER GENERATING PROJECT WORK BREAKDOWN STRUCTURE, CONCEPT 1. This WBS is reflective of the way contracts are awarded and engineering work is advanced in this industry. Phase 1 is usually preceded by feasibility studies, proposal engineering, or other preaward work paid for by the customer or a third party, e.g., the World Bank.

corporations often are obliged to carry out substantial amounts of design, development, and engineering activity for the client or with the client prior to commencing the actual work, as represented by the phases seen in Fig. 3.11.

The client organization may pay for this "predevelopment" or "preaward" work as part of the project feasibility study. The work may be part of the engineering corporation's proposal, or a third party, such as, the World Bank, may cover the cost. If these conditions apply, the work activities involved may be considered to be in a feasibility study phase, which would be a predecessor to the phase 1 activities shown in Fig. 3.11. If this is the case, the feasibility studies become phase 1, preliminary engineering becomes phase 2, and so on, and the hydro power project WBS as seen in Fig. 3.11 would become similar to the airport project WBS depicted in Fig. 3.10.

The work breakdowns drawn as examples for both the airport and the hydro projects are presented at the very highest levels of the WBSs, depending on the project or program makeup, at level 2 or level 3. Project phases, such as final drawings or construction are big ticket items. A hydro project construction phase could easily cost $1 billion, its drawings and specifications $200 million. For project management to control an undertaking of this size, much smaller, controllable components must be created. These control components are identified by the use of the basic systems of project management, (1) project definition and (2) project work breakdown.

In continuing the discussion of work breakdown based on generic phases, we will see and review the close relationship that exists between the two key systems, PDS and WBS, and depict further how they are interdependent. For example, each project phase listed in Fig. 3.11 is preceded by the area, function, or major component derived by definition. The power generating hydro project, for example, may have major elements or functional areas, as drawn in Fig. 3.12.

Each of the eight major elements seen in the graphic could be a project in its own right. Thus what we may be setting up is a multiproject control system. The major elements do not necessarily follow each other in a set pattern. They could be "staged" or "phased" in many different ways, using the two words in their generic sense as opposed to their formal usage in project management systems terminology. Having identified the major elements at level 2 of the definition structure, each is then processed through the WBS phases, as depicted in Fig. 3.11, namely, the proposed WBS for the power generating project.

Each phase is intended to identify activities pertaining to it. The activities may also be called work units. The activities or work units may be assembled into work packages or, simply, packages. When a package is bid or tendered, it may be awarded as a purchase order or contract.

The power generating project, seen as a PDS in Fig. 3.12, is redrawn as a WBS in Fig. 3.13. To illustrate the creation of a WBS using major element 3, spillway, the

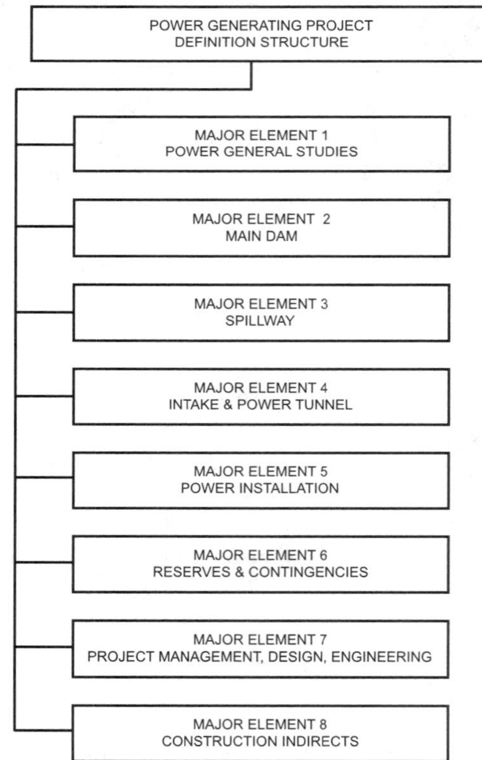

FIGURE 3.12 POWER GENERATING PROJECT DEFINITION STRUCTURE, LEVEL 2, CONCEPT 1. Every WBS must start with a PDS. The line at which project elements become activities is fine and variable. In this case the major elements shown are available for breakdown as activities, based on the way project work is carried out in this industry.

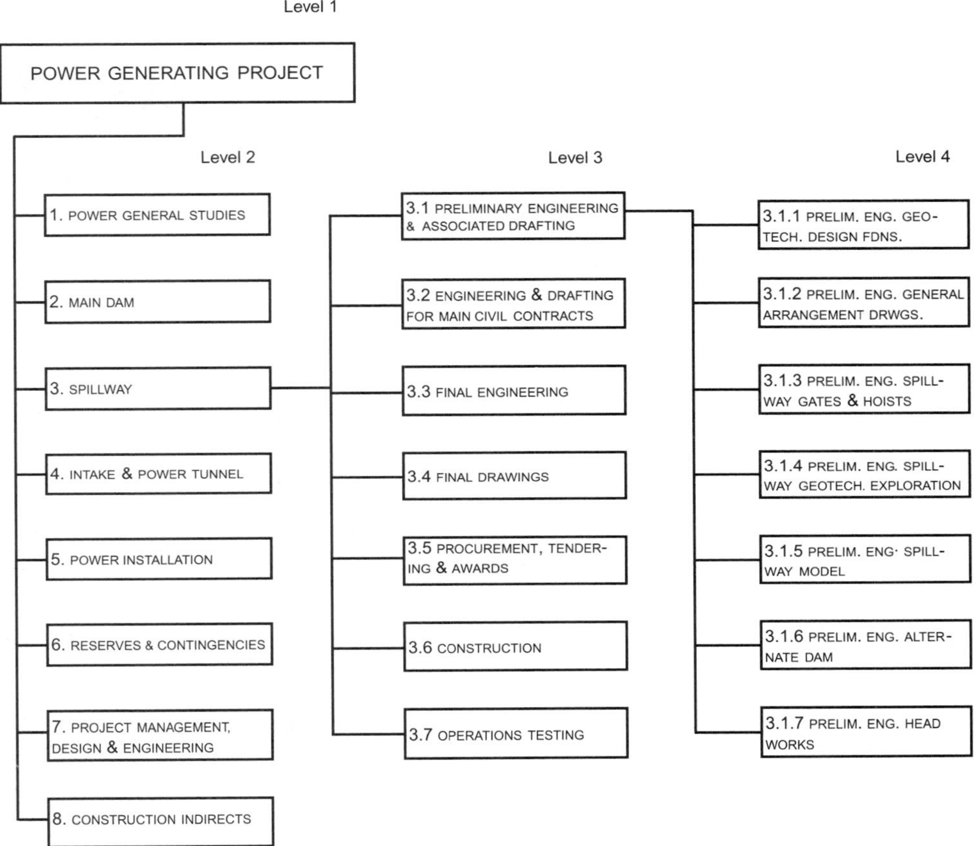

FIGURE 3.13 POWER GENERATING PROJECT, SPILLWAY WBS PHASE 1, PRELIMINARY ENGINEERING, ACTIVITIES. Rules of WBS as dicussed in relation to Fig. 3.11 are applied to the major element Spillway from the PDS in Fig. 3.12 to create and code packages of preliminary engineering activities at level 4 of the structure. The packages of activities are taken to level 5, as seen in Table 3.1.

rules of breakdown and code from the WBS in Fig. 3.11 are applied. The result is a list of spillway preliminary engineering tasks coded 3.1.1 to 3.1.7, as seen in Fig. 3.13. Applying the same rules to the other major elements and phases would create a WBS of the whole power generating project.

The tasks in Fig. 3.13 are at level 4 of the WBS. The spillway tasks and codes are illustrated as a list in Table 3.1. The "." separators in the code numbers have been left out to simplify the illustration. As the process of breakdown is continued to lower levels, the activities become more detailed, the code system more complex, and cost estimating more detailed. Considering the number of major elements, their subsets, and the seven or eight project phases, it is seen that the number of project activities can grow very quickly.

TABLE 3.1
Spillway Preliminary Engineering Breakdown from Fig. 3.12

Code	Description
311	Spillway: Preliminary Engineering, Geotechnical Design Fdns.
312	Spillway: Preliminary Engineering, General Arrangements Drwgs.
313	Spillway: Preliminary Engineering, Gates and Hoists
314	Spillway: Preliminary Engineering, Geotechnical Exploration
315	Spillway: Preliminary Engineering, Spillway Model
316	Spillway: Preliminary Engineering, Alternate Dam
317	Spillway: Preliminary Engineering, Head Works

Note: These activities are based on the WBS in Fig. 3.11 and the PDS in Fig. 3.12. Only the spillway structure is processed in this preliminary engineering exercise.

An example of a more complex power generating station is seen in the PDS depicted in Fig. 3.14. It contains more major elements, and the potential for work breakdowns into many work units or activities grows exponentially. The major elements in the graphic are meant to be representative only. There could be more or fewer, depending on the actual makeup of the project and, more important, on the proposed project management systems approach to be used.

It is most important that breakdown detail be limited to what can actually be used in the project control process. This means that an activity must be "hard" in terms of its scope measure, its cost parameters, and as a schedule activity. The test of the durability of an activity is the question of who in the project functional organization will recognize it for their own project purposes. Is it truly a coded project component? Can costs be allocated to it easily? Will costs be allocated to it? Is it a recognizable code item in a purchase order? a contract? a measurable task in the owners' own organization? a federal government agency?

Figure 3.14 depicts 21 major elements at level 2 of the power generating PDS. The project manager's next question is how these elements will be delivered, that is, what activities must be completed, and how the activities are coordinated and as parts of what packages. Is it enough to define a project to one or two levels below the project objective, for example, to level 2 in Figs. 3.12 and 3.14, and immediately go into a breakdown phase, as seen in Fig. 3.13? We can test this premise by referring to major element 9, Reservoirs & Channels, in Fig. 3.14.

Table 3.2 shows the next level elements in the PDS. Is it necessary to define the reservoirs and channels into the two-digit coded functions before the function goes into the breakdown phases. It may be that the additional definition breakdown does not add more controllability. The degree and amount of definition breakdown in all cases must be based on the approach that works, the integration of the design process if in the engineering phase, and on the packaging approach in any phase. In the preceding case it was not seen that the additional functional breakdown would help in developing activities for project control purposes. The subject major element could go into the work breakdown phases, to be followed by the creation of activities and work unit packages in the various phases.

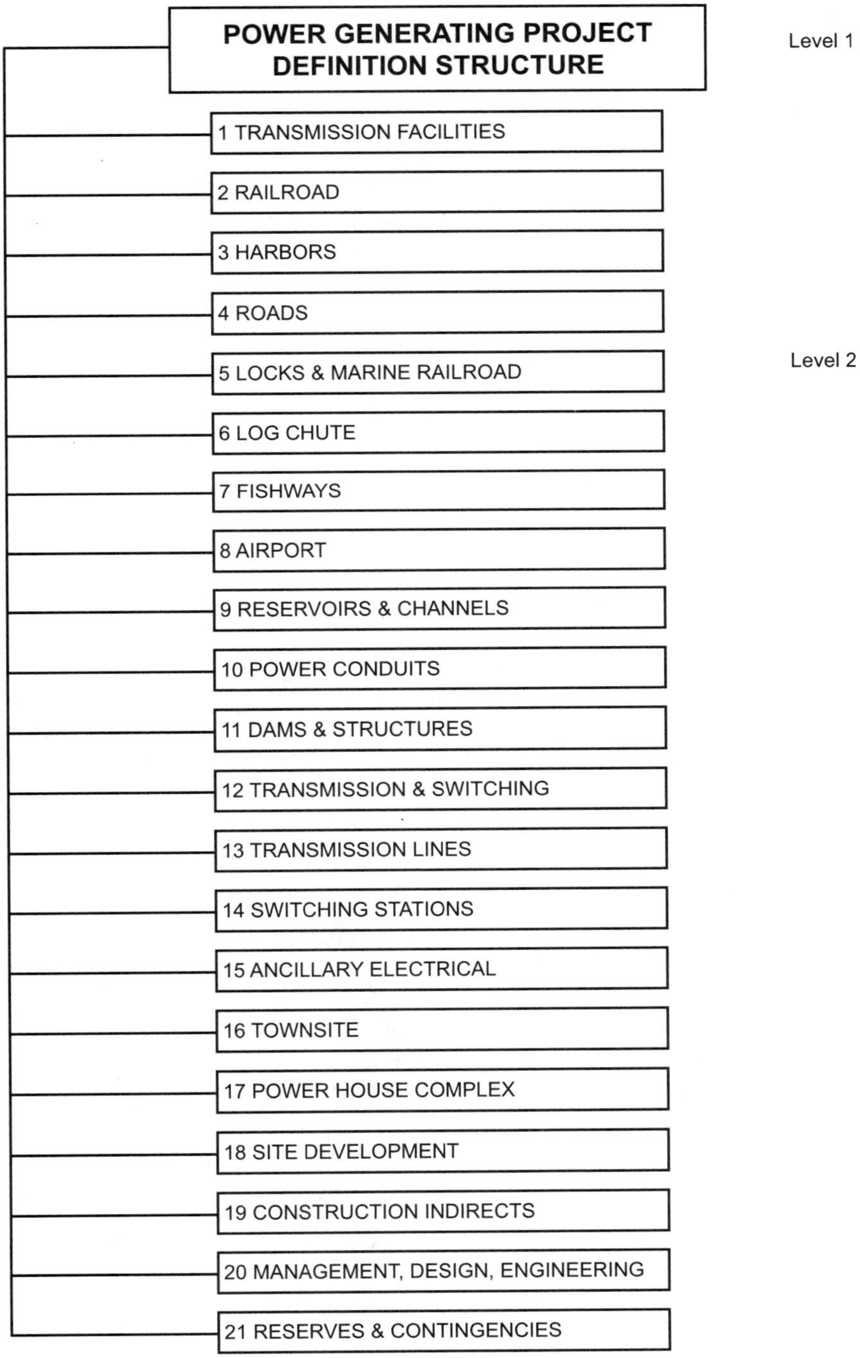

POWER GENERATING PROJECT DEFINITION STRUCTURE — Level 1

Level 2:

- 1 TRANSMISSION FACILITIES
- 2 RAILROAD
- 3 HARBORS
- 4 ROADS
- 5 LOCKS & MARINE RAILROAD
- 6 LOG CHUTE
- 7 FISHWAYS
- 8 AIRPORT
- 9 RESERVOIRS & CHANNELS
- 10 POWER CONDUITS
- 11 DAMS & STRUCTURES
- 12 TRANSMISSION & SWITCHING
- 13 TRANSMISSION LINES
- 14 SWITCHING STATIONS
- 15 ANCILLARY ELECTRICAL
- 16 TOWNSITE
- 17 POWER HOUSE COMPLEX
- 18 SITE DEVELOPMENT
- 19 CONSTRUCTION INDIRECTS
- 20 MANAGEMENT, DESIGN, ENGINEERING
- 21 RESERVES & CONTINGENCIES

FIGURE 3.14 POWER GENERATING PROJECT DEFINITION STRUCTURE. The intent of this PDs is to set up the project for the development of its phases, activities, codes, and contract packages. The 21 major elements at level 2 are representative of a complex power generating project. In this case, the 2-digit numbers will form the basis for the project code system. The WBS process will start at level 2, but this need not always be the case.

TABLE 3.2
Reservoirs and Channels from Fig. 3.14

Code	Description
9	Reservoirs and Channels
91	Reservoirs
92	Channels
93	Diversion Channel
94	Gauging Station

Note: The major element Reservoirs and Channels is broken down into its level 3 elements as an exercise of defining the project to an appropriate level of definition before applying the concept of phases to create activities. As discussed in the text, no additional functional definition was indicated before the WBS processing.

To expand this investigation of the conversion of definition elements to activities, major element 11, Dams & Structures, is defined from its level 2 position into level 3 functional elements as seen in Table 3.3. If the major element Dams & Structures is compared to the major element Reservoirs & Channels, it will become apparent to a student of project management structures that 11, Dams & Structures, requires the next or functional level of PDS breakdown before the work units are developed through the WBS phases. It is seen that Dams & Structures comprises six major functions, 111 to 116, and that they break out of major element 11.

One additional example to illustrate how experienced judgment is necessary in converting project definition to project breakdown may be seen in the tables listing major element 17, Power House Complex. In Table 3.4 Power House Complex, assumed to be at level 2 of the PDS, is broken down into three major functions.

Some major functions will immediately lend themselves to further definition breakdown before activities are considered. This can be illustrated through 171, Power House and Service Area, as seen in the Table 3.5. In project management terminology the coded items in this table are at level 4 of the PDS.

TABLE 3.3
Dams and Structures from Fig. 3.14

Code	Description
11	Dams and Structures
111	Earth Dikes
112	Concrete Dam
113	Spillway Structure
114	Diversion Structure
115	Coffer Dams
116	Protective Works

Note: The major element Dams and Structures is broken down into elements at level 3. Analysis shows that no additional functional breakdown is indicated for the level 3 elements before WBS type phases are applied.

TABLE 3.4
Power House Complex from Fig. 3.14

Code	Description
17	Power House Complex
171	Power House and Service Area
172	Control and Administrative Building
173	Ancillary Buildings

Note: The major element Power House Complex is shown developed into its three component parts and coded. Analysis shows that additional functional breakdown is indicated before WBS type processing into project management phases.

As discussed in Chapter 2 and using the terminology developed for process plants projects, the next levels of definition would be element types or element groups, after which the next level in the PDS would be individual elements.

In this structure, element types would occur at level 6 and individual elements at level 7. And the functional elements have not yet been broken down into project phases for the derivation of activities, work units, and work packages.

And there's the rub: the recognition and implementation of the point at which the element in the PDS is convertible into an activity in the WBS, its part in a work package, and finally the ownership of that work package by a member of the project functional organization.

TABLE 3.5
Power House and Service Area From Table 3.4

Code	Description
171	Power House and Service Area
17101	Access
17102	Transformer Deck
17103	Tail Race Deck
17104	Walls
17105	Equipment Foundations
17106	Foundations
17107	Superstructure
17108	Building Details
17109	Draft Tube
17110	Scroll Case

Note: Of the three major elements from Fig. 3.14 tested for the development of phased activities only 17, Power House Complex, needs to be taken beyond level 3 before applying the project management phases for the creation of activities. The degree of defining and breaking down of a project is presented on a "need to do" basis. Projects need to be structured for control purposes. But the degree of detail must be carefully managed. It is far easier to create paper codes.

Terminology in project work, as in all endeavors, plays an important role in grasping and understanding these systems concepts. As seen before, on a power project a major element is the highest level of definition, just below the project at level 1. It is a large slice of the project, which could be a project in its own right. On a process plant project, a similar level 2 definition component may be called an area, and the component at the lowest level may be called an element. In addition to recognizing the point of conversion from definition to breakdown, it is necessary to contend with inconsistencies in terminology from industry to industry, and between different computer applications.

In the Power House and Service Area example the PDS is considered to be convertible into work breakdown activities at level 5 of the structure, as may be seen in Fig. 3.15. This is the purpose of definition and breakdown: to create activities and tasks that account for the delivery of the finished project.

As a general rule the tasks are unique for the phase in which they exist. Whether a task is derived from a higher or a lower level of project definition is immaterial. The important consideration is that the derived tasks can fulfill their roles as hard project activities, which can be scoped, costed, scheduled, and packaged, and which are measurable not only in the eye of the scheduler but in all other respects and by all project team members.

Referring again to the power generating project PDS in Fig. 3.14, it is seen that 9, Reservoirs & Channels, can go into phases after level 3, as can 11, Dams & Structures. But 17, Power House Complex, is required to go to level 4, after which the phased activities may be constructed. As a summary of the power project WBS, the following general guidelines are seen to be applicable.

Phase 1, Concepts: Unique breakdown for scope development

Phase 2, Preliminary Engineering & Drafting: Unique breakdown for preliminary engineering and associated drafting

Phase 3, Final Engineering: Unique breakdown for final engineering

Phase 4, Final Drawings: Unique breakdown

Phase 5, Procurement, Tendering, & Awarding: Unique breakdown

Phase 6, Construction: Unique breakdown

Phase 7, Operations Testing: Unique breakdown for operations testing and startup

Although each phase of the breakdown is designated unique, making for seven breakdowns, the reality may be somewhat different. It may be possible to transfer or flow through some work units from phase to phase. The important consideration is that the results of each phase, the deliverables, are different and in that respect unique. Another main consideration in the design of breakdowns is that whole phases generally do not follow each other. Activities within phases may not follow each other in a predetermined, lockstep manner. The relationships of phases to each other, activities within phases to succeeding phases, and packaging are influenced by project procurement, bidding and awarding, contracting methods, and scheduling, to be discussed in later chapters.

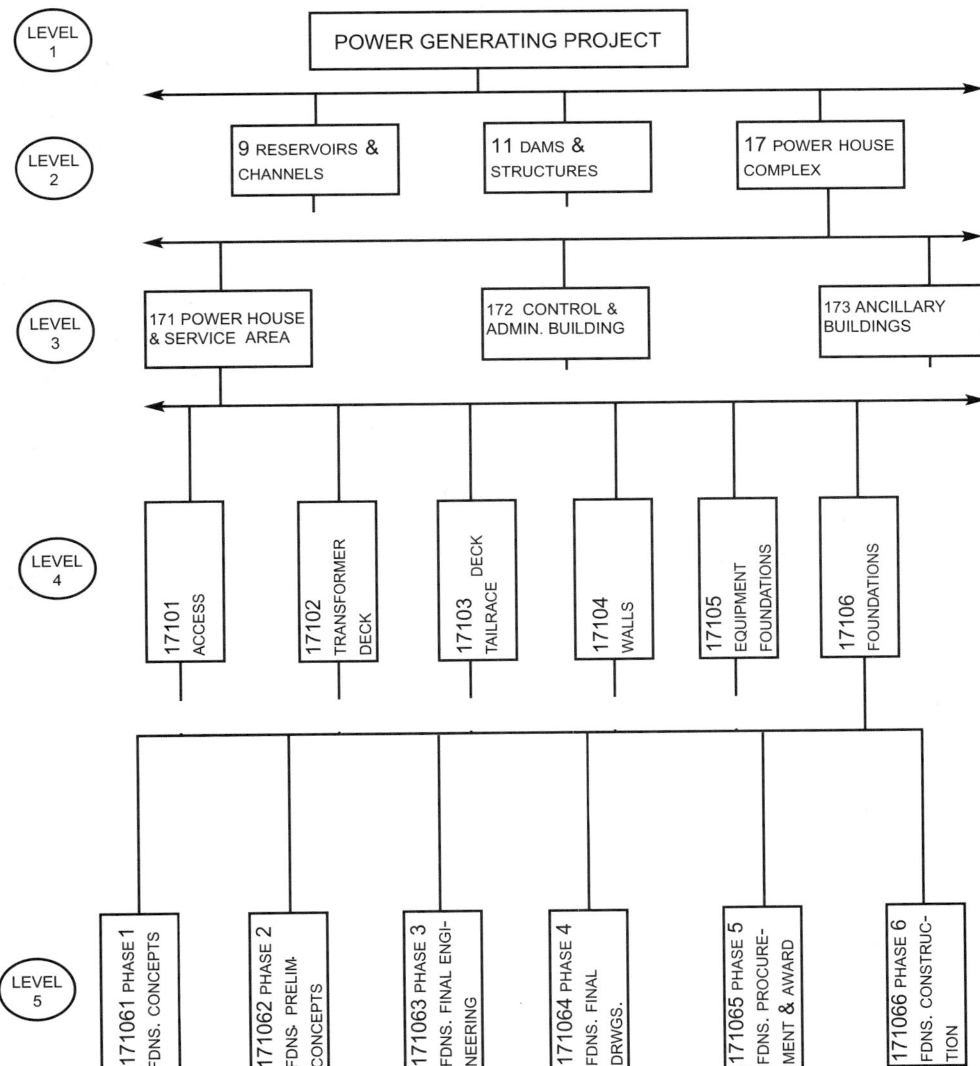

FIGURE 3.15 POWER GENERATING PROJECT, POWER HOUSE AND SERVICE AREA FOUNDATIONS, WBS AND CODE TO LEVEL 5. It is difficult to delineate the reference lines in project work at which project elements become activities. This figure shows the transition occurring at level 5. The previous illustrations showed transitions from elements to activities at other levels.

3.8 Examples of Activities from Phases and Stages

In project management language a phase is sometimes called a stage, or the stage may be called a phase. They are considered synonymous terms in this text. In the design of any project management system, it pays to go with accepted usage in the subject project environment. This is not always self-evident in many situations because of the generally fragmented multidisciplinary nature of most postmodern projects. As a rule it is necessary to consider issues such as the owner's preference or custom, the jargon to be used by the professional designers, vendors, manufacturers, contractors, subcontractors, trade contractors, specialist suppliers, government agencies, utilities, environmentalists, and of late the public interest and involvement in almost every project. All of them have an impact on how jobs are done and the way words are used in the delivery of projects. Some of this has already been seen in the way two key words, phase and stage, have been used in the examples from different industrial projects.

Structured project phasing or staging is an integral part of the systems of project management. When we use these two words in a breakdown structure, it is a meaningful, deliberate choice, which when applied leads to the development of coded tasks and activities aimed to achieve a distinct project deliverable as defined by a parallel coded definition structure. Before using either term, the project control system designer needs to be aware of the level of understanding of project management terminology. A pattern may be in place based on the use of proprietary software or because of previous project work. Imagine the confusion if you are marketing your services describing how you stage project work when the client has been previously taught that project work is phased. And your potential client considers that there is a fixed number of project phases, whereas we know that the number of stages may vary to suit specific conditions.

That is what will be discussed and demonstrated in this section of the text: the results of phasing or staging project work in terms of its place, terms, and usage in the control of projects. The discussion and demonstration will be based on more, rather than fewer, project phases so as to provide a range of scenarios from which the project manager can choose the kind and number of stages that may be used for actual project work. The phases and stages referred to in the following discussion flow from the WBS illustrations in Figs. 3.7–3.9.

Phase 1 WBS Activities

In some project environments the intent of phase 1 is to deliver a project memorandum. A project memorandum may also be a memorandum to accompany the appropriation request. A project memorandum is a document or a study, which is acceptable to the approving authority (the boss) and is suitable as the springboard for the future project stages or phases. If approval of funding is involved, it becomes the memorandum to accompany the appropriation request.

In large corporate environments or bureaucracies where many projects may be under consideration, the tendency is to create more rather than fewer project stages. This leads to a step-by-step approval process. It is very structured and intended to slow down the process so that projects do not run out of control. Fig. 3.8 illustrates this approach.

In fast moving, more communicative environments much of the work of the front-end stages may be merged as needed to progress the project. This approach reduces the number of distinct phases, but real control is exercised through the imposition of a capital approval stage, as seen in Fig. 3.7. What this approach may lead to is the combining of phases 1 and 2 in Fig. 3.8 into the stage 1, Project Definition, and the establishment of a stage 2, Concept Design, as seen in Fig. 3.7.

Figure 3.9, however, is representative of the classic breakdown phases wherein we identify the problem or look to grasp an opportunity as stage 1 of a potential project solution. This stage when looked at in isolation is seen as the first step leading to the project definition. There are a number of tasks or activities that are consistent from project to project which would flow from stage 1. Having first defined the project, as discussed both under the project definition concept and as part of the power project work breakdown example, into subprojects, areas, major elements, or even element types and elements—but only to the extent needed—the classic first set of stage 1 tasks may comprise the statements listed in Table 3.6.

The first-stage tasks are flexible to the extent that they are not necessarily consistent from project to project, nor from company to company. For that matter they may vary from department to department in the same corporate environment. Often the initial front-end work as represented by stage 1 or phase 1 is less readily definable as belonging to a distinct, separate phase, except perhaps in those corporate environments where large numbers of projects are concurrently being actively considered. More often than not, the first two or three project stages flow together, with just enough done in each stage to prove a point, or shoot down a premise.

TABLE 3.6
Project Beginning Model

Phase 1/Stage 1 Classic Tasks
Problem/opportunity identification
Mission or mandate statement
Project objectives
Risk analysis
User needs, e.g., systems, facilities, equipment
Functional requirements, e.g., systems, equipment, buildings
People requirements, e.g., systems, furnishings, buildings
Alternative solutions
Proposal statements, e.g., users, functions, people
Cost estimates, e.g., capital, lease, operating
Project schedule
Financial schedule, e.g., profit/loss, cash flow
Recommendations

Note: At the beginning there is a problem or an opportunity that must be fixed with a project. Some of the things that need to be considered to come up with the right project are identified.

Phase 2 WBS Activities

Phase 2, as in Fig. 3.8, is identified as the design criteria step. Design criteria flow from decisions made and approved, or accepted for progressing the project in the previous front-end work such as may occur in phase 1. Design criteria is defined by some project managers as the statement of technical understanding of the users' needs and functions by the project designers given to the client's project management. However, in Fig. 3.9 stage 2 is called Feasibility. Sometimes feasibility studies are thought to precede the development of design criteria. As design criteria is not a fully representative term to describe the stage of interaction between user needs and project front-end planning, the phase 2 or stage 2 activities are better described as feasibility steps. The phase 2 deliverables would be generally a refinement and accuracy improvement of the deliverables from phase 1, with perhaps the additional output listed in Table 3.7.

Referring to the airport example in Fig. 3.10, phase 2 is named Design Criteria. In Fig. 3.11, phase 2 is named Engineering & Drafting for Main Civil Contracts. It was explained that in the power generating project, the project phase numbering was influenced by the amount and kind of conceptual front-end activity that was carried out as part of a proposal. If the conceptual work was carried out as part of the project work breakdown, it would have fallen into phase 1, and the breakdown structure would be more in keeping with the other examples.

As may be seen in Table 3.7, the phase 2 activities are quite similar to the longer list shown in Table 3.6 under phase 1. In a real application, the quality, such as engineering, cost, and scope, of the information would be better, that is, more accurate, more reliable, and harder in phase 2. The phase 2 classic list when combined with the phase 1 classic list would define the project in a progressive way. When the total of the information is approved, the project hard information could be "frozen" and become the design criteria to set and thereby control future project phases.

Table 3.7
Design Criteria

Phase 2/Stage 2 Classic Tasks
Site identification
Real estate information
Environmental impacts
Alternative solutions
Capital cost estimates
Project schedule
Operating cost estimates
Financial analysis
Recommendation

Note: In the design criteria stage of a project the project team provides answers to problems and alternative solutions requiring decisions for project progress in conceptual design and engineering language. Some of the subjects are listed. Approvals become the basis for project progress.

Phase 3 WBS Activities

Using what may be called the maximum number of project stages, as depicted in Fig. 3.9, stage 3 is sometimes called Project Definition. As in this text project definition is the name of one of the systems of project management, and the most important in terms of scope, quality, and cost control, there may appear to be an inconsistency. What is meant here, in the phased development of project work, is that by phase 3 the project will have achieved a definitive form and structure, based on formal measurements and objective decisions in the previous two phases. In other words, we know that it is an apple that we are growing, and not an orange. And that is what is meant by the term "project definition" in this project life cycle.

It is important to keep in mind always that project terminology varies between industries and business sectors. Our intent is to provide the broadest picture and the widest discourse on the subject. The aim is to explore and provide relevance to the many different approaches used for the business of project management. The system of project definition aims to transcribe the user needs into project language. The system of project work breakdown identifies the activities that will deliver the project to the users. Within the system of work breakdown, phase 3 is called Project Definition in some industries, as shown in Fig. 3.9, and that is what is being demonstrated here.

In Fig. 3.9 stage 3 is intended as the successful culmination of the work and activities of the previous stages. It consolidates the results for approval, and when approved becomes the basis for the ongoing project. In some corporations the result of this phase may be called a "design transmittal." In other environments, public works departments, for example, the process may result in a coordination and control document called a "project brief." Building consultants, architects, and engineers may refer to the results as a "design report." The content of the design report might be called "design criteria." A comprehensive project brief would contain not only design criteria, but detailed cost estimates, contract packaging information, resource requirements, and full project management information.

Whatever the name, the target is to deliver documented information to manage and control ongoing project activities and stages. Having defined the project functions and elements and proceeded through stages 1 and 2, stage 3 work would produce the hard information listed in Table 3.8.

The comprehensive list in Table 3.8 has incorporated the results of stage 4, Conceptual Design, seen in Fig. 3.9, because, based on experience, a project cannot be defined with only words and numbers. Concept drawings, process flow diagrams, schematics, or sketches are also needed. But since the project team people who prepare the drawings are not always the same as those who do the words, numbers, and needs analysis, they should be required to receive first the words and numbers. If this is not the case, concept drawings may be offered as solutions before it has been proven that the drawing does indeed provide a solution.

Experience has shown that for accurate and meaningful project cost control it is best that the problem or opportunity, feasibility, and project definition stages, that is, stages 1 through 3, be augmented with stage 4, Conceptual Design, prior to applica-

TABLE 3.8
Project Definition Final Product as Paper Trail

Phase 3/Stage 3 Classic Tasks
1 Executive summary
1.1 Background
1.2 Proposal
1.3 Project cost summary
1.4 Special conditions
1.5 Risks
1.6 Recommendations
2 Capital (or lease) appropriation request
2.1 Financial data summary
2.2 Construction and financial summary
3 Project description
3.1 Major project components (site, building, equipment fixtures, landscaping, etc.)
3.2 Statement of requirements (organization, objectives, facilities, occupancy dates, assumptions, people and space requirements, functional concepts, special requirements)
3.3 Construction schedule
3.4 Key plans
3.5 Project program
4 Justification
4.1 Quantitative analysis
4.2 Qualitative analysis
4.3 Energy conservation
4.4 Present space/future requirements
4.5 Building space assumptions
4.6 Incentives
5 Financial
5.1 Capital needs
5.2 Expenses
5.3 Operating costs
5.4 Contingencies
5.5 Inflation assumptions
5.6 Lease/buy options
5.7 Cash flow
6 Alternatives
6.1 Do nothing alternative
6.2 Renovation alternative
6.3 Other alternatives
7 Risks
7.1 Consequences of nonapproval
7.2 Impact of delay
7.3 Risks in basic program justification
8 Bibliography
9 Appendices
9.1 Proposals
9.2 Facility project (project description, schematic drawings, outline specifications)
9.3 Facility project cost estimate details
9.4 Project schedule details
9.5 Project program details

Note: The tasks listed have resulted in a paper trail that proves the project feasibility, satisfies the functional requirements of the users of the project, complies with all corporate and legal obligations, and has enough detail to prove that the project can be delivered for the budget submitted for approval.

tion for capital project funds. There are many reasons why this is not always done. A common reason is that it, namely, project definition or conceptual design, is expensive and there is no time to do it.

Phase 4 WBS Activities

Stage 4 activities result in conceptual drawings. Project conceptual drawings may include site plans, site services, architectural plans, elevations, and sections along with supporting structural, mechanical, and electrical drawings. The drawings would reflect the functions that drive the project. For example, if the project definition information includes a function-related code system, the code should be reflected in the plans. As for the degree of detailing on conceptual drawings, it requires to be adequate enough to prove compliance with local building codes, user functionality, safety, and constructability. In the final reckoning the drawings and the outline specifications need to be advanced enough so that there is confidence in the cost estimate. This means that structural drawings define and depict the materials of construction as well as the design of the frame. Mechanical and electrical drawings would size, specify, and show power and safety services in place. Materials are specified. Heating, ventilating, and air-conditioning systems are calculated and balanced, as are electrical loads. All systems would be described in outline specifications.

The kind and contents of drawings and specifications depend on the project type. An airport project preliminary outline plan, for example, would show the location of buildings and other facilities, land use, roads, and service corridors. The medium would consist of plans, elevations, and sections. For a process facility the most important conceptual drawing would be the process flow and instrumentation diagram, supported by plans, elevations, sections, and outline specifications. A sample partial list of drawings for a complex industrial lab project is seen in Table 3.9.

The drawing list in the Table 3.9 flows out of and back into the list of deliverables named under item 3 in Table 3.8, phase 3/stage 3, Classic Tasks. The intent in showing linkage is to demonstrate the kind and quality of project information needed through stage 4 to prove the feasibility and confirm the cost of a project to appropriation-grade accuracy.

Phase 5 WBS Activities

The need for detailed working drawings and specifications, the result of phase 5 project work, needs to be well understood for all kinds of projects. General arrangement plans, sections, elevations, and specifications are used for final quantity takeoffs and detailed estimating, and as the basis for vendors' drawings, manufacturing shop drawings, and architectural, structural, mechanical, and electrical working drawings.

The timing, makeup, grouping, and packaging of detail drawings in this phase is a function of the project delivery process, which is sensitive to the arrangement of contracts and schedules. This is where another form of project complexity often arises. It is not easy to extract specific, narrow details for a single contract package without

TABLE 3.9
Drawings and Specifications

Phase 4/Stage 4 Classic Tasks	
Architectural	Electrical
Site plan	Site plan
First-floor plan	First-floor plan
Elevations	Third-floor plan
Systems interface	Typical lab lighting
Third-floor plan	Typical lab power
Second-floor plan, lab block	Electrical details
Sections	Single-line diagram
South axonometric	Distribution riser diagram
West axonometric	Fire alarm riser diagram
North axonometric	Security riser diagram
Outline specifications	Voice communication riser diagram
	Outline specifications
Mechanical	
Site plan	
First-floor plan	
Second-floor plan	
Third-floor plan	
Typical lab layout	
Typical mechanical room details	
First-floor mechanical room	
Second-floor mechanical room	
Air-flow diagram	
Heating/cooling piping flow diagram	
Outline specifications	

Note: Drawings and specifications are the final representations of project deliverables before they are cast in steel or stone.

at the same time creating a large amount of other project information. Problems of coordination arise in delineating the bits and pieces forming the whole project between the different contract packages.

Phase 6 WBS Activities

The stage 6 activities listed in Fig. 3.9 consist of procurement and bidding. This is a difficult project stage in that it frequently leads to jurisdictional problems between corporate departments such as engineering, operations, and purchasing. As project work is usually a high-profile activity, particularly in corporations that launch new projects infrequently, many groups will attempt to influence how the project will be delivered. As the awarding of project assignments, purchase orders, and contracts is seen as the exercise of corporate power, the project manager will have a difficult time in keeping the project on track, and in the making of objective decisions. The other thing that happens is that projects are often packaged before they are ready, meaning the contracts are issued on incomplete information. The biggest challenge for the project manager at this point in the project life cycle is to ensure that enough work is completed in stages 3, 4, and 5 before stage 6 is expedited to be started.

Unless a corporate owner is fixated on an approach, there are many ways to package and buy project work. Complex and large projects may be delivered in vertical slices or horizontally. Packages may consist of complete functional groupings, such as a turnkey process plant, or as elements, such as the structure, the building skin, the mechanicals, and so on. The problem is to know what the implications, benefits, and negatives are in the different approaches, and to select the one that is most beneficial to the project objective.

Procurement often entails ordering long-delivery elements early in the project life cycle, say, at the end of stage 4, Conceptual Design, and basing the final drawings and specifications on the design of the element ordered. Packaging is not only the identification of groups of activities to be contracted outside the client organization. It is essential to identify tasks to be carried out in the owner organization, project management organization, consultants, and approval agencies such as those at the municipality, state, province, and federal government. The results are depicted in Table 3.10.

A most important aspect of this phase is that it does not necessarily happen all at once, or in one continuous, single project time span. There are projects that lend themselves to a complete design and drawings mode, after which they are bid and awarded as one lump sum contract. They usually take a long time. Others are packaged and fast-tracked to save time. For effective, responsive project delivery, the smart project manager will establish early in the life cycle how the project is to be packaged, procured, and delivered.

The measurables will include time targets, package budgets, coded financial controls, and complete coordination and control of the functional organization responsible for the delivery of the undertaking.

TABLE 3.10
Packaging Activities and Tasks for Assignment, Contracting, and Procurement

Phase 6/Stage 6 Classic Tasks
Owner organization packages
Project team packages
Design packages
Procurement packages
Purchase requisitions
Internal organization charges packages
Contract packages
Supplier packages
Bidding documents
Memoranda of agreements with outside agencies
Bidding, tendering, and awarding all packages
Purchase orders
Consulting contracts
Construction contracts
Utilities agreements
Agencies approval packages

Note: Activities and tasks developed through breakdown structuring must be assigned and contracted for so that all activities leading to project deliverables are accounted for.

Phase 7 WBS Activities

Construction activities are different from planning and design activities in that they are usually the culmination of a long string of tasks leading up to the fabrication, delivery, and assembly of the hard project components. This applies to all kinds of project work, including facilities, planes, trains, and hardware and software systems. The construction phase is always the most fun, because it is action-packed and visible. Project visibility leads to happy events such as a ribbon cutting, a ground breaking, or a launching.

But there may be problems lurking in the background, generally the result of starting the construction delivery phase too soon. Too soon means that there may not be enough confirmed and detailed information in the form of final drawings. If at one time the only way to deliver a project was by the traditional lump sump contract, there are now many different fast-tracking approaches in which drawings and the digging of holes may overlap and parallel each other. Obviously the drawings for the hole for the foundations would have been finished before the hole was started, as would the foundation drawings and the structural drawings. In the fast-track approach the idea is to ensure that drawings are always ahead of the construction, so that the project does not run out of information.

Phase 8 WBS Activities

Phase 8 in Fig. 3.8 is named Operations Testing. It is called Commissioning in Figs. 3.7 and 3.9. As a project is completed it needs to be commissioned (debugged) and started. Project specifications provide for initial startup consumables such as filters, fluids, lamps, and so on. The delivery contracts normally require that the designers or installers start the facility and thereby prove that it works. Once started and signed off, it is then ready to be turned over to the customer.

With the advent of more complicated technology and the incorporation of energy conservation, environmental, life support, safety, security, computer control, and communication systems projects have become more difficult to start and put into operation. What all of this means to the project manager is that stage 8 needs its own breakdown planning, scheduling, and cost estimating to ensure that the last preoperation phase does not hold up the start of the operation of the completed facility. A generic list of possible activities in this phase is given in Table 3.11.

Phase 9 WBS Activities

In Fig. 3.9 stage 9 is the operations and maintenance stage of the project. This stage is not generally seen as the responsibility of the project management team, particularly if the owner and users have received a high-quality, trouble-free facility which does what it was meant to do. Trouble-free operation is helped with the provision of as-built drawings, operating manuals, and equipment maintenance documentation. It helps also if the users had the time, the expertise, and the inclination to actively participate in constructive decision making in the front-end project phases. However, it often happens in all kinds of project endeavors that the completed project is of poor

TABLE 3.11
Completed Project Startup List

Phase 8/Stage 8 Classic Tasks
Hazard and operability review procedure
Facility startup procedure
Starting systems
Testing, adjusting, and balancing systems
Mechanical systems
Piping systems
Air systems
Electrical equipment
Demonstrations
Startup schedule
Startup budget
Startup resources
Turnover procedure

Note: The startup or commissioning of a completed project is very important and needs to be planned, budgeted, and scheduled as carefully as the design and construction of the project itself.

quality; the users and the designers never saw each other during the course of the project; project definition has not been adequately prepared through a cooperative effort by the project team and the users, and the finished system has little or no relation to what the users expected; the cost is overrun; or the project is late and the competition has stolen away with the market. If any, some, or all of these bad things happen, the project manager had better be prepared to spend a lot more time and money, perhaps his or her own, to make good. And, as often happens on project work, there is the worst-case scenario in which everybody ends up in a court of law.

It needs to be clear to project managers that the users drive the project need. Their concerns are paramount in defining, designing, and delivering the system. Their needs and preferences must be dealt with at the beginning of the project. They must somehow be kept informed and be part of the decision making. Even then, if there are startup and operating problems, it is not the users who will take the fall. As is known in project work, success has many authors. But failure is the fault of the project manager.

Decommissioning and Disposal

Stage 9, Operations & Maintenance, in Fig. 3.9 is the last of the project life cycle steps listed, as is Phase 9, Operations, in Fig. 3.8. Project managers should not be surprised when smart clients now ask them to include a decommissioning and disposal phase in the project life cycle. Built projects, systems, and facilities have shorter life spans than ever. As a result the project life cycle may need to include a planned disposal phase—in other words, planned obsolescence to a predetermined scope, cost, and time frame. This kind of additional stricture places greater demands on the skills and decision-making capabilities of the project management team. Not only is the target to define, design, and deliver to suit operations, the market, and the bottom line, but to comply with an established decommissioning and environmentally driven cleanup target.

3.9 Summary

This chapter provides a method to break down a project using stages or phases to identify activities and tasks. The previous chapter identified a method to define the scope and quality of a project. The difficulty in finding the line that separates definition from breakdown was discussed at some length in both chapters. The answer is that the line varies from project to project. No one structure can answer both questions, and experience shows that more rather than fewer structures provide better means for project control systems.

Work breakdown structuring and its related coding system are seen to come from at least two project management schools. There is the WBS system from the PERT usage on military and industrial and NASA megaprojects. And there is the cost engineering methodology developed by the engineers of process industries to control project cost. This book shows that they both were looking to break down and code projects into elements, tasks, and organizations for cost control purposes. Both systems had the same objective.

Go one step further and use the system for *all* project control.

REFERENCES

CA-SuperProject Reference Guide for Microsoft Windows, 3.0 (Computer Associates International, Islandia, NY, 1992, p. 4.8.

Clark, F. D., and A. B. Lorenzoni, *Applied Cost Engineering* (Marcel Dekker, New York, 1978).

Hackney, J. W., *Control and Management of Capital Projects* (Wiley, New York, 1965).

Iannone, A. L., *Management Program Planning and Control with PERT, MOST and LOB* (Prentice-Hall, Englewood, Cliffs, NJ, 1967).

Microsoft Project, Version 3.0, Apple Macintosh or Windows Series, User's Reference (Microsoft Corp., Redmond, WA, 1992).

Open Plan 4.0, User Guide (Serious Project Management Software, WST Corp., Houston, TX, 1991).

Prestige PC User Manual (4.1) (Artemis Management Systems, Boulder, CO, 1991).

Primavera Project Planner 5.0, Project Management Handbook (Primavera Systems, Bala Cynwyd, PA, 1991), p. 601.

Project Management System/360 (360A.CP.04X) Version 2 Program and Operations Manual, 3rd ed. (IBM, White Plans, NY, 1968).

Rigney, R. A., and R. H. Campbell, "PMS: What Are You Getting for Your Money," *Proc. Project Management Inst.* (Newtown Square, PA, 1978).

3100, 3200, 3300, Computer Systems PERT/COST Reference Manual (Control Data Corp., Palo Alto, CA, 1966).

Wysocki, R. K., R. Beck, Jr., and D. B. Crane, *Effective Project Management* (Wiley, New York, 1995).

QUESTIONS AND EXERCISES

3.1 What is the principal purpose of the work breakdown structure (WBS)?

3.2 In this textbook, in discussing project definition and project breakdown, it was seen that there are two main streams of management thought in the development of project management systems based on structures. Describe the two main structural approaches and how they were joined to become the performance measurement system.

3.3 Using the principles presented in this chapter, prepare a concept 1 WBS to level 3 based on the following expressions:

> House, Concept design, Grounds, New house, Capital approval, Loan and mortgage approval, Procurement, Bid and contract award, Construction, Installation, Service areas, Utilities, Drawings and specifications

Add in any missing terms.

3.4 Based on the theories and examples presented in this chapter, prepare a concept 2 WBS to the lowest level possible, based on the following array of expressions:

> Phase 1, Exterior cladding, Phase 3, New house, Interior finishes, Final design and drawings, Substructure, Structure, Interior partitions and doors, Services, Stairs, Construction, Electrical, Plumbing and drains, Heating, ventilating, and air-conditioning, Site development, Services, Exterior doors, Partitions, Driveway and sidewalks

3.5. Describe the main difference between the preceding two WBSs, using words such as stage, phase, packages, activities.

4 PROJECT FUNCTIONAL ORGANIZATION

Traditional corporate departments (the matrix organization) were not capable of delivering modern projects because departments were and are sovereign. As projects were handed off from one department to another, they were fumbled because the departments had their own systems. This always led to delays, loss of scope control, poor quality, and cost overruns. Two main developments evolved out of this situation.

One was the invention of modern project management systems and their computerization, the subject of this book. These systems aim to provide a common project control language, which all project participants use.

The other development was the creation of the office of project manager, the project management office, and the identification and assignment of departmental and external human resources to project tasks through a system of project functional organization, the subject of this chapter.

As top management saw that departmental organizations were unable to deliver multistage and multidisciplinary-driven projects, they appointed project coordinators in matrix organizations with limited success. For big projects, persons with exceptional leadership qualities were appointed as project managers. These appointments were not always welcomed in corporate and public-sector enterprises. The imposition of a project manager was seen as criticism of the existing organization.

In the A/E/C industry, construction projects were notorious for being lengthy, almost always late, often of poor quality, and generally over budget. As a result new project management organizational concepts as well as new tools based on the critical-path method (CPM) were introduced to speed up project delivery and reduce cost.

In the postmodern age, projects are delivered by teams of skilled human resources who are not in hierarchical organizations. They are bound by contract to a project, but not necessarily to each other. Some have a legal role in the project based on the law of the place, or because they represent the public interest. A post-1990s phenomenon is the flattening out of the hierarchical structure, and the empowering of skilled individuals or small groups who have project roles.

This chapter identifies these individuals and groups as functional project organizations and shows their ties to the systems of project management.

4.1 Origins of Project Management

The concept of project management initially was closely linked with the personality of the project manager. If the project was under a super project manager, all would be well. It is difficult to argue against this tenet, as the concept of a strong leader taking on any endeavor is attractive in any walk of life. The personification of one such individual in the project management world was Admiral Hyman Rickover of the Bureau of Ordinance, U.S. Navy, who was the project manager of the Fleet Ballistic Missile Program (Polaris).

PERT was developed for the same project, at the same time. Thus the concept of modern project management very early involved both new-age management and new methodologies.

Other arguments for the application of project management principles used the idea of a central project office occupied by a skilled communicator. This individual would make a place for project management as a new approach to deliver projects within the corporation. The intent was not to replace traditional departments, but to coordinate existing departmental functions for project input.

Project management is still often viewed with disdain in manufacturing, retailing, and utilities companies. This is because the project organization may be superimposed over the operating organization. Corporate departments, bureaucracies, and institutions, such as, hospitals and school boards, normally have a vested interest in maintaining the organizational status quo in terms of the power and influence that has accrued to them. They will generally resist any changes that might detract from their corporate influence.

A project is so different from the day-to-day corporate activities that it is seen as a threat to many departments. They wish to maintain their hierarchical place in the corporate order, but they may not have the resources to take on a new project; they may not have the skills, or they may not have that much to gain from the new project, and therefore not give it the due diligence that it needs for success.

Before the advent of project management, most projects were carried out by existing corporate operations departments through a decentralized organizational process in which different departmental managers were responsible for the various project stages. Even now, with the concept of project management being well understood and accepted, at least on the surface, there are many corporations and institutions that continue to handle project work in a non-project-management manner, that is, decentralized project stages handed off from department to department, no common project code system, and no dedicated project staff whose loyalty is to the project, as opposed to a home department. This condition, using the project stages identified in Chapter 3, may be illustrated by Fig. 4.1.

In this approach, each department manager responds to that department head. No one has total responsibility for the entire project. In these situations, the only project coordination would be at the chief executive or the corporate general manager level. In effect, the chief executive officer may become the defacto project manager.

PROJECT STAGES AND RESPONSIBLE CORPORATE DEPARTMENTS IN A NON-PROJECT-MANAGEMENT ENVIRONMENT

Stage	Project Activity	Functional Department
1	Problem/Opportunity	Manufacturing, user or other functional department having responsibility.
2	Feasibility Study	Manufacturing, user or other functional department having responsibility, with other corporate groups brought in by user group.
3	Conceptual Design	In large corporations by corporate engineering, but under the control of the user group; often by outside consultants under user group, or under corporate engineers.
4	Project Definition	Functional department with the assistance of the engineering department and other corporate departments having a role as selected by the users and approved by corporate executive.
5	Capital/Lease Appropriation Request/Approval	Corporate CEO or Board, depending on approval limits.
6	Design, Drawings, Specifications and Contract Documents	Corporate engineering, by consultants, or by Works departments in cities, states, provinces, and federal governments.
7	Procurement, Tendering, Bidding and Awards	Central purchasing in large corporations, public institutions; user group if authorized, or by corporate engineering.
8	Construction	Construction contractors and subcontractors, major vendors, turnkey builders, under control of the user or corporate engineering.
9	Installation of Equipment and Moving	User department, construction contractors, or major vendors, often under direction of corporate engineers or Works department specialists.
10	Operations Testing	User department or as in 9 above.
11	Commissioning and Startup	User department or as in 9 above; most often, together.
12	Operation	User department.

FIGURE 4.1 PROJECT STAGES OR PHASES IN A NON-PROJECT-MANAGEMENT CORPORATE ORGANIZATION. In this kind of enterprise project work is handed off from department to department. Each department has its own systems, which are applied to the project when it is under that department's control.

In many large corporations, governments, and institutions, in particular those active in repeat project work, responsibility for projects may be vested in the corporate engineering or the public works department. Usually these departments share project authority with other corporate departments. Their roles also were often limited, with authority and responsibility divided among a number of managers and departments. In most of these situations there was initially little or no attempt made to develop distinct, project-oriented functional organizations, even though projects were taking a lot of time to deliver, and were generally over budget. It was a delicate situation in most corporate environments as the idea of a project management organization within a corporate or bureaucratic hierarchy would have upset the status quo.

Figure 4.1 provides an example of how project phases and stages were treated, controlled, and handed off from stage to stage by their various corporate departmental sponsors in pre-project-management corporate organizations.

The information in Fig. 4.1 is recognizable as project stages in a typical project work breakdown exercise. Stages 1 through 12 are listed and named as discussed in Chapter 3. The stages are shown as they may be assigned in a typical corporate or institutional organization. Under the project management concept of organization all the project stages would be under the direction and control of the project manager. In a non-project-management environment there may be a project coordinator without the responsibility and authority of a project manager. If this happens to be the case, the individual in the role may become the project messenger.

As no one ever likes the bearer of bad news, the project messenger never carries any as the project deteriorates. Sometimes in these situations, the project becomes the property of the strongest departmental manager, which may or may not be good for the corporate project objective.

In other cases the project becomes disrupted through inaction, lack of timely decisions, infighting, loss of scope control, no possibility of cost control, and general confusion, until eventually the chief executive officer is forced onto the scene to resolve the mess. And it is precisely these kinds of situations and conditions that led to the concept of project management in the first instance.

In many large corporations and institutions, the corporate engineers often take on the broader coordination role and assume overall guidance of the project stages. But they are by no means the master of the project. They may have no real authority and do not build separate project organizations. As long as they work in this way, they may be able to generate cooperation and the forbearance of the corporate departments.

This kind of corporate environment may have existed at a major electric power generating utility company as discussed by Stuckenbruck in *The Implementation of Project Management.*

This corporation had a power supply department responsible for operation, and an engineering department. The engineering department, organized by disciplines, could be very strong, depending on the number of new projects going through. There was no project management. Project leadership would be provided by the lead engineering discipline. For example, a nuclear generating project would be led by the nuclear engineer. An oil-fired generating station would have a mechanical engineer as the leader, and so on. But the lead engineers did not have overall authority. Some of the project problems that were reported included inadequate design criteria, lack of input by disciplines to suit schedules, no cost control, and no schedule control.

A simplified version of the organization in place at the time is seen in Fig. 4.2. As a measure to help resolve the problems of inadequate design and cost and schedule problems, the company decided to convert all projects in the engineering department to project management, including the appointment of project managers. The resulting engineering department organization with project management in place may be seen in Fig. 4.3. This is a classic matrix organization wherein personnel report functionally to a discipline head and at the same time to a project manager for a specific project, or to a number of project managers. People would have two or more bosses.

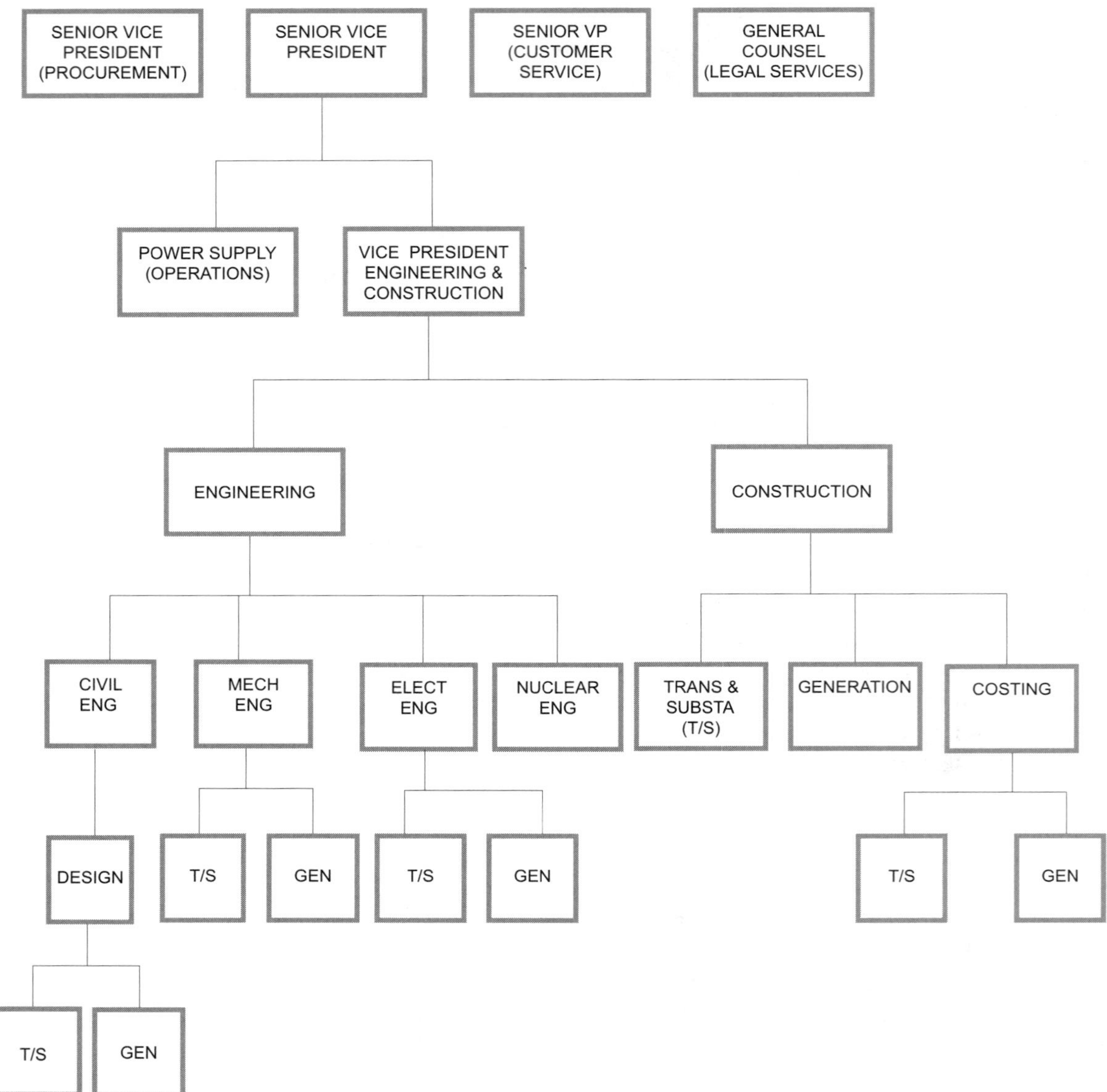

FIGURE 4.2 POWER GENERATING UTILITY FUNCTIONAL DEPARTMENTS, PRIOR TO PROJECT MANAGEMENT POSITIONS. This is a typical corporate organizational structure, prior to the recognition of the needs of project management principles for the delivery of projects.

It was concluded in this case that the introduction of project management helped in the delivery of projects by coordinating all projects, setting priorities, and allocating resources. Project managers developed their own reporting formats. Simple projects were scheduled by bar charts. Larger projects used critical-path scheduling.

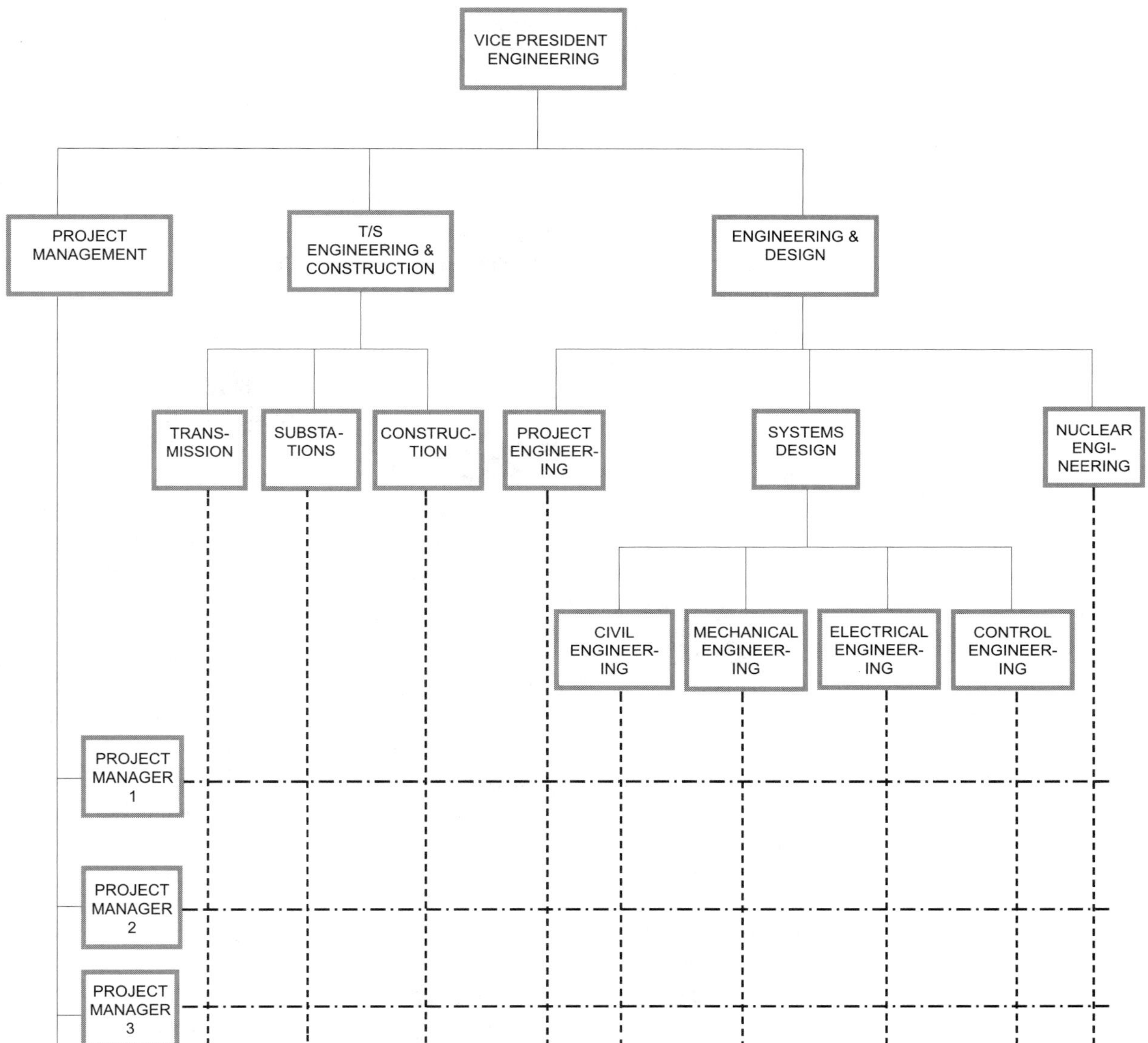

FIGURE 4.3 POWER GENERATING UTILITY MATRIX ORGANIZATION, INCORPORATING PROJECT MANAGEMENT POSITIONS. This illustrates a typical departmental organization augmented with project manager positions. A project manager would call on individuals or groups within departments to provide input to their project. Each discipline or group would have two or more offices to report to.

From a project management systems point of view, as presented in this book, projects were handled as before. But the concept of a matrix organization incorporating project management was a very important step, and a precursor to a system of project management applicable to all kinds of projects, not only those in engineering.

As discussed previously, the introduction of a project manager position would undoubtedly help the project coordination and control situation, but from a purely organizational and human resources perspective. There is still the question of the information systems, codes, and procedures that are needed to glue all the diverse project groups together and make them as one for the purposes of project control.

4.2 Systems of Project Management and the Matrix Organization

Project management is an idea, a concept, an approach. It is a group of coordinated systems which when applied to project work cause movement and progress. There are as many ways to apply ideas and systems to projects as there are people. Some ways are more effective than others. Some organizational concepts may work better than others, not because they are better, but because of the conditions and human interactions that occur at that time, in that place.

The idea of systems project management is not dependent on a "my way or the highway" organization of people. On the contrary, project management systems need to be flexible and applicable in all kinds of organizations, including the many different concepts of matrix organizations.

This textbook does not join in the discussion of the pros and cons of the matrix organization versus the dedicated project organization, or who has and who does not have power, or where people's loyalties should be. A key objective is to demonstrate that the concepts of project management systems works equally well in all kinds of project organizations. To understand project management is to be aware that people will be cast in many different organizational relationships.

In the North American business climate, project work, in particular the capital cost manufacturing and building sectors, is the most fragmented, individualistic, entrepreneurial, free-spirited, and competitive in the world. The systems of project management are not intended to collar these individualistic companies and people. The objective is to coordinate and control their activities as they impact on your project. This is to be done first by identifying their activities and deliverables, and second, by relating their resources to the project functional organization.

The capital goods and building facility delivery services (planners, designers, manufacturers, constructors) really belong to the ultimate matrix organization. When management scientists discuss matrix organizations in very large corporations, they often speak of people's loyalties: is it to the project, or to the functional department? This is no contest. It is definitely to the person's home department.

In the capital goods and building facilities projects, public works, and civil engineering jobs there is no doubt in the minds and hearts of the employees of contractors and subcontractors, vendors and installers as to where their loyalties are: to the project? No.

And that is the challenge of project management and the systems of project management: to coordinate and control the many diverse organizations and their people for the benefit of the project, because, in the final reckoning, if the program does not succeed, they all lose.

Modern project management systems came with the invention of the program evaluation and review technique (PERT) and CPM. Postmodern projects in the age of the PC are invariably delivered by teams of multidisciplinary individuals. In the past, project management organizations were almost always depicted as task forces or groups in very large and complex military or industrial style organizations. Although we can draw on the concepts from those developments and apply the theory to today's project management needs, the main commonality between those early concepts and today's computerized applications is that they both aim to deliver project control systems services.

Taking a modern capital project, for example, it is usually scoped by the client, designed by an architect, many consultants, and engineers, and constructed by a contractor and subcontractors, and all of them supported by many private sector vendors, manufacturers, agents, and individuals. These individuals and groups do not belong to a single organization. They could range from a one-person firm to a 1000-employee organization. The only thing they have in common is the project on which they are all working. The thing that binds them together is their contract with each other and the project owner. And the functional organization structure must reflect this and be made suitable for the code system that will lead to project control.

4.3 Construction Project Functional Organizations

The capital goods, building, public works, and engineering construction sectors are made up of small and large companies and groups of skilled people, such as architects, engineers, analysts, programmers, and so on. They provide a wide range of goods and services. They as well as the buyers of the products and services for projects are organized in many different ways. But they need to work together to deliver projects. When this happens, they do not change their internal organizations, but look to be brought together and organized as a project team. The thing they have in common is the project. As each project is unique, how are the human resources brought together as organizations to create that project?

Unique projects require unique methods to achieve their objectives. The methods are meant to reflect the main goal of the project. A project goal may be construction cost containment. It may be to meet a short timeline. It may be the method of financing from the owner's perspective. It may be complexity. Or it may be that the project process is proprietary, and the buyer is obliged to comply with the seller's terms of purchase.

A project objective is best achieved with an objective-oriented functional organization. As the project and its project delivery team are temporary associations, they are bound to each other by their contracts. It is essential to incorporate into the organization structure the contractual relationships between project buyers and sellers.

We have identified 16 ways to organize human resources and financing for all kinds of projects. A "way" to deliver a project may also be called a "mode," a "method," or an "approach," but the constant factor in all ways is the agreement, or the contract between the buyer of the project and the sellers of the services. The 16 ways to deliver projects are

1. Lump sum (general contract)
2. Phased packages (up to 10 packages)
3. Construction management of phased packages
4. Construction management of lump sum general contracts
5. Multiple packages (trades)
6. Project manager (project management)
7. Accelerated (sequential) scheduling
8. Overlapping design and construction
9. Fast track (fast tracking)
10. Design/build—developer
11. Design/build—lump sum or guaranteed maximum price
12. Design/build—cost plus fee
13. Design/build—turnkey
14. Lease/purchase, alternative 1 (standard approach)
15. Lease/purchase, alternative 2 (phased package conversion)
16. Lease/purchase, alternative 3 (design/build)

The 16 ways are just the tip of the project delivery methods iceberg. Buyers are always looking for a better way to procure projects. As the buyers are usually more powerful than the individual sellers, employing many business and legal specialists to take better advantage of their suppliers and professionals, the number of ways and modes to deliver projects is probably much higher.

The American Institute of Architects recognized the many new approaches to deliver building projects and issued a guide for its members to follow in connection with all the different project delivery methods. That guide covers the subject from the point of view of the architect. This discussion covers project delivery from the functional organizational perspective involving all project participants.

When we speak of the many ways, modes, or methods to deliver projects, the discussion invariably centers on organization. The different modes of delivery and their names are a means to cast the same players in different roles. Even though different results are expected to be achieved by each of the different ways, there are three important fundamentals that form the basis for each of the ways:

1. The project manager plays the lead role in each way. Organizationally speaking, the project manager is at the top of the project organizational pyramid.

2. There is to be no tinkering with the corporate organization (on account of the project) or any outside designers, construction contractors, subcontractors, or vendor organizations. There is no question of where people's loyalties lie: it is to the organizations that employ them.

3. The project organization is a reflection of the contract between the owner or buyer of the project and the deliverers. The organization needs to mirror the project objective. The contract needs to be agreed early, and the project functional organization structure must reflect it.

When a corporate owner, a public works unit, or a large government department engages in projects, it is incumbent on the senior executives of those entities to create project management organizations that can operate in the context of these three maxims. If this cannot be done because of internal considerations or statutory regulations, the executive would be well advised to appoint outside professional project management.

Professional project management people owe their allegiance to the project that employs them. The project is their home. They know that, and every other project participant knows that and is able to live and work within that context.

4.3.1 Lump Sum (General Contract) Project Organization

At one time the traditional lump sum general contract was the only way to acquire a capital project. It is still the preferred way for many corporations and public institutions. Indeed, it is so well established in North American capital project work that rules governing general contract public tendering or bidding by private-sector firms for public-sector projects are written into law in many jurisdictions.

In its earlier manifestation before the advent of project management, the design consultants, usually architects or engineers, played a "master builder" role in the process. The traditional approach was for the consultants to completely program, design, and specify the project. The owner would then call bids on the basis of completed drawings and specifications. A contract for construction eventually would be awarded, usually to the low bidder. The consultant would act as the arbiter of the contract between the owner and the contractor. Eventually the project was finished and the facility occupied or placed in service. Project management was unheard of and not really necessary according to the conventional wisdom of the day.

The traditional lump sum general contract approach normally followed a well-established corporate or bureaucratic procedure, usually comprising the following steps:

- Project functional requirements are prepared by the owner.
- The project definition is prepared by the owner.
- Design consultants are appointed by the owner.

- A project manager from the owner's own organization is sometimes appointed.
- Construction documentation is prepared by the consultants.
- A lump sum construction contract is awarded to the low bidder.

In a well-ordered business environment or a public bureaucracy, the lump sum general contract approach continues to be a favorite method to acquire not only capital building projects, but all sorts of hardware and software. The most attractive feature of the lump sum approach is that it does not unduly disrupt the corporate status quo. This means that a project may be treated as just another piece of business to be processed by the corporate divisions, departments, and functions. In this case there would not be a project management function.

The corporation may recognize that the project is different from the day-to-day business of the firm and appoint a project management function. The project management function may be filled by any one of a number of people or a committee.

In these examples of the 16 ways to deliver a project, a project management function is shown in a key role in each organization chart.

The selection of the mode of project delivery is dependent on many reasons. Objectively speaking, from the owner's perspective there are advantages and disadvantages to each of the 16 ways, and they are listed alongside the organizational charts. The lump sum general contract organization chart is depicted in Fig. 4.4. Its advantages and disadvantages are shown alongside the graphic.

4.3.2 Phased Packages (up to 10 Packages)

For many years the lump sum general contract way was the only game in town. Because of its established position in the business world and in public works, it continues to be used widely for the delivery of capital projects. As postmodern projects became technologically more complex, and factors such as the cost of money, the pressures of inflation, the volatility of the construction marketplace, and not least the market forces driving the owner's needs for the new facility all came into play, it became evident that the lengthy schedules required for the lump sum general contract approach were not viable.

The impetus for the new approach to project delivery services came from project managers or construction managers. One of the earlier efforts to speed up the delivery process was the phased packages approach, usually comprising not more than 10 packages, as illustrated in Fig. 4.5. The actions to invoke this approach by the corporate owner are not dissimilar to the general contract way, and are listed here as procedures:

- Project functional requirements are prepared by the owner and the users.
- The project definition is prepared by the owner.

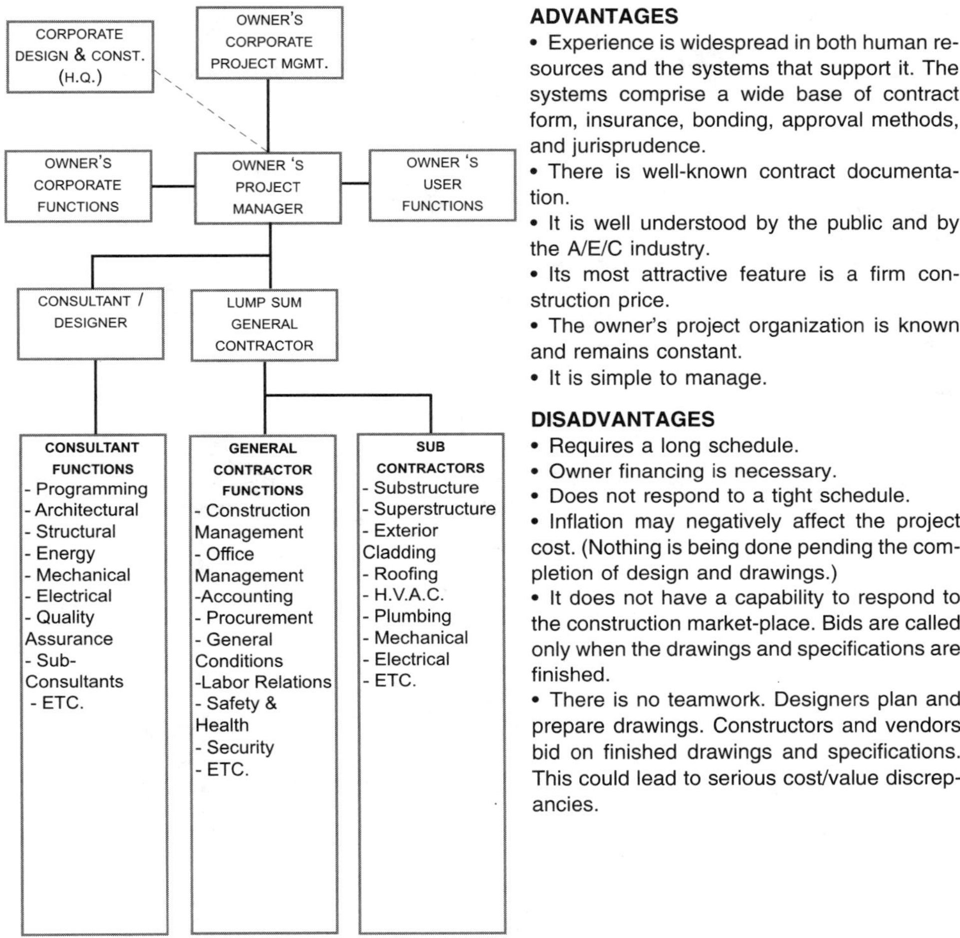

FIGURE 4.4 PROJECT FUNCTIONAL ORGANIZATION CHART, LUMP SUM GENERAL CONTRACT.

- Design consultants are appointed by the owner.
- A project manager from the owner's own organization is appointed.
- Construction documentation is prepared by the consultants.
- Construction management is by the owner.
- Lump sum construction contracts are awarded for the construction packages.

The advantages and disadvantages of this approach from the owner's aspect are listed alongside the organization chart in Fig. 4.5.

ADVANTAGES

- Reasonable depth of experience exists in most corporate owner organizations.
- This approach is reasonably well understood by the public, the A/E/C industry, and tenderers.
- It responds better to a tight schedule.

DISADVANTAGES

- Owner financing is necessary.
- More owner human resources are required. These project-specific skills are not always readily available within the organization.
- Construction costs are less well known as the project goes into the more expensive phases of project work earlier.
- As in the lump sum general contract way, there is still no teamwork. Linear responsibility is in place.

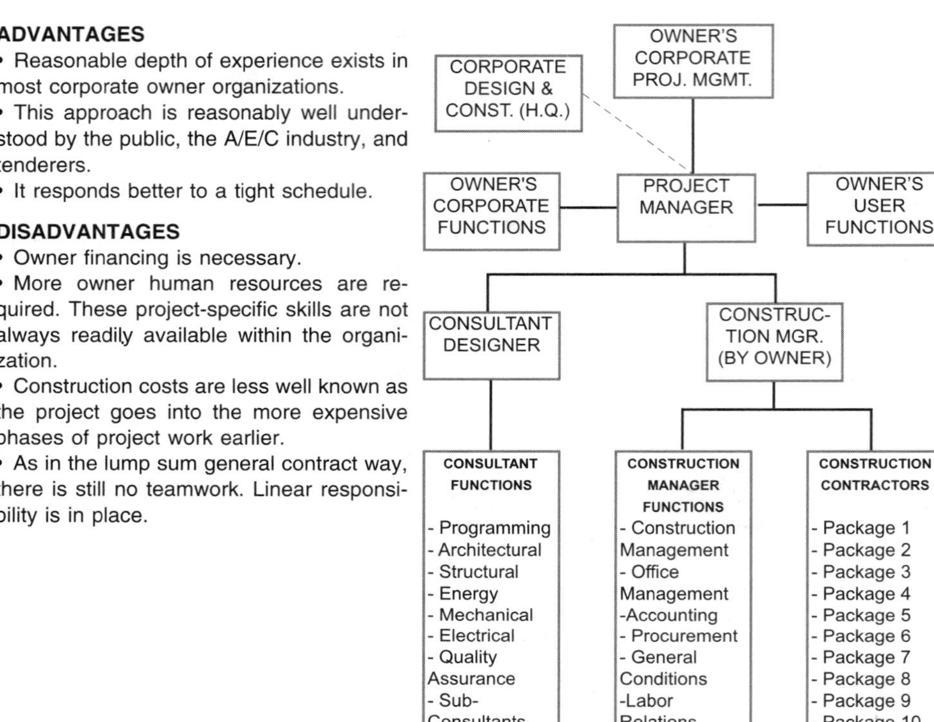

FIGURE 4.5 PROJECT FUNCTIONAL ORGANIZATION CHART, PHASED PACKAGES (UP TO 10 PACKAGES).

4.3.3 Construction Management of Phased Packages

Construction management is seen by many as a complete project delivery system, which encompasses all aspects of the project process. Often in the capital project business, the terms "project management" and "construction management" are seen as synonymous. Although that is not necessarily the case in this book, it is important to understand that many people have this perception, and as far as they are concerned, it works for them.

In this project organization example construction management is used to facilitate the construction process, rather than the project process. The construction process is traditionally thought to begin with the bidding and award stage of the project process. The project process is thought to begin with the "need" or the "opportunity or problem" stage of the process.

The construction management functional organizational chart is depicted in Fig. 4.6. The basic rules or procedures to invoke this method are approximately as follows:

- The project requirements are prepared by the corporate user department.
- The project definition (called "project brief" by some corporate owners or bureaucracies practicing project management) is prepared by the owner.
- Designers and consultants are appointed by the owner from outside the owner's own organization.

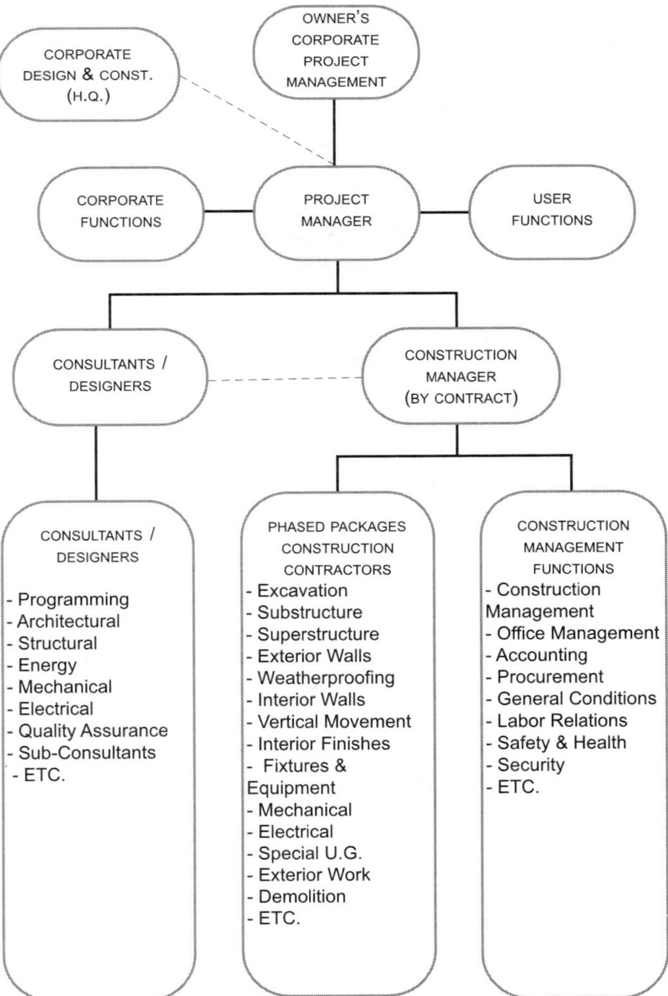

ADVANTAGES

- There is some depth of experience in owner organizations and the A/E/C industry.
- There is an inventory of tested and proven contract documentation.
- The CM approach is fairly well understood by the public and by construction industry vendors, contractors, and subcontractors.
- This method reduces or eliminates the need for the owner organization to grow its human resources for the life of the project.
- The CM method promises to reduce the project schedule.
- The CM method provides an opportunity for more teamwork, construction input during planning and design, and better cost control.
- CM responds best to a tight (short) schedule.

DISADVANTAGES

- The owner does not know the project cost until after the last contract is let.
- In some public agencies regulations do not permit delivery of projects by the CM method.
- Some corporations do not allow CM because of cost uncertainty.
- Owner financing is a disadvatage to some owners.

FIGURE 4.6 PROJECT FUNCTIONAL ORGANIZATION CHART, CONSTRUCTION MANAGEMENT (CM) OF PHASED PACKAGES.

- The project manager is appointed by the owner from within the owner organization. In this case the project manager is an employee of the corporate owner.
- The construction manager, appointed by the owner, is a professional individual or a firm from outside the owner corporate organization or the public agency. The appointment of the construction manager may be through a bidding, tendering, or prequalifying process. The key consideration in this case is that the construction manager (firm or individual) is a specialist from outside the owner organization.
- The construction contract documents are prepared jointly by the construction manager and the designers or consultants.
- Construction packages are bid and awarded by invitation, prequalification, or open advertising.

The advantages and disadvantages of the construction management way to deliver a project are listed alongside the graphic in Fig. 4.6.

Lump sum general contracts between owners and general contractors continue to be the most frequently used way to acquire projects in North America. With the introduction of professional construction management the approach gained even more credibility as a modern management approach that is suitable for big engineering jobs, public works, and industrial and commercial projects.

There are other ways, as described and as will be seen in the following pages. It may be useful at this point to touch upon the different ways there are to break down construction projects for packaging, bidding, and awarding contracts for construction. Two of the most widely used are (1) vertical breakdown and (2) horizontal breakdown.

The vertical breakdown may be seen in the discussion and depiction of the construction management of lump sum general contracts. In this method each facility, building or stand-alone unit is completely defined, designed, tendered, and constructed under a lump sum contract.

Horizontal breakdowns refer to project elements as they relate to trade contractors. For example, all the project concrete would be wrapped up into one package, bid and awarded as a lump sum trade contract. Structural steel, piping, insulation, and the other project element groups would be individually wrapped, documented, bid, and awarded. Bulk purchasing might be introduced also for materials such as cement, piping, reinforcing steel, electric wiring, and so on. The impact of horizontal construction breakdowns on project functional organizations is touched upon in the discussions of the different modes that follow.

It is important to understand that the delivery mode selected and the breakdown of construction, assembly, purchasing, and procurement will have a strong impact on the project quality, cost, and schedule.

4.3.4 Construction Management of Lump Sum General Contracts

There are projects comprising many elements of site works, services, buildings, functions, and processes. These often large undertakings, or megaprojects, may be delivered in many different ways. A favorite way is construction management of lump sum general contracts.

Figure 4.7 depicts the project functional organization structure for this method. It is seen that this organization structure is similar to the chart for construction management of phased packages. The difference is that the phased packages contracts are replaced by lump sum general contract packages. This obviously raises many questions regarding management actions in the design and procurement of the individual lump sum packages and the role of the construction manager. Some of these questions are answered by the project procedures listed:

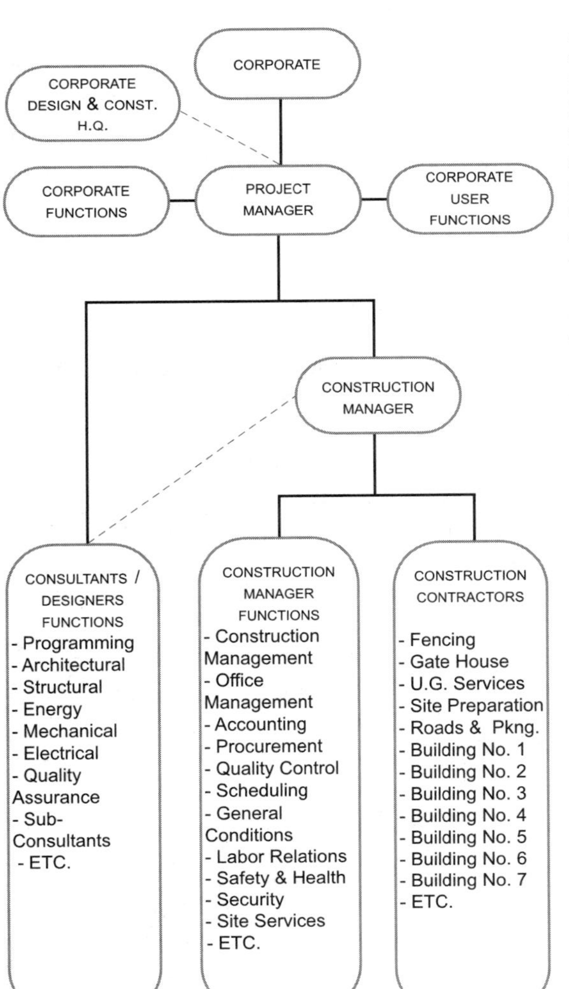

ADVANTAGES

- This method is mostly applicable to large projects comprising many buildings, like a university campus or a green field facility comprising a water pump house, a waste treatment plant, railroad siding, process plants, administration building, etc.
- For processing lump sum contracts there is a reasonable depth of experience in large organizations, along with proven contract documentation.
- The method is well understood by the public and the A/E/C industry.
- CM would provide construction input during the design process and generate more teamwork between owners, designers, and constructors.
- It responds to a tight schedule and requires a shorter schedule.

DISADVANTAGES

- Owner financing is necessary.

FIGURE 4.7 PROJECT FUNCTIONAL ORGANIZATION CHART, CONSTRUCTION MANAGEMENT (CM) OF LUMP SUM GENERAL CONTRACTS.

- Functional requirements are prepared by the owner or user.
- Project definition is prepared by the user.
- Consultants and designers are appointed by the owner.
- The project manager is an owner appointee.
- The construction manager could be a construction contractor, or the construction division of an engineering/procurement/construction (E/P/C) company. Usually the function is under contract to the owner.
- Construction documentation is prepared jointly by the construction manager and the designers and consultants.
- Lump sum construction contracts would be executed between the owner and the general contractors.

4.3.5 Multiple Packages (Trades)

The concept of multiple or trade packages is perhaps the true forerunner of the term "construction management."

Construction management was first seen as a new way to shorten the schedule and reduce the cost of the project to the owner. These two benefits could be achieved with phased packages and with construction management. Maximum benefits, according to "pure" construction management professionals, could only be achieved by breaking down the project into its individual trade packages and awarding contracts on that basis only. In this way no trade contractor employed on the project would be a subcontractor. All trades would be under the management of the construction manager. The construction manager in turn would have no subcontractors.

Since this way is remarkably different from the traditional lump sum way, the approach although attractive to many owners was seen to have potential for causing problems of quality, coordination, and responsibility for the project cost.

As for the project functional organizational structure for multiple packages (trade) it is similar to that for construction management of phased packages seen in Fig. 4.6. The difference is that each trade contract would be a prime contractor with the owner. The additional main disadvantage is the pronounced complexity of dealing with many more independent contractors.

4.3.6 Project Manager (Project Management)

The term "project manager" or "project management" initially became synonymous with the project organizational concept, whereby the project owner turned over the project completely to an outside individual or firm offering project management services. Some of the firms offering this new service came from the architectural and engineering professions. Some had their genesis in large, multinational accounting firms and general management consulting groups.

Project management as a complete service to major owners was first successfully marketed by the big E/P/C firms for megadollar defense, energy, and resource projects. The concept of project management and project manager became a metaphor for doing the job right, meaning on time and on budget. While initially "project manager" meant the person in the office of the project manager, it now more often signifies a total project delivery system, including the office of project manager and the systems of project management. The concept today is used by just about everybody, in every industry and every sector of economic life.

Although there are many variations on the project management theme, the general procedures to initiate the process are outlined next. Depending on the project and the owner's own capabilities to establish the project terms of reference, it is advisable for the owner to do a number of fundamental tasks before the project is turned over to an outside project management company. As a minimum, these tasks are as follows:

- Preparation of the functional requirements by the owner or user organization.
- Preparation of the project brief as part of the project definition.
- Appointment of the owner's own project manager. Sometimes this is a problem area in that the project becomes top heavy with an owner's project manager and an outside project manager. But it does work with proper terms of reference and professional attitudes all around.
- The outside project manager needs to be appointed early in the project, during the earliest front-end activities.
- The preparation of the contract documents is to be under the direction of the outside project manager in cooperation with the designers and consultants.
- Bidding of project and construction packages would be by invitation, or by public advertising for public works projects.
- Construction contracts would be based on lump-sum tenders.

The advantages and disadvantages of the project management approach are listed alongside the organizational chart in Fig. 4.8.

However, it needs to be reiterated that the project organization must be a reflection of the agreement between the owner organization and the outside project manager. The extent, quality, and viability of the project management services and the resulting positive influence on the completed project will vary directly with the powers vested in the project manager by the corporate owner.

4.3.7 Accelerated (or Sequential) Scheduling

The concept of construction management is sometimes referred to as accelerated or sequential scheduling. The procedures, the pros and cons, and the organizational chart are similar to those listed under construction management.

ADVANTAGES

- The outside project manger is to be an A/E/C professional. The project would benefit early from construction input.
- Outside consultants, designers, and construction contractors would be under the coordinating umbrella of a professional project manager from the outset.
- Project design would benefit by early construction input.
- A shorter project schedule is the expectation.
- This approach responds to a tight schedule.
- There is potential for real teamwork in the front-end stages.
- The project is in a better position to respond to market place conditions.
- Bid prices should have less contingency and risk.

DISADVANTAGES

- The main disadvantage is that the owner could lose control of the project.
- Changes are difficult, mostly because of the fast pace of the project under this method.
- As this is a new method, formal, proven owner/project manager agreement documentation is less available.
- Financing is by the owner corporation.

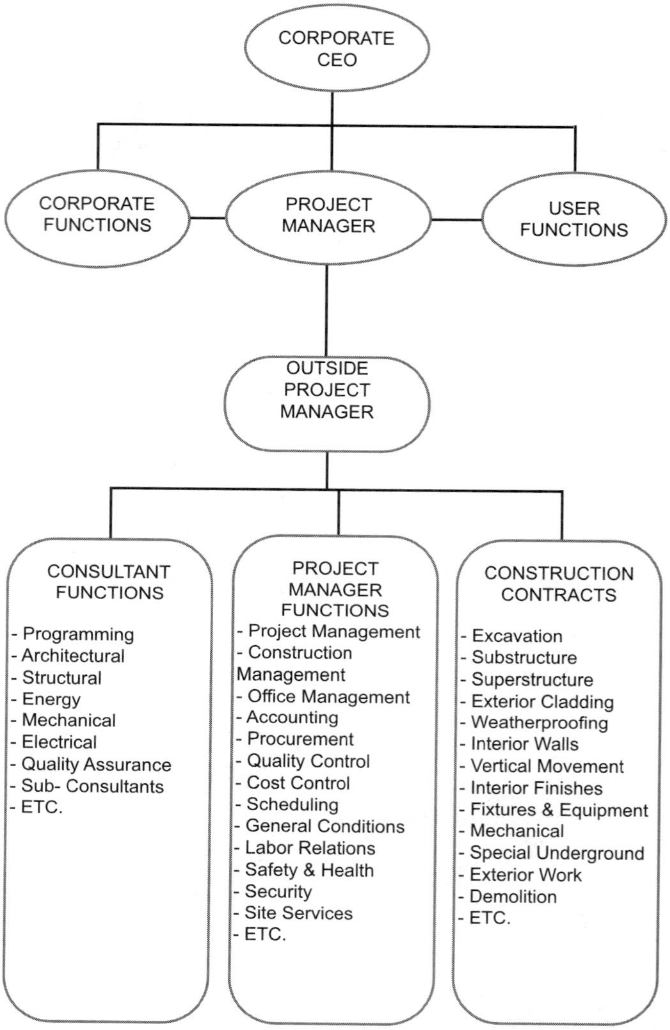

FIGURE 4.8 PROJECT FUNCTIONAL ORGANIZATION CHART, PROJECT MANAGER (PROJECT MANAGEMENT).

The whole idea of this approach is that the entire project does not need to be designed before some of it is processed into the manufacturing, assembly and construction phases.

Problems arise in selecting from the different construction management ways when a way is chosen without fully understanding and following through on all aspects of the impact of that way. For example, the way chosen affects owner decision making, consultant design process, contract documentation, bid packaging, procurement, and construction. Accelerated or sequential scheduling to work properly and deliver the accepted benefits must be reflected in all project phases.

Accelerated or sequential scheduling is similar to overlapping design and construction and to fast tracking discussed next.

4.3.8 Overlapping Design and Construction

The thrust of the overlapping design and construction organization is to shorten the project schedule and put the facility to earlier use. The functional organization, the procedures, and the advantages and disadvantages are similar to those shown for construction management and in some cases for project management.

4.3.9 Fast Track (Fast Tracking)

Perhaps the project management name that is most popular is "fast track way," or "fast tracking." Fast tracking has become a favorite term, as it applies not only to project management of construction, but also to jet-setting life styles and the style of business in high technology, the applied sciences, the arts, and indeed processing government legislation.

4.3.10 Design/Build—Developer

The design/build method is a competitive way for corporate owners and government agencies to acquire facilities and capital projects. The traditional owner need, architect design, and contractor build lump sum general contract method tended to offload more of the construction risk to the contractor.

The lump sum general contract method came under attack by the construction management method because of its slowness and inability to react to schedules and the construction marketplace. What happened quite often was that the entire project schedule float would be used up by owner decision making and the design process, leaving not enough time for the construction phase. Second the lump sum general contract method could lead to loss of cost control because of the lengthy design period and the fact that cost control methods were usually not in place during early planning and design.

The design/build approach aimed to improve upon not only the traditional lump sum general contract method, but also upon the construction management and project management methods by making the design/build firm responsible for the cost of the entire project, including design, construction, and in some cases financing as well. Whereas the traditional methods very rarely included land as part of the project process, the design/build method often incorporated the provision of land and its cost into the equation.

It can be said about the design/build practitioners that they are individualistic, competitive, entrepreneurial, and not averse to risk taking. The attractiveness of the service they offer to owners stems from its capability to remove more of the risk when launching a new product or service requiring capital facilities and equipment. If a corporate owner needs a new facility to launch a product line, should the owner place its capital in bricks and mortar or in the technology that drives the business? Are not most owners better equipped to manage their own business rather than the jungles that most construction projects become?

Design/build sprang out of the modern-day development industry. Initially involved in shopping centers, speculative office buildings, and residential developments, design/build groups sometimes led by merchant bankers also deal in high-technology research centers, schools, and institutional facilities.

If there is a negative aspect to the design/build process, it is that it is perceived as delivering poor quality. This could be because initially it operated at the low end of the facilities spectrum, such as strip malls and minimal warehouse type buildings. This aspect is negated by a knowledgeable owner who knows what is wanted and puts in the project management effort to ensure that the selected design/build group delivers.

A corporate owner or a public agency contemplating a design/build project needs to follow strict front-end procedures to ensure the delivery of the project that it wants. Owners must be aware that the design/build industry is intensely cost conscious. This attitude is prevalent during the bidding process, negotiating, and especially so after the award of the design/build contract. What this means to the owner organization is that it must know what it wants, state it clearly in the definition, and make no changes during the process.

The procedures to be followed by the owner organization to initiate a design/build process include the following:

- Functional requirements must be well prepared by the owner or users.
- The project brief prepared by the owner as part of the project definition must be a "tight" document in every respect.
- The owner appoints its own project manager.
- The owner prepares its own design/build proposal call, stipulating the method of payment. Bidding may be by invitation, or by open tenders for public works projects.

Figure 4.9 depicts the project organizational structure involving a design/build developer. Listed alongside are the general advantages and disadvantages to the owner of this way to deliver a project.

The matter of the contractual agreement and method of reimbursement between the buyer and the design/build contractor is discussed next. A typical way might be the cost of the project plus a fixed fee. This kind of arrangement could be suitable for a situation where the buyer wants a specific location and is obliged to deal with the owner of the site, who will only sell the project including land on a fee basis. The fee could be a fixed amount or a percentage or, indeed, a share of the profits forever. Other arrangements are touched upon in the following sections.

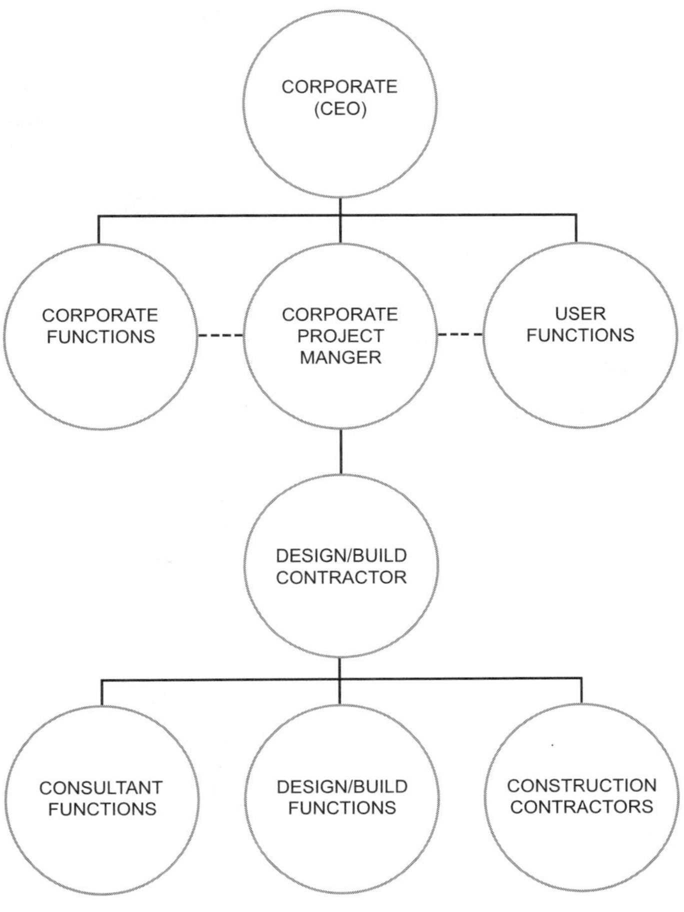

ADVANTAGES

- The owner human resources need not grow for the project.
- The project cost is set.
- The design/build contractor takes the risks.
- Current construction marketplace input is provided.

DISADVANTAGES

- Less well known as a process with a lack of proven documentation.
- Quality control is often a problem.
- Management is difficult. Not liked by A/E/C professionals.
- Owner/user changes are difficult and costly.
- Limited availability of biders. Not well understood by public.
- Payment may be required for unsuccessful proposals.

FIGURE 4.9 PROJECT FUNCTIONAL ORGANIZATION CHART, DESIGN/BUILD.

4.3.11 Design/Build—Lump Sum or Guaranteed Maximum Price

There are many ways to pay for a design/build project. A design/build contract between owner and contractor may be on the basis of a lump sum or a guaranteed maximum price.

The lump sum agreement would be perhaps the most difficult to structure, document, and negotiate. The buyer requires skill and resources to define, design, and structure the basis of the agreement and obtain bona fide proposals from experienced design/build contractors.

The guaranteed maximum price agreement is perhaps less stringent initially in that some of the project parameters may be firmed up as progress is made and costed at that time. There may be a provision for sharing savings between the owner and the contractor. But again for a business-like relationship to exist there is a firm project definition needed as the basis for the project scope.

The *advantages* of the lump sum approach include a stipulated price. A stipulated price is supposed to be a lump sum, a "hard" amount that is fixed, firm. There should be no extras. It is a "what you see is what you get" (WYSIWYG) type of deal. The problem is the extreme difficulty in taking the time and expending the energy and resources to come up with a foolproof project definition and, the corollary of that, a complete design transmittal by the proponent.

The *disadvantages* of the lump sum way are a most expensive project definition, more difficult changes, and a harsher business environment.

The *advantages* of the guaranteed maximum price agreement are that the terms of the definition are softer, changes are easier, and the business climate might be a little friendlier. If all goes well, there may even be some money left at project completion to share between buyer and seller.

The *disadvantages* of the guaranteed maximum price design/build way are fuzzier definitions, which could lead to downstream cost and quality problems.

Charts of the lump sum and the guaranteed maximum price design/build organizations would be similar to Fig. 4.7 But the contractual language would be harder for the guaranteed maximum price agreement and hardest for the lump sum contract.

4.3.12 Design/Build—Cost Plus Fee

Compared to a lump sum or guaranteed maximum price design/build approach, the cost plus fee method should lead to a friendlier business environment between the buyer and the seller. On the surface, the proponent's profit comes only from the fee that the buyer has agreed to pay. Presumably the successful proponent is selected on the basis of skill and success in the particular field of endeavor in which the buyer wishes to engage. It is assumed that the proponent has a similar working arrangement with the professional consultants, vendors, contractors, and subcontractors that will be engaged on the project. If this indeed is the case, the owner or buyer could anticipate a smooth project process and a high-quality trouble-free facility upon completion.

If, on the other hand, the proponent is interested in not only the fee, but an additional profit on every consultant and contractor, and is prepared to extract that amount from each contract and report it as cost, the result may be less than what the owner anticipated.

In terms of the fee itself, it could be a lump sum fee or a percentage of the cost of the work. The percentage fee seems unreasonable on the surface in that the higher the cost of the project, the higher the fee to the proponent.

The procedures to initiate a proposal for a design/build—cost plus fee agreement are similar to those listed for the two previous design/build methods. The organizational structure is similar to Fig. 4.9, with the proviso that the communications would be colored by the language of the cost plus fee agreement.

The *advantages* of this approach would be similar to those listed for the previous methods, but modified by the elimination of the discipline imposed by the lump sum and softened even more by the absence of the guaranteed maximum price arrangement.

The *disadvantages* are similar to those listed previously, again heightened by the absence of ceiling prices employed in lump sum and guaranteed maximum price agreement.

4.3.13 Design/Build—Turnkey

The design/build—turnkey way is a well-established method to deliver a proprietary project package to a corporate owner. The proprietary package may be part of a large undertaking, such as a plant that converts natural gas to ethylene as feedstock in a polyethylene process plant. It could be a fast-food outlet as part of a large mall, the operating theater in a hospital complex, or it could be an institutional facility. A turnkey project is one that may be off the shelf and is repeatedly constructed. The only differences between projects come about as a result of site conditions.

A design/build turnkey approach may also be sought by a corporate buyer on the basis of a customized performance specification prepared by the buyer. The intent would be to turn over responsibility for the delivery of the project completely to the contractor selected through a competitive bidding process, or on the basis of reputation.

The main *advantage* of the process is to offload responsibility to a reliable provider.

The main *disadvantage* is possible loss of control, with very little recourse except eventually through the courts.

4.3.14 Lease/Purchase, Alternative 1 (Standard Approach)

The lease purchase method has been used to acquire all kinds of facilities by both the private sector and public institutions. Public works agencies apply the process to reduce capital funding requirements for new facilities, and to put underutilized land holdings, development rights, and air and density rights to higher and better use.

Although many business and professional people do not like the concept of leasing, seeing it as a mortgage on the future and on future generations, others see it as a viable way to reduce the need for more capital to pay for bricks and mortar and to put the available financial resources into the business instead. Public bodies are often rich in land holdings. Placing these holdings into higher and better use through private-sector developers, using private-sector money through the lease purchase method could lead to lower taxes and less borrowing.

Because there are complexities when public lands are involved, the lease/purchase approach comes in a number of different alternatives. It is also possible to combine lease/purchase with more traditional approaches. For example, the owner may have a project designed and specified completely, as for a lump sum bid, and then instead of tendering for a conventional contractor, solicit lease/purchase proposals. Alternatives to this approach will include variations concerning the extent of the completeness of construction documentation and the breakdown of work between the owner as buyer and the lease/purchase proponents.

Typical procedures by a corporate or government owner may include these steps:

- The owner appoints its own project manager.
- Functional requirements are prepared by the owner or user organization.
- Professional consultants and designers are appointed by the owner.
- The project brief as part of the project definition is prepared by the owner or user consortium.
- Construction contract documentation is prepared by the owner project team.
- The owner prepares terms of reference and lease/purchase documentation.
- Lease/purchase bids are invited from prequalified proponents or open for public tendering for public works projects.

It is evident from these steps that the entire project is specified by the owner's project team. In this respect the front-end approach is similar to the traditional lump sum general contract approach, except that it becomes the basis for the lease/purchase alternative 1.

Figure 4.10 shows the project functional organization with its advantages and disadvantages as compared to other lease/purchase alternatives listed alongside.

4.3.15 Lease/Purchase, Alternative 2 (Phased Package Conversion)

There are a number of principal differences between alternatives 1 and 2. In alternative 1 the owner does no construction work. Under alternative 2 the owner does not only carry out the project front end and the design work, but tenders and has constructed a number of usually difficult project elements such as site preparation, site work, municipal services, difficult foundations, and possibly the substructure. The lease/purchase contractor is then obliged by agreement to take over the work completed so far, include it in the scope of the lease/purchase price, and complete the entire project.

Many construction contract problems are caused by owners, either deliberately or through omission, when the owner attempts to minimize the cost of the project by omitting to provide accurate and adequate subsurface information. Most often un-

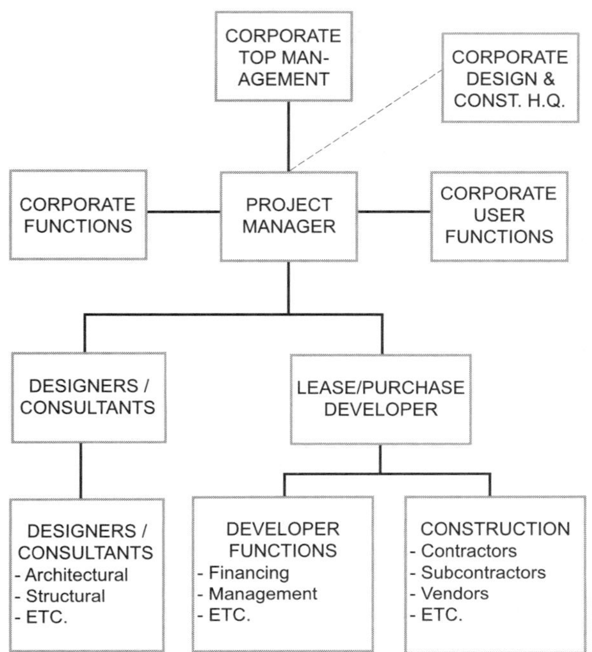

ADVANTAGES

- Because the project is designed by the owner's consultants the quality is known.
- Financing is by the lease/purchase developer/contractor.
- Construction risk is carried by the developer. (To ensure this condition, lease/purchase bidders are severely screened as to their financial stability.)
- As the construction documentation is fully completed, similar to a lump sum, general contract, the quality of the documentation should present fewer problems.
- Expect for the owner's project manager, who may not be on staff, the owner's human resources may not need to be increased for the new project.

DISADVANTAGES

- This alternative requires a longer schedule, similar to a lump sum, general contract way, as there is no overlapping of design and construction. Indeed, the entire delivery may be lengthened because of the possible complexity of the lease/purchase process.
- Because complete project documentation is bid by the lease/purchase developers, and the price tied to a long-term lease, owner changes would be difficult and could be very costly.
- As in a lump sum, general contract scenario, this approach would not be responsive to the construction marketplace.
- There is no teamwork in the project front end.

FIGURE 4.10 PROJECT FUNCTIONAL ORGANIZATION CHART, LEASE/PURCHASE, ALTERNATIVE 1.

derground conditions are assessed only to the extent needed by the structural engineers for foundation and substructure design information. A few soil borings on a site may be enough for foundation design, but may not tell the story of the underground conditions. Invariably, the owner, the owner's legal department, and the owner's consultants through contract "weasel" clauses make construction bidders responsible for underground conditions when the only subsurface information available is based on a few soil borings for foundation design.

In this lease/purchase alternative the owner constructs the site infrastructure and the foundations, and in this way removes a large slice of complexity from the lease/purchase bidding process.

The corporate procedures for the lease/purchase alternative 2 method are the same as for alternative 1 for the owner activities plus the handling of site preparatory work and other difficult conditions as early phased construction contracts.

Figure 4.11 illustrates the lease/purchase alternative 2 organization outline. Listed alongside are the advantages and disadvantages of this approach.

4.3.16 Lease/Purchase, Alternative 3 (Design/Build)

For this way to deliver a project, the owner's procedures are similar to those described for both the design build concepts and the two lease/purchase alternatives. Since the

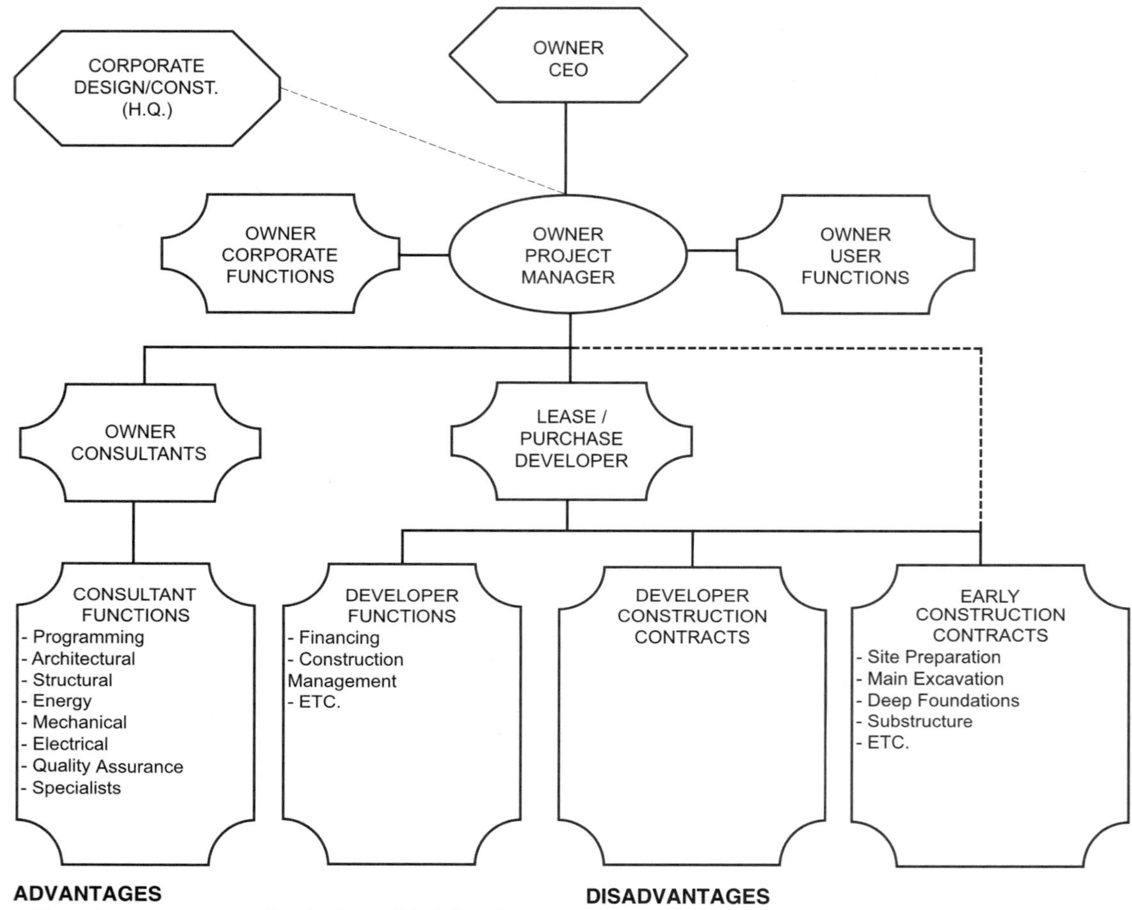

ADVANTAGES

- The advantages are similar to those listed for alternative 1, with these additions.
- It responds better to the construction marketplace.
- It responds better to a tight schedule by overlapping design with early construction.

DISADVANTAGES

- With fast tracking of the early construction, a number of difficulties creep in.
- Contract documentation becomes more difficult merging owner early contracts with developer jobs.
- More owner human resources are required.
- More difficult to manage.
- Owner changes are difficult.
- The structure does not allow for teamwork.

FIGURE 4.11 PROJECT FUNCTIONAL ORGANIZATION CHART, LEASE/PURCHASE, ALTERNATIVE 2.

outcome of the process is expected to be a lease, only the lump sum design/build scenario would apply. Also, this discussion will be based on the standard lease alternative under which the owner does no construction work. In this case the owner does not do any project design work either.

The advantages may be extrapolated from the previously described ways. There are a number of new disadvantages listed alongside the organizational chart depicted in Fig. 4.12.

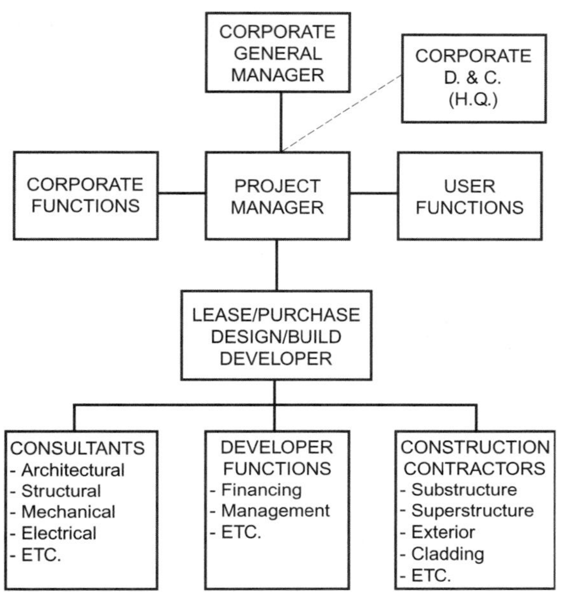

FIGURE 4.12 PROJECT FUNCTIONAL ORGANIZATION CHART, LEASE/PURCHASE, ALTERNATIVE 3.

ADVANTAGES

• See alternative 1 for a list of advantages to the owner.

DISADVANTAGES

• See alternative 1 for a list of disadvantages to the owner. The following additional disadvantages apply.
• Construction industry design professionals do not like design/build generally, and appreciate even less the concept of lease/purchase coupled with design/build.
• The assessment of proposals is very difficult because it is essential to measure not only the financial aspects of a long-term lease, but also the facility nuts and bolts.
• The corporate owner front-end planning and performance criteria are difficult. The conversion of the user requirements to design parameters and drawings is a tough row to hoe as the designers are removed from the users.
• As tenant, the owner has little say in project quality, except initially when the project performance specifications are prepared.
• Changes by the owner are really difficult, and could be very expensive.
• Because these kinds of proposals are expensive to prepare, proponents may require to be paid for unsuccessful proposals.
• The process is difficult and requires smart human resources to manage.
• There is limited experience in preparing performance specs for this way to deliver a project, and even less criteria for an objective, value-driven award procedure.
• The process is not that well understood by the public and bona fide tenderers.

4.4 Not a Project Management Organization

Project organizations are hierarchical by contract, but not always by functionality when applied to the individualistic, entrepreneurial, and creative A/E/C industry. Military style organizations may work for the military, and they may work for large, vertically integrated E/P/C firms. But they work to a lesser extent for the great numbers of projects undertaken year in year out by both the private sector and public works agencies.

The other new-age consideration is the hierarchical flattening out of postmodern project delivery services seen in the delivery of both hard goods and soft services. One of the features of breakdown structures is their capability to allow up to nine generally accepted levels of breakdown in organizational structuring. This has led to thinking that each lower level is subservient to the level above it. In most project management software, for example, tasks can be promoted or demoted, leading to subordinate tasks and summary tasks. A hierarchy comprises "parents" and "children." The parent represents a pool of resources (children). An individual resource, not a pool, becomes a "skill."

It may be that the concepts of summary and subservience and of parent and child are programming language. But for project functional organization building it may be counterproductive. It is indeed a given that for project definition, and for work breakdown, units make up elements, elements make up element groups, and element groups make up systems. This is structural, and activities and tasks become parts of packages, which become contracts. But there is no hint of a parent/child relationship.

The same hierarchical rationale (parent/child) may not be applicable to organizational structures. There needs to be much more flexibility in how they relate to each other and to the project. At the same time their input needs to be recorded into code structures, and it is these codes that are structured and organized.

The project management structures and charts illustrated for the 16 ways to deliver projects are drawn as hierarchies, as a way to show project functional relationships between people drawn from different companies. But that is not to say that they have a hierarchical relationship, except insofar as a client may be considered to be the superior of the vendor or contractor.

In project management the relationship is a function of the agreement between the parties to the contract. That is why in each of the ways discussed in this chapter there is so much emphasis placed on the contracts between the parties to the project. Each member is obliged to perform the terms of their agreement. Failure by even one of them may lead to a failed project. In most cases the only thing that project participants have in common is the project in question. Once the project is completed successfully, the relationships are ended.

The 16 ways discussed above are said to be driven by the objective-oriented contracts between owners, designers, and contractors, and in some cases between owners and developers, who in turn sign contracts with designers and contractors. The chapters following will discuss and illustrate how the organizations are the ultimate source of cost to the project. Project cost control is seen first as the establishment of the project budget on the basis of functions and elements, secondly through packages, and finally through contracts and purchase orders issued to contractors and vendors.

A project organization cannot always be seen as a vertical military line diagram. In some situations it may not be possible to draw the project as a hierarchy because of the complex nature of the owner organization. In these cases the functional organization may be considered in some other more functional mode, perhaps as a circle, as seen in Fig. 4.13.

The whole idea is to consider the project as the center of the universe. This would lead to the conclusion that in an organizational sense, the project manager would be the central focus of the organizational chart. As such the position would be the hub of the wheel, or the central point of the circular diagram.

This communications approach represents reality in the world of projects, perhaps more accurately, effectively, and fairly than any military line diagrams. It is also important in that this kind of diagram would tend not to upset people with whom the project managers have to deal in existing corporate organizations or governmental agencies. Further, drawn in this way the organigram can encompass every person, group, agency, activist, consultant, contractor, and vendor that has or could have an impact on the project.

If anybody can have a material impact on the project, this person could and will affect project cost, schedule, and quality. Although these persons do not necessarily

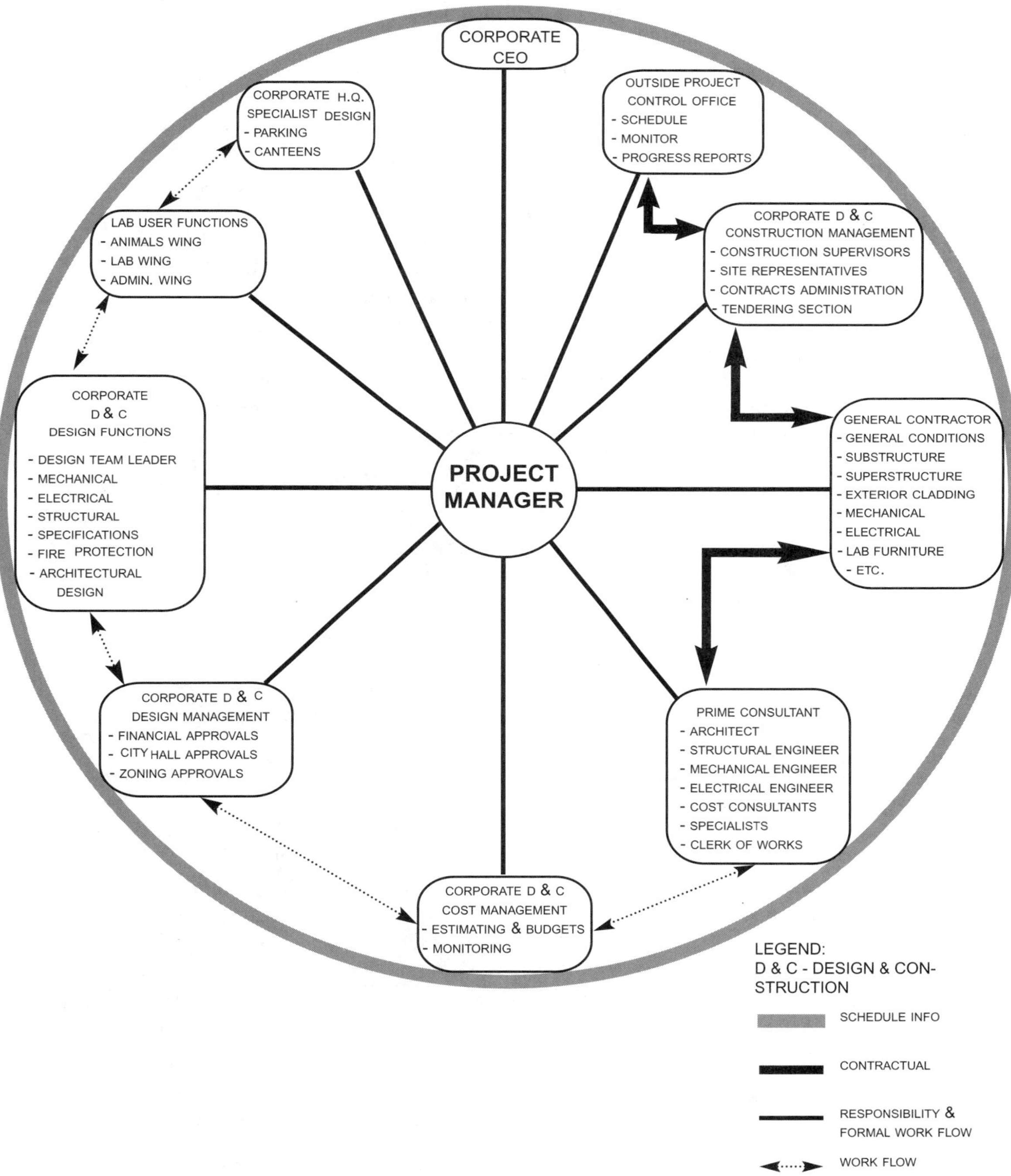

FIGURE 4.13 DIAGRAM FOR MULTIFACETED CORPORATE ORGANIZATION, NOT A PROJECT MANAGEMENT ORGANIZATION.

have a contract with the project, their public or regulatory position entitles them to a voice. If this indeed is the case, they belong in the non-project-management organization, and their potential for impact needs to be included as input or as a risk factor on project quality, cost, and schedule.

4.5 Project Functional Organization as Cost Code

A project is scoped, costed, coordinated, and initially controlled on the basis of its project definition structure comprised of functions and elements.

In Chapter 2 Fig. 2.8 illustrates a cost code system for project elements based on project definition. It shows what is considered to be one-half of a full project code system, the half generated by definition. The other half is derived from activities packages assigned to organizations. The organization is the source of cost to the project.

To review the process: following project definition, the project is broken down into packages of activities. The packages are molded into assignments, purchase orders, or contracts, which are given, allocated, awarded, or otherwise assigned to members of the owner's own organization, approval agencies, governmental bodies, designers, consultants, vendors, construction contractors, trade contractors, furniture suppliers and installers, startup specialists, and facility operators, to name a few, until all project elements are parts of assignments held by individuals or organizations.The organizational code is thus a function of work package codes.

In Chapter 3 Fig. 3.6 shows this relationship by explaining that a contract package code is eventually synonymous with the project functional organization code. Figure 3.6 shows an eight-part element code in the left barrel, and a five-part package or organizational code in the right, with the two sides comprising the double-barreled code system, deemed to be the cornerstone of the integration of elements and cost sources for project control purposes.

Thus the project code system first depicted by Fig. 2.8, expanded by the addition of a package code in Fig. 3.6, can now be completed with the addition of the organization code, as may be seen in Fig. 4.14. The code structure in this picture can accommodate a wide range of projects, from megaprojects to small undertakings. Basically it is the concept for coding individual projects, that is, one project at a time. To accommodate a multiple-project environment, the project codes are expanded with the inclusion of the project code and subproject code and other corporate information, as seen in Fig. 4.14.

4.6 Summary

The intent of this chapter is to show that projects are carried out in all kinds of organizational environments. Corporations exist to fulfill their destiny, which is to make a profit for their shareholders. When a project is necessary, the last thing a firm wants

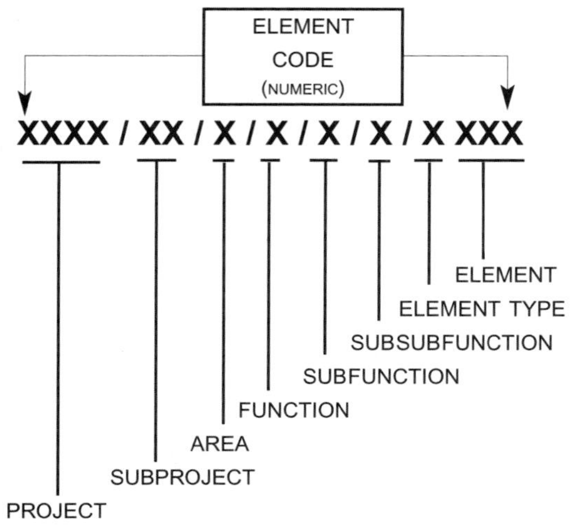

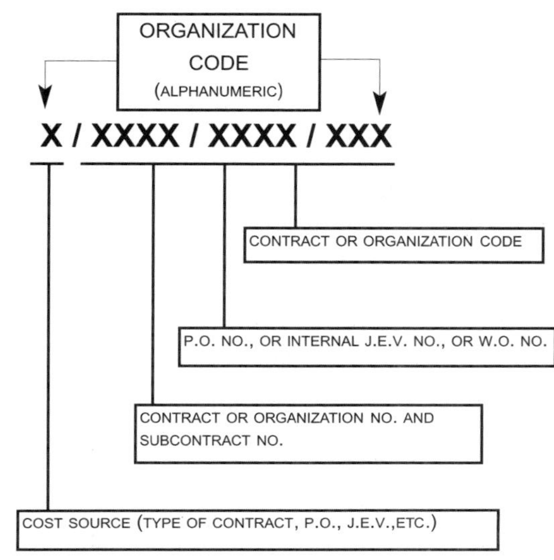

ELEMENT CODE Derives from the project definition structure (see Chapter 2.)
ORGANIZATION CODE Derives from the package code as discussed under WBS in Chapter 3 and under functional organization in Chapter 4.
COST SOURCE Individual, internal department, contractor, or vendor being paid for the fulfillment of an agreement in connection with a work order or a project.
J.E.V. Journal entry voucher, used by corporations for transferring charges from departments to a project or a work order.
P.O. Purchase order, a written order issued to a vendor or a supplier for hard goods, or a service pertaining to a work order or a project.
W.O. Work order, a written order issued to corporate engineers to study a problem or opportunity, that may lead to a project.

FIGURE 4.14 DOUBLE-BARRELED PROJECT CODE STRUCTURE BASED ON FULL PROJECT DEFINITION AND FUNCTIONAL ORGANIZATION.

is to change its structure until it becomes clear that the project is not achieving its objectives, thus causing losses to the owners. To preclude these situations, corporations will appoint coordinators and project managers.

Professional project managers know that successful projects require systems and organizations that create and control issues of project scope, quality, and cost. This can only happen through project definitions and work breakdowns, which lead to the development of tasks, activities, and packages of work for assignment to teams of people. It is seen that tasks become synonymous with the people that do them, and they are the source of cost to the project.

The systems of project management identify project elements from their inception to their completion. This is done through continuous coding as a deliverable, a task, and as an account code in a contract.

The chapter shows that projects are influenced by all kinds of people. It shows organizational structures for different kinds of projects. The bottom line is the identification of the person or group responsible for the task linked to the deliverable, and the ability to include the impact of that contribution on the project.

REFERENCES

Antill, J. M., and R. W. Woodhead, *Critical Path Methods in Construction Practice,* 4th ed. (Wiley, New York, 1990).

Fondahl, J. W., *A Non-Computer Approach to the Critical Path Method for the Construction Industry,* 2nd ed. (Stanford University, Stanford, CA, 1962).

Haviland, D. S., ed., *Project Delivery Approaches, an AIA Guide* (American Institute of Architects, Washington, DC, 1976).

Open Plan User Guide (Project Management Software, WST Corp., Houston, TX, 1993).

"Outlining," *Microsoft Project, Version 3.0, User's Reference* (Microsoft Corp., Redmond, WA, 1992), p. 296.

Salapatas, J. N., "Project Management: How Much Is Enough," *Proc. Project Management Inst.* (Newton Square, PA, 1978).

Stuckenbruck, L. C., Ed., *The Implementation of Project Management, The Professional's Handbook,* Project Management Institute (Addison-Wesley, Reading, MA, 1981).

QUESTIONS AND EXERCISES

4.1. Create a project functional organization breakdown structure (OBS) to manage, plan and design, and construct the house project referred to in Questions 2.3 and 3.4. The diagram is to be based on a matrix style organization. The organizational diagram is to be all inclusive, showing generically owners, users, bankers, financiers, permit issuers, utility providers, planners, designers, architects, engineers, construction managers, and trade contractors.

4.2. Draw a project functional organization for construction management of phased packages as presented in Section 4.3.3 to manage, plan and design, and construct the house project in Question 4.1.

4.3. Identify the project code systems based on the preceding OBS and the relevant work breakdown and project definition structures as developed for the questions in Chapters 2 and 3.

PROJECT BUDGET AND COST CONTROL SYSTEM

5

There is a public and business perception that projects always cost too much. Business leaders see it as a serious problem, with all the participants in the delivery process contributing to the malaise.

It starts with estimates. Inaccurate estimates lead to inadequate budgets, and that may be one of the reasons why projects are seen to cost too much: the estimate was inadequate to begin with. A hierarchy of estimates shows that budgets are as accurate as the information on which they are based.

Estimating based on project definition progresses from scope and quality statements to functional cost estimates. Using the research center project from Chapter 2 as the model, project issues such as contingencies and the relationship between corporate account codes and construction cost information are explored. The way a corporate financial manager sees project cost is not the same way as do project users. The way that the project management team cost and deliver the project is different still. Although everybody is involved in the same project, they speak different cost languages. The systems of project management pull them together for scope, quality, and cost.

Cost and expenditure report formats depicting columns and fields, and rows and records of database information from the research center model are presented. It is seen how information flows from a user-oriented functional cost depicted by the project definition structure (PDS) to the project-team-related tasks and packages driven by the work breakdown structure (WBS), to the contract-oriented source of project cost as coded by the organizational breakdown structure (OBS).

Computerized warehousing and mining of generic project cost information, including prices based on widely-used and standardized cost codes are discussed. A series of approaches and techniques used to monitor or model projects is presented. A visual tool to depict the cost and schedule progress of a project is the S curve. The S-curve concept led to the development of the cost/schedule control system criteria (C/SCSC), which is also called performance measurement system or earned value system. The intent of these techniques is to show the status of projects by graphics. Other quick tools are trend lines and productivity models.

5.1 Problem with Construction Project Cost

Project cost is a major problem in the construction industry according to a study and report by the Business Roundtable. The report concluded:

- Construction is important to the economy as a whole and therefore to everybody. It affects costs, prices, and our international competitiveness in both domestic and foreign markets.
- Construction dollars are not being used effectively.
- Declining cost-effectiveness is not the fault of any one group. Owners, managers, contractors, unions, workers, suppliers, and governments all share responsibility.
- Cost-effectiveness in construction can be improved to the advantage of all without inequity to any group if we recognize it as a national problem and seek cooperation instead of adversarial solutions.

Under the heading of what's wrong, the report cited many reasons including:

- A constant state of confrontation
- A bizarre lack of accurate information
- Construction productivity
- The perverse effect of scheduled overtime

The report's main conclusion was that construction costs too much, and everybody in the industry was to blame. The report highlighted the need to use computers for planning, design, scheduling, including use of the critical path method (CPM), procurement, and budgeting.

From an anecdotal perspective based on experience, project costs are always too high because:

- The estimate was wrong and way too low.
- The budget was too low.
- Design changes caused the problem.
- Construction changes caused the overrun.
- Bad weather was the problem.
- Labor costs were too high.
- Underground conditions were responsible.
- Government regulations caused the overrun.
- Poor-quality workmanship caused it.

- Bidders caused the problem.
- Inflation caused it.

The reasons are valid. They happen and will occur as long as projects are undertaken. Do these conditions cause serious cost overruns? Could a project cost overrun become so major that the benefits expected from the subject project are not achieved? Can a project cost overrun be so massive that the corporate owner is driven into bankruptcy? And can serious cost overruns be mitigated by better project definition; better conceptual design; more accurate and adequate estimating and budgeting? Or was it, as is often the case, that project cost was given short shrift, downplayed, or otherwise ignored for whatever reason.

The objective of the system of project cost control is to eliminate, or at least minimize, the effect of conditions like those named here on the cost overrun potential of the project. It does not mean that costs are not included for these influences. It follows that they need to be recognized, estimated, and budgeted.

Project cost control is about the identification of those elements, outside influences, and factors that can cause problems of cost escalation, and estimating their potential effect on the project cost. These costs are in addition to the costs of project functional areas, their inherent elements, and indirect costs, such as management, design, and other soft costs that are consumed in the delivery of the project.

5.2 Not All Estimates Are Equal

How many different types of cost estimates are there? As project cost control invariably starts with estimating, the first place to look is at project estimating, estimates, and estimators. There are almost as many versions, variations, and types of estimates as there are estimators. Here are some names of estimates, along with their approximate accuracy ranges, used by professional cost engineers and cost consultants, whose business it is to put together dollar numbers for projects.

Name of Estimate	*Aproximate Accuracy Range*
Appropriation	−5% to +15%
Back of the envelope	−30% to +50%
Ballpark	−30% to +50%
Blue sky	−30% to +50%
Budget	−15% to +30%
Conceptual	−30% to +50%
Definitive	−5% to +15%
Detailed	−5% to +15%
Final	−5% to +15%

Gross	−30% to +50%
Guesstimate	−30% to +50%
Horseback	−30% to +50%
Lump sum	−5% to +15%
Official	−15% to +30%
Order of magnitude	−30% to +50%
Orientation	−30% to +50%
Original	−30% to +50%
Parametric	−30% to +50%
Preliminary	−15% to +30%
Quickie	−30% to +50%
Ratio	−30% to +50%
Rough	−30% to +50%
Scope	−30% to +50%
Screening	−30% to +50%
Semidetailed	−15% to +30%
Study	−30% to +50%

These terms designating estimates, listed alphabetically, represent project cost based on the amount, degree, and quality of information available at the time of the estimate.

As seen in Chapter 2, an estimate designation may be used to describe the PDS itself. Sometimes, though the project definition is advanced, the owner may not wish to pay for a detailed estimate and will start the project with an order-of-magnitude type number. In general, the less detail available, the lesser the accuracy range of the estimate. As determined by the American Association of Cost Engineers, the degree of accuracy of a cost analysis is dependent on the extent of information available.

In *Applied Cost Engineering* Clark and Lorenzoni classified estimates into three categories based on their accuracy range. To complete the estimate classification picture, the estimates listed above are bundled into these categories.

1. *Order-of-magnitude estimates (−30% to +50%).* Prepared at the phases of project opportunity or problem and feasibility of a project, as discussed in Chapter 3, they are also known as: conceptual, screening, ratio, quickie, guesstimate, rough, gross, and scope.
2. *Budget estimates (−15% to +30%).* Prepared at the design criteria stage, phase 2 of the work breakdown, as discussed in Section 3.8, this estimate is also known as semidetailed and preliminary.
3. *Definitive estimates (−5% to +15%).* Definitive estimates are prepared as the project goes into detailed engineering and construction. They may also be

referred to as detailed, final, lump sum, and appropriation estimates in cost engineering circles. In this book, a definitive estimate is also called an appropriation-grade estimate, which is prepared at stage 3 of the work breakdown, as discussed in Section 3.8.

Schoemann and Bachynsky, in their paper on batch-operated plants, list five types of capital cost estimates in increasing order of accuracy, along with the basis for the estimates, as summarized:

1. *Order of magnitude.* Based on historical data from similar plants, $>>\pm 30\%$.
2. *Study.* Based on bench scale lab data, rough flow sheets, and major equipment, $\pm 30\%$.
3. *Preliminary.* Based on early pilot plant flow sheets, major equipment list, material balance, partial offsites—such as storage, warehousing, and power generation—and pollution control, $\pm 20\%$.
4. *Definitive.* Based on flow sheets, process and instrumentation diagrams, equipment specifications, major equipment quotes, layouts, site information, and all process streams characterized, $\pm 10\%$.
5. *Detailed.* Based on complete process and equipment specifications, $\pm 5\%$.

As far as project cost is concerned, on the one hand there is dissatisfaction with the cost of construction projects; on the other, as reported by cost engineers, there is real difficulty in establishing project cost estimates. If costs are so difficult to establish in the first place, and if construction projects are approved before their costs are known, there is a major problem between the buyers of construction (the owners) and the providers of construction cost estimates (the cost engineers).

James H. Black, one the founders of the American Association of Cost Engineers, in his discussion of parametric estimating recognized the difficulty of costing projects. Parametric estimating had its start in the aerospace industries. There was a problem with rapidly changing technology and performance standards and the impact on costs. Cost growth exceeded inflation on account of increased performance standards and in the increasing technological sophistication required. This meant that costs were driven by more than just project size. The condition occurred in construction as well as in defense industries.

For construction projects, causes of cost growth include the reasons listed, plus changing scope, changing design specifications, changing markets, changing politics, and changing schedules. The parametric estimating procedures aim to provide an estimate considered to be $>>\pm 30\%$ accurate. Of the 26 estimates named in this section, it is seen that 16 are in this category.

The North American economy, according to the Business Roundtable, considers that construction is too costly. North American cost engineers report on the technological difficulty in cost estimating more and more complex projects. It can be concluded that buyers of construction services do not really know what the cost of projects should be, and that they are not prepared to pay for and carry out enough design, engineering, and estimating to prove the cost of any project before starting it. And once a project is started, it goes to completion almost at any cost, including paying for such things as the "perverse effect of scheduled overtime."

There is a serious cost information gap between buyers and providers of project services. This is difficult to understand because the cost of cost estimating is insignificant in relation to total project cost.

In the *Project and Cost Engineers' Handbook,* published by the American Association of Cost Engineers, the cost of making definitive estimates (accuracy range of −5% to +15%) was estimated at about 1.3% for $1 million projects, 0.35% for $10 million projects, and 0.30% for $20 million projects. For a budget estimate (accuracy range of −15% to +30%) the costs of making estimates were set at 0.30%, 0.09%, and 0.045%, respectively, for similarly sized projects. For order-of-magnitude estimates (accuracy range of −30% to +50%) the costs to make estimates were significantly lower.

It is not intended in this chapter to cover the subject of quantity surveying and estimating. In its own right, the subject is complex and difficult, requiring schooling and experience to acquire proficiency.

The intention here is to explore the place of estimating, particularly as practiced by cost engineers, including value engineering, all as part of the system of cost control in the systems of project management, and to discuss how cost numbers are assigned to deliverables resulting from the PDS, the WBS, and the OBS.

From experience, project cost estimates often were done in a vacuum, that is, if they were done at all. As a result the numbers were a mystery to everybody on the project, except the estimators. The intent of this text is to bring estimating and cost engineering out into the open through the systems of project management. The basis for this to happen will be seen to be the definition of scope and quality parameters, the development of activities and tasks, the identification of functional organization team members responsible for the tasks, and the integration of cost with time through scheduling.

5.3 Hierarchy of Project Cost Estimates

Project structuring, starting with definition, is all important in the cost estimating, budget setting, and cost control of a project.

In practice, although there are many ways to define a project, there are two basic and completely opposite ways to set a project budget. The first way is simplicity itself. The owner sets an amount and delivers the project for that amount. This is accomplished by trade-offs, cajolery, threats, haggling, and bargaining. No systems, no definitions, no code structures, no fancy names for degrees of accuracy. There is just toughness, shrewdness, and knowing what is wanted, based on what has been provided previously on other mostly similar projects. Simple, repetitive, small, local, owner-financed, and owner-operated facilities may be done using this approach.

The owner/builders of these kinds of projects think they have all the project control systems in their heads. Perhaps it is these kinds of projects that cost "too much," according to the Business Roundtable, when it said " . . . (the economy) no longer gets its money's worth in construction . . ."

This same way was also being used to deliver industrial projects. The problems engendered by the traditional approaches to deliver projects reported by the Business Roundtable were seen also by cost engineers among others, who created a system of cost estimating and cost control.

The systems of project management presented in this book respond to the need to improve cost estimating, cost control, and productivity. The approach invokes the rule that the more we know about a project, the more accurately we can establish its cost through estimating. If the estimating exercise is related to a code system derived from a PDS, the cost estimate, or budget, when approved becomes suitable for project cost control after first serving as an accurate measure of the project scope and quality.

A project definition does not just happen, and neither does its cost estimate or budget. As we define a project through its subprojects, areas, functions, subfunctions, element types, and eventually elements and activities, its costs become progressively more accurate.

A project manager always needs to be aware of the kind of cost number he or she is talking about. The manager must know that the accuracy of the number depends on the level of detail in the project definition. This not only is needed to reflect the accuracy of the estimate fairly, but is worthwhile for the project manager as a defense strategy for those times when the project manager may be unfairly blamed for cost overruns. One should only be blamed for an overrun if one first agreed to the numbers or, worse, prepared the numbers that lead to the overrun. If you agree to numbers based on no solid definition, no levels of detail, you deserve to be blamed.

Project definition for cost control purposes may start with the preparation of a ratio estimate. This is one of the most common approaches to produce an estimate and is based on comparing a proposed project to a completed similar project, with allowances for differences in site conditions, inflation, and other easily visible variations.

A parametric estimate is similar to a ratio estimate, as are others named earlier, in the order-of-magnitude accuracy range of −30% to +50%.

The project definition relates to an order-of-magnitude type estimate at only the highest levels of a top-down hierarchical PDS, that is, level 2 or perhaps level 3. If an owner sets a project budget on the basis of a parametric or a ratio estimate and then imposes it as a working budget or the basis for cost control, one of two things will happen. Either the budget will be seriously overrun, or the scope and quality will become unknown. Experience shows that this condition happens again and again.

Project developers by nature are optimistic. Their optimism is contagious, especially at the initial project stages. This attitude is invariably passed on to the project team members, simply because project people want to see the project go ahead. As a result professional project practitioners have a difficult time convincing owners that there are different levels of accuracy of cost estimates, and that the accuracy is a function of detail information.

A set of simple easily understood rules is a useful tool to demonstrate the relationship between the accuracy of the estimate and the amount and quality of the information that is available. Rule 1 sets the relationship between a top-down project definition and the accuracy of an order-of-magnitude estimate.

Order-of-Magnitude Estimate
Rule 1

> At level 1 of the PDS the accuracy of the cost information is on the order of −30% to +50%, that is, it is a conceptual estimate, a ratio estimate, a parametric estimate, a quickie, or a horseback estimate. It is sometimes called a guesstimate. If the owner dictates the cost, it is none of these, and there should be no expectation as to what the project may cost, or what the project may end up as in terms of its scope and quality.

This rule applies when working from the beginning of a project, that is, in the highest project stage with no lower stage detail information available. The same rule applies to the three succeeding rules.

However, the converse of the rule does not apply. When lower level project elemental information is developed and cost is estimated, budgeted, and rolled up to the higher levels of definition, the accuracy of the rolled up information is similar to the accuracy at the level worked.

The next level of estimating accuracy, comprising estimates termed scope, preliminary, budget authorization, and official, ranges between −15% and +30%. Some cost engineers consider these types of estimates to be in the ±20% accuracy range. In these cases the project definition information may consist of the following quality of detail:

- Early pilot plant data to prepare flowsheets
- Major equipment lists
- Material balance
- Partial definition of offsites and pollution control

The major elements depicted by this class of engineering information could be considered to be at about level 2 to 3 of the PDS. Rule 2 demonstrates the relationship between the cost estimates within this range of accuracy and the PDS.

Budget Estimate
Rule 2

> At level 2 of the PDS the project has definition to the subproject level, meaning that major aras are defined, as are a preliminary flow diagram and ma-

jor equipment. The estimate may be considered a budget authorization estimate, and its accuracy may be on the order of −15% to +30%. It may be in the ±20% accuracy range according to some cost engineers.

The aim of project definition is to take the project concept represented by level 1 of the PDS and support it with connected information. At levels 1 and 2 the cost information is largely based on comparing this proposed project to similar completed projects. If the indicators are favorable and the green light is given to proceed, more planning, design, and engineering are authorized and carried out. This information is considered to be at level 3 of the PDS. Some aspects of it may be at level 4.

The project information is now adequately detailed and advanced enough for the preparation of an estimate that is considered suitable for the appropriation of funds for the entire project. Variously named definitive, final, and most often appropriation-grade, an estimate of this kind is considered to be accurate to within −5% and +15%. Rule 3 provides for this condition.

Definitive Estimate
Rule 3

At level 3 (with some aspects at level 4) of the PDS the project has subprojects, major areas, functions, and some subfunctions defined, and its estimate may be considered to be an appropriation-grade estimate, accurate to within −5% and +15%.

Once the project is approved for funding on the basis of the details produced at levels 3 and 4 of the PDS, the estimating activities continue at the same rate as the progress of the work. At levels 4 and 5 the quality of the information is now suitable for the preparation of detailed and cost control information, which will then be used as the yardstick against which actual commitments and expenditures will be compared. Rule 4 relates the cost estimate to the PDS.

Detailed Estimate
Rule 4

At level 4 of the PDS the project is advanced to the conceptual drawings stage, with many elements at level 5, and the cost estimate is considered by some cost engineers to be accurate within ±5%.

A project definition cost hierarchy based on the accuracy ranges of its top-down estimates or budgets therefore might be drawn as seen in Fig. 5.1. This figure is a way for the project manager to illustrate to the owner the need for detail information on which to base project cost information. However, this is a one-way structure. It works from the top down only.

Once the information is prepared at, say, level 4, its wrap-up to levels 3, 2, and 1 is of the same accuracy as the level 4 information.

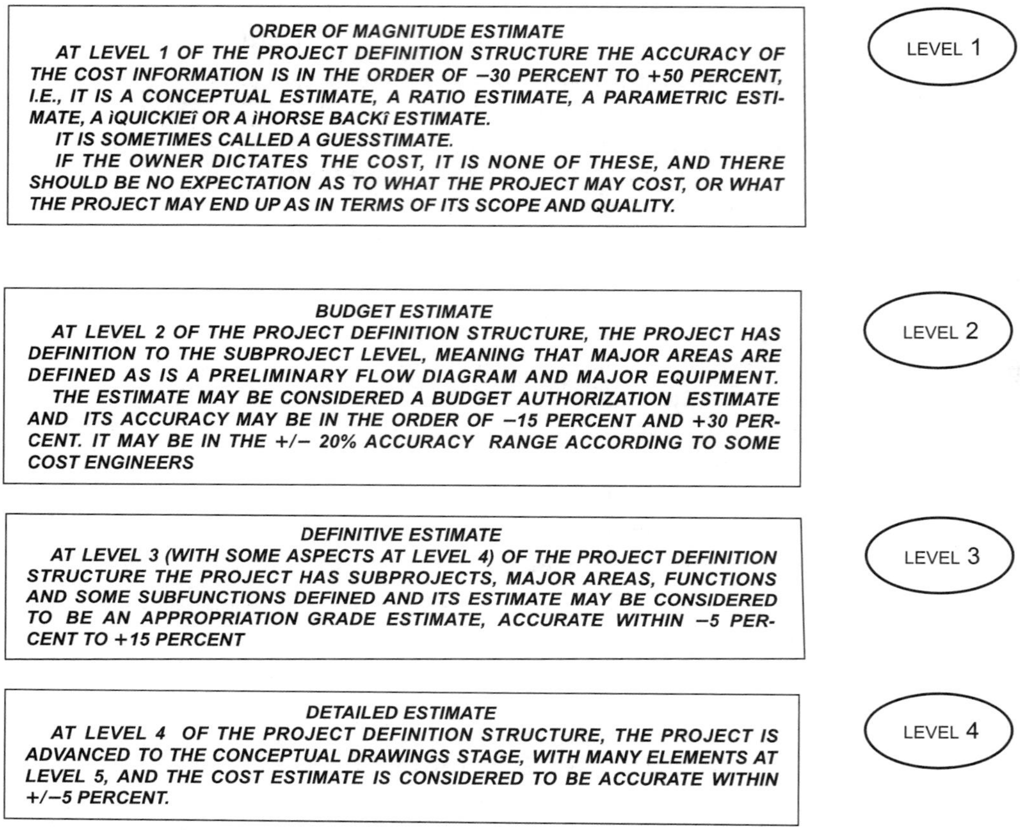

LEVEL 1

ORDER OF MAGNITUDE ESTIMATE

AT LEVEL 1 OF THE PROJECT DEFINITION STRUCTURE THE ACCURACY OF THE COST INFORMATION IS IN THE ORDER OF −30 PERCENT TO +50 PERCENT, I.E., IT IS A CONCEPTUAL ESTIMATE, A RATIO ESTIMATE, A PARAMETRIC ESTIMATE, A ìQUICKIEî OR A ìHORSE BACKî ESTIMATE.

IT IS SOMETIMES CALLED A GUESSTIMATE.

IF THE OWNER DICTATES THE COST, IT IS NONE OF THESE, AND THERE SHOULD BE NO EXPECTATION AS TO WHAT THE PROJECT MAY COST, OR WHAT THE PROJECT MAY END UP AS IN TERMS OF ITS SCOPE AND QUALITY.

BUDGET ESTIMATE

AT LEVEL 2 OF THE PROJECT DEFINITION STRUCTURE, THE PROJECT HAS DEFINITION TO THE SUBPROJECT LEVEL, MEANING THAT MAJOR AREAS ARE DEFINED AS IS A PRELIMINARY FLOW DIAGRAM AND MAJOR EQUIPMENT.

THE ESTIMATE MAY BE CONSIDERED A BUDGET AUTHORIZATION ESTIMATE AND ITS ACCURACY MAY BE IN THE ORDER OF −15 PERCENT AND +30 PERCENT. IT MAY BE IN THE +/− 20% ACCURACY RANGE ACCORDING TO SOME COST ENGINEERS

DEFINITIVE ESTIMATE

AT LEVEL 3 (WITH SOME ASPECTS AT LEVEL 4) OF THE PROJECT DEFINITION STRUCTURE THE PROJECT HAS SUBPROJECTS, MAJOR AREAS, FUNCTIONS AND SOME SUBFUNCTIONS DEFINED AND ITS ESTIMATE MAY BE CONSIDERED TO BE AN APPROPRIATION GRADE ESTIMATE, ACCURATE WITHIN −5 PERCENT TO +15 PERCENT

DETAILED ESTIMATE

AT LEVEL 4 OF THE PROJECT DEFINITION STRUCTURE, THE PROJECT IS ADVANCED TO THE CONCEPTUAL DRAWINGS STAGE, WITH MANY ELEMENTS AT LEVEL 5, AND THE COST ESTIMATE IS CONSIDERED TO BE ACCURATE WITHIN +/−5 PERCENT.

FIGURE 5.1 HIERARCHY OF COST ESTIMATES AS A STRUCTURED DEFINITION. The development of more accurate cost estimates and the establishment of budgets follow the creation of project definition structures into detailed elements through design and engineering. More detail equals better accuracy.

It should become obvious even to the most rigid developer or corporate chief executive officer that the only way to prove the project budget is through detail estimating. To draw a parallel, it is a given that the three rules for success in selling real estate are location, location, location. In project cost control, the three rules for success are detail, detail, detail. And detail only comes from the effort, time, and resources placed in the development of definition.

Each of the four rules stated relate the degree of detail to the accuracy of the estimate, from a ±5% range to a −30% to +50% range. Estimating and accuracy ranges are the purview of cost engineers. Clark and Lorenzoni show in *Applied Cost Engineering* how estimates fall into the plus and minus categories based on the amount of detail on which the estimate is based, which in this book is illustrated as a hierarchy of estimates, tied to project definition.

Hackney describes estimating accuracy in *Control and Management of Capital Projects* as the deviation of estimated from actual values. The deviation is developed through probability plotting and development of a distribution curve. Thus once the estimating effort is known to be centered, that is, neither always too low nor always too high, a straight-line probability plot will show the deviation of the estimate from the actual cost.

5.4 Project Definition to Cost Estimate—Research Center

Chapter 2 provides examples of the application of the system of project definition on a number of projects, including a research center project, used here as a model to illustrate the transition of project definitions to cost estimates.

The research center project definition in Fig. 2.12 is seen as a list of user functional areas A through P and project consumable areas Q through Z. These areas in turn are made up of functions and coded as lab spaces, other spaces, and offices. The spaces are based on equipment and functions as developed by the project manager and the facility users. The process and results of the definition exercise are depicted in Figs. 2.13 through 2.18 and discussed in related pages.

The information is both qualitative and quantitative, defining both the scope and the quality of the project as a concept and in architectural and engineering terms. The quality parameters drive the unit prices of the work, and the quantities establish the overall project cost. The research center facility space summary for a cost estimate is seen in Fig. 5.2.

5.4.1 Budget Process—Level 2 Budget Estimate

In the hierarchy of cost estimates an order-of-magnitude estimate identifies the project definition in terms of a ballpark number. The research center is well beyond that in terms of its conceptual design and engineering, as reflected by the work seen in Figs. 2.12 through 2.18 and 5.2.

Comparing the scope and quality information to the cost hierarchy places the information for cost estimating at about level 2 or better, that is, at −15% to +30% accuracy.

Often level 2 cost accuracy can be obtained by the project manager working with design architects and engineers, and using cost engineering experience and square foot (sf) or square meter (m^2) cost figures available as purchased information in the A/E/C industry.

Pricing the sf or m^2 quantities, and factoring in design and management costs and contingencies, the corporate owner now has a project scope and a −15% to +30% budget estimate, which is suitable in most cases to support a decision to either pro-

RESEARCH CENTER PROJECT
CODED PDS FUNCTIONAL AREAS
IN SQUARE FEET (SF) FOR CODES A -N

PDS FUNCTION OR AREA CODE	FUNCTION OR AREA DESCRIPTION	FUNCTION LAB AREA SF	FUNCTION OFFICE AREA SF	FUNCTION OTHER AREA SF
A	PHYSICS AND ENGINEERING	4920	2000	1280
C	MATERIALS AND EXPLORATORY RESEARCH	9140	2400	340
E	COLLOIDS AND INTERFACE	5180	1225	340
G	MATERIALS & CONTROL ENGINEERING	1620	400	-
H	POLYMERIZATION	2465	925	100
I	COMMON RESEARCH	350	500	2640
J	FUTURE RESEARCH	0	-	-
K	ADMINISTRATION & TECHNICAL SERVICES	-	1675	2900
M	SHIPPING/RECEIVING/STORAGE	-	-	4700
N	MAINTENANCE (BUILDING)	-	75	6800
O	MECHANICAL & ELECTRICAL SERVICES	-	100	1400
P	OUTSIDE SERVICES	-	-	-
Q	PROJECT MANAGEMENT	-	-	-
R	DESIGN/DRAWINGS/SPECS/CONTRACT DOCS.	-	-	-
T	MOVING & OCCUPANCY	-	-	-
Z	RESERVES AND CONTINGENCIES	-	-	-
	TOTAL	23675	9300	20500

Figure 5.2 Research Center Project Definition Structure, Functional Areas and Sizes for Cost Estimating. The scope of the project is stated as a square-foot summary of spaces to which unit prices are applied to create a construction cost estimate, plus the cost of areas Q through Z.

ceed with the next project step or cancel it as not feasible, too expensive, too complex, or too risky.

In addition to the facility spaces, the exercise also provides for the identification and specification of equipment normally included as part of the facility space functions, such as kitchen equipment, fitness center equipment, storage shelving, built-in refrigerators, security equipment, safety and life support, and communications systems. For a research center there is the laboratory equipment itself, including fume hoods, lab benches, and tables. Other requirements are fixtures and furnishings, such as office furniture, conference rooms, work stations, and computer terminal rooms, as well as landscaping.

5.4.2 Budget Process—Level 3 Definitive Estimate

A −15% to +30% level 2 estimate is not accurate enough for prudent corporate executives to appropriate funds. But it is enough to go to the next step, which involves expanding the project information through design, engineering, and procurement planning. In the research center project example the information was improved to include

PROJECT FUNCTIONAL AREAS		BUDGET
CODE	DESCRIPTION	$
A	PHYSICS AND ENGINEERING	)
C	MATERIALS AND EXPLORATORY RESEARCH	)
E	COLLOIDS AND INTERFACE	)
G	MATERIALS & CONTROL ENGINEERING	)
H	POLYMERIZATION	)
I	COMMON RESEARCH	) 12,973,000
J	FUTURE RESEARCH	)
K	ADMINISTRATION & TECHNICAL SERVICES	)
M	SHIPPING/RECEIVING/STORAGE	)
N	MAINTENANCE (BUILDING)	)
O	MECHANICAL & ELECTRICAL SERVICES	)
P	OUTSIDE SERVICES (landscaping only)	100,000
Q	PROJECT MANAGEMENT	1,654,000
R	DESIGN/DRAWINGS/SPECS/CONTRACT DOCS.	1,654,000
T	MOVING & OCCUPANCY	1,654,000
Z	RESERVES AND CONTINGENCIES	1,700,000
	TOTAL	16,427,000

FIGURE 5.3 RESEARCH CENTER APPROPRIATION-GRADE COST ESTIMATE. A facility project cost is driven by its square-foot size and unit prices, which incorporate the project quality, allowances for site conditions, soft costs, and contingencies.

schematic architectural, mechanical, and electrical engineering drawings and outline specifications.

The schematic drawings were subjected to quantity takeoff and pricing by professional quantity surveyors. Acting in a cost engineering role the project manager converted the quantity surveyors' estimates into the project functional estimate and the corporate coding system. He factored in escalation numbers based on inflationary trends at the time of the project and priced lab equipment, fixtures, and furnishings not included in the base construction project. The project manager calculated cash flow, carried out currency conversions where required, priced out the contingencies, including risks, and prepared the submission for approval by the chief executive officer's staff and the corporate board.

A level 3 definitive estimate with an accuracy range of -5% to $+15\%$ is also referred to as an appropriation-grade estimate. An appropriation-grade estimate in this case was required by the corporate staff to be $\pm 10\%$. Thus the target was met.

Some cost engineers report that for industrial construction a $\pm 10\%$ estimate requires that the average design be 40% completed. In the case of the subject industrial research center, the design was considered to be 16% completed for the $\pm 10\%$ estimate. The research center estimate is depicted in Fig. 5.3.

5.5 Functional Cost, Construction Cost, and Corporate Cost

Cost control requires the project manager to control the project scope. For example, in Fig. 5.2 lab PDS function code area A is 4920 sf and lab PDS function code area

C is 9140 sf. That is their defined scope as reflected in the 16% completed (schematic) drawings. The other physical areas are also defined as sf numbers. When those numbers were set, the project scope was defined.

In the cost estimate of Fig. 5.3 the coded functional areas are individually listed again, but their dollar numbers are included in a global amount. Other amounts appear against the soft cost PDS function code areas Q–Z.

Where do the numbers come from? They are assembled by the project manager from different sources. The way in which project scope is controlled is not necessarily the way in which project cost is estimated. Quantity surveyors, cost engineers, and cost estimators track costs on "bricks and mortar." Cost information providers track costs by building elements, such as substructure, structure, exterior cladding, interior partitions, electrical, plumbing, heating, and so on. As these elements are all quantity and quality driven, their cost is not available until drawings and specifications are done. A project is approved for funding long before the drawings are available. In the research center example experience dictated that the drawings needed to be 16% completed to prove the estimate in the ±10% range.

When a project is scoped, converted to drawings and specifications, and given to professional consulting quantity surveyors and estimators for a detailed estimate, the expected result is a classical elemental construction cost estimate. In this case the form of the estimate is an elemental building cost breakdown using the Canadian Institute of Quantity Surveyors (CIQS) measurement and pricing method.

The application of this method on the research center example is depicted in Fig. 5.4. It is seen, however, that only the construction component of the total project is included in this estimate. The construction cost, modified and expanded, is incorpo-

Building Element	Description of Element	Estimate $
1	Substructure	190,700
2	Superstructure	1,100,000
3	Exterior Enclosure	1,409,200
4	Interior Construction-	-
4.a	- Partitions	268,900
4.b	- Doors	156,100
4.c	- Fittings	148,900
4.d	- Finishes	373,500
5	Vertical Movement	97,600
6	Plumbing	963,000
7	HVAC	2,094,000
8	Electrical	1,464,300
	BASIC BUILDING COST	8,266,200
9	Fixed Equipment	-
10	Special Foundations	-
	TOTAL BUILDING COST	8,266,200
11	Site Construction	521,850
	CONSTRUCTION COST	8,788,050
12.a	Construction Overhead & Profit	884,761
12.b	Contingency for Above Items	486,632
	Total Construction Estimate	10,159,443
	Inflation Contingency	2,813,557
	TOTAL for Appropriation	12,973,000

FIGURE 5.4 RESEARCH CENTER SUMMARY OF ELEMENTAL CONSTRUCTION COST FOR APPROPRIATION-GRADE ESTIMATE. Construction estimates are prepared on the basis of building elements using estimating units maintained as databases by providers of construction cost information. This estimate has been extended by the project manager to provide for inflation contingencies.

rated into the project functional cost estimate alongside the other project areas, as seen in Fig. 5.3.

With the project scope under control, schematic drawings and specifications and the construction cost estimate in hand, and with the user's approval, the project manager is now ready to go to corporate staff for project approval and the appropriation of funds.

Corporate financial staff see proposals for projects every day. Proposals must be in the approved, corporate finance standard format. Approved projects will be monitored for cash flow and cost control on the basis of the approved format.

This subject of function cost to elemental cost to corporate cost and eventually to construction cost is an area of great difficulty in project work for the following reasons:

- The definition and function exercise is necessary for scope and quality control.
- The professional estimators cost the whole project in another totally different way.
- The conversion to corporate cost language is mandatory for approvals.
- The construction industry then bids and invoices in a different way.

When it comes to project cost control, it needs to be understood that the way in which construction contractors price and build projects, and estimators prepare estimates and budgets, is different from the way that project managers manage projects, which is different from the way in which the owner's corporate managers look at budgets for presenting them to the corporate board of directors for approval of funding. That is, assuming that each party to the determination of the project cost is doing the job with integrity and objectivity, and in the absence of personal agendas and subjective preferences.

Figure 5.5 introduces the corporate financial code system on which project cost will be controlled after approval. The major item in a facility construction project is construction. Appearing as line item 30 in Fig. 5.5, it is backed by a quantity surveyor's cost summary of building systems, as presented in Fig. 5.4. The line items in Fig. 5.4 in turn are backed by quantity takeoffs and unit prices or factors of cost to make up the total building project cost estimate. There are apparent differences between the numbers in Figs. 5.4 and 5.5 because the former is only construction cost-related, whereas the latter is the total project, including all soft costs, three types of contingencies, nondepreciable landscaping, and fixtures and furnishings, allocated into the corporate code of accounts. The Fig. 5.5 total number, now cast in stone as the project budget, is the baseline for cost control.

The following additional comments explain how cost numbers are developed and justified for a major facility project.

Item 10, Design, Project Management, and Contract Documents The details of the the design and management component of the appropriation request include the following items:

CODE	DESCRIPTION	BUDGET $
10	Design, project management, and contract documents	1,654,000
20	Land	-
30	Facility construction	11,750,000
40	Bid contingency	582,000
50	Construction contingency	1,223,000
60	Equipment	119,000
70	Occupancy contingency	699,000
80	Landscaping	100,000
90	Fixtures and furnishings	300,000
	TOTAL PROJECT	**$16,427,000**

FIGURE 5.5 RESEARCH CENTER APPROPRIATION-GRADE ESTIMATE AS CORPORATE COST CODE PROJECT BUDGET. A corporation codes its facilities and equipment to suit its business information needs. A project control system must be able to generate data for this system, while providing project scope and cost control information for the project manager, based on the way the construction industry delivers projects.

Architect/engineer fee

Project management fee

Construction administration and quality control

Internal corporate fees to project

Permits

Photographs

Testing

Site office, staff, and printing

Miscellaneous

Inflation allowance

Item 20, Land In this case land is not included. The facility was on an existing site.

Item 30, Construction See Fig. 5.4.

Item 40, Bid Contingency The makeup of the bid contingency includes various provisions. First the construction contract amount was calculated. Because of market conditions at the time, because construction was scheduled to start in the middle of winter, and due to labor shortages that were anticipated at that time, the bid contingency was estimated at 5% of the contract amount. This figure was then inflated based on inflation expectations.

Item 50, Construction Contingency This item was forecast at 7% of the construction contract to provide for unforeseen field conditions, such as, underground rock, underground water, foul weather conditions, a tight construction schedule, and to allow for connecting to an existing pilot plant. Providing for serious inflationary pressures at that time, the amount was factored up based on inflation projections.

Item 60, Equipment In a full-service facility project, such as an industrial research center, equipment comprises owner or user-purchased equipment and user-specified equipment normally designed by the architects and engineers and provided as part of the construction contract. For example, the owner or user would buy such equipment as CCTV cameras and monitors, a card access system, an ethernet system, a master clock system, audiovisual equipment, lockers, library equipment, and coat racks. The construction contract may include kitchen equipment, dining room, and all built-in equipment. Both owner-purchased and contract-provided equipment was carried in the appropriation request.

Item 70, Occupancy Contingency The occupancy contingency is strictly to pay for owner-initiated change orders when the owners or users start to really see what it is that the designers have planned, and have now taken the extra time to look at the spaces they are to occupy. Alternately, the user requirements have changed, requiring new building services or revamped spaces. Owner- or user-initiated changes can be very destructive not only to the cost of the project, but to the quality and the project schedule of the completed work, not to say project team productivity. The amount was calculated as 5% of the construction cost figure in item 30.

Item 80, Landscaping The amount of landscaping was estimated from design drawings and operational criteria. It is carried separately in the appropriation for corporate capital cost allowance purposes, but is delivered under the construction contract.

Item 90, Fixtures and Furnishings These items include lab and office fixtures and furnishings.

5.6 From Approved Budget to Project Cost Control Reporting

Discussed here is how a project cost control system arises out of the earliest project budget estimates through the PDS and code system; how on a building project, functional areas as seen by the facility users convert to construction elements as seen by the building designers and constructors; how the level of detail is a function of the element itself, and the need for detail.

For some corporate people, and indeed for some project designers, an approved project budget is nothing more than a control estimate, meaning: "OK, that's the budget, but what has that got to do with me?" This type of attitude is particularly prevalent where a project is not well mandated as to its ownership and sponsorship. Publicly funded projects may receive this kind of treatment.

For others an approved project budget means that now is the time for them to get in on the project. Managers, department heads, and vice presidents who were virtually impossible to be reached for their input during the planning process now demand a piece of the project. It is at this point in the project life cycle, when the money has been approved by the board of directors, that the project managers have their work cut out for them, fending of project raiders to maintain not only the integrity and the scope of the project, but the validity of the budget.

A cost control system looks to keep costs in line with the budget funds made available by the approval process. To do this it is necessary to initiate a number of actions to monitor and report the current status of the budget and to "predict" or forecast the cost of the project at completion. What we are talking about is a cost control monitoring and reporting system.

A cost control reporting system is driven by an array of information consisting of columns and fields and rows and records. The question is, however, what is it that is to be monitored and reported? and, at whom is the information aimed?

The cost situation at this point in the research center project life cycle is as follows:

1. The project definition and scope are set and confirmed by conceptual drawings and outline specifications.
2. The project has been estimated on the basis of quantities taken off from the schematic drawings and market unit prices. This estimate is considered to be accurate within $\pm 10\%$.
3. The project budget, after much massaging and fine-tuning of the submissions, has been approved, and the project is now funded.
4. The project may now proceed into final drawings, construction packaging, bidding, awards and procurement, construction, and installation of equipment.
5. A project cost control system is needed to ensure that the project budget is not exceeded.

A cost control system aims first of all to relate actual costs to budget amounts, not so much to individual line items in the budget, but to the budget bottom line. As the project is approved on the basis of the corporate cost code line items, the cost control system must reflect actual amounts versus budget amounts. And it is this code system that becomes the basis for the cost control code system at its highest level.

A reporting system with this feature incorporated can be introduced with a description of the columns and fields that would be applied to the rows and records comprising the budget line items, as will be seen in the formats that follow.

Column 1: Code. Code known by such names as code of accounts, chart of accounts, account code, or code. This line represents both the level and the type of information.

Column 2: Description. Project definition description as provided by the project program, for each code item.

Column 3: Amount Authorized. Budget amount for the code line item.

Column 4: Approved Changes. An approved change alters the amount authorized in column 3 by adding or deducting budget dollars. The amount must come from or go to some other line item in the project budget.

Column 5: Expenditures and Commitments to Date. A commitment is made when a contract is signed or a purchase order is placed and accepted. Every contract and purchase order is coded by the project definition code of accounts.

Column 6: Forecast Final Cost. Current estimate of the line item.

Column 7: Amount Authorized Redistributed. Current budget for the code line item. It includes approved changes from column 4. An addition to a code line item must be a deduction from another code line item. The project bottom line is not a variable.

Column 8: Over or Under Budget. The amount is obtained by subtracting the forecast final cost (column 6) from the amount authorized redistributed (column 7).

Some projects, depending on the requirements of project management and the way in which a cost control system is used, may have additional columns. For example, one additional column may be Estimate to Complete. An estimate to complete amount may be obtained by subtracting expenditures and commitments to date (column 5) from the forecast final cost (column 6).

A cost control report may be simplified by eliminating the expenditures and commitments to date column (column 5) and using instead the commitments column, which will be seen in the discussion on project expenditures. This is possible because the amounts are the same in both cases. The difference is that commitment dollars have not left the company treasury, whereas expended dollars have.

A cost control report may show even more information. For example, over and under numbers may be converted to percentages based on columns 7 and 8.

If there are eight columns in the cost control report format, what are the rows and records? A row may comprise a cost code item at any level of the PDS code system. In the research center example, the structure is represented by codes 10 through 90, or any breakdown of each. A record is the value in the field identified by the row and column.

Cost Control Reporting

Using the research center example budget numbers, a summary project cost control report based on the columns and rows described is depicted in Fig. 5.6. This report

1 CODE	2 DESCRIPTION	3 AMT. AUTHO-RIZED	4 APPROVED CHANGES	5 EXP. & CMTS. TO DATE	6 FORECAST FIN. COST	7 AMT. AUTH. REDISTRIB.	8 OVER / UNDER
10	DESIGN & MANAGEMENT	1654000	0	1617000	1654000	1654 000	0
30	CONSTRUCTION	11750000	250000	3330483	12000000	12000000	0
40	BID CONTINGENCY	582000	0	0	582000	582000	0
50	CONST. CONTINGENCY	1223000	-250000	250000	973000	973000	0
60	EQUIPMENT	119000	0	0	119000	119000	0
70	OCCUPANCY CONTINGENCY	699000	0	0	699000	699000	0
80	LANDSCAPING	100000	0	0	100000	100000	0
90	FIXTURES & FURNISHINGS	300000	0	0	300000	300000	0
*	COST CONTROL GRAND TOTALS	16427000	0	5,197,483	16427000	16427000	0

FIGURE 5.6 RESEARCH CENTER COMPUTER COST CONTROL REPORT, SUMMARY OF AREAS. This is a system report. The line items are level 2 area summaries based on coded detail input at lower levels. The information represents a snapshot of a project in progress.

reflects the corporate cost codes (10 through 90) developed for the appropriation request in Fig. 5.5.

The numbers seen in the report are based on the postapproval "massaged," fine-tuned status of the project. After approval of the project by the board of directors and the appropriation of funding, the project went into final design and drawings. This process was scheduled to take four months. During that time a number of major scope changes were made to the project functions, resulting in major reductions.

The numbers in the report in Fig. 5.6 are the result of computer processing of a cost and expenditure control database. The database was formulated using the rules of project definition, work breakdown, and organizational breakdown presented in this book. The other feature of the numbers in Fig. 5.6 is that they represent a "snapshot" taken as the project is in progress. That means that the design and final drawings, procurement, shop drawings, and construction are all underway.

More detailed cost reporting is seen in Fig. 5.7, which shows design and management, code 10, broken down as A architectural cost, B mechanical engineering, C electrical engineering, D cost consultant, and so on. These code items are then detailed further as AA, AB, AC; BA, BB; and so on.

Construction, cost code 30, as seen in Fig. 5.6, is the major component of the project budget. The construction cost is broken down into elements, as seen in Fig. 5.8. The elements are similar to the elemental breakdown for the appropriation estimate prepared by the cost estimators. There are differences because the breakdown is now oriented in the way in which the construction contractor and subcontractors will invoice the owner. (It is reiterated that the way estimators estimate is not necessarily the way the project is packaged, bid, and awarded for construction.)

1 CODE	2 DESCRIPTION	3 AMOUNT AUTHORIZED	4 APPROVED CHANGES	5 EXP. & CMTS. TO DATE	6 FORECAST FIN. COST	7 AMT. AUTH. REDISTRIB.	8 OVER / UNDER
10AA	ARCHITECTURAL FEE	515000	0	515000	515000	515000	0
10AB	ARCHITECTURAL EXPENSES	5000	0	5000	5000	5000	0
10AC	ARCHITECT CONSULTANTS	10000	0	10000	10000	10000	0
10BA	MECHANICAL ENGINEER FEE	200000	0	200000	200000	200000	0
10BB	MECH. ENG. EXPENSES	3000	0	3000	3000	3000	0
10CA	ELECT. ENGINEER FEE	100000	0	100000	100000	100000	0
10CB	ELECT. ENG. EXPENSES	2000	0	2000	2000	2000	0
10DA	COST CONSULTANT FEE	80000	0	80000	80000	80000	0
10DB	COST CONSLT. EXPENSES	1000	0	1000	1000	1000	0
10FF	SPECIALIST CONSULTANT	15000	0	15000	15000	15000	0
10GB	PROJ. MGMT. EXPENSES	6000	0	6000	6000	6000	0
10GS	PROJECT MGMT. FEE	340000	0	340000	340000	340000	0
10GT	PROJECT MGMT. OFFICE	34000	0	34000	34000	34000	0
10GX	PROJECT MGMT. PAYROLL	120000	0	120000	120000	120000	0
10MI	MISC.	10000	0	10000	10000	10000	0
10PA	COMPUTER	1000	0	1000	1000	1000	0
10XC	CORPORATE HEAD OFFICE	5000	0	5000	5000	5000	0
10XR	CORPORATE DES. & CONST.	95000	0	95000	95000	95000	0
10XX	FEASIBILITY CHARGE	112000	0	75000	112000	112000	0
*	DESIGN & MGMT. TOTALS	1654000	0	1617000	1654000	1654000	0

FIGURE 5.7 RESEARCH CENTER COMPUTER COST CONTROL REPORT, AREA 10, DESIGN & MANAGEMENT. This system report is a snapshot of the design and management area of the project in progress. Expenditure information is input at lower levels and summarized into the code items shown. The detail is seen as a line item in Fig. 5.6.

1 CODE	2 DESCRIPTION	3 AMOUNT AUTHORIZED	4 APPROVED CHANGES	5 EXP & CMTS TO DATE	6 FORECAST FIN. COST	7 AMT. AUTH. REDISTRIB.	8 OVER / UNDER
30AA	SUBSTRUCTURE	191000	0	182000	191000	191000	0
30AB	MASONRY BELOW GRADE	4000	0	4000	4000	4000	0
30AC	THRML./MOIST. PROTECT.	8000	0	8000	8000	8000	0
30BA	CONCRETE STRUCTURE	801000	0	1026000	680000	680000	0
30BB	STR. STEEL & ROOF DECK	224000	0	224000	224000	224000	0
30CA	EXTERIOR CLADDING	674617	0	0	800417	800417	0
30CB	PORCELAIN METAL WALL	693383	0	693383	693383	693383	0
30CC	LOADING DOCK	3000	0	3000	3000	3000	0
30DA	INTERIOR PARTITIONS	489000	0	0	599500	599500	0
30EA	VERTICAL MOVEMENT	106000	0	0	96300	96300	0
30GA	INTERIOR FINISHES	353000	0	0	353000	353000	0
30HA	FITTINGS & EQUIPMENT	875000	0	0	929200	929200	0
30JA	ELECTRICAL	1746817	0	0	1712317	1712317	0
30JB	ELECTRICAL UNDERGROUND	15183	0	15183	15183	15183	0
30KA	MECHANICAL	3076700	0	0	3317700	3317700	0
30KB	MECHANICAL UNDERGROUND	238300	0	238300	238300	238300	0
30LA	GC OVERHEAD & PROFIT	230383	0	0	102283	102283	0
30LB	INSPECTION & TESTING	10000	0	10000	10000	10000	0
30LC	GC MANAGEMENT EXPENSES	325000	0	325000	325000	325000	0
30LD	GC GENERAL EXPENSES	369617	0	369617	369617	369617	0
30NA	SITE DEVELOPMENT	756000	0	182000	928200	928200	0
30PA	DESIGN CONTINGENCY	560000	250000	50000	399600	399600	0
*	CONSTRUCTION TOTALS	11750000	250000	3330483	12000000	12000000	0

FIGURE 5.8 RESEARCH CENTER COMPUTER COST CONTROL REPORT, CONSTRUCTION AREA. This is a snapshot of the construction area in progress. The line items are summaries of the code items at the indicated levels or their elements at lower levels.

Sometimes in planning project cost control there is a propensity for too much detail, particularly in the use of codes derived from computerized breakdowns. In reality, it is easier to code items in planning stages than to pick up actual costs for those items. In addition, just how much micro detail is necessary for cost control?

This issue is demonstrated in Fig. 5.9, using code item 30DA, Interior Partitions. The information shows 0 against individual line items in the amount authorized, forecast final cost, and amount authorized redistributed columns.

An amount of $489,000 for the sum of the items, was entered as a line item into the amount authorized column. As the project was started up, an approved change of $110,500 as one line item was entered to make up the budget shortfall. (This amount comes from the $250,000 design contingency, code item 30PA.)

A code item such as 30DA, Interior Partitions, is made up of diverse elements forming this building system. The amounts are code items from general contract progress billing, or from subcontracts and purchase orders that are part of the general contract. They are coded as 30DA, the match looked for when invoices are paid.

The individual dollar amounts are not entered for cost control purposes, since that is being taken care of by the authorized budget amount as one line by itself. The system works without becoming embroiled in difficult detail. Indeed, even the amount of detail shown may be too much.

The cost control report in Fig. 5.6 shows code items 10 through 90 as single line items. Code items 10 and 30 are shown broken down as detail items in the reports in Figs. 5.7 and 5.8. Construction item 30DA is broken down into the next level of detail, as seen in Fig. 5.9. To complete the picture, code items 40 through 90 are depicted in Fig. 5.10.

What is in a cost control reporting system? There are detail reports and there are summary reports. Then there are action reports, exception reports, trend reports, cash-flow reports, and, graphic reports such as pie charts, bar charts, and histograms. There

1 CODE	2 DESCRIPTION	3 AMOUNT AUTHORIZED	4 APPROVED CHANGES	5 EXP & CMTS TO DATE	6 FORECAST FIN. COST	7 AMT. AUTH. REDISTRIB.	8 OVER / UNDER
30DA	SLIDING DOOR	0	0	0	0	0	0
30DA	TOILET PARTITIONS	0	0	0	0	0	0
30DA	BLAST-RESISTANT DOORS	0	0	0	0	0	0
30DA	ROLLING SHUTTER DOOR	0	0	0	0	0	0
30DA	FINISHING HARDWARE	0	0	0	0	0	0
30DA	HM DOORS, FRAMES, SCREENS	0	0	0	0	0	0
30DA	ROUGH & FINISH CARPENTRY	0	0	0	0	0	0
30DA	INTERIOR MASONRY PARTITIONS	0	0	0	0	0	0
30DA	DRYWALL PARTITIONS	0	0	0	0	0	0
30DA	FOLDING PARTITIONS	0	0	0	0	0	0
30DA	INTERIOR PARTITIONS	489000	110500	0	599500	599500	0
*	SUB-TOTAL FOR 30D	489000	110500	0	599500	599500	0

FIGURE 5.9 RESEARCH CENTER COMPUTER COST CONTROL REPORT, CONSTRUCTION CODE ITEM 30DA DETAILS. This computer snapshot shows detail input for code item 30DA, Interior Partitions. The details would comprise subcontracts or elements of the general contract. The individual details are not coded beyond the 30DA code.

1 CODE	2 DESCRIPTION	3 AMOUNT AUTHORIZED	4 APPROVED CHANGES	5 EXP & CMTS TO DATE	6 FORECAST FIN. COST	7 AMT. AUTH. REDISTRIB.	8 OVER / UNDER
40	BID CONTINGENCY	582000	0	0	582000	582000	0
*							
50	CONST. CONTINGENCY	1223000	-250000	250000	973000	973000	0
*							
60	EQUIPMENT	119000	0	0	119000	119000	0
*							
70	OCCUPANCY CONTINGENCY	699000	0	0	699000	699000	0
*							
80	LANDSCAPING	100000	0	0	100000	100000	0
*							
90	FIXTURES & FURNISHINGS	300000	0	0	300000	100000	0
*	*	*	*	*	*	*	*

Figure 5.10 Research Center Computer Cost Control Report, Code Items 40, 50, 60, 70, 80, 90. This summary report shows the nondesign and nonconstruction project items.

are weekly, monthly, quarterly, and annual usage curves and cumulative curves. They come in every color and all densities of black and white hatches and shades. What they all need, without exception, is a database of accurate information. And that is what the columns and fields, rows and records discussed here are all about: the making and recording of accurate cost control information.

The depictions so far have been summary cost control reports. The line items coded 30DA in Fig. 5.9 represent code amount items from the general construction contract progress billing, or amounts carried under this code for individual subcontractors or purchase orders. These items thus represent commitments and eventual expenditures, generated by the expenditure control system.

It is seen in the foregoing figures that cost control reporting has incorporated information from an expenditure control system. There is also a statement to the effect that the reports are driven by a database.

5.7 From Cost Control to Expenditure Control Reporting

When people speak of cost control they usually mean that there is an attempt being made to control a cost versus a budget. In knowledgeable repeat project-experienced corporate organizations it is a given that the best available estimate used to set a project budget is about 10% accurate. They know from experience that an estimate cannot be more accurate. Nevertheless some construction project managers claim that a definitive cost estimate can be accurate within ±5%. Accuracy is an indication of the probability of overrunning or underrunning an estimate.

For the research center model, the cost of design leading to schematic drawings to enable a ±10% estimate amounted to 16% of the architectural engineering budget. To achieve that kind of accuracy, a corporation must take the time and pay for the resources to prepare preliminary drawings that can be quantified and estimated.

Figures 5.1 through 5.10 show the development of a system of reports to facilitate comparing actual costs to budgets. As budget approval is tied to the corporate account code, the root codes 10 through 90 are the ultimate account codes for the project elements. They do not, however, identify the source of the actual costs for the deliverables covered in account codes 10 through 90.

The source of the actual costs are the organizations and people who are contracted to carry out the project tasks that result in the delivery of the project. For the research center project used as the model in this chapter, the tasks are carried out by groups of organizations which may be classified as follows:

A Consultants, designers, and project managers

C Construction contractors

E Vendors and suppliers with purchase orders

M Miscellaneous charges to the project

X Owner internal charges to the project

Z Reserves and contingencies

If code items 10 through 90 provide the budget amounts, the cost source codes A through Z are the sources of actual costs. In Figs. 5.6 through 5.9 the numbers in column 5, Expenditures & Commitments to Date, result from contracts and agreements with the organizations coded as A through M. Contingencies, code Z, receives special treatment as a source of internal project funds.

A cost control system requires a parallel expenditure control system. It consists of a series of columns and fields and rows and records as follows:

Column 1: Cost Source Type. Classification of the organization or service being provided, and level of expenditure information.

Column 2: Description. Name of the class of organization, or name within a class, or type of service within a class.

Column 3: Original Commitment. Amount of the agreement between the project and the organization, which may be a purchase order, contract, handshake, or a predetermined fee.

Column 4: Approved Commitment Change. Amount to be added to or deducted from the original commitment.

Column 5: Current Period Expenditures. In project work a current period has been traditionally a month. It could be daily, weekly, or the period since the last update. In this model a current period represents one month, as invoices and progress billings were paid monthly.

Column 6: Expenditures to Date. Sum of money actually paid out, that is, a check has been issued, or an invoice has been approved, or a check requisition has been issued.

Column 7: Current Outstanding Commitment. Amount calculated by the system as the difference between original commitment (column 3) and expenditures to date (column 6).

Column 8: Expenditures and Commitments to Date. Amount calculated by the system by adding expenditures to date (column 6) to current outstanding commitments (column 7); should be equal to original commitments (column 3).

Figure 5.11 depicts the project expenditure report for the research center model project illustrated in the preceding cost control reports.

This is a classic project expenditure report as the companion to the project cost control report. It is seen that the reports perform different functions. Cost control is a comparison against the budget. Expenditure control is a "money committed versus money expended" tracking system. It may be said that if a project is 100% committed to contracts and purchase orders, and the total commitments are under budget, the cost control system could be redundant. This is true, except that projects usually reach that stage of commitment on about the same day that the project is completed, or later.

Figure 5.12 provides the next level of expenditure detail for consulting contracts, cost source A. The abbreviated headings of the eight columns are explained as follows:

CST TYP	Cost source type
DESCRIPTION	Description
ORIG CMT	Original commitment

1 CST TYP	2 DESCRIPTION	3 ORIGINAL COMMITMENT	4 APPROVED CMTMT. CHANGE	5 CURRENT PERIOD EXPEND.	6 EXPENDI- TURE TO DATE	7 CURRENT O/S CMTMT.	8 EXPEND. & 0/S CMTMT TO DATE
A	CONSULTING CONTRACTS	1473000	0	44413.29	947811.25	524895	1473000
C	CONSTRUCTION CONTRACTS	3330483	0	157112.30	517512.30	2812971	3330483
E	PURCHASES	34000	0	10912.99	23787.30	10213	34000
M	MISCELLANEOUS	10000	0	240.89	2580.29	7420	10000
X	INTERNAL CHARGES	100000	0	93.63	14102.40	85897	100000
Z	RESERVES & CONTINGENCIES	250000	0	.00	250000.00	0	250000
*	EXPENDITURE PROJECT TOTALS	5197483	0	212773.10	1755793.54	3441396	5197483

FIGURE 5.11 RESEARCH CENTER COMPUTER PROJECT EXPENDITURE REPORT, COST SOURCES A, C, E, M, X, Z. This is a summary report of the commitments by task assignment, contract, and purchase order made by the corporate owner for the research center project to the individuals and firms classified.

1 COST SOURCE TYPE	2 DESCRIPTION	3 ORIG CMT	4 AP CMT CHG	5 CUR PRD EXP	6 EXP TO DATE	7 CUR O. CMTS.	8 E & C TO DATE
A	ARCHITECTURAL FEE	515000	0	17711.36	362594.45	152406	515000
A	ARCHITECTURAL EXPENSES	5000	0	11342.34	17958.24	-12958	5000
A	ARCHITECT CONSULTANTS	10000	0	.00	10417.04	-417	10000
A	MECHANICAL ENGINEER FEE	200000	0	.00	150000.00	50000	200000
A	MECH. ENG. EXPENSES	3000	0	.00	2603.43	101	3000
A	ELECT. ENGINEER FEE	100000	0	.00	75000.00	25000	100000
A	ELECT. ENG. EXPENSES	2000	0	.00	1535.89	464	2000
A	COST CONSULTANT FEE	80000	0	.00	79500.00	500	80000
A	COST CONSLT. EXPENSES	1000	0	.00	.00	1000	1000
A	SPECIALIST CONSULTANT	15000	0	1786.64	10549.68	4450	15000
A	PROJ. MGMT. EXPENSES	6000	0	323.71	2037.41	3963	6000
A	PROJECT MGMT. FEE	340000	0	7885.00	149045.00	190955	340000
A	PROJECT MGMT. PAYROLL	120000	0	5349.14	27151.25	92849	120000
A	COMPUTER	1000	0	15.10	185.40	815	1000
A	FEASIBILITY CHARGE	75000	0	.00	59233.46	15767	75000
* TOTALS	CONSULTING CONTRACTS	1473000	0	44413.29	947811.25	524895	1473000

FIGURE 5.12 RESEARCH CENTER COMPUTER PROJECT EXPENDITURE REPORT, COST SOURCE A, CONSULTING CONTRACTS. This is a snapshot of the consulting contract awards and expenditures. Each line represents a consultant contract or a purchased item. This report is system-produced from the project cost database.

AP CMT CHG	Approved commitment change
CUR PRD EXP	Current period expenditure
EXP TO DATE	Expenditure to date
CUR O. CMTS	Current outstanding commitments
E & C TO DATE	Expenditures and commitments to date

Figure 5.13 is an illustration of the expenditure report for cost source C, Construction Contracts. In both cost source types A and C, the aim of the reporting is toward a reflection of the contract breakdown either into subconsultants, subcontracts, or trade packages, or into a scheduled progression of how the work is to be delivered.

For example, it is seen in Fig. 5.13 that both electrical underground and mechanical underground are line items with their own expenditure progressions. That is the result of packaging these elements ahead of the main electrical and mechanical contracts to accommodate construction of the substructure.

To complete the expenditure reporting scenario, cost source types E, Purchases; M, Miscellaneous; X—Internal Charges; and Z—Reserves & Contingencies are illustrated in Fig. 5.14. In real life they most likely would be individual reports.

5.8 Database Drives Project Cost and Expenditure Control

The project cost and expenditure control reports for the research center project were produced by a computer project expenditure and cost control system which functions

1 COST SOURCE TYPE	2 DESCRIPTION	3 ORIG CMT	4 AP CMT CHG	5 CUR PRD EXP	6 EXP TO DATE	7 CUR O. CMTS.	8 E & C TO DATE
C	LANDSCAPING	0	0	.00	.00	0	0
C	SUBSTRUCTURE	182000	0	17386.00	26485.00	155515	182000
C	MASONRY BELOW GRADE	4000	0	.00	.00	4000	4000
C	THRML./MOIST. PROTECT.	8000	0	.00	.00	8000	8000
C	CONCRETE STRUCTURE	1026000	0	91414.00	139265.00	886735	1026000
C	STR. STEEL & ROOF DECK	224000	0	.00	.00	224000	224000
C	EXTERIOR CLADDING	0	0	.00	.00	0	0
C	PORCELAIN METAL WALL	693383	0	.00	.00	693383	693383
C	LOADING DOCK	3000	0	.00	.00	3000	3000
C	INTERIOR PARTITIONS	0	0	.00	.00	0	0
C	VERTICAL MOVEMENT	0	0	.00	.00	0	0
C	INTERIOR FINISHES	0	0	.00	.00	0	0
C	FITTINGS & EQUIPMENT	0	0	.00	.00	0	0
C	ELECTRICAL	0	0	.00	.00	0	0
C	ELECTRICAL UNDERGROUND	15183	0	.00	3400.00	11783	15183
C	MECHANICAL	0	0	.00	.00	0	0
C	MECHANICAL UNDERGROUND	238300	0	.00	30600.00	207700	238300
C	OVERHEAD & PROFIT	0	0	12750.00	155550.00	−155550	0
C	INSPECT & TEST	10000	0	2412.30	2412.30	7588	10000
C	GC MANAGEMENT EXPENSES	325000	0	15300.00	30600.00	294400	325000
C	GC GENERAL EXPENSES	369617	0	.00	.00	369617	369617
C	SITE DEVELOPMENT	182000	0	17850.00	129200.00	52800	182000
C	DESIGN CONTINGENCY	50000	0	.00	.00	50000	50000
* TOTALS	CONSTRUCTION CONTRACTS	3330483	0	157112.30	517512.30	2812971	3330483

FIGURE 5.13 RESEARCH CENTER COMPUTER PROJECT EXPENDITURE REPORT, COST SOURCE C, CONSTRUCTION CONTRACTS. This is a snapshot of the construction contract awards and expenditures. Each line represents a subcontract or an element of a general contract. This report is system-produced from the project cost database.

1 COST SOURCE TYPE	2 DESCRIPTION	3 ORIG CMT	4 AP CMT CHG	5 CUR PRD EXP	6 EXP TO DATE	7 CUR O. CMTS.	8 E & C TO DATE
E	EQUIPMENT	0	0	.00	.00	0	0
E	F & F	0	0	.00	.00	0	0
E	OFFICE EXPENSES	34000	0	10912.99	23787.30	10213	34000
* TOTALS	PURCHASES	34000	0	10912.99	23787.30	10213	34000
*	*	*	*	*	*	*	*
M	MISCELLANEOUS	10000	0	240.89	2580.29	7420	10000
* TOTALS	MISCELLANEOUS	10000	0	240.89	2580.29	7420	10000
*	*	*	*	*	*	*	*
X	CORPORATE H. O.	5000	0	93.63	5075.66	-76	5000
X	CORPORATE D. & C.	95000	0	.00	9026.74	85973	95000
* TOTALS	INTERNAL CHARGES	100000	0	93.63	14102.40	85897	100000
*	*	*	*	*	*	*	*
Z	BID CONTINGENCY	0	0	.00	.00	0	0
Z	OCCUP CONTINGENCY	0	0	.00	.00	0	0
Z	CONST CONTINGENCY	250000	0	.00	250000.00	0	250000
* TOTALS	RESERVES & CONTIN.	250000	0	.00	250000.00	0	250000
*	*	*	*	*	*	*	*

FIGURE 5.14 RESEARCH CENTER COMPUTER PROJECT EXPENDITURE REPORT, COST SOURCE E, M, X, Z ITEMS. This is a snapshot of the purchases, assignments, and awards and expenditures against the coded items. This report is system-produced from the project cost database.

as a database management system utilizing a set of master records and commands specifically designed for the purpose. For the research center model the master records contained the following information, listed as column headings in a two-module system:

PROJ ELEM.	Project element or number
CST	Cost source type
DESCRIPTION	Description
ORIG CMT	Original commitment
CMT CHG	Commitment change
AMT AUTH	Amount authorized
APPRV CHG	Approved change to amount authorized
REDIST AMT	Amount authorized redistributed
FOFCST	Forecast final cost
ECDT	Expenditures and commitments to date
COC	Current outstanding commitments
CURR EXP	Current period expenditures
EXP TO DTE	Expenditures to date
EST TO COMP	Estimate to complete
O/U$-BDGT	Over / under $ budget

A representative snap shot of the records in module 1 is seen in Fig. 5.15. Module 2 is shown in Fig. 5.16. It is from this database that the research center project cost and expenditure reports illustrated so far, and others to be named, are prepared by the system.

5.9 Rationalizing Project Cost Control with PDS/WBS/OBS

The PDS exercise scopes the project in language and code that the users can relate to, and prepares it for design and engineering. Estimates at this point in time are order-of-magnitude numbers. The WBS breaks the project down into tasks for design and construction, which can be estimated to budget or preliminary-grade accuracy.

A definitive or detailed project estimate is only possible after the preparation of preliminary drawings and specifications and the resulting takeoff and pricing by professional estimators. From experience, this estimate is suspect in its detail. Reliable estimators will say that although line items may vary significantly, the bottom line is trustworthy within the $\pm 10\%$ accuracy level.

Activities resulting from the WBS are not usually stand alone, but are formed into packages. The packages may or may not be estimated and assigned budgets.

1 PROJ ELEM	2 CST	3 DESCRIPTION	4 ORIG CMT	5 CMT CHG	6 AMT AUTH	7 APRV CHG	8 REDIST AMT	9 FOFCST
10AA00000	A	ARCHITECTURAL FEE	515000	0	515000	0	515000	515000
10AB00000	A	ARCHITECTURAL EXPENSES	5000	0	5000	0	5000	5000
10AC00000	A	ARCHITECT CONSULTANTS	10000	0	10000	0	10000	10000
10BA00000	A	MECHANICAL ENGINEER FEE	200000	0	200000	0	200000	200000
10BB00000	A	MECH. ENG. EXPENSES	3000	0	3000	0	3000	3000
10CA00000	A	ELECT. ENGINEER FEE	100000	0	100000	0	100000	100000
10CB00000	A	ELECT. ENG. EXPENSES	2000	0	2000	0	2000	2000
10DA00000	A	COST CONSULTANT FEE	80000	0	80000	0	80000	80000
10DB00000	A	COST CONSLT. EXPENSES	1000	0	1000	0	1000	1000
10FF00000	A	SPECIALIST CONSULTANT	15000	0	15000	0	15000	15000
10GB00000	A	PROJ. MGMT. EXPENSES	6000	0	6000	0	6000	6000
10GS00000	A	PROJECT MGMT. FEE	340000	0	340000	0	340000	340000
30AA00000	C	SUBSTRUCTURE	182000	0	191000	0	191000	191000
30AB00000	C	MASONRY BELOW GRADE	4000	0	4000	0	4000	4000
30AC00000	C	THRML./MOIST. PROTECT.	8000	0	8000	0	8000	8000
30BA00000	C	CONCRETE STRUCTURE	1026000	0	801000	0	801000	801000
30BB00000	C	STR. STEEL & ROOF DECK	224000	0	224000	0	224000	224000
30CA00000	C	EXTERIOR CLADDING	0	0	674617	0	674617	674617
30CB00000	C	PORCELAIN METAL WALL	693383	0	693383	0	693383	693383
30CC00000	C	LOADING DOCK	3000	0	3000	0	3000	3000
30DA00000	C	INTERIOR PARTITIONS	0	0	489000	0	489000	489000
30EA00000	C	VERTICAL MOVEMENT	0	0	106000	0	106000	106000
30GA00000	C	INTERIOR FINISHES	0	0	353000	363400	716400	381246
30GA09300	C	MOSAIC & QUARRY TILE	49329	0	0	0	0	0
30GA09650	C	RESILIENT FLOORING	98400	0	0	0	0	0
30GA09680	C	CARPET & BROADLOOM	105652	0	0	0	0	0
30GA09890	C	PAINTING	110365	0	0	0	0	0
30GA10270	C	COMPUTER ACCESS FLR	17500	0	0	0	0	0
30HA00000	C	FITTINGS & EQUIPMENT	0	0	875000	0	875000	875000
30JA00000	C	ELECTRICAL	0	0	1746817	0	1746817	1746817
30JB00000	C	ELECTRICAL UNDERGROUND	15183	0	15183	0	15183	15183
30KA00000	C	MECHANICAL	0	0	3076700	0	3076700	3076700
30KB00000	C	MECH. UNDERGROUND	238300	0	238300	0	238300	238300
40AA00000	Z	CONTINGENCIES	0	0	582000	0	582000	582000
50AA00000	Z	CONST. CONTINGENCY	250000	0	1223000	0	1223000	1223000
60AA00000	E	EQUIPMENT	0	0	119000	0	119000	119000
70AA00000	Z	OCCUPANCY CONTINGENCY	0	0	699000	0	699000	699000
80AA00000	C	LANDSCAPING	0	0	100000	0	100000	100000
90AA00000	E	FIXTURES & FURNISHINGS	0	0	300000	0	300000	300000

Figure 5.15 Research Center Cost and Expenditure Control System, Module 1 Database Information. This is a snapshot of the database of project cost and expenditure control information. Reports are produced from this and the module 2 database.

Keeping in mind what the estimators say about the validity of individual line item numbers, the package budgets may or may not be reliable. However, in a professionally managed project, packages are usually assigned budgets.

As activities are packaged, the packages take on generic organizational names, such as, design packages, construction packages, purchase packages, and internal charges. As they are bid and awarded, they take on the names of the companies and people that will carry them out, thus forming the OBS.

Except for changes to be paid for by the reserves and contingencies amounts, the project is now totally committed, and it may be said that its cost is firm.

What happens though is that in the process both the PDS code and the WBS code seem to disappear out of the cost control equation. The line item codes in the database and report examples above are coded by project elements or project numbers,

1 PROJ ELEM	2 CST	3 DESCRIPTION	4 ECDT	5 COC	6 CURR EXP	7 EXP TO DTE	8 EST TO COMP	9 O/U$-BDGT
10AA00000	A	ARCHITECTURAL FEE	515000	152406	171711.36	362594.45	0	.00
10AB00000	A	ARCHITECTURAL EXPENSES	5000	-12958	11342.34	17958.24	0	.00
10AC00000	A	ARCHITECT CONSULTANTS	10000	-417	.00	10417.04	0	.00
10BA00000	A	MECHANICAL ENGINEER FEE	200000	50000	.00	150000.00	0	.00
10BB00000	A	MECH. ENG. EXPENSES	3000	101	.00	2603.43	0	.00
10CA00000	A	ELECT. ENGINEER FEE	100000	25000	.00	75000.00	0	.00
10CB00000	A	ELECT. ENG. EXPENSES	2000	464	.00	1535.89	0	.00
10DA00000	A	COST CONSULTANT FEE	80000	500	.00	79500.00	0	.00
10DB00000	A	COST CONSLT. EXPENSES	1000	1000	.00	.00	0	.00
10FF00000	A	SPECIALIST CONSULTANT	15000	4450	1786.64	10549.68	0	.00
10GB00000	A	PROJ. MGMT. EXPENSES	6000	3963	323.71	2037.41	0	.00
10GS00000	A	PROJECT MGMT. FEE	340000	190955	7885.00	149045.00	0	.00
30AA00000	C	SUBSTRUCTURE	182000	155515	17386.00	26485.00	9000	.00
30AB00000	C	MASONRY BELOW GRADE	4000	4000	.00	.00	0	.00
30AC00000	C	THRML./MOIST. PROTECT.	8000	8000	.00	.00	0	.00
30BA00000	C	CONCRETE STRUCTURE	1026000	886735	91414.00	139265.00	−346000	.00
30BB00000	C	STR. STEEL & ROOF DECK	224000	224000	.00	.00	0	.00
30CA00000	C	EXTERIOR CLADDING	0	0	.00	.00	800417	.00
30CB00000	C	PORCELAIN METAL WALL	693383	693383	.00	.00	0	.00
30CC00000	C	LOADING DOCK	3000	3000	.00	.00	0	.00
30DA00000	C	INTERIOR PARTITIONS	0	0	.00	.00	599500	.00
30EA00000	C	VERTICAL MOVEMENT	0	0	.00	.00	96300	.00
30GA00000	C	INTERIOR FINISHES	0	0	.00	.00	.00	335154.00
30GA09300	C	MOSAIC & QUARRY TILE	49329	49329	.00	.00	.00	.00
30GA09650	C	RESILIENT FLOORING	98400	98400	.00	.00	.00	.00
30GA09680	C	CARPET & BROADLOOM	105652	105652	.00	.00	.00	.00
30GA09890	C	PAINTING	110365	110365	.00	.00	.00	.00
30GA10270	C	COMPUTER ACCESS FLR	17500	17500	.00	.00	.00	.00
30HA00000	C	FITTINGS & EQUIPMENT	0	0	.00	.00	929200	.00
30JA00000	C	ELECTRICAL	0	0	.00	.00	1712317	.00
30JB00000	C	ELECTRICAL UNDERGROUND	15183	11783	.00	3400.00	0	.00
30KA00000	C	MECHANICAL	0	0	.00	.00	3317700	.00
30KB00000	C	MECH. UNDERGROUND	238300	207700	.00	30600.00	0	.00
40AA00000	Z	CONTINGENCIES	0	0	.00	.00	582000	.00
50AA00000	Z	CONST. CONTINGENCY	250000	0	.00	.00	723000	.00
60AA00000	E	EQUIPMENT	0	0	.00	.00	119000	.00
70AA00000	Z	OCCUPANCY CONTINGENCY	0	0	.00	.00	699000	.00
80AA00000	C	LANDSCAPING	0	0	.00	.00	.00	.00
90AA00000	E	FIXTURES & FURNISHINGS	0	0	.00	.00	.00	.00

Figure 5.16 Research Center Cost and Expenditure Control System, Module 2 Database Information. This is a snapshot of the database of project cost and expenditure control information. Reports are produced from this and the module 1 database.

tied to the corporate code, and always matched with the cost source (organizational) code.

The project numbers in the database seen in Figs. 5.15 and 5.16 also have taken on a five-digit extension 00000. For example, 30BA00000 is the code for concrete structure. The extension feature was designed into the system to accommodate the code system of Masterformat's Master List of Section Titles and Numbers for the construction industry. In the research center model there was no need to use the Masterformat numbers, and as a result they do not appear in any cost control reports.

To conclude this rationalization, the results of WBS are activities that become packages that are awarded as contracts. The contract amount is compared to the package budget for cost control purposes. In the process, however, both the original PDS code and the WBS code disappear from the cost control system and are replaced by the construction element code and the code for the organization delivering the work.

What then is the purpose of the WBS? The WBS represents the development of actions or activities. It is the link between deliverables and the organizations that carry them out. If the PDS defines and codes the "completed" project deliverables, the WBS establishes the act of completing them as standard construction packages of activities for individuals and organizations.

The packages as contracts are delivered by the organizations coded as OBS. A WBS package code is ultimately synonymous with its OBS code.

5.10 Construction Project Cost Databases and Standards

The development of a PDS aims to scope the completed project as it will be seen by the users and owners of the project and to form the basis for planning and design by the A/E/C industry. It is not yet a construction project at the PDS stage, and the order-of-magnitude estimate is based on cubic foot (cf), sf, m^2, or user units, such as, an auditorium seat, a hospital bed, or a nursing home bed, for parametric or ratio cost estimating. Although the resulting cost estimate is known to be unreliable at this stage, it is all that is available until the project is approved to proceed to preliminary design and drawings, with the resulting $\pm 10\%$ accuracy definitive cost estimate.

Definitive estimates are based on quantity takeoffs, the application of normal percentages for construction overhead and profit, escalation, and the application of current prices from historical cost information databases kept by the corporations themselves or by industry professionals.

Construction industry cost professionals maintain and apply construction cost information in many different ways. A preferred method is on the basis of building elements, as seen in Fig. 5.17. This figure is based on the research center example at a stage of its development to better illustrate this concept of estimating.

This estimating approach is based on breaking down a building project into eight building systems (elements) as listed, with item 8 subdivided into mechanical and electrical. Additional items provide for overhead and profit, site, and contingencies.

ELEMENT NO.	ELEMENT NAME	ESTIMATE $
1	Substructure	193,000
2	Superstructure	1,037,000
3	Exterior Cladding	1,369,000
4	Interior Partitions	489,000
5	Vertical Movement	106,000
6	Interior Finishes	353,000
7	Fittings and Equipment	875,000
8(a)	Electrical	1,762,000
8(b)	Mechanical	3,315,000
9	Overhead & Profit	935,000
	Net Building Cost	10,434,000
10	Site Development	756,000
11	Contingencies	560,000
*	Progressive Cost	11,750,000
**	Cost per Square Foot (Gross Floor Area: 88,125 SF)	133.33

FIGURE 5.17 ESTIMATING APPROACH, QUANTITY SURVEYORS CONCEPT BASED ON BUILDING SYSTEMS. This quantity surveyors estimating system was used on the research center project. The eight elements are based on using historical cost figures and applying them to the specific quality/quantity takeoffs for the research center project.

This particular breakdown in use by professional quantity surveyors is historically the most mature.

To illustrate further how estimating is a progressive, detailed information-gathering exercise, the type of detail backing the estimate for 3, Exterior Cladding, is shown in Fig. 5.18. The other building systems would be similarly detailed.

It becomes evident from the information shown that the only way that this degree of detail is available is through quantity takeoffs of drawings and specifications, and through the pricing of the resulting units based on historical and current cost information.

The storing and delivery of parametric and detailed cost information to the A/E/C industry is gathered, organized, and maintained in a number of different ways by commercial cost services providers. For example, the Means company, a major publisher of construction cost information, breaks down a building project into 12 systems or element groups, with each system broken down into elements, plus the cost of general conditions and the architect's fees.

3. EXTERIOR CLADDING	QUANTITIES	UNIT RATE	SUB-TOTAL	TOTAL
(A) ROOF FINISH	24,635 SF	9.58	236,000	
(B) WALLS BELOW GROUND FLOOR	6,640 SF	9.94	66,000	
(C) WALLS ABOVE GROUND FLOOR	31,260 SF	27.32	864,000	
(D) WINDOWS	9,600 SF	17.29	166,000	
(E) EXTERIOR DOORS AND SCREENS	-	-	17,000	
(F) BALCONIES AND PROJECTIONS	-	-	20,000	
				1,369,000

FIGURE 5.18 QUANTITY SURVEYORS CONCEPT BASED ON BUILDING SYSTEMS, SYSTEM 3, EXTERIOR CLADDING. This provides a detailed breakdown of element 3, Exterior Cladding, in Figure 5.17. It shows a professional method of keeping unit costs that make up the eight building systems maintained as cost databases by professional quantity surveyors.

The third and perhaps most current approach to construction project estimating and pricing is to use the Masterformat 16-division approach. Masterformat invokes the following 16 divisions for all project control purposes, including estimating and cost control:

1. General requirements
2. Sitework
3. Concrete
4. Masonry
5. Metals
6. Wood and plastics
7. Thermal and moisture protection
8. Doors and windows
9. Finishes
10. Specialties
11. Equipment
12. Furnishings
13. Special construction
14. Conveying systems
15. Mechanical
16. Electrical

Each division in turn is broken down into subdivisions, which in turn are divided into element types and individual elements, as discussed at length in Chapter 2.

There is now more availability of cost information in the 16-division format. This is particularly true of commercially available computerized cost databases. The Masterformat breakdown will gain momentum in terms of its usage, both for project elemental breakdown and for estimating and cost control as elements and their quantities are planned, designed, drawn, and calculated by computer-aided design systems. Once an item is quantified by computer, its cost will be readily calculated through the importation and application of unit prices to the quantities.

5.11 S Curves, Earned Value, and Performance Measurement

5.11.1 S Curves

With the advent of postmodern computerized project management it was anticipated that hard copy (paper) reports would become obsolete. The mantra went something like this:

Paper reports: Bad. Computer screens: Good.

Columns and rows: Bad. Curves and pie charts: Good.

Trend lines: Good. Reports: Bad.

A curve, a bar, a pie segment, a histogram is only as good as the information that drives it. The information presented in the columns, rows, and fields in the preceding reports aims to be as good (accurate) as the cost of management and data allows. Once entered into the system, the computer can produce curves, bars, and trend lines. It needs to be understood, however, that the graphics would come after the fact. The work that goes into producing accurate cost and schedule information is needed in whatever form management sees it.

On the negative side of computerized S-curve usage, computer systems can produce information that looks like accurate data, but in fact may be order-of-magnitude quality or worse. For example, consider the 5% classical project S curve, as depicted in Fig. 5.19. Assuming a start date, a finish date, and a total project cost figure, a computer system can produce detailed weekly, monthly, or quarterly cash-flow reports on the basis of the S curve. The detail would be impressive. But the assumptions on which the detail is based could be grossly inaccurate.

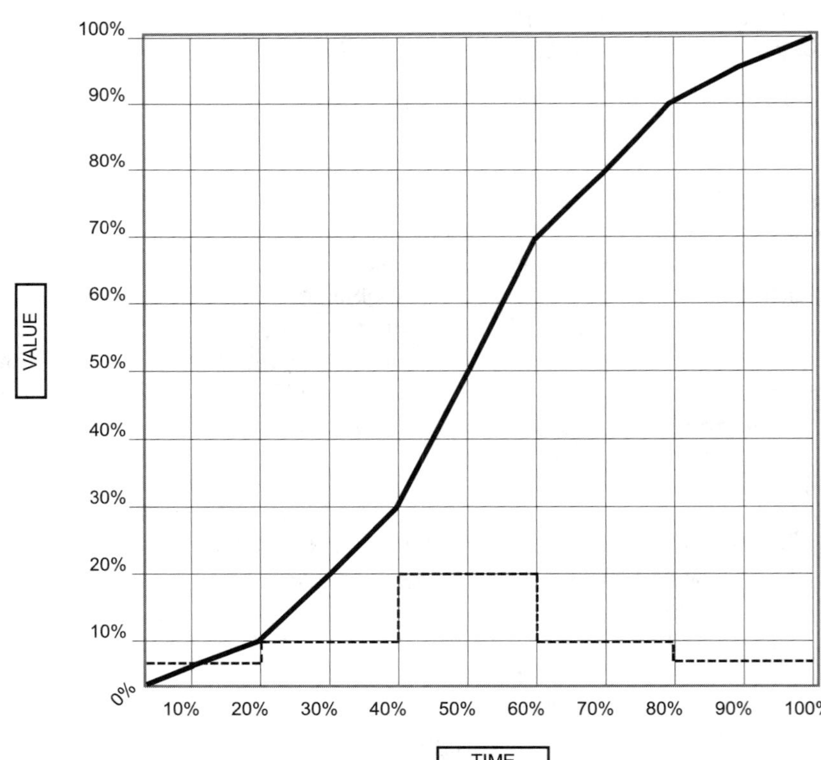

FIGURE 5.19 5% S-SHAPED DISTRIBUTION (OPTIMUM S CURVE). From experience, of about 10 commonly used S curves, the 5% cumulative S curve is the distribution used most often by professional project managers for order-of-magnitude cost or schedule projections for "green field" projects.

However, S curves are used for project modeling, monitoring, and reporting by being adaptable in the planning and measuring of earned value and performance. The S curve in Fig. 5.19 is one of ten classical S curves widely used in project work. Some project management systems have the capability to accommodate up to 40 client-generated S curves for the management of industrial, construction, and business projects.

5.11.2 Earned Value Performance Curves

A valid use of an S curve is as a front-end planning tool to forecast cash flow, materials, or human resources requirements. It can provide the basis for a master schedule of major milestones, and a launching pad for detail planning and estimating. The target in this kind of usage is to replace the order-of-magnitude S curve with the computer-calculated S curve based on resource-loaded activities scheduled by CPM. It is this kind of S curve that can form the basis of earned value reporting.

By definition, earned value is the value in base budget units of the actual work performed, regardless of the actual cost incurred. The project is thus estimated in detail in base budget units, which form the baseline S curve when the units are coupled with scheduling activities to form time-phased budgets.

It is important to understand that use of the earned value analysis method must be agreed upon by contract between the project owner and the contractor. Experience has shown two contract forms as being most amenable to this approach: a fixed price contract and a target or incentive type contract. Cost-plus contracts cause more complexity in that they require client-approved budgets or revised budgets due to changes. Constantly changing conditions in a cost-plus contract environment would make trend analysis difficult.

An earned value performance analysis chart is seen in Figure 5.20. The baseline S curve may be constructed on the basis of time-phased budgets of project areas, quantities of direct materials, human resources person-hours, or budget dollars. As the individual areas are quantified or scheduled, the results of all the areas are accumulated to form the cumulative S curve. To do it this way may be found expensive and difficult to implement. Another way to achieve the S curve at less cost is through the application of experiential or historical information.

It may be seen that the development, management, and implementation of an earned value performance system is not an insignificant undertaking, and it is perhaps for that reason that the method is not widely used in nongovernmental projects.

5.11.3 Earned Value, Bar Charts, and CPM

The benefits of linking payments to performance using bar charts, CPM, and the earned value concept have been discussed widely by project management software vendors and project managers. A concern of many project owners is overpaying the

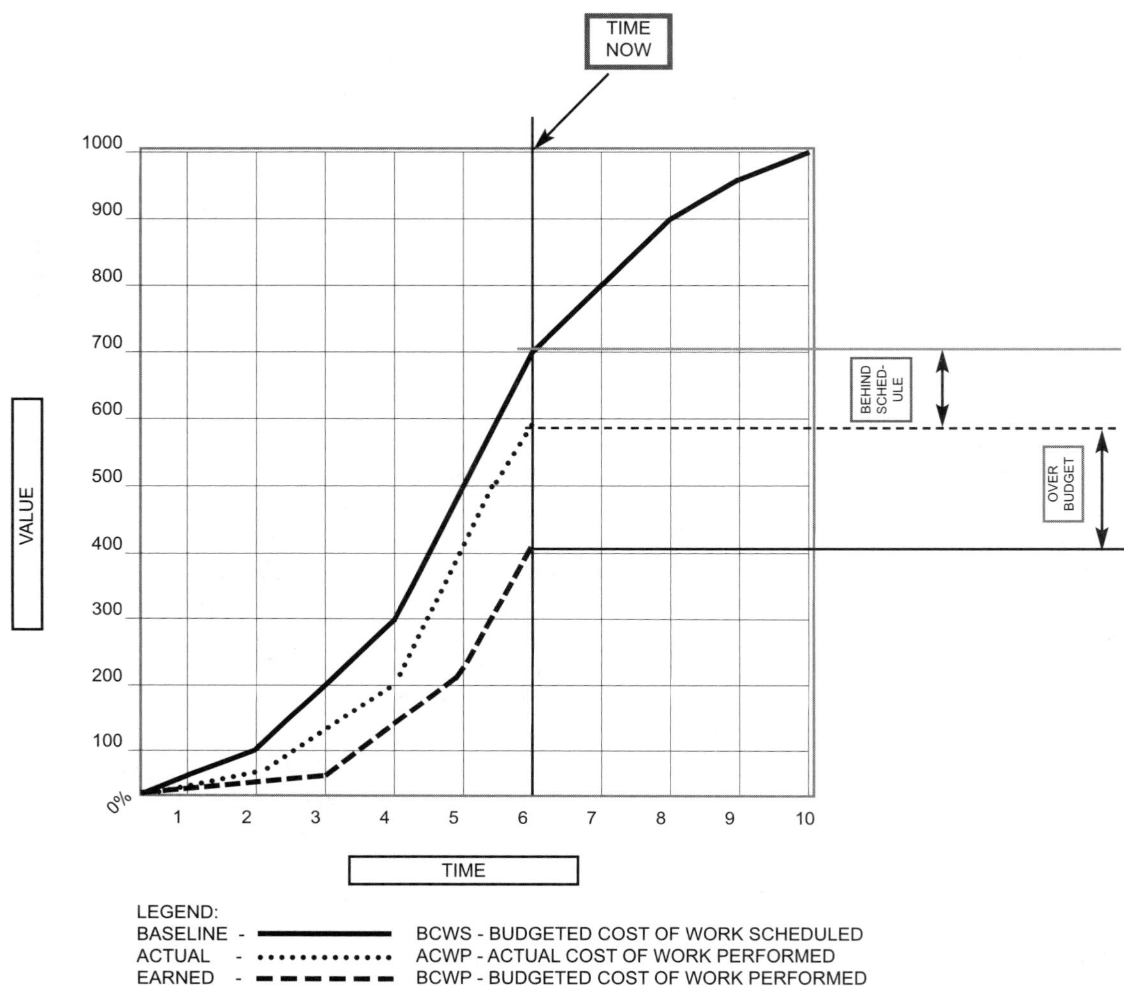

FIGURE 5.20 EARNED VALUE PERFORMANCE CURVE. This S curve of scheduled units of work is the baseline, or BCWS line. To earn value, a unit must be completed as scheduled and awarded BCWP points. Progress is measured by comparing units, as depicted.

contractor. The deployment of a form of earned value performance measurement technique to generate a "planned value" project baseline is seen by some software providers as the solution for better cost and schedule control. This approach mainly aims to eliminate construction contract front-end loading. (Front-end loading is the attempt by contractors to overprice the elements of the project that must be done first in order to inflate their early invoices.)

The idea of comparing earned value to planned value would generate early warning signals about project status. In this kind of a scenario, earned value performance measurement may be applicable to three types of construction contracts: (1) cost reimbursable, (2) firm fixed price with payments based on actual costs, and (3) lump sum.

The main advantage in combining contract type (1) with performance measurement is that the owner can be alerted as early as 15% into the construction cycle as to the project cost direction. This is achieved by comparing achievement to expenditures.

Under contract type (2) the aim is to deter payment of incurred costs without a corresponding achievement in performance, particularly on U.S. federal government contracts.

To make the earned value system applicable to these kinds of contracts requires these essential elements:

- All major tasks are listed on the schedule.
- Each task is scheduled.
- Each task has a weighted value, and the sum of these values is 100% of the project value.

The tasks are depicted on a bar chart, and the project is monitored monthly. The contractor is still paid the actual costs incurred, but now there is also a comparison of actual costs versus the planned or baseline cost as depicted by the bar chart to ascertain performance. By using the progress bar chart, the owner is now able to ascertain if there are indications of a cost overrun, before it happens.

Construction contract type (3), lump sum, is the most widely used form of agreement in the construction industry. As a general rule, payments are made monthly on the basis of physical progress achieved as set out in an agreed list of values. The basis for progress payments in commercial construction is most often American Institute of Architects (AIA) documentation. The big fear for owners in using this approach is front-end loading, as mentioned.

To improve upon the perceived discrepancies in this method, some suggest that the contractor prepare a cost-loaded or resource-loaded CPM, which is then converted into a list of time-phased budgets. The sum of the budgets equals the value of the contract. The schedule leads to the required project completion date. The result is a project baseline (cumulative S curve) to monitor performance on the basis of earned value.

5.11.4 Performance Measurement System

The S curve is an experienced quick tool to plan a project cost and schedule profile. Computerization of bar charts and CPM activities and the application of values to those activities led to the concept of the earned value S curve. The earned value approach requires that the planned curve or baseline be compared to an earned value and the actual cost curve. The result is the performance measurement system, a cost and schedule monitoring system used mostly by government for megaprojects.

Some performance measurement system technical language is provided here.

- The result of the resource (or cost) loaded CPM network, the performance baseline, is called the budgeted cost of work scheduled (BCWS).
- The contractor's work effort is measured against the baseline and assigned a value, which is called budgeted cost of work performed (BCWP).
- The contractor's work effort has an actual cost, which is called the actual cost of work performed (ACWP).
- Schedule status, known as schedule variance (SV), is the difference between BCWS and BCWP.
- Cost status, known as cost variance (CV), is the difference between ACWP and BCWP.

From experience, the performance measurement system is not used for lump sum commercial construction work. If it were used, and its cost may mitigate against this happening, the benefits to the owner would be an early warning of possible downstream cost overruns and the elimination of overpayment for completed work. The benefits to the contractor would include early indications of possible losses. This results from seeing early the direction that the cost is taking.

Use of the earned value within a performance measurement system in the private sector is not common. Experienced cost engineers report that its use on large-scale industrial construction projects is expensive and difficult. The difficulty of measuring project progress using the S curves as a performance measurement tool may be seen in Fig. 5.21.

The basis for earned value language comes from the U.S. Government Department of Defense (DoD) C/SCSC, which was introduced to government defense contract work. Although not as widely used in private-sector work, C/SCSC, also known as performance measurement system, was normally applied to megaprojects by the Atomic Energy Commission (AEC), DoD, Department of Energy (DoE), and the General Accounting Office (GAO).

Cost variance reports only on the deviation from the budget. This can be done for any level of the project cost: total project, an area, a package, or a task; a contract or a subcontract; an organization, a division, a department, or a discipline.

Cost variance, calculated as CV = BCWP − ACWP, may show an under or over condition. An overrun is a negative number. The cost variance may be expressed as a percentage, CV% = CV/BCWP × 100).

Schedule variance, showing deviation from a plan, is stated as SV = BCWP − BCWS. A negative result indicates a behind-schedule condition. Schedule variance may also be expressed as a percentage, SV% = SV/BCWS × 100.

The concept of earned value and performance measurement is attractive because it aims to reduce the very difficult task of cost and schedule measurement to the lowest common denominator. Its use is costly and difficult.

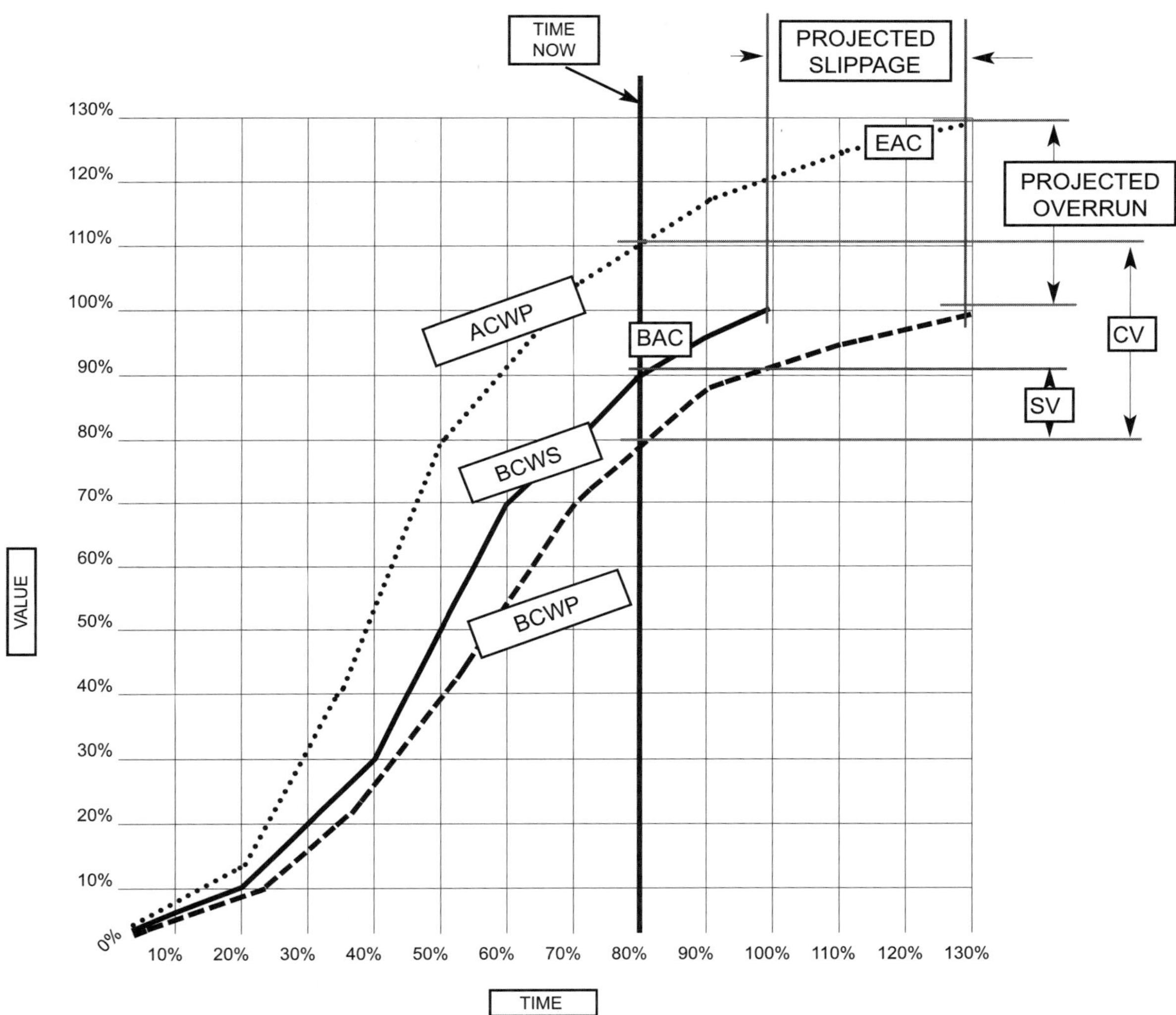

Legend: ACWP-actual cost of work performed; BAC-budget at completion; BCWP-budgeted cost of work performed; BCWS-budgeted cost of work scheduled; CV-cost variance (CV = BCWP – ACWP); EAC-estimate at completion; SV-schedule variance (SV = BCWP – BCWS); projected overrun = cost overerun; project slippage = schedule slippage

FIGURE 5.21 PERFORMANCE MEASUREMENT S CURVE. The use of this system requires that the units of work be costed and scheduled. Each unit of project time would take on value. Their cumulative sum would create the S curve. Project cost or schedule performance and progress would be measured and reported as depicted.

To transform cost-loaded scheduled activities into a baseline S curve is fraught with complexity and uncertainty on account of the dynamic and invariably changing nature of a construction project. If this is recognized, and project management agrees to the measure, a practical solution may be the application of standard or historical S curves to shape the baseline against which the project is monitored.

5.11.5 Trending and Trend Lines

The traditional project S curve is the result of experience showing that a project starts slowly, accelerates rapidly, and finishes slowly. This experience has created the classical 5% S curve depicted in Fig. 5.19. Other curves have been developed by cost engineers to illustrate desired or planned approaches to deliver projects.

If a project is planned in detail on a bar chart or CPM network, which is then converted to a costed or resource-loaded bar chart, and the bars are stacked and converted to a cumulative S curve, the result is the basis of a performance measurement baseline, as was discussed at length. The cost and difficulty of creating these baselines is only the beginning of the measurement process. Equally difficult is the measurement and comparison of actual performance to the baseline so that apples are compared to apples.

In *Project Management* Lock discussed this issue at length and illustrated the relationship of achievement to expenditure. In the process he provided an extensive introduction to the use of trend lines. Lock relates the three most important factors for a successful project as the budget, the actual (or incurred) cost, and the relationship of progress to budget and actual costs. He considers the making of a budget as not problematical (assuming repeat experienced departmental projects). Cost recording is also considered routine (in any well-run firm). It is achievement analysis that is difficult, simply because it had not been done as a normal routine, and as discussed by many cost engineers, it continues not to be the norm.

Lock used the example of a design engineering department being responsible for the delivery of drawings and specifications for a project. The design work is broken down into activities, which are estimated in person-weeks. The total person-weeks in the example is 450, as seen in Figure 5.22.

The S curve seen is a plot of actual person-weeks plotted every second week.

The departmental budget is depicted as a flat line at the 450 person-week marker.

The trend line is a plot of the prediction of the budget at completion, plotted each two-week period.

Achievement is measured by comparing the number of drawings completed against the number that should be completed at the point in time and converting the result to person-weeks achieved. On a straight-line distribution the number to be achieved would be a function of project time, that is, 20% of drawings completed at 20% of time, 50% at 50% of time, and so on.

The application of an equation to predict the budget at completion in person-weeks (PW) is as follows:

$$\frac{\text{Actual PW} \times \text{Budget PW}}{\text{Achievement PW}} = \text{estimated PW at completion.}$$

The S-curve concept can also be used as a trending tool to depict productivity and to measure earned value or achievement. From experience, construction project

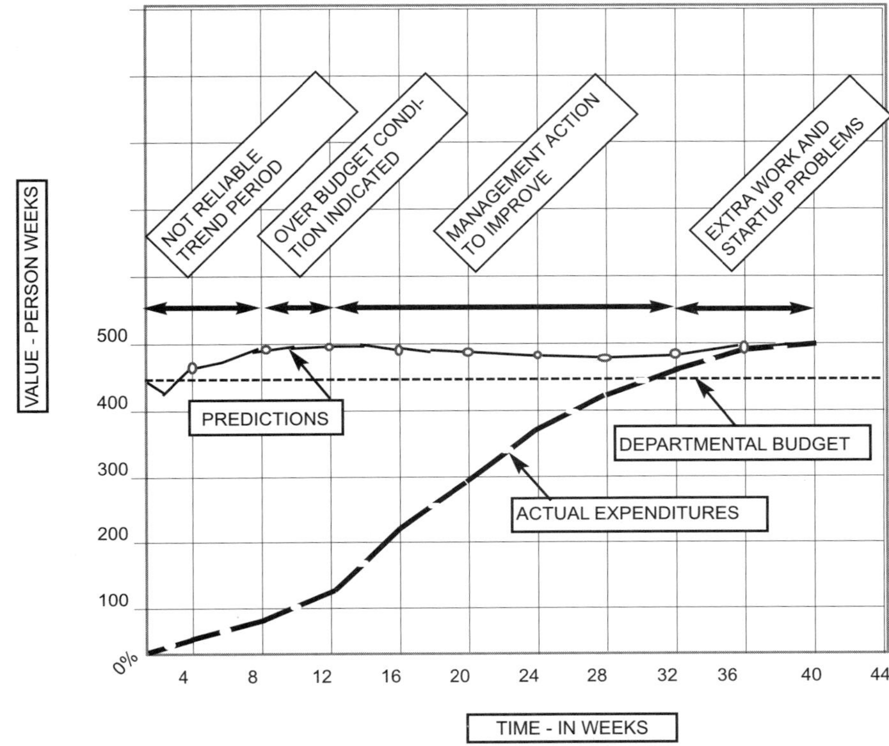

FIGURE 5.22 RELATING ACHIEVEMENT TO EXPENDITURE, TRENDING. An S plot of actual expenditures as a measure of project progress needs to be adjusted by trending information based on experience.

productivity varies with the project life cycle. For example, productivity does not remain constant throughout a project but varies according to well-established curves, or more appropriately as productivity profiles. Typically, productivity for any activity starts out poorly, reaches a maximum somewhere between 30% and 80% completion, and then tapers off to final completion, according to Clark and Lorenzoni in *Applied Cost Engineering.*

Two formulas are provided for calculating productivity:

$$\text{Productivity} = \text{QAB person-hours/actual person-hours} \qquad (1)$$

$$\text{Productivity} = \text{\% physical completion/\% QAB Person-hours used.} \qquad (2)$$

where QAB is quantity-adjusted budget.

A theoretical productivity profile as a trending curve (labeled formula) is shown in Fig. 5.23. A productivity profile is best based on experience. Experiential information is often substituted by conventional or standard formulaic data, which may have been adopted in various businesses or industries.

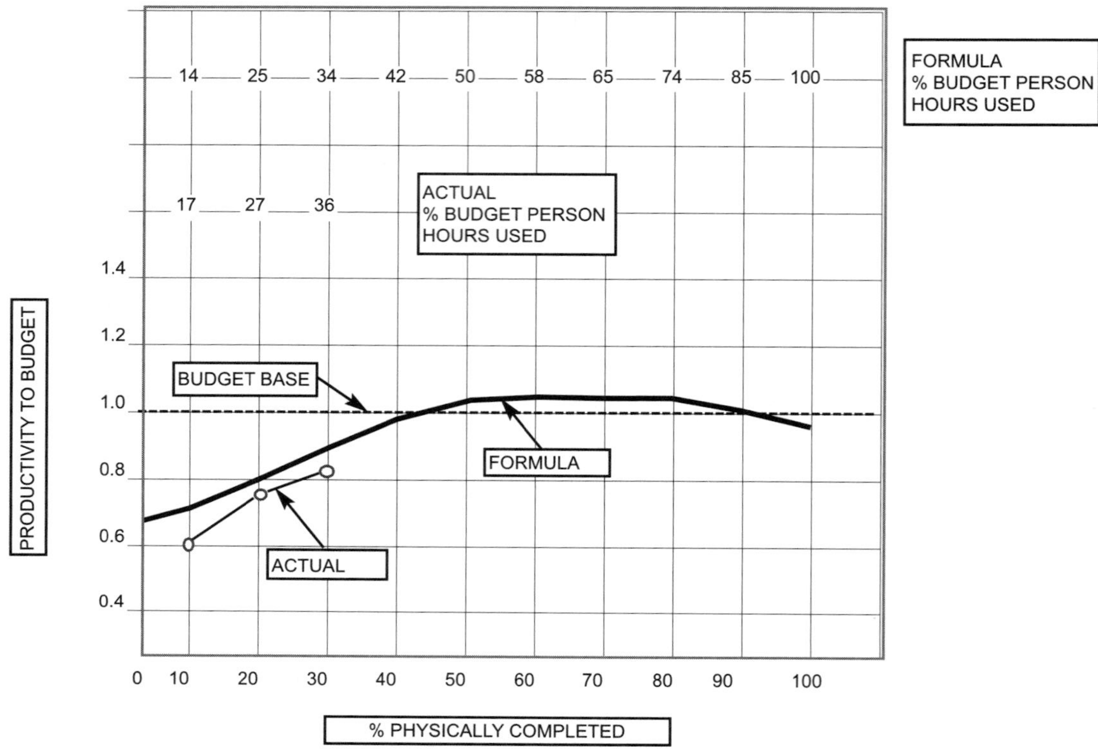

FIGURE 5.23 PRODUCTIVITY PLOT, % PHYSICALLY COMPLETED/% BUDGET PERSON-HOURS USED VS. ACTUAL PERSON-HOURS. This figure shows that project productivity varies. Thus any trend lines would be skewed accordingly and provide misleading information, unless adjusted for this condition.

In this example, at 10% of project time the formulaic productivity is shown as 0.7. Dividing the physical percent complete (10%) by the productivity (0.7) results in a percentage of 14% of budgeted person-hours. In the meantime, reports indicate that 17% of actual person-hours has been used. This indicates an actual productivity of

$$\frac{\%\ \text{physical completion (10)}}{\%\ \text{actual person-hours (17)}} = 0.59.$$

In reading trends, caution needs to be exercised because the trending results may be skewed in the earliest days of the project life cycle.

At 30% physical completion of the project depicted in Fig. 5.23 the data show that 36% of the budgeted person-hours has been used. Based on this condition, what is the forecast overrun at project completion? The actual productivity is

$$\frac{\%\text{ physical completion (30)}}{\%\text{ budgeted person-hours used (36)}} = \text{productivity.}$$

$$\frac{30}{36} = 0.83.$$

The formulaic (theoretical) productivity from Fig. 5.23 is 0.88 at 30% completion. The percent difference in productivity is then

$$\left(\frac{0.88 - 0.83}{0.88}\right) \times 100 = 5.7\%.$$

Therefore the forecast overrun, based on these projections, is expected to be 5.7%.

The percent budget person-hour information seen in Fig. 5.23 can also be converted into a cumulative S curve, as seen in Fig. 5.24.

The cumulative S curve becomes the calibration against which actual cumulative information is measured to gauge performance. Called a trend chart, it is used to compare person-hours expended against person-hours achieved as related to physical percentage completed.

Referring to Fig. 5.24, what will be the project overrun at the point where 43,000 person-hours have been charged to achieve 30% completion against a budget of 120,000 person-hours, as plotted by the calibration graph?

Actual person-hours expended for 30% completion, 43,000.

Formula-based hours available for 30% completion, 40,700.

Overrun person-hours:

$$43{,}000 - 40{,}700 = 2300.$$

Percent overrun:

$$2300/40{,}700 \times 100 = 5.7.$$

The answer is a 5.7% overrun, or 6840 person-hours, against a budget at completion of 120,000 person-hours.

Also to be noted from Fig. 5.24 is that 30% completion was achieved on April 1. As the S curve shows 30% completion on March 1, the project is behind schedule by one month as well as being overrun.

5.11.6 Computerized Performance Measurement

Most higher end commercial project management software packages have the capability to process performance measurement data, including the following formulas:

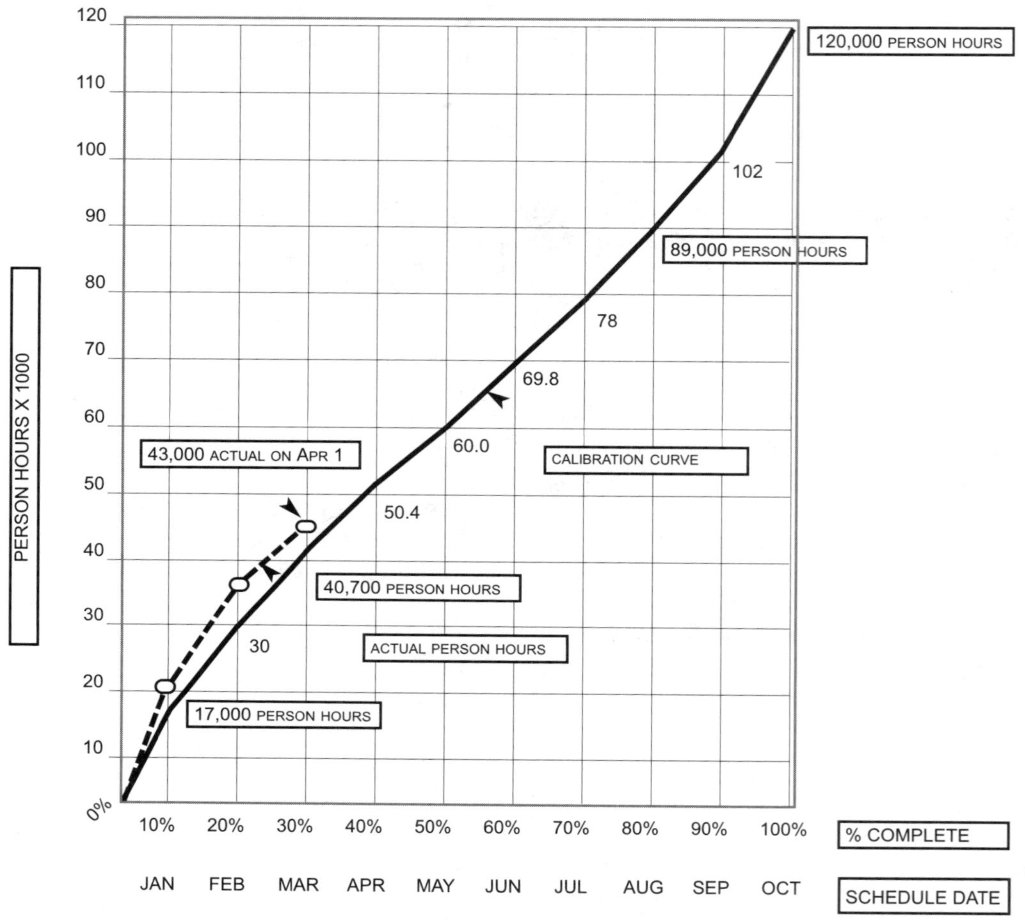

FIGURE 5.24 S TREND CURVE BASED ON % BUDGET PERSON-HOURS IN FIG. 5.23 AND A BUDGET OF 120,000 PERSON-HOURS. A formula S curve shows the deployment of 120,000 person-hours on a project. By April 1, 43,000 actual hours were reported used. What is the time and cost status of the project based on the system described in this section?

BAC Budget at completion (project budget, area budget, or contract amount)

BCWS Budgeted cost of work scheduled,

$$\text{BCWS} = \text{planned \% completed} \times \text{BAC}$$

BCWP Budgeted cost of work performed,

$$\text{BCWP} = \text{actual \% completed} \times \text{BAC}$$

ACWP Actual cost of work performed (time now is same as % completed for BCWS and BCWP)

ETC — Estimate to complete (from time now, estimate to complete remaining work)

EAC — Estimate at completion,

$$EAC = ACWP + ETC$$

FTC — Forecast to complete (in some cases same as FAC; in others same as ETC; in others same as EAC)

FAC — Forecast at completion,

$$FAC = ACWP + FTC$$

CV — Cost variance,

$$CV = BCWP - ACWP$$

SV — Schedule variance,

$$SV = BCWP - BCWS$$

Not all software vendors use the same terminology. Artemis Prestige, a predecessor of Artemis Views, calls for the creation of a baseline version of the project, including the original project budget estimates and schedules, which are then compared with the current schedule.

A report of actual quantities and an earned value percentage for actual time periods as activities are progressed are required for each resource. The earned value percentage is applied to the baseline budget estimate to derive an earned value quantity, which can then be estimated.

The terms used by this software package are compared to the performance measurement system descriptions in the preceding list (in parentheses):

- Actual work performed (ACWP)
- Estimate to complete (ETC)
- Estimate at completion (EAC)
- Budget at completion (BAC)
- Variance at completion (BAC - EAC)
- Budgeted work performed (earned value) (BCWP)
- Budgeted work scheduled (BCWS)
- Schedule variance (SV)
- Cost variance (CV)
- Schedule performance index (SV/BCWS)
- Cost performance index (CV/BCWP)

The program is designed to show the foregoing values as activity listing tables, cost curves, hard copy, or on screen. The system can produce summaries of resources,

VARIANCE ANALYSIS - SUMMARY

PAGE NUMBER:
TIME NOW:

ACTIVITY IDENTIFIER.	DESCRIPTION	EARNED VALUE	BUDGET SCHEDULED	ACTUAL TO DATE	ESTIMATE TO COMPLETE	ESTIMATE AT COMPLETION	BUDGET AT COMPLETION	VARIANCE AT COMPLETION
1001	INITIAL DESIGN	7000.00	7000.00	7000.00	.00	7000.00	7000.00	.00
1002	FINAL DESIGN	12000.00	12000.00	13200.00	.00	13200.00	12000.00	1200.00
1003	SET-UP	160.00	160.00	600.00	2800.00	3400.00	3000.00	400.00
1004	PRODUCTION	.00	.00	.00	4000.00	4000.00	4000.00	.00
1005	INTEGRATION	.00	.00	.00	1600.00	1600.00	1600.00	.00
1006	TESTING	.00	.00	.00	600.00	600.00	600.00	.00
1007	PKGE SET-UP	.00	.00	.00	1700.00	1700.00	1700.00	.00
1008	COMPLETE PACKAGING	.00	.00	.00	600.00	600.00	600.00	.00

FIGURE 5.25a BUDGET/ESTIMATE, VARIANCE ANALYSIS, SUMMARY LIST BY ACTIVITY IDENTIFIER. This shows the use of performance measurement terminology in conjunction with a computerized CPM schedule of activities.

resource categories, activities, or code categories at any level of the WBS. Examples of a number of performance measurement hard copy reports based on the Artemis Prestige user's manual are provided in Figs. 5.25 and 5.26.

The cost control features in another PC-based software package, Open Plan Professional, are capable of performance measurement processing and reporting. The requirements are baseline dates (original schedule dates), budgeted cost estimates for activities, physical percent complete of activities, and actual cost on the same date as the physical percent complete.

With this information, this software can define the three principal elements of cost control—BCWS, BCWP, and ACWP. Its standard reports can calculate these three costs as cumulatives to date or for a specified time period, for the project, for individual activities, or for a group of activities. The standard reports assume a single budgeted cost for each activity, which will be expended evenly between the start and the finish of the activity.

BUDGET/ESTIMATE - VARIANCE ANALYSIS - SUMMARY

PAGE NUMBER:
TIME NOW:

	DESCRIPTION	EARNED VALUE	BUDGET SCHEDULED	ACTUAL TO DATE	ESTIMATE TO COMPLETE	ESTIMATE AT COMPLETION	BUDGET AT COMPLETION	VARIANCE AT COMPLETION
WBS=PDWBS DESIGN	LEVEL=02 CODE=100	19000.00	19000.00	20200.00	2200.00	22400.00	21200.00	1200.00
WBS=PDWBS MANUFAC-TURING	LEVEL=02 CODE=200	160.00	160.00	600.00	6800.00	7400.00	7000.00	400.00
WBS=PDWBS MARKETING	LEVEL=02 CODE=300	.00	.00	.00	2300.00	2300.00	2300.00	.00
	GRAND TOTALS	19160.00	19160.00	20800.00	11300.00	32100.00	30500.00	1600.00

FIGURE 5.25b BUDGET/ESTIMATE, VARIANCE ANALYSIS, SUMMARY LIST BY WBS CODE, LEVEL 2. This shows the use of performance measurement terminology in conjunction with a computerized CPM schedule of activities. The line items are summaries of WBS code items.

VARIANCES & INDICES - SUMMARY

PAGE NUMBER:
TIME NOW:

ACTIVITY IDENTIFIER.	DESCRIPTION	ACTUAL TO DATE	EARNED VALUE	BUDGET SCHEDULED	SCHEDULE VARIANCE	COST VARIANCE	SCHEDULE PERF. INDEX	COST PERF. INDEX
1001	INITIAL DESIGN	7000.00	7000.00	7000.00	.00	.00	1.00	1.00
1002	FINAL DESIGN	13200.00	12000.00	12000.00	.00	-1200.00	1.00	.91
1003	SET-UP	600.00	160.00	600.00	-440.00	-440.00	.27	.27
1004	PRODUCTION	.00	.00	.00	.00	.00		
1005	INTEGRATION	.00	.00	.00	.00	.00		
1006	TESTING	.00	.00	.00	.00	.00		
1007	PKGE SET-UP	.00	.00	.00	.00	.00		
1008	COMPLETE PACKAGING	.00	.00	.00	.00	.00		
	GRAND TOTALS	20800.00	19160.00	19600.00	-440.00	-1640.00	.98	.92

Figure 5.26*a* Earned Value, Variances and Indices, Summary List by Activity Identifier. This is the companion report to Fig. 5.25*a*, showing the balance of the earned value information and performance tied to activity identifiers.

The program calculates cost and schedule variances, BAC, and EAC using the formulas introduced in this section.

A third program, CA-SuperProject for Microsoft Windows, contains a wide array of activity cost types, from hourly costs to total costs. These costs can appear in different types of cost fields, including scheduled, baseline, actual, and remaining. For earned value and performance measurement calculations and reporting this software uses the following terminology, which is compared to the more standard terms first introduced, in parentheses:

- Assignment actual total cost (ACWP)
- Assignment baseline total cost (BAC)

EARNED VALUE - VARIANCES & INDICES - SUMMARY

PAGE NUMBER:
TIME NOW:

	DESCRIPTION	ACTUAL TO DATE	EARNED VALUE	BUDGET SCHEDULED	SCHEDULE VARIANCE	COST VARIANCE	SCHEDULE PERF. INDEX	COST PERF. INDEX
WBS=PDWBS DESIGN	LEVEL=02 CODE=100	20200.00	19000.00	19000.00	.00	-1200.00	1.00	.94
WBS=PDWBS MANUFAC-TURING	LEVEL=02 CODE=200	600.00	160.00	600.00	-440.00	-440.00	.27	.27
WBS=PDWBS MARKETING	LEVEL=02 CODE=300	.00	.00	.00	.00	.00		
	GRAND TOTALS	20800.00	19160.00	19600.00	-440.00	-1640.00	.98	.92

Figure 5.26*b* Earned Value, Variances and Indices, Summary List by WBS Code, Level 2. This is the companion report to Fig. 5.25*b*, showing the balance of the earned value information and performance tied to the WBS code items.

- Assignment earned value (BCWP)
- Assignment budgeted cost of work scheduled (BCWS)

  BCWS calculations vary according to the accrual method used as follows:

  1. For start/end types BCWS is the baseline total cost at the start or the end of the assignment.
  2. For prorate types

$$\text{BCWS} = \left(\frac{\text{baseline duration to time now}}{\text{total baseline duration}}\right) \times \text{baseline total cost}$$

- Assignment scheduled variance (SV)
- Assignment cost variance (CV)
- Assignment variance at completion (VAC),

$$\text{Total baseline cost} - \text{total scheduled cost}$$

- Assignment cost variance percent (CV%),

$$\frac{\text{Cost variance} \times 100}{\text{BCWP}}$$

- Assignment schedule variance percent (SV%),

$$\frac{\text{Schedule variance} \times 100}{\text{BCWS}}$$

- Assignment cost performance index percent (CPI),

$$\frac{\text{BCWP} \times 100}{\text{ACWP}}$$

- Assignment calculated EAC,

$$\frac{\text{BAC} \times 100}{\text{CPI}}$$

- Assignment scheduled performance index (SPI),

$$\frac{\text{BCWP} \times 100}{\text{BCWS}}$$

- Assignment actual performance index (API),

$$\frac{\text{ACWP} \times 100}{\text{BCWS}}$$

5.12 Summary

Project cost starts life as a ballpark number. As its definition is scoped, it takes on a budget estimate based on parameters from previous similar projects. A definitive budget requiring design and engineering, which ensures that the project will be delivered for the requested amount, is essential for the appropriation of funds.

Cost estimating and budgeting is driven by definitions of functions and elements, the breakdown of work into tasks and packages, and the assignment of packages to individuals and organizations. The process leads to more accurate cost pictures at each transition point. Control requires that the project scope be maintained throughout each stage.

Interested project participants see cost differently. The project cost and expenditure control system must be able to relate to all of them. This is achieved through breakdowns and codes that capture cost at its source and deliver the information to the corporate financial manager as well as to the project manager responsible.

Cost control is difficult at the best of times. Quick tools such as formulaic S curves and trend lines aim to provide graphic methods to predict cost direction and initiate management action. The performance measurement system aims to reduce cost and schedule to their lowest common denominator to measure progress and control both.

Computerization is carrying out more and more of the roles of estimating, budgeting, and cost control. For this to happen, the systems of project management comprising definition, breakdown, and organization need to be tied to cost, as discussed in the preceding section, and to schedule, to be discussed in the next chapter.

REFERENCES

Black, J. H., "Application of Parametric Estimating to Cost Engineering," *Trans. Am. Assoc. of Cost Engineers* (*Proc. 8th Int. Cost Engineering Congr.,* Montreal, PQ, 1984).

Blough, R. M., "More Construction for the Money," Summary Report of the Construction Industry Cost Effectiveness Project (The Business Roundtable, New York, 1983).

CA-SuperProject Reference Guide for Microsoft Windows, 3.0, 1st ed. (Computer Associates International, Islandia, NY, 1992).

Charette, W., and W. Halverson, "Tools of Project Management," in *The Implementation of Project Management, The Professional's Handbook,* L. C. Suckenbruck, Ed. (Addison-Wesley, Reading, 1981), chap. 8, p. 118.

Clark, F. D., and A. B. Lorenzoni, *Applied Cost Engineering* (Marcel Dekker, New York, 1978).

Copes Cost Planning and Evaluation System, McAuto Version 3.0 (McDonnell Douglas Automation Co., St. Louis, MO, 1976).

"Cost Management," in *Primavera Project Planner 5.0, Project Management Handbook,* (Primavera Systems, Bala Cynwyd, PA, 1991), pp. 601, 606.

Cox, B. J., and F. W. Horsley, "Square Foot Estimating" (R. S. Means Co., Kingston, MA, 1983).

Fleming, W. Q., and J. M. Koppelman, "Linking Contractor Payments to Contractor Performance," *Cost Engineering* (Dec. 1995).

Hackney, J. W., *Control and Management of Capital Projects* (Wiley, New York, 1965).

Hackney, J. W., "Design of a Viable System for Process Plant Estimating," *Trans. Am. Assoc. Cost Engineers* (Washington, DC, 1980).

"Hanscomb's Yardsticks for Costing, Cost Data for the Canadian Construction Industry" (Southam Business Information and Communications Group, Toronto, ON, annual).

Humphries, K. K., Ed., *Project and Cost Engineers' Handbook,* 2nd ed., revised and expanded, American Association of Cost Engineers (Marcel Dekker, New York, 1984).

Humphries, K. K., and S. Katell, *Basic Cost Engineering* (Marcel Dekker, New York, 1981), p. 1.

Hurlburt, B. D., "Project Conceptual Estimating: A Systematic Approach," *Trans. Am. Assoc. of Cost Engineers* (Washington, DC, 1980), p. B-1.

Kerzner, H., *Project Management, a Systems Approach to Planning, Scheduling, and Controlling,* 3rd ed., (Van Nostrand Reinhold, New York, 1989), p. 805.

Lock, D., *Project Management,* 2nd ed. (Gower Press, Farnborough, UK, 1981).

Mahler, F., and M. Mazina, "Earned Value Reporting Earns Its Keep," *Cost Engineering,* vol. 24, no. 1 (1982).

Mahler, F., and M. Mazina, "Implementing Earned Value Reporting," *Trans. Am. Assoc. of Cost Engineers* (Washington, DC, 1982).

"Masterformat, Master List of Section Titles and Numbers," Construction Specifications Inst., Alexandria, VA; Construction Specifications Canada, Toronto, ON, 1988.

"Means Square Foot Costs, Residential, Commercial, Industrial, Institutional" (R. S. Means Co., Kingston, MA, 1984).

Microsoft Project, Version 3.0, Apple Macintosh or Windows Series, User's Reference (Microsoft Corp., Redmond, WA, 1992).

Open Plan 4.0, Reference Manual Serious Project Management Software, WST Corp., Houston, TX, 1989).

Prestige PC User Manual (Artemis Management Systems, Boulder, CO, 1991), p. 30.1 and App. A.

Rigney, R. A., and R. H. Campbell, "PMS: What Are You Getting for Your Money," *Proc. Project Management Inst.* (Newtown Square, PA, 1978).

Ritz, G. J., *Total Construction Project Management* (McGraw-Hill, New York, 1994).

Schoemann, F. H., and M. J. Bachynsky, "Shortcut Capital Cost Estimating for Low-Volume Batch-Operated Plants," *Trans. Am. Assoc. of Cost Engineers* (Washington, DC, 1980).

Stuckhart, G., "Cost Management Report: The Business Roundtable Project," *Trans. Am. Assoc. of Cost Engineers* (*Proc. 8th Int. Cost Engineering Cong.,* Montreal, PQ, 1984), p. C.1.1.

Texim Project 2.0, Windows Version (Serious Project Management Software, WST Corp., Houston, TX, 1993).

The Richardson Rapid System, General Construction Estimating Standards" (Richardson Engineering Services, San Marcos, CA, 1984).

QUESTIONS AND EXERCISES

5.1. Prepare an order-of-magnitude estimate based on the project definition structure (PDS) of the house depicted in Question 2.3.

5.2 Prepare an appropriation-grade estimate based on the answer to Question 5.1. Price the following phases:

Conceptual

Preliminary design

Final design and drawings

Construction

Break down the construction cost as follows:

Substructure	3.0%
Structure	12.7
Exterior cladding	29.9
Interior doors and partitions	3.5
Vertical movement (stairs)	0.2
Interior finishes	6.0
Fittings and equipment	3.4
Electrical	9.0
Mechanical	21.1
Construction soft costs	11.2

5.3. Prepare a project functional organization based on the concepts depicted in the exercises in Chapter 4 and packaged and costed in Question 5.2.

5.4. Prepare a cost control report.

5.5. Prepare an expenditure control report.

6 PROJECT PLANNING AND SCHEDULE CONTROL SYSTEM

Modern project management is based on the concept of the office of project manager using the computerized critical path method (CPM) and the program evaluation and review technique (PERT). CPM was invented for planning and scheduling construction activities. PERT had its start on defense megaprojects. Of the two systems, CPM was more forgiving in that activities were done as they had always been, except that schedules were now drawn as arrows on a diagram, scheduled by computer, and presented as bar charts. PERT demanded management changes through the use of organizational and work breakdown structuring as well as coding, computer processing of scheduling networks, and bar charts.

Computerized networks create communications problems requiring the use of bar charts as visual tools to present schedule results. In the postmodern PC era, computers are used to create bar charts without the benefit of networks. In essence, this means scheduling work without first planning it. A computerized bar chart is incapable of showing logical relationships to the same degree as a network. But marketing of postmodern graphic user interface (GUI) project management systems is based on computerized bar charts.

In the project management systems environment presented in this textbook, project activities are to be planned and scheduled by CPM/PERT. The creation of CPM/PERT activities is an extension of the process of defining scope and quality, staging and phasing activities, code allocating, cost estimating, budgeting, and assigning functional responsibility.

Networks at one time were drawn as arrow diagrams. Arrow diagrams are still employed in construction, but the precedence diagram method is used more widely.

As schedule control is one of the five key systems of project management, rules and terminology applicable to the use of CPM/PERT, along with specific project management system rules, labeled "SPM rule," are presented.

6.1 Introduction to CPM and PERT

It is almost impossible to meet anyone in project work who does not believe in planning and scheduling. This makes it difficult to understand why so many projects do not finish on time. One of the reasons may be that although people believe in planning and scheduling, they usually mean somebody else's work. This is evident from literature on the subject.

In *Critical Path Methods in Construction Practice,* for example, Antill and Woodhead in providing a model to introduce the use of CPM/PERT in construction, depict a project starting with two activities: "fence site" and "erect site workshop." In a project management systems environment, the question is, why is the site to be fenced and the site workshop to be erected? How long did it take to decide to fence the site? Who was involved, and were their activities planned and scheduled by CPM/PERT? The conclusion in this case may be that the planning and engineering work preceding these two activities was not planned by CPM/PERT. But the construction activities, being somebody else's, are to be so treated. This is not an incidental observation.

This generalization is further evident in the many construction project specifications prepared by owners, architects, and engineers aimed at controlling the work of contractors and subcontractors during the project construction phase. What happens is that many capital projects go through lengthy and complex feasibility, planning, design, and drawing phases without the use of formal planning and schedule control, and then impose tough construction schedule deadlines using language similar to that reported by Trauner in *Construction Delays, Documenting Causes, Winning Claims, Recovering Costs,* which says in part: "If the contractor is delayed by any act or neglect of the owner or by changes in the work, no claim for any damages or any claim other than for extensions of time as provided shall be made or asserted against the owner."

Sometimes penalties may be levied on contractors who finish behind schedule. In fair project contracts, time penalty clauses are offset with bonus clauses for early completions. Often when working for large corporate owners, and certainly for many government departments, contractors are obliged to employ formal, computerized planning and scheduling methods, even though they (the contractors) do not normally use these methods.

Project participants such as consultants and construction contractors are paid monthly as progress is made. The project owner uses its own money or borrows it. Whether borrowed or not, money has a time cost. Until the project is completed and started up, it has no value. It is just a drain for money. The sooner the project is completed, the sooner the money sinkhole is plugged.

Most project construction contracts state that time is of the essence. The old saying has it that "time is money." This statement was obviously invented for the construction industry.

There are other reasons why projects must be scheduled. In boom times, materials and equipment may be in short supply. This condition makes it essential to plan ahead. Scheduling is also necessary to ensure that resources such as skilled workers and management personnel are made available as needed, "or just on time" to progress the project. The most important project resource is money, and cash-flow control is not possible without scheduling.

On another level, planning and scheduling are important to measure and monitor productivity. Construction labor productivity is one of the principal reasons behind the invention of CPM for planning and scheduling.

CPM was developed for the express purpose of utilizing a computer to schedule construction. New chemical process plants as well as turnaround projects, consisting of the installation of new equipment and piping systems in existing plants, were the first targets of CPM. The objective of computerized CPM was to reduce construction time and improve labor productivity. To achieve that, the network included construction activities and some material deliveries and design.

The process at the same time had an impact on design, starting after the issuance of preliminary drawings, and on material procurement activities. To improve construction time and productivity, it was obvious that there had to be improvements in the project front-end activities.

Some of the benefits of CPM expected by project owners and the construction industry are as follows:

- CPM pinpoints the activities whose completion times are responsible for establishing the overall project duration. With these critical operations clearly identified, major attention may be directed toward keeping them on schedule in order that the planned completion date may be met.
- CPM gives a quantitative evaluation of the amount of float that each activity has. Within the limits of float time the activities with float may be started and finished later than the earliest dates, or they may be shifted in time to smooth labor or equipment requirements.
- CPM shows the most economical scheduling for all activities for each possible project completion date. This allows consideration of both time and cost in choosing methods, equipment, materials, crews, and work hours.
- CPM provides the necessary data for choosing the best project completion date.
- CPM offers a means for assessing the effect of adding activities, making changes, and adding extra work.

As CPM was invented for construction, early network examples are based on typical construction activities, as seen in Figs. 6.1 and 6.2. It is also seen from the two figures that there are a number of variations in drawing networks. Figure 6.1*a* shows an activity-on-arrow network, whereas Fig. 6.1*b* depicts an event-labeled arrow diagram.

Early users of CPM eventually concluded that precedence or activity-on-node diagramming is a simpler method of drawing and calculating CPM networks. Figure 6.2 depicts two precedence diagrams. Figure 6.2*a* is an activity-labeled network, Fig. 6.2*b* an event-labeled network.

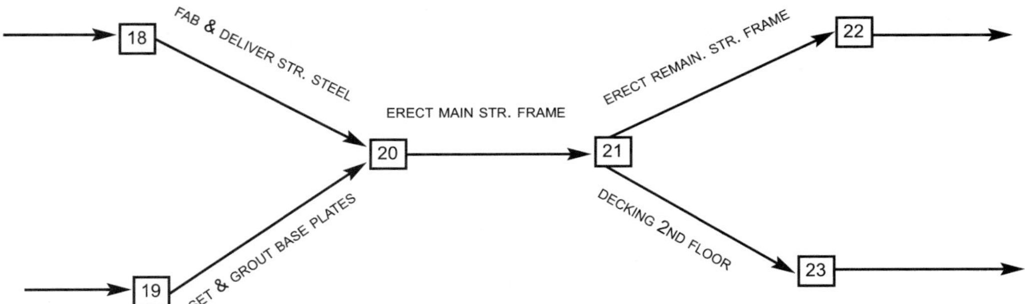

FIGURE 6.1*a* CPM ARROW DIAGRAMMING METHOD, ACTIVITY-ON-ARROW NETWORK. This shows an excellent way to represent activities as labeled arrows. The method, used mostly in construction, shows flow of work and the relationship of activities.

While CPM was aimed at improving schedule performance and labor productivity in the industrial project construction phase, PERT had its genesis in the U.S. Navy Polaris Missile program. Although CPM set a precedent for PERT, the two systems were seen to be related from the start.

The progress of PERT from a management theory to a computerized management system was based on applications and usage in the U.S. defense industry.

In *Management Program Planning and Control with PERT, MOST, and LOB* Iannone provides a source of definitions and insights into its application by military and industrial contractors. PERT was seen as having the following management, planning, and scheduling attributes:

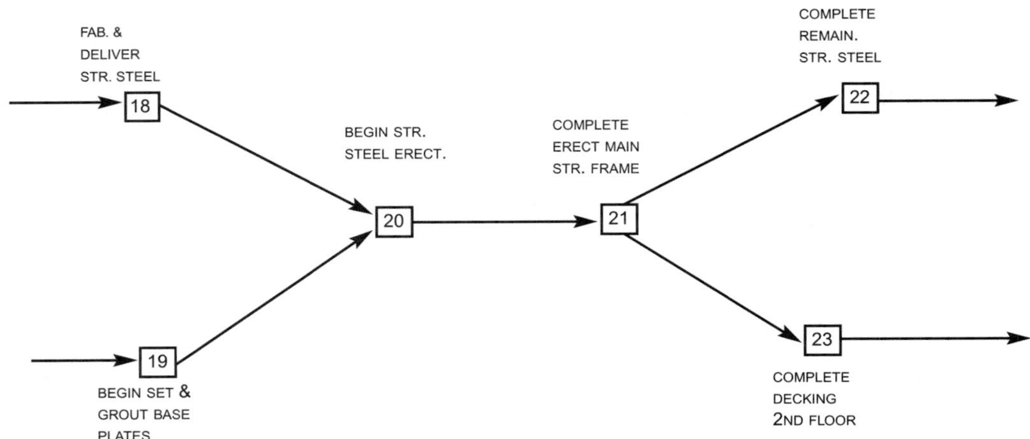

FIGURE 6.1*b* CPM ARROW DIAGRAMMING METHOD, EVENT-LABELED NETWORK. This shows another way to represent activities as labeled events. The arrows show the flow of work and the relationship of the events. This approach is the forerunner to the precedence diagram method.

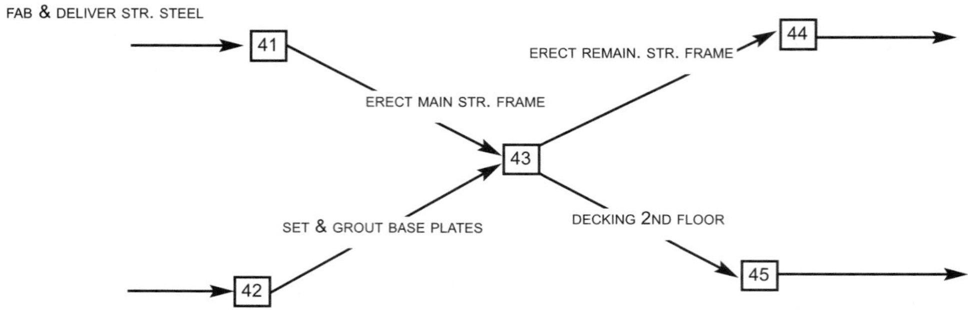

FIGURE 6.2*a* CPM PRECEDENCE DIAGRAMMING METHOD, ACTIVITY-LABELED NETWORK. This diagram shows that arrow diagrams and precedence diagrams were closely related from the start. Figure 6.1*a* is similar to this figure.

- PERT is a management tool for defining and integrating events that must be accomplished on a timely basis.
- PERT is a management control tool that reflects the complex interrelationships of a large number of activities which make up an integrated network of events.
- PERT assists the manager in estimating, budgeting, and controlling the schedule, cost, and technical performance of a project.
- The PERT network becomes a means of showing the Christmas tree type of planning to visualize an engineering end item assembly drawing broken down as a work breakdown structure (WBS).

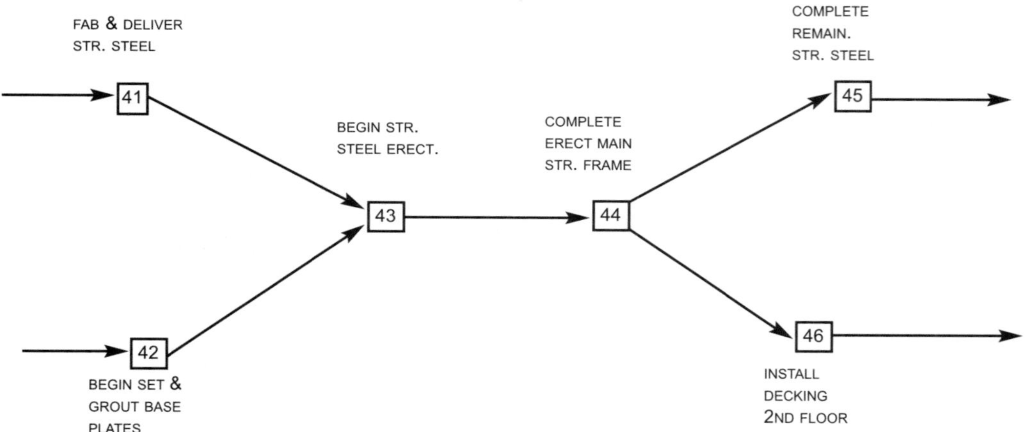

FIGURE 6.2*b* CPM PRECEDENCE DIAGRAMMING METHOD, EVENT-LABELED NETWORK. The events are numbered and labeled. Their predecessors are shown by arrows. Although called a precedence diagram, it is seen to be similar to the event-labeled arrow diagram in Fig. 6.1*b*.

- PERT activities are the work efforts of a project representing the actions of the network such as designing and building.
- PERT events are specific, definable accomplishments in a project plan recognizable at a particular instant in time. An event does not consume time or resources and is shown on a network as a square, circle, or other geometric design. An event is the start or completion of a task. (This rule is true for an arrow diagram or activity-on-arrow networks, but is not applicable for activity-on-node or precedence diagram networks, as will be discussed. However, an event can exist on any kind of network to signify an achievement, a point in time, or the confluence of a number of activities.)
- PERT constraints are used to indicate the relationship of an event to a succeeding activity or activities. An event cannot occur until its preceding activities have been completed.
- PERT time estimating is determining the time required to perform each activity in the network based on customary levels of human resources working normal shifts.
- The PERT critical path in a network is the particular sequence of activities from the start event that has the greatest negative or least positive slack or float, that is, consumes the longest time in reaching the end event.
- PERT time duration: PERT was originally conceived as using three time estimates: *m*—most likely, *a*—optimistic, and *b*—pessimistic. The expected time for an activity is calculated from the formula

$$\text{Time} = \frac{(a + 4m + b)}{6}.$$

  Most applications today are based on a single time duration.

Whereas early CPM networks were based on construction activities, early PERT diagrams were related to manufacturing and production jobs. One of the earliest measures of the credibility of a PERT network was to compare it to the conventional bar chart, as seen in Fig. 6.3. This depiction illustrates that the PERT system is event oriented, whereas the earliest CPM system was activity oriented. Figure 6.3 shows the development of interrelationships between PERT events, which is not possible with a conventional bar chart without the use of special symbols. It needs to be noted that whereas bar charts are drawn to coincide with calendar dates, network diagrams are rarely suitable for time scaling.

Having determined that a PERT network is event oriented, what happened in practice is that the events became the start and finish nodes of an activity, and it is the activity that was labeled a task, and the nodes became identifiers.

In other words, the PERT network took on a similar appearance as the CPM network, as may be seen in Fig. 6.4. Figure 6.4*a* shows a Christmas tree type structure

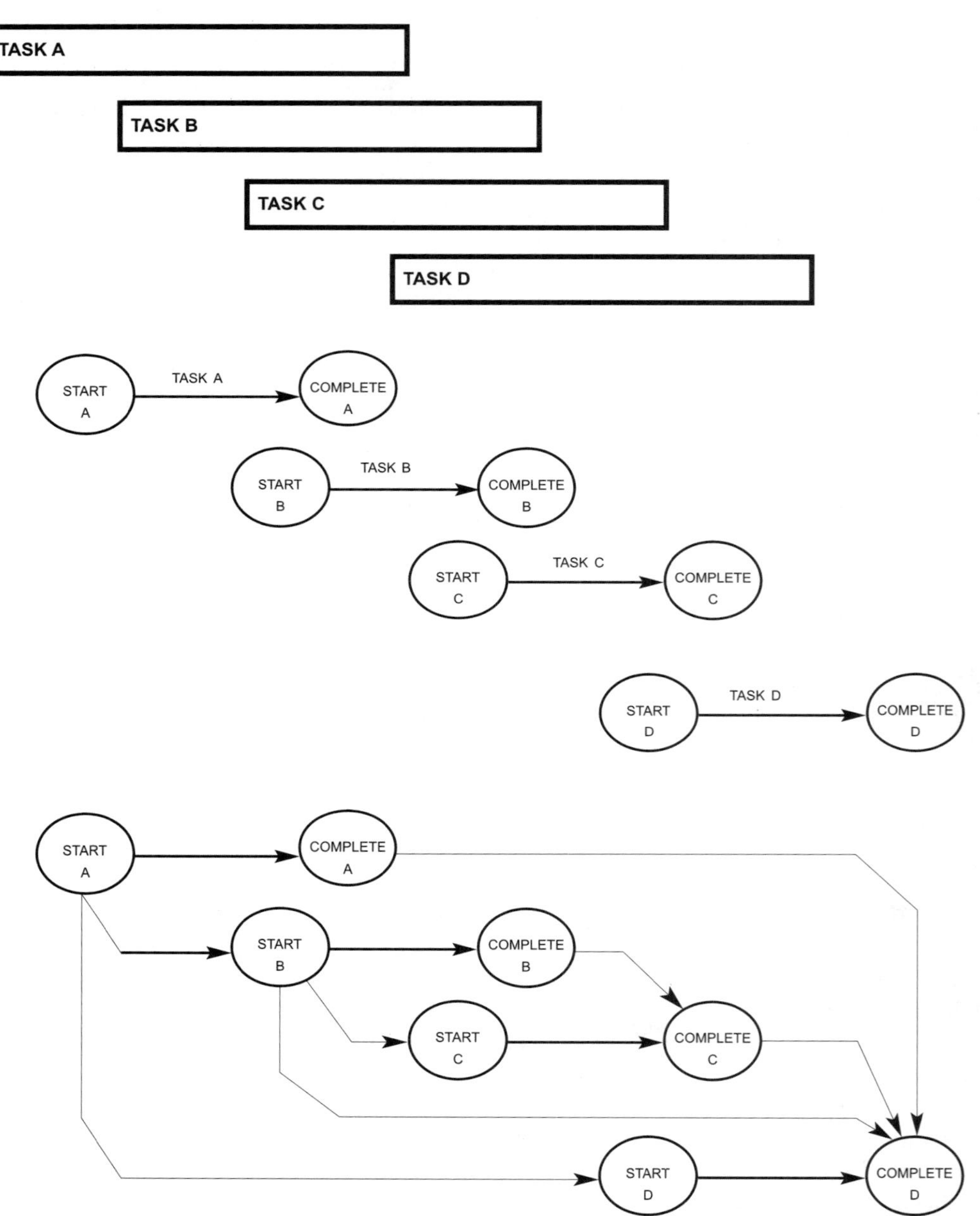

FIGURE 6.3 PERT VERSUS, BAR CHART, EVENT-LABELED NETWORK. The bar chart shows positioning of four tasks as a schedule. The arrow diagram first labels each task with a start and a complete event and then creates logical relationships between the eight events.

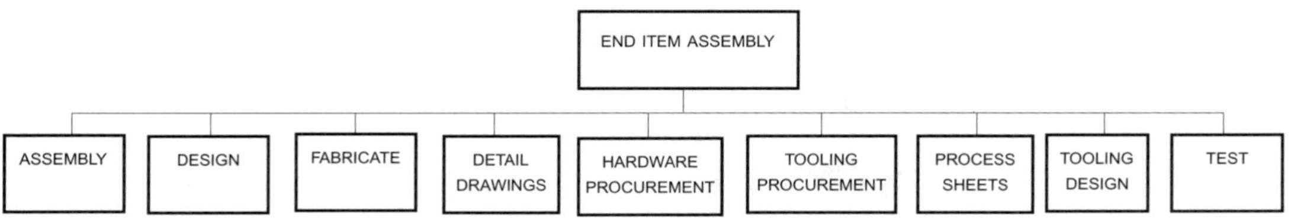

FIGURE 6.4*a* END ITEM ASSEMBLY, CHRISTMAS TREE TYPE STRUCTURE. This is a classic breakdown of an end-time assembly for the purpose of creating the PERT network shown in *b*.

for the end item assembly to be delivered. This is an important depiction of a main feature of the PERT system as it is the precursor to the concept of WBS.

Figure 6.4*b* is the PERT network for the end item assembly. Having established a treelike structure of subassemblies or components and drawn a PERT network, there remain the tasks of event identifiers, time estimates based on one duration or three durations for each activity, the resulting calculations of the critical path, slack, or float for all activities, and the requisite management actions.

The term PERT now means the charting and scheduling of activities and the control of progress by computer processing. The original term was PERT/Time. Under PERT/Time a treelike structure would be prepared and drawn as a network. This structure was not used for cost control.

PERT/Cost in its original manifestation aimed to create a network for planning and scheduling, and a WBS for controlling cost.

For schedule control, an activity must relate to a work package derived from the WBS. A work package in PERT/Cost exists approximately at level 4 or level 5 of the WBS, with level 1 being the end item assembly (the top of the structure). Estimating and cost recording in PERT/Cost is limited to work packages. Scheduling activities are not assigned costs. The intent is to ensure that cost-significant packages as well as schedule-significant activities both receive management attention and do not lead to too much detail.

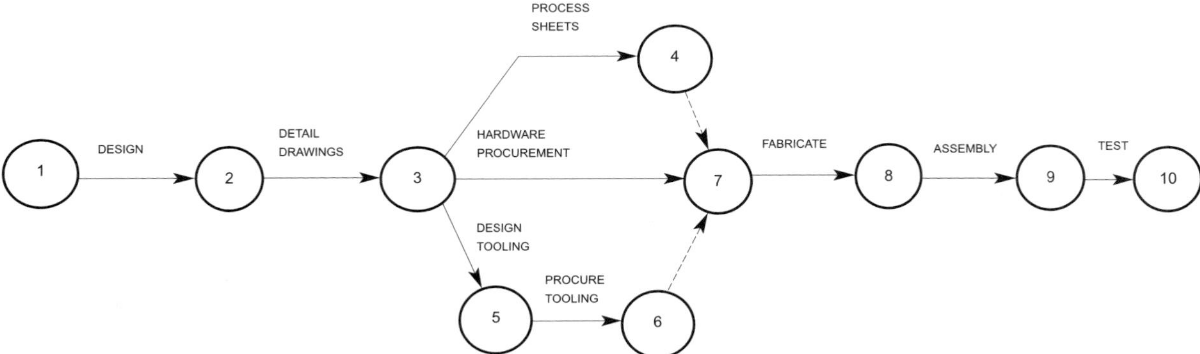

FIGURE 6.4*b* END ITEM ASSEMBLY, PERT ACTIVITY-LABELED NETWORK. This is the PERT network of the breakdown of the end-item assembly shown in *a*.

Treelike structures of end items or WBSs may have many levels, as discussed in Chapter 3 and depicted in Figs. 3.1 and 3.2. Large WBSs would lead to the creation of large networks of activities.

Some projects may be simpler with fewer levels. One such example is drawn in Fig. 6.5. In this case the treelike structure is simplified to show the relationship between the WBS and the scheduling network.

To summarize modern scheduling methods, a project manager may prepare a CPM network, a PERT/Time network, or a PERT/Cost network. CPM as a rule did

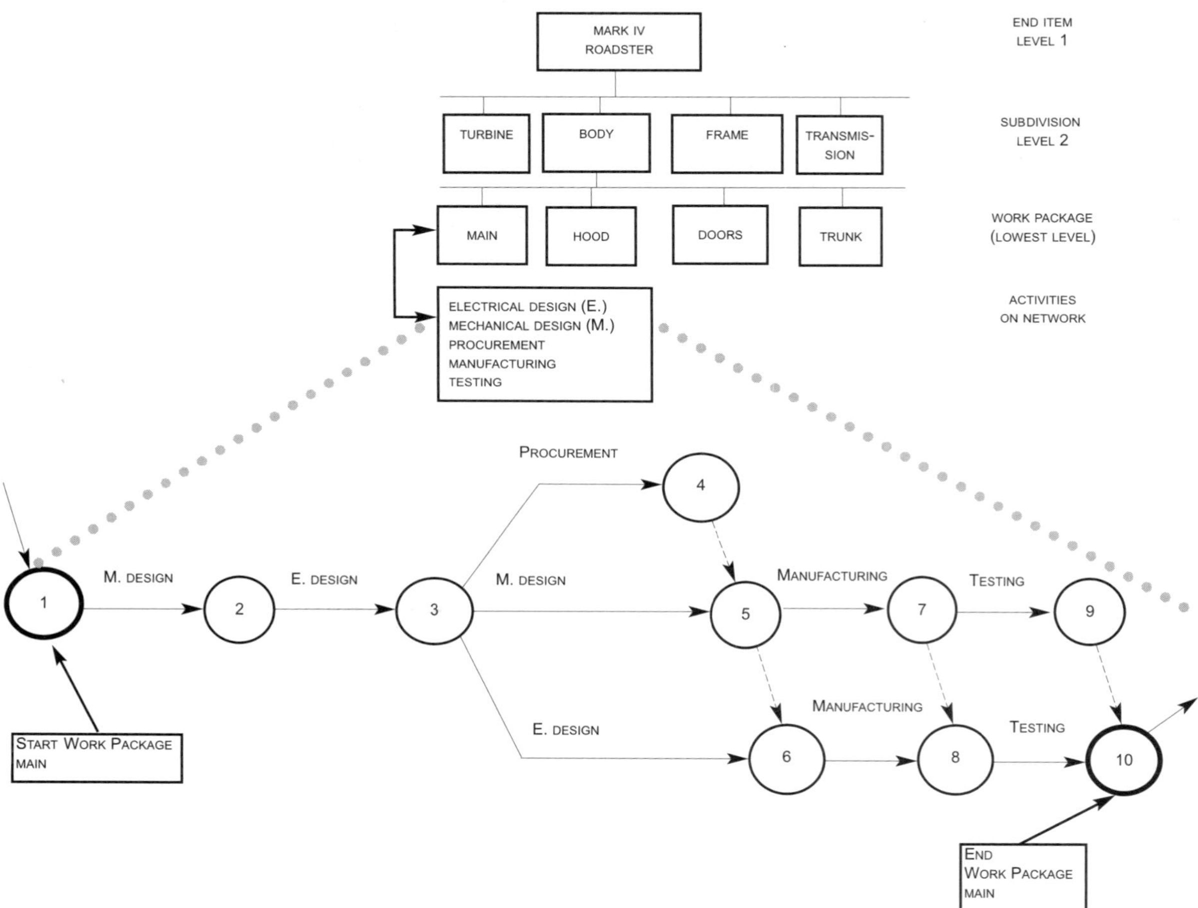

FIGURE 6.5 PERT/COST WORK-PACKAGE-BASED PLANNING NETWORK. Under PERT/Cost rules, work packages, generally at level 5 of the WBS, were cost estimated, budgeted, and cost controlled. Schedule activities at about level 6 were neither coded nor budgeted but had to be applicable to specific packages. This figure shows the end-item assembly, Mark IV Roadster, at level 1 in a simplified WBS with packages at about level 3 and schedule activities at about level 4. If the entire WBS were drawn to show the coprorate hierarchy, the packages would occur at lower levels.

not require a formal WBS. PERT/Time recommended a treelike structure, and considered that the PERT network is really another look at planning the structured project. PERT/Cost aimed at a formally coded WBS for cost control of packages only, with the network activities created for schedule only.

In this book the systems of project management require the compulsory preparation and coding of PDSs, WBSs, and OBSs. Their results go to both cost control and schedule control. For scheduling this means that there are no stand-alone networks of activities, and that every activity has a place in the project hierarchy.

In current usage less and less of the networking process is done manually. As a result, this book does not provide a primer on manually calculating CPM/PERT networks.

Although very few project managers would calculate a network manually, there is inevitably a creative process required in its construction. Creativity is invariably enhanced by computerization, but computerization could also be detrimental to the quality of the process and the results if the rules concerning the application of the systems of project management to CPM/PERT networking are not applied or insufficiently understood.

6.2 Rules and Terminology for CPM/PERT Networks

CPM and PERT are now one and the same. In *Project Management, a Systems Approach to Planning, Scheduling, and Controlling* Kerzner links PERT to CPM with the term PERT/CPM. The rules and conventions that follow, largely based on current commercially available project management software and current literature, are applicable to both CPM and PERT. In some usage the term CPM will be used. In others, PERT will be used. More often, the terms CPM/PERT or network will be used.

Second, where warranted a rule will be augmented or modified so that it complies with the fundamental rules of the systems of project management as presented and discussed throughout this book. This additional rule will be identified as the SPM rule.

Common Terms

activity Discretely defined task. Activities are specified by an activity number, description, duration, and type.

> *SPM rule* An activity must exist as a hard activity in that it has been defined and coded through the PDS, the WBS, and the OBS. It has a scope, a cost, and a place in time. It cannot disappear. It can only be canceled or eliminated through a scope change or through a change order. An activity that does not meet the SPM rule is an event, milestone, or target.

activity description Defines the activity scope of work.

SPM rule An activity description generally contains no action verb such as Start, Continue, Complete, Place, Set, Install, and so on. If these or similar verbs or qualifiers are imposed, the activity is a milestone or special event. But there are exceptions to the rule if the principal rule of what is a hard activity is not broken.

activity identifier Unique identification number.

activity type An activity may be one of the following:

- Begin activity
- End activity
- Hammock activity
- Special event activity
- Milestone activity

arrow diagramming method Method of graphically representing network logic in which activities are depicted by an arrow or line between two nodes or events. Relationships are shown by broken (or dotted) lines or arrows between the activities or by the impingement of the arrow head of one activity on the tail node of the succeeding activity. This method is sometimes called the activity-on-arrow (AOA) method or the *i–j* or *I–J* method. Here *i(I)* represents the tail node and *j(J)* represents the head of the arrow. The arrow method is the original method for both CPM and PERT. Computer systems were programmed to support arrow networks, and many users developed expertise in it. That is one of the reasons why users did not switch away from arrows when the precedence method was thought to be superior. Most high-end current personal computer (PC) project management software packages have the capability to process arrow networks, or to convert arrows to precedence. Users may see the advantage of arrow networking when creating complex networks.

critical path Longest path through a schedule network, or the chain or sequence of activities that takes the longest time, or the longest irreducible sequence of events. The critical path determines the project duration.

duration Duration of an activity is normally expressed in elapsed, working days. It may also be expressed in weeks or hours. Although PERT allows for the formulaic calculation of duration based on three time estimates, this is rarely used in construction project management. But it can be if required, and most top-end PC project management applications have the capability to handle this requirement.

SPM rule Activity durations in systems project management are aimed to be agreed on by the team member responsible, through consensus, or by contract. In the case of project influencers such as government approval agencies, the durations for their activities are based on their own input, to which they are not contractually bound. In both cases the durations will be set in a framework of management-imposed milestones or “drop dead” dates. Management decisions severely limit and restrict durations, thus influencing resource usage and project cost.

early finish date (EF) The earliest that an activity can finish based on its duration, and the durations of all the activities that are its predecessors. If management imposes the early finish date, the imposed date governs.

early start date (ES) The earliest that an activity can start based on the durations of all the activities that are its predecessors. If management imposes the early start date, the imposed date governs.

finish to finish (FF) Network relationship whereby the finish of a preceding activity is a condition for the finish of the succeeding activity.

finish to start (FS) Most common network relationship. The preceding activity must finish before the succeeding activity can start.

float Amount of leeway (in days if durations are measured in days) that an activity has in the schedule before it adversely affects the critical path. This is also called "total float." Free float is the amount of leeway an activity has before it adversely affects another activity. Called slack in some PC project management applications.

forward pass A network is first calculated from beginning to end. This is called forward pass, which calculates the early start and early finish dates for all activities. The longest sequence of activities sets the critical path and the project completion date.

backward pass Calculates late start and late finish dates for all activities by calculating backwards from the project end date, set by the forward pass calculation, to its beginning. Activities that have the same start and finish dates on both passes are on the critical path. The others have float values.

lag Establishes the relationship between activities. Lag may have a value based on the percentage completion of an activity's duration, or on units similar to the activity duration units. (See also precedence diagramming.)

late finish (LF) Latest finish date calculated for an activity on the backward pass. Late finish is the activity latest date allowed so as not to delay the project completion date. Late finish can be set by management as an imposed date. The imposed date takes precedence.

late start (LS) Latest start date calculated for an activity on the backward pass. Late start is the activity latest start date allowed so as not to delay the project completion date. Late start can be set by management as an Imposed Date. The Imposed Date takes precedence.

milestone (activity) Can be used to represent an achievement in the project, such as, the installation of a final piece of equipment in a complex computer installation. It could be used to flag an event, such as, finish the roof (which then allows all interior work to start). A project network could have a number of milestone activities or events, which are representative of the project schedule status.

node Synonym for event in CPM/PERT terminology. It is usually a circle, but could be an oval.

precedence diagramming method (PDM) A precedence diagram is a derivative of an arrow diagram as developed for both CPM and PERT network scheduling methods. In the activity-on-arrow method the event or node was initially used to delineate the start and finish of the activity, so that each activity was labeled three ways: start node, activity arrow, and finish node. Experientially, the network evolved in an activity-on-node representation. Thus there is one node per activity, with all activities connected by arrows. A node could be a square, a circle, a rectangle, an oval, and so on.

precedence relationships Activities in a network may relate to each other as:

- Finish to start (FS)
- Start to start (SS)
- Finish to finish (FF)
- Start to finish (SF)

predecessor activity One that goes before this activity, either completely (e.g., FS 100%), or partially (e.g., FS 50%).

start to finish (SF) Activity can only finish if its predecessor activity has started.

start to start (SS) Activity can only start if its predecessor activity has started.

successor activity One that goes after (follows) this activity, either completely (e.g., FS 100%), or partially (e.g., FS 50%). A successor is dependent on a predecessor.

This book looks to orient the reader toward computerized project management, including creating and calculating CPM/PERT networks with PCs or whatever combination of computer power may be available to the user. For a more in-depth understanding of network scheduling, which may only come with a better understanding of manually creating and calculating networks, the reader may wish to refer to literature that predates current PC project management applications. A partial list is provided in the references at the end of this chapter.

The listed references refer to the development and application of manual CPM and PERT methods as modern tools, without the use of postmodern PCs. Postmodern PC project management applications have computerized many of the manual tasks. But the process of creating, calculating, monitoring, and reporting plans, networks, and results discussed by the authors, practitioners, and teachers cited requires human actions before, during, and after computer interfacing and processing, as is discussed throughout this textbook.

6.3 Scheduling by CPM in Construction

Modern projects are assembled from many different systems, equipment arrangements, and materials, employing many different design, planning, and building professionals. The more plug-in systems there are, the more essential is planning and scheduling. Projects have become big. As megaprojects grew from millions of dollars to billions, the planning and scheduling systems needed to keep pace in terms of sophistication, complexity, application, and computerization.

The need for effective planning and scheduling systems has not diminished. If anything, it is a growth industry, now used in business sectors such as software development, banking, insurance, and the conceptualization, design, and manufacturing of new automobiles. As scheduling became more sophisticated in terms of its application to larger and more complex projects, and as computers played a larger role, there were movements to integrate scheduling systems with other systems of project management such as project definition, breakdown, and cost control. The strongest links were first seen in the relation with project work breakdown. From a project management systems point of view, PERT was seen to be more effective than CPM in terms of its capability to integrate project scope, cost, and time. Although not necessarily meant as such by its inventors, the CPM first was considered by many to be a time scheduling tool, and not a forerunner of a project management system. Over time, as discussed, CPM and PERT networks have become interchangeable and are seen almost as one by experienced users and project management software developers.

Before demonstrating the integration of planning and scheduling networks into the concept of project management it may be instructive to demonstrate early standalone usage of CPM for construction. CPM in its earliest manifestation was thought to have magic powers and the ability to cure the problems of low productivity and long schedules. However, there were many difficulties in applying expensive network techniques in the competitive, often low-profit construction industry. A major concern was the lack of understanding between the construction industry professionals and the network innovators.

As with many new techniques, in the rush to get on the bandwagon, persons unfamiliar with construction but trained in CPM were called in, often with disastrous results.

If at the beginning networks were being made in a vacuum, that is, as stand alone, without being related to and integrated with the other systems of project management, they still are being done that way. Bad networks, that is, networks without meaning except in the narrowest sense, are still being produced.

A sometimes excuse for bad networks is that any planning network is better than no network at all. As network planning is often seen as a demanding exercise, a bad network could detract from systems planning altogether. To ease the complexity of creating networks, many new PC project management systems are based on the creation of schedules with connected bar charts, which may then be converted to PERT networks automatically. This is not network planning.

There are great expectations from network planning, and even more so now that the procedure is resident on many PC project management systems. What with increasing project complexity and demand for better productivity, major builders became interested in scheduling by CPM shortly after its appearance on the scene. Early users of CPM expected that it would improve construction operations through better information such as:

- Knowing the time by which a detailed drawing is required
- Knowing the day on which a delivery must be made
- Being able to avoid the cost of expediting all operations should some fall behind, because the critical path is known

It was anticipated that these expectations would be met through schedule networks similar to the one illustrated in Fig. 6.6. This figure shows a network of familiar steps in the construction of a structural concrete slab, including logic relationships, task durations, node numbers, and the use of dummies. The critical path can be calculated manually or by computer. When applied to a project calendar, the network would result in a time schedule for the planned activities.

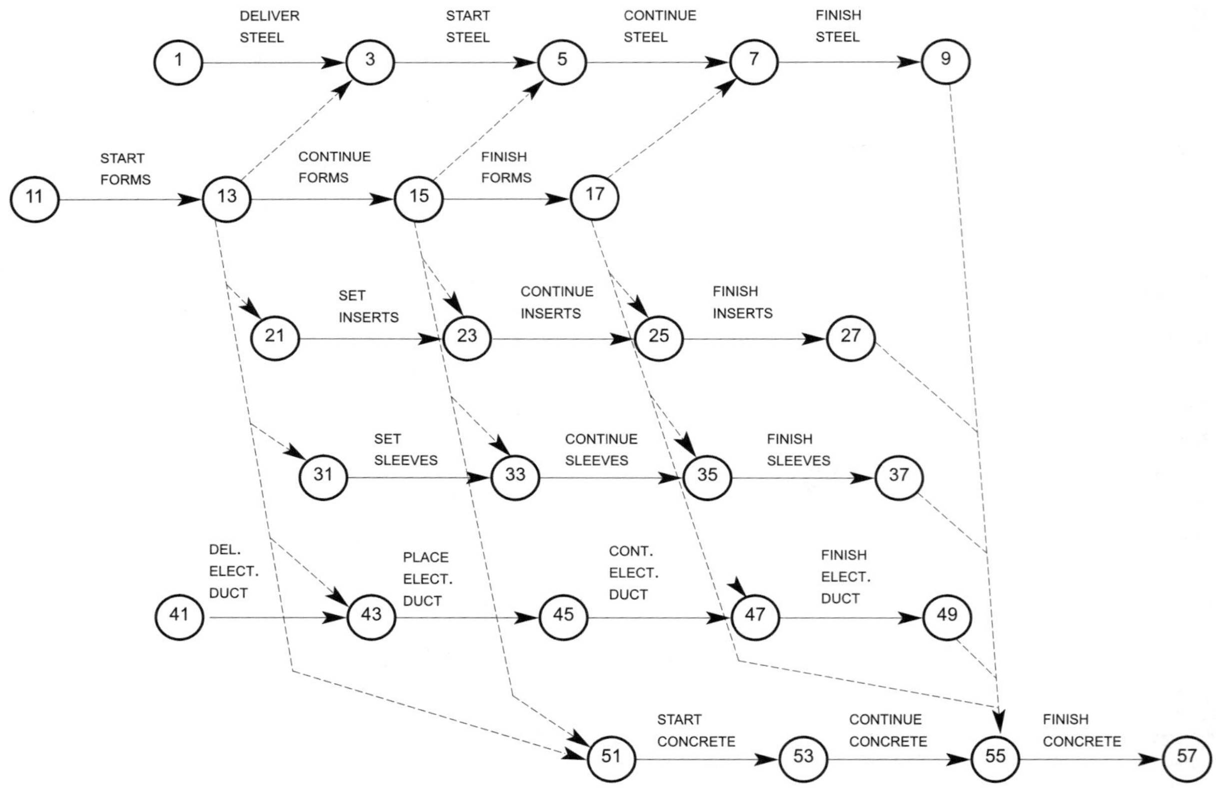

FIGURE 6.6 VERY EARLY CPM CONSTRUCTION NETWORK BASED ON CPM/PERT RULES.
1. This is considered to be a stand-alone network.
2. These kinds of activities are only valid for establishing a time frame.
3. The activities themselves are most difficult to scope or quantify.
4. A network of these kinds of activities may be considered a network of events.
5. This would not be considered a project management systems network.

The approach runs into difficulty when the sequence of construction changes, for whatever reason. When this happens, the network is put in the position of trying to catch up with the progress of the work. In practice it never does catch up. And that was the first problem with networks for construction: they invariably became obsolete in relation to the way in which the work was being done.

The second main problem was with the activities themselves. The tasks seen in Fig. 6.6 just do not have any relation to any other management functions on the job. They are not quantified. They do not relate to any cost code. Except for the scheduler, it is doubtful that any one else in the construction organization knows what an activity means, except in the broadest, generic sense. The names of the activities themselves lead to misrepresentation. For example, names such as "start" and "continue" are open invitations to misleading progress reports on the status of the work. If the progress reporter wishes to show better progress, a start activity could be reported complete with only a modicum of work done. Even to apply quantities to activities such as start and continue is unsatisfactory in that their quantification could only be for scheduling purposes.

The conclusion to be reached on a network of these kinds of activities is that as the activities are only recognizable to the scheduler, and have little or no meaning for the rest of the project organization, the network and schedule will have little credibility and may be considered not meaningful. But networks of these kinds of activities are still being created.

A CPM/PERT network is nothing if not accommodating in that anything may be networked. If the network exists in a stand-alone environment, such as, not as an element of an integrated project management system, it may be that "soft" activities similar to those in Fig. 6.6 are acceptable. As the systems of networking matured and experience was gained, changes started to be put into place. The most important of these changes relate to the inclusion of hard activities as compared to those deemed to be soft. In CPM/PERT network planning there are degrees of hardness of activities. The hardest activity is the one developed through project definition, work breakdown, and functional organization breakdown. If a project manager does not practice full-bore project management, the activities may still have a degree of hardness somewhere between those in Fig. 6.6 and project management systems activities tied to definition, breakdown, and organization. Figure 6.7 illustrates these systems activities.

The designer of the network in Fig. 6.7 argued that network activities must not be seen to have been created in a vacuum. For this to happen, it needs also to be recognized that network building is an iterative process, a condition not always acknowledged by planners and managers.

The activities in Fig. 6.6 are bad from a project management systems aspect, because they are not quantifiable and therefore not relatable to resources and costs. They may be useful to establish milestones and event dates, but that would tend to keep the networking activity as an isolated scheduling exercise without integration into the systems of project management.

The activities in Fig. 6.7 are somewhat better from a systems perspective. For example, the activity Site Preparation can have a scope, cost, and resource compo-

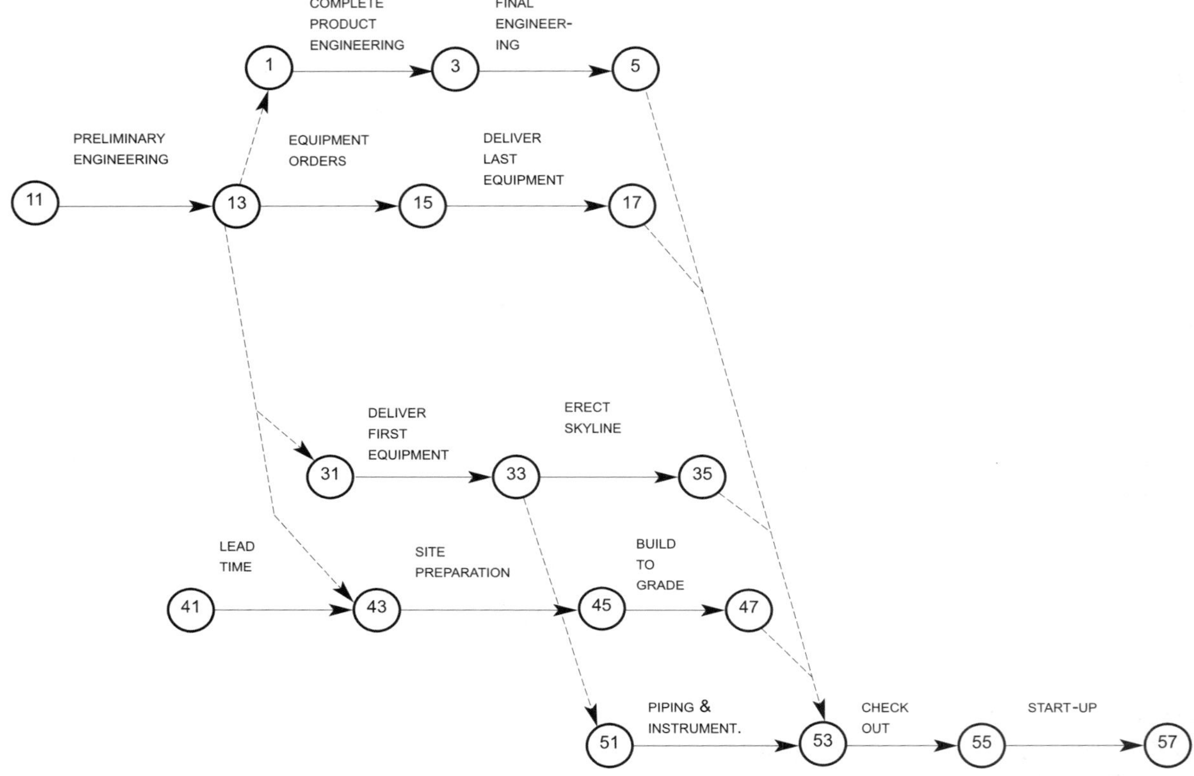

FIGURE 6.7 EARLY CPM CONSTRUCTION NETWORK BASED ON CPM/PERT RULES.

1. This is considered to be a better but still stand-alone network in that some activities have more "hardness".
2. These kinds of activities are still basically only valid for establishing a time frame.
3. The activities themselves are still difficult to scope or quantify.
4. A network of these kinds of activities may be considered a network of events.
5. This still would not be considered a project management systems network.

nent. It can exist on the monthly progress billing. So can activities such as Preliminary Engineering and Piping & Instrumentation. But others, such as Complete Product Engineering, Erect Skyline, and Deliver First Equipment, generally are not quantifiable. They are mainly useful as events or milestones.

The main message from this exercise is that bad networks are easy to make; that networks made in a vacuum by schedulers may have little or no credibility; and that activities must have some hardness in that they are relatable to scope, breakdown, and organization. In general unless the intent is to create a network of events or milestones, activities such as "start," "continue," and "complete" should not be used.

Project managers look to CPM/PERT network schedules to achieve results such as better utilization of work force; to show the relationship of jobs and the effects of delay; to indicate expediting action; to evaluate the need for overtime; and to carry out more careful and thorough planning. The question is, do they achieve these objectives with activities such as those depicted in Figs. 6.6 and 6.7?

These two examples of critical path networks are to show that those kinds of activities are suitable only as stand-alone scheduling exercises. Other project management functions would have difficulty relating to the individual activities, except as events, milestones, deadlines, constraints, and imposed dates. If a system such as CPM serves only a narrow, isolated purpose, and is at the same time complicated and expensive to operate, its chances of success and benefit to the project are limited at best. At worst, it may have a negative impact on the project and its organization. The result may be that although many successful engineering, construction, and project management companies adopted the approach, they eventually concluded that it was worth it only because "it forces us to plan better."

If those early networks and activities were not fully meaningful as systems, are those now being made more suitable? Current practice would seem to indicate that many are not. They are somewhat more meaningful in that the activities are better related to other project management functions, networks are cleaner in terms of fewer drawings, and network drawings are generally easier to read and understand.

6.4 CPM versus PERT Networks for Scheduling Construction

As CPM was invented for construction scheduling, the engineering and construction project industry gravitated more to it than to PERT as a way to fix the problem of productivity. As with many innovations, a solution to fix problems of schedule control and productivity in construction was not forthcoming from within the industry itself, but from its customers.

Although PERT played a major role in the management and control of projects in the defense and energy industries, it was virtually ignored by both public and private-sector building and engineering construction industries. The PERT concept was completely geared to big projects. Private-sector construction contractors, generally engaged in public works and building projects for the private sector, neither needed nor could afford the massive management system that was PERT. But neither was CPM, as it was being learned and applied, the answer.

Would the construction industry have been better served if it had been introduced to PERT first? The essential difference between CPM and PERT is that CPM is a scheduling system.

CPM does not demand any management changes and the possible resulting upheaval. Whereas PERT was developed for use in well-funded defense industry projects, CPM was intended to control less well-funded construction contractors, who were not required to change their management methods, but simply were to adopt the new tool and apply it in their construction operations.

While PERT requires the development of activities through WBSs, CPM does not stress work breakdown. A negative result was that network activities were not necessarily relatable to other project functions. CPM was often prepared in a vacuum, often by a junior scheduler. A prerequisite for a construction scheduler being that the scheduler be versed in computer usage, the advent of cheaper computers lead to situations where people had some computer competence but little or no construction skills. The results often were less than useful CPM scheduling networks. If not openly reviled, the function of network preparation for scheduling was at best tolerated.

PERT on the other hand was based on a structured and systematic process governing the development of activities, as illustrated in Fig. 6.8.

From a project management systems point of view, the CPM activities not being based on a breakdown structure was the essential missing ingredient in the CPM network. As a result, CPM networks continued to be unsatisfactory in depicting project work for more than scheduling purposes.

From a project planning and scheduling perspective, the CPM networks seen in Figs. 6.6 and 6.7 were not capable of responding to the needs of the construction industry to improve its productivity and schedule performance. The criticism of CPM, perhaps without knowing it, was looking for a system that if not PERT, would have been similar to it.

If the stand-alone schedule activities were unsuitable, what were the desirable attributes for schedule control by CPM?

From experience, people were looking for a system that could start delivering some or all of the following values in a network of activities:

- The units of work establish the work to be done and develop the relationship between project objective and functional organization.
- The units become the activities on the planning and scheduling network.
- They establish the framework for integrating cost and schedule.
- They establish the framework for reporting cost and progress.
- There is created only one database for cost and schedule.

As CPM was not capable of delivering the values listed, and as PERT criteria were not being applied, it can be concluded that systems project management was not being used in the delivery of projects in the construction industry.

6.5 The Politics of CPM Scheduling in Construction

The introduction of CPM was not welcomed with open arms in the construction industry, nor is it necessarily welcomed today. Following its invention and first application on process plant turnaround projects, there was generally a great deal of dissatisfaction with it. There was much consternation about what it was to do, who would apply it, and who would pay for it.

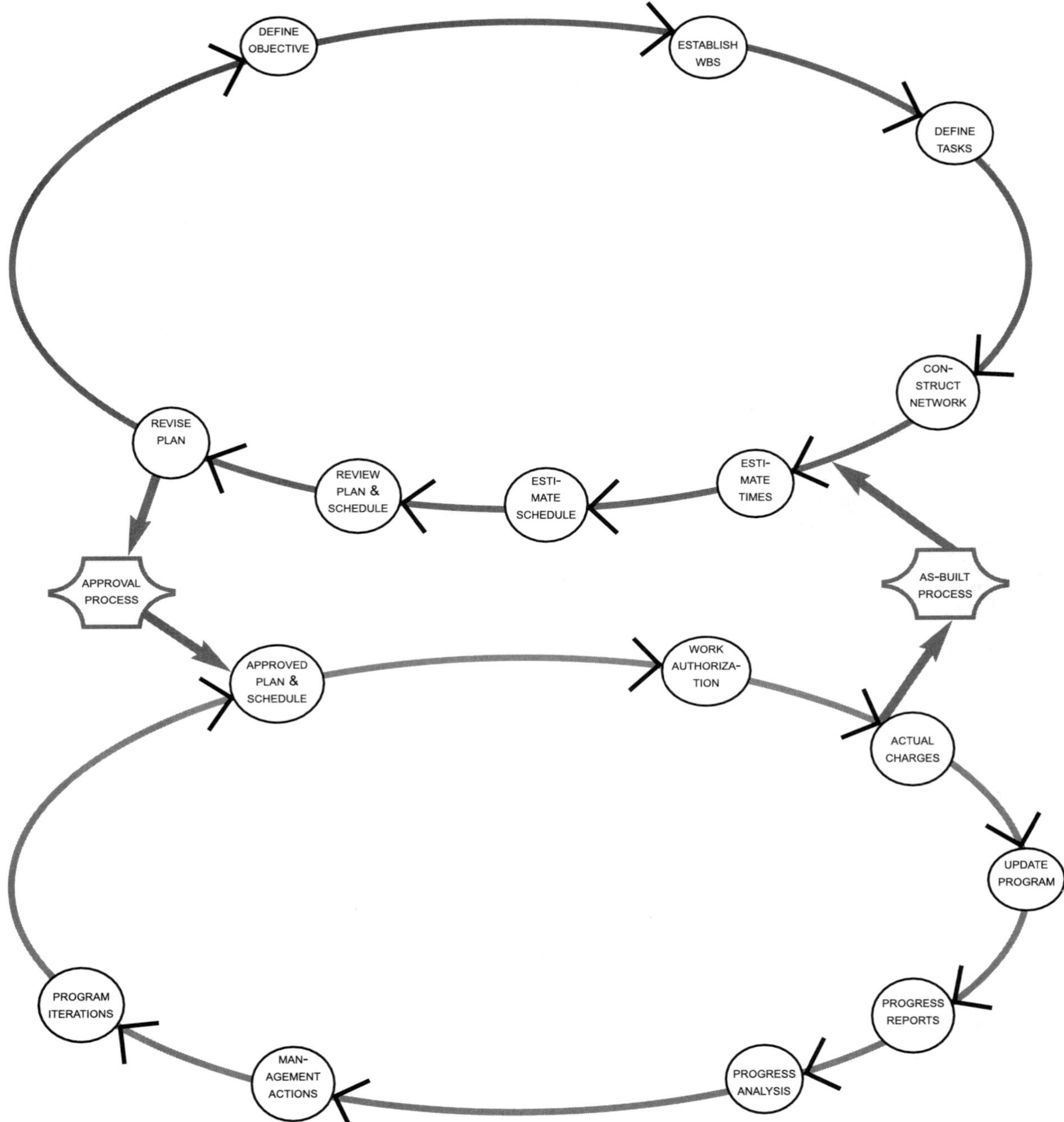

FIGURE 6.8 DEVELOPMENT AND PROCESSING OF PERT ACTIVITIES. PERT activities, when compared to CPM activities, are created and developed in a more formal way, largely as depicted above. Although there was no rule mitigating against doing CPM activities in this way, it was not the usual approach.

Criticism of CPM in construction took many forms, from outright rejection of the technique to barely tolerating it because the client wanted it.

In discussing the application of CPM to design and engineering, managers reported that the major problem was the massive amount of information generated as computer printout and the difficulty in reading it, never mind being able to understand it. Some managers conceded that CPM planning did help set time parameters for decision making.

Architectural designers thought that the CPM approach had very little merit in the traditional building delivery mode of owner need, architect design, and contractor build. On the other hand, many architects believe that there is merit in using CPM on construction management projects. Designers generally concede that they do not like CPM, because they perceive it as an attack on their creativity, that is, "you can't schedule creativity" (the thinking process). At the same time the designers who have had experience with CPM have criticized it on the grounds that many CPM activities are just not meaningful. For example, the activity "Prepare floor plans and elevations" as a single activity represents no real change from the intuitive method of working. (From a scheduling perspective, however, as this activity would have both predecessors and successors, its place in a time schedule would be visible, and its impact on the project schedule discernible.)

As might be expected, the most support for using networks to control design comes from large purchasers of design services. One corporate engineering manager had been an enthusiastic supporter and user of CPM for some time. But his corporation devised a different approach for its projects, one that would ensure for the owner "the earliest practicable return on investment." As such it was seen not as a means to reduce cost, but to control engineering design time so as to give procurement and construction, both seen as less controllable, the maximum amount of time to do their thing.

Sometimes computer processing of CPM networks may create its own problems. Unless the output is subjected to very careful and informed analysis, the resulting information can be not very useful, or in some cases considered nearly misleading. One result was that some corporate managers adopted other methods to monitor project progress, including an approach that concentrated on analyzing and measuring work remaining rather than depending on computer output to predict a completion date. Experienced project managers often saw problems with only concentrating on the critical path. The fear was that other important activities having "float" or "slack" might be ignored in the monitoring process, leading to a condition called "end of job pileup."

Experience teaches that a project critical path can and will shift and change often and sometimes drastically as the job progresses. The changes may be a result of management decisions, field conditions, technical problems, or bad scheduling. What this means is that the negative or zero float path and the total float of chains of activities are constantly under attack and subject to change.

The corporate engineering manager referred to recognized this as a problem area and adopted a technique that measured the "rate of work" using a unit known as a job-week. This approach largely ignored the concept of float and the importance of the critical path.

Initially many construction contractors saw CPM as a tool to be used as a "weapon in their fight against architects, engineers, and owners, "and this continues to be often the case. The attitude of some general contractors was that "here was a way to prove mathematically, with a computer, that the other fellow was wrong." This was in many respects the natural outcome of a condition where project owners and their professional consultants specified that general contractors must use a CPM system to plan and schedule the contractor's work, and then used the CPM information in any contract dispute against the contractor.

In civil engineering construction, senior executives saw CPM planning and scheduling as an unwanted development. Major heavy engineering builders saw the system as intrusive and unhelpful. Bar charts were used widely, and were seen as adequate for planning and scheduling purposes.

Mechanical and electrical construction contractors were generally aghast that a new planning technique would be applied to their work. One reason they gave is that there is not enough time to produce a network. Second, people would not use it because networks are too confusing. Most important, in the eyes of successful mechanical and electrical contractors "it is people and not networks that make a job successful."

In all the cases on which the preceding commentary is based, CPM was being introduced into traditional workplaces with the intent that it would affect and improve the output of the skilled and experienced project people that were targeted. Without exception, the concept was rejected. None of them wanted it or saw a need for it in their operations, although everyone agreed that planning is important. In the case of general contractors, they saw the tool being used as a weapon in adversarial situations by the owner and the consultants.

If CPM did not work for the groups and types of organizations identified here, whom did it work for? The most successful applications seem to be those in which the owner organization provides professional project management encompassing the entire project and all project team members from project concept to completion. People who understand project management will agree that that there is invariably a serious lack of communication between project owner, designers, suppliers, and contractors, and those who wish to address this problem will agree that a system such as CPM could become the common language of communication for the entire project industry.

6.6 State of the Art of CPM Network Scheduling

At one time there were discussions on whether or not CPM networks should be computerized. Computerization won. Having said that, it does not mean that CPM is necessarily better or more effective or better loved than it was originally. The question is, how meaningful are networks, in particular now that they are produced by computer? Are the current activities more relatable to project scope, quality, cost, and functional organization, or are they still mostly stand-alone activities prepared in a vacuum?

The problem is that too often when one looks at a company, one sees the schedulers in one corner furiously cranking out schedules and in the other corner, cost engineers setting up and controlling budgets. Too often there are examples of networks of activities which are understandable only to the scheduler. Such activities do not have much relevance to other project control parameters.

Has the current cheap availability of PC project management application packages offering project control, including planning and scheduling, done anything to improve the quality of network activities?

First, the PC project management packages are economical to buy and are advertised as easy to use.They offer to turn projects into profits. But the CPM network activity examples provided with the PCs are similar to the types of activities shown on networks 30 years earlier. Examples are:

- First review of floor plan
- Redraft floor plans
- Finalized floor plan review

Although these kinds of activities can lead to the creation of a critical path and a schedule, it is obvious that they are events or project snapshot points, and have no validity or standing in the quality or cost measure of the project.

Activities like the ones following are examples of nonsystem activities and need to be avoided in a project management systems environment:

- Purchase and deliver piping
- Run in electrical cabling
- Wire building
- Connect piping
- Procure building material
- Excavate and pour foundations
- Connect suction line to pump
- Bolts and plates

These kinds of schedule activities are not relatable to scope, quality, and cost measures, which are the other measures of project work, quantifiable in precise units. If it is wished to use names similar to those above, it is better to refer to them as events. What would be created would be a network of events. To achieve an event it is necessary to carry out activities. Therefore it may be futile to create event networks when it is activities that must be measured.

If there is a rule to be followed in building networks, it is that the use of event names, as above, and the use of verbs, as in start, continue, finish, pour, or procure, should be avoided. The intent is to create networks of hard activities that are recognizable across all project control parameters. In this way scheduling becomes a part of the systems of project management as opposed to it being a stand-alone exercise.

To sum up, a schedule should be prepared as if it were a part of a project management system. Recognize that project scheduling must take the scope and cost control disciplines into account.

6.7 Age of Computer-Aided CPM/PERT Scheduling

With the advent of PC project management systems, networks are being produced by computers and processed as they are made. With the introduction of local area networks (LANs), and the client/server configuration, networks are now made interactively, processed and used for project scheduling, scope control, and the assignment of resources.

The objective here is to look at the process of making networks of activities and to demonstrate the differences between good and bad activities. In general, a bad activity is one that is not relatable to the other project parameters. A good activity is hard in that it exists for more than just the scheduling exercise. It is just as easy to make a bad network with a GUI package as it is to make it manually. Indeed, it may be easier to make with a PC, because with a GUI package there is instant gratification with the availability of PERT, Gantt, or Tables screen views, as well as hard copy. The exercise here is to look at examples of networks of bad activities, easily made by PC packages. These are some examples of bad network activity names:

"Select building from options". This is not an activity. It is an event or a milestone.

"Approve outside contracts." It is an event, a point in time.

"First review of floor plan." How would this be quantified. It would be more reasonable to convert it into a marker or a milestone as a point in time that would terminate a number of activities leading into it.

"Production begins." This is an event. It is best as a network of events.

"Agency approvals." It is difficult to label this. At best, for any undertaking, it is an ongoing process, happening from time to time during the progress of the project.

"Finalize intro plan." This would be suitable to mark a point in time, either at the beginning or at the end of a group of activities.

Figure 6.9 is an illustration of a number of these above activities as a PC GUI-screen generated network plan.

The descriptions of good and bad activities are meant to help differentiate between what may be termed hard project management system types of activities, and

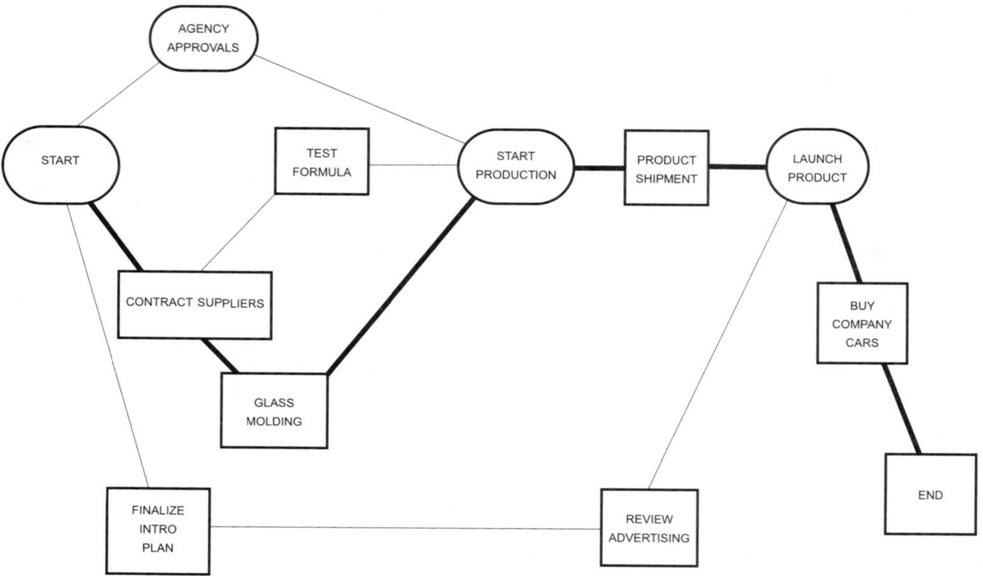

FIGURE 6.9 TYPICAL PC PROJECT MANAGEMENT APPLICATION PACKAGE, DEPICTION OF CPM/PERT NETWORK OF ACTIVITIES. Computers are used to create networks such as this one. The computer works just fine. It is the activity that is not suitable for project control purposes because these activities are not relatable to scope, quality, and cost measures.

others deemed soft schedule type activities. The intent is to make scheduling a mainstream project management function, and not a back room exercise in futility. (For the beginning scheduler, who may be a wizard on the PC, nothing could be more frustrating than to have a line manager say: "I didn't follow your schedule; you didn't check with me, and anyway I don't understand your network.")

From an architect's, engineer's, or job superintendent's point of view there is no merit in seeing reams of printout of the date and time status of activities, with the activities themselves only existing in the schedule. They must be part of the project database. And that is what systems project management is about.

The activities have a life outside of the time plan. They have a unique identification. The relationships between activities may change, but the activities only change if the scope of the work changes. And they are created long before the network is formatted.

6.8 CPM/PERT Scheduling Networks Based on the SPM Rule

The SPM rule was introduced in Section 6.2. Systems project management aims to integrate project definition, work breakdown, functional project organization, cost budgeting and control, and scheduling. The systems create a common language for the control and coordination of the project as it progresses through the different stages. The language consists of project deliverables, their codes, their organizations, their cost, and their time.

The systems approach expects that there will be no stand-alone activities for planning and scheduling purposes only, except those that are generated by the systems for the other project purposes. This is a generalization, and as for any generalization, there are exceptions to the rule. The exceptions will become self-evident in the planning process and in the examples that follow. Besides the inclusion of events and milestone markers required for any schedule, systems planning activities frequently need to be either combined or merged from smaller project elements, or split or fragmented into smaller elemental activities.

Previously activities labeled "start" and "finish" were seen as nonactivities because they had no other project measurement, such as, no scope, therefore no quantity, and obviously no cost. However, a start or a finish could become a project milestone or an event. Milestones and events may be created by management, or by the conjunction of a number of activities. They may have an imposed date, a contract date, or a naturally occurring time frame, such as, weather freeze up.

An important feature of systems networks is that unless they are quite small, they are better thought of as being written in machine language. The machine in this case is the computer. Currently the computer most often is a PC, a server/client system, or a LAN. CPM/PERT planning networks are connected groups of paths that can very quickly become a maze. To follow the paths becomes tedious and difficult. An understanding of the network maze only comes with computer processing, reporting tables, and graphics. High-quality graphics and color drawings help to understand the message being delivered by the results of the planning process and the resulting schedule.

Some of the rules to follow to create these kinds of systems planning and scheduling networks are the following:

1. An activity exists as a deliverable from the PDS and the WBS.
2. Each activity belongs to a group or member of the functional organization.
3. The activity has a code developed by the PDS and the OBS.
4. Each activity has a cost based in the project cost control system.
5. An activity may be a fraction or a summary of an element.
6. Terms such as Start, Continue, Complete, Review, Approve, Finalize are OK to use, but as events or Milestones.
7. Events have no cost or resources associated with them (although they could have as the summary of the activities that terminate in the event).

A network of model activities having these characteristics is provided in Fig. 6.10. Drawn as an arrow diagram, the illustration aims to portray a classic network of hard

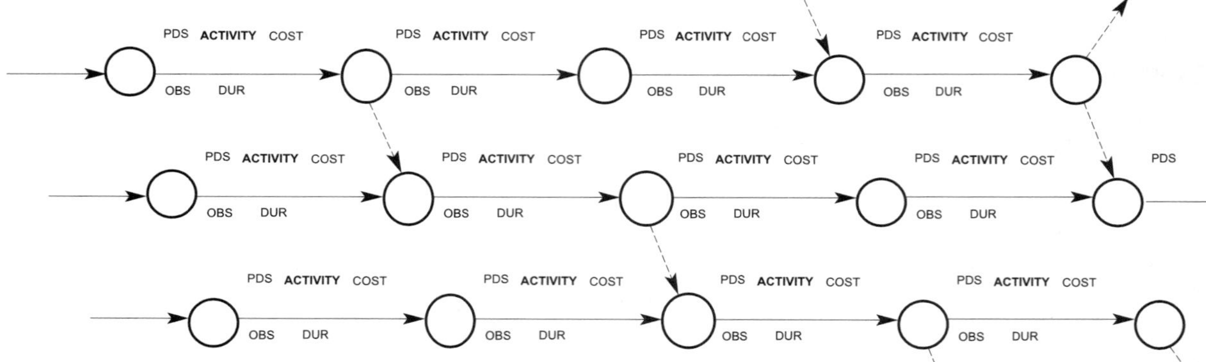

FIGURE 6.10 PROJECT MANAGEMENT SYSTEMS NETWORK ARROW DIAGRAM.

activities. As most current PC project management programs are based on precedence diagrams, the model arrow diagram network in Fig. 6.10 is reconstructed as a precedence diagram in Fig. 6.11. Any project management systems activity appearing in a CPM/PERT network is required to be identified not only with its logical relationships, duration, lag, and lead values for scheduling purposes, but also from time to time any or all of its project PDS, WBS, and OBS codes and values. At the same time, the network may be assigned constraints, milestones, and events by management, or forces beyond the control of management.

The activities in both figures comply with rules 1 through 5. As no events or milestones are shown in the figures, rules 6 and 7 are not tested in this model.

Current practice and PC project management marketing literature are filled with examples of both good and bad activities, but generally there are more bad than good. The types of activities that should be avoided have already been named.

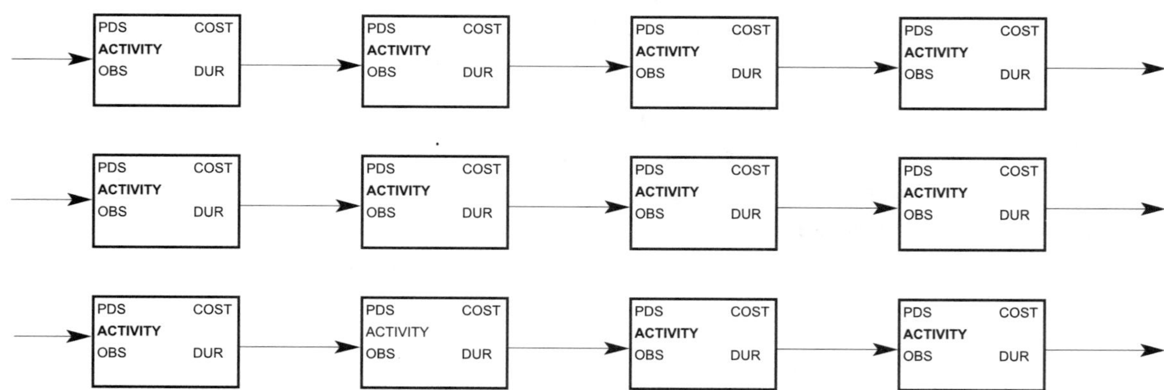

FIGURE 6.11 PROJECT MANAGEMENT SYSTEMS NETWORK PRECEDENCE DIAGRAM.

Examples of suitable activities that would meet the test of rules 1 through 5 above for a building project network would be similar to the following:

- Soil Stabilization
- Concrete slab on grade
- Windows
- Bathroom Tile
- Painting
- Resilient Flooring and Base
- Plumbing Fixtures

The consistent property of each of these is that they exist in the project as scope, quality statements, specifications, quantities, budget items, progress billing line items, and accounts payable. Therefore they must be there as schedule activities.

For scheduling purposes, in response to test 5, they might be broken down by areas, floors, or walls. For example, Windows might appear as these activities on a network:

- Windows, fourth floor
- Windows, third floor
- Windows, second floor
- Windows, first floor

Although it is unlikely that the budget for the project windows would be broken down floor by floor, windows as an item may be broken down for scheduling purposes. Other examples of names suitable as network activities may be similar to the following:

- Repair old roof
- Paint exterior of building
- Interior wall construction
- HVAC installed and tested

6.9 CPM Network Example Airport Project Passenger Terminal

The objective in this textbook is to promote the project management process as an integrated group of five systems: PDS, WBS, OBS, cost, and schedule. Each system has a distinct role and its own deliverable. None is a stand-alone system. The output of each system acts as input to the others. The preceding chapters define the purpose

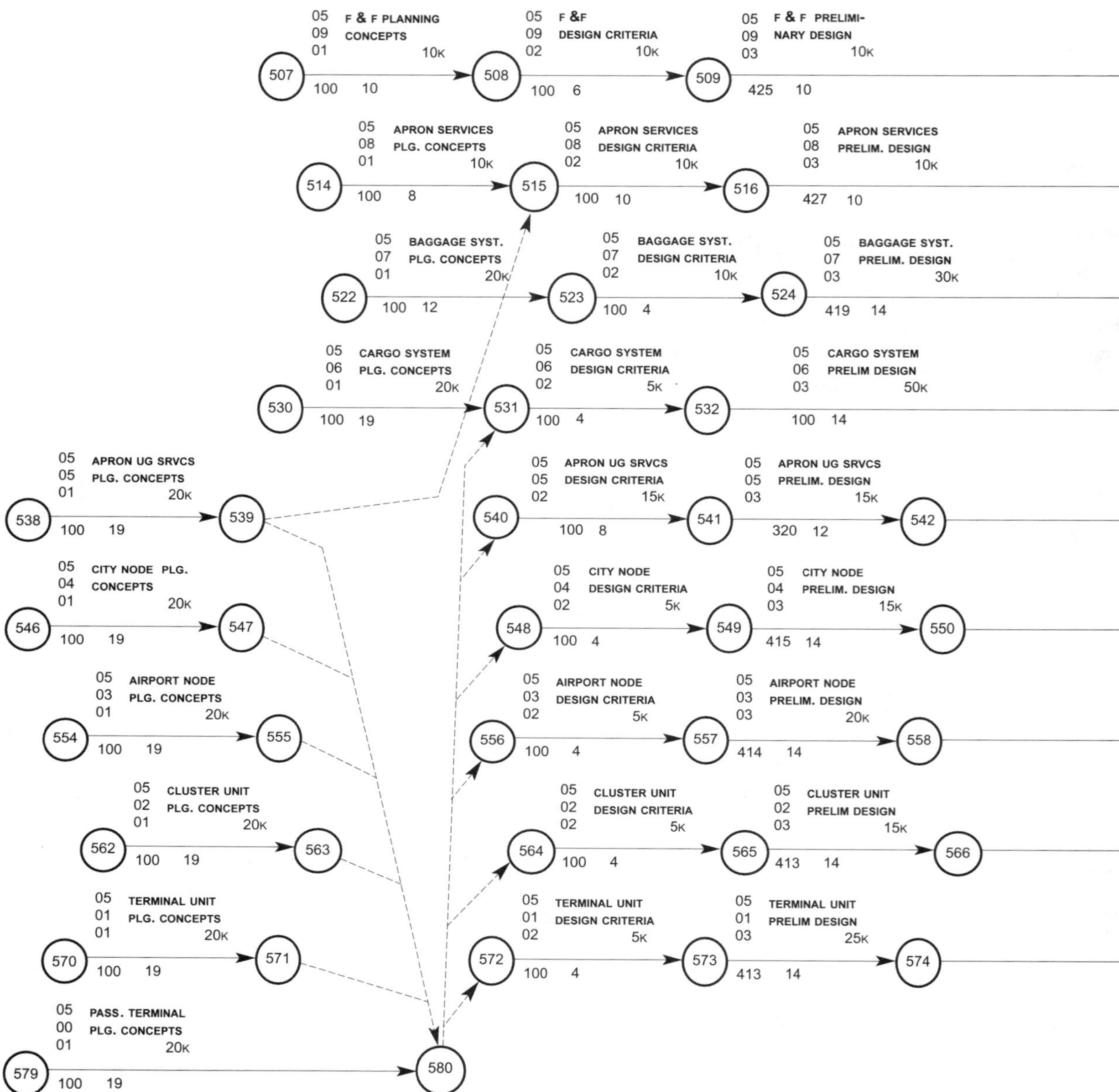

FIGURE 6.12 PROJECT MANAGEMENT SYSTEMS NETWORK, AIRPORT PROJECT PASSENGER TREMINAL. This is a cut of a large CPM scheduling network to show the application of project codes and scheduling values to activities created by the project management systems approach.

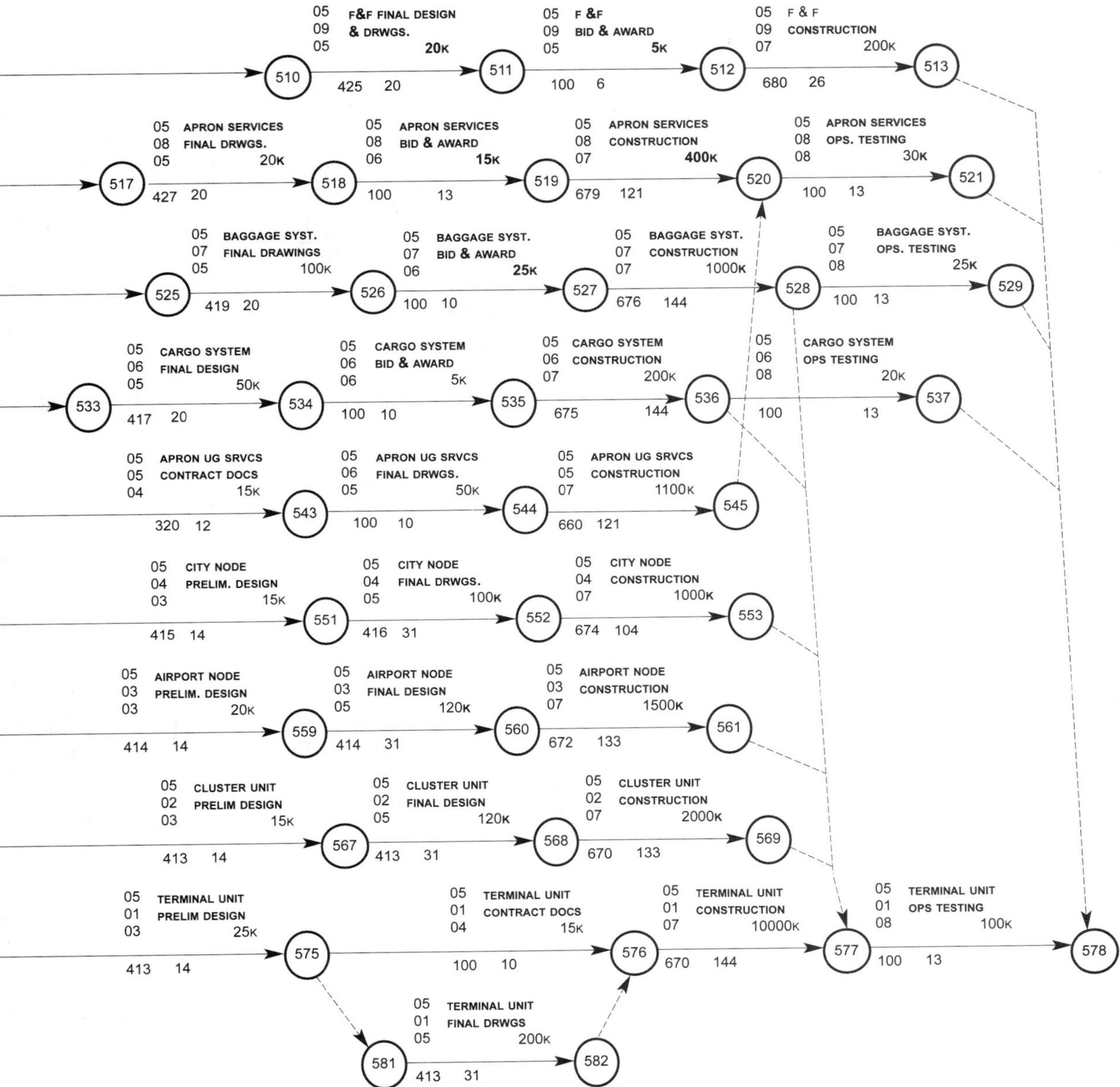

FIGURE 6.12 (CONTINUED).

of the systems covered and discuss their applications to different projects, including an airport project example.

In Chapter 2 Fig. 2.9 illustrates the basis for an airport project definition structure, and the resulting code system is seen in Fig. 2.10.

Chapter 3 discusses the relationship of PDS and WBS, and introduces the concept of project phases. Figure 3.10 depicts a classic WBS of nine project stages and uses the airport project to illustrate it.

In Chapter 4 the discussion introduces a code system incorporating all three measures of a project, PDS (scope and budget), WBS (task and budget), and OBS (package and cost). The code that incorporates all three project parameters is seen in Fig. 4.14.

In this chapter the aim is to construct schedules based on project management systems rules, as depicted in Figs. 6.10 and 6.11.

Accordingly, a network of activities for the passenger terminal of the airport project is depicted in Fig. 6.12. The activities are cast as systems of project management tasks. Each activity has a project definition code, a functional organization code, a cost number, and a single time duration. The activities are developed through the project WBS of typical project phases. The cost number assigned to each activity is for demonstration purpose only. In practice the accuracy of the cost would be in accordance with the rules of cost estimating, as discussed in Chapter 5.

The activities depicted in Fig. 6.12 could be very large in terms of their scope, cost, and time requirements. The purpose of the type of network seen in Fig. 6.12 is to act as a master time plan or master schedule network to set the milestones and targets for more detailed schedules.

The network of activities in Fig. 6.12 may seem complicated. In fact, it has been simplified for illustration purposes. In practice the passenger terminal activities would be related to other project areas, such as airport roads, the transportation system, and taxiways and runways.

A logic network containing as few as 50 to 100 activities with up to 100 to 200 relationships, such as finish to start, start to start, and finish to finish, with various lead and lag values, becomes complex to follow. The calculations and iterations necessary to create a valid schedule are only possible with a computer program.

Project planners make networks on an activity-by-activity basis. As a network is compiled, it seems to grow exponentially, quickly becoming complicated. An experienced planner reduces complexity by keeping the predecessor/successor relationships to a minimum and limiting the lead and lag values. Less experienced planners are prone to create more complex networks, giving rise to complaints of too much information, too much paper, and too much complexity for little or no gain. Indeed, bad networks and computer output can throw scheduling networks into disrepute.

The network in Fig. 6.12 has built into it a number of structural problems, which should be avoided in real applications. It is drawn as an activity-on-arrow diagram, which is a preferred method for construction. Current project management software is based on the activity-on-node or precedence diagram method. However, high-end software will process both arrow and precedence methods.

Second, some node numbers are shared by activities. Although each activity has a unique *i–j*, the *j* of one activity is the *i* of a succeeding activity. If the succeeding activity is deleted, the *j* may also have to be scrapped, meaning that the preceding activity will have new *i–j* identifiers. This may be overcome by unique identifiers for all activities, no shared node numbers, or by drawing precedence diagrams.

In systems project management the systems depend on and support each other. A change in one drives changes in the others. This is illustrated in the airport passenger terminal example by coding each activity with a definition code, a work breakdown code, an organizational or source of cost code, and a duration for time scheduling purposes, thus creating the relationship between scheduling, cost, definition, and organization.

The large, complex network in Fig. 6.12 is computer created and processed for scheduling purposes, resources management, and cash-flow planning and monitoring. The network is not in itself a presentation tool. Invariably the results of network planning are represented by bar charts. The companion bar chart in this case is seen in Fig. 6.13. The graphic has been grossly oversimplified for the purposes of this book, showing only the calendar time frames for some of the activities in the network.

Using the features and properties of the network and the computer capability of PC project management packages, other bar charts may be created to show critical tasks only, milestones, early starts and finishes, late starts and finishes, baseline starts and finishes, and actual starts and finishes.

The bars may be cost bars or human resources person-hours for the entire project, for individual project phases, or for selected time frames, such as weekly, monthly, quarterly, or yearly.

The network and computer-processed information may be used to establish the budgeted cost of work scheduled and performed as well as the actual cost of work performed for performance measurement, as discussed in Chapter 5.

6.10 Summary

The project planning and scheduling system is the fifth system of the five systems of project management presented in this book. It is not a stand-alone system. A scheduling activity derives from and is a close relative of the other four systems. If it is not, it is not an activity but an event, a milestone, or a timeline target, such as start or finish. An effective schedule is a combination of both activities and events.

In this book planning and scheduling are recommended to be done by computerized network planning, which may be CPM or PERT. In current usage both are seen to be one and the same, and are most often referred to as CPM/PERT or, simply, network. A network may be an arrow diagram, preferred for construction, but it is most often a precedence diagram. As networks are created and calculated by computer, this book is not a primer on manual calculations.

Networks are poor communication tools. The results of network planning and scheduling are invariably presented by bar or Gantt charts. Because of the ease of using bar charts, postmodern PC project management applications promote scheduling by bar charts. It must be recognized that bar charts do not have the power of networks as logical planning tools.

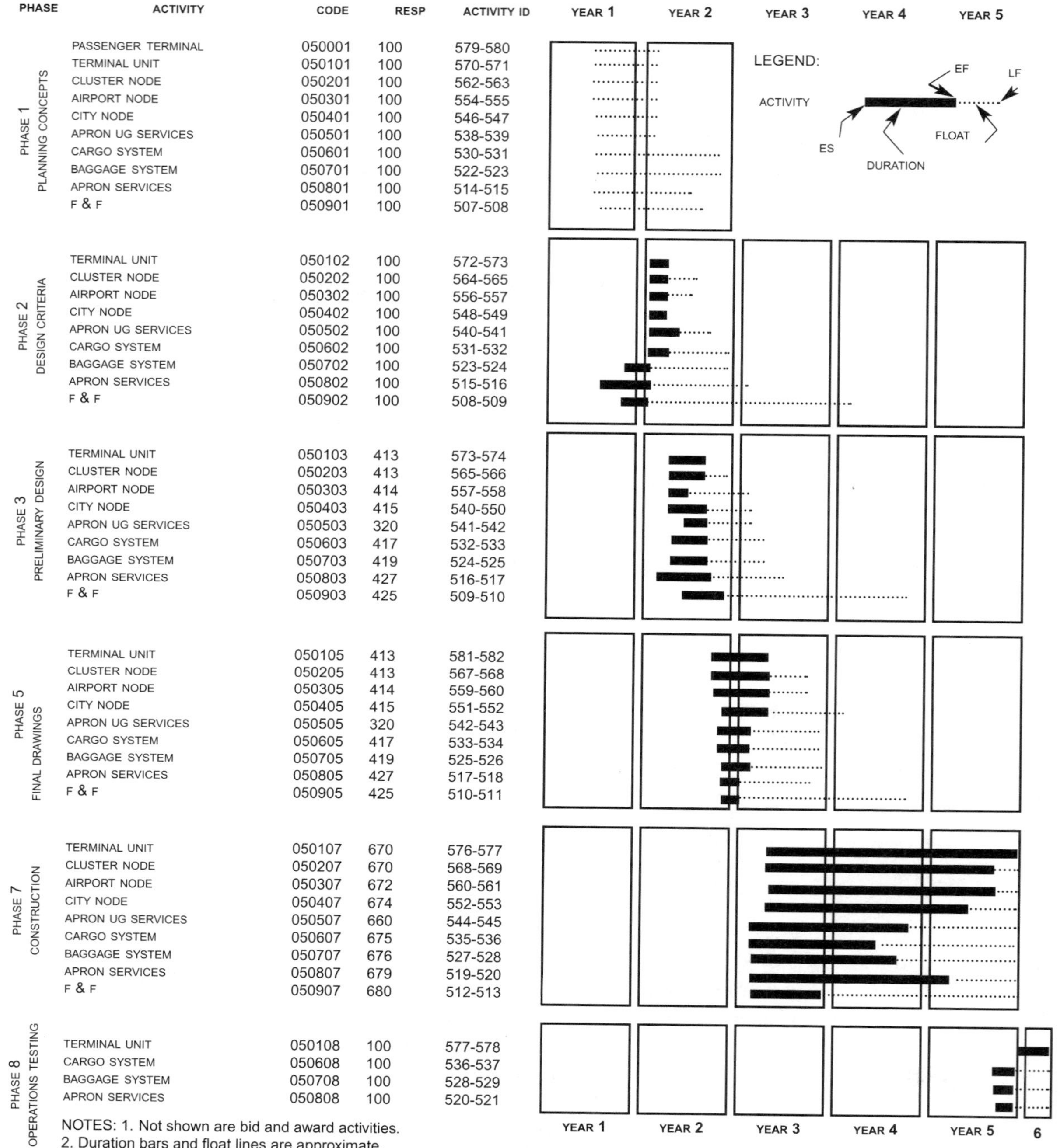

PHASE
ACTIVITY
CODE
RESP
ACTIVITY ID
YEAR 1
YEAR 2
YEAR 3
YEAR 4
YEAR 5
LEGEND:
ACTIVITY
ES
DURATION
EF
LF
FLOAT
PHASE 1 PLANNING CONCEPTS
PASSENGER TERMINAL 050001 100 579-580
TERMINAL UNIT 050101 100 570-571
CLUSTER NODE 050201 100 562-563
AIRPORT NODE 050301 100 554-555
CITY NODE 050401 100 546-547
APRON UG SERVICES 050501 100 538-539
CARGO SYSTEM 050601 100 530-531
BAGGAGE SYSTEM 050701 100 522-523
APRON SERVICES 050801 100 514-515
F & F 050901 100 507-508
PHASE 2 DESIGN CRITERIA
TERMINAL UNIT 050102 100 572-573
CLUSTER NODE 050202 100 564-565
AIRPORT NODE 050302 100 556-557
CITY NODE 050402 100 548-549
APRON UG SERVICES 050502 100 540-541
CARGO SYSTEM 050602 100 531-532
BAGGAGE SYSTEM 050702 100 523-524
APRON SERVICES 050802 100 515-516
F & F 050902 100 508-509
PHASE 3 PRELIMINARY DESIGN
TERMINAL UNIT 050103 413 573-574
CLUSTER NODE 050203 413 565-566
AIRPORT NODE 050303 414 557-558
CITY NODE 050403 415 540-550
APRON UG SERVICES 050503 320 541-542
CARGO SYSTEM 050603 417 532-533
BAGGAGE SYSTEM 050703 419 524-525
APRON SERVICES 050803 427 516-517
F & F 050903 425 509-510
PHASE 5 FINAL DRAWINGS
TERMINAL UNIT 050105 413 581-582
CLUSTER NODE 050205 413 567-568
AIRPORT NODE 050305 414 559-560
CITY NODE 050405 415 551-552
APRON UG SERVICES 050505 320 542-543
CARGO SYSTEM 050605 417 533-534
BAGGAGE SYSTEM 050705 419 525-526
APRON SERVICES 050805 427 517-518
F & F 050905 425 510-511
PHASE 7 CONSTRUCTION
TERMINAL UNIT 050107 670 576-577
CLUSTER NODE 050207 670 568-569
AIRPORT NODE 050307 672 560-561
CITY NODE 050407 674 552-553
APRON UG SERVICES 050507 660 544-545
CARGO SYSTEM 050607 675 535-536
BAGGAGE SYSTEM 050707 676 527-528
APRON SERVICES 050807 679 519-520
F & F 050907 680 512-513
PHASE 8 OPERATIONS TESTING
TERMINAL UNIT 050108 100 577-578
CARGO SYSTEM 050608 100 536-537
BAGGAGE SYSTEM 050708 100 528-529
APRON SERVICES 050808 100 520-521
YEAR 1
YEAR 2
YEAR 3
YEAR 4
YEAR 5
6
NOTES: 1. Not shown are bid and award activities.
2. Duration bars and float lines are approximate.
3. Start, finish dates are approximate.

FIGURE 6.13 AIRPORT PROJECT PASSENGER TERMINAL, BAR CHART. This is a bar chart of the cut of a large CPM scheduling network to show the application of project codes and scheduling values to activities created by the project management systems apporach.

REFERENCES

Ahuja, H. N., *Project Management, Techniques in Planning and Controlling Construction Projects* (Wiley, New York, 1984).

Antill, J. M., and R. W. Woodhead, *Critical Path Methods in Construction Practice,* 4th ed. (Wiley, New York, 1990).

Clough, R. H., and G. A. Sears, *Construction Project Management,* 3rd ed. (Wiley, New York, 1979).

Faulkner, *Project Management with CPM* (R. S. Means Co., Kingston, MA, 1973).

Fondahl, J. W., *A Non-Computer Approach to the Critical Path Method for the Construction Industry,* 2nd ed., (Stanford University, Stanford, CA, 1962).

Fondahl, J. W., *Methods for Extending the Range of Non-Computer Critical Path Applications* (Stanford University, Stanford, CA, 1962).

Horsley, W. F., *Means Scheduling Manual* (R. S. Means Co., Kingston, MA, 1981).

Iannone, A. L., *Management Program Planning and Control with PERT, MOST and LOB* (Prentice-Hall, Englewood Cliffs, NJ, 1967).

Kast, W. G., "Critical Path Planning," *Trans. Am. Assoc. of Cost Engineers* (San Francisco, CA, 1963).

Kerzner, H., *Project Management, a Systems Approach to Planning, Scheduling, and Controlling,* 3rd ed. (Van Nostrand Reinhold, New York, 1989, p. 337).

Mason, D., "The CPM Technique in Construction: A Critique," *Trans. Am. Assoc. of Cost Engineers* (*Proc. 8th Int. Cost Engineering Cong.,* Montreal, PQ, 1984).

Moder, J. J., and Phillips, *Project Management with CPM and PERT,* (Reinhold, New York, 1964).

O'Brien, J. J., Ed., *Scheduling Handbook* (McGraw-Hill, New York, 1969).

Prestige PC Release (4.1), (Artemis Management Systems, Boulder, CO, 1991).

Priluck, H. M., and P. M. Hourihan, *Practical CPM for Construction* (R. S. Means Co., Kingston, MA, 1968).

Primavera Project Planner 5.0 (Primavera Systems, Bala Cynwyd, PA, 1991).

Shiring, P. B., Jr., "Integration of Cost and Scheduling Systems", *Trans. Am. Assoc. of Cost Engineers* (Toronto, ON, 1981).

3100, 3200, 3300, Computer Systems PERT/COST Reference Manual (Control Data Corp., Palo Alto, CA, 1966).

Trauner, T. J. Jr., *Construction Delays, Documenting Causes, Winning Claims, Recovering Costs,* (R. S. Means Co., Kingston, MA, 1993).

Tyas, J. P. I., "Pertaining to PERT," Government of Canada, Ottawa, ON, 1971.

QUESTIONS AND EXERCISES

House Project

6.1. Prepare a CPM/PERT network of milestone events based on the project definition structure (PDS) of the house depicted in the exercises in Chapter 2. The target completion date is 50 weeks from the project start date of October 1, 2000.

Begin event.

Apply for funding.

Complete living conceptual drawings.

Complete grounds conceptual drawings.

Complete common areas concepts.

Prepare an appropriation-grade estimate.

6.2. Prepare a CPM/PERT network of activities based on the work breakdown structure (WBS) of the house depicted in the exercises in Chapter 3. Activities exist in the following stages:

Conceptual

Preliminary design

Final design and drawings

Construction
- Substructure
- Structure
- Exterior cladding
- Interior doors and partitions
- Vertical movement (stairs)
- Interior finishes
- Fittings and equipment
- Electrical
- Mechanical
- Construction soft costs

6.3. Apply the PDS, WBS, and OBS codes to each activity.

6.4. Apply the budget amount to each activity.

Airport Passenger Terminal Project

6.5. Convert the network in Fig. 6.12 into a precedence logic diagram. Assume one begin event as a predecessor to the multiple start events seen in Fig. 6.12. Assume one end event. Follow the logic sequences established in Fig. 6.12. Apply the PDS, WBS, and OBS codes and the durations from Fig. 6.12 to the new precedence diagram activities.

Download or obtain an available educational or commercial project management computer application, and process the network to prove the logic as you create it. The logic is proven when there is only one begin event, one end event, and tasks follow each other in a logical sequence. Assume the program default calendar for a 5-day, 40-hour workweek and apply the statutory holidays for your country, province, or state.

Develop a critical path based on the path that may be detected from the bar chart in Fig. 6.13. Create the following series of computer reports:

Only the critical path report

A report of all activities in ascending order of criticality

PDS code reports based on early starts and early finishes as well as bar charts

A WBS code report based on the ascending order of activity identifiers as well as bar charts

An OBS code report based on criticality as well as bar charts.

PART 3

CASE HISTORIES AND EXERCISES

CORPORATE ENGINEERING DEPARTMENT CASE HISTORY 7

7.1 Introduction

Traditionally corporate engineering departments are repeat project builders. They are the repository of project management skill and experience. Corporate engineers and project managers may not communicate project status adequately with top management and other functional and user departments because, in their eyes, the projects are their responsibility, and they have the authority to deliver them. User departments, on the other hand, are sometimes reluctant or do not have the time to provide information to the project engineers, and to make the decisions needed to launch and progress the project. These conditions often lead to slow projects, late projects, and poor-quality and overbudget projects.

In this case history, with many projects under way, the corporate engineering department president decided to break this cycle of poor communications and bad projects by ordering the development and implementation of a project control system that would inform him of the status of all projects. It is important to accept that the corporate engineering department had experienced engineers and managers who had delivered many successful projects. Computers were in use for accounting, design and engineering, drafting, and scheduling, but on an individual basis. And the systems were not generating the project-planning and status-reporting S curves that the chief engineer wanted.

The different sections in this chapter reflect the approach used for the progressive development of the project control system. First we need to learn what was in place, and how it must be used to achieve the aim of the project control system set by the chief engineer. At the same time we want to build the bridge between the systems of project management presented in the first six chapters of this book and this case history of a corporate engineering department. The student will see the reflection of the five systems of project management presented in Chapters 2 through 6 in the case that follows. If there are differences in terms here and there, this is normal in project work and in project management systems.

7.2 Foundation of the Project Control System

The corporate engineering department had in place a project delivery process comprising a cost code system which, although not stated as such, related to the work breakdown structure (WBS) concept of project phases, as discussed in earlier chapters. The project control system developer saw the cost code as a natural component of the project control system. The code had features that recognized project definition, tasks, packages, people skills, and the organizations that deliver the project.The cost code could be extended and used as a code for all project control purposes.

The bottom line was the recognition and adoption of the components in place as the foundation for the computerized project control system. This was achieved by first recognizing that the existing approach was based on five project control phases.

Five Project Phases

Project phases are the result of the application of the concept of the WBS, which in this case history identified five project phases. Each phase was responsible for a number of deliverables, that is, classes of products or work units, as seen in Fig. 7.1. The figure identifies 24 products or deliverables. For example, phase 2, Design, delivers drawings and specifications. Phase 4, Construction, delivers the typical facility elements, which in this case make up a process plant.

The names of the deliverables are important because they are not just subjective, randomly selected words. They are standard coded descriptions in this case history of a corporate engineering department.

To touch upon project complexity, the work of the individual phases is invariably overlapped. If overlapping is planned and scheduled, the process may be called "fast tracking." An example of fast tracking on a project is when the building architectural drawings may be under way as a phase 2 activity, whereas the building structure may be under construction as a phase 4 activity, while the air-conditioning system compressor is being prepurchased as a phase 3 activity.

In the lexicon of project control, WBS is a much used term. There is the idea that if one breaks down a project, one will automatically get project control. Nothing could be further from the truth. A breakdown structure is meaningless if the result is a subjective, stand-alone structure that does not have credibility and value beyond its author's office.

Project Objective

Many people who work on projects do apply the concept of WBS. Its application may not provide project control if the idea is not reflected in a formal project coding system. In this case history the unstated WBS concept was seen to be developed and used for project delivery work.

If Fig. 7.1 shows a table of phases, the concept may also be presented as a more typical WBS, as depicted in Fig. 7.2.

PROJECT CONTROL SYSTEM
FIVE PROJECT PHASES

PROJECT PHASES	DESCRIPTION	CLASS OF PRODUCTS, OR WORK UNITS	DELIVERABLE NO.
1	ASSESSMENT AND DEFINITION	Design Brief	1
		A.R. (Scope, Budget, Schedule)	2
2	DESIGN	Drawings	3
		Specifications	4
		Requisitions	5
		Bid Packages	6
		Construction Guidelines	7
		Hazard & Operability Reports	8
3	PROCUREMENT	Purchase Orders	9
		Contracts	10
		Shop Drawings	11
		Equipment & Supplies	12
		Labor & Materials	13
4	CONSTRUCTION	Civil Engineering Elements	14
		Building Elements	15
		Mechanical Equipment	16
		Piping	17
		Electrical	18
		Instrumentation	19
		Vessels	20
		Heat Transfer Equipment	21
		Other	22
5	STARTUP AND OPERATIONS	Startup	23
		Saleable Product	24

Notes:
1. Item 8 in phase 2, Hazard and Operability Studies, also occurs in phase 1 and phase 3.
2. The names in phase 4 are based on the construction cost code in place in the case history corporate engineering department.

Figure 7.1 Project Control System, Five Project Phases. An analysis of the corporate engineering department project procedures identified the 24 deliverables from the five classical phases depicted. The phases were formalized as the foundation of the computerized project control system, and the associated cost codes were promoted to project codes. The work units terminology is formal and tied to the project code.

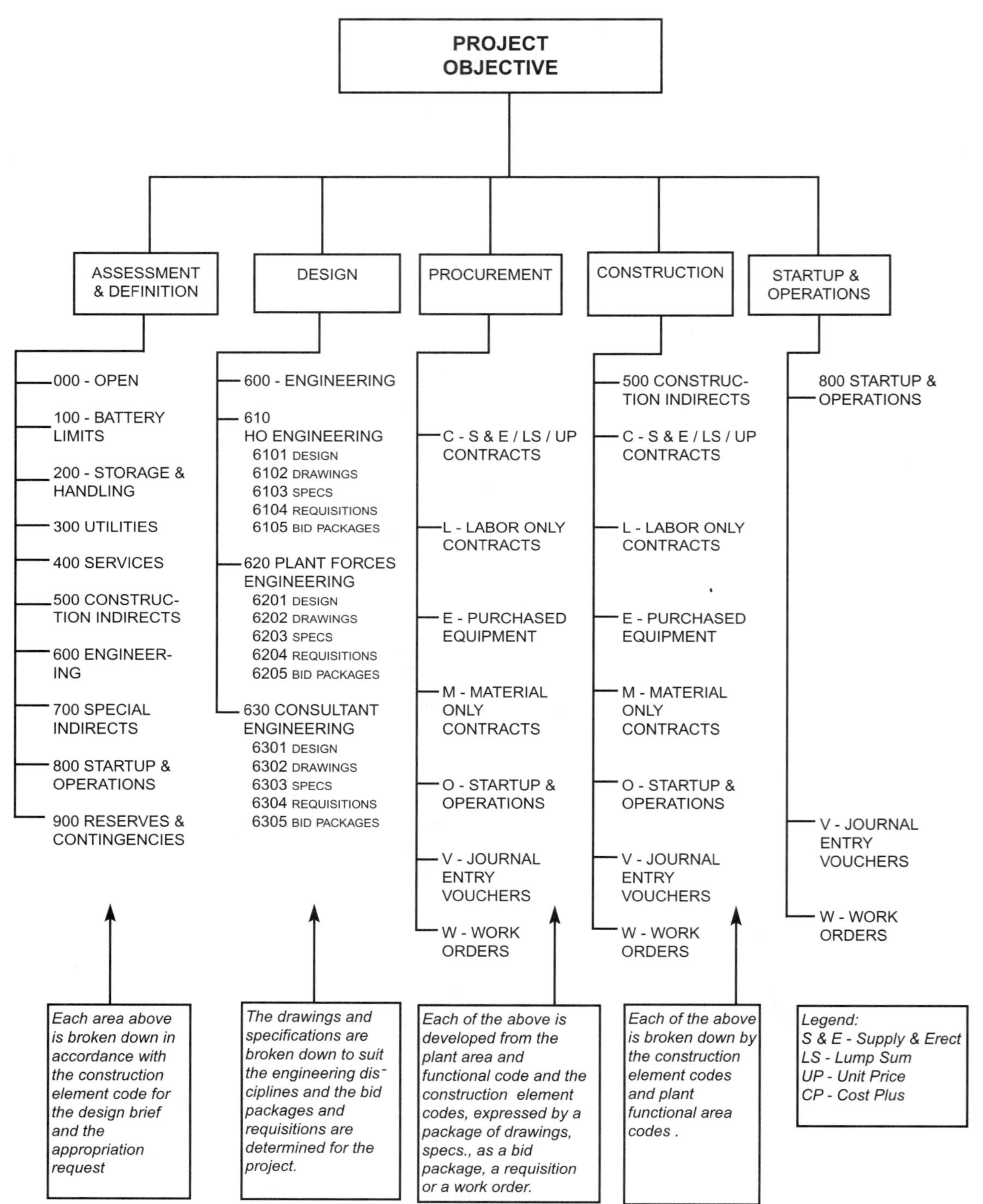

PROJECT OBJECTIVE
ASSESSMENT & DEFINITION
DESIGN
PROCUREMENT
CONSTRUCTION
STARTUP & OPERATIONS
000 - OPEN
100 - BATTERY LIMITS
200 - STORAGE & HANDLING
300 UTILITIES
400 SERVICES
500 CONSTRUCTION INDIRECTS
600 ENGINEERING
700 SPECIAL INDIRECTS
800 STARTUP & OPERATIONS
900 RESERVES & CONTINGENCIES
600 - ENGINEERING
610 HO ENGINEERING
6101 DESIGN
6102 DRAWINGS
6103 SPECS
6104 REQUISITIONS
6105 BID PACKAGES
620 PLANT FORCES ENGINEERING
6201 DESIGN
6202 DRAWINGS
6203 SPECS
6204 REQUISITIONS
6205 BID PACKAGES
630 CONSULTANT ENGINEERING
6301 DESIGN
6302 DRAWINGS
6303 SPECS
6304 REQUISITIONS
6305 BID PACKAGES
C - S & E / LS / UP CONTRACTS
L - LABOR ONLY CONTRACTS
E - PURCHASED EQUIPMENT
M - MATERIAL ONLY CONTRACTS
O - STARTUP & OPERATIONS
V - JOURNAL ENTRY VOUCHERS
W - WORK ORDERS
500 CONSTRUCTION INDIRECTS
C - S & E / LS / UP CONTRACTS
L - LABOR ONLY CONTRACTS
E - PURCHASED EQUIPMENT
M - MATERIAL ONLY CONTRACTS
O - STARTUP & OPERATIONS
V - JOURNAL ENTRY VOUCHERS
W - WORK ORDERS
800 STARTUP & OPERATIONS
V - JOURNAL ENTRY VOUCHERS
W - WORK ORDERS
Each area above is broken down in accordance with the construction element code for the design brief and the appropriation request
The drawings and specifications are broken down to suit the engineering disciplines and the bid packages and requisitions are determined for the project.
Each of the above is developed from the plant area and functional code and the construction element codes, expressed by a package of drawings, specs., as a bid package, a requisition or a work order.
Each of the above is broken down by the construction element codes and plant functional area codes .
Legend:
S & E - Supply & Erect
LS - Lump Sum
UP - Unit Price
CP - Cost Plus

Like most WBSs, the case history WBS is an imperfect instrument. It comprises five project phases:

1. Assessment & Definition
2. Design
3. Procurement
4. Construction
5. Startup & operation

The assessment and definition phase comprises 10 functional areas, including project consumables such as engineering and project reserves. In WBS parlance the 10 areas are said to be at level 3 of the WBS (with the project objective at level 1 and the phases themselves at level 2).

The design phase shows engineering at level 3, broken down as three coded engineering organizations at what may be called level 4. The procurement and construction phases are similarly broken down at level 3 of the structure. The startup and operations phase shows code 800 at level 3, broken down into services carried out by operations workforces, coded V, Journal Entry Vouchers, and W, Work Orders, at level 4.

Why is the case history WBS imperfect? The design phase is only broken down into engineering and perhaps could be called "engineering" instead of introducing a phase called "design" and then only breaking it down into engineering. Also, under Assessment & Definition, area 600, Engineering, exists to measure not only engineering, but also design. Furthermore, under Assessment & Definition there are two areas for indirect accounts: 500, Construction Indirects, and 700, Special Indirects.

The boxed notes at the bottoms of the phases in Fig. 7.2 state that the functional areas under Assessment & Definition, the bid packages under Procurement, and the contracts under Construction are broken down and coded as construction elements.

The basis for coding the construction elements as well as the project areas, functions, and subfunctions is seen as a generic cost code in Fig. 7.3. Although the alphanumeric code characters in Figs. 7.2 and 7.3 are based on the present case history, the code concept discussed in Section 3.5 is widely utilized by cost engineers and is applicable to all kinds of projects.

The application and use of the structures and codes as integral parts of the computerized project management system developed for the case history of the corporate engineering department will be illustrated further in this chapter.

◄

Figure 7.2 Corporate Engineering Department Project Control Structure. The procedures in the case history were recognizable as WBS phases, as may be seen in this figure. There is a cost code system tied to the procedures. Further, they can facilitate other project structures such as PDSs, WBSs, and OBSs, and the cost code becomes the project code. The legends in the boxes describe the intent and result of each vertical breakdown.

CORPORATE ENGINEERING PROJECT COST CODE

PLANT AREA AND FUNCTION CODE **XXX**			CONSTRUCTION ELEMENT CODE **XXXX**		COST SOURCE **A**	SUB-SOURCE **SSSSSSSSSSS**
AREA **X**	**FUNCTION** **X**	**SUB-FUNCTION** **X**	**ELEMENT GROUP** **X**	**SPECIFIC ELEMENT** **XXX**	**TYPE OF SOURCE** **A**	**PURCHASE ORDER, OR CONTRACT, ETC.** **SSSSSSSSSSS**
0 OPEN **1** BATTERY LIMITS **2** STORAGE AND HANDLING **3** UTILITIES **4** SERVICES **5** OPEN **6** OPEN **7** OPEN **8** OPEN **9** RESERVES	**0** TO **9** TO BE USED TO IDENTIFY FUNCTION CODE	**0** TO **9** TO BE USED TO IDENTIFY SUBFUNCTION CODE	**0000** TO **0999** **1000** TO **1999** **2000** TO **2999** **3000** TO **3999** **4000** TO **4999** **5000** TO **5999** **6000** TO **6999** **7000** TO **7999** **8000** TO **8599** **8600** TO **8799** **8800** TO **8899** **8900** TO **8999** **9000 TO 9099** **9100 TO 9199** **9200 TO 9299** **9300 TO 9399** **9400 TO 9499** **9500 TO 9599** **9600 TO 9699** **9700 TO 9799** **9800 TO 9899** **9900 TO 9999**	VESSELS HEAT TRFR. EQUIPMENT MECHANICAL EQUIPMENT BUILDINGS CIVIL WORKS ELECTRICAL INSTRUMENTATION PIPING PROTECTIVE COVERING SVCE. & MTCE. EQUPMNT. CATALYSTS & CHEMICALS SPECIAL DIRECTS PROJECT MANAGEMENT TEMPORARY FACILITIES TEMPORARY SERVICES OPEN OPEN OPEN OPEN OPEN OPEN RESERVES /CONTINGENCIES	**C** - S& E / LS / UPSET PRICE CONTRACTS **L** - LABOR ONLY COST PLUS CONTRACTS **E** - PURCHASED EQUIPMENT **M** - MATERIAL ONLY COST PLUS CONTRACTS **O** - STARTUP & OPERATIONS	**S** - CONTRACT NOS. **S** - PURCHASE ORDER NOS. **S** - INTERNAL CHARGES **S** - CHANGE ORDERS (ANY COMBINATION OF UP TO 11 ALPHANUMERIC & SPECIAL CHARACTERS)

Legend:
"X" - Numeric character
"A" - Alpha character
"S" - Alphanumeric or special character

FIGURE 7.3 CORPORATE ENGINEERING DEPARTMENT PROJECT COST CODES. The corporate engineering department had in place the above project cost code system. As seen in the previous figures, the codes were tied to project phases, and then related and promoted to project structures and project codes. The importance of structures and codes for project management is discussed in Chapters 1 through 6.

7.3 Introductory and Input Sessions

This large corporate engineering department has a long tradition of planning, designing, engineering, procuring, constructing, and starting up new process plants and retrofitting existing plants in the chemical and petrochemical product field. Many processes are complex and hazardous, requiring a high degree of engineering and the procurement of specialized process and manufacturing equipment.

The work is handled by experienced designers and specialized project, process, and discipline engineers. New product lines are particularly difficult as the process may be understood only by its inventor, but the facility must be designed and built by the experienced project managers, engineers, and project support staff. Often there are many projects under way at the same time, with project teams using different project management approaches. They all compete for their share of corporate and departmental resources and services.

Top corporate management is looking for a project control system to inform them on the status of all projects. If the project status is known, top management can take timely steps to solve any problems that might surface.

To put in place a project control system requires that corporate management understand the kinds of problems that plague the delivery of projects. What became quickly apparent to the control system designers is that for corporate management to get this kind of a system, the system first must have the capability to help the project participants in their work. While top management wants a control system, the project people are in need of tools to help deliver their work. The control system needs to benefit the project people in terms of helping them do better work, improve their productivity, keep them coordinated and informed, and in the process provide corporate management with the project information that they need.

A key precept in the development and implementation of a project control system is that the development of such a system be not a stand-alone event. Even the introduction of a relatively simple tool such as a personal computer (PC)-based scheduling system may lead to concern and fear on the part of the people whose work will now be scheduled by computer.

Any effort by corporate management to impose control measures by computer systems must eventually lead to the development of systems that act as work tools for the individuals and functions that the corporation wishes to "control." The computer-based project management systems, for example, must therefore become the tool of the people doing the work. Since the expectation is that productivity will be improved by the new tool or system, management will be on the way to better control through higher productivity.

An attempt to develop a project control system must incorporate the systems and procedures already in place. This is not to say that you computerize only what is in place, but the new system should include the procedures and practices that have worked in the past and that need to be available for future projects, albeit as part of the new systems approach. There is no "magic bullet" in project management systems. Although prior to the systems initiatives, projects were delivered by professional project managers and by project and discipline engineers using personalized project management techniques, it is these same people who will deliver the jobs in the future. Now there will be a system in place as a tool to help them in their work, and to inform other corporate functions of their project input, impact, and status. At the same time the system acts to inform corporate management, which at the outset was the sole reason for the system.

The scene is thus set like this:

- The corporation is a repeat builder of projects.
- The corporation needs to monitor and better control project work, as the current procedures for monitoring and reporting are not informing corporate manage-

ment adequately. Clients are unhappy with the quality of the projects, costs are more often than not over budget, and schedules are not being met.

• A system of project control is proposed. Corporate management appoints the system facilitators and designers, who call in and inform all project participants of the need for a system, explain why a system is needed, and ask participants what they want from such a system, what their concerns are, and so on.

• The approach used is a series of kick-off introductory and input meetings with small groups of project participants. The groups often comprise different disciplines and skills, which creates opportunities for cross-fertilization.

Meetings Are Called

Up to about this point in time, corporate engineering department staff may have heard that senior management is contemplating the development and implementation of a system to manage future projects. The various section managers have been kept informed by senior management, and they have heard from the systems facilitators and designers that a new project control system is being contemplated. The section managers have informed their people, and the facilitators and designers are now going around assessing the diverse and stand-alone systems that are in place.

This approach has led to a working paper which states the corporate objectives, discusses the shortfall in the current environment, and proposes the new systems concept, as follows:

• The largely manual and personalized systems to control projects and services are inadequate to carry out the modern departmental mandate.

• The new departmental computer-aided project control systems are being designed to improve productivity; to provide management with information to control the cost, schedule, quality, and scope of work; to facilitate and speed up more accurate transfer of accounting, capital cost, and accounts payable data; to convert engineering information into a database for management and business information; to create estimating and budgeting files of easily accessible current information; and, generally, to integrate project engineers and discipline engineers through a system designed to help them meet project objectives of cost, quality, scope, and schedule.

Using the series of discussion and working papers and the stated objectives as guidelines, the purpose of the meetings may be outlined as follows:

• The discussion and working papers have been circulated and we have an idea as to the intent of the new system.

• The system objectives have been stated and agreed to by senior management, project management, and section managers.

• Essentially, senior management requires project information that is not being made available by the current way of operation. Senior management understands that control systems do not carry out projects. Professional people and skilled designers and discipline engineers are responsible for the delivery of high-quality projects. The new computerized system is seen as a tool for use by the project delivery teams and will aid them in doing better projects. At the same time the system will be capable of providing project information to all levels of project and corporate management.

• The system operators will be the project managers, designers, engineers and project support staff. There is no intention of creating a systems information department, except for the personnel responsible for the design, development, and smooth operation of the computer hardware, communication linkages, and the software that makes it all possible. It is not expected that the project participants will send their work for processing anywhere. In essence the work will be processed as each individual does it, but the results of this work will flow to other team members as well as to a reporting function for project, senior, and corporate management.

• Since this is a systems development and implementation exercise, there is not really any impact on the engineering department organization. The system is designed to be flexible, so that it responds to different organizational structures.

• The project control system is not seen as one large system, but the integration of a number of systems. Each system is designed to operate in its own area, but they are supportive of each other.

After the tone for the meetings, objectives, and roles had been set and the shortcomings in the old approach discussed, the groups were introduced to the system components and expectations, in the following order.

Project Definition

Of all the complaints about problems with the old approach to doing project work, the most consistent one was about the lack of a means to define the project. There was no systematic way to do it. This missing link in project management was identified very early in the investigations and put forth as a key feature of the new system. Its purpose, objectives, and uses were seen to be along the following lines:

• Project definition is seen as a new system.

• A principal feature of project definition is the establishment of a project scope.

• Project definition will set the project code of accounts.

• Project definition is driven by phases, which are developed through breakdown structures.

• The making of a project definition structure (PDS) is facilitated with a team think-tank approach or brain-storming session, where the project team develops project units, and discipline work units, thereby scoping the work.

• Under the old approach many of these steps and exercises were carried out, but not necessarily widely disseminated to project team members. Under the new project control system the system would have the capability to set up the project definition, change it, update it, and maintain it as a central recording device.

• The project engineer would be the custodian of the PDS.

• The code of accounts or code breakdown would be an important part of the PDS.

Cost Estimating and Cost Control

In the discussions during the introductory and input sessions cost estimating was seen as one of the more mature systems in this case history. There were a number of techniques used to forecast project cost, based on applying parameters of similar projects as well as the use of as-built cost figures. To put estimating and cost control in the context of the new systems of project management, the following points were highlighted:

• If cost estimating is seen as a mature discipline, cost control is less so. There is a particular need to tie together early project scope definition with cost.

• The new systems approach will stress earlier front-end definition and design phase cost control.

• The corporate engineering department in this case history had in place a well-understood and widely used cost code, or code of accounts system. It was expected that the cost code would be an integral part of the new system. The PDS and the WBS are expected to follow closely the code system in place.

• There was, however, a need seen to separate the accounting function from the cost control activity. The main problem was that accounting information was always behind project status. For example, an engineering department purchase requisition was in fact a project commitment. But accounting would not pick it up as a commitment until a purchase order was issued. This made accounting reports late, and not representative of the status of the project cost.

Planning and Scheduling Control

• Planning and scheduling are seen as very important to many of the systems, for example, to project definition. The brain-storming or think-tank approach, wherein a multidisciplinary team conceptualizes the project definition as a series of functions, elements, activities, and constraints, in the process of creating documentation that looks like a precedence diagram, may be the basis for the project plan and schedule.

• It was recognized by the new system designers that planning and scheduling activities are to be tied closely to the work units developed from project definition. The concept is that the unit of work to develop a project function is to be suitable for its scope control, cost control, and schedule control. The glue that binds them together is the code of accounts.

• Planning and scheduling is to be computer driven. Planning is to be based on pure logic, that is, the critical path method (CPM) or the program evaluation and review technique (PERT) precedence diagramming method, coupled with the practicalities of "drop dead" dates, firm milestones, and event dates set by management decisions.

• Project schedules are to be dynamic and flexible, but within the parameters of fixed milestones and committed completion dates.

Accounting

The corporate engineering department had its own accounting section. The accounting section produced engineering time analysis reports and after-the-fact project expenditure reports. The time analysis reports were produced monthly and the information was up to 6 weeks old when it reached the project managers. Project expenditures such as time charges, major and minor purchases, and travel expenses were sometimes up to 8 weeks old when transmitted to project managers through the old system.

The accounting codes used to accumulate engineering expenditures were not directly relatable to those used to control project engineering costs. The accounting system was bulky and difficult to read as it had no exception reporting features.

The new system would look to resolve these shortcomings and provide project management with new information including:

- Cash flows
- Target costs
- Exception reporting
- Coded cost information for project management

Human Resources Allocation and Leveling

This topic was introduced as a new system. Previously there was no systems approach to allocate, level, and monitor the assignment of people to projects. The departmental resources stayed fairly constant. People would be added as projects were initiated. But there was inevitable conflict as projects competed for resources. The objectives of the new system were discussed along the following lines:

• It would be designed to provide data on human resources requirements based on known, existing jobs; to provide engineering service on demand to corporate operational divisions, the department's "clients"; and to be able to allocate human resources for new business, generated by new projects.

• For the system to be able to handle these requirements, the first order of business would be to develop a new, improved human resources coding system.

• To be able to schedule and level human resources requires that the human resources coding system be integrated with the planning and scheduling system.

Procurement

Modern project management changes the old concept of purchasing by casting it in the middle of the engineer–procure–construct project delivery mode. There are three principal areas of change that must be picked up by the project control system:

• Modern procurement is considered to be an integral part of a seamless design and construction process. As overlapping of the process causes difficulties in cost control, schedule control, and scope control, the procurement function influences the project delivery process and needs to be integrated.

• Procurement control is difficult because it crosses many departmental, functional, and discipline lines before, during, and after the writing and issuance of an engineering requisition and the placement of a purchase order.

• Any system of project management must incorporate procurement control for scope and schedule control.

Materials Control

Materials control is an important issue in project work, and in this case was seen as requiring its own control system as part of the systems of project management. The topic was presented along the following lines:

• Materials control is different from procurement in that it starts long before procurement is initiated, and it continues into and after delivery as well as during installation and, indeed, startup.

• A project materials control system is seen to comprise these main elements of material takeoff by:

Drawings
Startup system
Purchase order
Bid package
Equipment number
Inspection system
Expediting system by purchase order
Expediting system by startup system

• The concept of materials control is to ensure that it is not overlooked from the earliest through the last phase of project work. Procurement, on the other hand, ensures its assignment to a vendor, after competitive bidding or other consideration such as sole sourcing.

Disciplinary Technical Programs

All planning, design, and engineering disciplines have their own computer programs. In a corporate engineering department these application programs do civil engineering, architectural planning, building engineering, design, drawings, process piping, instrumentation, and so on.

The issue in the development and implementation of a project control system is to ensure that the application programs relate to and tie into the systems of project management. This is to be done through the assimilation and widespread usage of project definition codes, work breakdown codes, organizational codes, account codes, cost codes, and resource codes in project and corporate databases.

Project Control Graphics

Senior corporate management as a rule has no time to read reports. It was decreed early in the development phase that the system must deliver computer graphics that accurately reflect the project status in some of the following forms:

- S curves
- Trend curves
- Productivity curves
- Bar charts
- Planning networks

The objective of the project control system is that based on high-quality human input, these requirements would be produced by computer systems.

Corporate Systems Tie-In

A corporate engineering department works for all the corporate divisions requiring expanded or new facilities. At the same time it is subject to corporate accounting, depreciation, financial, legal, and other rules and regulations. As a result the project control system needs to be able to communicate with and accommodate the systems in effect in corporate headquarters and in other divisions. As the divisions and headquarters are in effect clients of the project managers and engineers, being able to satisfy their requirements is not taken lightly.

As the delivery of a project depends on the availability of information that is specific to project management needs, it was clear that the system first and foremost had to control projects. At the same time it was to be a part of and tied into the corporate systems.

7.4 Summary of Input

The introductory and input sessions in Section 7.3 evolved into a summary of the main features and attributes that project participants would look for in the project control system. From these discussions, project control is seen as an integrator of traditional corporate functions, such as accounting and procurement, with new features, such as a system of project definition, planning, and scheduling and the use of computer graphics for management information and reporting.

The recurring theme from these discussions is that there is no one stand-alone control system. A project control system is nothing if not an integrator of information that drives functions and activities. It was seen that the new system must become a part of the company culture when it comes to project work, influencing and being influenced by the methods and procedures already in place. The difference now is that the computerized system captures the information and disseminates it faster and better to those who need to know.

The following is a summary of the project control system user inputs, as well as their concerns and fears concerning the elements of the systems of project management identified in Section 7.3.

Project Definition (Scope and Quality)

- Project engineers consider that a system of project definition could lead to too rigid an approach. They fear that it could stifle freedom and flexibility.

- There is a concern by project engineers that there is never enough time to develop and define the scope of a project before having to get on with it.

- Would all jobs have to be entered into the system?

- Discipline engineers consider it essential that projects be defined better (than in the past) and sooner.

- A fear of both design engineers and project engineers is that the integration factor, inherent in a system, will take away responsibility from people and vest it in the system operators, or in the system itself.

- People expressed a fear that every little design change would have to be plugged in.

- It was proposed by the designers, discipline engineers, and support groups that the custodian of the project definition system would be the project engineer.

- The discussions pertaining to a system of project definition uncovered misunderstandings between the various groups as to the meaning of widely used engineering department terms, such as "design brief" and "memo to accompany an appropriation request (AR)." (A design brief is a definitive statement of the project before it goes from a concept to design and engineering. A memo to accompany an AR is sometimes similar to a design brief. It may be less definitive in those cases when a rush AR is in the works.)

- There is a consensus that the most difficult job in project work is controlling the scope of the project.

- In a corporate engineering department service advice and consulting form a large part of the workload. Advice is provided freely to "old" clients and potential new "customers." How would this kind of work be entered into the system? At what point in providing advice would the advice be converted into a project?

It was thought that a system would tend to impose controls on the way services are provided.

• In project work, drawings are the main technical communication tool. As the design progresses from concept to feasibility to preliminary drawings, the information needs to flow from the designers to the discipline engineers. Discipline engineers complained that they were often working with obsolete arrangement drawings.

• Design and engineering are seen by many of the practitioners as proprietary and, in some ways, mysterious. The fear was that if early project information is "published," it somehow loses its professionalism.

• A main concern in all project work is change. The question for the system designers is, how would the system handle "168 design changes," which is exactly what happened on a recent job.

• The early project stages are the most confusing in that the project is not adequately defined. There is an information gap between the project users, the project leaders, and the engineering disciplines. The feasibility has not yet been proven, and the project codes are uncertain. In general, how will a system resolve these conundrums?

Cost Estimating and Cost Control

• Estimates for a project appropriation request are now prepared without reference to the discipline engineers and the support groups. If it is intended that groups will work according to budgets, will they be given an opportunity for input to the budgets?

• The single biggest problem in the preparation of estimates is defining the scope of the job.

• Site resident engineers often make field changes, which lead to increased costs, without consulting the project engineer back in corporate engineering. The point is: who is responsible for project cost?

• It should be made mandatory to reestimate jobs frequently in the early project stages and at least when design engineering is about 60% completed.

• A cost control system should receive top priority in the development of a project control system.

• In high-quality project work the most important aspect is scope control according to some project engineers. They say, once the project scope is set, forget cost.

• Cost control needs to be more closely tied to project planning and schedule control.

• Cost control reporting should be separated from accounting (expenditure) reporting.

• Some discipline engineers wish to make their own estimates; more time is needed to evaluate bids when they come in over budget; a tax exemption system is needed. More cost breakdown information is desirable from lump sum contract bids, which are not forthcoming under the current system.

Planning and Schedule Control

• A planning and schedule control system should receive top priority in the project control system development work.

• A better handle is needed on scheduling design engineering and the production of drawings.

• Planning and scheduling need to be integrated with cost estimating and cost control for project management purposes. At the same time, many project managers and project engineers consider that cost activities and schedule activities are not relatable.

• Planning networks should be based on CPM. Once plans and schedules are made, it is important that they be updated to reflect job status and progress.

Human Resources Allocation and Leveling

The input from both project engineers and discipline engineers indicated that human resources would be in three main categories: (1) consulting services, (2) projects, and (3) new business.

• Under consulting services some of the department's capability goes into providing advice to operating divisions, giving "snap" estimates, participating in feasibility studies, and generally being available as a corporate in-house resource. The engineers consider that it was not possible to plan and schedule this service work. Generally the thinking was that this work forms the basis for the department's existence. The question is, how would this activity fit in with a project control system which as a fundamental rule requires the allocation of human resources.

• Formal studies and projects may require dedicated multidisciplinary teams for long periods of time. In these cases human resources requirements would need to be identified well into the future.

• New business would need to be identified in terms of future human resources needs. The human resources would be classified by discipline and allocated to future project and consulting service work.

• In dealing with the human resources question for project work the burning question is how many people with what kind of skills are needed when. The answer is doubly confusing in that the scope of projects is very difficult to define, particularly in the early stages when the corporation is most pressed to know how soon and how much. And, the usual response is too much and not soon enough.

Accounting

• A main weakness in the old system is that it provides unfiltered information on the basis of account codes. It does not have the capability to provide cost information by contracts and purchase orders.

• The new system should be able to track commitments and expenditures as well as providing cost control information. Important elements of cost control are commitment amounts on purchase orders and contracts as compared to expenditure amounts to date.

• An engineering department project is subject to input and influences from other corporate functions, such as corporate accounting. For timely cost and expenditure control, project accounting and corporate accounting will need to be integrated.

• A problem on corporate projects is that of charges being rung up to a project by "unknown persons."

Procurement

The project leaders and project engineers cited the following information needs with regard to purchase orders (POs) as a way to improve procurement:

- By PO numbers
- By PO vendor name, number
- By PO value
- By contract and account code
- By materials control system

Materials Control

Besides information control, the other main insufficiency in project work is the timely availability of materials and equipment. A materials control system is seen as an essential feature of a project control system, as may be seen from the following input:

• In the development of any project control system, a materials control system should receive top priority.

• Quantity takeoffs of materials and equipment are very important for successful projects. The new system must be capable of both bulk takeoffs and detailed takeoffs.

• The materials control system needs to be able to control project materials on the following basis:

Drawings
Startup systems
Purchase orders
Bid packages
Equipment

• Inspection (quality control) needs to be a part of the materials control system.

• Expediting should be formalized under the materials control system and have capability to provide information sorted by purchase orders and startup systems.

• A materials control system would inevitably be tied to a labor estimating system and eventually form the basis for an estimating system.

• As materials control is a new system, it needs a "home." Who would be the custodian of the materials control system?

• In corporate project work, the construction phase is often delivered under a lump sum contract arrangement. The question for the corporate engineers is at what point does materials control stop for those projects that may go this route.

• As projects become more technically complex, and are tied to specific preengineered equipment and systems, it is often necessary to preorder components. This requires that materials control start earlier in the project life cycle.

• Projects are more and more comprised of equipment, systems, components, and materials from diverse sites. Design engineering is handled at the head office or in consultants' offices, with equipment installation at the site. The system thus needs comprehensive communication links.

Disciplinary Technical Programs

Designers, specialists, consultants, manufacturers, vendors, engineers, and architects invariably create or have created for them their own computer-aided design (CAD) and manufacturing (CAM) packages. This was the situation within the corporate engineering department of this case history. And the burning question was, would the disciplines keep their own systems, or would these systems become a part of the project control system.

• Who would be the custodian of the disciplinary technical programs?

• How many technical programs were out there?

• At what point does a disciplinary technical program become a material control program, and when does it tie into the project control system?

None of these questions were answered at the input sessions.

Project Control Graphics

It was known to the project managers and engineers that senior management wished to be informed, and thereby control projects through graphics. The input was split about equally as follows:

- Project graphics are not useful for project control purposes.
- Of all project control graphics, the S curve is the most useful.
- Some said, the graphics should have the lowest priority.
- Some wanted graphics to have a top priority.

Corporate Systems Tie-In

In a large corporation or a government agency, even small projects are impacted by many groups, departments, and divisions. A project control system needs to be able to relate to all of these other interests, inputs, and information needs if it is to be effective, indeed if it is to survive. In the narrowest sense, these other concerns may involve:

- Operating division systems for maintenance, statutory inspections, capital and operating spare parts, cost, and progress reports
- Corporate and divisional fixed assets systems
- Functional, area, equipment, and elemental numbering systems used for design, development, and control.

7.5 System Development Graphics

Systems more often than not are designed after the fact, that is, work is done with the tools at hand until a better tool, or a new system, is introduced. The usual approach is to take what is prosaically referred to as a manual procedure and computerize it. This approach may lead to computerizing inefficient and unproductive methods. Second, it may be that the existing procedures may not be able to provide the systems control information expected by senior management.

In the development of the project control system for this case history, it was agreed early that the system would act first as a tool for the project management and design functions, and that they would be the custodians and operators of the system. Second the system would have the capability to provide senior management with the control information not otherwise previously available. This was not necessarily evident at the beginning of the process, but evolved through the introductory and input sessions, with senior management becoming convinced of the validity of this approach in the process.

The process of computer control system design involves taking the work of individual and workgroup skillsets, identifying information interdependencies, needs, and conflicts, and illustrating the flows of information through graphics and reports. In some respects it is a top-down process, meaning that the system developer needs to know what the final result should be, what is needed in the process, and what parts of the process can be delivered by computer hardware and software configurations.

Project Control System Overview

One of the earliest system graphics for this case history is Fig. 7.4. Although the assignment is to develop a project control system for the corporate engineering department, the implications of the exercise will reverberate throughout the corporation. The intent is not only to ensure that the system will be effective in the narrowest sense

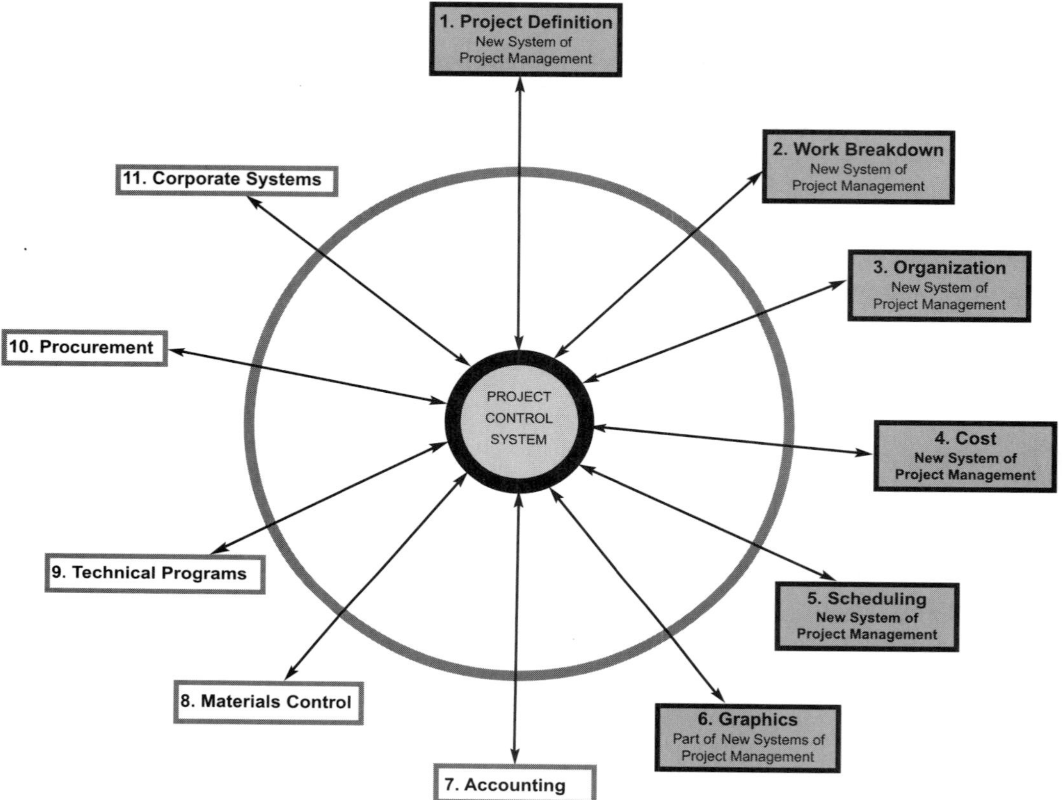

FIGURE 7.4 CORPORATE ENGINEERING DEPARTMENT PROJECT CONTROL SYSTEM. This graphic illustrates the statement that a project control system is not a stand-alone system. Other corporate systems are shown tying into project control, and project control feeds other corporate information needs.

for project control purposes, but to give it credibility in other departments who may impact the project work, or whose activities or functions may in turn be impacted by the work of the project.

Figure 7.4 is drawn as a circle with individual systems emanating from it and feeding into it, as depicted by the two-way arrows. This diagram is neither an organizational structure nor a work breakdown. Its purpose is to show the possible effect on and the implications for an organization's undertaking to design and implement a project control system. Some or all of the connections and impacts may occur, whether or not planned, in any control system development undertaking. In this case history the impacts were recognized and developed as part of the system, which would make for a broad-based and comprehensive project control system. The alternative approach is a narrow-cast system in which few if any functions or impacts outside of the project engineering sphere of influence are recognized and included.

Project Control System and Subsystems

If Fig. 7.4 is an overview of the project control systems at the highest level, each of the systems in its turn is a wrap-up of a number of systems or subsystems, as may be seen in Fig. 7.5. At best a graphic such as this aims to depict information flows and dependencies that go beyond the immediate project team. Very few projects are totally stand alone. Accordingly it is more effective to recognize and make allowances for all the inputs and impacts that go into the makeup of any project, as depicted by these two systems graphics.

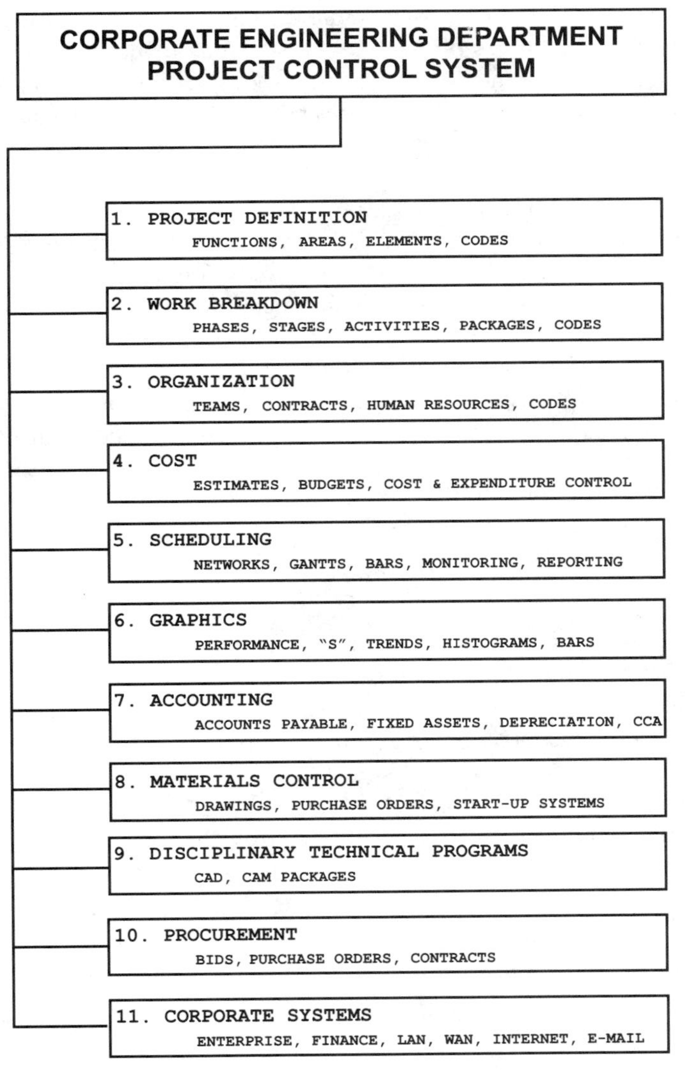

FIGURE 7.5 CORPORATE ENGINEERING DEPARTMENT PROJECT CONTROL SYSTEM AND SUBSYSTEMS. A project control system is dependent on a range of management, corporate, and engineering systems and subsystems as depicted. Very few of the systems are proprietary to the project team running the project control system. But without linkages between the project control system and the disciplinary and corporate systems, project control would not be possible.

Project Control System Summary Data

The development of a project control system involves the compilation of the old, the new, and a combination of the two as a system. The system brings a new dimension into the picture. The new dimension consists of the computer's capability to process old information in a new way, retain agreed and approved corporate and project information, and use it as the base for data to progress project work. A depiction of the process linking the old as input with the new as the database resident on a computer, and the result as information output, may be seen in Fig. 7.6.

Project Control Database System

The development of a project control system requires that the human activities of the project be interfaced with computer processors. The processors may be desktop PCs for immediate input and information, or the PCs may be in communication with mainframes, client/server arrangements, the Internet, wide-area networks, or local-area networks. In this case the development of the human/computer interfaces created the linkages seen in Fig. 7.7.

Figure 7.7 shows an overall database comprising two main sectors: Engineering Cost Control driven by activity codes and Project Expenditure and Cost Control driven by project codes. The rest of the graphic depicts two types of information needs, immediate and nonimmediate. The computer systems are meant to depict a distributed computing system comprising large-volume processing in a central location, and subsets of database information for immediate processing.

Information is delivered in two ways: on screen and as hard copy reports.

It will be seen that in this case the concept of project management and control became vested in the two systems shown at the top of the database in Fig. 7.7—Engineering Cost Control (ECCO) and Project Expenditure and Cost Control (PECCO) and their respective activity and project codes.

Project Database

A project control system is largely dependent on the development and faithful maintenance of the database of information that is used for project management and control purposes. The concept for the project database maintenance system for the case history is depicted in Fig. 7.8. The names and descriptions introduced in Fig. 7.8 are defined as follows:

EMPLOYEE	Departmental employee who is preapproved to charge time and expenses to a job or project.
JOB	Departmental work or project that has been assigned a job number in the system, and to which employees may charge time and expenses.
ACT	Short for activity. Activities are defined and coded, as will be seen later.

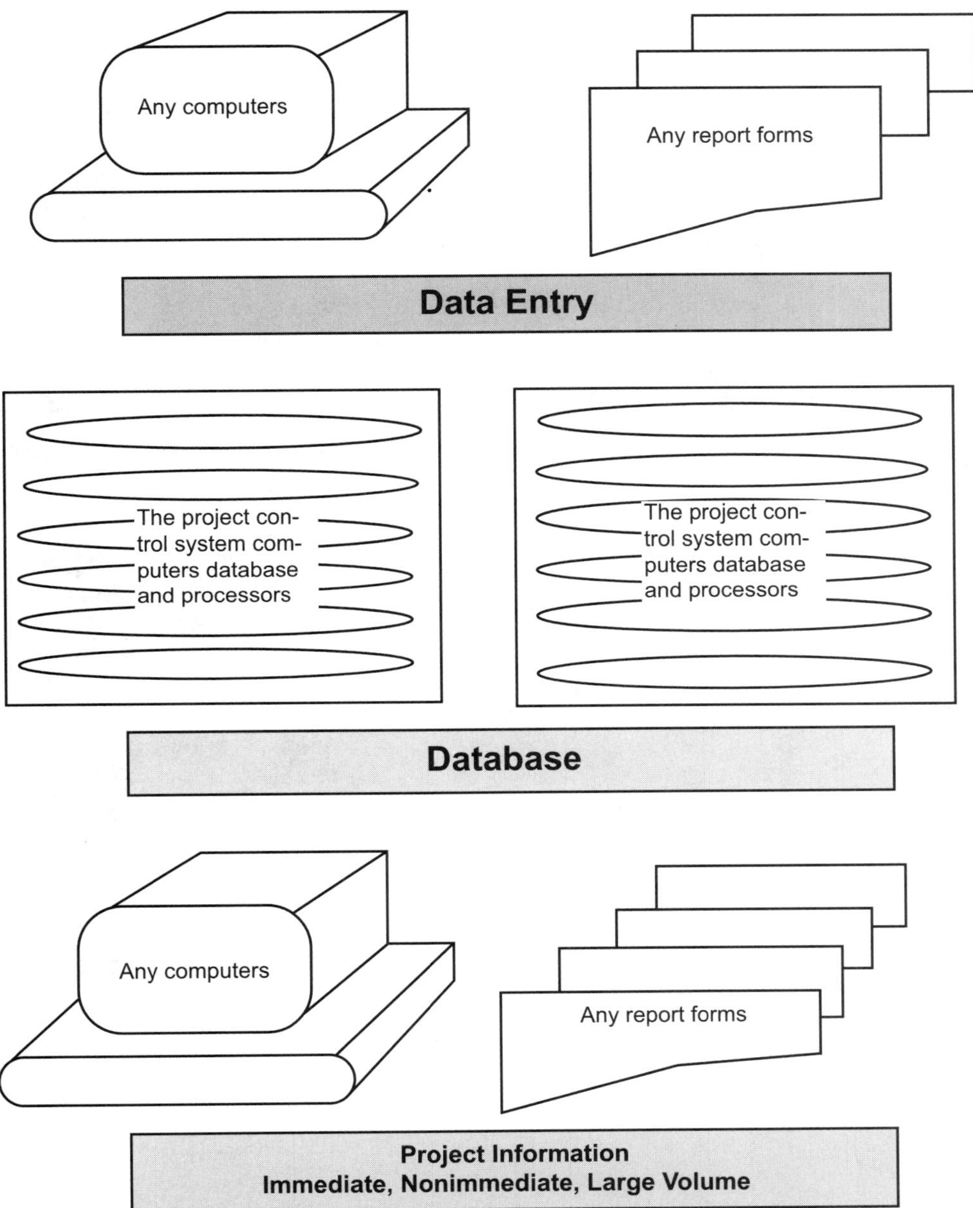

FIGURE 7.6 CORPORATE ENGINEERING DEPARTMENT SUMMARY DATA. Data entry is made by on line computer or from report forms. It is matched to and verified by the database on disk, and processed to create project information, which can be immediate on line, reports or nonimmediate or large-volume reports.

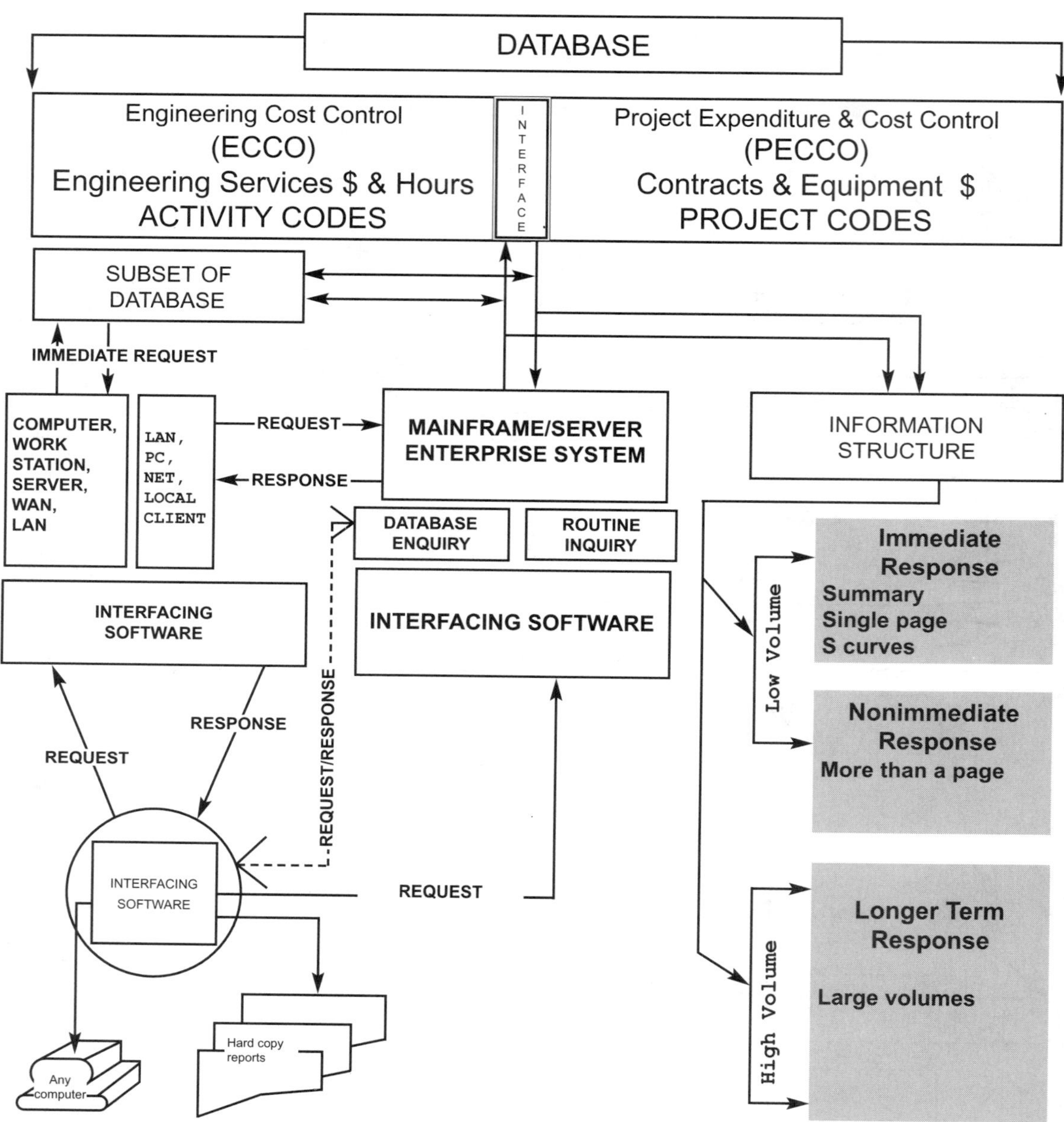

FIGURE 7.7 CORPORATE ENGINEERING DEPARTMENT DATABASE SYSTEM. The database drives the project control system. The depiction shows human/computer interfaces and computer processing of predetermined data. The data comprise two kinds: engineering cost control (ECCO) and project expenditure and cost control (PECCO). Project and engineering activities are an integral part of the system, to be discussed later for this case.

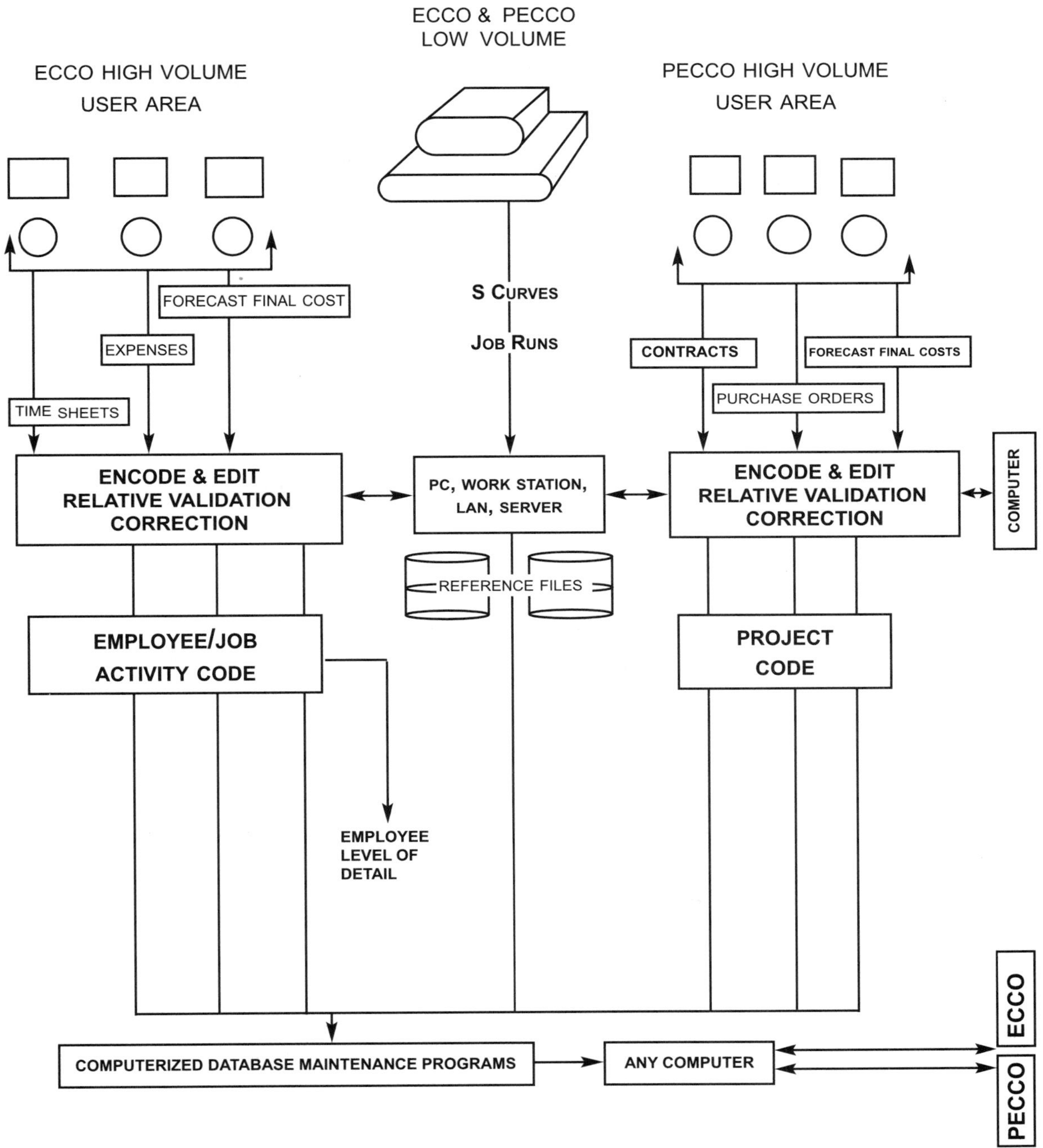

FIGURE 7.8 CORPORATE ENGINEERING DEPARTMENT PROJECT DATABASES. The flow diagram shows the human/computer interface concerning the input of engineering time and expense, and forecast cost data for ECCO reports, and contracts, purchase orders, and forecast cost data for PECCO reports.

S CURVES	Traditional *X/Y* plots of cost over time, human resources over time, utilization of a resource over time, or progress over time. Project work may be planned on the basis of a series of empirical S curves. Progress is measured by comparing actual utilization to planned utilization.
ENCODE	To apply project code numbers to activities and expenditures.
RELATIVE VALIDATION	Computer comparison of codes with approved codes in data base.
CORRECTION	Computer correction of incorrect codes.
TIME SHEETS	Submitted by personnel charging activity time to jobs and projects, and to overhead accounts, such as, vacation or illness. All time must be accounted for.

PECCO Database Maintenance

When one says that for project control purposes it is necessary to maintain a project control database, and then it is seen that data comprise an interdependent series of information modules or sets of data, it follows that if the database is to be valid, the subsets also must be dependable and accurate. In this case the most important system was seen to be PECCO. The actions pertaining to the maintenance of PECCO are illustrated in Fig. 7.9. The abbreviations and acronyms that appear in the graphic are defined as follows:

PROJ DEF	Project definition. The importance, concept, and use of the term is discussed at length in its own chapters. The discussion here is to show it being generated on line, and as an integral part of PECCO.
STANDARD COST CODES	Codes of accounts used for project cost control.
ON-LINE PROJECT DEFINITION	Representation of a computer process assisting in project definition.
S-CURVE PARAMETERS	Criteria for S curve to be applied to project in question.
XACTS	Transactions.
A.P.	Accounts payable on a current project.
XFER DATA	To transfer data.
VALIDATE	To compare to an approved list and continue process, if validated.
DATA BASE	Project control system database.
BATCHES	Computer batches of data for processing or validation.

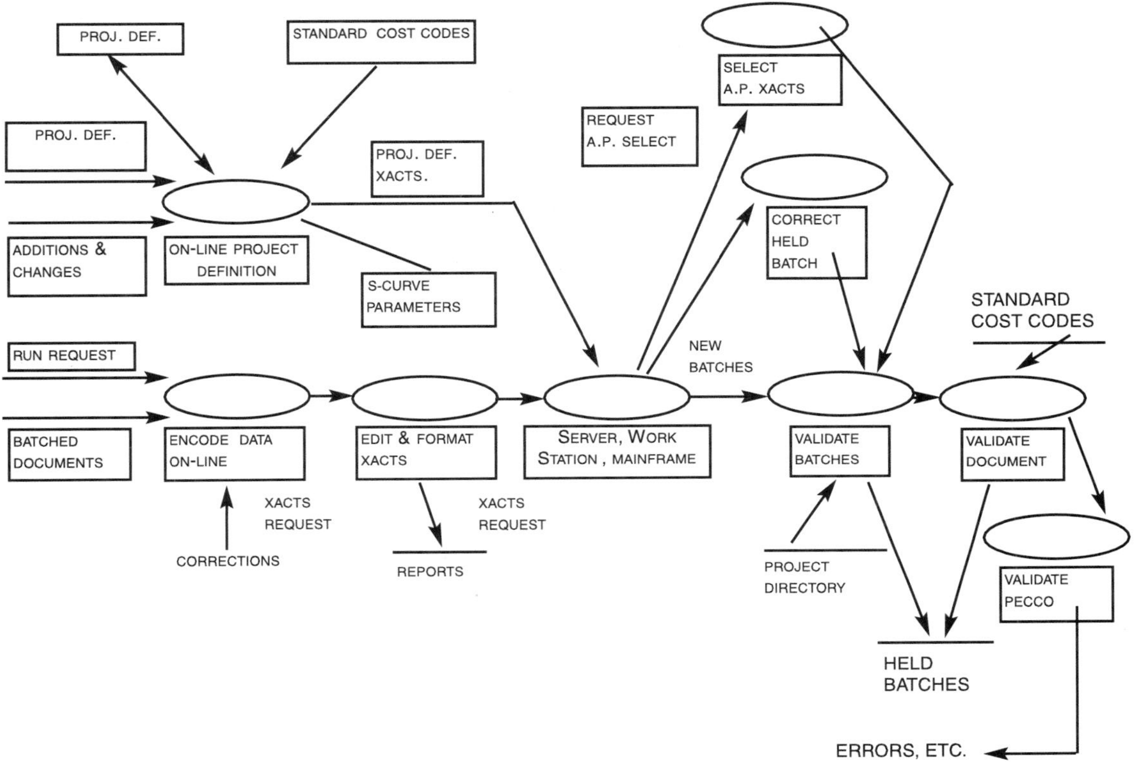

FIGURE 7.9 CORPORATE ENGINEERING DEPARTMENT PECCO DATABASE MAINTENANCE. Project cost and expenditure information is encoded and maintained in computer modules as depicted. Inputs, updates, and information requests are handled by the system as batches and on line.

ECCO Flow Diagram

The engineering cost control system is one of the two most important systems in the case history project control system. This is so because project work, including architecture, engineering, product development, systems design, research and development, or any other human activity, invariably starts with an idea, a problem, or an opportunity, which is first conceptualized and then progressed through activities, which may be described as feasibility studies, risk analysis, preliminary design, preliminary engineering, final design, drawings, specifications, procurement, and so on, until these front-end creative activities are done and other processes take over.

A project environment is nothing if not dynamic, meaning that every day the project looks a little different than it did the day before. The expectation is that it is different in a better way, that is, that progress has been made toward achieving the stated objective. What ECCO is expected to do is to help the multidisciplinary project design and engineering team achieve the stated project objectives by acting as their tool, and at the same time provide corporate management with information as to the status of the project in terms of cost and progress. The information flows and the person/computer interfaces are depicted in Fig. 7.10. The new acronyms and abbreviations are defined as follows:

DISC. HEAD	Manager of a design or service group, such as civil engineering or cost estimating.
COST ENG.	Cost engineer, in this case responsible for project cost estimates and the accumulation, synthesizing, and reporting of cost information throughout the project duration.
PROJ. MGR.	Person named by the corporate manager as being in charge of the project. The implication of being in charge varies from corporation to corporation and in governmental agencies. In this case history the project manager was a highly experienced and competent individual with both people skills and project knowledge, to say the least.
PROJ. ENG.	Project engineer; in this case the leader of the multidisciplinary process design and engineering group. This person is the project creative head and the coordinator and compiler of all project documentation pertaining to the scope and quality of the undertaking.
ACCTG.	Project accounting section.
TIME SHEETS	Time records submitted by project employees in connection with their activities.
ENG.	Engineers.
DRF.	Drafters.
CLRK.	Clerical or support personnel.
TRAVEL EXP.	Travel expenses.
CORP. A.P.	Corporate accounts payable function. In many corporate environments, all accounts are paid by a central corporate function. Problems arise in linking project accounts to payments, timeliness, or the check writers taking on a project function (for example, Monday morning quarterbacks) where none is warranted.
G.L.	Corporate general ledger of plant and equipment.

FIGURE 7.10 CORPORATE ENGINEERING DEPARTMENT PROJECT COST CONTROL, ECCO FLOW DIAGRAM. Engineering cost control consists of information inputs, e.g., time sheets, processing by computer against targets and standards, e.g., S curve, and output of status reports, e.g., single-job S curve.

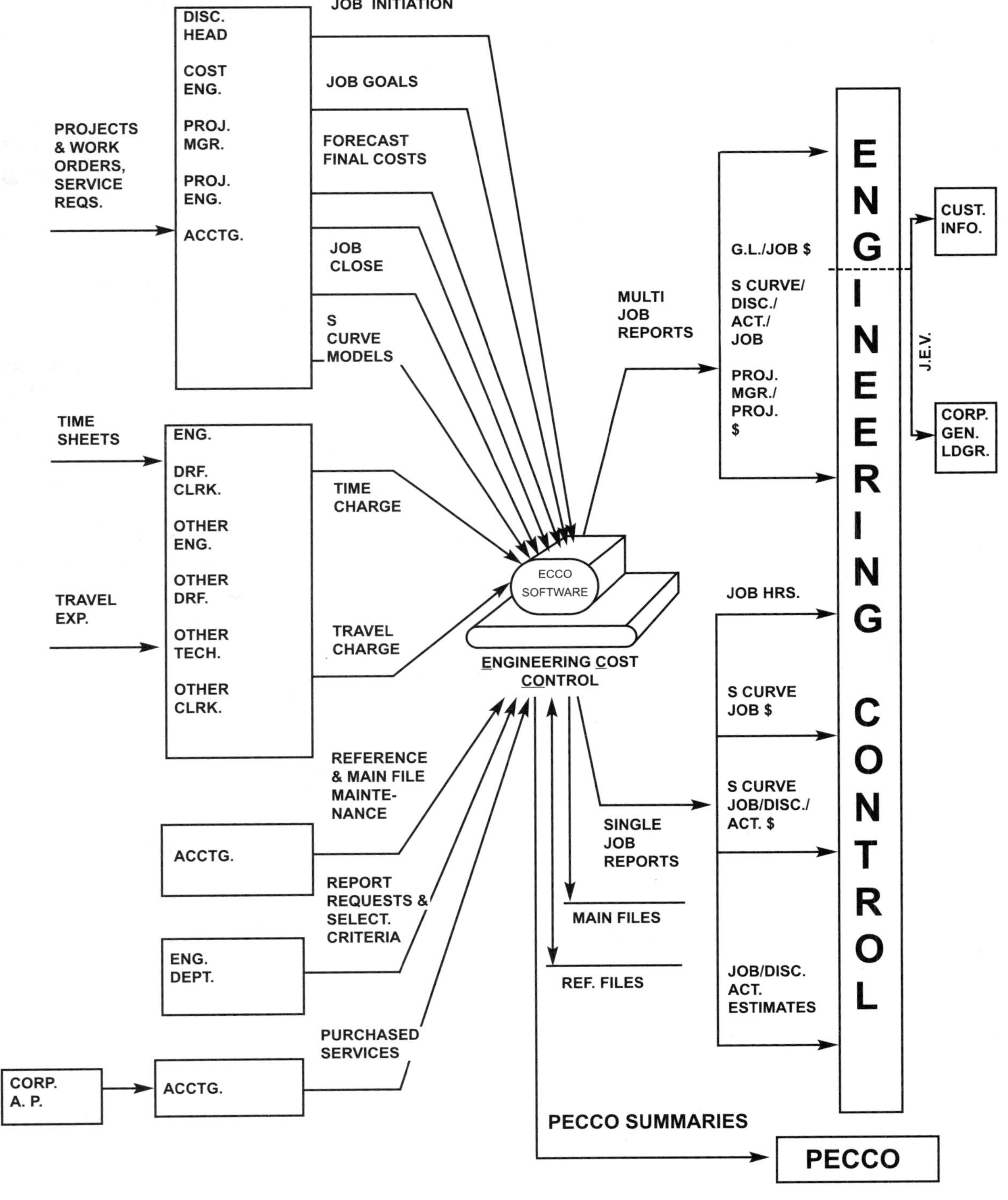

JOB INITIATION
DISC. HEAD
COST ENG.
PROJ. MGR.
PROJ. ENG.
ACCTG.
PROJECTS & WORK ORDERS, SERVICE REQS.
JOB GOALS
FORECAST FINAL COSTS
JOB CLOSE
S CURVE MODELS
TIME SHEETS
ENG.
DRF. CLRK.
OTHER ENG.
OTHER DRF.
OTHER TECH.
OTHER CLRK.
TRAVEL EXP.
TIME CHARGE
TRAVEL CHARGE
ECCO SOFTWARE
ENGINEERING COST CONTROL
MULTI JOB REPORTS
G.L./JOB $
S CURVE/ DISC./ ACT./ JOB
PROJ. MGR./ PROJ. $
ENGINEERING CONTROL
CUST. INFO.
J.E.V.
CORP. GEN. LDGR.
JOB HRS.
S CURVE JOB $
S CURVE JOB/DISC./ ACT. $
JOB/DISC. ACT. ESTIMATES
REFERENCE & MAIN FILE MAINTE- NANCE
ACCTG.
REPORT REQUESTS & SELECT. CRITERIA
ENG. DEPT.
PURCHASED SERVICES
CORP. A. P.
ACCTG.
SINGLE JOB REPORTS
MAIN FILES
REF. FILES
PECCO SUMMARIES
PECCO

J.E.V.	Journal entry voucher, an accounting technique to transfer interdepartmental and interaccount costs.

PECCO Flow Diagram

The other equally if not more important system in the project control system is PECCO. Whereas ECCO concerns itself with the project front end or a range of soft costs, PECCO handles the entire project, including the ECCO costs. ECCO and PECCO thus work together in the corporate environment. They share information, but they perform different and distinct functions. The linkages between the two are seen in Figs. 7.10 and 7.11. Many of the abbreviations and acronyms in the two figures were explained previously. The new terms are described next:

PROJECT INITIATION (CODES)	Creation or development and input of coded project elements. Codes are representative of predetermined and approved project functions, elements, and activities, generally input as line items.
AUTHORIZED $	Approved budget amount for a line item. A line item is a coded project element.
REDIST. AUTH. $ AMT.	$ amount resulting from a management cost action pertaining to a line item. The sum of the authorized dollar amounts is the project budget. Project management may recast line item amounts as redistributed dollar amounts. If the total of the redistributed amounts is less than the project budget total, the project is under budget. If the total is over, the project may be over budget.
S CURVE MODELS	Computer-generated standard models used as visual tools to depict the project cost/time plan.
COMMITMENTS	Corporate purchase orders or contracts which have been acknowledged and accepted by vendors and contractors. A commitment represents a binding contract between the two contracting parties.
EST. TO COMPLETE	Cost estimated as remaining to complete a line item or job.
REF. FILE & MAIN FILE MAINTENANCE	Ongoing housekeeping of corporate and project files.

FIGURE 7.11 CORPORATE ENGINEERING DEPARTMENT PROJECT CONTROL SYSTEM, PECCO FLOW DIAGRAM. Projects are initiated by participants, e.g., project manager, and input into the system, e.g., as authorized $ amount, for processing by the software and delivering information, e.g., single-project forecast versus authorized report.

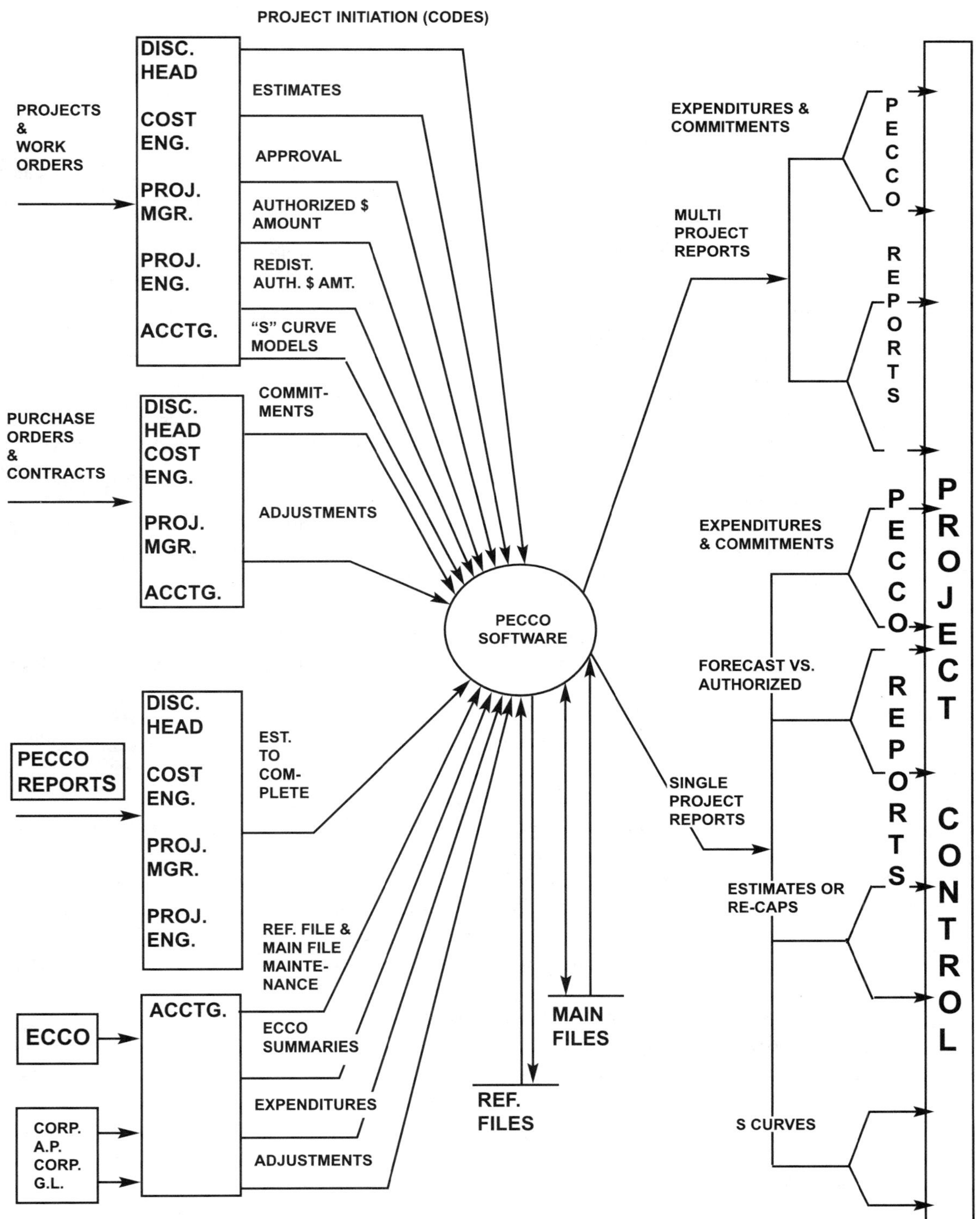
PROJECT INITIATION (CODES)
PROJECTS & WORK ORDERS
DISC. HEAD
COST ENG.
PROJ. MGR.
PROJ. ENG.
ACCTG.
ESTIMATES
APPROVAL
AUTHORIZED $ AMOUNT
REDIST. AUTH. $ AMT.
"S" CURVE MODELS
PURCHASE ORDERS & CONTRACTS
DISC. HEAD
COST ENG.
PROJ. MGR.
ACCTG.
COMMIT- MENTS
ADJUSTMENTS
PECCO REPORTS
DISC. HEAD
COST ENG.
PROJ. MGR.
PROJ. ENG.
EST. TO COM- PLETE
ECCO
CORP. A.P. CORP. G.L.
ACCTG.
REF. FILE & MAIN FILE MAINTE- NANCE
ECCO SUMMARIES
EXPENDITURES
ADJUSTMENTS
PECCO SOFTWARE
REF. FILES
MAIN FILES
MULTI PROJECT REPORTS
EXPENDITURES & COMMITMENTS
PECCO REPORTS
SINGLE PROJECT REPORTS
EXPENDITURES & COMMITMENTS
FORECAST VS. AUTHORIZED
ESTIMATES OR RE-CAPS
S CURVES
PECCO REPORTS
PROJECT CONTROL

7.6 Project Control System Development Tasks

There is no successful stand-alone project control system. This means that one cannot go to the local computer vendor and buy a package that provides all that is needed in a project control system.

The way one company works is invariably different from the way other companies do the same kind of work. It is not enough to say that one can customize a purchased package. The effort to coordinate and control project activities invariably involves the management of work being carried out by many diverse agencies, companies, departments, disciplines, and individuals.

To effectively coordinate and control the delivery of the inputs that make up a project requires that the people who provide these inputs participate in the development and implementation of the project control system. In the project owner's own organization, their participation is best enlisted by making the project control system their own tool.

As their tool, it needs to help them in the execution of their work. While acting as their tool, the system also has the capability to provide corporate management with information for its purposes, namely, project scope, cost, schedule, and status information. In the case of project participants such as outside agencies, consultants, contractors, and vendors, their input is solicited and acquired by various means and plugged into the system as project activities, which makes them integral parts of the project control system.

Even the most simple projects require the creative effort and input of many individuals. No one individual or single company can work on their own on a project. They are dependent upon and require the support and input of others. Others in their turn are dependent on them. And that is where the system comes in. It acts as the keeper and disseminator of project information. The system serves to coordinate and control activities for the benefit of the project, as well as for the people and companies doing the work. People will participate and support a project control system if they derive benefits from it. The benefits include being made aware of the project scope, quality measures, cost parameters, and schedule requirements. They will know when their work is required to be delivered, and others will be made aware of their information needs and time constraints.

The previous sections of this chapter identified up to eleven corporate engineering department and enterprise systems as impacting, or being impacted by, the project control system. These systems are broken down and expanded here as tasks to be carried out by the project users and system operators to enable these systems to be analyzed and coded by the computer analysts and programmers.

The tasks are listed more or less in order of priority as seen at the time of the development, rather than as subsystems of the systems named in the figures in Section 7.5. The tasks developed were closely related to the existing project processes and methods already in place. This may be because the engineering department of this case history is an experienced project management group with systems already in place, as discussed in Section 7.2.

The building of the new computerized system on the foundations of the existing methods is a very important consideration because, as said earlier, there is no stand-alone system.

1. Project Definition (PD) Tasks

1.1 PD procedure, preliminary estimate stage
1.2 PD procedure, appropriation request stage
1.3 PD procedure, minimum prerequisites for an appropriation request procedure
1.4 Scope breakdown procedure
1.5 Project coordination manual, procedure for preparation
1.6 Procedure for preparation of equipment lists
1.7 Procedure for estimating and monitoring engineer hours
1.8 Procedure for estimating and monitoring drafter hours
1.9 Procedure for preparation of technical specifications
1.10 Procedure for constructability review
1.11 Procedure for startup review
1.12 Cost-plus contracting procedure
1.13 Unit price contracting procedure
1.14 Design/build contracting procedure
1.15 Work order procedure to request plant services
1.16 Procedure to establish construction plan
1.17 Procedure to set up site security
1.18 Procedure to set up site safety
1.19 Weekly construction report procedure
1.20 Startup procedure
1.21 Design change procedure
1.22 Turnover procedure

2. Estimating and Cost Control

2.1 Computerized estimating system
2.2 Procedure for factor estimate preparation
2.3 Procedure for definitive estimate preparation
2.4 Procedure for control estimate preparation
2.5 Cost control system procedure

2.6 Project tax treatment procedure
2.7 Cost feedback procedure
2.8 Engineering and drafting cost control procedure
2.9 Lump sum contract cost control procedure
2.10 Cost-plus contract cost control procedure
2.11 Commitments control procedure
2.12 Exposure control procedure

3. Planning and Scheduling

3.1 Procedure for definition of planning terms
3.2 Startup schedule procedure
3.3 Contractors' construction schedule procedure
3.4 Project milestone schedule procedure
3.5 Detail engineering schedule procedure
3.6 Appropriation request schedule procedure

4. Cost Accounting

4.1 Review and amend engineering cost reporting system
4.2 Review and amend engineering time reporting system
4.3 Interface engineering cost reporting and accounts payable
4.4 Interface engineering cost reporting and fixed assets

5. Human Resources Allocation and Leveling

5.1 Development of resources coding procedure
5.2 Development of backlog projection procedure

6. Procurement

6.1 Procedure to list project purchase orders by PO numbers
6.2 List of project purchase orders by vendor name and PO numbers
6.3 List of purchase orders by contract and account code

7. Materials Control System

7.1 CAD and CADD as basis for materials control
7.2 Expediting procedure
7.3 Field stores control procedure for contracts
7.4 Computerized materials control tracking
7.5 Inspection procedures for quality assurance

7.6 Vendor data, e.g., shop drawings, control procedure
7.7 Monitoring procedure for contractors' purchase orders

8. Disciplinary Technical Programs

8.1 Catalogue disciplinary technical programs
8.2 Interface disciplinary technical programs with project control system

9. Project Control Graphics

9.1 Define project control graphics

10. Corporate Systems Tie-In

10.1 Define corporate systems tie-in

7.7 Project Control System Schedule of Tasks

Section 7.6 provides a list of tasks to be developed by the users and operators of the new project control system at the same time as the computer analysts and programmers do the coding for computer processing. Most of the tasks are seen to be departmental procedures, some of which have been in place and now require to be updated to form the base for the new system. Many of the procedures refer to project cost control. Others, particularly those listed under project definition, are new and are seen to be extensive and far reaching.

The delivery of these tasks is important to the development and implementation of the project control system, as their content is the driving force behind the computer software boxes depicted in the figures in Section 7.5.

To plan and schedule the delivery of the tasks, a CPM precedence style network was drawn and run on a CPM application. The intent of the network is to show the logical flow of tasks as CPM logic is aimed to be a function of logical dependencies. Invariably, the logic is influenced by resources availability, people's preferences, and management decisions. When planning and scheduling creative management activities such as these tasks, there are a number of considerations that come into play:

- It is difficult to know predecessor/successor relationships.
- Too many logical relationships lead to complexity and hurt the credibility of the exercise.
- Often a small amount of work on an activity will permit its successor to begin, thus hanging up the predecessor activity and in the process throwing the logic plan into disrepute.

A sample cut, comprising 12 activities plus the start event from the case history drawing is seen in Fig. 7.12. The tasks as activities contain the initials of the re-

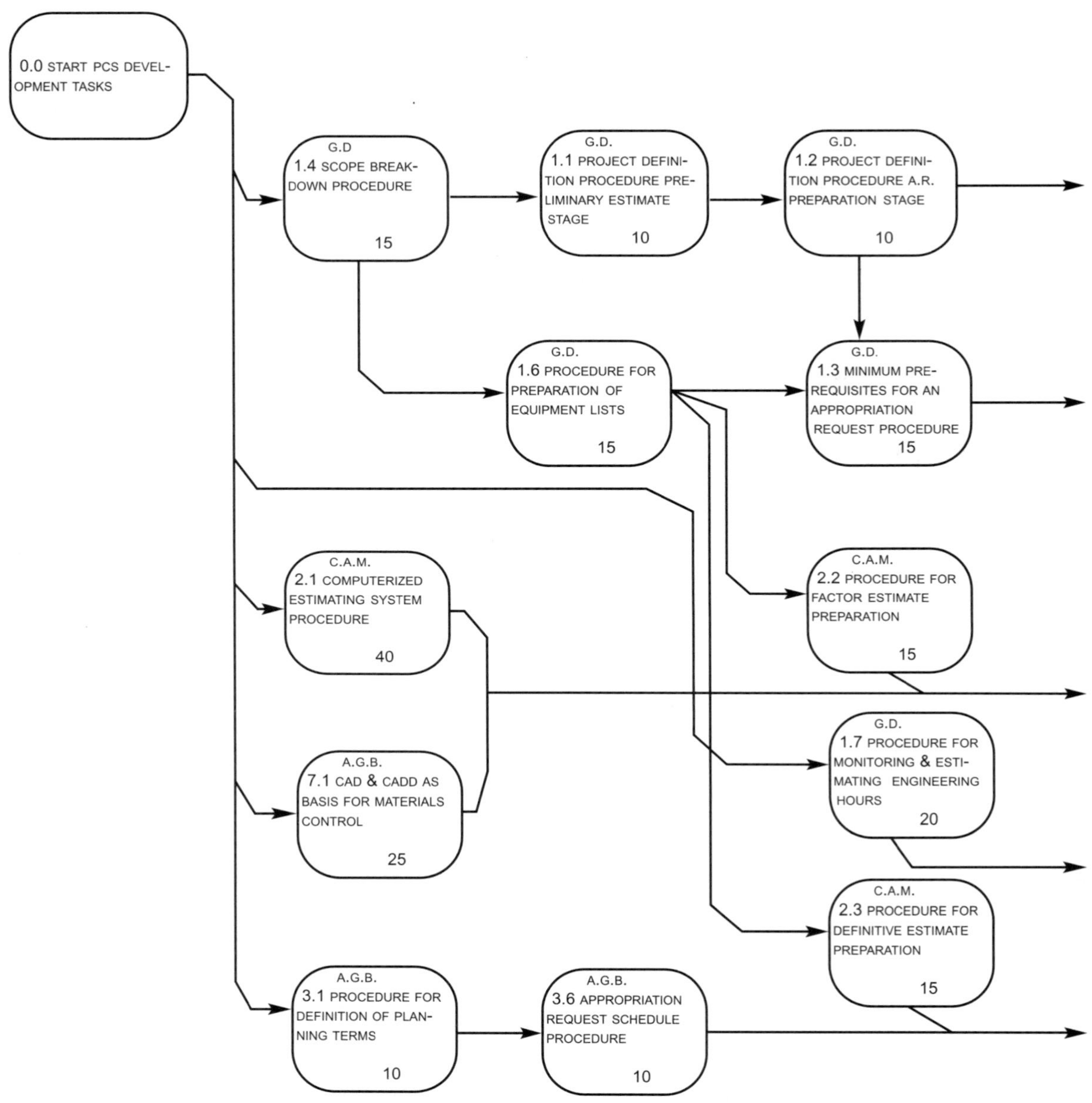

FIGURE 7.12 CORPORATE ENGINEERING DEPARTMENT CPM NETWORK OF DEVELOPMENT TASKS. This is an example of 12 activities from the logical network of the 64 activities listed as tasks by the engineering department engineers and managers for the development of the project control system. The completed tasks would form the basis for computer analysis and programming.

sponsible manager (A.G.B.), the task number (7.1), the task name (CAD & CADD as basis for materials control), and the task duration in working days (25). The network logic is represented by orthogonal lines and arrows.

It is noted that the tasks in Section 7.6 are listed in order of priority. But in drawing the tasks as a logic-ordered CPM network in Fig. 7.12, it may be seen that priorities have been changed. For example, task 1.4 precedes tasks 1.1 and 1.2, and task 1.6 is a predecessor to task 1.3.

The actual case network consisted of the 60 tasks listed in Section 7.6 as activities. To show how that network would be processed by a postmodern project management software application, 24 of these tasks were selected and processed for scheduling purposes by Microsoft Project 4.0 for Windows.

Figure 7.13 shows a report of the project as 24 tasks. Seen are the task ID, task name, duration in working days, start and finish dates, dollar cost estimates and person-hours of work.

Figure 7.14 is a Gantt view of the activities as developed in Microsoft Project. Information consists of the task ID, task name, logic relationships shown by arrows, and a calendar in weeks over a 3-month time window.

Figure 7.15 is a typical GUI-produced PERT view showing tasks, task codes and descriptions, durations, and start and finish dates. The activities on the critical path are connected by bold lines.

ID	TASK NAME	DURATION	START	FINISH	% COMP.	COST	WORK
1	0.0 START PCS DEVELOPMENT	1d	8/29/95	8/29/95	0%	$0.00	0h
2	1.4 SCOPE BREAKDOWN PROCEDURE	15d	8/30/95	9/19/95	0%	$4,900.00	120h
3	2.1 COMPUTERIZED ESTIMATING SYSTEM	40d	8/30/95	10/24/95	0%	$12,880.00	320h
4	7.1 COMPUTERIZED DRAWINGS PROCEDURE	25d	8/30/95	10/3/95	0%	$8,100.00	200h
5	3.1 SCHEDULE TERMS DEFINITION PROCEDURE	10d	8/30/95	9/12/95	0%	$3,300.00	80h
6	5.1 RESOURCE CODING PROCEDURE	10d	11/8/95	11/21/95	0%	$3,300.00	80h
7	8.1 CATALOGUE DISCP. TECH PROGRAMS	30d	8/30/95	10/10/95	0%	$19,400.00	240h
8	3.8 INTEGRATION OF PCS DEVELOPMENT TASKS	10d	10/4/95	10/17/95	0%	$3,300.00	80h
9	3.7 SPEC PLANNING & SCHED. PROCEDURE	5d	10/18/95	10/24/95	0%	$1,700.00	40h
10	3.4 PROJECT MILESTONES PROCEDURE	10d	9/13/95	9/26/95	0%	$3,300.00	80h
11	7.8 VENDOR DATA CONTROL PROCEDURE	15d	9/27/95	10/17/95	0%	$4,900.00	120h
12	1.1 PDS PROCEDURE PRELIM. EST.	10d	9/20/95	10/3/95	0%	$3,300.00	80h
13	1.6 PROCEDURE TO PREP. EQUIPT. LISTS	15d	11/1/95	11/21/95	0%	$4,900.00	120h
14	1.2 PDS PROCEDURE FOR AR PREP. STAGE	10d	10/4/95	10/17/95	0%	$3,300.00	80h
15	1.3 MINIMUM AR REQMTS. PROCEDURE	15d	11/1/95	11/21/95	0%	$4,900.00	120h
16	2.2 FACTOR ESTIMATING PROCEDURE	15d	10/4/95	10/24/95	0%	$4,880.00	120h
17	2.3 DEFINITIVE ESTIMATING PROCEDURE	10d	10/25/95	11/7/95	0%	$3,280.00	80h
18	1.7 ESTIMATING & MONITORING ENGINEER HOURS PROCEDURE	20d	10/4/95	10/31/95	0%	$6,500.00	160h
19	3.5 DETAIL ENGINEERING SCHEDULE PROCEDURE	15d	11/1/95	11/21/95	0%	$4,900.00	120h
20	3.6 SCHEDULE FOR AR APPROVAL PROCEDURE	10d	10/18/95	10/31/95	0%	$3,300.00	80h
21	3.3 CONTRACTORS' CONST. SCHEDULE PROCEDURE	10d	10/25/95	11/7/95	0%	$3,300.00	80h
22	1.21 DESIGN CHANGE PROCEDURE	10d	9/27/95	10/10/95	0%	$3,280.00	80h
23	1.9 TECHNICAL SPECS. PREPARATION PROCEDURE	20d	8/30/95	9/26/95	0%	$6,480.00	160h
24	9.9 FINISH PCS DEVELOPMENT TASKS	1d	11/22/95	11/22/95	0%	$0.00	0h

FIGURE 7.13 CORPORATE ENGINEERING DEPARTMENT DEVELOPMENT TASKS, REPORT OF TASKS.

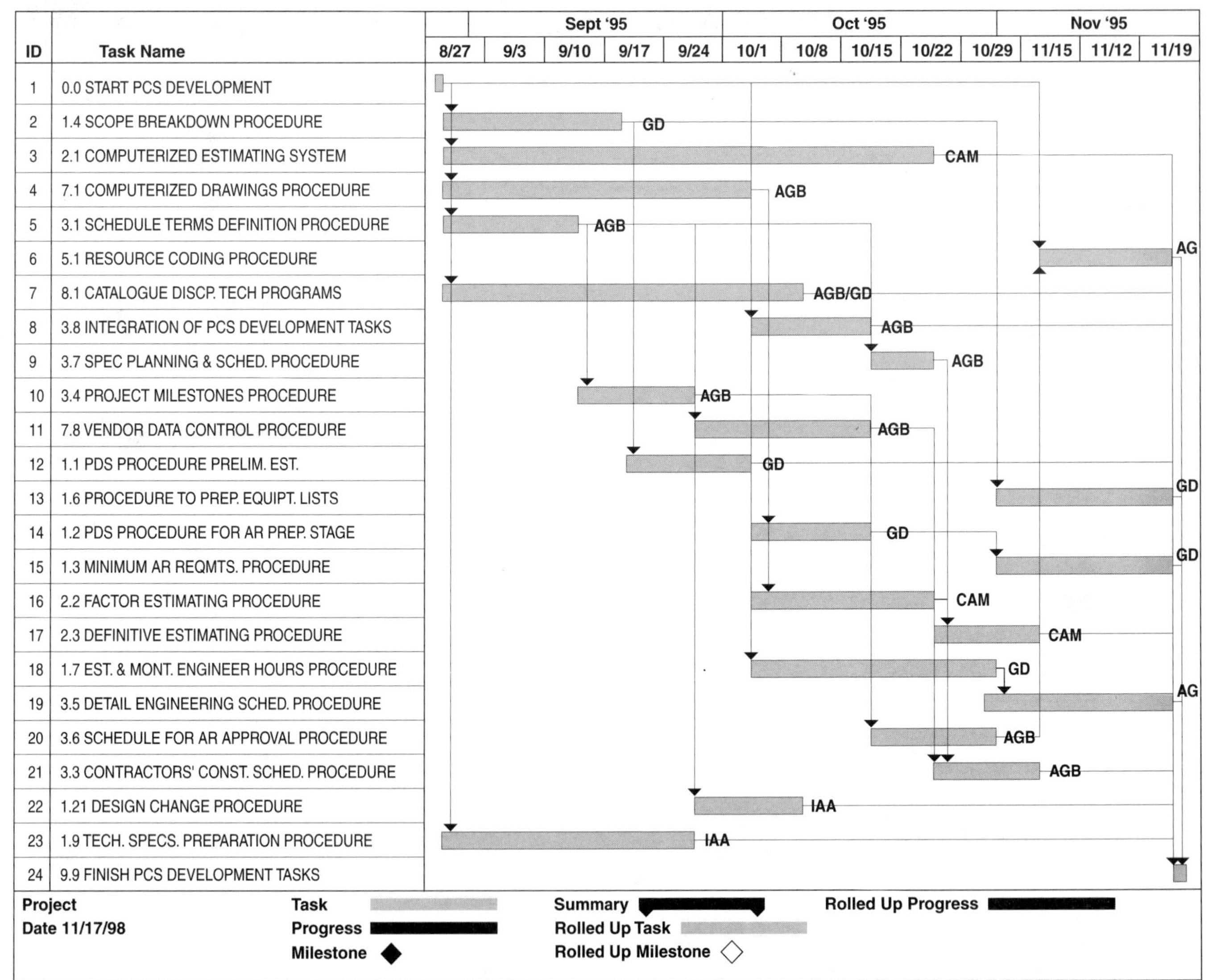

FIGURE 7.14 CORPORATE ENGINEERING DEPARTMENT NETWORK OF DEVELOPMENT TASKS, GANTT CHART.

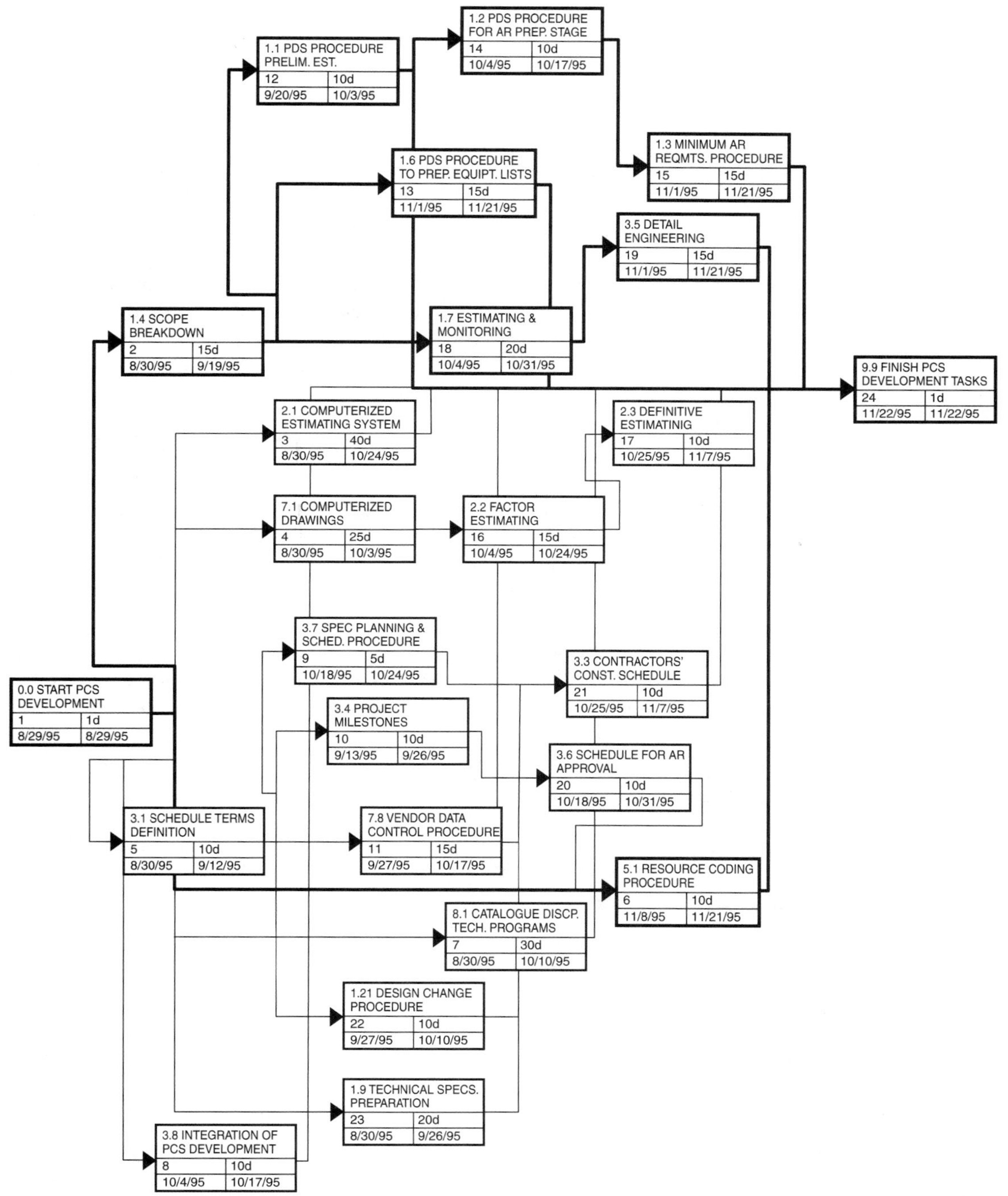

FIGURE 7.15 CORPORATE ENGINEERING DEPARTMENT DEVELOPMENT NETWORK OF DEVELOPMENT TASKS, PERT VIEW.

Figure 7.16 is a list of the critical activities, their successors, their logic relationships, lag types, and values, their predecessors, and the initials of the resource persons.

7.8 Engineering Cost Control System

The way corporate projects are delivered may depend on the project manager or on other circumstances if there is no project control system in place in the organization. It could be that there are no formal templates to define projects, no systematic element codes, no formal cost and scheduling systems, and only ad hoc ways to monitor and report status and progress. It may be that the project manager must depend on the operations department to develop the project scope and quality, on functional departments to provide procurement services, and on outside services for cost information.

Before the advent of project management and CPM type project logic, projects were done in this fragmented, nonteam way, where every department took a turn owning the project as it touched upon its turf. Most continue to be delivered in this way.

Although CPM/PERT-based techniques had many positive attributes, they were never complete project management systems in that they were used by corporate owners to control outside construction contractors. They were not recognized as helpful in the corporate owner's own organization, nor were they popular in smaller, independent companies serving the project industries. The CPM/PERT systems, however, evolved into computer software packages, which were purchased by firms to apply to project work as it came up. As corporate projects were most often carried out by engineers, the engineers were invariably the first to buy and apply the computerized packages for scheduling.

The evolution of a project control system may go from being nonexistant, that is, project managers do it their way, to the use of planning networks based on CPM thinking, to computerized CPM, and finally to a mandatory comprehensive project control system, as presented here based on the corporate engineering department in this case history.

How is a project control system developed and applied, and when and where is it started? A project management system to be effective must start at the beginning of the project. When does a project start?

- A project starts when a problem is uncovered, or
- A project starts when an opportunity arises.

As a corporate or other project owner looks to solve the problem or seize the opportunity, the project is considered started.

The inputs at the beginning of a project, the project front end, are creative, consisting of risk analysis, feasibility studies, design concepts, financial inputs, "blue sky" estimates, and so on. A common difficulty at the project front end is that corporate management may not spend enough time and money on the project analysis.

ID	Task Name		Duration		Start	Finish	Predecessors	Resource Names
1	0.0 START PCS DEVELOPMENT		1d		8/29/95	8/29/95		
	ID	Successor Name	Type	Lag				
	2	1.4 SCOPE BREAKDOWN PROCEDURE	FS	0d				
	3	2.1 COMPUTERIZED ESTIMATING SYSTEM	FS	0d				
	4	7.1 COMPUTERIZED DRAWINGS PROCEDURE	FS	0d				
	5	3.1 SCHEDULE TERMS DEFINITION PROCEDURE	FS	0d				
	6	5.1 RESOURCE CODING PROCEDURE	FS	0d				
	7	8.1 CATALOGUE DISCP. TECH. PROGRAMS	FS	0d				
	8	3.8 INTEGRATION OF PCS DEVELOPMENT TASKS	FS	0d				
	23	1.9 TECHNICAL SPECS. PREPARATION PROCEDURE	FS	0d				
2	1.4 SCOPE BREAKDOWN PROCEDURE		15d		8/30/95	9/19/95	1	GD
	ID	Successor Name	Type	Lag				
	12	1.1 PDS PROCEDURE PRELIM. EST	FS	0d				
	13	1.5 PROCEDURE TO PREP. EQUIPT LISTS	FS	0d				
	18	1.7 ESTIMATING & MONITORING ENGINEER HOURS PROCEDURE	FS	0d				
6	5.1 RESOURCE CODING PROCEDURE		10d		11/8/95	11/21/95	1,20	AGB
	ID	Successor Name	Type	Lag				
	24	9.9 FINISH PCS DEVELOPMENT TASKS	FS	0d				
12	1.1 PDS PROCEDURE PRELIM. EST.		10d		9/20/95	10/3/95	2	GD
	ID	Successor Name	Type	Lag				
	14	1.2 PROCEDURE FOR AR PREP. STAGE	FS	0d				
	24	9.9 FINISH PCS DEVELOPMENT TASKS	FS	0d				
13	1.6 PROCEDURE TO PREP. EQUIPT. LISTS		15d		11/1/95	11/21/95	2	GD
	ID	Successor Name	Type	Lag				
	24	9.9 FINISH PCS DEVELOPMENT TASKS	FS	0d				
14	1.2 PDS PROCEDURE FOR AR PREP. STAGE		10d		10/4/95	10/17/95	12	GD
	ID	Successor Name	Type	Lag				
	15	1.3 MINIMUM AR REQMTS. PROCEDURE	FS	0d				
15	1.3 MINIMUM AR REQMTS. PROCEDURE		15d		11/1/95	11/21/95	14FS+10d	GD
	ID	Successor Name	Type	Lag				
	24	9.9 FINISH PCS DEVELOPMENT TASKS	FS	0d				
18	1.7 ESTIMATING & MONITORING ENGINEER HOURS PROCEDURE		20d		10/4/95	10/31/95	2	GD
	ID	Successor Name	Type	Lag				
	19	3.5 DETAIL ENGINEERING SCHEDULE PROCEDURE	FS	0d				
19	3.5 DETAIL ENGINEERING SCHEDULE PROCEDURE		15d		11/1/95	11/21/95	18	AGB
	ID	Successor Name	Type	Lag				
	24	9.9 FINISH PCS DEVELOPMENT TASKS	FS	0d				
24	9.9 FINISH PCS DEVELOPMENT TASKS		1d		11/22/95	11/22/95	22,17,19,21, 12,23,3,6,1	

FIGURE 7.16 CORPORATE ENGINEERING DEPARTMENT DEVELOPMENT TASKS, REPORT OF CRITICAL TASKS.

Top management in the best of times is unwilling to spend money on a project that may not go ahead. On the other hand the project that is approved on skimpy, incomplete, or inaccurate scope, quality, cost, and time information invariably ends up as a disaster.

The most detrimental aspect of project work is the unavailability of project definition information in the project front-end stages. Although the corporation has decided to proceed with the project, its scope, its quality, and its cost have not been established in hard enough parameters, resulting in confusion and wasted effort.

To overcome the identified front-end and the resulting downstream problems, the corporate engineering department in this case history developed project control concepts ultimately referred to as the ECCO and PECCO systems to be used by all project managers and project and discipline engineers who have the authority and responsibility for the delivery of projects.

What this meant is that the method to be used to manage a project was no longer the personalized approach of a senior project manager. As the system was to serve both as a tool for project management and as the basis for control information by corporate management, all work was now to be entered into the new system.

ECCO and PECCO were developed simultaneously as both play a project role from the beginning. The start of any project first involves creativity and ideas, which are then expanded into concepts, designs, drawings, cost estimates, and time frames by skilled people. ECCO captures the creative effort as activities and packages of tasks by the engineering department disciplines and skills required to achieve the project. To do this it was necessary to identify and code the functions that people carried out as activities. The activities were reported on time sheets, as seen Fig. 7.17. The time sheet has provision for the names and numbers of jobs, projects, subprojects, functions, activity codes, and drawing numbers. All corporate engineering department work would now be entered and incorporated into the ECCO system.

Figure 7.17 is the basis for charging time to jobs and projects handled by the corporate engineering department. To account for all of a person's available time it acts as a time report incorporating all chargeable time, vacation, personal time, and so on. As far as project work is concerned, the most important aspect is the section called "project activities."

The bulk of the project front-end cost would be made up of these time charges. The two-digit activity charge numbers are based on discipline numbers, with the first digit representing a departmental discipline, that is, 0 represents project managers and project engineers, 1 represents chemical engineers and process engineers, 4 represents civil engineers, and so on.

The second digit of the two-digit activity code represents the skill or subskill provided by the discipline.

Thus the job or project undertaken by the corporate engineering department is produced by the disciplines and skills carrying out the described activities and producing the drawings, documents, and output needed to deliver the project.

To demonstrate the system, examples of ECCO reports are provided. ECCO reports provide both hours worked and dollars spent on a project. The hours charged

ENGINEERING COST CONTROL SYSTEM TIME SHEET

PERSONAL

DATE & PERIOD

CATEGORY OF WORK
1 Projects
2 Work Orders
3 Service
6 Eng. Dept. Service
9 Non-Chargeable

JOB NUMBERS
Cat. 1 - 4 digit numeric project no.
Cat. 2 - 4 digit numeric work order no.
Cat. 3 - 4 digit service order no.
Cat. 6 - 0000
Cat. 9 - Personal 9100
- Vacation 9200
- Illness 9300
- No Work 9900

SUBPROJECTS OR SUBJOBS
This is a further breakdown of the job into subjobs, subprojects, or site components, e.g.,
01 - Site Component 1
02 - Site Component 2

JOB DESCRIPTION

PROJECT ACTIVITIES
01 Project Management/Engineering
11 Chemical & Process Engineering
12 Environmental
13 Computer Application
21 Materials of Construction
22 Maintenance
23 Material Handling
24 Power House (Equipment & Housing)
25 Other Specialists (Energy Conservation)
31 Models
32 Equipment Design & Procurement
33 Piping Design & Procurement
41 Civil Design (Roads, etc.)
42 Structural Engineering
43 Architectural
44 Underground Piping
45 Fire Protection
46 Building HVAC& Plumbing
51 Electrical
61 Instrumentation
71 Cost Estimating
72 Accounting
73 Contracts & Construction Supervision
74 Schedule, Cost, Progress Control
75 Inspection
76 Drafting Support
81 Field Supervision & Support

NONPROJECT
91 Personal
92 Vacation
93 Illness
99 No Work

DRAWING NUMBERS
Drawing numbers are to be 7 alphanumeric characters.
Only drafters may charge time to drawing numbers.
Drafters are to charge their time to specific drawing numbers or to one of the following pro-forma drawing numbers:
XXX-00000 - All work other than drafting or drafting supervision
ISO-00000 - Isometric Piping detail drawings
EXD-00000 - Revising existing drawings from other projects
SUP-00000 - Drafting supervision used by squad leaders and deputies

CATEGORY	JOB NO.	SUB NO.	JOB TITLE OR DESCRIPTION	ACTIVITY	DRWG. NO.	HRS.	DATE
XX	XXXX	XX	The name of the project	XX	AAA-XXXXX	X.X	XXAAAXX

Figure 7.17 Corporate Engineering Department Engineering Cost Control System, Time Sheet. The engineering cost control system is driven by the application of codes, which represent projects, jobs, disciplines, and activities, to person-hours and dollar expenses. Use of the coding system is mandatory for all jobs and all personnel.

are processed by ECCO, and the dollars spent are handled by the PECCO system and cross-referenced into ECCO.

Hours Charged to a Project

The first example in Fig. 7.18 is a report of hours charged to a project for a customer. A report of hours worked on managing, designing, and engineering a project for a customer would only be provided if the customer were entitled to this kind of infor-

CHARGE - OUT REPORT

HOURS CHARGED
(BY CUSTOMER)

CUSTOMER NAME:

JOB NO./ ACTIVITY	DESCRIPTION	CURRENT PERIOD HOURS	CURRENT MONTH HOURS	YEAR TO DATE HOURS	JOB TO DATE HOURS
15186 00	**PURCHASE ETHYLENE**				
01	PROJECT MANAGEMENT/ENGINEERING				
	ENGINEER	0.0	0.0	3.5	3.5
	01 ACTIVITY TOTAL	0.0	0.0	3.5	3.5
09	TIME AUDIT CONVERSION				
	ENGINEER	0.0	0.0	0.0	0.0
	09 ACTIVITY TOTAL	0.0	0.0	0.0	0.0
12	ENVIRONMENTAL ENGINEERING				
	ENGINEER	20.0	20.0	20.0	20.0
	12 ACTIVITY TOTAL	20.0	20.0	20.0	20.0
61	INSTRUMENTATION AND CONTROL				
	ENGINEER	3.5	3.5	7.0	7.0
	61 ACTIVITY TOTAL	3.5	3.5	7.0	7.0
72	ACCOUNTING				
	CLERICAL	25.5	25.5	65.5	65.5
	72 ACTIVITY TOTAL	25.5	25.5	65.5	65.5
	15186 00 SUBJOB TOTAL	49.0	49.0	96.0	96.0
	CUSTOMER TOTAL	49.0	49.0	96.0	96.0
	JOB TOTAL	49.0	49.0	96.0	96.0

FIGURE 7.18 CORPORATE ENGINEERING DEPARTMENT HOURS CHARGED TO A PROJECT. This report accumulates person-hours by skill and activity charged to a project for a customer.

mation. This may happen on a feasibility study or for a cost-plus project. This report is strictly for information as there are no cost control data shown.

Hours Charged to Drawings

Drawings are the principal means to communicate information for complex projects. The production of diagrams, drawings, and specifications uses skilled human resources. To assist in the management and control of any project, a classic procedure is to develop a list of project drawings as early in the schedule as possible, closely followed by an estimate of the hours to produce them. This is followed by the allocation of hours worked by drawing numbers, as depicted in Fig. 7.19.

HOURS CHARGED TO DRAWINGS

ALL SKILLS

CUSTOMER NAME:

JOB NO.	DESCRIPTION	ACTIVITY CODE	DRAWING NO.	CURRENT PERIOD HOURS	CURRENT MONTH HOURS	JOB TO DATE HOURS
15262 00	**TANK CAR LOADING**					
		32	NDD23465	6.0	6.0	32.0
		32	NDG26906	0.0	0.0	15.0
		32	ZZZ99999	7.5	7.5	7.5
		33	PCD23390	0.0	0.0	5.0
		33	PDG26264	0.0	0.0	10.0
		33	PDG26445	0.0	0.0	15.0
		33	XXX00000	0.0	0.0	15.0
		SUB-JOB TOTAL		13.5	13.5	99.5
15280 00	**PROJECT EDMONTON**					
		SUB-JOB TOTAL		0.0	0.0	0.0
15280 01						
		31	MOD00004	0.0	0.0	25.5
		31	MOD00005	0.0	0.0	4.0
		32	ISO00000	30.0	30.0	30.0
		32	NDD40123	0.0	0.0	11.0
		32	NDD40301	0.0	0.0	11.5
		32	NDD40303	0.0	0.0	7.5
		32	NDD40311	0.0	0.0	22.5
		32	NDD40980	0.0	0.0	10.0
		32	NDD40981	0.0	0.0	25.5
		32	NDD40983	0.0	0.0	7.5
		32	NDD40984	0.0	0.0	15.0
		32	NDD40986	0.0	0.0	17.0
		32	NDG40980	0.0	0.0	7.5

Note: The three alpha characters in the drawing numbers represent plant locations, in addition to the pro-forma numbers listed in Figure 7.17

Figure 7.19 Corporate Engineering Department Hours Charged to Drawings, (All Skills). The creation and production of drawings for projects is a high-cost time-consuming process which is difficult to coordinate and control. This report lists project skills including model making, equipment design and piping design, that have been charged to the project.

The intent of this report is to track the production of all job drawings by the organization. The report is a record of hours worked on drawings by drafters and the engineers responsible for the design of the systems and their equipment configurations.

Project Engineer Report

The project engineer is primarily responsible for the design and drawings of the project. This person often works in a matrix style organization, meaning that the disciplines and skills do not report directly to the project engineer, but to their own functional managers. Nevertheless, the engineer is responsible for the quality of the project documentation, its budgets, and its schedule. In this case history, the project engineer has the ECCO system in place as a principal resource management tool. An example of the kind of management information available to the project engineer is seen in Fig. 7.20.

This report provides information on the hours charged, dollars expended, and budget control information provided by such features as forecast cost, budget amount, and an indication of the dollar under or over budget condition.

PROJECT ENGINEER REPORT

ENGINEERING EXPENDITURES

PROJECT BY DISCIPLINE

PROJECT NO. 15186 00
DESCRIPTION: ________________ PROJECT ENGINEER: ________________

DISCIPLINE SKILL	PERIOD HOURS	TO DATE HOURS	PERIOD $	TO DATE $	FORECAST $	BUDGET $	UNDER/ OVER-
00 PROJECT MANAGEMENT/ENGINEERING							
ENGINEER	0.0	3.5	0	124	0	0	0
OTHER	0.0	0.0	0	103000	0	216000	216000
00 TOTAL	0.0	3.5	0	103124	0	216000	216000
10 CHEMICAL ENGINEERING							
ENGINEER	20.0	20.0	710	710	0	0	0
10 TOTAL	20.0	20.0	710	710	0	0	0
60 INSTRUMENTATION & CONTROL							
ENGINEER	3.5	7.0	124	248	0	0	0
60 TOTAL	3.5	7.0	124	248	0	0	0
70 SUPPORT							
CLERICAL	25.5	65.5	408	1048	0	0	0
70 TOTAL	25.5	65.5	408	1048	0	0	0
SUBJOB TOTAL	49.0	96.0	1242	105130	0	216000	216000

FIGURE 7.20 CORPORATE ENGINEERING DEPARTMENT PROJECT ENGINEER REPORT, ENGINEERING EXPENDITURES. This single project report shows the hours charged by discipline skills, and the costs for the period and to date. Also shown are forecast costs and budget amounts for the line items. A comparison of budget amount to forecast amount generates an under/over figure.

Project Manager Report

A project engineer may handle only one project at a time. If the project engineer is responsible for a number of projects, the corporation may name the person project manager. A project manager may handle only one project at a time if the project is big. It often happens that a project manager is responsible for a number of jobs at various stages of progress, each of which may be under the leadership of a project engineer. In these cases the project manager may have available project control system reports, as seen in Fig. 7.21.

Skill Hours by Job/Activity/Subskill

The cost of design and engineering person-hours is a big ticket item on any project. Input is required from many engineering disciplines, skills, and subskills. In this case, to accommodate both person-hour costs and other associated expenses, the skill codes were set as follows:

1. Engineers
2. Drafters
3. Clerks
4. Travel expenses
5. Other expenses

Figure 7.22 lists only the engineer (skill 1) person-hours for job number 15280 01. Also shown are subskills by activity. A subskill is a breakdown of an activity that designates a specific person's skill or a type of expenditure in connection with the activity.

The preceding sample reports are to illustrate only parts of the system. Some other report types are listed below. This is by no means a complete list of reports available from the system, or that may be required by project or corporate management.

Accumulation and Charge Out Reports

Index of jobs

Hours charged

Engineering expenditure, current period and to date

Monthly charge out report details

Automatic journal entry voucher (JEV) for charge outs

Charging jobs, purchased services, and employee travel

Charging project, corporate engineering

Charging work orders (WOs) and service charges, corporate engineering

Drafting report

Audit trail

PROJECT MANAGER REPORT

ENGINEERING EXPENDITURES
BY PROJECT ENGINEER

PROJECT MANAGER CODE:

PROJECT NO./ PROJECT ENG.	PERIOD HOURS	TO DATE HOURS	PERIOD $	TO DATE $	FORECAST $	BUDGET $	UNDER/OVER $
15128 00 PROJECT							
CLERICAL	0.0	20.0	0	320	0	0	0
OTHER EXP.	0.0	0.0	0	0	0	0	0
SUBJOB TOTAL	0	20.0	0	320	0	0	0
15128 01 PROJECT OFFSITES							
OTHER EXP.	0.0	0.0	0	745373	0	627645	627645
SUBJOB TOTAL.	0.0	0.0	0	745373	0	627645	627645
15128 02 PROJECT BATTERY LIMITS							
OTHER EXP.	0.0	0.0	0	448731	0	389240	389240
SUBJOB TOTAL.	0.0	0.0	0	448731	0	389240	389240
15128 TOTAL.	0.0	20.0	0	1194424	0	1016885	1016885

FIGURE 7.21 CORPORATE ENGINEERING DEPARTMENT PROJECT MANAGER REPORT, ENGINEERING EXPENDITURES. This report is for the multiproject manager. Each project is under the direction of a project engineer. The projects comprise subprojects identified and coded above as project offsites, e.g., storage and utilities, and project battery limits, i.e., the process. The system gathers and presents person-hours charged and dollars as forecasts and budgets.

Input/output control report
Control report

Project Engineering Reports

Project engineer report
Project manager report
Manager, projects group summary report
Project engineer report work orders
S Curves, projects, work orders
Engineer hours by job/activity

ENGINEER HOURS
BY JOB/ACTIVITY

JOB NUMBER: **15280 01**
NAME:
SKILL: **1-ENGINEER**

PROJECT ENGINEER: ______________________

DISCIPLINE ACTIVITY/SUBSKILL	CURRENT PERIOD HOURS	TOTAL TO DATE HOURS	ESTIMATE TO COMPLETE HOURS	FORECAST FINAL HOURS	BUDGET HOURS	UNDER/OVER HOURS
00 PROJECT MANAGEMENT/ENGINEERING						
01/1000 PROJECT MGT.	456.5	5010.5	5010.5-	0.0	0.0	0.0
00 TOTAL	456.5	5010.5	5010.5-	0.0	0.0	0.0
10 CHEMICAL ENGINEERING						
11/1000 CHEMICAL	0.0	14.0	14.0-	0.0	0.0	0.0
12/1000 ENVIRONMENTAL	0.0	9.0	9.0-	0.0	0.0	0.0
13/1000 COMPUTER PRG.	0.0	97.0	97.0-	0.0	0.0	0.0
10 TOTAL	0.0	120.0	120.0-	0.0	0.0	0.0
20 SPECIALIST						
21/1000 MATLS OF CONST	11.5	743.5	743.5-	0.0	0.0	0.0
23/1000 MATL HANDLING	4.5	73.5	73.5-	0.0	0.0	0.0
24/1000 POWER HOUSE	0.0	9.5	9.5-	0.0	0.0	0.0
25/1000 OTHER SPECIAL.	33.0	38.5	238.5-	0.0	0.0	0.0
20 TOTAL	49.0	1065.0	1065.0-	0.0	0.0	0.0
30 EQUIPMENT & PIPING						
31/1000 MODELS	0.0	75.0	75.0-	0.0	0.0	0.0
32/1000 EQUPMT. DESIGN	0.0	607.0	607.0-	0.0	0.0	0.0
33/1000 PIPING DESIGN	0.0	634.0	634.0-	0.0	0.0	0.0
30 TOTAL	0.0	1316.0	1316.0-	0.0	0.0	0.0
40 CIVIL ENGINEERING						
41/1000 CIVIL DESIGN	0.0	49.0	49.0-	0.0	0.0	0.0
42/1000 STRUCTURAL	31.5	273.0	273.0-	0.0	0.0	0.0
43/1000 ARCHITECTURAL	0.0	11.5	11.5-	0.0	0.0	0.0
45/1000 FIRE PROTECT.	0.0	74.0	74.0-	0.0	0.0	0.0
46/1000 BUILDING MECH.	0.0	44.5	44.5-	0.0	0.0	0.0
40 TOTAL	31.5	452.0	452.0-	0.0	0.0	0.0
JOB /SKILL TOTAL	537.0	7963.5	7963.5-	0.0	0.0	0.0

FIGURE 7.22 CORPORATE ENGINEERING DEPARTMENT, ENGINEER HOURS BY JOB ACTIVITY. This view aims to gather and present engineer hours worked on a single project. The engineer hours are charged by engineering discipline, e.g., 10, Chemical Engineering, and subskill, e.g., 12/1000, Chemical Environmental Engineering.

Drafting

Drafting supervisor report

Drafting hours by discipline

Drafting hours, Small WOs

Drawings S curves

Miscellaneous

Absenteeism report

Vacation report

Hours charged by individuals

7.9 Project Expenditure and Cost Control System

PECCO aims to control the whole project, including the cost of design and engineering. In construction project work there is too much made of the separation of the stages of work. Design, procurement, manufacturing, assembly, such as construction, are often treated as individual and sovereign stages, instead of as a project continuum. For all projects these stages should have only one aim: to play their prescribed role in the delivery of the completed job or a facility to serve the intended purpose. This means that no one stage is an entity unto itself. A project cannot be built until it is procured. Procurement is not possible without scope definitions. Drawings can only follow design, and so on. But because of historical custom, convention, specialization, and fragmentation, the constructors were separated from the designers. More often than not, the roles were adversarial.

PECCO aims to pull these disparate but essential actions together. In developing the system for the case history, both ECCO and PECCO were designed, developed, and implemented concurrently, as discussed and depicted in the preceding sections. Their interdependence will become apparent very quickly through the computerized reports provided in the figures that follow.

It starts with the pull-down windows menus. The system's main address is (P)ECCO. The following (P)ECCO reports will reflect in broad strokes how the systems merge, grow, interact, and serve all aspects of project control. They will be of service to the chief engineer, who may want a snapshot of the status of all projects, or where any project is today, or is going to be tomorrow, or was yesterday, as well as fulfilling the information needs of the enterprise.

System Control Main Menu

The project control system is addressed as (P)ECCO in the client/server computer configuration. This is seen in Fig. 7.23, a simplified rendering of the on-line actions available on the system menu screens. Its purpose here is to illustrate system inputs and interdependencies

(P)ECCO 0100 V1.1
SYSTEM MENU

SYSTEM CONTROL
MAIN MENU

REPORTS:
1. Project Expenditure Cost Control
2. Engineering Service Cost Control
3. Display a Report (See Options)
4. DMINQ - On-Line Inquiry

S CURVES
5. Hardcopy
6. Screen

SYSTEMS
7. Job Definition or Change
8. S Curve Plan Definition or Revision
9. Data Entry, Proj. Exp., Cmmits., Etc.
10. Data Entry, Eng. Services, Time, Etc.
11. System Management Functions

OPTIONS:
*.REP/L1 List of Files
XXXXXX.REP Shows Report
. REP;/DE Deletes files
SHOW Transmit Status

JOB CODE:
S CURVE CODE: (1 TO 8 FOR PECCO, 9 FOR ECCO)
SELECT: Original, Current and Original or No Plan Curves (O, C, N)
Whole or Partial Display (W,P)

FIGURE 7.23 CORPORATE ENGINEERING DEPARTMENT SYSTEM CONTROL, SYSTEM MENU. The server-resident project control system is programmed to output the report and S curves listed as items 1 to 6. Jobs may be initiated or changed, planned as S curves, or data entered and updated as listed in items 7 through 10. The options window provides a list of reports and has provision to delete files. A number of S curves are available for display.

Job Definition, Job Listing—Job Directory

A project control system is invariably a multiple-job control system. No organization is ever just a single-job organization. This is because enterprises stay in business and jobs are never finished. They just go through stages, and new jobs are added. All jobs in the organization of this case history would go through the system and be identified as seen in Fig. 7.24

Job Definition, Job Listing—Cost Code Structure

Each job in the system is processed in accordance with the job code structure, as highlighted in Fig. 7.25.

Project Expenditure Report—Summary of Projects

Project control requires that the project manager know early and often what has been spent, and what has been committed for which project or subproject. That is why an early report is the project expenditure report, summary of projects, seen in Fig. 7.26.

(P)ECCO 0300 V1.1	JOB DEFINITION JOB LISTING JOB DIRECTORY
JOB CODE	:1 0024 00
JOB STATUS	:1 OPEN
JOB INDICATOR	: IMPROVE WASTE GAS
SITE/WORKS	: ABERCROMBIE
BUSINESS AREA	: FERTILIZER
LOCATION	: WINDSOR
JOB RESP/CUST NAME	: PLANT MANAGER
DATES - START	: 95/02/03
- COMPLETION	: 95/10/30
- APPROVAL	: 95/01/31
- DEFINITION	: 95/06/30
GL MAIN/SUB/CLASS	:
CHARGE OUT	: 1 - CHARGED OUT
ECCO BUDGET $	:
ECCO EXP JOB-TO-DATE	:
ECCO EXP YEAR TO DATE	:
ECCO CHARGED OUT	:
AUTH. AMT. APPROVED	:
AA MAJOR SCOPE CHANGE	:

FIGURE 7.24 CORPORATE ENGINEERING DEPARTMENT JOB DEFINITION, JOB LISTING–JOB DIRECTORY. The initiation of a job is handled on line with responses to the menu-driven questions listed above. The opening of a job would be signaled with the assignment of the job number. An open status would allow charging hours worked and expenditures. The 6 ECCO amounts, including authorized amount (AA) approved and AA major scope change, would be system-driven numbers.

In this case the project manager is responsible for a number of projects, requiring information on many projects. The project control system therefore must be able to process multiple projects. The report in Fig. 7.26 provides a single bottom line for each project. The report numbers are produced by the system based on timely input to show approved and generated commitments and actual expenditures. An actual expenditure is one where a corporate check has been written for an invoice approved for payment by the project manager.

Project Expenditure Report—Project Summary by Areas

Each project is individually cost controlled on the basis of its own line items and coded project functional areas, as seen in Fig. 7.27. This is a difficult report to generate because of the kind of corporate dedication and project discipline needed to define, code, and monitor a project on a functional area basis, as depicted by this report example.

Project Expenditure Report—Project Details by Element Group

A typical project may be broken down into its subprojects, functional areas, element groups, and elements. Figures 7.26 and 7.27 show a project as subprojects and as

(P)ECCO 0330 V1.1

JOB CODE: 1 0024 00

JOB DEFINITION

JOB LISTING

COST CODE STRUCTURE

JOB CODE	AREA	ELE-MENT	COST SOURCE	AREA/ELEMENT DESCRIPTION	AUTH AMT. APPROVED	AUTH SCOPE CHANGE	AMOUNT REDISTR.	FORECAST FINAL COST	CCA CLASS
1	110	0100	E	HYPO SYSTEM MODS ABSORPTION TOWER	0	0	0	0	0
1	110	0100	V	HYPO SYSTEM MODS ABSORPTION TOWER	0	0	0	0	0
1	110	0520	E	HYPO SYSTEM MODS PUMP TANK & PUMPS	0	0	0	0	0
1	110	0520	V	HYPO SYSTEM MODS PUMP TANK & PUMPS	0	0	0	0	0
1	110	4300	C	HYPO SYSTEM MODS FDN. & EQPMT. SUPP.	0	0	0	0	0
1	110	5000	V	HYPO SYSTEM MODS ELECTRICAL	0	0	0	0	0
1	110	7300	E	HYPO SYSTEM MODS PLASTIC PIPE & FTGS.	0	0	0	0	0
1	110	7300	V	HYPO SYSTEM MODS PLASTIC PIPE & FTGS.	0	0	0	0	0
1	910	9900	X	RESERVES & CONTINGENCIES	0	0	0	0	0
				GRAND TOTAL					

FIGURE 7.25 CORPORATE ENGINEERING DEPARTMENT JOB DEFINITION, JOB LISTING COST CODE STRUCTURE. The result of on line input, this report shows a project (job code 1), the full project no. (1 0024 00), the process area (110), the elements as 4-digit code items, the cost sources (E, V, C, and X) for the elements, four cost control columns, and a fifth colunm for the capital cost allowance (CCA) classification.

functional areas. Each area is further broken down and defined as element groups. Element groups are hardware components or major equipment types carrying out specific mechanical functions in a process system. This functional breakdown generates a fairly high degree of detail, as may be seen in Fig. 7.28, which depicts the following mechanical equipment element groups:

PROJECT EXPENDITURE REPORT

SUMMARY OF PROJECTS

PROJECT MANAGER NAME:

PROJECT NO.	DESCRIPTION	COMMITMENTS APPROVED	COMMITMENTS GENERATED	EXPENDITURES CURRENT	EXPENDITURES TO DATE	CURRENT O/S CMTS.	EXP. & CMTS. TO DATE
5305 00	PETN PARTICLE SIZING COMP. SYSTEM	0	0	0	0	0	0
5305	TOTAL	0	0	0	0	0	0
5317 00	DOPE HOUSE	1386373	519203	6805	1699966	205610	1905576
5317	TOTAL	1386373	519203	6805	1699966	205610	1905576
5354 00	CONTROL FOR BOIL-ERS AT POWERHOUSE	19120	58047	127	60627	16540	77167
5354	TOTAL	19120	58047	127	60627	16540	77167
5355 00	BOILER FEED H20 DEMINERALIZER	0	0	0	0	0	0
5355	TOTAL	0	0	0	0	0	0
5362 00	A/C & HEATING BUILD-ING P12	0	0	0	0	0	0
5362	TOTAL	0	0	0	0	0	0

FIGURE 7.26 CORPORATE ENGINEERING DEPARTMENT PROJECT EXPENDITURE REPORT, SUMMARY OF PROJECTS. This is a typical project expenditure bottom-line report for a project manager handling a number of projects. This report tracks commitments and expenditures only. Commitments are of two kinds: those that are approved and those that are generated. A generated commitment is one where the formal paperwork follows the action of committing an amount.

Group 2300 Filters, separators, silencers, dust collectors, and cyclones in project number 5280 01.

Group 2400 Solids handling equipment in the same project.

The four-digit codes in the groups identify individual pieces of equipment.

PROJECT EXPENDITURE REPORT

PROJECT SUMMARY BY AREAS

PROJECT CODE: 5280 01
PROJECT NAME:
PROJECT ENGINEER:

AREA CODE	DESCRIPTION	COMMITMENTS APPROVED	COMMITMENTS GENERATED	EXPENDITURES CURRENT	EXPENDITURES TO DATE	CURR.O/S CMTS.	EX+O/S TO DATE	CHANGES IN E+C
000	GENERATED DESCR.	0	0	0	0	0	0	0
100	BATTERY LIMITS	18274379	63006	0	14596244	3741159	18337403	0
200	STORAGE AND HANDLING	375196	2883	0	313637	64442	370079	0
300	UTILITIES	4076142	2113	0	3077164	1001191	4078255	0
400	SERVICES	2354999	75008-	0	2106206	173785	2279991	0
500	INDIRECTS	743269	1100191	35373	1682649	161171	1843820	35373
600	ENGINEERING	218723	8981745	67983	9057553	142915	9200460	67983
700	SPECIAL INDIRECT	24926	335829	0	330221	30534	360755	0
SUB-TOTAL	(000-700) FIXED ASSETS	26068012	10410759	103356	31163674	5315097	36478771	103356
800	OPERATIONS	440975	44654	0	478753	6876	485629	0
900	RESERVES	0	0	0	0	0	0	0

Figure 7.27 Corporate Engineering Department Project Expenditure Report, Project Summary by Areas. Project 5280 01 comprises areas 100 to 900, seen as the first column. Commitments and expenditures made and paid by contracts and purchasse orders have been allocated to the project areas. This report accumulates the allocated costs.

Project Expenditure Report—Summary

The two expenditure reports in Figs. 7.27 and 7.28 have detailed project 5280 01 by its area codes, such as, codes 100 through 900, and a selection of element group codes, such as, codes 2301 through 2403. These codes are known as project functional or project elemental codes. Except for code 500 and 600 items and other soft cost or op-

PROJECT EXPENDITURE REPORT

PROJECT DETAILS BY ELEMENT GROUP

PROJECT CODE: 5280 01
PROJECT NAME:
PROJECT ENGINEER:

ELEMENT CODE	DESCRIPTION	COMMITMENTS APPROVED	COMMITMENTS GENERATED	EXPENDITURES CURRENT	EXPENDITURES TO DATE	O/S CMTS.	EX+ CMTS TO DATE
2301	FILTERS, SEPARATORS	25155	11901	0	37056	0	37056
2302	FILTERS, SEPARATORS	390379	0	0	323778	66601	390379
2303	FILTERS, SEPARATORS	17095	0	0	15091	2004	17095
2304	FILTERS, SEPARATORS	10910	0	0	10910	0	10910
2305	FILTERS, SEPARATORS	19737	0	0	17879	1858	19737
2306	FILTERS, SEPARATORS	19046	0	0	17166	1880	19046
2307	FILTERS, SEPARATORS	7480	0	0	5017	2463	7480
2308	FILTERS, SEPARATORS	939	0	0	939	0	939
2401	SOLIDS HANDLING EQUIP.	89660	0	0	89660	0	89660
2402	SOLIDS HANDLING EQUIP.	51524	0	0	50532	992	51524
2403	SOLIDS HANDLING EQUIP.	23216	0	0	23216	0	23216
2404	SOLIDS HANDLING EQUIP.	9090	0	0	9090	0	9090
2405	SOLIDS HANDLING EQUIP.	18462	4690	0	23152	0	23152
2406	SOLIDS HANDLING EQUIP.	59590	0	0	57156	1924	59590
2407	SOLIDS HANDLING EQUIP.	2431	0	0	2431	0	2431
2408	SOLIDS HANDLING EQUIP.	10197	0	0	10197	0	10197
2409	SOLIDS HANDLING EQUIP.	6355	0	0	6355	0	6355
2410	SOLIDS HANDLING EQUIP.	133019	949	0	133968	0	133968

FIGURE 7.28 CORPORATE ENGINEERING DEPARTMENT PROJECT EXPENDITURE REPORT, PROJECT DETAILS BY ELEMENT GROUP. Project 5280 01 comprises many major element groups as part of its process battery limits, including groups 2300 and 2400. The elements in these two groups are listed in the above report. As purchases are made and contracts issued for the supply and installlation of these elements, amounts are allocated to their codes to create a record of commitments and expenditures.

erational items which are consumed in the creation of the project, the functional areas and elements are representative of the way the facility users or the owners receive the completed project. In other words, they are what is left in place after the project manager and the engineers and constructors finish their work and leave the site.

The functional areas and elements are designed, procured, and constructed by the corporation's own forces and/or by consultants, vendors, and construction contractors. They provide their services to a project via an internal work order, a purchase order, or a contract. As such, they are the sources of cost for the project areas and elements.

Project Expenditure Report—Sum of Contracts, POs, and Internal Charges

Figure 7.29 is a cost source summary expenditure report for project 5280. A cost source summary report may also be described as a summary report by project functional organization. In the engineering department of this case history the coding system for the traditional project functional organizations was as follows:

- C Construction contractors
- E Vendors hired under purchase orders
- S Consultants retained under consulting contracts

PROJECT EXPENDITURE REPORT

PROJECT SUMMARY
BY SUM OF CONTRACTS/P.O. s/INTERNAL CHARGES

PROJECT CODE: 5280 01
PROJECT NAME:
PROJECT ENGINEER

COST SOURCE	DESCRIPTION	COMMITMENTS		EXPENDITURES		CURR. O/S. CMTS.	EXP. & CMTS. TO DATE
		APPROVED	GENERATED	CURRENT	TO DATE		
C	CONSTRUCTION CONTRACTS	11925285	144809-	0	8941398	2839078	11780476
E	CORPORATE H.O. PURCHASES	14546756	333715	0	12426012	2454459	14880471
S	CONSULTING CONTRACTS	0	414929	0	414929	0	414929
V	INTERNAL CHARGES	36946	9851578	103356	9860008	28436	9888524
X	RESERVES AND CONTINGENCIES	0	0	0	0	0	0
5280 01	PROJECT CODE TOTALS	26508987	10455413	103356	31642427	5321973	36934400
5280	PROJECT TOTALS	28001820	10469837	103356	32744282	5727375	38471657

FIGURE 7.29 CORPORATE ENGINEERING DEPARTMENT PROJECT EXPENDITURE REPORT, PROJECT SUMMARY BY SUM OF CONTRACTS, POs AND INTERNAL CHARGES. Project 5280 01, a subproject of project 5280, is under way. This snapshot report shows commitments made and expenditures paid to construction contractors, C, vendors under H.O. purchase orders, E, consulting contracts, S, etc. The project 5280 01 code totals are shown. Expenditures are being generated by other 5280 subprojects. They are reflected in the 5280 project totals.

V Internal work carried out by the corporation's own forces

X Project cost reserves and contingencies

The concept of functional organization codes was introduced previously and discussed most recently in Section 7.2.

Figure 7.29 is a system-generated project expenditure summary report made by selecting lower level detail information within the cost source codes representing construction contractors, purchase orders, consulting contracts, and the internal organization.

An example of the required code detail is seen in Fig. 7.30. Listed are a number of construction contracts, such as 80C02-000, a number of construction material contracts, such as 80M03-000, and a number of purchase orders, such as LEE 0656000. The contracts and purchase orders listed make up two of the cost sources for area code 119.

The PECCO reports described and illustrated to this point are expenditure reports. Expenditure reports concern themselves with commitments, such as contracts and purchase orders, and expenditures, such as approved invoices and actual checks issued as payment for services or goods received. Expenditure reports track project reality. They do not relate to estimates or budgets. Estimates and budgets are the purview of cost control reports to be discussed in the following PECCO report series examples.

Project Cost Control Report—Summary of Projects

This report, shown in Fig. 7.31, is similar to the expenditure report in Fig. 7.26 in that it provides a listing of projects being handled by the project manager. The report shows six columns solely for cost control purposes, named:

1. Amount authorized
2. Approved scope changes
3. Estimate to complete
4. Forecast final cost
5. Amount authorized redistributed
6. Amount over or under

The other column from the expenditure reporting system is

7. Expenditures and outstanding (O/S) commitments to date

Six of these seven columns are cost control input, based on estimating, budgeting, and management decisions. Cost control requires the action of comparing expenditures with budgets for the line item in question. A line item may be a project, an area, an element, a contract, or a purchase order. A line item must be scoped and coded and exist for the life of the project, or until completed, unless it is canceled as the result of a scope change.

PROJECT EXPENDITURE REPORT

PROJECT DETAILS BY
AREAS/ELEMENTS
CONTRACTS / P.O. s / INTERNAL CHARGES

PROJECT CODE: 5280 01
PROJECT NAME:
PROJECT ENGINEER:

AREA MAIN: 1 BATTERY LIMITS
FUNCTION: 11 POLYMERIZATION
SUBFUNCTION: 119 PROCESS EQUIPMENT & MATERIAL

CONTRACT/P.O. INTERNAL CHARGE CODE	DESCRIPTION	COMMITMENTS		EXPENDITURES		CURR. O/S COMMITS	EXP. + CMTS. TO DATE
		APPROVED	GENERATED	CURRENT	TO DATE		
2097	MECHANICAL EQUIPMENT						
C	CONSTRUCTION CONTRACTS						
80C02-000		13469	0	0	13469	0	13469
80C02-036		9590	0	0	9590	0	9590
80C02-044		2070	0	0	2070	0	2070
80M03-000		1903	0	0	1903	0	1903
80M03-135		1114	0	0	947	167	1114
C	TOTAL COST SOURCE	28146	0	0	27979	167	28146
2097	TOTAL ELEMENT	28146	0	0	27979	167	28146
2101	PUMPS AND DRIVES						
E	HEAD OFFICE PURCHASES						
LEE 0656000		129553	0	0	91259	38294	129553
LEE 0656001		4205	0	0	0	4205	4205
E	TOTAL COST SOURCE	133758	0	0	91259	42499	133758
2101	TOTAL ELEMENT	133758	0	0	91259	42499	133758

FIGURE 7.30 CORPORATE ENGINEERING DEPARTMENT PROJECT EXPENDITURE REPORT, PROJECT DETAILS BY AREAS/ELEMENTS, CONTRACTS, POs AND INTERNAL CHARGES. Area code 119 has elements, including 2097, Mechanical Equipment, and 2101, Pumps and Drives, being constructed under a number of construction contracts and purchase orders, as listed. The report shows commitments and expenditures in a number of contracts and purchase orders made on behalf of these elements.

PROJECT COST CONTROL REPORT

SUMMARY OF PROJECTS

PROJECT MANAGER NAME:

PROJECT NO.	DESCRIPTION	AMOUNT AUTHO-RIZED	APPRVD SCOPE CHANGES	EXP. + O/S CMTS. TO DATE	ESTI-MATE TO COMPL.	FCST. FINAL COST	AMOUNT AUTH. RE-DISTR.	AMOUNT OVER / UNDER
5305 00	PETN PARTICLE SIZING COMP SYSTEM	0	0	0	0	0	0	0
5317 00	DOPE HOUSE	2376000	0	1905576	228050	2133626	2376000	242374
5317	TOTAL	2376000	0	1905576	228050	2133626	2376000	242374
5354 00	POWERHOUSE CONTROL FOR BOILERS	116200	0	77167	52433	129600	116200	13400-
5354	TOTAL	116200	0	77167	52433	129600	116200	13400-
5355 00	BOILER FEED H2O DEMINERALIZER	0	0	0	0	0	0	0
5355	TOTAL	0	0	0	0	0	0	0
5362 00	A/C AND HEATING BUILDING P12	0	0	0	0	0	0	0
5362	TOTAL	0	0	0	0	0	0	0
5373 00	ADMINISTRATION OFFICES AND LABORATORY	0	0	0	0	0	0	0
5373	TOTAL	0	0	0	0	0	0	0
5407	REFRIGERATION SYSTEM	517000	0	251210	265790	517000	517000	0
5407	TOTAL	517000	0	251210	265790	517000	517000	0

FIGURE 7.31 CORPORATE ENGINEERING DEPARTMENT PROJECT COST CONTROL REPORT, SUMMARY OF PROJECTS. This is a multiple-project cost control report for the responsible project manager. The project manager is in charge of projects 5305 00 through 5407. The system-produced report provides project totals for the designated cost and expenditure columns.

But, what the cost and expenditure control reports have in common, the glue that binds them together, is the cost code system. Figure 7.31 aims to depict this feature of merging expenditures and budgeting and estimating inputs for cost control purposes.

Project Cost Control Report—Summary by Areas

A project bottom line is only as good as the sum of the line items that add up to the bottom line. Line items for project cost control are code driven. In the systems of project management approach for this case history the line items represent hard functional areas. To create a project cost control system, each project area in its turn is scoped, value engineered, estimated, and budgeted through each project stage, until all aspects of the project are converted to purchase orders, contracts, or owner tasks. To achieve an on-budget condition, the sum of the costs of all tasks must equal the sum of the costs of all the components that make up the cost of the functional area. And the sum of all the areas makes up the project bottom line. Figure 7.32 illustrates that concept.

Project Cost Control Report—Details by Element Group

If a project comprises a number of functional areas, as seen in Fig. 7.32, the areas are represented the way the completed project will be operated after its turnover to the owners and users. To manage the delivery of the project, a number of areas were added to the coded structure to accommodate project consumables, such as 500, Indirects; 600, Engineering; 700, Special Indirect, and 900, Reserves, as seen in Fig. 7.32.

The definition structure does not stop with areas because each area in turn is defined by its elements or element groups. As this case history illustrates process plants, the plant areas are defined by element groups such as mechanical equipment, as seen in Fig. 7.33.

A point of concern. The development of project control systems often leads to the proliferation of detailed information, particularly coded information at the project front end. If a project is "cost overcoded," it may be difficult to apply the codes during the many project delivery stages. This could cause frustration and lead to corrupt data to the extent that although there are mounds of information, it becomes suspect. What happens in these cases is that the system continues to be used, but there is little confidence in it.

The content of Fig. 7.33 is perhaps an illustration of this conundrum. On one hand there are many coded element groups. On the other, the elements are the product of many design and engineering activities, procurement, assembly, and construction. The question is, can the costs attributed to the elements be gathered from the many different cost sources, and second, do they really need to be?

PROJECT COST CONTROL REPORT

PROJECT SUMMARY BY AREAS

PROJECT CODE: 5280 01
PROJECT NAME:
PROJECT ENGINEER:

AREA CODE	DESCRIPTION	AMOUNT AUTHO-RIZED	APRVD SCOPE CHANGES	EXP. + OS CMTS TO DATE	ESTI-MATE TO COMPL.	FCST. FINAL COST	AMOUNT AUTH. RE-DISTR.	AMOUNT OVER / UNDER
000	GENERATED DESC.	0	0	0	0	0	0	0
100	BATTERY LIMITS	28684690	0	18337403	4160770	22498173	28694690	6196517
200	STORG. & HANDLG.	966400	0	378079	206436	584515	966400	381885
300	UTILITIES	3418400	267500	4078255	1059814	5138069	3418400	1719669-
400	SERVICES	2107900	214600	2279991	196397	2476388	2097900	378400-
500	INDIRECTS	3402600	0	1843820	1316645	3160465	3402600	242135
600	ENGINEERING	8406800	84400	9200468	1133232	10333700	8689800	1643900-
700	SPECIAL INDIRECT	1355210	0	360755	780345	1141100	1072210	68890-
SUBTOTAL 000-700	FIXED ASSETS	48342000	566500	36478771	8853639	45332410	48342000	3009590
800	OPERATIONS	514000	12000	485629	61241	546870	514000	32870-
900	RESERVES	5658000	0	0	0	0	5658000	5658000

FIGURE 7.32 CORPORATE ENGINEERING DEPARTMENT PROJECT COST CONTROL REPORT, PROJECT SUMMARY BY AREAS. This is the project cost control report for the responsible project engineer in charge of project 5280 01. The database system-produced report provides cost totals of the line item codes 100 through 900 for the designated cost and expenditure control columns.

Project Cost Control Report—Summary by Contracts/POs/Internal Charges

In some respects the project cost control system illustrated by this case history may be referred to as a "double-barreled" system. Indeed for successful project control there are usually many control barrels required. The three immediately preceding PECCO reports provided a cost control look through the PDS, namely, project, subproject, area, element group, and element. These items all have the cost control attributes ascribed to them by the report column headings. The costs ascribed to them come from cost sources, which are contracts, purchase orders, and internal charges, such as time charged by employees or consultants.

The way it works is that each coded functional or elemental line item is delivered by a person or company working under a PO or contract. Thus each item is dou-

PROJECT COST CONTROL REPORT

PROJECT DETAILS BY ELEMENT GROUP

PROJECT CODE: 5280 01
PROJECT NAME:
PROJECT ENGINEER:

ELEMENT CODE	DESCRIPTION	AMOUNT AUTHORIZED	APPROVED SCOPE CHANGE	EXP + OS CMTS TO DATE	ESTIMATE TO COM-PLETE	FCST. FINAL COST	AMOUNT AUTH. REDISTR.	AMOUNT OVER / UNDER
2301	FILTERS, SEPARATORS	28950	0	37056	0	37056	34250	2806-
2302	FILTERS, SEPARATORS	391950	0	390379	15093	405473	400700	4772-
2303	FILTERS, SEPARATORS	17300	0	17095	0	17095	17300	205
2304	FILTERS, SEPARATORS	15120	0	10910	0	10910	15620	4710
2305	FILTERS, SEPARATORS	17750	0	19737	0	19737	21800	2063
2306	FILTERS, SEPARATORS	19500	0	19046	0	19046	19500	454
2307	FILTERS, SEPARATORS	8350	0	7480	0	7480	8350	870
2308	FILTERS, SEPARATORS	1000	0	939	0	939	1000	61
2401	SOLIDS HANDLING EQUIP.	90200	0	89660	0	89660	94700	5040
2402	SOLIDS HANDLING EQUIP.	53550	0	51524	214	51738	52950	1212
2403	SOLIDS HANDLING EQUIP.	24500	0	23216	0	23216	26800	3584
2404	SOLIDS HANDLING EQUIP.	7600	0	9090	0	9090	10000	910
2405	SOLIDS HANDLING EQUIP.	17050	4690	23152	0	23152	19850	3302-
2406	SOLIDS HANDLING EQUIP.	59550	0	59590	0	59590	61700	2110
2407	SOLIDS HANDLING EQUIP.	2500	0	2431	0	2431	2500	69
2408	SOLIDS HANDLING EQUIP.	10400	0	10197	495	10692	10400	292-
2409	SOLIDS HANDLING EQUIP.	6500	0	6355	0	6355	6500	145
2410	SOLIDS HANDLING EQUIP.	137250	949	133968	4326	138294	137150	1144-

FIGURE 7.33 CORPORATE ENGINEERING DEPARTMENT PROJECT COST CONTROL REPORT, PROJECT DETAILS BY ELEMENT GROUP. Project 5280 01 includes a process area which is driven by process machinery, including the filter and separators coded as 2301 to 2308 and solids handling machines coded as 2401 to 2410. The items have authorized amounts. They are code items in contracts and purchase orders. As progress is made, commitments and expenditures are tracked, amounts are redistributed, and the amount authorized redistributed is compared to forecast final cost to establish over/under budget status of the project.

ble coded both as to function and as to cost source. That is where the term "double barrel" comes from. This second barrel is seen in the project cost control report—project summary by sum of contracts / PO / internal charges, as shown in Fig. 7.34.

At the very least it is a burden to run a single-barrel cost control system. A double barrel is more than twice the complexity. Why a double barrel? No project should ever be conceptualized just as the sum of its time charges, purchase orders, and contracts. If the corporate owners are to know what they will be getting, the project requires to be first conceived, designed, scoped, engineered, and costed as functions and elements. These coded and costed elements then become the cost and quality control mechanisms as cost code items for the people and organizations that will deliver the project. That is what is seen in Fig. 7.34 for project 5280 01.

PROJECT COST CONTROL REPORT

PROJECT SUMMARY BY
SUM OF CONTRACTS / P.O. /
INTERNAL CHARGES

PROJECT CODE: 5280 01
PROJECT NAME:
PROJECT ENGINEER:

COST SOURCE	DESCRIPTION	AMOUNT AUTHO-RIZED	APRVD SCOPE CHANGES	EXP. + OS CMTS TO DATE	ESTI-MATE TO COMPL.	FCST. FINAL COST	AMOUNT AUTH. RE-DISTR.	AMOUNT OVER / UNDER
C	CONSTR. CONTRACTS	18362730	482100	11780476	3713781	15494257	17412393	1910676
E	PURCHASE ORDERS	19141270	0	14880471	2073160	16953631	19512319	258688
S	CONSLTG. CONTRACTS	361500	0	414929	233571	648500	628500	200000-
V	INTERNAL CHARGES	10990500	96400	9888524	2894368	12782892	11302248	1480644-
X	RESERVES & CONTING.	5658000	0	0	0	0	5658000	5658000
5280 01	PROJECT CODE TOTAL	54514000	578500	36964400	8914880	45879280	54514000	8634720
5280	PROJECT TOTALS	56000000	578500	38471657	8893623	47365280	56000000	8634720

FIGURE 7.34 CORPORATE ENGINEERING DEPARTMENT PROJECT COST CONTROL REPORT, PROJECT SUMMARY BY SUM OF CONTRACTS, POS AND INTERNAL CHARGES. Project 5280 01, a subproject of Project 5280, is under way. Contracts, purchase orders, and consulting contracts have been issued. Internal teams are responsible for a big part of the project, as seen under internal charges. A sum has been set up as a reserve and as a contingency. The report, created from the project database by the system, is a project cost snapshot of the project cost sources C, E, S, V, and X and the two bottom lines.

Project Cost Control Report—Details by Areas/Elements/Contracts/PO/Internal Charges

Figure 7.35 shows project 5280 01 area 119 broken down into two elements, 2097, Mechanical Equipment, and 2101, Pumps and Drives. These elements are work package line items in a number of contracts and purchase orders, as listed. The report has estimating and budget numbers in a number of columns, which aim to facilitate cost control of the subject elements, code items 119 2097 and 119 2101.

Does this illustration show complexity? Yes, it does. Is this type of complexity warranted? From a corporate viewpoint, the creation and maintenance of this kind of reporting system is expensive. What is the return on the investment? From a project management perspective, is this effort just too much detail to handle? Only the corporate owner and the experienced project manager should attempt to answer this question.

We know from experience that most projects are not adequately cost controlled. When the inevitable problems of over budget, unacceptable quality, and late delivery occur, the money that was saved through inadequate design and engineering is spent many times over.

The other side of the coin is too much detail, which no one can assimilate or use effectively, as may be construed from the information overload seen in Fig. 7.35.

7.10 System-Based Cost Estimating

Computerized estimating is difficult. It is not as if computer spread sheets and databases cannot manage formulas, units, codes, numbers, and extensions. They can, if they have quantities to work with. But project budgets are set long before there are quantities, indeed before owners and their project managers know the scope of the project. The problem lies in converting early decisions into design parameters, the parameters into drawings and specifications, and drawings into quantities, which are relatable to units of person-hours, or elements manufactured by vendors and components assembled by construction companies.

Project estimating is particularly difficult in the earliest conceptual or feasibility project stages. The biggest problem is in pulling the team players together and reaching consensus on the project scope and quality, and eventually a cost number. When a scope agreement is reached and approved by senior management, there is still the time and skill needed to develop the information so that the project may be quantified and costed. If the project is seen as time critical, it may be approved long before enough cost information is available. These kinds of early approvals, sometimes based on skimpy information, invariably lead to disastrous cost overruns. (In some instances the corporate owners may say that it will cost what it will cost. The completed project benefits override all cost considerations.)

In this case computerized estimating was the least advanced of the corporate and engineering department project control systems. This is not because the estimating skills and computer technology were not available. The cost engineering and esti-

PROJECT COST CONTROL REPORT

PROJECT DETAILS BY
AREAS / ELEMENTS
CONTRACTS / P.O. S / INTERNAL CHARGES

PROJECT CODE: 5280 01
PROJECT NAME:
PROJECT ENGINEER:

AREA MAIN: 1 BATTERY LIMITS
FUNCTION: 11 POLYMERIZATION - COMPRESSION
SUB-FUNCTION: 119 PROCESS EQUIPMENT & MATERIAL

CONTRACT/P.O. INTERNAL CHARGE CODE	DESCRIPTION	AMOUNT AUTHORIZED	APPROVED SCOPE CHANGES	EXPENDS. + O/S CMTS. TO DATE	ESTIMATE TO COMPLETE	FORECAST FINAL COST	AMOUNT AUTH. REDISTR.	AMOUNT OVER/ UNDER
2097	MECHANICAL EQUIPMENT							
C	CONSTRUCTION CONTRACTS							
80C02-000		46000	0	13469	25158	38627	46000	7373
80C02-036		0	0	9590	9590-	0	0	0
80C02-044		0	0	2070	2070-	0	0	0
80M03-000		0	0	1903	1903-	0	0	0
80M03-165		0	0	1114	1114-	0	0	0
C	TOTAL COST SOURCE	46000	0	28146	10481	38627	46000	7373
2097	TOTAL ELEMENT	46000	0	28146	10481	38627	46000	7373
2101	PUMPS AND DRIVES							
E	HEAD OFFICE PURCHASES							
LEE 0656000		60000	0	129553	129553-	0	0	0
LEE 0656001		0	0	4205	4205-	0	0	0
E	TOTAL COST SOURCE	60000	0	133758	133758-	0	0	0

Figure 7.35 Corporate Engineering Department Project Cost Control Report, Details by Areas/Elements, Contracts, POs and Internal Charges. For project 5280 01 an element/resource group, e.g., 119 2097/80C02-000, or 119 2101/LEE 0656000, is reported as to its status in relation to the cost control columns depicted. A resource group may be a contractor, a vendor, or an owner's team member. As a project comprises many contracts and purchaes orders as cost sources, which in turn include many elements, there may be difficulty in tracking expenditures and costs. For this reason it is important not to overallocate in the planning stages. At the same time, this report shows that cost control is not being exercised in that expenditures are being made beyond the amounts authorized.

mating skills are reflected in the project control code systems seen in the ECCO and PECCO report examples. Computer technology consisted of computer-aided design and drawing applications capable of drawing and quantifying process piping and instrumentation, as well as project cost and time information databases.

In early project stages, estimates are made by comparing the proposed project to a previously completed similar job, and making allowances for factors such as size, product output, cost escalation, site conditions, and other risks. These parameters are quantified and costed to the limits of accuracy allowed by circumstances such as the time allowed by senior management and the availability of design information. The cost numbers are only estimates until senior management says that they are the budget. Then the numbers are broken down into functional areas, element groups, and elements. Activities are created and assigned to work packages, which are procured through contracts and purchase orders. The activities and packages of work are coded as database information and input into (P)ECCO for current project cost and expenditure control. As projects are carried out, the (P)ECCO actual costs become historical cost information for future projects.

Engineering Estimate and Budget

As a project is identified to seize an opportunity or solve a problem, the process starts with the creative effort of conceptualization, feasibility studies, program analysis, preliminary design, coding, estimating, and budgeting. These activities form a large part of the cost of the project if the project goes ahead, or they are corporate sunk costs if it does not proceed.

This mostly engineering effort identified by disciplines and skills is charged to the project as seen in Fig. 7.36. The person-hours and expenses are accumulated by the system, and can form the basis for estimating engineering for future similar projects.

Summary of Estimate by Project Areas

The most difficult estimate to make in the world is an estimate by project function. This is because people do not build functions. They build bricks and mortar, or wires and motors, or piping and pumps, or hardware and software. As a result, historical cost data by project functions are difficult to come by.

Do we need cost information by project functions? Yes, absolutely, because when a project is conceptualized, it is done so not as bricks and mortar but as functions that house people, or a manufacturing facility, computer space, a laboratory, a transportation system.

In designing a project function the project manager aims to set the quality standards and scope of the function as a top-down quality control exercise. This means that every component that goes into that function is specified by the functional user, as coached by the project manager and not, as most often happens, by designers who may have an agenda and want to see only bricks and mortar as the most important part of the project criteria.

ENGINEERING ESTIMATE AND BUDGET

PROJECT CODE: 5280 01
PROJECT NAME:
PROJECT ENGINEER:

DISCIPLINE / ACTIVITY	DESCRIPTION	ENGINEERS / ANALYSTS HOURS	ENGINEERS / ANALYSTS DOLLARS	TECHNICIANS / PRGRMRS. HOURS	TECHNICIANS / PRGRMRS. DOLLARS	EXPENSES TRAVEL	EXPENSES OTHER
00 / 01	PROJ. MGMT. / PROJ. ENG.	0	0	0	0	0	0
10 /11	CHEMICAL ENGINEERING	0	0	0	0	0	0
10 / 12	ENVIRONMENTAL ENG.	0	0	0	0	0	0
10 /13	COMPUTER APPLICATION	0	0	0	0	0	0
20 /21	MATERIALS OF CONSTR.	0	0	0	0	0	0
20 /24	POWER HOUSE EQUIPMT.	0	0	0	0	0	0
30/32	EQUIPMT. DESIGN & PROC.	0	0	0	0	0	0
40 /41	CIVIL ENG. DESIGN	0	0	0	0	0	0
40 /43	ARCHITECTURAL	0	0	0	0	0	0
40 /46	BUILDING HVAC & PLBG.	0	0	0	0	0	0
50 /51	ELECTRICAL	0	0	0	0	0	0
60 /61	INSTRUMENTATION	0	0	0	0	0	0
70 /71	COST ESTIMATING	0	0	0	0	0	0
70 /72	PROJECT ACCOUNTING	0	0	0	0	0	0
70 /73	CONTRACTS SUPERVISION	0	0	0	0	0	0
70 /74	COST/SCHEDULE CONTROL	0	0	0	0	0	0
00 TO 70	TOTAL H.O. ENGINEERING	0	0	0	0	0	0
80 / 81	SITE SUPERVISION	0	0	0	0	0	0
00 TO 80	TOTAL PROJECT ENG.	0	0	0	0	0	0

Figure 7.36 Corporate Engineering Department Engineering Estimate and Budget. As a project is planned, designed, and engineered, the engineering cost control system stores in the database the actual person-hours and expenses charged to the disciplines and skills seen in this report. Similar future projects can be estimated on the basis of these units.

This means that a cost control system starts with estimates and budgets coded by completed project functions, including soft costs such as engineering. The function codes are treated as cost allocations or line items in all purchase orders, contracts, and project work carried out by the owner's own organization. Besides providing cost control on a functional basis, that is how cost estimating information can be gathered for estimating future project areas. The concept is depicted in Fig. 7.37.

It is understood that areas 500, 600, 700, 800, and 900 are deemed to be consumed in the delivery of areas 100, 200, 300, and 400.

SUMMARY OF ESTIMATE
BY PROJECT AREAS

PROJECT CODE: 5280 01
PROJECT NAME:
PROJECT ENGINEER:

AREA CODE	AREA DESCRIPTION	CONTRACTS (C)	LABOR (L)	MATERIAL (M)	PURCHASES (E)	TOTAL (C+L +M+E)	AS % OF TOTAL
100	BATTERY LIMITS	0	0	0	0	0	0
200	STORAGE & HANDLING	0	0	0	0	0	0
300	UTILITIES	0	0	0	0	0	0
400	SERVICES	0	0	0	0	0	0
500	CONSTRUCTION INDIRECTS	0	0	0	0	0	0
600	ENGINEERING	0	0	0	0	0	0
700	SPECIAL INDIRECTS	0	0	0	0	0	0
800	OPERATIONS & STARTUP	0	0	0	0	0	0
900	RESERVES & CONTINGENCY	0	0	0	0	0	0
100 TO 900	TOTAL ESTIMATE	0	0	0	0	0	0

Figure 7.37 Corporate Engineering Department Summary of Estimate by Project Areas. The earliest look at a project is by its funcitons. That is the way projects are scoped and their quality is established. That is the way they are delivered to the users. But they are not built that way. They are built through contracts and purchase orders. Therein lies the difficulty. And that is why cost estimating information gathered on the basis of functions and areas is so imporant, as depicted by this report. Only through cross-referenced cost coding of cost sources and areas is it possible to know the cost of areas for cost control, and to estimate future projects.

Summary of Estimate by Project Elements

As a project is made up of functional areas, the areas consist of subfunctions, element groups, and elements. A subfunction, for example, could be a set of vessels for raw material storage, or a separate building housing special equipment. Elements, for example, can be single components, such as windows or doors in a building. They in turn could belong to the element group exterior wall. Or elements could be mechanical components forming part of the heating, ventilating, and air-conditioning system, the refrigeration compressor, for example.

A summary of the estimate by project elements is illustrated in Fig. 7.38. It indicates that the element groups coded 0000 through 8100 are all part of functional area 100. Area 100 in this case is the process heart of the project, or the "battery limits." The battery limits function, before being defined as element groups, could be defined by subfunctions. The subfunctions in turn could comprise element groups and elements.

If project area functions and subfunctions are project specific, they relate only to the project in question. The element groups shown in Fig. 7.38 may be seen to be

SUMMARY OF ESTIMATE
BY PROJECT ELEMENTS

PROJECT CODE: 5280 01
PROJECT NAME:
PROJECT ENGINEER:

AREA /ELMT CODE	AREA DESCRIPTION	CONTRACTS (C)	LABOR (L)	MATERIAL (M)	PURCHASES (E)	TOTAL (C+L +M+E)	AS % OF TOTAL
100 / 0000	PROCESS VESSELS	0	0	0	0	0	0
100 / 2000	PROCESS MECHANICAL	0	0	0	0	0	0
100 / 3010	BUILDING ARCHITECTURAL	0	0	0	0	0	0
100 / 3020	BUILDING SERVICES	0	0	0	0	0	0
100 / 4000	CIVIL ENGINEERING	0	0	0	0	0	0
100 / 5000	ELECTRICAL	0	0	0	0	0	0
100 / 6000	INSTRUMENTATION	0	0	0	0	0	0
100 / 7000	PROCESS PIPING	0	0	0	0	0	0
100 / 8100	PROCESS INSULATION	0	0	0	0	0	0
100 0000 - 8100	TOTAL ESTIMATE	0	0	0	0	0	0

FIGURE 7.38 CORPORATE ENGINEERING DEPARTMENT SUMMARY OF ESTIMATE BY ELEMENTS IN AREA 100. Projects are scoped and designed by area functions and elements. This figure shows the element groups of area 100. The elements are parts of many contracts and purchase orders, as depicted by the colunm headings showing the sources of cost for the elements. Only through cross-referenced cost coding of cost sources and elements is it possible to know the cost of elements for cost control, and to form the estimating database for futrue projects.

generic in that they are recognizable as being of the building industry. For example, all buildings have building services (3020) and electrical (5000). But only the battery limits, area 100, would have specific services and electrics. Therefore the cost information gathered by the estimating report in Fig. 7.38 would only be suitable for a similar project.

Element groups are arrangements of like elements. For example, all the doors in a project, all the windows, all the pumps, all the compressors, the roof system, and the concrete structure form element groups. Within a group, even on a small project, the differences between like elements may be substantial. A door, for example, may be an overhead door, a fire door, a security door, a blast door, and so on. Each type of door (element) has its own code. For project scope and quality control the doors are specified for specific functions as design progress is made. Their cost forms a part of the budget for the functional area in question.

This process applies to all elements. A generic list of elements and their codes used by the corporate engineering department of this case history was given in Section 7.2.

7.11 Summary

The corporate engineering department in this case was the repository of project engineering skill and experience. Project managers were usually recruited from the ranks of project engineers. The way a project was managed depended on the project manager. Although there were many computer systems in use, they were operated by their custodians as stand-alone applications for accounting, design, or scheduling. If project managers wanted to benefit from these systems, they had to apply to the owners of the systems, and from time to time the systems would deliver specific project information to the project managers and engineers.

There were many projects under way at any given time, but their status was unknown as there was no multiple-project tracking system. At the same time projects were often late, of poor quality, and over budget. To address this situation, the chief engineer ordered that a project control system be put in place. Every project would be in the system. Projects would be planned graphically, using S curves. The cost and schedule status of every project would always be available on line.

In responding to the chief engineer's order, the system developers interviewed a core of highly experienced and skilled project engineers using project management methods that could form the foundation of the project control system, as presented in Section 7.2. The developers discovered that the project and discipline engineers' biggest concern was the difficulty of defining project scope and quality. The other major concern was cost estimating and budgeting, and the issue of communicating information for project control purposes, discussed in Sections 7.3 and 7.4.

To implement an on-line multiple-project control system, it was agreed by the chief engineer that the system become a computer tool of the project engineers, and that all projects be in the system. Although the chief engineer only wanted to view projects as S curves, to have validity the curves had to be based on the quality of information presented in Sections 7.5 through 7.9.

Finally the project control system of the corporate engineering department in this case history is fully representative of the fundamentals of the systems of project management presented in the chapters in Part 2 of this book.

Note: This chapter is based on my experience as a systems engineer for the corporate engineering department of a large multiplant corporation in the process industry. The corporate engineers and engineering department project managers were highly skilled and experienced repeat designers and builders of all kinds of manufacturing and process plants for the firm's own account. The corporation wanted an information technology–based information system to track projects on line and in real time. My assessment of their needs led me very quickly to the conclusion that for a management information system to be useful it must at the same time be a tool for the engineers and project managers who deliver the projects. The result was the ECCO system to control in-house design, engineering, and administration, and PECCO to control jobs and projects. Both systems were computer based and aimed to be tools for the project teams as well as on-line information systems for management.

The project files are the references. These files are replicated as the systems of project management throughout this book. This chapter aims to represent the task of capturing proven in-house project design, engineering, and management processes as practiced by experienced engineers, and incorporating them into a new computerized project control system.

QUESTIONS AND EXERCISES

7.1. Write a 500-word textbook-referenced thesis on what is the single most important concern of project managers, project engineers, and discipline engineers in a corporate engineering environment. How does this concern manifest itself and what effect does it have on projects?

7.2. Explain with words and graphics the development of the project control system.

7.3. Assume that you are the project manager. Your professor is the head of the class, and the class is your customer. Working on behalf of your customer, apply the project management concepts learned in the example case of the corporate engineering department when considering, contemplating, and studying the feasibility and risks associated with planning, designing, financing, procuring contractors, constructing, and moving into a new house. For scope, quality, tasks, and organizational inputs refer to the house questions in previous chapters. Write a scenario and defend it to the class.

7.4. Assume that you are the project control system development manager in your corporation. The corporation can be in any line of business. Your task is to develop and implement an enterprise-wide computer-based project control system. Write a 500-word essay, based on the lessons learned in this chapter, on how to introduce new computer tools in your company, and how they will serve people as working tools and at the same time provide project control information to management. As project management software is extensively marketed, refer to specific software that is available on the Internet or for downloading. A few Web sites are listed here as references:

Artemis Views	www.artemispm.com
CA-SuperProject	www.cai.com
Open Plan Professional	www.wst.com
Primavera Project Planner	www.primavera.com

RAPID TRANSIT EXPANSION PROJECT (RTEP) CASE EXERCISE 8

8.1 Introduction

This chapter develops a concept to manage and control the delivery of a multiple-project subway program. The exercise is based on the the Rapid Transit Expansion Program Consulting and Construction Information Packages, issued by the Toronto Transit Commission (TTC) between 1993 and 1995. The RTEP phase 1 was a proposal to design and construct five rapid transit projects in Toronto.

The TTC developed the feasibility studies, order-of-magnitude estimates, design criteria, design and construction packaging, and procurement strategies, which were published in the information package as a precursor to hiring design and construction services to deliver the projects.

To simplify the concept for the purpose of this book, the RTEP phase 1 program is referred to as a project. Of the five projects in phase 1, only one, the Eglinton West subway line, is developed for project management purposes. However, to accommodate future projects, provision is made for a multiple-project hierarchy breakdown and coding system. Thus the Eglinton West subway structures and codes were developed and designed to accommodate future projects. This feature is reflected in Fig. 8.1.

The project definition structure (PDS) discussion shows how to set the project scope and quality from the perspective of the project owners and customers in project management code-driven language. The customer-driven project code is seen to be based both on cost engineering and on work breakdown structure (WBS) and organizational breakdown structure (OBS) principles. The project definition code is the glue that binds elements for scope and cost control from phase to phase, from concept to completion. As a project is defined and its scope frozen, thousands of functional elements take on scalable code identities that both the customer and the project team relate to and communicate with.

Each deliverable coded element becomes a repository for its scope, quality, and cost estimate. When defined and approved, the estimate becomes the budget. The sum

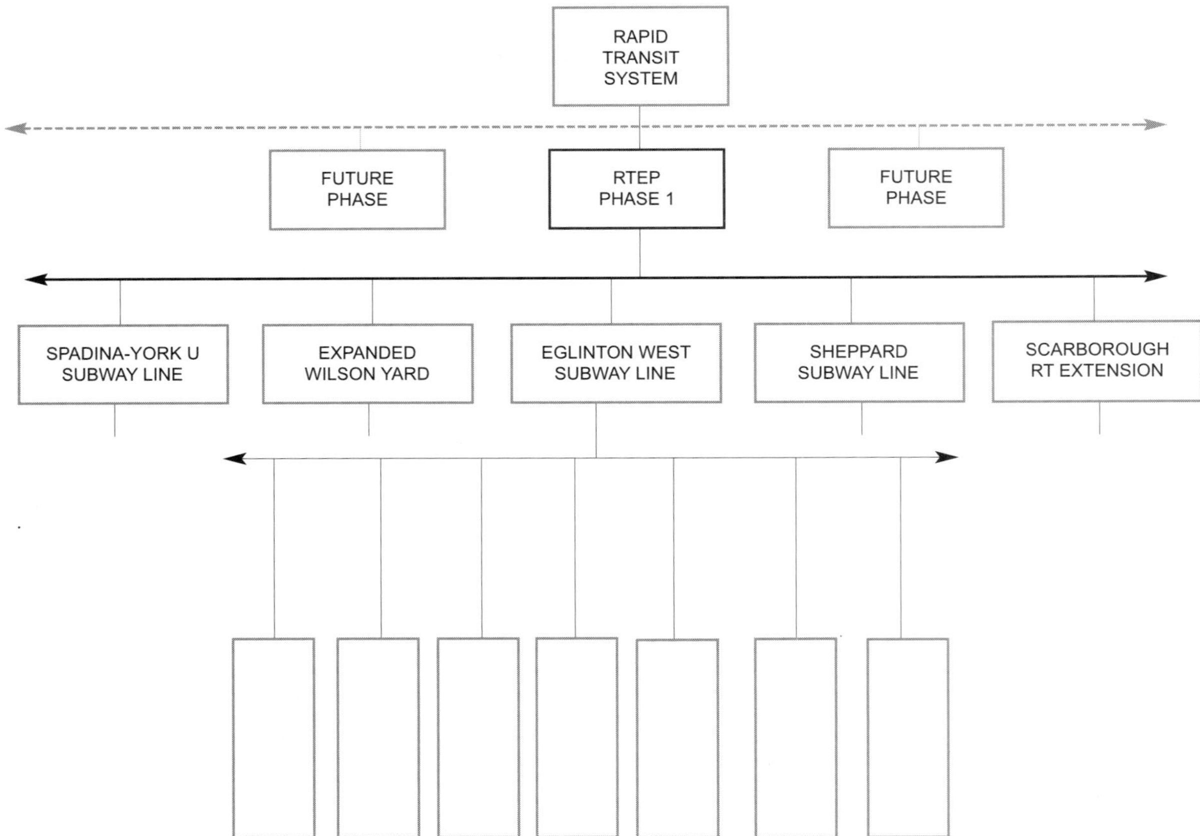

FIGURE 8.1 RAPID TRANSIT EXPANSION PROGRAM (RTEP) PROJECT DEFINITION OUTLINE STRUCTURE. A rapid transit expansion program is announced. Phase 1 will comprise the projects named. The intent of this exercise is to create a project definition structure and associated code system to be used as the basis for a project scope, quality, and cost control system. The PDS is the first among equals of the systems of project management presented in this book. RTEP phase 1 is designated as the level 1 objective. The phase 1 projects named are assigned at level 2. The system is designed to accommodate future phases.

of all the elemental budgets forms the project budget. The project definition budget is the only source of funds for the project.

As the project is influenced by both the customer and the project delivery team, it is important that both sides develop and agree on project code language.

In this case the owner's information package expressed a number of management concepts for a design and construction strategy. This means that decisions had been taken as to how project deliverables will be packaged, bid, awarded, manufactured, and constructed. These early decisions set the basis for definition codes, breakdown codes, and functional organization codes, as will be reflected in the development of the definition structure and the derived PDS code system.

First every effort must be made to accommodate the approach already in place, and at the same time create a viable project management structure. Second the code structure needs to be made simple, through the use of acronyms and abbreviations, to facilitate communication. To achieve these features, different concepts are considered and demonstrated using the Eglinton West subway as a model.

In the project industry there is often confusion concerning project definitions and work breakdowns. For many people a PDS looks like a WBS. They are and they are not one and the same. The first defines finished deliverables; the second activities. There is a huge difference.

This difference will be illustrated in this chapter, along with an introduction to computer usage in the creation of project phases and coded activities. A work breakdown, similar to a project definition, needs to be a derivative of current thinking in the customer/project team matrix. In other words, the project management system developer has to use what is there. What often happens is that computer systems reorder the presentation of information in out-of-sequence rows. This needs to be understood and accounted for in system design.

It will also be seen how a WBS code develops provisions for five levels of breakdown, with the fifth level tied to the North American construction industry-wide Masterformat divisions. This computer-processed feature illustrates the use of structured code as the foundation for project databases.

The basis for the development of a project functional organization from the perspective of "team project" will be presented. In a team project environment every individual, work group, department, firm, corporation, public agency, and even a public interest group who has a role, a contract package, a purchase order, or an activity in the project is included as a member of the functional organization. The activity has a scope, code, cost, and time: once assigned to a member, it takes on the member's functional organization identity. The activity/member relationship exists for the life of the activity. It can only be completed and paid for. It can only disappear if it is canceled through a scope change.

The derivation of project code systems in the light of computer programming, as project glue, rounds out the systems of definition, breakdown, and functional organization. Alphabetic versus numeric identities are compared. Based on the fundamentals of project management, and the RTEP phase 1 discussions, a code system is recommended and adopted for the exercise. The code is very simple in that it uses structures and abbreviations for the RTEP phase 1 project. The five projects that make up RTEP phase 1 are coded at level 2 of the structure and augmented with three other level 2 "projects," vehicles, soft costs, and contingencies.

The concept of cost control is based on the Eglinton West subway as the model. Code-driven cost control is seen to emanate from estimates and budgets based on definitions, to estimates and budgets based on breakdowns, to budgets for packages awarded by contracts or purchase orders, to members of the functional project organization. After developing the codes for the Eglinton West subway, cost and expenditure control monitoring and reporting formats are based on the use of classical cost terms as column labels and the code items themselves as row labels.

Planning and scheduling by CPM networking is based on the Eglinton West subway. The planning activities are those developed through the formal breakdown structure. An activity not so identified and coded can only be an event, a milestone, a target date, imposed date or other external constraint, or an imposition. Examples of time impositions on project scheduling are management decisions, acts of God, acts of nature, force majeure, strikes, third-party actions, and so on.

8.2 Project Definition

An early realization in project work is that there are very few totally stand-alone projects. Projects invariably are upgrades, expansions, or retrofits of existing facilities. This means that an early consideration is that what is already there will need to be accommodated and incorporated in one way or another. Similarly, many of the people and large segments of the organization that will have a role in the project are also in place. A typical project organization is thus a hybrid of people who may already be in place augmented by ad hoc project professionals, secondments, contract personnel, and members drawn from matrix organizations.

The first result of this condition may be total confusion. All the different groups will have their own systems, methods, and procedures to carry out their different mandates and, first of all, protect their own interests. And that is why the project must have a dedicated project control system, or a system of project management.

In this case exercise we will look at a number of ways to set up a project management system for a subway megaproject. The systems of project management comprise five distinct, integrated control modules: definition, breakdown, organization, cost, and schedule. All systems are related, and each has an objective to fulfill. This exercise will demonstrate all five systems using a number of basic computer project management application packages, graphics, and boiler plate reporting formats.

A project starts with the effort needed to scope it and establish its quality parameters. That is achieved through the use of the PDS. It aims to define the project in the way that the users of the finished project will see it. To make it more than a laundry list, the definition exercise incorporates provision for project management consumables such as soft costs and contingencies. As a PDS resembles a WBS, the approach to its creation is similar. A first exercise in the definition of the RTEP is the project definition code structure in Fig. 8.2.

Figure 8.2 demonstrates the beginning of the definition structure and code for one line of the RTEP, the Eglinton West subway. Taken only to level 3 of the definition structure, the fundamental features to look for are the following:

- The definition and code structure aim to identify the project as it will be seen in its completed form.
- The project consumables of soft costs and contingencies are included as part of the definition.

RTEP PHASE 1
EGLINTON WEST SUBWAY
PROJECT DEFINITION CONCEPT 1

LEVEL	CODE	DESCRIPTION
1	01	RTEP Phase 1
2	EW	Eglinton West Subway Line
3	EWAS	Eglinton West/Allen Station
3	EWCC	York City Center Station
3	EWCS	Caledonia Station
3	EWDS	Dufferin Station
3	EWKS	Keele Station
3	EWSU	Eglinton Subway 4.8 km
3	EWWY	Wilson Yard Component
3	EWXA	Soft Costs/Design/Mgmt
3	EWZZ	Contingencies

FIGURE 8.2 EGLINTON WEST SUBWAY LINE PROJECT DEFINITION STRUCTURE, CONCEPT 1, TABLE. The project definition concept in this case starts as a table. The intent is to use acronyms as codes to the extent possible, as an inheritance of the structure and the breakdown levels. It is seen that the level 3 elements are projects as they will be delivered to the users. But to make the definition more than a laundry list, project consumables such as soft costs and contingencies are included.

- The code system aims to make it easier to relate code to function by using acronym type characters. For example, EW represents Eglinton West and EWDS stands for the Eglinton West Dufferin station.

Because this is the first run at developing the code, this structure is labeled concept 1.

If this code were adopted and used in the management of the project, a stand-alone code developed in the database might be 01EWDS, representing the Dufferin station on the Eglinton West line as part of the phase 1 program. The code format being used in this concept is based on a computer application that allows alphanumeric and special characters in its syntax. This type of feature is important because it allows the generation of meaningful code structures and better facilitates reading and understanding reports and output.

Figure 8.3 is a stylized plot of the information of the code structure developed in Fig. 8.2 as concept 1.

A problem in project management systems development is that people look for instant solutions. On the other hand, sometimes they just do not look for solutions, allowing the various multidisciplinary team members to work on their own, or to their own stand-alone systems without developing a project-specific language and code system. This eventually leads to confusion and loss of quality control and provides for virtually no cost control. Therefore it is incumbent on project management to look at the different definition and code concepts.

For complex projects or projects that are a tight fit or that may require a shutdown of an existing process, it would not be unrealistic to consider a number of structures and code exercises before one is adopted. That is why a second concept of definition is proposed, as seen in Fig. 8.4.

Figure 8.5 is based on a computer-produced plot of the structured and coded definition illustrated in Fig. 8.4. There are not that many differences between the plots shown

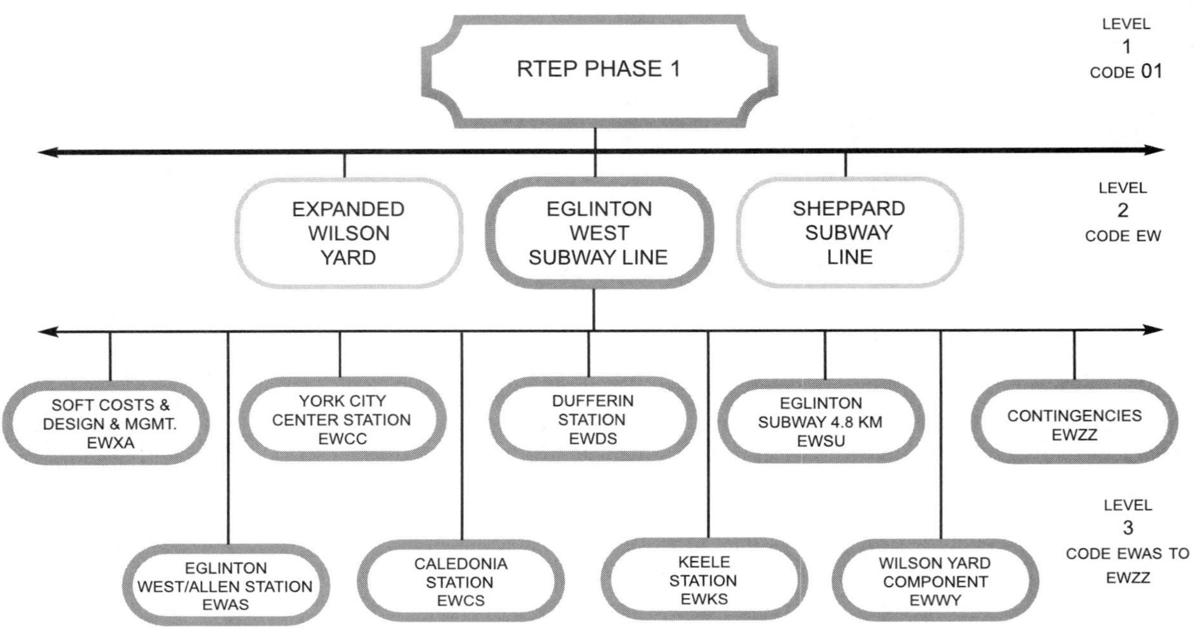

FIGURE 8.3 EGLINTON WEST SUBWAY LINE PROJECT DEFINITION STRUCTURE, CONCEPT 1, DRAWING. This is a stylized drawing of the project definition concept presented in Fig. 8.2. The drawing shows the elements of the Eglinton West subway line and their proposed codes, as already discussed. The structure levels are indicated. Also shown are two of the other phase 1 projects.

in Figs. 8.3 and 8.5. It comes down to selecting a definition and code structure that can act as a management tool, be accepted by most team members, and be suitable for a database system. In developing this kind of project management system in conjunction with a personal computer (PC)-based package, it is important to look for flexibility in the package to ensure that it will allow easy-to-use codes and database formats.

FIGURE 8.4 EGLINTON WEST SUBWAY LINE PROJECT DEFINITION STRUCTURE, CONCEPT 2, TABLE. The best way to describe the code concept presented here is by comparing it to concept 1. In concept 1 each major deliverable is seen to be immediately relatable to Eglinton West through EW being part of the code. In concept 2 the code for each major deliverable first identifies a specific major element, e.g., STACA for the station at Dufferin, XAEW for the soft costs for Eglinton West project, etc. Which concept is better? That depends on project and corporate management needs. From a project management perspective, the intent of the code is to track the quality and cost of an element as it morphs from a sketch into a working subway platform through hundreds of tasks, skills, purchase orders, and contracts.

RTEP PHASE 1
EGLINTON WEST SUBWAY
PROJECT DEFINITION CONCEPT 2

LEVEL	CODE	DESCRIPTION
1	RTEP	RTEP Phase 1
2	EWS	Eglinton West Subway
3	4800M	4.8 km Subway
3	STACA	Caledonia Station
3	STADU	Dufferin Station
3	STAEA	Eglinton/Allen Station
3	STAKE	Keele Station
3	STAYC	York City Center Station
3	XAEW	Soft Costs/Design/Mgmt.
3	ZZEW	Contingencies

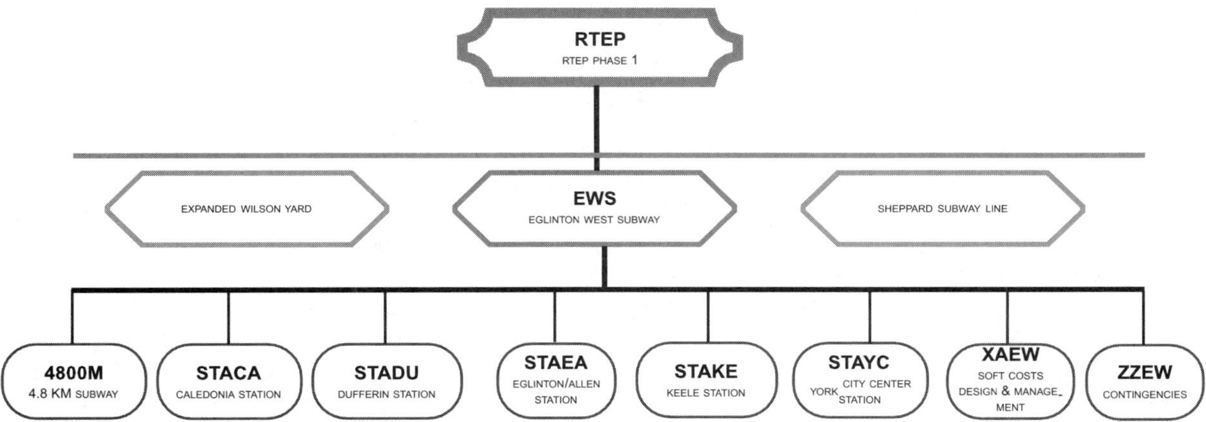

Figure 8.5 Eglinton West Subway Line Project Definition Structure, Concept 2, Drawing. This is a computer-based drawing of the project definition concept presented in Fig. 8.4. The drawing shows the elements of the Eglinton West subway line and proposed alternative codes. Also shown in faint outine are two of the other phase 1 projects. In this drawing the codes are driven first by elements of the Eglinton West subway, e.g., STACA is the Caledonia station, ZZEW is the contingencies amount for Eglinton West. In the concept 1 code in Fig. 8.3 the code was ordered to reflect first Eglinton West and then the major element.

The perceding two simplistic project definition concepts are presented to demonstrate beginning principles and possible variations of coded definition structures, but only to level 3 in this exercise. The features to look for in a project definition system are as follows:

- Codes should relate to the actual project, rather than simply consisting of a coded numbering system.
- The definition structure itself should reflect the completed project, as it will be delivered to the project owners and users.
- The definition and code system should incorporate and fully utilize the concept of project consumables such as soft costs, design, management, engineering, architecture, and all project contingencies.

8.3 Work Breakdown

The most widely used "buzz" word in project management circles is WBS: work breakdown structure. WBSs aim to break down a project into tasks and activities.

What is it that we have done in Section 8.2? Isn't that a work breakdown? It is and it is not. It is a project definition, but it looks like a breakdown. As can be seen, however, the role of the definition structure is to define and code the project as it will be delivered to the owners and users. On the other hand, the breakdown structure is to establish the tasks and activities to be carried out by the project team members.

Tasks, activities, and packages of work are carried out within project phases. In the systems of project management there are a number of classic project stages or phases that are generally applicable to most projects. This does not mean that they are applicable totally to all projects, nor can a professional project manager assume that they are to be applied automatically. In this case, as for most projects, the undertaking would go through a long process before it becomes a managed multiple project. As a result project concepts, codes, and language are developed that take on a great deal of credibility. Eventually these assumptions need to be tested for validity as a true project management language.

To illustrate this condition, Fig. 8.6 shows the project work breakdown of the case exercise which illustrates just such a situation, that is, the adoption of terms already in place on a specific project for use as permanent project management code. The table codes and names specific project stages, such as, CONST for construction phase, RFP for request for proposals phase, and so on. These stage names are very similar to the standard stages presented in this text. If anything, the RTEP stage names may be too specific and could generate problems of structure and code. From experience, easily structured codes, other than numeric digits, should be acronym-like and somewhat less specific than the examples named in Fig. 8.6.

Where Fig. 8.6 is a typed table of the WBS, Fig. 8.7 is based on a computer application–produced list. The features to be noted in the computer report in Fig. 8.7 are:

- The software accepts a code syntax of 8 alphanumeric and special characters such as /, ., etc., shown as SSSSSSSS.
- The importance of this kind of feature is the capability to generate codes that are flexible and most visually meaningful.

A problem area for the project management system designer may be that although the code is initiated as a sequence based on the project chronological time frame, the

RTEP PHASE 1
PROJECT WORK BREAKDOWN CONCEPT 1

LEVEL	CODE	DESCRIPTION
1	RTEP	RTEP Phase 1
2	CONST	Construction Phase
2	DESIGN	Design Phase
2	INSTALL	Installation Phase
2	MFGDLVR	Manufacture & Deliver Phase
2	PREDEV	Predevelopment Phase
2	RFP	Request for Proposals Phase
2	S/I	Supply and Install Phase
2	SELECT	Select Consultants Phase
2	TENDER	Tender Construction Phase

Figure 8.6 RTEP Phase 1 Eglinton West Subway Line Work Breakdown Structure, Concept 1, Table. This table shows a work breakdown structure based on concepts and terms in use during the feasibility and conceptual stages. The intent of a work breakdown structure is to create tasks and packages tied to the phases named and coded above. Although the terms are close to the standard WBS terminology presented in this text, the above names may be too restrictive and narrow if adopted as the basis for creating tasks and packages.

```
Format - SSSSSSSS Table Lookup - N

1....RTEP        RAPID TRANSIT EXPANSION PHASE 1
     2....CONST         CONSTRUCTION PHASE
     2....DESIGN        DESIGN PHASE
     2....INSTALL       INSTALLATION PHASE
     2....MFGDLVR       MANUFACTURE AND DELIVER PHASE
     2....PREDEV        PREDEVELOPMENT PHASE
     2....RFP           REQUEST FOR PROPOSAL PHASE
     2....S/I           SUPPLY AND INSTALL PHASE
     2....SELECT        SELECT CONSULTANTS PHASE
     2....TENDER        TENDER CONSTRUCTION PHASE
```

FIGURE 8.7 RTEP PHASE 1 EGLINTON WEST SUBWAY LINE WORK BREAKDOWN STRUCTURE, CONCEPT 1, COMPUTER REPORT. This is a computer report of the predetermined work breakdown phases presented as concept 1 and seen in Fig. 8.6. The computer application accepts alphanumeric and special characters as codes. The intent of this work breakdown structure is to create a computerized project framework for all project activities, tasks, and packages.

software may list and sort numerically, alphabetically, or as a combination of characters. This is a standard feature in software, and it may be disconcerting when seen in reports. For example, it is known that design precedes construction, but since C, the code for construction, precedes D, the code for design, in a standard computer-generated report, listed alphabetically, construction is invariably listed ahead of design. These kinds of anomalies must be programmed out.

Figure 8.8 is a CAD drawing of the concept 1 breakdown structure and code seen as a computer report in Fig. 8.7, and as a typed list in Fig. 8.6.

It would be a rare undertaking indeed, that does not have the makings of a structure for project control purposes. For example, Chapter 7 described at length the importance of using the existing methods as the basis for the new project control system. In this chapter the basis for the RTEP project management system was the extensive work that had gone into the owner's predevelopment effort. An example of a rare undertaking might be a major natural disaster, such as a river flooding, or a monstrous airplane accident. There would be nothing there before emergency action had to be taken to save lives, and recover victims. The project manager for normal circumstances needs to recognize and capture the concepts and features that are recognizable to project participants and incorporate them into the project coordination and management information system, as discussed in relation to the concept 1 work breakdown. The achievement of this aim requires consensus and tough decisions with regard to the purpose and extent of the project management system.

The intent of the RTEP case exercise is to explore and develop a project-specific breakdown structure concept, hopefully based on what may already be in use. The concept 1 WBS and code may be a viable solution, but there were suggestions that based on experience, the phase names may be too specific, which could cause downstream problems of allocation. At the same time the codes based on phase names may be awkward. Looking at other approaches, another possible WBS for this project is depicted in the computer report in Fig. 8.9. Figure 8.9 shows that some phase names have been carried over from concept 1. Some phases have been broken down to lower levels. The construction phase is carried down to level 5.

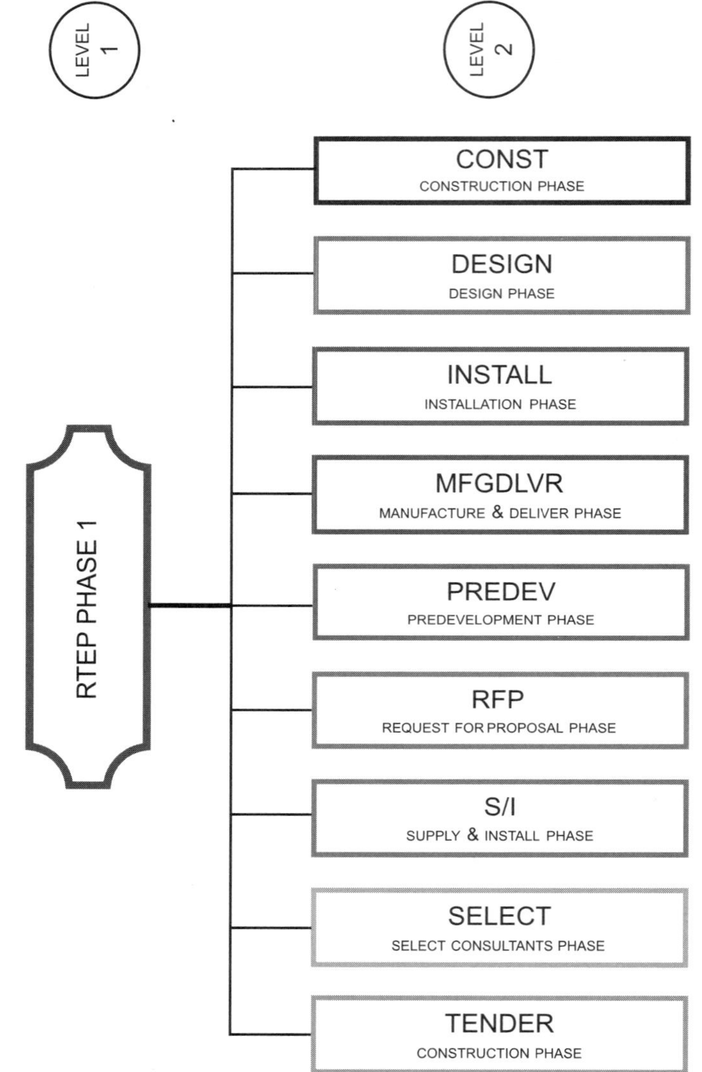

Figure 8.8 RTEP Phase 1 Eglinton West Subway Line Work Breakdown Structure, Concept 1, CAD Drawing. This is a stylized CAD drawing of the project phases listed in the computer report in Fig. 8.7 and the list in Fig. 8.6. All project activities would be breakdown items of the phases shown above. The bold type represents the code for the item named. This figure represents the first of a number of breakdown concepts considered for the case exercise. Note that the software reordered the phases in alphabetical order.

To generate more flexibility, the codes have been expanded to alphanumeric characters. Level 1, RTEP phase 1, is coded as 001. Although level 2 comprises a number of subway links, only the Eglinton West subway system, coded as 1, is demonstrated. At level 3 the standard project phases are coded numerically, as seen in the typical managed project, with 01 being the predevelopment phase code. At level 4 alphabetic characters are introduced to represent the various stations and links of the Eglinton West subway. The alpha characters may be seen to be along the lines of the acronyms discussed as concept 1, and may be maintained across all project phases.

It is evident that what is being developed is the basis for a structured and logical database management system. For example, in this case the level 3 code for the construction phase of the Eglinton West subway line would be 001 01 07. The level 4 code for the construction of the Eglinton West/Allen station is 001 01 07 AS.

Construction project coding cascades easily through the fifth, sixth, and seventh project levels. The recognized construction breakdown follows the Masterformat system of elemental coding and costing. As seen in Fig. 8.9, the full program code for the construction of the element group Siteworks for the Eglinton West /Allen subway station would be 001 01 07 AS 02. At the next level the element group Siteworks may be broken down into its elements.

Full computerized database code systems very easily may become large, complex, and difficult. Strings of integers or alpha characters may become so difficult that users are turned off. When special characters such as /, ., or : are incorporated, even more complexity may be introduced. The ultimate difficulty occurs when structures are imposed by software systems, and the structures and the resulting codes are not fully representative of typical project management fundamentals, local usage, agreed terminology, or a truly meaningful computerized project management system.

Computer software systems are designed using both specific and nonspecific placement of characters. They may be designed using breakdown structures, or they may be nonbreakdowns. There are examples of both usages in this book. A powerful project management code is one in which the full code exists only at the lowest database level, with reporting at all levels by computer. Once a project element is coded, the system takes care of all reporting needs, at all levels of the project cost and expenditure control systems, and for all levels of the project functional organization.

Producing project codes with or without the use of breakdown structures is at best a difficult process. It is not simply a matter of applying a library style decimal system of numbering. Structures and codes must be flexible and able to accommodate the progressive development of tasks, activities, and packages that derive from the progressive management of a project. Structures can become complex very quickly. For an illustration of the beginnings of complexity, Fig. 8.10 shows a CAD drawing of the computer WBS listed in Fig. 8.9.

Figure 8.10 depicts a classic WBS. It may be atypical in that it is structured on the basis of the principles promoted as fundamentals of the systems of project management. What this means is that there are no stand-alone activities; that activities derive from known and planned phases; that activities lead to a deliverable; that they are or will become a part of a package; and that they are or will be assigned to a member of the project functional organization.

8.4 Functional Organization

A project control system, or a system of project management, needs to coordinate and control not only the enterprise owner's organization, departments, and resources, but

Figure 8.9 RTEP Phase 1 Eglinton West Subway Line Work Breakdown Structure, Concept 2, Computer Report. The RTEP phase 1 project is the objective at level 1 of the structure. It is coded as 001. Of the multiple projects that make up RTEP phase 1, only the Eglinton West subway, coded as 01, is shown to keep it simple. No other level 2 projects are shown. Of the phases named in the concept 1 discussion only PREDEV, DESIGN, and CONST are used. To fit the new structure and code they are shown at level 3. PREDEV is broken down as subway stations at level 4. CONST is broken down into level 4, which shows only the construction phase of the Eglinton West/Allen station, code 0107AS. At level 5 the Eglinton West/Allen station is broken down into Masterformat construction elements.

Format - SSSSSSSS	Table Lookup - N
1....001	RAPID TRANSIT EXPANSION PHASE 1
2....01	EGLINTON WEST SUBWAY LINE
3....0101	PREDEVELOPMENT PHASE EGLINTON WEST
4....0101AS	PREDEV. PHASE EGLINTON W./ALLEN STATION
4....0101CS	PREDEV. PHASE CALEDONIA STATION
4....0101DS	PREDEV. PHASE DUFFERIN STATION
4....0101KS	PREDEV. PHASE KEELE STATION
4....0101SU	PREDEV. PHASE EGLINTON W. SUBWAY
4....0101WY	PREDEV. PHASE WILSON YARD COMPONENT
4....0101YC	PREDEV. PHASE YORK CITY CENTER STATION
3....0102	DESIGN PHASE EGLINTON WEST SUBWAY
3....0103	FINAL DRAWINGS EGLINTON WEST SUBWAY
3....0104	TENDER & AWARD PHASE EGLINTON WEST SUBWAY
3....0105	SUPPLY & DELIVER PHASE EGLINTON WEST SUBWAY
3....0106	SUPPLY & INSTALL PHASE EGLINTON WEST SUBWAY
3....0107	CONSTRUCTION PHASE EGLINTON WEST SUBWAY
4....0107AS	CONSTRUCTION PHASE EGLINTON WEST/ALLEN STATION
5....0107AS01	CONST. EGLINTON W./ALLEN STA. GEN. REQMTS.
5....0107AS02	CONST. EGLINTON W./ALLEN STA. SITEWORKS
5....0107AS03	CONST. EGLINTON W./ALLEN STATION CONCRETE
5....0107AS04	CONST. EGLINTON W./ALLEN STATION MASONRY
5....0107AS05	CONST. EGLINTON W./ALLEN STATION METALS
5....0107AS06	CONST. EGLINTON W./ALLEN STA. WOOD & PLASTICS
5....0107AS07	CONST. EGLINTON W./ALLEN STA. THERMAL & MOIST.
5....0107AS08	CONST. EGLINTON W./ALLEN STA. DOORS & WINDOWS
5....0107AS09	CONST. EGLINTON W./ALLEN STATION FINISHES
5....0107AS10	CONST. EGLINTON W./ALLEN STA. SPECIALITIES
5....0107AS11	CONST. EGLINTON W./ALLEN STA. EQUIPMENT
5....0107AS12	CONST. EGLINTON W./ALLEN STA. FURNISHINGS
5....0107AS13	CONST. EGLINTON W./ALLEN STA. SPECIAL CONST.
5....0107AS14	CONST. EGLINTON W./ALLEN STA. CONVEYING SYSTEMS
5....0107AS15	CONST. EGLINTON W./ALLEN STATION MECHANICAL
5....0107AS16	CONST. EGLINTON W./ALLEN STATION ELECTRICAL
3....0108	STARTUP PHASE EGLINTON W./ALLEN STATION
3....0109	OPERATIONS PHASE EGLINTON W./ALLEN STATIONZ

the entire project functional organization. The project functional organization constitutes the owner, consultants, contractors, regulatory agencies, vendors, subcontractors, managers, purchasers, and everybody else who is an implicit or explicit stakeholder in the project. As long as somebody may have an influence on the project, they are a part of the functional organization, like it or not.

Project work, to be successful, must be structured. That means definition structures, breakdown structures, and organizational structures. The organization structures aim to identify and code the groups and teams and the people that will commit to carry out the activities and tasks, either as a corporate assignment, as a legal requirement, such as, issuance of a building permit, or by proposal and contract, subcontract, or purchase order.

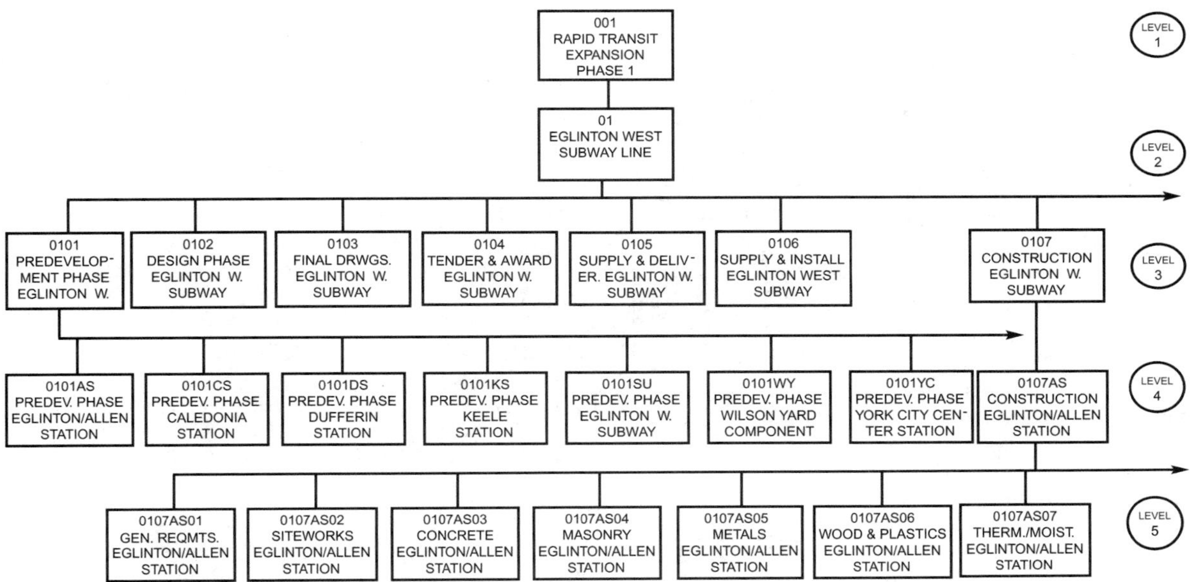

Figure 8.10 RTEP Phase 1 Eglinton West Subway Line Work Breakdown Structure, Concept 2, CAD Drawing. This is a stylized cut of a CAD drawing plotted by computer from the structured information in Fig. 8.9. A full drawing like this could fill a wall or consist of many pages, showing codes, descriptions, and structural levels. Element names and their codes would be exactly the same in drawings and computer reports.

Figure 8.11 shows a computer-produced functional organization structure for the Eglinton West subway. Seen as a beginning exercise, the organizational breakdown structure (OBS) type hierarchy depicts and codes the development of a structure of companies, firms, and organizations that will carry out assigned, contracted, or legal packages of project activities as developed through the WBS exercise. The packages become the organization.

The features to look for include an understanding of the growth of the structure from the RTEP exercise at level 1, coded as a double digit numeric 01, down to a type of organization coded as EWC04T02 to designate twin tunnel 2 from EW (Eglinton West) to BC (Black Creek) consultants at level 5 of the organization structure.

Another feature to observe is the apparent speed with which a lot of complexity appears at level 5 of the structure, where the code is already eight characters long, and this only identifies the type of organization, with the individual companies still to be identified.

Figure 8.12 is a CAD drawing of the data in Fig. 8.11. To keep it simple, only the codes are depicted in the drawing. As a project develops into thousands of coded packages and tasks, a computer system needs to be able to generate both drawings and reports to aid the process.

Perhaps the most noteworthy feature of the case exercise structures developed thus far is their similar appearance. Although a definition structure may look like a

FIGURE 8.11 RTEP PHASE 1 EGLINTON WEST SUBWAY LINE FUNCTIONAL ORGANIZATION STRUCTURE, COMPUTER REPORT. This is a view of the project as a functional organization structure. Assignments have been made and coded using acronym-like alphanumeric characters in significant positions. The application allows for the use of special characters, as seen in the S designation. As this is a first run at the organizational structuring, there is no provision to look up the structure in a table, as designated by N for No. Only parts of five levels of breakdown are illustrated.

Format - SSSSSSSS   Table Lookup - N

1....01	RAPID TRANSIT EXPANSION PROGRAM PHASE 1
2....EW	EGLINTON WEST SUBWAY LINE
3....EWA	EGLINTON WEST PROGRAM MGMT. TEAM
4.... EWA1	PROGRAM TEAM MEMBERS
3....EWB	EGLINTON WEST PROJECT TEAM
4.....EWB1	EGLINTON WEST PROJECT TEAM MEMBERS
3....EWC	DESIGNERS & CONSULTANTS
4.... EWC04	EGLINTON WEST DESIGNERS & CONSULTANTS
5....EWC04S01	EW STATION & RUNNING STRUCTURE CONSULTANTS
5....EWC04S02	DUFFERIN STATION CONSULTANTS
5....EWC04S03	CALEDONIA STATION CONSULTANTS
5....EWC04S04	KEELE STATION CONSULTANTS
5....EWC04S05	YORK CITY CENTER STATION CONSULTANTS
5....EWC04T01	TWIN TUNNEL 1 EW TO BC CONSULTANTS
5....EWC04T02	TWIN TUNNEL 2 EW TO BC CONSULTANTS

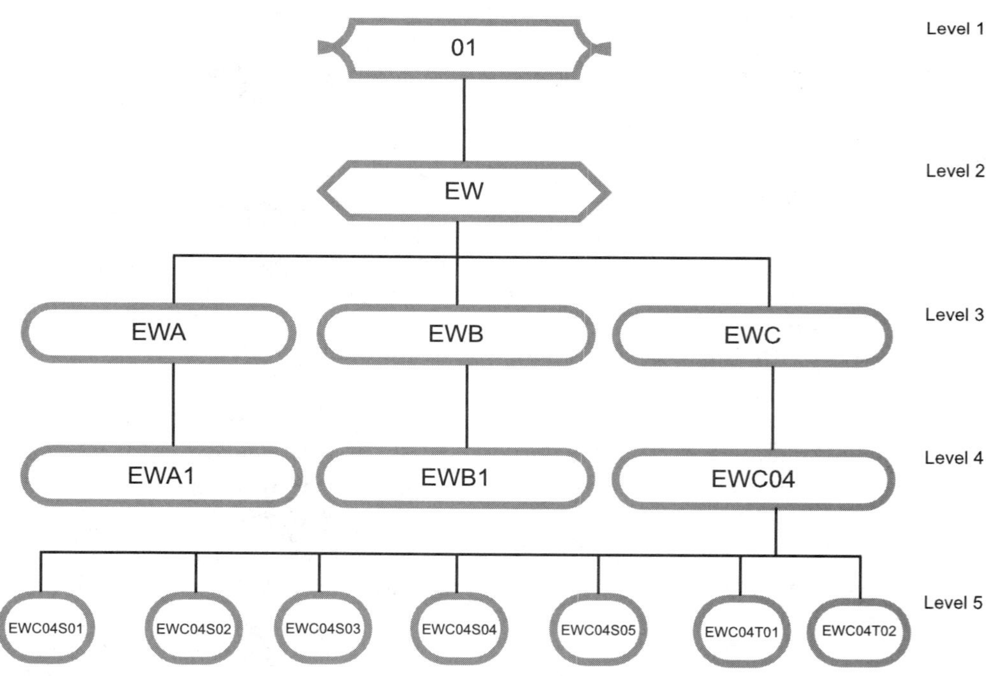

FIGURE 8.12 RTEP PHASE 1 EGLINTON WEST SUBWAY LINE FUNCTIONAL ORGANIZATION STRUCTURE, CAD DRAWING. This is a drawing of only the code structure of the project functional organization developed by computer, as seen in Fig. 8.11. To keep it simple, only the codes are shown. An important feature of this OBS is that it reflects the project as an organization based on packages. When the packages are assigned and awarded, the package names are replaced by company names.

breakdown, and both may seem similar to the organization structure, each performs a totally different and distinct project function.

The OBS is the assignment matrix of companies and individuals committed by contract to deliver activities and packages. It identifies the ultimate project cost sources and is the basis for the final cost and expenditure control system.

Arguably the most important message to be delivered in this part of the book is that no two project organizations are the same. Projects are by nature the domains of individualists, developers, haughty professionals, ensconced bureaucrats, and driven entrepreneurs. They are all members of the project organization and must be accommodated by the system.

To illustrate organizational complexity based on this case, further, another organizational concept is considered. During the feasibility study stages the project owner established a procurement and construction packaging strategy, including consulting services, bulk materials purchases, major equipment procurement, and construction contracts. The systems project management assignment is to consider the approach adopted by the project owner and develop a computer project control system to handle the proposed functional organization.

Figure 8.13 is a two-level computer report of the resulting functional OBS adopting the plan to allocate consulting and supply contracts. The rationale for the code

Format - SSSSSSSS	Table Lookup - N
1....RTEP	RAPID TRANSIT EXPANSION PROGRAM PHASE 1
2....CONCORCO	CORROSION CONTROL (PROGRAM) CONSULTANT
2....CONFILIP	FIRE/LIFE SAFETY (PROGRAM) CONSULTANT
2....CONGEOP	GEOTECHNICAL SERVICES (PROGRAM) CONSULTANT
2....CONGEOS	GEOTECH./HYDROLOGICAL SURVEYS CONSULTANT
2....CONNOVI	NOISE & VIBRATION (PROGRAM) CONSULTANT
2....DESSTA1	DESIGN STATION 1 EGLINTON WEST
2....DESSTA2	DESIGN STATION 2 EGLINTON WEST
2....DESSTA3	DESIGN STATION 3 EGLINTON WEST
2....DESTCC1	DESIGN STA. & C & C RNG. STRUCTURE EGLINTON W.
2....DESTCC2	DESIGN STA. & C & C RNG. STRUCTURE EGLINTON W.
2....DESTUN	DESIGN TUNNELS EGLINTON WEST
2....S/ICOMM	SUPPLY & INSTALL COMMUNICATION SYSTEM
2....S/ICSUB	SUPPLY & INSTALL COMMUNICATION SUBSYSTEM
2....S/IEL&ES	SUPPLY & INSTALL ELEVATORS & ESCALATORS
2....S/IFARE	SUPPLY & INSTALL FARE COLLECTION
2....S/IS&G	SUPPLY & INSTALL SIGNAGE & GRAPHICS
2....S/ISCADA	SUPPLY & INSTALL SCADA
2....S/ITCS	SUPPLY & INSTALL TRAIN CONTROL SIGNALING
2....SITREW	INSTALL TRACKWORK EGLINTON WEST
2....SITRPWR	INSTALL TRACTION POWER
2....STR1EW	SUPPLY TRACKWORK MATERIALS EGLINTON WEST
2....STR2EW	SUPPLY TRACKWORK MATERIALS EGLINTON WEST
2....STR3EW	SUPPLY TRACKWORK MATERIALS EGLINTON WEST
2....STR4EW	SUPPLY TRACKWORK MATERIALS EGLINTON WEST
2....STR5EW	SUPPLY TRACKWORK MATERIALS EGLINTON WEST
2....STRPOEW	SUPPLY TRACTION POWER EQUIPMENT EGLINTON W.
2....SVENTEW	SUPPLY VENTILATION EQUIPMENT EGLINTON WEST

FIGURE 8.13 RTEP PHASE 1 EGLINTON WEST SUBWAY LINE FUNCTIONAL ORGANIZATION STRUCTURE, CONCEPT 2, COMPUTER REPORT. This computer application aims to convert management decisions on project packaging of engineering, design, supply and install contracts, and purchases into a coded project functional organization breakdown structure. The computer applet shows by the S designation that the code can be alphanumeric and special characters. N denotes that there is no lookup table. The leftmost digits 1 and 2 denote the level of the breakdown. Level 3 would accommodate subsets of level 2 packages. The codes are set as close as possible to acronyms, simply to aid communication.

appearance is that codes should approximate closely the names they represent. It is useful if the code can be seen as an acronym for the representative group of companies. The intent is that the codes will become database records and will serve as the basis for cost control, commitment control, change order control, expenditure control, resources allocation, scheduling, and progress monitoring.

The code devised in this exercise may seem awkward, but the project management systems developers must keep in mind that the organizational breakdown is already considered to be in place, and suggestions for changes by systems designers, for example, into numerics, may be unwelcome and could be deemed to be unfriendly.

Figure 8.14 is a two-level CAD drawing of the code information in Fig. 8.13. The breakdown structure is incomplete, as only those consultants and vendors listed are identified. Levels 3, 4, and so on would expand the structure into specific names, which would grow the code structure.

8.5 Code Category Development

The previous sections of this chapter discussed approaches in the development of definition structures, work breakdowns, and project functional organizations. The exercises introduced concepts that adopt decisions already made by project ownership and

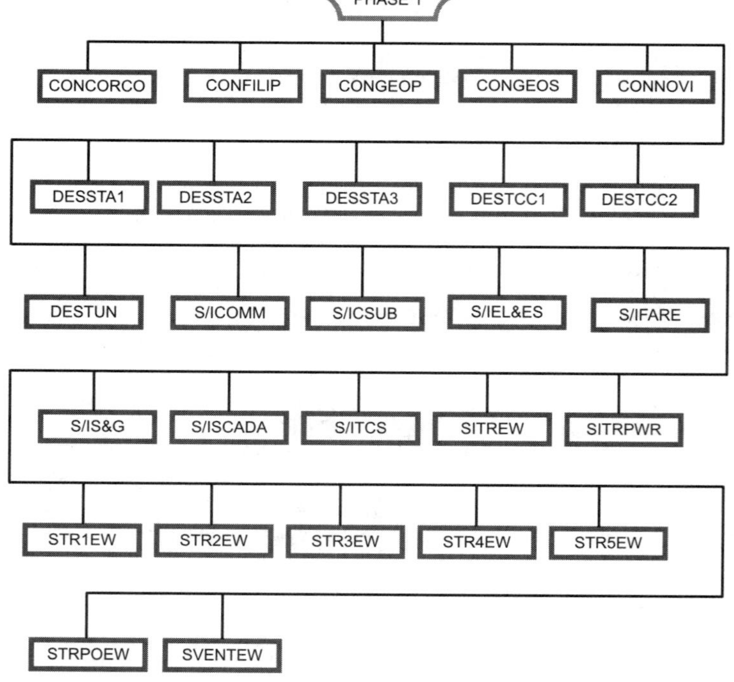

FIGURE 8.14 RTEP PHASE 1 EGLINTON WEST SUBWAY LINE FUNCTIONAL ORGANIZATION STRUCTURE, CONCEPT 2, CAD DRAWING. This is a stylized rendering of a CAD drawing generated by the applet described in Fig. 8.13. To keep it simple only the package codes at level 2 of the structure are shown. If a level 2 package is assigned to a single organization, the code becomes synonymous with that organization. If a level 2 package is assigned to a number of organizations, each of the organizations is coded as a breakdown of the level 2 code.

develop them into computer-based project management systems. The premise is that systems have to accommodate project decisions, rather than project decisions needing to be bent to accommodate a computer system.

A code structure is expected to approximate in a project-meaningful way that which it aims to codify in a database and subsequently uses in project management monitoring and reporting tasks. It may be perceived from the foregoing discussion that codes can become fairly complex, even at higher project levels; that alphabetic characters are preferable to numeric characters; that alphanumerics are more than likely most desirable, and that the bases for most code structures are more than likely hierarchical, that is, pyramids or Christmas trees. It may also be concluded that computer project management systems may have limiting syntax strings, making some of them somewhat inflexible.

The preceding exercises are examples of the type of review and development activities that may be required at the launch of any but the most simplistic project management system. Based on these exercises, the structures that were eventually adopted for the purposes of this book, and that would be recommended to project ownership, are the following.

Figure 8.15 depicts the project definition code structure seen to be suitable for the case exercise. The RTEP phase 1, at level 1 of the project structure, is coded as 01, if only for the simple reason that we wish it to appear at the top of the pyramid.

The phase 1 projects are placed at level 2 and coded alphabetically so that the code has some visual relationship to the subway line it represents. EW is the code for Eglinton West; RT stands for the Scarborough Rapid Transit link, and so on.

As a basic tenet of project definition, the definition structure needs to represent the finished facility as it will be delivered to the users upon completion, plus the project soft costs, including the cost of money, management, engineering, design, inflation, and contingencies.

Figure 8.15 is the product of a project management package. The code structure provides for up to eight alphanumeric and special characters. Including the two digits at level 1, the code comprises four characters at level 2, and at level 3 there are an additional two characters for a total of six.

The information listed in Fig. 8.15 is plotted as a simplified CAD drawing in Fig. 8.16. The CAD drawing may be more useful for some management purposes than a tabular report. In these project management demonstrations, the exercises are taken to only two or three levels, with the result being fairly simple drawings of simplistic structures. When these structures are taken to lower levels, the results are much more complex drawings and codes.

What is the purpose of the definition structure, and how is that purpose achieved? The goal is a structured code system for the purposes of project scope, quality, and cost control. And this is best achieved through the project definition lists and drawings. The lists and drawings come first and are immediately followed by the systems of cost control.

Figure 8.17 depicts a computer cost control list using the definition structure and code system developed here. The report cost control columns are the paradigmatic

Format - SSSSSSSS Table Lookup -Y

Code	Description
1....01	RAPID TRANSIT EXPANSION PHASE 1
2....EW	EGLINTON WEST SUBWAY LINE
3....EWAS	EGLINTON WEST/ALLEN STATION
3....EWCS	CALEDONIA STATION
3....EWDS	DUFFERIN STATION
3....EWKS	KEELE STATION
3....EWSU	4.8 KM SUBWAY LINE
3....EWWY	WILSON YARD COMPONENT
3....EWYS	YORK CITY CENTER STATION
2....RT	SCARBORO RT EXTENSION
3....RTBY	BELLAMY YARD
3....RTIS.	MILNER STATION
3....RTMS	MARKHAM STATION
3....RTRT	3.2 KM RT LINE
3....RTSS	SHEPPARD STATION
2....SS	SHEPPARD SUBWAY
SSBS	BAYVIEW STATION
SSDS	DON MILLS STATION
SSDY	DAVISVILLE YARD
SSLS	LESLIE STATION
SSSU	6.4 KM SUBWAY LINE
SSYS	SHEPPARD/YONGE STATION
2....SU	SPADINA/YORK U LINE
3....SUSS	STEELES WEST STATION
3....SUSU	5.1 KM YORK SUBWAY LINE
3....SUWS	FINCH WEST STATION
3....SUWY	WILSON YARD COMPONENT
2....VE	VEHICLES
2....WY	EXPANDED WILSON YARD
2....YY	PROGRAM SOFT COSTS
2....ZZ	PROGRAM CONTINGENCIES

FIGURE 8.15 RTEP PHASE 1 CODE CATEGORY, PROJECT DEFINITION. This figure represents the project definition code structure deemed most suitable for project managment and administration purposes. It is based on the rules of breakdown presented in this book. It incorporates decisions made by the project owners and construction management. The codes are as close to acronyms and abbreviations as possible, and the aim is to create and process the information by computer, including lookup tables as templates.

project cost control measures defined in Chapter 6. The records and fields in this prototypical cost control report are designed to be driven by the code systems developed by and for the project definition system. Cost estimating input would be expected at the lowest level of the database. A report such as that seen in Fig. 8.17 would be generated by the system at the appropriate working level. An appropriate level of detail is that level at which hard information, which can be measured, exists.

There are many ways to deliver large projects. They may be handled in their entirety, in a top-down arrangement, where all aspects of the project are integrated vertically as one system, with reporting aimed at level 1, in this case the RTEP phase 1.

This approach is illustrated in Fig. 8.17, which is seen to incorporate a number of major lines and facilities, including Eglinton West, Scarborough RT, Sheppard subway, Spadina/York U line, and vehicles, as well as the project soft costs and contingencies. This definition and its system is a top-down approach.

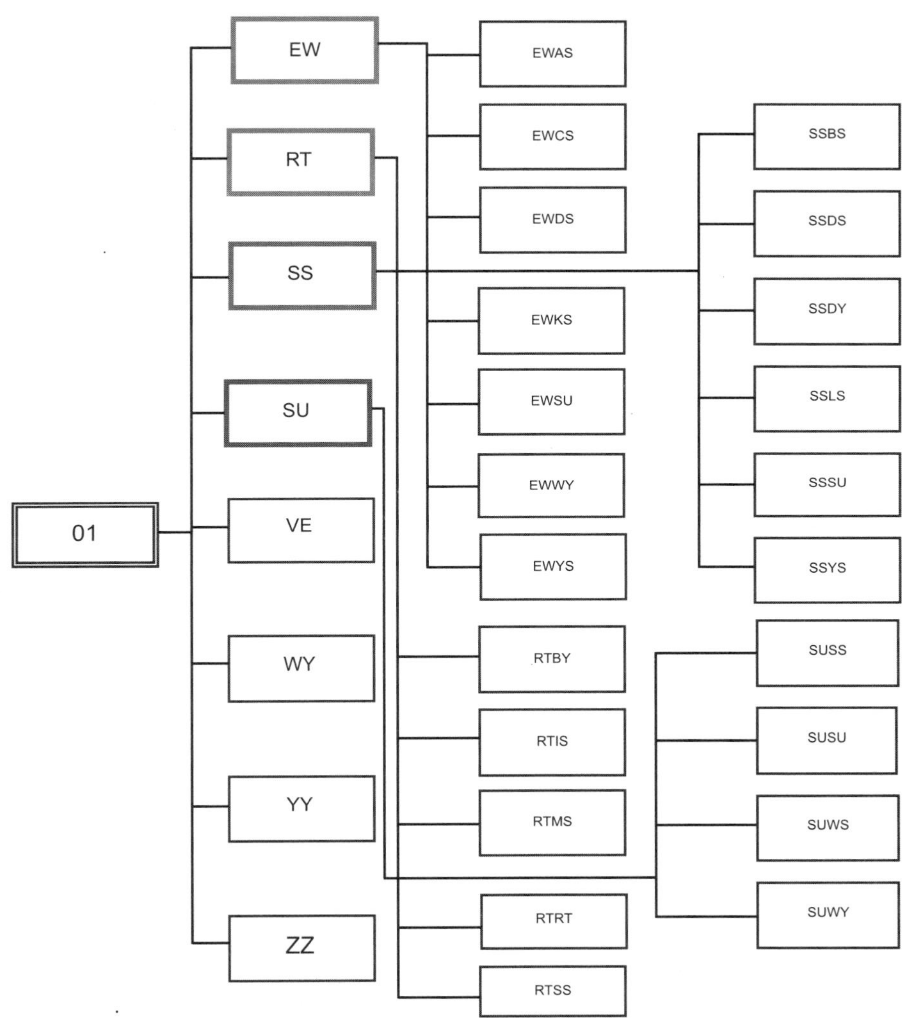

FIGURE 8.16 RTEP PHASE 1 CODE CATEGORY, PROJECT DEFINITION, CAD DRAWING. This is a simplified CAD drawing of the computer-generated definition list and code system depicted in Fig. 8.15. Only the codes are shown, and only to level 3 for four lines, EW, RT, SS, and SU.

On the other hand, the program may comprise a number of stand-alone projects, with only the project bottom lines being reported to phase 1 program management, as depicted in Fig. 8.18. The definition and code system in Fig. 8.18 provides for its own soft costs, which generally include administration, legal, financing, management, design, engineering, and contingencies.

The definition and code system depicted as a list in Fig. 8.18 is converted to a CAD drawing in Fig. 8.19. The structure is taken down to level 3 only. The format in this particular application is based on the use of only eight alphanumeric characters shown in a computer menu as SSSSSSSS. It may be that this array may be insufficient to code the project elements at the lower levels of the definition, so that

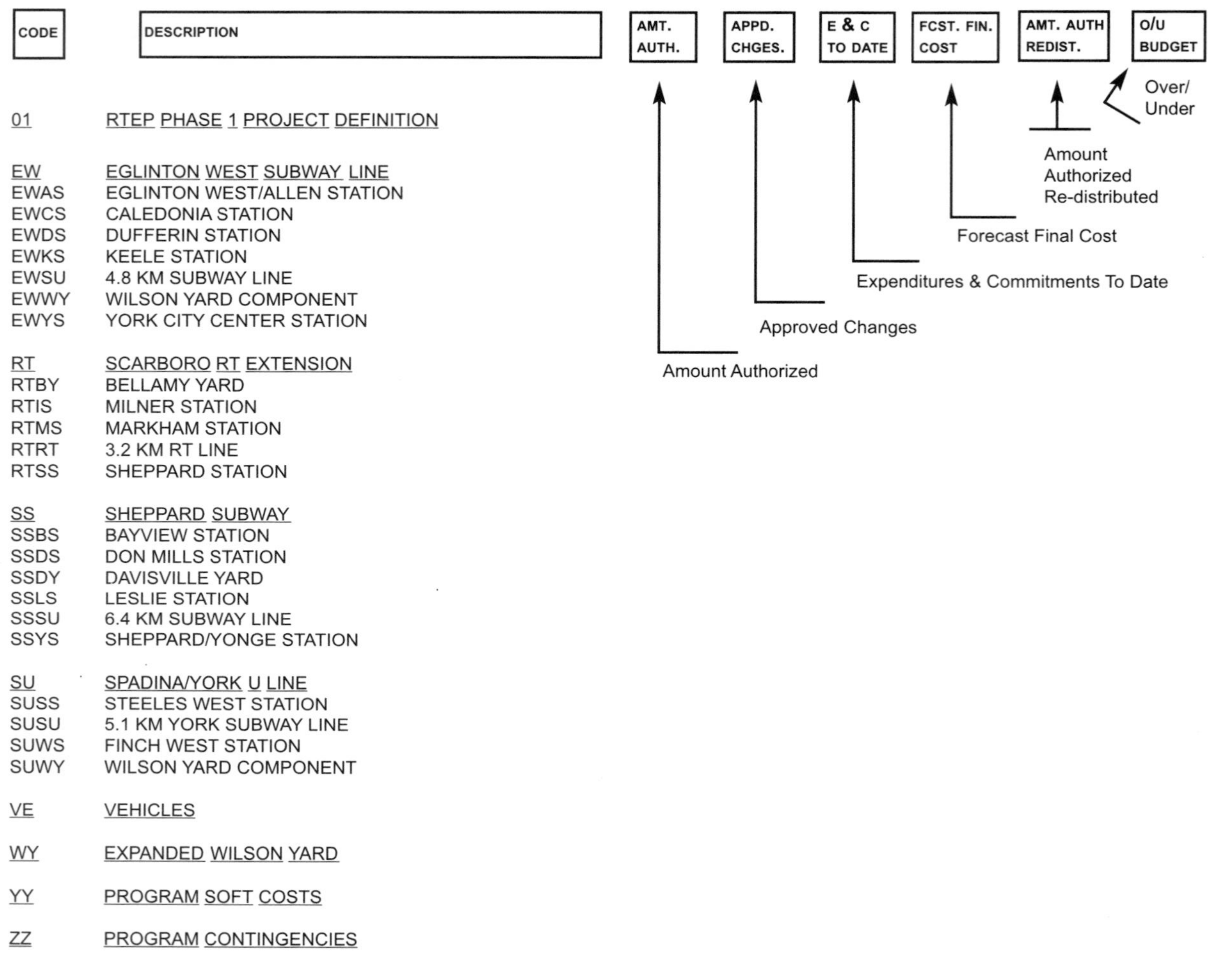

CODE
DESCRIPTION
AMT. AUTH.
APPD. CHGES.
E & C TO DATE
FCST. FIN. COST
AMT. AUTH REDIST.
O/U BUDGET
Over/ Under
Amount Authorized Re-distributed
Forecast Final Cost
Expenditures & Commitments To Date
Approved Changes
Amount Authorized
01 RTEP PHASE 1 PROJECT DEFINITION
EW EGLINTON WEST SUBWAY LINE
EWAS EGLINTON WEST/ALLEN STATION
EWCS CALEDONIA STATION
EWDS DUFFERIN STATION
EWKS KEELE STATION
EWSU 4.8 KM SUBWAY LINE
EWWY WILSON YARD COMPONENT
EWYS YORK CITY CENTER STATION
RT SCARBORO RT EXTENSION
RTBY BELLAMY YARD
RTIS MILNER STATION
RTMS MARKHAM STATION
RTRT 3.2 KM RT LINE
RTSS SHEPPARD STATION
SS SHEPPARD SUBWAY
SSBS BAYVIEW STATION
SSDS DON MILLS STATION
SSDY DAVISVILLE YARD
SSLS LESLIE STATION
SSSU 6.4 KM SUBWAY LINE
SSYS SHEPPARD/YONGE STATION
SU SPADINA/YORK U LINE
SUSS STEELES WEST STATION
SUSU 5.1 KM YORK SUBWAY LINE
SUWS FINCH WEST STATION
SUWY WILSON YARD COMPONENT
VE VEHICLES
WY EXPANDED WILSON YARD
YY PROGRAM SOFT COSTS
ZZ PROGRAM CONTINGENCIES

FIGURE 8.17 RTEP PHASE 1, PROJECT DEFINITION, COST CONTROL SUMMARY REPORT. To set up project cost control, the project is estimated. When the estimate is approved, it becomes the project budget. The budget is made up of many elements as identified by the code structure. The exercise of cost control requires the comparison of dynamic cost information to the fixed budget amounts for the coded line items, as illustrated. It is not possible to exercise cost control without coding both budgets and expenditures. To compare apples to apples, both must be coded.

more systems and database design may be required to achieve the aim of structured and coded project definition systems.

Project definition systems aim to scope, code, and cost a project. Figures 8.18 and 8.19 demonstrate the procedure to level 3 of the Eglinton West subway. The activities of defining, listing, structuring, and coding lead to the development of a database for project cost control. The resulting cost control framework for the subject

CODE CATEGORY - RTEPPRODEF2

Format - SSSSSSSS Table Lookup -Y

Code	Description
1 01	RTEP PHASE 1
2 . . . . EW	EGLINTON WEST SUBWAY
3 . . . . EWAS	EGLINTON/ALLEN STATION
3 . . . . EWCS	CALEDONIA STATION
3 . . . . EWDS	DUFFERIN STATION
3 . . . . EWKS	KEELE STATION
3 . . . . EWSU	4.8 KM SUBWAY LINE
3 . . . . EWWY	WILSON YARD COMPONENT
3 . . . . EWYS	YORK CITY CENTER STATION
3 . . . . EWYY	SOFT COSTS
3 . . . . EWZZ	CONTINGENCIES

FIGURE 8.18 EGLINTON WEST SUBWAY LINE CODE CATEGORY, PROJECT DEFINITION COMPUTER LIST. This is the basis for the project coded definition. Created by a menu-driven computer, the structure accepts alphanumeric inputs to level 3 as shown, and up to a predetermined number of lover levels as allowed by the program. This particular package has a lookup table facility.

project is illustrated in Fig. 8.20. The columns and fields are based on the classic systems of project management presented in this book.

There are three faces to cost control in the systems of project management. It starts with cost based on PDS, as demonstrated in this case exercise for the Eglinton West subway. Cost estimates based on definitions lock in scope and budgets. Or, put another way, they establish quality and cost. The accuracy of the budget is a function of the completeness of the design and engineering information. The less information there is to measure, the less reliable the estimates.

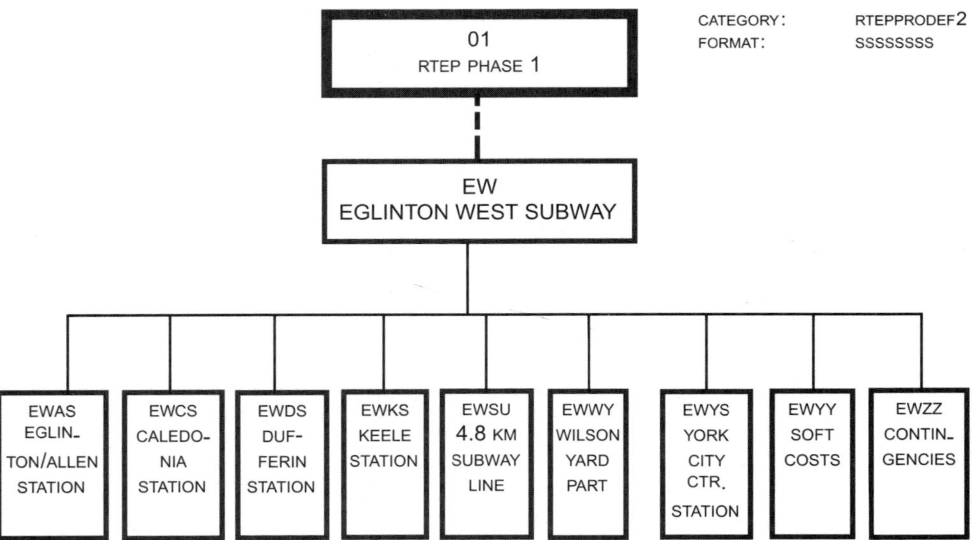

FIGURE 8.19 EGLINTON WEST SUBWAY LINE CODE CATEGORY, PROJECT DEFINITION CAD DRAWING. This is a CAD drawing of the computer list generated in Fig. 8.18. The form of definition is optional. After the third level, both lists and drawings become unwieldy as codes are extended and decisions made as to the location of elements.

CODE CATEGORY	DESCRIPTION	AMT. AUTH.	APPD. CHGES.	E & C TO DATE	FCST. F. COST	AMT AUTH REDIST.	O / U BUDGET
01	RTEP PHASE 1						
EW	EGLINTON WEST SUBWAY						
EWAS	EGLINTON/ALLEN STATION						
EWCS	CALEDONIA STATION						
EWDS	DUFFERIN STATION						
EWKS	KEELE STATION						
EWSU	4.8 KM SUBWAY LINE						
EWWY	WILSON YARD COMPONENT						
EWYS	YORK CITY CENTER STATION						
EWYY	SOFT COSTS						
EWZZ	CONTINGENCIES						

FIGURE 8.20 EGLINTON WEST SUBWAY LINE CODE CATEGORY, PROJECT DEFINITION, COST CONTROL COMPUTER REPORT. This is a computer-generated cost control report of the project elements developed as a computer list and shown as a CAD drawing in Fig. 8.18 and 8.19. The cost columns are classic project cost control measures.

If the PDS codes and estimates establish budget amounts, the WBS codes and estimates redefine the project along a different breakdown, providing codes and estimates of the activities, tasks, and packages required.

To illustrate the breakdown code for the present case exercise refer to Fig. 8.21. In this demonstration the information is cast along project stages or phases set up for formal project cost and expenditure control. As the intent is to illustrate the design and development of a WBS, and as structures may be designed both graphically and as report formats, the WBS for the case exercise is shown in Fig. 8.21 as a computer-produced list and in Fig. 8.22 as a CAD drawing plotted from this list.

Format - SSSSSSSS Table Lookup -Y

```
1 . . . . EW        EGLINTON WEST SUBWAY LINE
 2 . . . . EW01           PREDEVELOPMENT PHASE
 2 . . . . EW02           DESIGN PHASE
 2 . . . . EW03           FINAL DRGS. & SPECS. PHASE
 2 . . . . EW04           TENDER & AWARD PHASE
 2 . . . . EW05           SUPPLY & DELIVER PHASE
 2 . . . . EW06           SUPPLY & INSTALL PHASE
 2 . . . . EW07           CONSTRUCTION PHASE
  3 . . . . EW07AS               CONST. EGLINTON/ALLEN STA.
  3 . . . . EW07CS               CONST. CALEDONIA STA.
  3 . . . . EW07DS               CONST. DUFFERIN STA.
  3 . . . . EW07KS               CONST. KEELE STA.
  3 . . . . EW07SU               CONST. 4.8 KM SUBWAY LINE
  3 . . . . EW07WY               CONST. WILSON YARD PART
  3 . . . . EW07YC               CONST. YORK CITY CTR. STA.
 2 . . . . EW08           STARTUP PHASE
 2 . . . . EW09           OPERATIONS PHASE
```

FIGURE 8.21 EGLINTON WEST SUBWAY LINE CODE CATEGORY, WBS CODE COMPUTER LIST. The WBS looks at a project as activities based on classical phases. The phases are broken down into activities, and eventually into packages, which have the responsibility to deliver elements of the project. The phases have their own codes, which are then attributed to the activities. The phase codes for eight phases at level 2 are shown. Phase 7, Construction, is shown broken down by major elements at level 3.

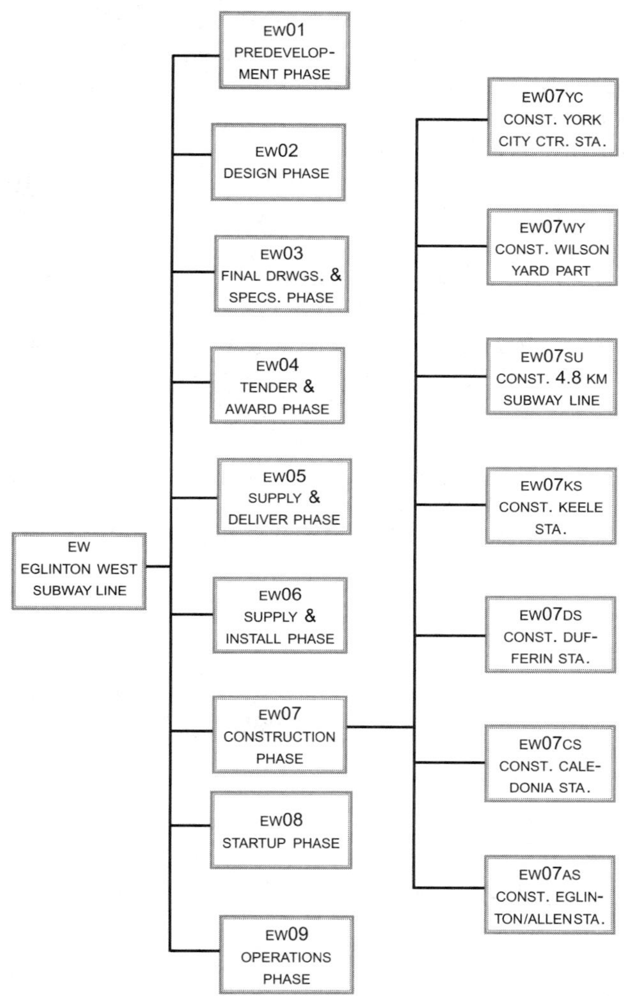

FIGURE 8.22 EGLINTON WEST SUBWAY LINE CODE CATEGORY, WBS CODE CAD DRAWING. This is a CAD drawing of the computer-generated information in Fig. 8.21.

The third face of project control is based on OBS, which is directly linked to the derivation of packages from WBS activities.

8.6 Cost Control

Of the five systems of project management cost control is seen by many to be the most important. Project horror stories invariably relate to runaway costs. Thus cost control is essential in every aspect and every phase of a project.

The results of the systems of definition, breakdown, and organization must be estimated, budgeted, committed, and expended as progress is made. All cost control starts with estimating and establishing budgets. The budgets can only be as reliable as the information on which the estimates are based. Cost information is driven by scope and quality decisions, documentation, design and drawings resulting from activities, and packaging, which after assigning and awarding represents organizational breakdown and resources loading.

The immediately preceding sections of this chapter covered the concepts of definition, breakdown, organization, and codes. The driving consideration was to define and code the project work with a view to set up codes as repositories for project money. The intent is to budget across two breakdowns, PDS and WBS, and then commit to organizations through the OBS. There is no single structure that can achieve this. Three structures are probably a minimum. In real life, the more structures, the better, as long as the structures follow the rules and requirements of project management.

The following figures show pro forma spreadsheet reports for various levels of project management. The information is intended to be produced by database systems. Thus an element in a database is expected to be coded and costed in the PDS system, the WBS system, and the OBS system, if it is expected that the system will produce the reports seen in the graphics that follow.

Cost Control Reports

The intent in this section is to demonstrate the details of cost control visuals. These are not pie charts, histograms, trend lines, S curves, or colored segments, but tables of hard numbers in rows and columns. Those come after the creation of these data-based reports.

The first of these, a PDS cost control report is seen in Fig. 8.17. It represents a summary of all the major areas of the RTEP phase 1. Those line items cover all aspects of costs as authorized, as changed and approved from time to time, and as updated by new cost estimates and expenditures during the progress of the project. But there is no additional money, except that shown as the bottom line in Fig. 8.17.

Figures 8.23 and 8.24 are cost control reports for the Eglinton West line only. Figure 8.23 represents all nine phases of the Eglinton West project as broken down and coded in Figs. 8.21 and 8.22. Figure 8.24 shows the construction phase only, broken down into its standard construction elements for packages EW07AS and EW07SUA.

As developed in the discussion pertaining to Fig. 8.17, each row in a cost control report has the following standard column descriptions or field names:

Column 1	Code
Column 2	Description
Column 3	Amount Authorized
Column 4	Approved Changes
Column 5	Expenditures and Commitments to Date

RTEP PHASE 1 - THE EGLINTON WEST SUBWAY
PROJECT WORK BREAKDOWN TO LEVEL 4
PROJECT COST CONTROL SUMMARY

CODE	DESCRIPTION
EW	EGLINTON SUBWAY BREAKDOWN
EW01	PREDEVELOPMENT PHASE
EW01AS	EGLINTON/ALLEN STATION
EW01CS	CALEDONIA STATION
EW01DS	DUFFERIN STATION
EW01KS	KEELE STATION
EW01YC	YORK CITY CENTER STATION
EW01SU	4.8 KM EGLINTON SUBWAY
EW01WY	WILSON YARD COMPONENT
EW02	DESIGN PHASE
EW02AS	EGLINTON/ALLEN STATION
EW02CS	CALEDONIA STATION
EW02DS	DUFFERIN STATION
EW02KS	KEELE STATION
EW02YC	YORK CITY CENTER STATION
EW02SU	4.8 KM EGLINTON SUBWAY
EW02WY	WILSON YARD COMPONENT
EW03	FINAL DRWGS & SPECS PHASE
EW03AS	EGLINTON/ALLEN STATION
EW03CS	CALEDONIA STATION
EW03DS	DUFFERIN STATION
EW03KS	KEELE STATION
EW03YC	YORK CITY CENTER STATION
EW03SU	4.8 KM EGLINTON SUBWAY
EW03WY	WILSON YARD COMPONENT
EW04	TENDER & AWARD PHASE
EW04AS	EGLINTON/ALLEN STATION
EW04CS	CALEDONIA STATION
EW04DS	DUFFERIN STATION
EW04KS	KEELE STATION
EW04YC	YORK CITY CENTER STATION
EW04SU	4.8 KM EGLINTON SUBWAY
EW04WY	WILSON YARD COMPONENT
EW05	SUPPLY & DELIVER PHASE
EW05AS	EGLINTON/ALLEN STATION
EW05CS	CALEDONIA STATION
EW05DS	DUFFERIN STATION
EW05KS	KEELE STATION
EW05YC	YORK CITY CENTER STATION
EW05SU	4.8 KM EGLINTON SUBWAY
EW05WY	WILSON YARD COMPONENT
EW06	SUPPLY & INSTALL PHASE
EW06AS	EGLINTON/ALLEN STATION
EW06CS	CALEDONIA STATION
EW06DS	DUFFERIN STATION
EW06KS	KEELE STATION
EW06YC	YORK CITY CENTER STATION
EW06SU	4.8 KM EGLINTON SUBWAY
EW06WY	WILSON YARD COMPONENT
EW07	CONSTRUCTION PHASE
EW07AS	EGLINTON/ALLEN STATION
EW07CS	CALEDONIA STATION
EW07DS	DUFFERIN STATION
EW07KS	KEELE STATION
EW07YC	YORK CITY CENTER STATION
EW07SU	4.8 KM EGLINTON SUBWAY
EW07WY	WILSON YARD COMPONENT
EW08	STARTUP PHASE
EW08AS	EGLINTON/ALLEN STATION
EW08CS	CALEDONIA STATION
EW08DS	DUFFERIN STATION
EW08KS	KEELE STATION
EW08YC	YORK CITY CENTER STATION
EW08SU	4.8 KM EGLINTON SUBWAY
EW08WY	WILSON YARD COMPONENT
EW09	OPERATIONS PHASE
EW09AS	EGLINTON/ALLEN STATION
EW09CS	CALEDONIA STATION
EW09DS	DUFFERIN STATION
EW09KS	KEELE STATION
EW09YC	YORK CITY CENTER STATION
EW09SU	4.8 KM EGLINTON SUBWAY
EW09WY	WILSON YARD COMPONENT

FIGURE 8.23 EGLINTON WEST SUBWAY LINE COST CONTROL REPORT. The line items in the rows are derived from the computer exercises depicted in Fig. 8.21 and 8.22. Each row would contain the records and fields identified as columns 1 through 8 in the lead-in discussion. Columns 1 and 2 are filled in above.

Column 6	Forecast Final Cost
Column 7	Amount Authorized Redistributed
Column 8	Over/Under Budget

Not shown in these reports are line items for contingencies and soft costs other than those coded as phases 01 through 04.

RTEP PHASE 1 - THE EGLINTON WEST SUBWAY
CONSTRUCTION PHASE WBS TO LEVEL 5
PROJECT COST CONTROL SUMMARY

CODE	DESCRIPTION
EW07	EGLINTON W. CONSTRUCTION PHASE
EW07AS	EGLINTON/ALLEN STATION
EW07AS01	GENERAL REQUIREMENTS
EW07AS02	SITEWORK
EW07AS03	CONCRETE
EW07AS04	MASONRY
EW07AS05	METALS
EW07AS06	WOOD & PLASTICS
EW07AS07	THERM. & MOIST. PROTECT.
EW07AS08	DOORS & WINDOWS
EW07AS09	FINISHES
EW07AS10	SPECIALITIES
EW07AS11	SUBWAY EQUIPMENT
EW07AS12	STATION FURNISHINGS
EW07AS13	SPECIAL CONSTRUCTION
EW07AS14	CONVEYING SYSTEMS
EW07AS15	MECHANICAL
EW07AS16	ELECTRICAL
EW07AS17	CONTROLS
EW07CS	CALEDONIA STATION
	same as above to suit code
EW07DS	DUFFERIN STATION
	same as above to suit code
EW07KS	KEELE STATION
	same as above to suit code
EW07SU	4.8 KM SUBWAY LINE

CODE	DESCRIPTION
EW07SUA	CUT & COVER RNG. STR. PKGE. 1
EW07SUA01	GENERAL REQUIREMENTS
EW07SUA02	SITEWORK
EW07SUA03	CONCRETE
EW07SUA04	MASONRY
EW07SUA05	METALS
EW07SUA06	WOOD & PLASTICS
EW07SUA07	THERM & MOIST PROTECT.
EW07SUA08	DOORS & WINDOWS
EW07SUA09	FINISHES
EW07SUA10	SPECIALITIES
EW07SUA11	SUBWAY EQUIPMENT
EW07SUA12	STATION FURNISHINGS
EW07SUA13	SPECIAL CONSTRUCTION
EW07SUA14	CONVEYING SYSTEMS
EW07SUA15	MECHANICAL
EW07SUA16	ELECTRICAL
EW07SUA17	CONTROLS
EW07SUB	CUT & COVER RNG. STR. PKGE. 2
	same as above to suit code
EW07SUC	CUT & COVER RNG. STR. PKGE. 3
	same as above to suit code
EW07SUD	SUBWAY TUNNEL
	same as above to suit code

FIGURE 8.24 EGLINTON WEST SUBWAY LINE CONSTRUCTION PHASE ONLY, COST CONTROL REPORT. The line items in the rows are derived from the computer exercises depicted in Figs. 8.21 and 8.22. Only the construction phase, code EW07, is presented. Each row would contain the records and fields identified as columns 1 through 8 in the lead-in discussion on cost control, above and in Figs. 8.17 and 8.20. Columns 1 and 2 are filled in. Code EW07AS has been expanded based on the Masterformat construction index. Code EW07SUA is added as a package. The package is then broken down based on Masterformat.

Expenditure Control Reports

Cost control is only possible with expenditure control. To control cost against a line item budget it is essential to capture expenditure information against that package line item. Expenditure control information is depicted by the eight columns listed next. Columns 1 and 2 are alike for both reports. Column 5 in cost control is fed by column 8 in the expenditures control report.

Column 1	Code
Column 2	Description
Column 3	Original Commitment
Column 4	Approved Commitment Change
Column 5	Current Period Expenditures
Column 6	Expenditures to Date
Column 7	Current Outstanding Commitments
Column 8	Expenditures and Commitments to Date

Figures 8.25 and 8.26 are set up as project expenditure budgets for the packages of work identified. Figure 8.25 depicts selected packages from the Eglinton West subway line. These packages would be assigned or awarded to the project team members, firms, and organizations. The packages and firms could be considered synonymous after the award, so that the name of the package could become the name of the firm. The development of this rationale of package/firm is seen in Figs. 8.11 and 8.12.

Figure 8.26 demonstrates the construction of standard Masterformat line items of item EWF04ST2 in Fig. 8.25, the York City Center station of the Eglinton West subway line. The expenditure columns would apply to the line items.

For project cost control the approved budget is cast along the project functional lines as depicted in Fig. 8.17. It is the cost of the finished project, as it will be delivered to the users of the facility.

The delivery of the project is based on activities and packages which become assignments and contracts for people and firms. The packages take on phase codes. But the package line items are funded from the functional budget. This is depicted in Figs. 8.23 and 8.24.

When the packages are awarded to firms and resources, the packages are renamed with the names of their resources teams. Figure 8.27 demonstrates a report format based on coded project functional organizations. Org. Code identifies the team members, firms, contractors, vendors, and subcontractors who are responsible for or have a contract to produce the work identified in the description.

Whereas in Figs. 8.25 and 8.26 the work packages are linked to WBS/PDS code items, in this concept organizations are identified generically, and their work assignments would then be associated back through the WBS packages to the PDS code. Every row in the expenditure report would have the classical expenditure control

RTEP PHASE 1 - THE EGLINTON WEST SUBWAY
CONTRACT PACKAGES - WBS TO LEVEL 5
PROJECT EXPENDITURE SUMMARY

01 RTEP PHASE 1

EW EGLINTON WEST SUBWAY

EWA EW PROGRAM MANAGEMENT PACKAGES
work packages to be developed

EWB EW PROJECT MANAGEMENT
work packages to be developed

EWC DESIGN & CONSULTANT PACKAGES

EWC04 EW DESIGN & CONSULTANT PACKAGES

EWC04S01	EW STA. & RUNNING STRUCTS.
EWC04S02	CALEDONIA STATION
EWC04S03	DUFFERIN STATION
EWC04S04	KEELE STATION
EWC04S05	YORK CITY CENTER STATION
EWC04T01	TUNNEL 1 EW TO BLACK CREEK
EWC04T02	TUNNEL 2 EW TO BLACK CREEK
EWC04C12	VEHICLES DESIGN FOR EW
EWC04C14	GEOTECH. SERVICES
EWC04C16	GEOTECH./HYDROLOG. SRVYS.
EWC04C18	NOISE & VIBR. DES. PKGES.
EWC04C20	CORROSION DESIGN PKGES.
EWC04C22	SURVEYS CONTROL PKGES.
EWC04C24	SURVEYS PROPERTY PKGES.

EWD EW SUPPLY PACKAGES

EWD02	TRACKWORK MATLS. PKGE.
EWD04	VENTILATION MATLS. PKGE.
EWD06	VENTILATION EQUPMT. PKGE.
EWD08	TRACTION POWER PKGE.
EWD10	TRACTION POWER PKGE.

EWE EW SUPPLY & INSTALL PACKAGES

EWE02	S & I TRACKWORK PACKAGE
EWE04	S & I TRACTION POWER PKGE.
EWE08	S & I TRAIN CONTROL & SIGNL.
EWE10	S & I COMMUNICATION SYST.
EWE12	S & I COMM. SUBSYS. PKGE.
EWE16	S & I TRAIN CONTROL & SIGNL.
EWE20	S & I SCADA PACKAGE
EWE30	S & I ELEVATORS/ESCALATORS
EWE40	S & I SIGNS & GRAPHICS

EWF04 EW CONSTRUCTION PACKAGES

EWF04CR1	C&C RNG. STR. 1 PKGE
EWF04CR2	C& C RNG. STR. 2PKGE.
EWF04ET1	TUNNEL 1 EW TO BLACK CRK.
EWF04ET2	TUNNEL 2 EW TO BLACK CRK.
EWF04ST1	EW/ALLEN STATION PKGE.
EWF04ST2	YCC STATION PACKAGE
EWF04CR3	C&C RNG. STR./SPECIAL PKGE.
EWF04ST3	DUFFERIN STATION PACKAGE
EWF04ST4	CALEDONIA STATION PACKAGE
EWF04ST5	KEELE STATION PACKAGE

EWG EW DESIGN/BUILD PACKAGES
work packages to be developed

EWH STARTUP PACKAGES
work packages to be developed

EWJ OPERATIONS PACKAGES
work packages to be developed

Note: See Figures 8.11 and 8.12.

FIGURE 8.25 EGLINTON WEST SUBWAY LINE EXPENDITURE CONTROL REPORT. The line items in the rows are derived from the computer exercises depicted in Figs. 8.11 and 8.12. Those figures depict the project as project management, consultant, vendor, supply, contractor, and startup packages. Once the packages are bid and awarded, expenditures would be charged to the project as a result of contracts and purchase orders. Each line item in the rows is associated with the expenditure control columns 1 to 8 as discussed.

RTEP PHASE 1 - EGLINTON WEST SUBWAY/YORK CITY CENTER STATION
CONTRACT PACKAGES - WBS TO LEVEL 6
PROJECT EXPENDITURE REPORT OF CONTRACT & SUBCONTRACT PACKAGES

CODE	DESCRIPTION
01	RTEP PHASE 1
EW	EGLINTON WEST SUBWAY
EWF	EGLINTON WEST CONSTRUCTION PHASE
EWF04	EGLINTON WEST CONSTRUCTION PKGES.
EWF04ST2	EW YCC STATION CONST. PKGES.
EWF04ST201	GENERAL REQUIREMENTS
EWF04ST202	SITEWORK
EWF04ST203	CONCRETE
EWF04ST204	MASONRY
EWF04ST205	METALS
EWF04ST206	WOOD & PLASTICS
EWF04ST207	THERM. & MOIST. PROTECT.
EWF04ST208	DOORS & WINDOWS
EWF04ST209	FINISHES
EWF04ST210	SPECIALITIES
EWF04ST211	SUBWAY EQUIPMENT
EWF04ST212	STATION FURNISHINGS
EWF04ST213	SPECIAL CONSTRUCTION
EWF04ST214	CONVEYING SYSTEMS
EWF04ST215	MECHANICAL
EWF04ST216	ELECTRICAL
EWF04ST217	CONTROLS

Figure 8.26 Eglinton West Subway/York City Center Station Construction Packages, Expenditure Control Report. The line items in the rows are derived from the summary item code EWF04ST 2 in Fig. 8.25. They depict construction contract packages only. Once the packages are bid and awarded, either as stand-alone contracts or as parts of general contracts, expenditures would be charged to the code items. Each line item in the rows is associated with the expenditure control columns 1 to 8 as discussed.

columns and fields listed as follows. Each line item would relate to the database through the triple-barrel code system of OBS/WBS/PDS.

Column 1	Code
Column 2	Description
Column 3	Original Commitment
Column 4	Approved Commitment Change
Column 5	Current Period Expenditures
Column 6	Expenditures to Date
Column 7	Current Outstanding Commitments
Column 8	Expenditures and Commitments to Date

RTEP PHASE 1
FUNCTIONAL OBS BASED ON DUTIES AND TASKS
PROJECT EXPENDITURE REPORT

ORG CODE	DESCRIPTION
A	PROGRAM MANAGEMENT ORGANIZATION
A02	EA COORDINATION & REVIEW
A04	DESIGN STANDARDS & TECHNOLOGY
A06	PROGRAM ENGINEERING
A08	PROGRAM CONSTRUCTION
A10	PROGRAM CONTROL
A12	QUALITY ASSURANCE
A14	PROGRAM PROCUREMENT
A16	FINANCE
A18	ADMINISTRATION
B	PROJECT MANAGEMENT ORGANIZATION
BEW	EGLINTON WEST SUBWAY
BEWA	PROJ. MGR. EGLINTON/ALLEN STATION
BEWC	PROJ. MGR. CALEDONIA STATION
BEWD	PROJECT MGR. DUFFERIN STATION
BEWK	PROJECT MANAGER KEELE STATION
BEWU	PROJ. MGR. 4.8 KM SUBWAY LINE
BRT	SCARBORO RAPID TRANSIT LINE
BSS	SHEPPARD SUBWAY LINE
BSU	SPADINA YORK UNIVERSITY LINE
BVE	VEHICLES
BWY	WILSON YARD COMPONENT
C	DESIGNERS & CONSULTANTS
C02	SPADINA/YORK UNIVERSITY LINE
C04	EGLINTON WEST
	etc.

ORG. CODE	
D	SUPPLY FIRMS
D02	TRACKWORK MATERIALS
D04	VENTILATION MATERIALS
D06	VENTILATION EQUIPMENT
E	SUPPLY & INSTALL FIRMS
E02	TRACKWORK
E04	TRACTION POWER
E08	TRAIN CONTROL & SIGNALIZATION
E10	COMMUNICATION SYSTEM
F	CONSTRUCTION FIRMS
F02	SPADINA YORK UNIVERSITY LINE
F02CC1	CUT & COVER STATION FIRM
F02CC2	CUT & COVER STA. & RNG. STR.
F02CC3	CUT & COVER STA. & RNG. STR.
	etc.
F04	EGLINTON WEST CONSTRUCT. FIRMS
F04CR1	CUT & COVER RNG. STR. 1
F04CR2	CUT & COVER RNG. STR. 2
F04ET1	EARTH TUNNEL 1
F04ET2	EARTH TUNNEL 2
F04R1	CUT & COVER RNG. STR. 1
F04R2	CUT & COVER RNG. STR. 2
F04S1	EGLINTON/ALLEN STA. FIRM
F04S3	CALEDONIA STATION FIRM
F04S4	KEELE STATION FIRM
F04S5	YORK CITY CENTER STATION FIRM
F04S6	YORK CITY CENTER STRUCTURE
G	DESIGN/BUILD FIRMS
H	STARTUP FIRMS
J	OPERATIONS TEAMS

FIGURE 8.27 RTEP PHASE 1 EGLINTON WEST SUBWAY LINE FUNCTIONAL OBS. The project is broken down by management duties, responsibility assignments, and packages, as depicted and coded above. Once the assignments are made, individual and firm names replace the duty and package names. But the breakdown of the individuals' and package assignments would be WBS coded line items depicted throughout this exercise. Figures 8.11 and 8.12 relate further how a project organization is developed through packaging and conversion to OBS.

8.7 Schedule Control

A project in its earliest conceptual form has a time frame or timeline. This might be just a future date. A date may be based on a commitment, it may be tied to a product launch, or it may relate to weather constraints for an isolated site. If it is a disaster, the disaster date is the start of the project. Activities would flow to minimize damage and relieve suffering.

For a planned engineering, construction, or business project, it is activities, tasks, and packages that form the basis for the timeline and for schedule control. The rationale for effective project management requires that a project be defined by its deliverables, and it is the activities leading to deliverables that are scheduled.

Many project management software packages are based on CPM / PERT techniques of planning and scheduling. Computerized CPM/PERT is the most widely marketed and the most popular of all project management tools. Its popularity has led to widespread usage. CPM/PERT methods were designed as successors to the Gantt chart, because the Gantt chart was not suitable for logical planning networks. But CPM/PERT networks are difficult to make and do not communicate well. To overcome this weakness, the Gantt or bar chart became the means to communicate the results of network planning and scheduling.

To make computerized scheduling more attractive and marketable, postmodern software designers bypassed the CPM/PERT logic planning networks and in the process converted the Gantt chart into the principal planning tool. Although Gantt has capability for simple logic relations, a Gantt schedule is not a network plan. In the systems of project management promulgated in this book, scheduling must be based on logical network planning.

The intent of network planning is to introduce logical connections between dependent activities. To make the logic visually understandable, computer systems convert the planning results to Gantt charts.

In this part of the case exercise the aim is to explore and demonstrate scheduling and progress control using the RTEP phase 1 Eglinton West subway line. This is done using the hard information and activities developed through the definition, breakdown, and organization exercises. Once a network is created, its application for project control purposes is shown through a series of CAD drawings, bar charts, and tabular reports.

The scheduling network seen in Fig. 8.28 consists of project activities from the work breakdown. To keep this demonstration simple, activities are picked at level 3 as named and coded in Figs. 8.21, 8.22, and 8.23. To facilitate understanding the concept of WBS levels, the RTEP phase 1 is considered to be level 1. The Eglinton West subway is at level 2, and the project phases from 01, Predevelopment, to 09, Operations, are considered to be at level 3.

In designing the network it was reckoned that project management planning may comprise a number of different schedule versions, made at different times. At some future point in time, management may wish to run them all together for a reason that may not be apparent initially. That is why the Eglinton West network activities are

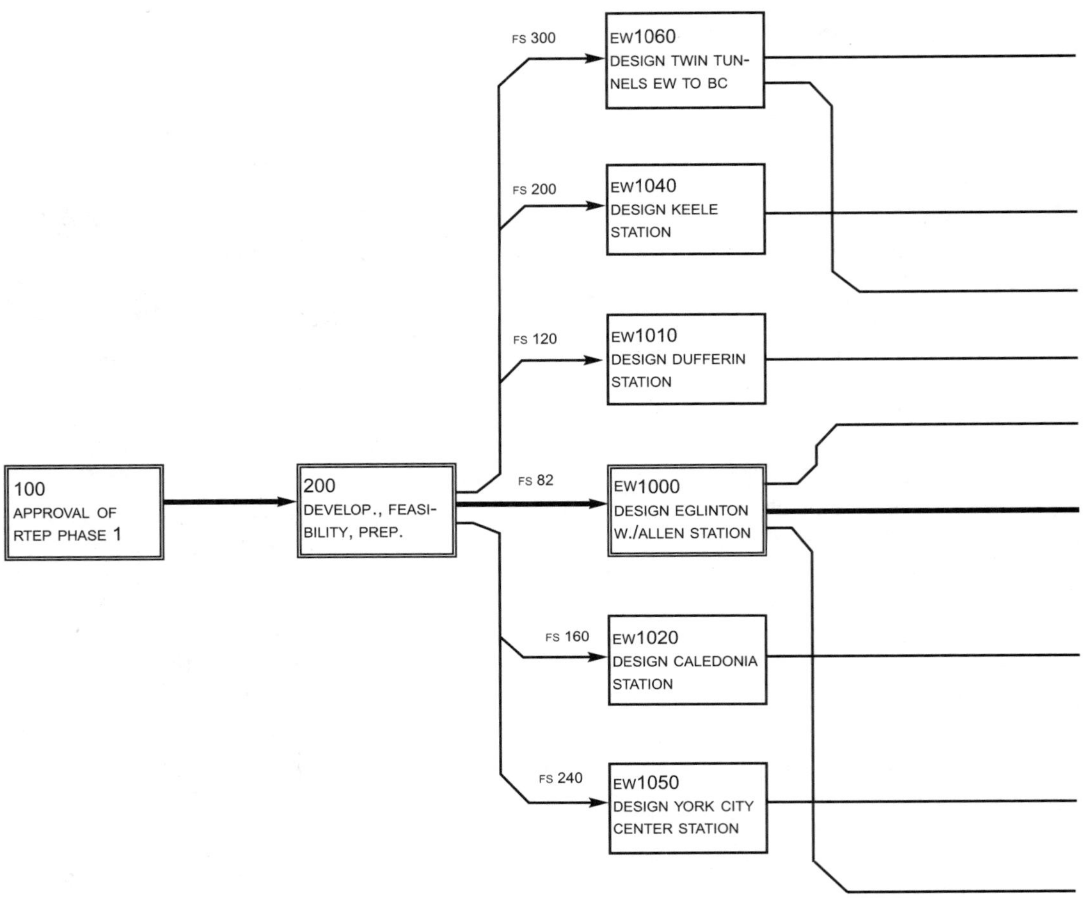

FIGURE 8.28*a* RTEP PHASE 1 EGLINTON WEST SUBWAY LINE CPM NETWORK, CAD DRAWING. The activities are based on the work breakdown structure in Fig. 8.23. The activity IDs relate to the Eglinton West line, except for a begin event, ID 100, and the development phase ID 200. Shown are logical relationships as well as activity relationships, which are finish to start unless otherwise shown. This page shows the start, developmnet, and design activities. In designing a large scheduling network it is good practice to group like activities when useful.

identified as EWnnnn. The Sheppard line (see Fig. 8.15) may be coded SSnnnn, and so on. It may be concluded that the larger the project, the more flexibility in codes and activities is required. On the other hand, too much flexibility could lead to large complex codes and activity numbers.

Figure 8.28 is based on a CAD drawing by a PC project management software application. The features include a planning network based on logic; activities that derive from the project scope and breakdown; the use of network features such as lead and lag values; and different relationships, including finish to start (FS); start to start (SS), and finish to finish (FF).

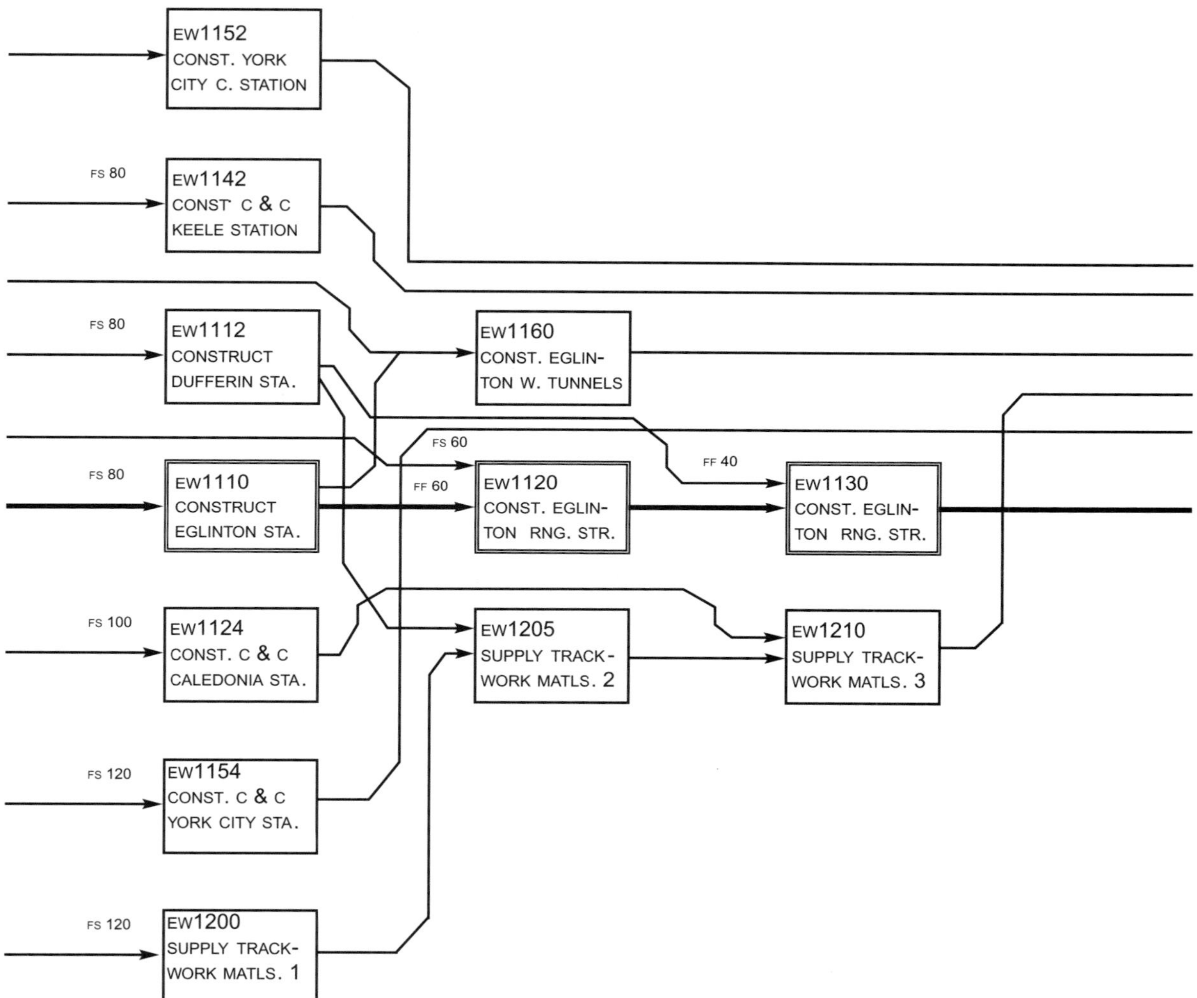

FIGURE 8.28b RTEP PHASE 1 EGLINTON WEST SUBWAY LINE CPM NETWORK, CAD DRAWING. Construction and supply activities.

A most important feature of network planning is the creation of the project critical path. The critical path sets the sequence, relationship, and logic, as well as the durations for those activities that establish the time that the project requires for its completion. It ties together and relates all activities to each other and to the critical path. The critical path network and the resulting schedule are then used for resources planning and cash-flow projections.

Figure 8.29 shows the activities in the network for the Eglinton West subway that are on the critical path, and which establish the project duration. If the logic, the activity duration values or the relational lag values are changed, the critical path will

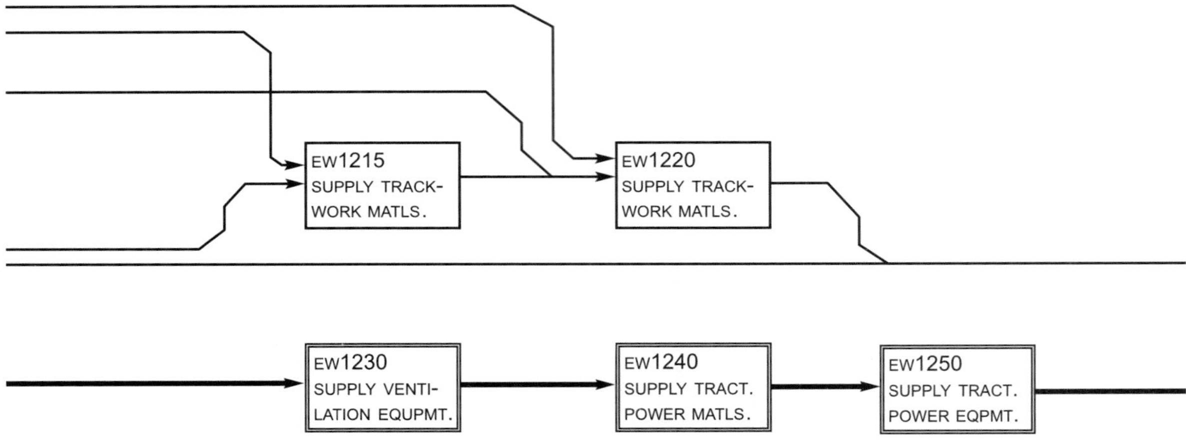

FIGURE 8.28c RTEP PHASE 1 EGLINTON WEST SUBWAY LINE CPM NETWORK, CAD DRAWING. Supply activites.

FF 80
EW1260
TRACTION
POWER INSTALL.
FF 00
EW1290
TRACKWORK
EGLINTON W.
EW1313
SIGNAGE &
GRAPHICS S & I
EW1311
ELEVATORS &
ESCALATORS S&I
EW1380
COMMUNICATION
SYSTEM S & I
EW1370
TRAIN SIG-
NALING S & I
EW1310
SCADA SUPPLY &
INSTALL
EW1312
FARE COLLEC-
TION S & I

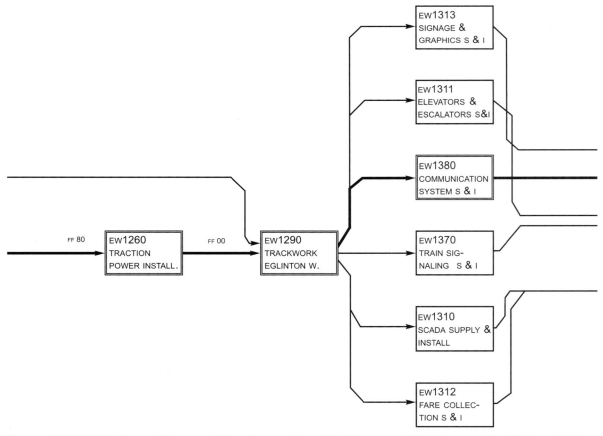

FIGURE 8.28d RTEP PHASE 1 EGLINTON WEST SUBWAY LINE CPM NETWORK, CAD DRAWING. Installation activities.

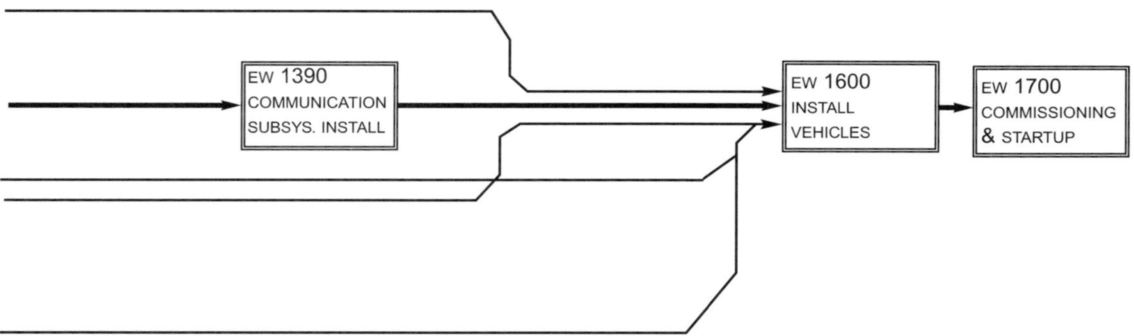

FIGURE 8.28e RTEP PHASE 1 EGLINTON WEST SUBWAY LINE CPM NETWORK, CAD DRAWING. Installation and starup activities.

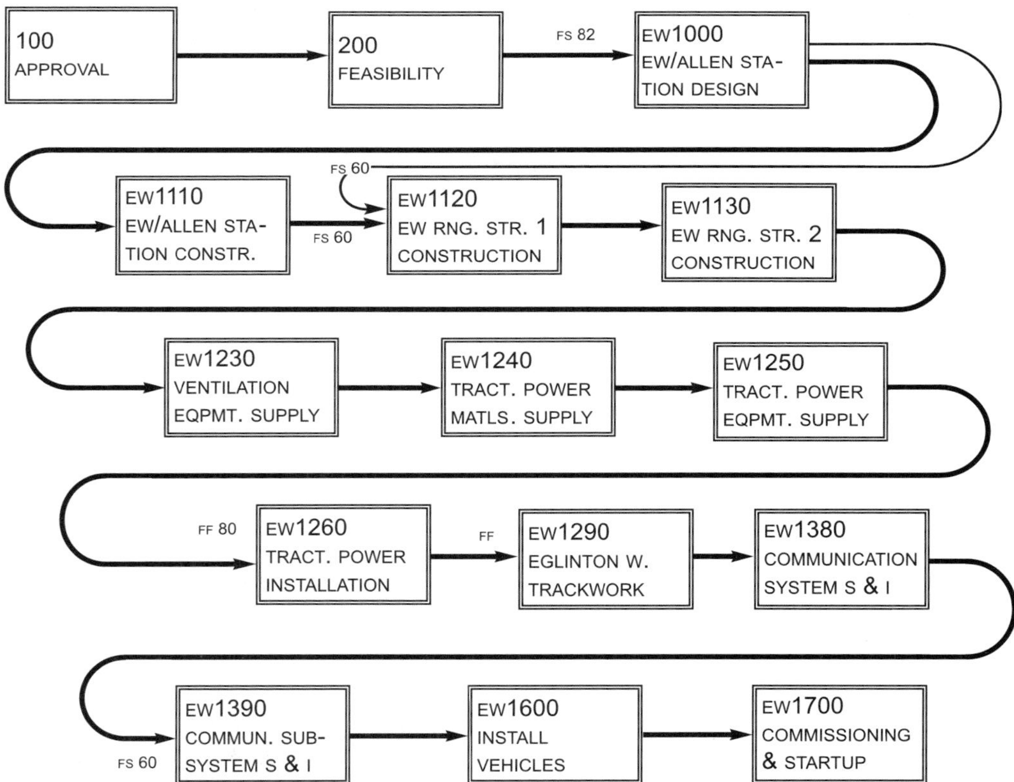

FIGURE 8.29 RTEP PHASE 1 EGLINTON WEST SUBWAY LINE CPM NETWORK, CRITICAL PATH, CAD DRAWING. The above activities form the critical path of the network of activities in Fig. 8.28. The critical path forms the longest irreducible sequence of events when calculated by computer on the forward and backward passes. A critical activity has zero float. The early and late start and finish dates are the same. All other activities' float values are related to the critical path. There are two kinds of float. Free float is amount of float before another activity is affected. Total float is amount of float before the critical path is affected.

also change. Considering the full case exercise network seen in Fig. 8.28 and the chain of critical activities drawn in Fig. 8.29, the entire project schedule is driven by the values of the critical path activities as seen in the computer-generated information in Fig. 8.30.

Another key feature of computerized network planning is the facility to plan the project quickly many times, and to run and analyze "what if" iterations. It is most unusual for the first project logic diagram to be the basis for the approved scheduling

ACTIVITY IDENTITY	ACTIVITY DESCRIPTION	ORIG. DUR.	REM. DUR.	EARLY START	EARLY FINISH	LATE START	LATE FINISH	TOTAL FLOAT
100	APPROVE RTEP	1	1	08FEB93	08FEB93	08FEB93	08FEB93	0
200	DEVELOP, FEASIBILITY, PREP.	60	60	09FEB93	04MAY93	09FEB93	04MAY93	0
EW1000	EGLINTON W. / ALLEN STA-TION DESIGN	480	480	26JUL93	22JUN95	26JUL93	22JUN95	0
EW1110	EW/ALLEN STATION CONSTR.	320	320	11SEP95	13DEC96	11SEP95	13DEC96	0
EW1120	EW RNG. STR. 1 CONSTRUC-TION	320	320	06NOV95	11FEB97	06NOV95	11FEB97	0
EW1130	EW RNG. STR. 2 CONSTRUC-TION	300	300	12FEB97	20APR98	12FEB97	20APR98	0
EW1230	VENTILATION EQPMT. SUPPLY	280	280	21APR98	17MAY99	21APR98	17MAY99	0
EW1240	TRACT. POWER MATLS. SUP-PLY	250	250	18MAY99	01MAY00	18MAY99	01MAY00	0
EW1250	TRACT. POWER EQPMT. SUP-PLY	300	300	02MAY00	25JUN01	02MAY00	25JUN01	0
EW1260	TRACTION POWER INSTALLA-TION	400	400	03MAR00	13SEP01	03MAR00	13SEP01	0
EW1290	EGLINTON W. TRACKWORK	400	400	03MAR00	13SEP01	03MAR00	13SEP01	0
EW1380	COMMUNICATION SYSTEM S & I	250	250	14SEP01	29AUG02	14SEP01	29AUG02	0
EW1390	COMMUNICATION SUBSYS-TEM S & I	250	250	18NOV02	31OCT03	18NOV02	31OCT03	0
EW1600	INSTALL VEHICLES	280	280	03NOV03	26NOV04	03NOV03	26NOV04	0
EW1700	COMMISSIONING & STARTUP	200	200	29NOV04	02SEP05	29NOV04	02SEP05	0

FIGURE 8.30 RTEP PHASE 1 EGLINTON WEST SUBWAY LINE CPM NETWORK, CRITICAL ACTIVITIES LIST, COMPUTER REPORT. This report lists all the critical activities in the network in Fig. 8.28. The report has been sorted in ascending order by AI number, second by early start, third by early finish. Also shown are original and remaining duration. At the beginning of a project both durations are the same. Once the project gets under way, the remaining duration may be changed based on progress, or for other reasons. It is important to accept that an activity's original duration is the result of many factors such as network logic, single or probabilistic time estimates, risk analysis, and resources allocation and leveling. At best it is an estimate for an activity at a point in time. All this is to say that a duration can change and probably will, thus changing the critical path.

plan. The logic diagram in Fig. 8.28 is the result of many iterations, and it can be expected that more runs will be needed.

Networks have exceptional capability to set down, test, measure, and calculate logical relationships between activities. The exercise consists of arranging, connecting, and processing activities seen as predecessors and successors. A hard-copy example of the kind of information that must be considered for planning and scheduling is seen in Fig. 8.31, which shows a few sample activities from the Eglinton West line network.

CPM/PERT project planning and scheduling is driven by the idea of the critical path and the related float values for all project activities. To achieve a zero-float path, the durations are calculated on the forward pass and then backward. The result is a classical computer report that lists two sets of early dates, start and finish; two sets of late dates, start and finish; and the total float value for each activity. As computer programs became more advanced, and more information was input, other values became available. But the classical boiler-plate computer information comprises the key

PREDECESSOR	LAG TYPE	LAG DUR	CAL ID	ACTIVITY/DESCRIPTION	FLOAT	SUCCESSOR	LAG TYPE	LAG DUR
			00	100 APPROVAL OF THE RTEP	0	200	FS	0
			00	200 DEVELOP, FEASIBILITY, PREP.	0			
100	FS	0				EW1000 EW1020 EW1040 EW1060 EW1050 EW1010	FS FS FS FS FS FS	82 160 200 300 240 120
			00	EW1000 DESIGN EGLINTON W./ALLEN STATION	0			
200	FS	82				EW1110 EW1120 EW1200	FS FS FS	80 60 120
			00	EW1110 CONSTRUCT EGLINTON STATION	0			
EW1000	FS	80				EW1160 EW1120	FS FS	0 60
			00	EW1120 CONSTRUCT EGLINTON W. RNG. STR.	0			
EW1000 EW1110	FS FS	60 60				EW1130	FS	0

Figure 8.31 RTEP Phase 1 Eglinton West Subway Line CPM Network, Precedence Relationship, Computer Report. The creation of a CPM network requires computer calculations to test and prove assumptions and logic as well as to remove errors, such as loops. As logical relationships are resolved, scheduling decisions are input, lead and lag values are assigned, and the computer iterates the process until the output is deemed acceptable. If the schedule is subjected to resources allocation and leveling, or to computerized risk analysis, which is not the case here, the iterations become more complex. In this event the process is driven by predecessor/successor relationships, as depicted in this computer report.

early/late, start/finish, and float information, as seen in Fig. 8.32, which shows 20 sample activities from the case exercise.

However, for many project planners and schedulers the most popular scheduling technique is the Gantt or bar chart. The reason for its popularity is its visual simplicity and ease of use. Early computerized CPM/PERT networks were difficult to read and impractical to use as communication tools. As a result computer applications were programmed to make simple bar charts by driving printers and using typewriter characters to represent network-derived information. With the advent of more advanced computer printers and plotters, they too were able to deliver scaled bar charts to reflect the results of network planning, as seen in Fig. 8.33, which shows a few selected activities from the case exercise.

As PC project management and graphics applications were further integrated, the results were more professional charts, as illustrated in Fig. 8.34, a bar chart of the Eglinton West project. With color plotters, laser printers, and three-dimensional renderings, the output would be better looking still. However, the efficacy of the scheduling exercise may not necessarily be improved just because of better and better looking printer output and graphics.

8.8 Cost and Schedule Integration

To show how project cost and the scheduling of activities may be integrated, the case exercise activities already developed are processed by Primavera Project Planner (P3). P3 is an activity-based system. What this means is that the project is broken down into activities or tasks. The activities are assigned account codes, responsibility codes, durations, resources, and cost estimates. In this book activities, account codes, and responsibilities are the result of definition, breakdown, packaging, and assignment to organizations. To illustrate the integration of cost and schedule, the case exercise activities are processed for logic and schedule, and then for cost. The graphics and tables that follow are based on P3 processing.

Figure 8.35 is a CAD drawing of a number of representative activities of the logic diagram developed for the case exercise. The activities are labeled with ID number (activity number), truncated description, PDS code, WBS code, and OBS code. Other labels may be selected and shown on the drawing.

The activities in Fig. 8.36 are on the critical path. Based on their logic, their durations in workdays, the lag values assigned to the FS SS FF relationships, and the project calendar employed, these activities have zero float or slack. Activities on the critical path have the same early/late, start/finish dates.

Figure 8.37 is a view of selected activities from the project network. The activity labels include ID, duration, float, early start, and late finish. Figure 8.37*a* depicts 15 activities with zero float, Fig. 8.37*b* depicts an assortment of representative activities together with a number of logic lines.

To reiterate, a computer-processed planning network creates a project schedule based on the logical progression of activities. Experience in project planning teaches

ACTIVITY IDENTITY	ACTIVITY DESCRIPTION	ORIG. DUR.	REM. DUR.	EARLY START	EARLY FINISH	LATE START	LATE FINISH	TOTAL FLOAT	IMPOSED DATE
100	APPROVE RTEP	1	1	08FEB93	08FEB93	08FEB93	08FEB93	0	08FEB93
200	DEVELOP, FEASIBILITY, PREP.	60	60	09FEB93	04MAY93	09FEB93	04MAY93	0	
EW1000	DESIGN EGLINTON W. / ALLEN STATION	480	480	26JUL93	22JUN95	26JUL93	22JUN95	0	
EW1010	DESIGN DUFFERIN STATION	320	320	02SEP93	12DEC94	11OCT94	19JAN96	277	
EW1020	DESIGN CALEDONIA STA-TION	360	360	12OCT93	17MAR95	14JUN95	15NOV96	420	
EW1040	DESIGN KEELE STATION	300	300	22NOV93	01FEB95	18MAR96	26MAY97	583	
EW1050	DESIGN YORK CITY CEN-TER STATION	360	360	31DEC93	06JUN95	15JUL96	17DEC97	638	
EW1060	DESIGN TWIN TUNNELS EW TO BC	360	360	01MAR94	03AUG95	27NOV96	30APR98	691	
EW1110	CONSTRUCT EGLINTON STA.	320	320	11SEP95	13DEC96	11SEP95	13DEC96	0	
EW1112	CONSTRUCT DUFFERIN STA.	300	300	03MAR95	09MAY96	09APR96	17JUN97	278	
EW1120	CONST. EGLINTON RNG. STR. 1	320	320	06NOV95	11FEB97	06NOV95	11FEB97	0	
EW1124	CONST. C & C CALEDONIA STA.	280	280	26JUN95	02AUG96	24FEB97	02APR98	419	
EW1130	CONST. EGLINTON RNG. STR. 2	300	300	12FEB97	20APR98	12FEB97	20APR98	0	
EW1142	CONST. C & C KEELE STA-TION	340	340	24APR95	27AUG96	15AUG97	10DEC98	583	
EW1152	CONST. YORK CITY C. STA-TION	360	360	04AUG95	09JAN97	01MAY98	16SEP99	691	
EW1154	CONST. C & C YORK CITY STA.	370	370	05OCT95	24MAR97	17APR98	16SEP99	639	
EW1160	CONST. EGLINTON W. TUN-NELS	200	200	16DEC96	01OCT97	28MAY99	02MAR00	627	
EW1200	SUPPLY TRACKWORK MATLS. 1	200	200	23OCT95	06AUG96	03SEP96	17JUN97	218	
EW1205	SUPPLY TRACKWORK MATLS. 2	200	200	07AUG96	22MAY97	18JUN97	02APR98	218	
EW1210	SUPPLY TRACKWORK MATLS. 3	180	180	23MAY97	09FEB98	03APR98	10DEC98	218	

FIGURE 8.32 RTEP PHASE 1 EGLINTON WEST SUBWAY LINE CPM NETWORK, CRITICAL ACTIVITIES LIST, COMPUTER REPORT. The start event has been assigned a date. Based on the date and the network in Fig. 8.28 the computer has calculated the schedule dates listed. The report lists only the first 20 activities in ascending order by ID number. Shown are the orginal duration, remaining duration, and total float in workdays based on a 5-day workweek. Also shown are early and late start and finish dates. For activities with zero float the early and late start and finish dates are the same.

ACTIVITY IDENTIFIER	EARLY START	TOTAL FLOAT	1993 FMAMJJASOND	1994 JFMAMJJASOND	1995 JFMAMJJASOND	1996 JFMAMJJASOND
100	08FEB93	0	C			
APPROVE RTEP						
200	09FEB93	0	CCCF			
DEVELOP, FEASIBILITY, PREP.						
EW1000	26JUL93	0	CCCCCC	CCCCCCCCCCC	CCCCCF	
EGLINTON W. / ALLEN STATION DESIGN						
EW1110	11SEP95	0			CCCC	CCCCCCCCCCCF
EW / ALLEN STATION CONSTR.						
EW1120	06NOV95	0			CC	CCCCCCCCCCCC
EW RNG. STR. 1 CONSTRUCTION						
EW1130	12FEB97	0				
EW RNG. STR. 2 CONSTRUCTION						
EW1230	21APR98	0				
VENTILATION EQPMT. SUPPLY						
EW1010	02SEP93	277	XXXX	XXXXXXXXXXX	...........................F	
DESIGN DUFFERIN STATION						
EW1112	03MAR95	278			XXXXXXXXXX	XXXXXX................
CONSTRUCT DUFFERIN STA..						

FIGURE 8.33 RTEP PHASE 1 EGLINTON WEST SUBWAY LINE CPM NETWORK-BASED SCHEDULE, BAR CHART. Although CPM networks are powerful logical planning tools, they are inadequate communication tools. They do not lend themselves to time scaling and calendarizing. To overcome this deficiency, the results of network plans were invariably converted to bar charts, first using simple computer printers and typed characters, as shown.

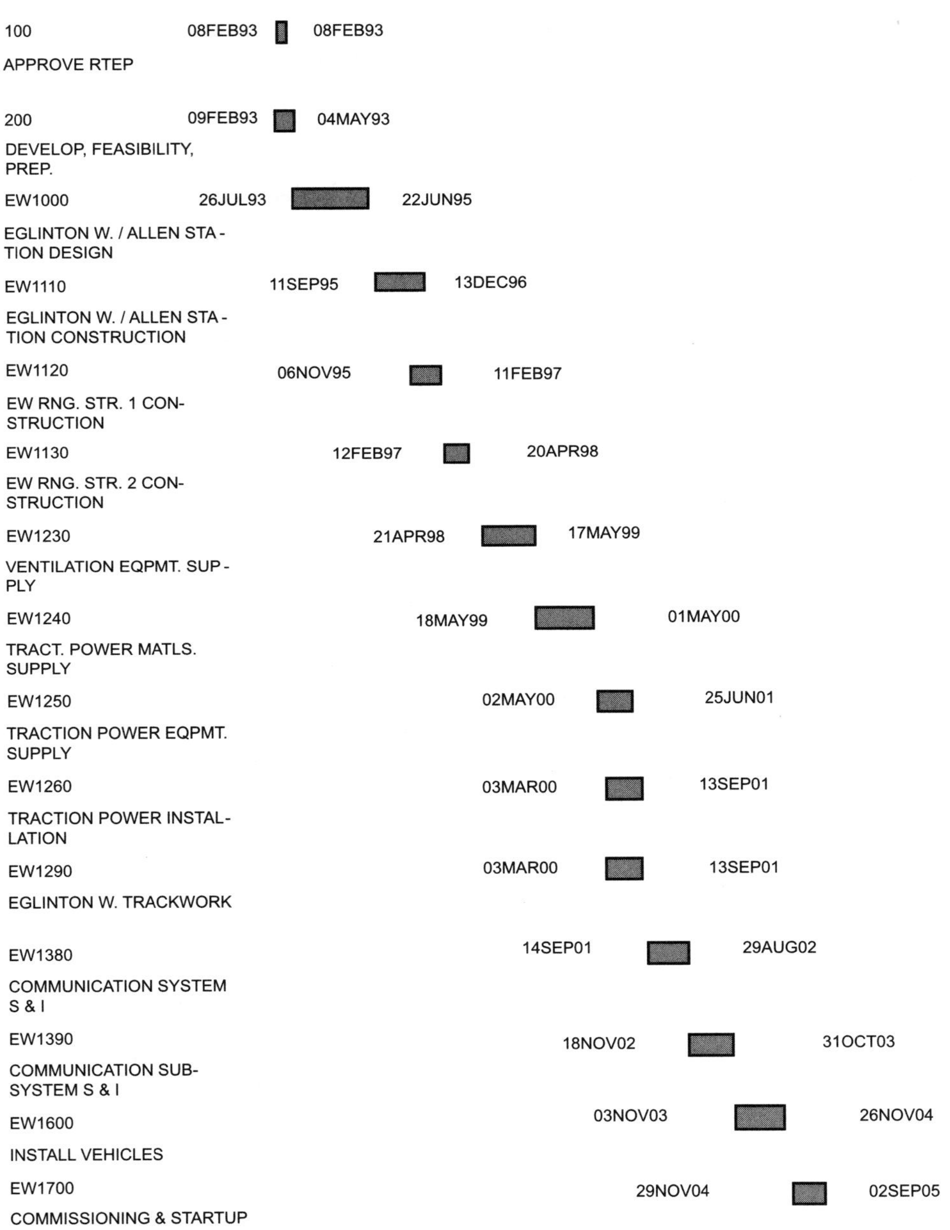

FIGURE 8.34 RTEP PHASE 1 EGLINTON WEST SUBWAY LINE CPM NETWORK-BASED SCHEDULE, CRITICAL PATH BAR CHART. This is a computer-produced graphical bar chart of the critical path information presented in tabular form in Fig. 8.30. Shown are activity identities, descriptions, and start and finish dates. The durations are represented by the calendar-related bars. The key to the efficacy of the bar chart is that it is backed by the CPM logic-based network of all the activities that form the case project.

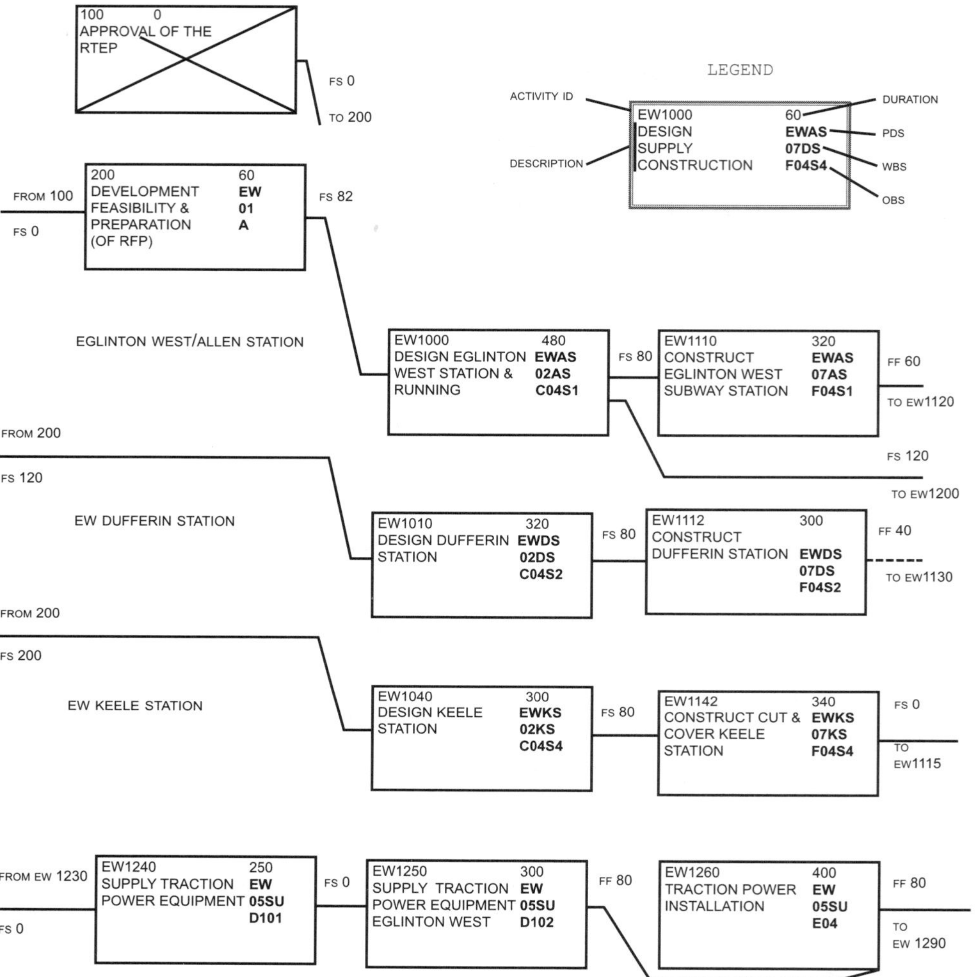

FIGURE 8.35 RTEP PHASE 1 EGLINTON WEST SUBWAY LINE LOGIC DIAGRAM, CAD DRAWING, SAMPLE ACTIVITIES ONLY. This is a simplified rendering of a CAD drawing of a logic diagram. The intent is to show an array of activities, their logical relationships, and some of their values. The drawing also aims to exhibit the inherent complexity of CPM/PERT style networking, meaning that computers can process, calculate, and draw logic diagrams, but their results must be read on other reports and by other means, e.g., bar charts.

that initial computer runs are trial runs only, and that many iterations are needed for meaningful results. Planning consists of a series of repetitive, iterative steps. A planner can assemble and set down a number of activities and durations, arrange their relationships, lags, and values, and then see the results of computer processing on screen and as hard copy.

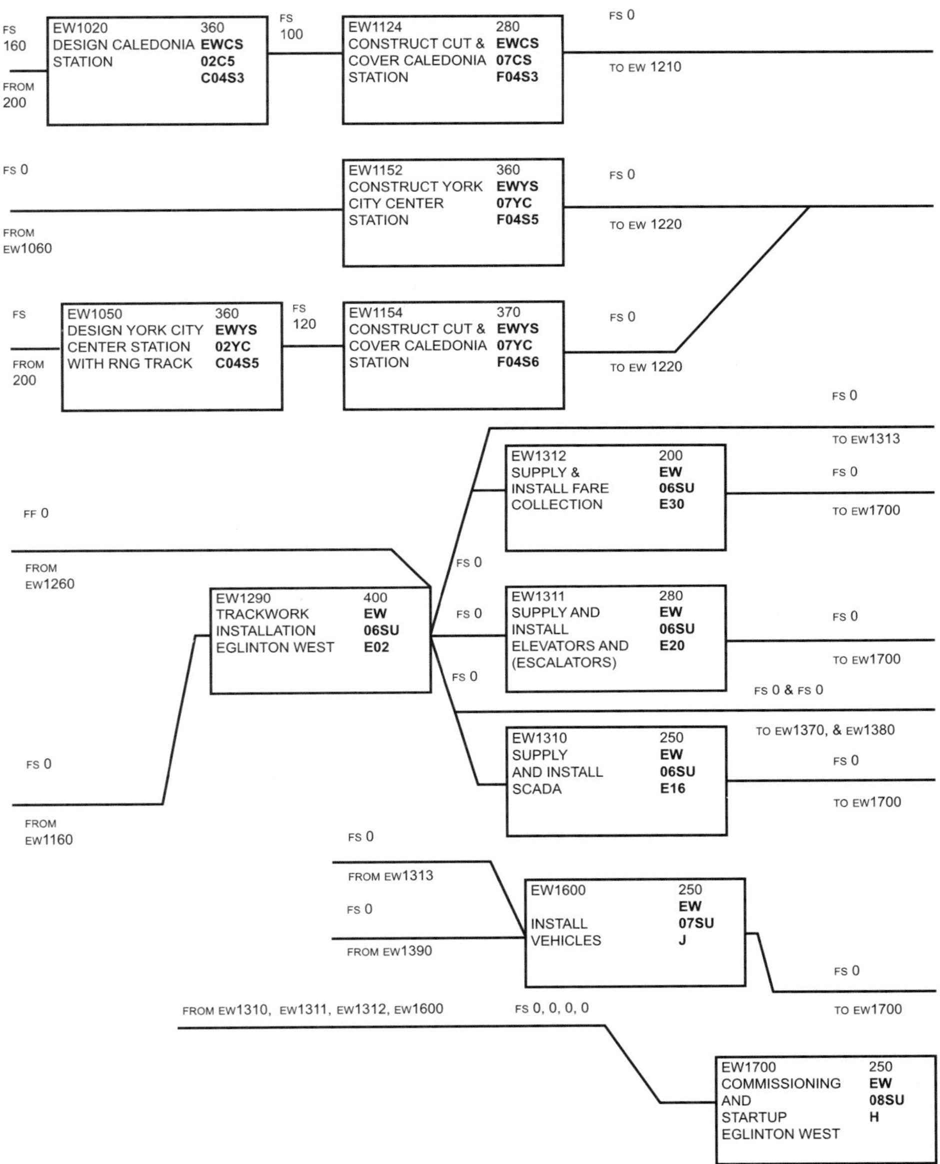

FIGURE 8.35 (CONTINUED).

Figure 8.38 is an example of a tabular report of predecessor and successor relationships between activities and their values. It is an important report in the design, development, and massaging of a network of activities. This report is a means to bridge the gap in the person/computer interface. Hard copy, as seen in this report example, is useful in communicating the information to team members, and

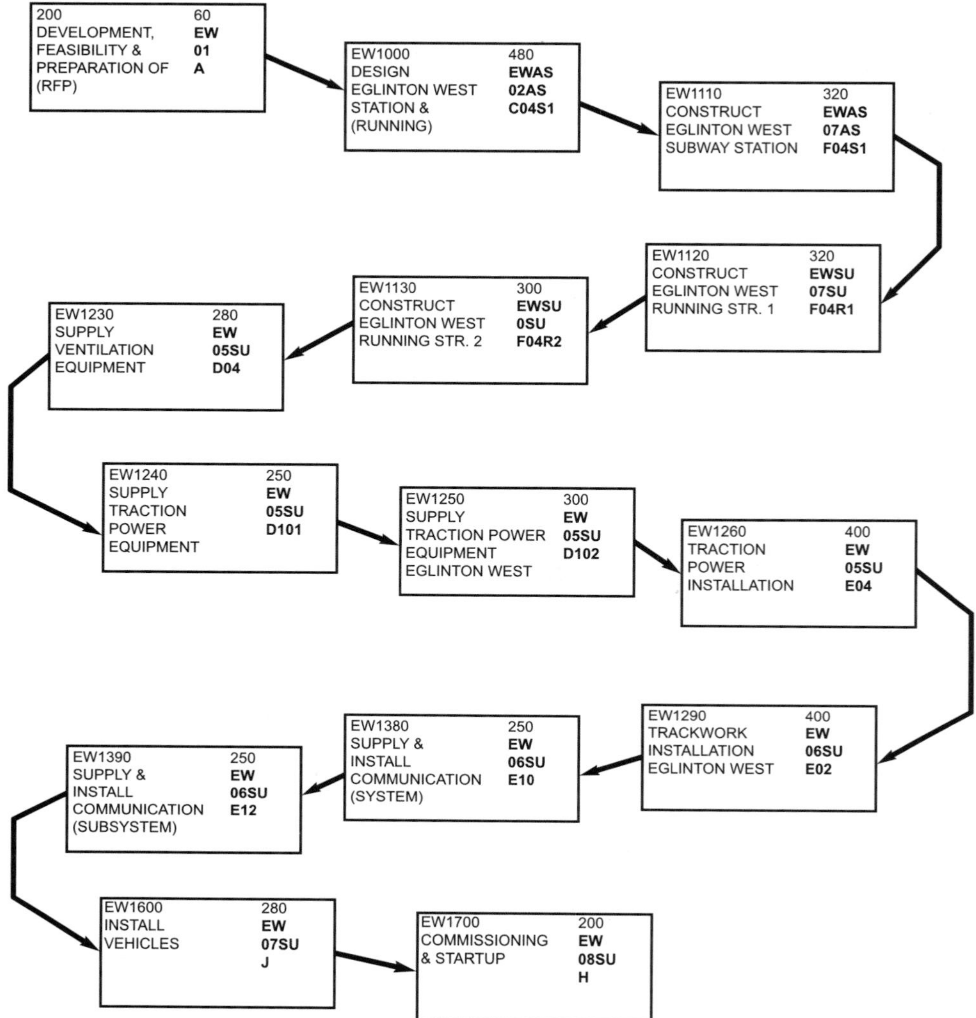

FIGURE 8.36 RTEP PHASE 1 EGLINTON WEST SUBWAY LINE LOGIC DIAGRAM, CAD DRAWING, CRITICAL PATH ACTIVITIES. This diagram shows only the activities on the project critical path. Shown are activity ID, activity description, duration in workdays, PDS code, WBS code, and OBS code. Essentially these would be very large activities, costing millions of dollars, and requiring many months to carry out. This kind of logic diagram may be called a master schedule or summary schedule.

to facilitate the analytical process. The information in Fig. 8.38 is explained as follows:

- P.L.D.F. stands for predecessor, lag, duration, float.
- For example, the P.L.D.F. values for activity ID 200 are activity ID 100, FS lag (0 days), duration (0 days), float (0 days).

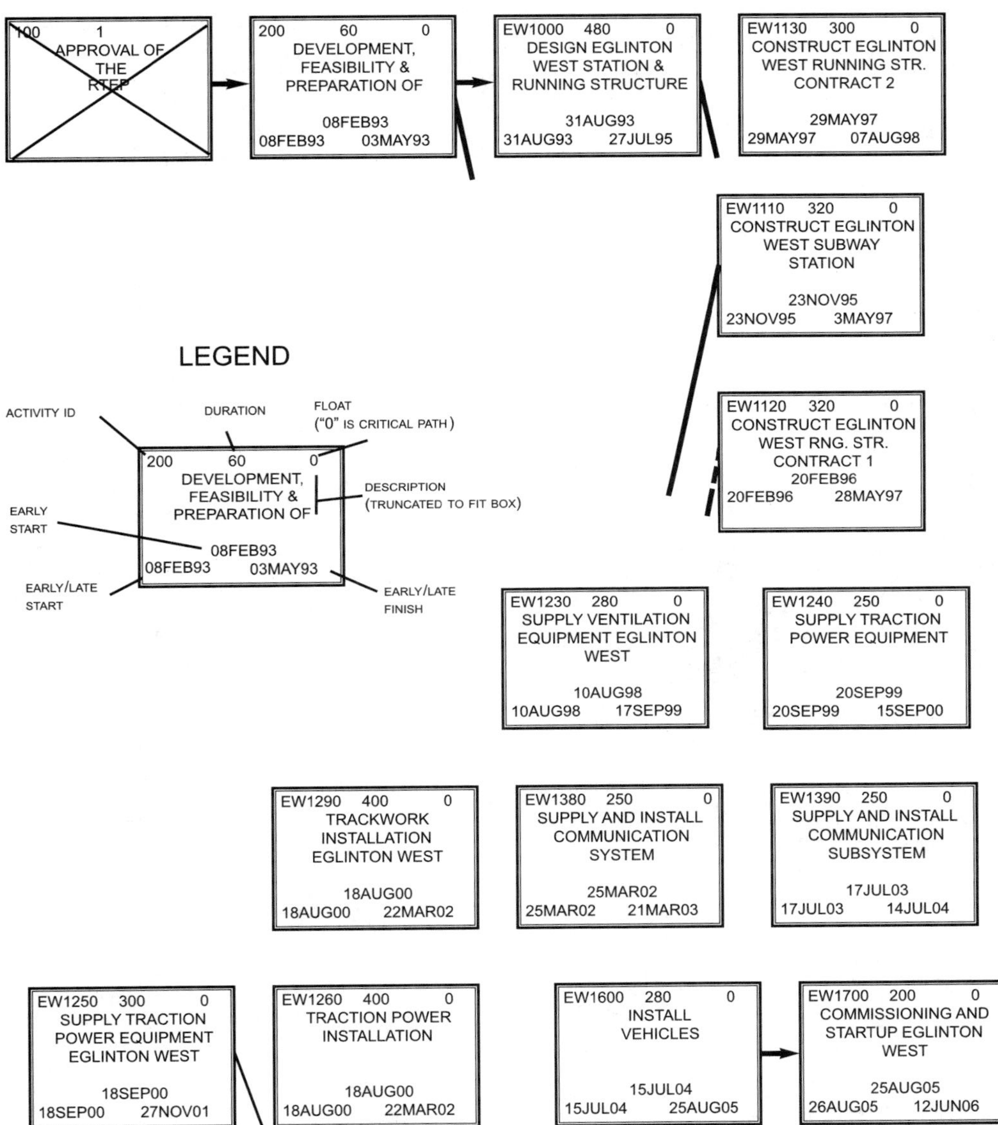

FIGURE 8.37*a* RTEP PHASE 1 EGLINTON WEST SUBWAY LINE LOGIC DIAGRAM, CAD DRAWING, SCHEDULE DATES. A CAD drawing of activities may be selected and filtered to show different kinds of information. Only critical activities are shown. Each activity is labeled with the information shown in the legend. Shown are also a number of logic lines for illustration purposes.

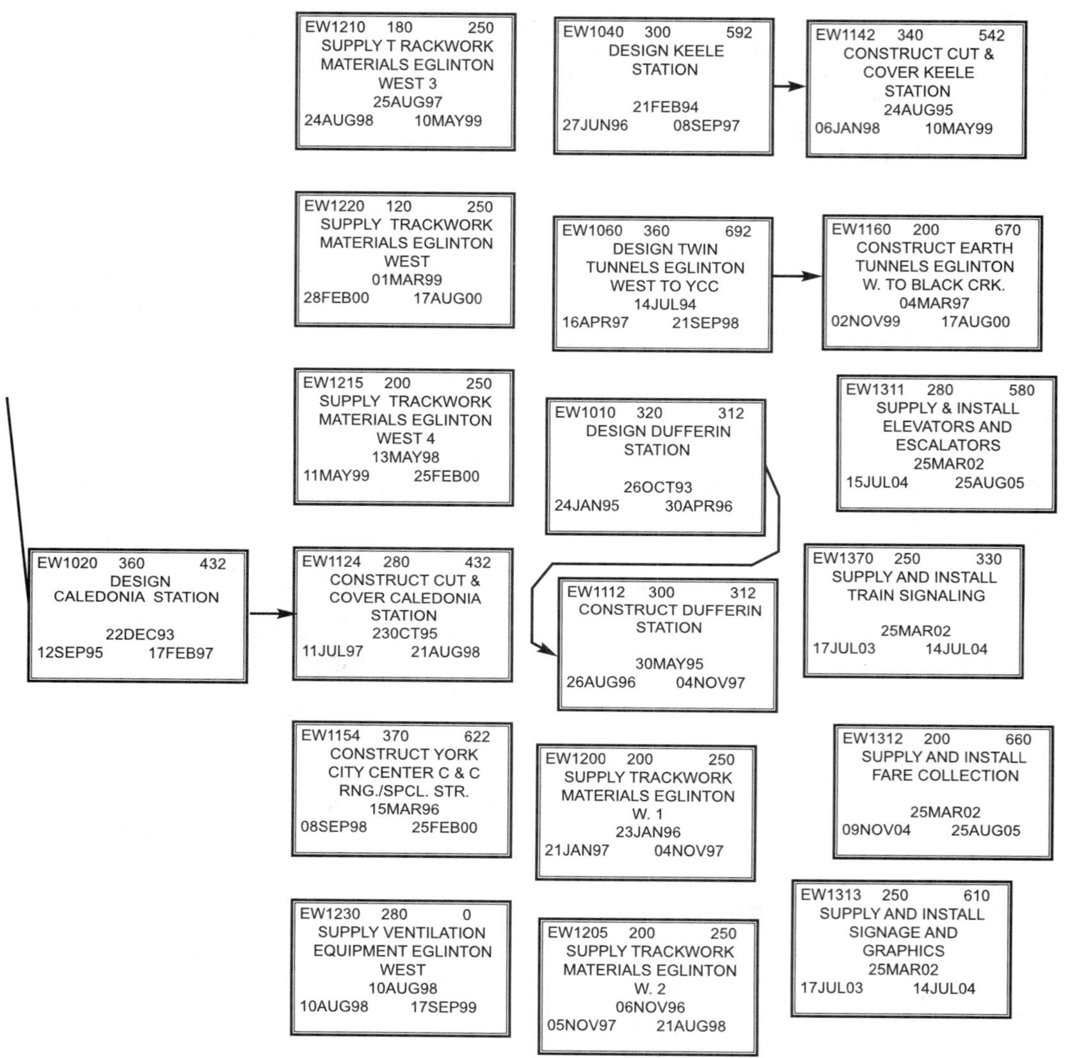

FIGURE 8.37*b* RTEP PHASE 1 EGLINTON WEST SUBWAY LINE LOGIC DIAGRAM, CAD DRAWING, SCHEDULE DATES. Information similar to *a* for a selection of other activities.

- S.L.D.F. stands for successor, lag, duration, float.
- For example, the successors to activity ID 200 are EW1000, EW1020, EW 1050, EW1010, EW1040, EW1060. The L.D.F. values are those listed.
- As another example, the predecessor to activity ID EW1000 is activity ID 200. The L.D.F. values are FS lag = 82 days, D. = 60 days for activity ID 200, and F. = 0 days.

Figure 8.39 represents a cut from a quintessential project planning and scheduling computer report. This kind of information is the essence of computerized

ACTIVITY ID	ORIG DUR	REM DUR	CAL	%	ACTIVITY DESCRIPTION	ES	EF	LS	LF	TOTAL FLOAT
		P.L.D.F.,	100,	FS	0 0 0					
200	**60**	**60**	**2**	**0**	**DEVELOPMENT, FEASIBILITY**	**8FEB93**	**3MAY93**	**8FEB93**	**3MAY93**	**0**
		S.L.D.F.,	EW1000,	FS	82 480 0	EW1010,	FS	120	320	312
		S.L.D.F.,	EW1020,	FS	160 360 432	EW1040,	FS	200	300	592
		S.L.D.F.,	EW1050,	FS	240 360 622	EW1060,	FS	300	360	692
		P.L.D.F.,	200	FS	82 60 0					
EW1000	**480**	**480**	**2**	**0**	**DESIGN EGLINTON WEST STA-TION & RUNNING STRUCTURES**	**31AUG93**	**27JUL95**	**31AUG93**	**27JUL95**	**0**
		S.L.D.F.,	EW1110	FS	80 320 0	EW1120	FS	60	320	0
		S.L.D.F.,	EW1220	FS	120 250					
		P.L.D.F.,	200	FS	120 60 0					
EW1010	**320**	**320**	**2**	**0**	**DESIGN DUFFERIN STATION**	**26OCT93**	**2FEB95**	**2FEB95**	**30APR96**	**312**
		S.L.D.F.,	EW1112	FS	80 300 312					
		P.L.D.F.,	200	FS	160 60 0					
EW1020	**360**	**360**	**2**	**0**	**DESIGN CALEDONIA STATION**	**22DEC93**	**29MAY95**	**12SEP95**	**17FEB97**	**432**
		S.L.D.F.,	EW1124	FS	100 280 432					
		P.L.D.F.,	200	FS	240 60 0					
EW1040	**300**	**300**	**2**	**0**	**DESIGN KEELE STATION**	**21FEB94**	**28APR95**	**27JUN96**	**08SEP97**	**592**
		S.L.D.F.,	EW1142	FS	80 340 592					
		P.L.D.F.,	200	FS	240 60 0					
EW1050	**360**	**360**	**2**	**0**	**DESIGN YORK CITY CENTER STA-TION WITH RNG. TRK.**	**19APR94**	**21SEP95**	**8OCT96**	**16MAR98**	**622**

FIGURE 8.38 RTEP PHASE 1 EGLINTON WEST SUBWAY LINE COMPUTER REPORT, PREDECESSORS AND SUCCESSORS, EXAMPLE ACTIVITIES ONLY. The creation of a CPM logic diagram involves arranging activities which reflect the logical flow of project work. Even a few activities, when comblined with the array of values required to make a project schedule, lead to a maze. A predecessors and successors report, as depicted, is essential to solve the maze, follow the logic, and create a useful schedule network.

CPM/PERT network planning and scheduling. The only way it is made available to the project planner is through a network of activities.

Computer reports of CPM networks are sometimes confusing. The confusion arises from computer calculations giving rise to large amounts of information, as may be seen in this report. As this example shows, there are four sets of dates, two sets of durations, a percent complete column, and a float column. Provision for more information, such as imposed dates, baseline dates, scheduled dates, free float, to name

ACTIVITY ID	ORIG DUR	REM DUR	%	DESCRIPTION	EARLY START	EARLY FINISH	LATE START	LATE FINISH	TOTAL FLOAT
100	1	1	100	APPROVAL OF THE RTEP PHASE 1					
200	60	60	0	DEVELOPMENT, FEASIBILITY, PREPARATION	08FEB93	03MAY93	08FEB93	03MAY93	0
EW1000	480	480	0	DESIGN EGLINTON W. STATION & RUNNING	31AUG93	27JUL95	31AUG3	27JUL95	0
EW1010	320	320	0	DESIGN DUFFERIN STATION	26OCT93	02FEB95	24JAN95	30APR96	312
EW1020	360	360	0	DESIGN CALEDONIA STATION	22DEC93	29MAY95	12SEP95	17FEB97	432
EW1040	300	300	0	DESIGN KEELE STATION	21FEB94	28APR95	27JUN96	08SEP97	592
EW1050	360	360	0	DESIGN YORK CITY CENTER STATION/RNG	19APR94	21SEP95	08OCT96	16MAR98	622
EW1060	360	360	0	DESIGN TWIN TUNNELS EGLINTON W. TO YCC	14JUL94	18DEC95	16APR97	21SEP98	692
EW1110	320	320	0	CONSTRUCT EGLINTON WEST SUBWAY STA.	23NOV95	03MAR97	23NOV95	03MAR97	0
EW1112	300	300	0	CONSTRUCT DUFFERIN STATION	30MAY95	07AUG96	26AUG96	04NOV97	312
EW1120	320	320	0	CONSTRUCT EGLINTON W. RNG. STR. CONTR. 1	20FEB96	28MAY97	20FEB96	28MAY97	0
EW1124	280	280	0	CONSTRUCT CUT & COVER CALEDONIA STA.	23OCT95	02DEC96	11JUL97	21AUG98	432
EW1130	300	300	0	CONSTRUCT EGLINTON W. RNG. STR. CONTR. 2	29MAY97	07AUG98	29MAY97	07AUG98	0
EW1142	340	340	0	CONSTRUCT CUT & COVER KEELE STATION	24AUG95	02JAN97	06JAN98	10MAY99	592
EW1152	360	360	0	CONSTRUCT YORK CITY CENTER STATION	19DEC95	26MAY97	22SEP98	25FEB00	692
EW1154	370	370	0	CONS. YORK CITY CTR. C & C RNG/SPCL . STR.	15MAR96	03SEP97	08SEP98	25FEB00	622
EW1160	200	200	0	CONST. EARTH TUNNELS EGLINTON W. TO B.C.	04MAR97	17DEC97	02NOV99	17AUG00	670
EW1200	200	200	0	SUPPLY TRACKWORK MATLS. EGLINTON W. 1	23JAN96	05NOV96	21JAN97	04NOV97	250
EW1205	200	200	0	SUPPLY TRACKWORK MATLS. EGLINTON W. 2	06NOV96	22AUG97	05NOV97	21AUG98	250
EW1210	180	180	0	SUPPLY TRACKWORK MATLS. EGLINTON W. 3	25AUG97	12MAY98	24AUG98	10MAY99	250
EW1215	200	200	0	SUPPLY TRACKWORK MATLS. EGLINTON W. 4	13MAY98	26FEB99	11MAY99	25FEB00	250
EW1220	120	120	0	SUPPLY TRACKWORK MATLS. EGLINTON WEST	01MAR99	19AUG99	28FEB00	17AUG00	250
EW1230	280	280	0	SUPPLY VENTILATION EQPMT. EGLINTON WEST	10AUG98	17SEP99	10AUG98	17SEP99	0
EW1240	250	250	0	SUPPLY TRACTION POWER EQUIPMENT	20SEP99	15SEP00	20SEP99	15SEP00	0
EW1250	300	300	0	SUPPLY TRACT. POWER EQPMT. EGLINTON W.	18SEP00	27NOV01	18SEP00	27NOV01	0
EW1260	400	400	0	TRACTION POWER INSTALLATION	18AUG00	22MAR02	18AUG00	22MAR02	0
EW1290	400	400	0	TRACKWORK INSTALLATION EGLINTON W.	18AUG00	22MAR02	18AUG00	22MAR02	0
EW1310	250	250	0	SUPPLY AND INSTALL SCADA	25MAR02	21MAR03	27AUG04	25AUG05	610
EW1311	280	280	0	SUPPLY AND INSTALL ELEVATORS AND ESCAL.	25MAR02	5MAY03	15JUL04	25AUG05	580
EW1312	200	200	0	SUPPLY AND INSTALL FARE COLLECTION	25MAR02	10JAN03	09NOV04	25AUG05	660
EW1313	250	250	0	SUPPLY AND INSTALL SIGNAGE AND GRAPHICS	25MAR02	21MAR03	17JUL03	14JUL04	330
EW1370	250	250	0	SUPPLY AND INSTALL TRAIN SIGNALING	25MAR02	21MAR03	17JUL03	14JUL04	330
EW1380	250	250	0	SUPPLY AND INSTALL COMMUNICATION SYST.	25MAR02	21MAR03	25MAR02	21MAR03	0
EW1390	250	250	0	SUPPLY AND INSTALL COMM. SUBSYSTEM	17JUL03	14JUL04	17JUL03	14JUL04	0
EW1600	280	280	0	INSTALL VEHICLES	15JUL04	25AUG05	15JUL04	25AUG05	0
EW1700	200	200	0	COMMISSIONING AND STARTUP EGLINTON W.	26AUG05	12JUN06	26AUG05	12JUN06	0

FIGURE 8.39 RTEP PHASE 1 EGLINTON WEST SUBWAY LINE COMPUTER REPORT, ACTIVITY LISTING, SORTED BY AI, ES, EF. Typical CPM computer report listing all the activities contained in the network as well as their scheduling parameters based on the logic, and values calculated by computer. As the idea is to create the basis for a true schedule, there are no constraints shown. The intent is to meet the schedule objective without imposing preferences or artificial inputs. That all comes later with fine-tuning and other management decisions.

a few, is readily available. It should be up to the project manager and the project scheduler to establish the type, quality, and amount of scheduling information that the project needs or requires. The quality of the scheduling information should not be a computer systems decision. It is not something that should be imposed by the limitations of a PC project management application package, but needs to be a management decision.

Figure 8.40 is a full listing of the case exercise project critical path activities. When considering the boring information being communicated by the critical path list and the full list of activities seen in the previous figure, it cannot be stressed enough that these kinds of reports are the final result of the intensive, iterative computerized network planning exercises.

ACTIVITY ID	ORIG DUR	REM DUR	%	DESCRIPTION	EARLY START	EARLY FINISH	LATE START	LATE FINISH	TOTAL FLOAT
200	60	60	0	DEVELOPMENT, FEASIBILITY, PREPARATION	8FEB93	9MAY93	8FEB93	3MAY93	0
EW1000	480	480	0	DESIGN EGLINTON WEST STA. & RNG. STR.	31AUG93	27JUL95	31AUG93	27JUL95	0
EW1110	320	320	0	CONSTRUCT EGLINTON W. SUBWAY STA.TION	23NOV95	3MAR97	23NOV95	3MAY97	0
EW1120	320	320	0	CONSTRUCT EGLINTON W. RNG. STR. CONTR. 1	20FEB96	28MAY97	20FEB96	28MAY97	0
EW1130	300	300	0	CONSTRUCT EGLINTON W. RNG. STR. CONTR. 2	29MAY97	7AUG98	29MAY97	7AUG98	0
EW1230	280	280	0	SUPPLY VENTILATION EQUPMT. EGLINTON W.	10AUG98	17SEP99	10AUG98	17SEP99	0
EW1240	250	250	0	SUPPLY TRACTION POWER EQUIPMENT	20SEP99	15SEP00	20SEP99	15SEP00	0
EW1250	300	300	0	SUPPLY TRACTION PWR. EQPMT. EGLINTON W.	18SEP00	27NOV01	18SEP00	27NOV01	0
EW1260	400	400	0	TRACTION POWER INSTALLATION	18AUG00	22MAR02	18AUG00	22MAR02	0
EW1290	400	400	0	TRACKWORK INSTALLATION EGLINTON W.	18AUG00	22MAR02	18AUG00	22MAR02	0
EW1380	250	250	0	SUPPLY & INSTALL COMMUNICATION SYSTEM	25MAR02	21MAR03	25MAR02	21MAR03	0
EW1390	250	250	0	SUPPLY & INSTALL COMM. SUBSYSTEM	17JUL03	14JUL04	17JUL03	14JUL04	0
EW1600	280	280	0	INSTALL VEHICLES	15JUL04	25AUG05	15JUL04	25AUG05	0
EW1700	200	200	0	COMMISSIONING & STARTUP EGLINTON WEST	26AUG05	12JUN06	26AUG05	12JUN06	0

FIGURE 8.40 RTEP PHASE 1 EGLINTON WEST SUBWAY LINE COMPUTER REPORT, CRITICAL ACTIVITY LISTING, SORTED BY AI, ES, EF. Typical CPM computer report listing activities on the critical path as well as their scheduling parameters based on the logic, and values calculated by computer.

As can be seen in Fig. 8.40, there are 14 activities on the critical path, out of a total of 36 listed in Fig. 8.39. Activity 100 is deemed completed and is not listed in the critical path report.

There are no imposed dates shown—no "must start," "must finish" dates. The results are based on network logic. If the logic is changed, the critical path will be changed. The imposition of a "finish not later than" date may destroy the planning logic. Keeping these kinds of considerations in mind, hard decisions are necessary as to the kind and quality of planning that will be applied on a job.

8.9 Summary

Network planning establishes the basis for the project schedule. Project management sets the time for the project. Project time may consist of a start date and a finish date. A start date is influenced by such circumstances as the availability of capital, cash flow, an action, such as a disaster, forcing the start of a project, a market need, a market opportunity, or an event such as an election year. A completion date may be set by management, or it may result from careful planning and competitive tendering. Completion dates may be set as the result of an arbitrary decision. But all projects have completion dates, with the dates made contractually binding between the project owner and the various parties involved in the delivery of the project.

In addition to the project completion date, a project often has a number of milestone dates and event dates that may be agreed upon or imposed. A schedule based on a network of hard activities must respond to the event dates and the completion dates. The whole idea of scheduling activities is to establish a system that measures deliverables and not effort. Having set the schedule, the next steps are to monitor progress. Progress monitoring of computerized network-based activities involves measuring every value associated with the activity. This means that parameters such as activity durations, logic relationships, lag types, lag durations, and percent completions are all open to analysis not only to establish the status of the project progress, but to reestablish the schedule and to make up any slippages.

Figure 8.41 illustrates a hard copy form that facilitates progress monitoring. This can be done on screen or on line and at any time. The example form shows minimal information, but customization can convert it to specific needs. The activities selected in the example all happen to be on the critical path, that is, they have zero float.

Scheduling has come full circle. The birth of modern scheduling is said to have occurred with the invention of the Gantt chart, more often referred to as the bar chart. The bar chart fell into some disrepute with the introduction of CPM and PERT. Although both CPM and PERT are logically elegant and analytically powerful tools, they are visual disasters. As a result, no sooner had the network been invented, than the bar chart was reinstated to act as the communications medium between the network plan and the users of the network as schedule. With the proliferation of PC-based project scheduling software and the continuing difficulty with networks of activities as visual tools, project management software now generally encourages planning by bar chart, with the system having the capability to convert the Gantt charts to PERT charts, once the bars are linked.

To do the project schedule as a bar chart–driven exercise requires that the project manager believe that there is no difference in the quality of the resulting schedule. It is necessary to be convinced that the same logical conclusions are available from both methods. This is simply not the case. If bar charts are all that is necessary to plan a project, why would the planner need a PERT chart. Logical planning is only achieved with networks. Once satisfied that the logic is correct for the time being,

ACTIVITY ID	ORIG DUR	REM DUR	CAL	COMPL. %	CODE	ACTIVITY DESCRIPTION	EARLY START	EARLY FINISH	TOTAL FLOAT
EW1110	320	320	2	0	CODE 07AS	EW =02AS =C04S1 CONSTRUCT EGLINTON W. SUBWAY STATION	23NOV95	3MAR97	0
EW1120	320	320	2	0	CODE 07SU	EWAS =07AS =F04S1 CONSTRUCT EGLINTON W. RNG. STR. CONTRACT 1	20FEB96	28MAY97	0
EW1130	300	300	2	0	CODE 07SU	EWSU =07SU =F04R1 CONSTRUCT EGLINTON W. RNG. STR. CONTRACT 2	29MAY97	7AUG98	0

FIGURE 8.41 RTEP PHASE 1 EGLINTON WEST SUBWAY LINE COMPUTER REPORT, TURNAROUND FORM FOR SCHEDULE, SAMPLE ACTIVITIES. The activities are picked from a computer report of the incomplete activities as seen in Fig. 8.39. On line, at a cutoff date or at any time, each activity is subject to measurement of its remaining duration, percentage completion, actual start, or actual completion dates. The values are input, computer processed, and the results used for project management purposes.

the planner then converts the network to bar charts for communication purposes, and only for communication purposes.

Figure 8.42 is a computer-generated bar chart of a part of the case exercise network seen in a tabular report in Fig. 8.39. Most CPM software packages can produce this type of bar chart graphic on screen and as hard copy. In this figure the bars are presented as E, plotting the early starts and durations. The better the hardware/software package and the better the printer or plotter, the better the graphic depiction of the Gantt chart.

The aim of this section is to depict the planning of activities by computerized CPM networking, using computer reports and graphics in the process, and creating the project schedule as sets of calendar information and bar charts. As this is done, cost estimates are being applied to the activities. The combinations of activity cost and time lead to the creation of useful information for project management purposes. The ideal is a database of cost and time information that can be cast to suit any control need that project management may have. In this case exercise, to integrate the activities for cost and schedule, budget dollars have been applied to the activities in the planning network.

Figure 8.43 depicts a typical cost control activity report available as a standard feature in the software application package. In this graphic, to simplify the illustration, only the 12 activities ID 200 to ID EW1130 have been selected. The sorting criteria are EW for the Eglinton West subway, ES for early start, and EF for early finish.

ACTIVITY DESCRIPTION ACTIVITY ID ES	 EF	SCHEDULE LS	01 JUL 93 · 01 JAN 94 · 01 JUL 94 · 01 JAN 95 · 01 JUL 95 · 01 JAN 96 · 01 JUL 96 · 01 JAN 97
DESIGN EGLINTON W. STA.. & RNG. STR. EW1000 ES = 31AUG93	 EF = 27JUL95	EARLY LS = 31AUG93	EEEEEEEEEEEEEEEEEEEEEEE LF = 27JUL95
DESIGN DUFFERIN STATION EW1010 ES = 26OCT93	 EF = 2FEB95	EARLY LS = 24JAN95	EEEEEEEEEEEEEEEE LF = 30APR96
DESIGN CALEDONIA STATION EW1020 ES = 22DEC93	 EF 29MAY95	EARLY LS = 12SEP95	EEEEEEEEEEEEEEEEE LF = 17FEB97
DESIGN KEELE STATION EW1040 ES = 21FEB94	 EF = 28APR95	 LS = 27JUN96	EEEEEEEEEEEEEEEEE LF = 8SEP97
DESIGN YORK CITY CTR. STA. WITH RNG. EW1050 ES = 19APR94	 EF = 21SEP95	EARLY LS = 8OCT96	EEEEEEEEEEEEEEEEEEEE LF = 16MAR98

FIGURE 8.42 RTEP PHASE 1 EGLINTON WEST SUBWAY LINE COMPUTER REPORT, BAR CHART, SORTED BY AI, ES, EF, SAMPLE ACTIVITIES. These activities are selected from the full project network listed in Fig. 8.39. Shown are their early/late start and finish dates based on the network logic and the values of all the other parameters. The durations are plotted as E signifying early starts and early finishes. This kind of bar chart is useful to apply human resources and to carry out cash-flow projections.

ACTIVITY ID	RESOURCE	COST ACCOUNT	ACCOUNT CATEGORY	UNIT MEAS	BUDGET	PCT CMP	ACTUAL TO DATE	ACTUAL THIS PER	EST TO COMPL.	FORE-CAST
200	DEVELOPMENT, FEASIBILITY & PREPARATION OF RFPS									
	RD 60 ES 8FEB93 EF 3MAY93 LS 8FEB93 LF 3 MAY93 TF 0									
	BUDGET $	01EWD		BD	100000	0	0	0	100000	100000
	TOTAL				100000	0	0	0	100000	100000
EW1000	DESIGN EGLINTON WEST STATION & RUNNING STRUCTURE									
	RD 480 ES 31AUG93 EF 27JUL95 LS 31AUG93 LF 27JUL95 TF 0									
	BUDGET $	01EWD		BD	4000000	0	0	0	4000000	4000000
	TOTAL				4000000	0	0	0	4000000	4000000
EW1010	DESIGN DUFFERIN STATION									
	RD 320 ES 26OCT93 EF FEB95 LS 24JAN95 LF 30APR96 TF 312									
	BUDGET $	01EWD		BD	2000000	0	0	0	2000000	2000000
	TOTAL				2000000	0	0	0	2000000	2000000
EW1020	DESIGN CALEDONIA STATION									
	RD 360 ES 22DEC93 EF 29MAY95 LS12SEP95 LF 17FEB97 TF 432									
	BUDGET $	01EWD		BD	2000000	0	0	0	2000000	2000000
	TOTAL				2000000	0	0	0	2000000	2000000
EW1040	DESIGN KEELE STATION									
	RD 300 ES21FEB94 EF 28APR95 LS27JUN96 LF SEP97 TF 592									
	BUDGET $	01EWD		BD	2500000	0	0	0	2500000	2500000
	TOTAL				2500000	0	0	0	2500000	2500000
EW1050	DESIGN YORK CITY CENTER WITH RNG. TRACK									
	RD 360 ES 19APR94 EF 21SEP95 LS8OCT96 LF 16MAR98 TF 622									
	BUDGET $	01EWD		BD	3000000	0	0	0	3000000	3000000
	TOTAL				3000000	0	0	0	3000000	3000000

FIGURE 8.43 RTEP PHASE 1 EGLINTON WEST SUBWAY LINE COMPUTER REPORT, COST CONTROL, SAMPLE ACTIVITIES. This report depicts the intergration of the cost and schedule measures of the 12 activities selected. The activties were scheduled by computerized CPM and the costs applied as budget $. The budget $ were allocated to the activity's cost account. This standard report shows a number of columns including ACTIVITY ID, RESOURCE, in this case Budget $, COST ACCOUNT, in this case 01EWD, ACCOUNT CATEGORY (not used in this case), UNIT MEAS, in this case BD, BUDGET, the amount in Budget $, PCT CMP, percent complete, ACTUAL TO DATE, the amount of Budget $, allocated to the line item by the system, ACTUAL THIS PER (Actual this period), an amount allocated to the line item since the last period, or update, EST TO COMPL., an amount calculated as the difference between the FORECAST (Forecast final cost), and the ACTUAL TO DATE for the line item.

ACTIVITY ID	RESOURCE	COST ACCOUNT	ACCOUNT CATEGORY	UNIT MEAS	BUDGET	PCT CMP	ACTUAL TO DATE	EST TO COMPL.	FORECAST
EW1060	DESIGN TWIN TUNNELS EGLINTON WEST TO YCC								
	RD 360	ES 14JUL94	EF 18DEC95		LS 16APR97		LF 21SEP98	TF 692	
	BUDGET $	01EWD		BD	2000000	0	0	2000000	2000000
	TOTAL				2000000	0	0	2000000	2000000
EW1110	CONSTRUCT EGLINTON WEST SUBWAY STATION								
	RD 320	ES 23NOV95	EF 3MAR97		LS 23NOV95		LF 3MAR97	TF 0	
	BUDGET $	01EWD		BD	30000000	0	0	30000000	30000000
	TOTAL				30000000	0	0	30000000	30000000
EW1112	CONSTRUCT DUFFERIN STATION								
	RD 300	ES 30MAY95	EF 7AUG96		LS 26AUG96		LF4NOV97	TF 312	
	BUDGET $	01EWD		BD	32000000	0	0	32000000	32000000
	TOTAL				32000000	0	0	32000000	32000000
EW1120	CONSTRUCT EGLINTON WEST RNG. STR. CONTRACT 1								
	RD 320	ES 20FEB96	EF 28MAY97		LS 20FEB96		LF28MAY97	TF 0	
	BUDGET $	01EWD		BD	45000000	0	0	45000000	45000000
	TOTAL				45000000	0	0	45000000	45000000
EW1124	CONSTRUCT CUT & COVER CALEDONIA STATION								
	RD 280	ES 23OCT95	EF 2DEC96		LS 11JUL97		LF 21AUG98	TF 432	
	BUDGET $	01EWD		BD	30000000		0	30000000	30000000
	TOTAL				30000000		0	30000000	30000000
EW1130	CONSTRUCT EGLINTON WEST RUNNING STR. CONTRACT 2								
	RD 300	ES 29MAY97	EF 7AUG98		LS 29MAY97		LF 7AUG98	TF 0	
	BUDGET $	01EWD		BD	35000000		0	35000000	35000000
	TOTAL				35000000		0	35000000	35000000
	REPORT TOTAL				187,600,000			187,600,000	187,600,000

FIGURE 8.43 (CONTINUED).

The features to look for in Fig. 8.43 are these. The activities are created through the systems of project management and exist across all parameters, including scope, quality, scheduling, cost, and organizational packaging. The activities are costed in "project definition budget dollars," shown as BD in the report. The cost account 01EWD is derived from the PDS and is meant to represent the basis for the project definition code. This is a level 3 code. Level 1 is the RTEP phase 1, code 01; level 2 is the Eglinton West subway, code EW, and D is intended to identify the definition budget.

Each activity would also be costed into its phases (WBS) code and into the organizational (OBS) code. These additional cost control reports are not shown. Another control measure available in this series of reports is based on the assignment of resources to the activities such as designers, builders, trade contractors, and equipment.

The columns in this standard report also provide for account category, unit of measure "unit meas," percent complete "pct cmp," and the self-explanatory actual to date, actual this period, estimate to complete, and forecast. As no two project management companies work in the same way, the column headings shown may not be suitable for all applications. It is usually necessary to customize the cost report for specific applications.

As this particular software system is schedule driven, the cost control report includes range-of-time information for each activity, including remaining duration RD, early start ES, early finish EF, late start LS, late finish LF, and total float TF.

To demonstrate other features of this project management software using the same 12 activities ID 200 to ID EW1130, Fig. 8.44 represents a tabular cost control report, detailed by resource. The resource in this case is budget dollars, and the unit of measure is BD. The fields and columns are as before, except that the activity descriptions are not provided. Also worthy of note is that this report (Fig. 8.44) as well as the previous report (Fig. 8.43) provides a Totals line of the activities selected. Figure 8.45 is a stylized cost curve illustration of the activities selected for this demonstration, based on early start dates and the tabular information in Fig. 8.44.

One of the most popular features of PC-based project management software is its capability to deliver graphic information. Depending on the quality, cost, and sophistication of the software and hardware, the packages produce networks, bar charts, histograms, S curves, "banana" curves, and pie charts of all sorts and in all colors. These visual products are excellent communication tools. To make them true management tools, the graphics need hard information backing them. The only way to develop hard information is by taking the difficult and bumpy road via the project management systems techniques to establish project quality, identify the tasks and packages, and assign the work to the project functional organization that is to deliver the project.

There is difficulty and hard work in relating individual projects and ad hoc organizations to modern software products. It is not necessarily easy to adapt new software tools to old project problems. Depending on project complexity, organizational difficulty, and budget considerations, the application of project management software may require a longer learning curve than may be considered reasonable.

ACTIVITY ID	RES-SOURCE	COST ACCOUNT	UNIT MEAS	BUDGET	PCT CMP	ACTUAL TO DATE	ACTUAL THIS PERIOD	ESTIMATE TO COMPL.	FORECAST FINAL COST	VARI-ANCE
200	BUDGET $	01EWD	BD	100000	0	0	0	100000	100000	0
EW1000	BUDGET $	01EWD	BD	4000000	0	0	0	4000000	4000000	0
EW1010	BUDGET $	01EWD	BD	2000000	0	0	0	2000000	2000000	0
EW1020	BUDGET $	01EWD	BD	2000000	0	0	0	2000000	2000000	0
EW1040	BUDGET $	01EWD	BD	2500000	0	0	0	2500000	2500000	0
EW1050	BUDGET $	01EWD	BD	3000000	0	0	0	3000000	3000000	0
EW1060	BUDGET $	01EWD	BD	2000000	0	0	0	2000000	2000000	0
EW1110	BUDGET $	01EWD	BD	30000000	0	0	0	30000000	30000000	0
EW1112	BUDGET $	01EWD	BD	32000000	0	0	0	32000000	32000000	0
EW1120	BUDGET $	01EWD	BD	45000000	0	0	0	45000000	45000000	0
EW1124	BUDGET $	01EWD	BD	30000000	0	0	0	30000000	30000000	0
EW1130	BUDGET $	01EWD	BD	35000000	0	0	0	35000000	35000000	0
TOTAL	BUDGET $			187600000				187600000	187600000	0

FIGURE 8.44 RTEP PHASE 1 EGLINTON WEST SUBWAY LINE COMPUTER REPORT, COST CONTROL, BUDGET $ COST CURVE. This figure depicts the selection and processing of cost-loaded, scheduled activities to produce S curves or other graphical depictions of project cost and schedule status, cash-flow information, resource usage, and similar project progress information. The column headings are explained in Fig. 8.43.

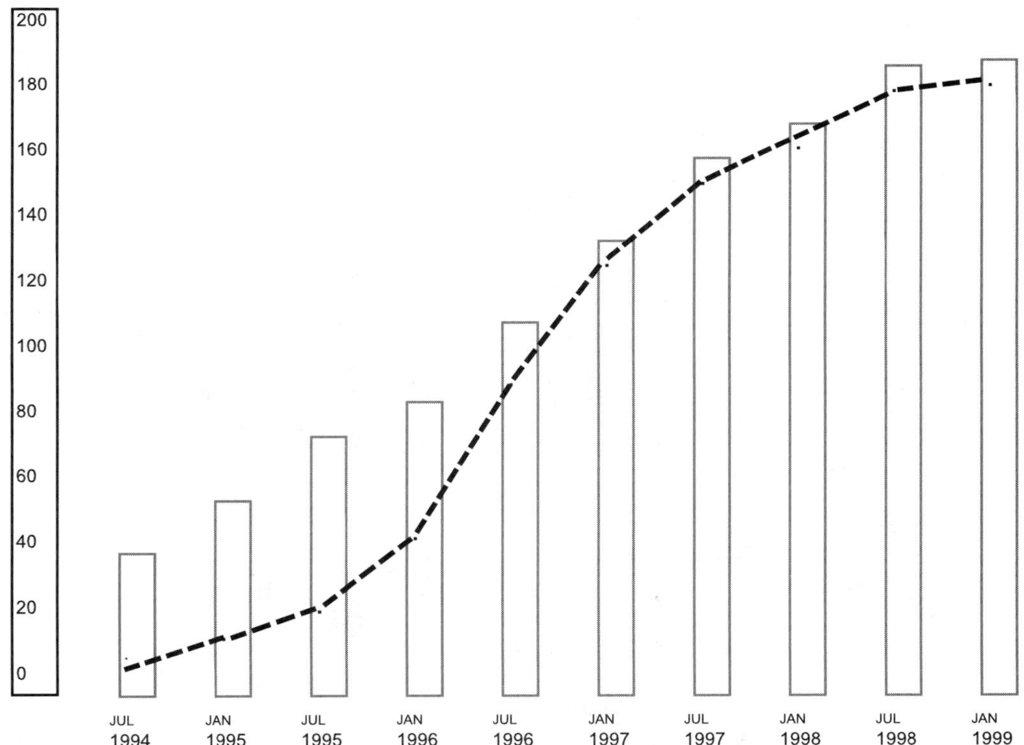

FIGURE 8.45 RTEP PHASE 1 EGLINTON WEST SUBWAY LINE COMPUTER REPORT, COST CONTROL, STYLIZED COST CURVE BASED ON ES. This is a computer-generated cumulative S curve based on the cost data presented in Fig. 8.44. The time profile is presented in Fig 8.43 and the preceding CPM reports.

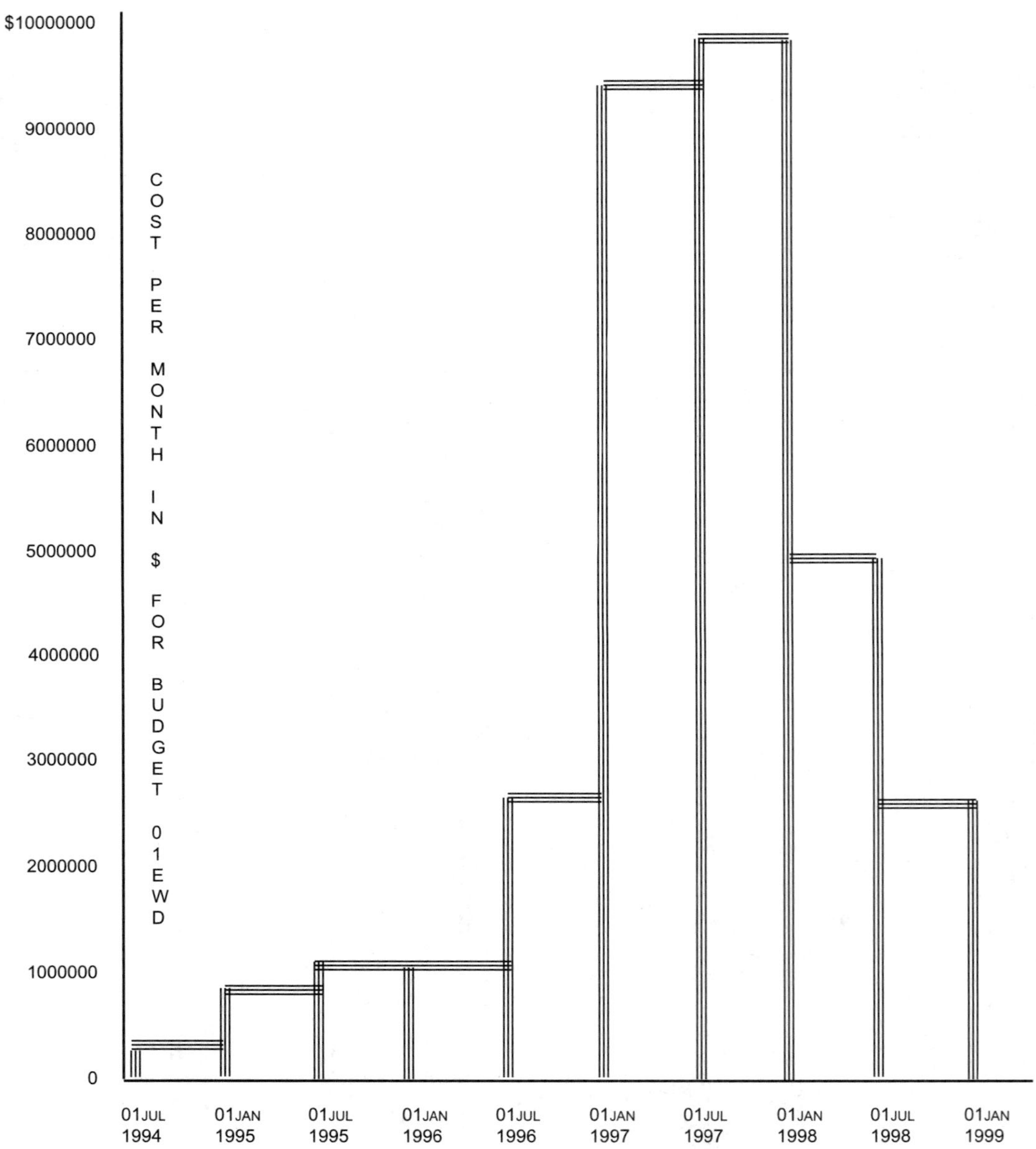

FIGURE 8.46 RTEP PHASE 1 EGLINTON WEST SUBWAY LINE COMPUTER REPORT, STYLIZED COST PROFILE, CASH FLOW. This is a computer-generated histogram depicting monthly cash flow, plotted at six-month intervals from about July 1994 through December 1998.

PERIOD BEGINNING	— EARLY SCHEDULE — USAGE	CUMULATIVE	— LATE SCHEDULE — USAGE	CUMULATIVE
RESOURCE/COST ACCOUNT = EQA BUDGET $01EWD				
1MAR97	3046875	146974999	5636875	96058335
1APR97	2953125	149928124	5604236	101662571
1MAY97	2905208	152833332	5611875	107274446
1JUN97	2450000	155283332	5156667	112431112
1JUL97	2566667	157849999	7009365	119440477
1AUG97	2333332	160183332	7053969	126494446
1SEP97	2450000	162633334	7273334	133767779
1OCT97	2566667	165199999	7576032	141343811
1NOV97	2216667	167416666	4729603	146073414
1DEC97	2450000	169866666	4991667	151065080
1JAN98	2450000	172316666	4991667	156056747

FIGURE 8.47 RTEP PHASE 1 EGLINTON WEST SUBWAY LINE COMPUTER REPORT, MONTHLY AND CUMULATIVE CASH USAGE, BASED ON ES AND LS. This is a computer-generated tabular report depicting monthly and cumulative cash flow based on the activities scheduled to occur over the period March through December 1997. The numbers, being computer-generated, are not rounded.

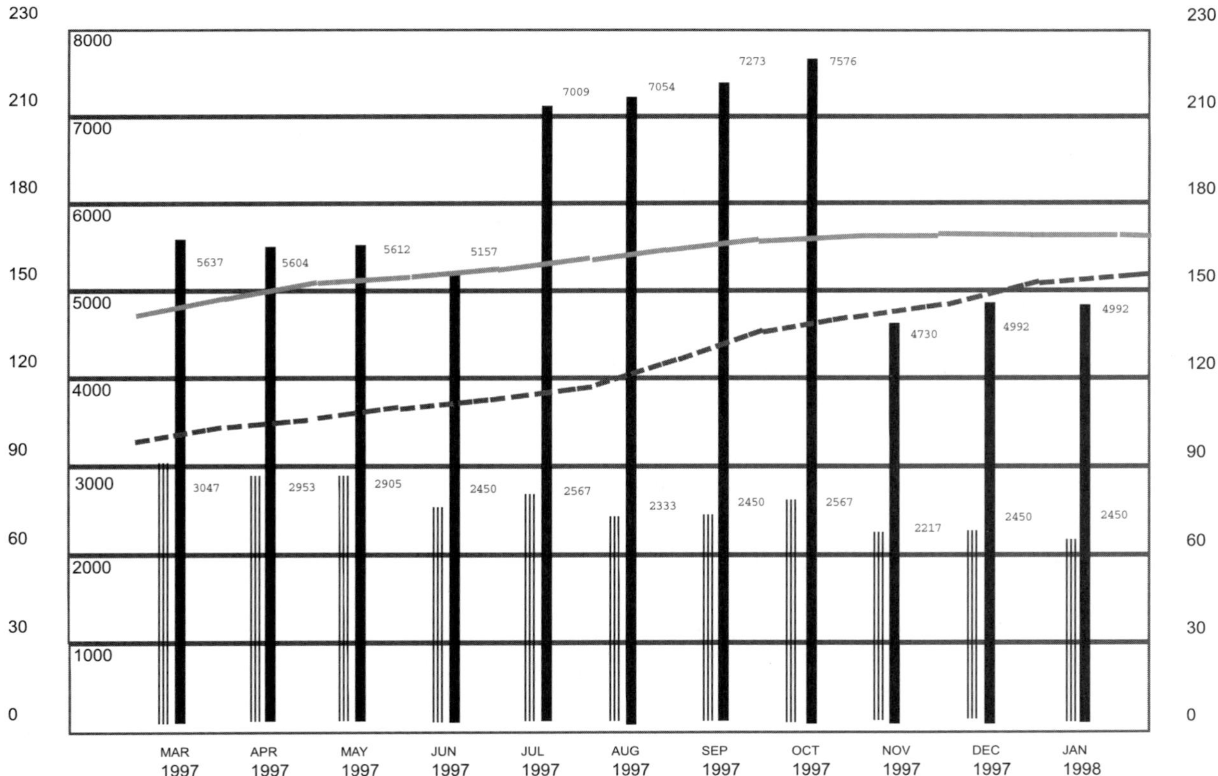

FIGURE 8.48 RTEP PHASE 1 EGLINTON WEST SUBWAY LINE COMPUTER REPORT, COST CONTROL, CURVES AND HISTOGRAMS. This figure is based on the data in Fig. 8.47. The light solid line shows cumulative cash folow based on the earyl schedule. The open vertical bar is monthly usage based on the early schedule. The dark broken line shows cumulative cash flow based on the late schedule. The solid vertical bar represents monthly usage based on the late schedule. The scale for the histograms is $n \times 1000$. The scale for the cumulative curves is $n \times 1000000$.

To illustrate the foregoing discussion, the graphics that follow are depictions of typical time-related cost control information produced by the software application selected for the current case exercise.

Figure 8.46 is a cost profile of the 12 selected activities. Depicted is monthly cash usage plotted in 6-month intervals for budget 01EWD, based on early starts from July 1, 1994 to January 1, 1999. Figure 8.47 is a tabular cost report showing monthly usage and cumulative cash flow, based on early/late starts for the period March 1997 through January 1998. Figure 8.48 is a graphic illustration of the data in Fig. 8.47. This kind of information may be seen in many different ways, including colored depictions on screen, filled histograms, and so on, over different time scales, and in all kinds of selections, sorts, and filters.

Computer-generated graphs, curves, bars, pie charts, especially on screen and in color, are visually pleasing and provide snap shots of the status of the project. The most difficult aspect of project work is its planning and costing. The depictions so far have been aimed to show the setups, that is, the targets. Once project work is under way, monitoring and measuring of cost and schedule is necessary to establish the status and initiate corrective measures as necessary. Measurements consist of percentage completions, actuals this period, actuals to date, estimates to complete, forecast final costs, variances on a line-by-line basis, and project bottom line. As these measurements are established, they are in turn plotted against their targets to illustrate visually the status of the subject item.

REFERENCES

Prestige PC Software, Release 4.1 (Artemis Management Systems, Boulder, CO, 1991).

Priimavera Project Planner (P3) Software, Version 5.0 (Primavera Systems, Bala Cynwyd, PA, 1991).

Rapid Transit Expansion Program Preliminary Consulting and Construction Information Package, Toronto Transit Commission, 1900 Yonge Street, Toronto, Ontario M4S 1Z2 (1993).

Rapid Transit Expansion Program, Consulting and Construction Information Package, Toronto Transit Commission, 1900 Yonge Street, Toronto, Ontario M4S 1Z2 (1995).

QUESTIONS AND EXERCISES

8.1. Refer to the discussion leading to the development of Fig. 8.12 and expand Fig. 8.12 on the basis of further discussions as concluded by the information in Fig. 8.25.

8.2. Refer to Fig. 8.35.

a. What is the source of the PDS code? Name the tables, figures, and page numbers, starting with the earliest numbers, in this book and discuss.

b. What is the source of the WBS code? Name the tables, figures, and page nnumbers, starting with the earliest numbers, in this book and discuss.

c. What is the source of the OBS code? Name the tables, figures, and page numbers, starting with the earliest numbers, in this book and discuss.

8.3. Prepare a one-page development of each of the following systems of project management:

Project definition structure

Work breakdown structure

Organizational breakdown structure

Cost estimate based on the PDS code

Pert network or Gantt chart based on the WBS

The results are to be based on the methods and theories presented in this textbook.

8.4. Based on a work environment selected by your instructor, write a short paper, with simple graphics and charts, to show how you would apply the systems of project management as presented in this textbook to manage the scope, quality, organization, and cost and schedule performance of project work in the workplace selected. How would computers be utilized?

9 RESEARCH CENTER CASE HISTORY

9.1 Introduction

The chapters in Part 2 of this textbook used among other projects an industrial research center to model and develop the concepts of scope definition, work breakdown, and organizational structure and their respective codes; to cost estimate and budget the project, and to schedule it.

The research center deliverables were seen to be functionally coded conceptual sketches (e.g., Fig. 2.15 and its associated discussions), a definitive budget (e.g., Fig. 5.3), and a range of cost control and expenditure control reports (e.g., Fig. 5.6). These references are specific to the research center project. Those chapters aimed to show the progression of a project from a functional or user engineering and architectural design concept through to corporate approval and presentation for financing.

This chapter will highlight the process of converting the project from an architectural and engineering look to the corporate view needed to navigate and communicate the project through the departmental, divisional, and corporate hierarchy to the office of the chief executive officer for financial approval. It will be seen how project management data are converted to the corporate financial information necessary for corporate approval.

The discussion revolves around the use of a key corporate document called the capital/lease appropriation request (C/LAR). Corporate enterprise systems, which is what the C/LAR document represents in this case, are invariably in place when new projects are considered. Project management needs are not necessarily the same as corporate management information. But corporate information needs and project needs cannot be mutually exclusive. That is why bridges must be built between enterprise systems and project management systems. The bridge building starts with a picture of the project, as seen in Fig. 9.1. Shown are stage numbers, stage names and bullets highlighting the stage deliverables.

The nine stages in Fig. 9.1 are based on the classic project management principle presented in this book for the creation and management of activities. The successful completion of these activities results in the delivery and operation of the defined project.

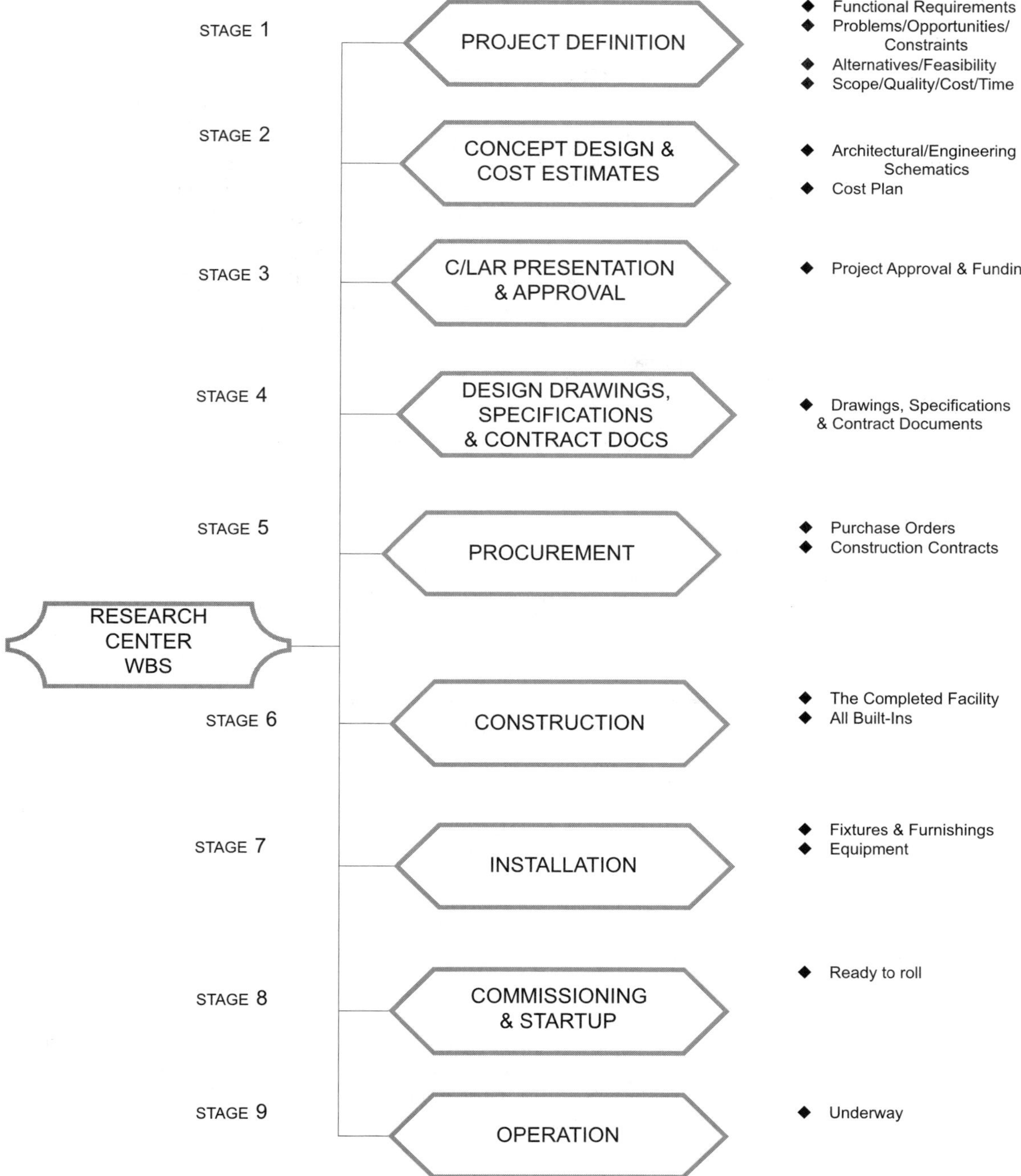

FIGURE 9.1 RESEARCH CENTER, THE 9 STAGES OF THE PROJECT LIFE CYCLE. This figure shows that the project has nine lives. If any one life is more important then the others, it is stage 1, Project Definition. That is when the project scope, quality, and function are set as they will be delivered to the users of the completed project. This is not necessarily the way corporate controllers want to see the project, but it is the way project managers deliver it. The discussion will build a bridge between the corporate information needs and the project delivery process. The intent is a seamless process, satisfying everyone.

9.2 Stage 1, Project Definition

All project stages are important. If any one is more important than the others, it is stage 1, Project Definition. That is where project quality, scope, and function are set as they will be delivered to the users of the completed project. The research center stage 1 was used to discuss fundamentals of project definition in Chapter 2, Section 2.6. That discussion explains the process of developing the research facility the way the researchers want it. At the same time it sets up the project codes and establishes criteria for project control purposes. It may be said that the project definition process needs to be very well communicated and agreed between those who will use the facility and the professional project managers.

9.3 Stage 2, Concept Design and Cost Estimates

The development of the research center concepts and design criteria is discussed in Sections 2.6.1, 2.6.2, and 2.6.3. Although Fig. 9.1 illustrates nine distinct project stages, the delivery process often merges parts of stages, as presented in the referenced sections. The discussion of stage 1 leads to the development of design concepts as stage 2, which flow out as concept drawings and cost estimates.

The cost estimating and budgeting of the research center are used to model the fundamentals of cost control in Sections 5.4.1, 5.4.2, and 5.5.

Corporate management is only marginally involved in defining, conceptualizing, and estimating the project in the work of the stages discussed. But their requirements for corporate coding must be met, and the project management code structures set up to accommodate those requirements, as will be seen in C/LAR, the subject of the stage 3 discussion.

9.4 Stage 3, Capital/Lease Appropriation Request (C/LAR) Presentation and Approval

Stage 3 required the formal compilation of the coded scope and cost information for senior corporate management to appropriate funds to deliver the project. A list of project tasks and the deliverables associated with this stage may be seen in Chapter 3, Table 3.8, which presents phase 3/stage 3 classic tasks.

The preparation of a C/LAR document is expensive, complex, and comprehensive. There must be a real need for the project for it to reach the stage where it is being presented formally for approval, as in this case. Obviously the project is being driven by the people who need it or want it. But in the final reckoning every corporate project has to be accepted and approved by people who have other corporate roles in the organization than those who want it, such as the chief executive officer, the board of directors, marketing, manufacturing, research and development, finance, and others.

To get their approval requires at the very least that the proposal be feasible, technically sound, and ultimately based on strict corporate financial presentation standards.

The contents of the subject C/LAR presentation document are included in the following listing. Although the entire contents of the C/LAR document are presented here, only highly summarized financial data aimed at corporate management are illustrated further in the figures that follow.

I. Executive Summary
   1. Background
   2. Proposal
   3. Project Cost Summary
   4. R & D Tax Incentives
   5. Risks
   6. Recommendation

II. C/LAR Forms
   1. Capital/Lease Appropriation Request (see Fig. 9.2)
   2. Financial Data Summary Form (see Fig. 9.3)
   3. Construction and Financial Schedule (see Figs. 9.4 and 9.5)

III. Description
   1. Facility Statement of Requirements
      a) Organization
      b) Mission
      c) Facilities
      d) Occupancy Dates
      e) Assumptions
      f) Functional Concept
      g) Special Requirements
   2. Major Components of the Investment
      a) Introduction
      b) Site
      c) Building
      d) Equipment
      e) Fixtures and Furnishings
      f) Landscaping
   3. Construction Schedule
   4. Key Plans
   5. Project Program
      a) Summary
      b) Personnel and Space Requirements

CAPITAL/LEASE APPROPRIATION REQUEST	C/LAR ITEM 2.1

OPERATING GROUP	PROJECT NO.	PROJECT TITLE	ORIGINATING MANAGER
RESEARCH UNIT		**RESEARCH CENTER**	

	CAPITAL ($ X 1,000)			EXPENSE ($ X 1,000)		
	BUDGETED	NOT BUDGETED	TOTAL	ASSOCIATED EXPENSES	LEASE PER YEAR	LEASE TOTAL
PRIOR APPROVALS	-	-	-	-	-	-
THIS REQUEST	16,471	-	16,471	323	NA	NA
FUTURE REQUESTS	-	-	-	-	-	-
TOTAL PROJECT	16,471	-	16,471	323	NA	NA

	CASH FLOW THIS REQUEST ($ X 1,000)					
	YEAR 1	YEAR 2	YEAR 3	YEAR 4	YEAR 5	TOTAL
CAPITAL	-	1,535	9,186	5,750	-	16,471
EXPENSE	-	-	-	-	-	323

RESEARCH UNIT
CONCURRENCE OR APPROVAL **NAME** **SIGNATURE**

Facilities Manager __________
Administration Manager __________
Controller __________
Vice President, Director Research Unit __________

CORPORATE RESEARCH GROUP
CONCURRENCE OR APPROVAL **NAME** **SIGNATURE**

Controller Research Group __________
Vice President Corporate Research __________

CORPORATE
CONCURRENCE OR APPROVAL **NAME** **SIGNATURE**

Corporate, Vice President Finance __________
Corporate Executive Vice President Finance __________
Corporate President & COO __________
Corporate Chairman & CEO __________

COMMENTS/QUALIFICATIONS

FIGURE 9.2 RESEARCH CENTER, C/LAR. This document shows the transition of a project from concepts and budget estimates prepared by the project manager, the users, and consultants into the highest summary level financial document for corporate approval of funding.

FINANCIAL DATA SUMMARY FORM	**C/LAR ITEM 2.2**

PROJECT TITLE	PROJECT NO.:
RESEARCH CENTER	DATE:

CAPITAL ITEMS — **$ AUTHORIZED**

ITEM NO.	DESCRIPTION	BUDGET TO DATE	TO DATE	THIS REQUEST	ANTICIPATED FUTURE	TOTAL ITEM
10	DESIGN	-	-	1,812,000	-	1,812,000
20	LAND	-	-	-	-	-
30	CONSTRUCTION	-	-	10,924,000	-	10,924,000
40	BID CONTINGENCY	-	-	604,000	-	604,000
50	CONSTRUCTION CONTINGENCY	-	-	846,000	-	846,000
60	EQUIPMENT	-	-	1,083,000	-	1,083,000
70	OCCUPANCY CONTINGENCY	-	-	546,000	-	546,000
80	LANDSCAPING	-	-	115,000	-	115,000
90	FIXTURES & FURNISHINGS	-	-	541,000	-	541,000
	TOTAL CAPITAL			16,471,000	-	16,471,000

LEASE AND ASSOCIATED EXPENSES — **($ X 1,000)**

Budget Center Acct. Nos	Description		Expenses Prior Year	Current Year Budget	Current Year Expenses	Future Annualized Expenses	Expense Over Lease Period
	Lease Expense		(not applica-ble)			(not applicable)	
	Associated One-Time Expense						
	F & F (Items < $300.)	223,000					
	Moving	100,000					
	TOTAL	323,000					

OPERATING EXPENSES (ANNUAL) — **($ X 1,000)**

		Year 1	Year 2	Year 3	Year 4	Year 5
-	UTILITIES	40	175	192	212	223
-	JANITORIAL	20	87	96	106	117
-	TELEPHONES	29	125	138	152	167
-	PROPERTY & BUSINESS TAXES	26	112	124	135	151
-	MAINTENANCE	33	138	303	332	364
-	INSURANCE	5	23	25	28	30
-	SECURITY	15	63	70	77	84
-	CONSTRUCTION & ALTERATIONS	4	17	38	42	46
-	CHEMICAL RECYCLING	13	58	3	70	77
	GROUNDSKEEPING	3	14	30	34	37
	TOTAL	188	812	1,019	1,188	1,296

FIGURE 9.3 RESEARCH CENTER, FINANCIAL DATA SUMMARY. The C/LAR documentation includes financial data which are summarized in this form. The features to look for include items 10 through 90, which first appeared as project definition codes in Sections 5.4.1, 5.4.2, and 5.6, the discussion of the budgeting and cost control process based on the research center project.

CONSTRUCTION AND FINANCIAL SCHEDULE **C/LAR ITEM 2.3**

PROJECT TITLE
RESEARCH CENTER

PROJECT NO.: ____________

DATE: ____________

PROPOSED DESIGN, CONSTRUCTION, COMMITMENT, AND CASH PAYMENT SCHEDULES HAVE BEEN ESTABLISHED FOR THIS PROJECT AS SHOWN BELOW. DOLLAR AMOUNTS ARE SHOWN AS THOUSANDS.

YEAR 1

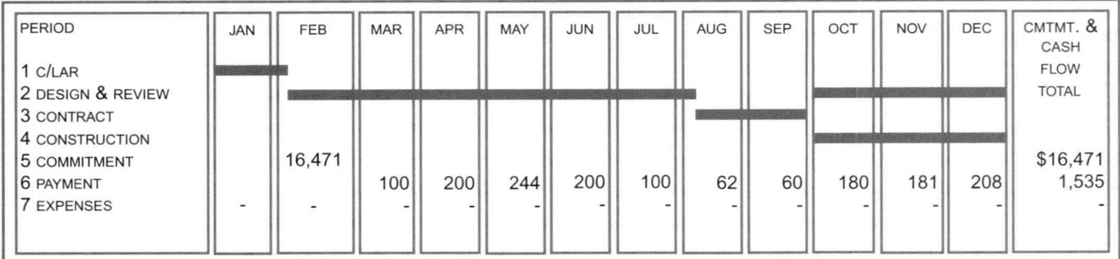

PERIOD	JAN	FEB	MAR	APR	MAY	JUN	JUL	AUG	SEP	OCT	NOV	DEC	CMTMT. & CASH FLOW TOTAL
1 C/LAR													
2 DESIGN & REVIEW													
3 CONTRACT													
4 CONSTRUCTION													
5 COMMITMENT		16,471											$16,471
6 PAYMENT			100	200	244	200	100	62	60	180	181	208	1,535
7 EXPENSES	-	-	-	-	-	-	-	-	-	-	-	-	-

YEAR 2

PERIOD	JAN	FEB	MAR	APR	MAY	JUN	JUL	AUG	SEP	OCT	NOV	DEC	CMTMT. & CASH FLOW TOTAL
1 C/LAR													
2 DESIGN & REVIEW													
3 CONTRACT													
4 CONSTRUCTION													
5 COMMITMENT													-
6 PAYMENT	430	596	520	520	492	838	876	1,126	1,185	909	849	845	9,186
7 EXPENSES	-	-	-	-	-	-	-	-	-	-	-	-	-

YEAR 3

PERIOD	JAN	FEB	MAR	APR	MAY	JUN	JUL	AUG	SEP	OCT	NOV	DEC	CMTMT. & CASH FLOW TOTAL
1 C/LAR													
2 DESIGN & REVIEW													
3 CONTRACT													
4 CONSTRUCTION													
5 COMMITMENT													-
6 PAYMENT	905	978	758	865	457	365	312	373	368	169	200	-	9,186
7 EXPENSES	-	-	-	-	-	-	-	-	75	100	65	83	323

PROGRAM TOTALS
COMMITMENTS
$16,471

PAYMENTS
$16,471

EXPENSES
$323

FIGURE 9.4 RESEARCH CENTER, CONSTRUCTION AND FINANCIAL SCHEDULE. Although there is difficulty and frustration in making project schedules, when it comes to presenting the schedule and cash flow to top corporate management, the look has to be simplicity itself, much as depicted by the above form. It is noted how the C/LAR leads to design and review, commitments, and payments. The cash-flow numbers are calculated in Fig. 9.5.

RESEARCH CENTER				CASH FLOW EXERCISE

CODE ITEM NO.	DESCRIPTION	$ (1,000)	CURVE TYPE	SCHEDULE
10	DESIGN	1,812	S3	START: 3/1 YEAR 1 FINISH:9/30 YEAR 3
30	CONSTRUCTION	10,924	S2	START: 10/1 YEAR 1 FINISH: 9/30 YEAR 3
40 50 70	)) CONTINGENCIES)	1,996	S2	START: 10/1 YEAR 1 FINISH: 9/30 YEAR 3
60	EQUIPMENT	1,083	S1	START: 6/1 YEAR 2 FINISH: 11/30 YEAR 3
80	LANDSCAPING	115	S10	START: 8/1 YEAR 3 FINISH 11/30 YEAR 3
90	FIXTURES & FURNISHINGS	541	S4	START: 2/1 YEAR 3 FINISH 11/30 YEAR 3

"S" CURVE VALUES

"S" CURVE NAME	% TIME VS. RATE (R) AND CUMULATIVE VALUE (C)										
		10	20	30	40	50	60	70	80	90	100
S1 5% S-SHAPED DISTRIBUTION	R	5	5	10	10	20	20	10	10	5	5
	C	5	10	20	30	50	70	80	90	95	100
S2 3% S-SHAPED DISTRIBUTION	R	3	7	10	13	17	17	13	10	7	3
	C	3	10	20	33	50	67	80	90	97	100
S3 FRONT LOADED DISTRIBUTION	R	30	20	10	10	5	5	5	5	5	5
	C	30	50	60	70	75	80	85	90	95	100
S4 BACK LOADED DISTRIBUTION	R	5	5	5	5	5	5	10	10	20	30
	C	5	10	15	20	25	30	40	50	70	100
S10 LINEAR DISTRIBUTION	R	10	10	10	10	10	10	10	10	10	10
	C	10	20	30	40	50	60	70	80	95	100

FIGURE 9.5 RESEARCH CENTER, CASH-FLOW CALCULATION. As cash flow is invariably of great interest to project bankers and funders, and as it is always necessary in the project approval process, the process that created the cash-flow projections for this case is illustrated here. These cash-flow calculations are applied to time frame in Fig. 9.4.

IV. Justification

1. Quantitative Analysis
2. Qualitative Analysis
3. Energy Conservation
4. Present Space/Future Requirement
5. Space Assumptions
6. Government Incentives for R & D

V. Financial
  1. Total Amount of Capital
  2. Total One-Time Associated Expenses
  3. Estimated Annual Operating Expenses
  4. Included Contingencies
  5. Inflation Assumptions
  6. Lease versus Buy Option
  7. R & D Tax Incentives
  8. Cash Flow

VI. Alternatives
  1. Do Nothing
  2. Renovate and Expand Existing Facility
  3. Other Leased Facilities

VII. Risks
  1. Consequences of Nonapproval
  2. Impact of Delay
  3. Risks in Basic Program Justification

VIII. Bibliography

IX. Appendices
  1. Sale/Leaseback Proposal
  2. Facility Project
    a) Project Description
    b) Color Photographs
    c) Schematic Drawings
      A Architectural
      M Mechanical
      E Electrical
    d) Outline Specifications
      A Architectural
      M Mechanical
      E Electrical
  3. Facility Project Cost Estimate
    a) C/LAR Cost Breakdown
    b) Building Cost Breakdown
  4. Facility Project Construction Schedule
  5. Long-Range Site Plan
  6. Facility Project Program

Each chapter of the C/LAR approval document listed here is the result of the project management and planning activities defined and illustrated in this book. Obviously every project would address its own mission thrust and specifics. To detail further the research center project specifics as outlined by this content list would not necessarily contribute to the readers' grasp of project management methodology, except to remind them of the many skills that projects need.

However, as every project requires funding and approval by top management before it can go further, the intention here is to illustrate the bridge between a specific project and a corporate financial approval process using the C/LAR financial documentation referenced in item II, which may be seen in Figs. 9.2 through 9.5.

9.5 Stage 4, Design, Drawings, Specifications, and Contract Documents

This stage does not occur unless and until the C/LAR is approved and the project money is in the treasury. The present project was approved and proceeded into the stage 4 activities and beyond. The method selected to deliver this construction project is best described as "construction management of phased packages," listed in Chapter 4 as the third of the 16 ways to deliver a project. It is illustrated in Fig. 4.6 in Section 4.3.3.

This method requires that the drawings, specifications, and contract documents be prepared to suit this way of delivering a project. Specifically the design and drawings were aimed to satisfy the following bid packages:

Bid package 1: Site and structure
Bid package 2: Mechanical
Bid package 3: Electrical
Bid package 4: General contract

The drawings and specifications varied for each package to reflect the scope of work of the specific package, but each package had to have a fairly comprehensive range of project drawings to ensure that errors and omissions did not occur through oversight. Thus the drawings and specifications included the following design, drawings, specifications, and contract documents:

Site
Architectural
Structural
Mechanical
Electrical
General conditions

In this case, bid package 1 (site and structure) was scoped to include also construction management of all construction activities to be carried out by the future packages.

In the process of developing the construction sequence in this case, control of schedule and cost was always in the forefront. This means that construction market conditions were being monitored, delivery time frames of major equipment and building systems were ascertained, and risks associated with preordering were assessed. As a result bid packages other than those named before were considered for preordering, including:

Exterior cladding

Refrigeration equipment

Air handling

Variable-volume control systems

Electric power package

Sprinklers

Building automation system

To preclude possible construction delays and cost escalation, a number of these packages, including exterior cladding and the refrigeration equipment, were preordered and eventually made part of the general contract package.

9.6 Stage 5, Procurement

In most cases, following project approval and the availability of funds, it is full speed ahead. As the design, drawings, and construction package requirements are set in the stage 3 approval process, procurement, tendering, and awards proceed automatically, as in this case.

As this project was delivered using construction management, there was programmed overlapping of design, bidding, and construction. Because the schedule was set, and as construction management allowed it to happen, project elements such as the exterior cladding and refrigeration compressors, which were seen as long-delivery items, were ordered in advance to be assigned to designated trade contractors for coordination and installation as part of their planned scope of work. Thus procurement in this type of project delivery environment is generally positive in that decisions are made to save time and therefore cost.

Procurement is positive in another way in that as small instead of very large packages are being procured, there is more room to maneuver if bids are high on individual packages or suspect in some other respect.

9.7 Stage 6, Construction

For an appreciation of the place of the construction stage in the overall project life cycle refer to the stylized project CPM diagram in Fig. 9.6. Although the construc-

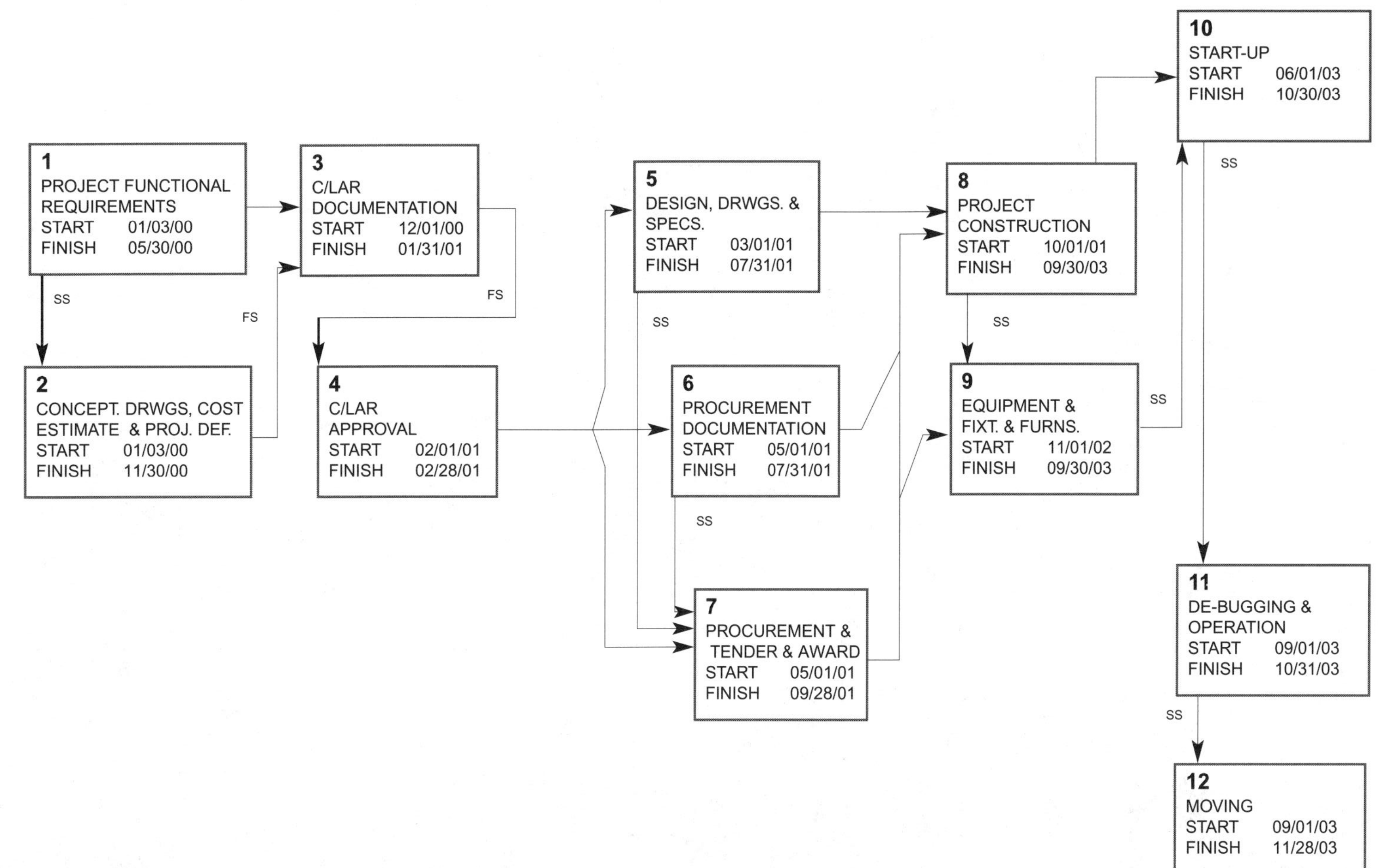

FIGURE 9.6 RESEARCH CENTER, PROJECT CPM. This is a stylized CPM summary network of the project. Only key events such as start and finish are shown. The dates have been cast into the future and the durations would be estimates of the time that would be needed to carry out the various stages. To reflect the process of CPM networking more accurately, a number of finish to start and start to start relationships are indicated.

tion stage accounts for up to 66% of the cost of the complete project and about 75% of project time, it can be troublefree if the previous stages are well founded in functional definition, breakdown into packages, cost estimating and control, and assignment to organizations, as was the situation in this case.

A successful construction project is one where the many diverse trade contractors pull together, start as needed, and finish as required by the schedule and in the process deliver high-quality work.

Given that the project front-end parameters in stages 1 through 5 are met, what is the essence of a well-scheduled construction stage? A well-scheduled job is one where the activities on the scheduling network are organized so that float value increments are very small between the activities on the zero-float critical path and other activities. In this case the maximum float was 57 days on a construction schedule that was 15 months long. Another important consideration is the size of the incremental float value increases. To illustrate:

- The critical path had 0 days of float.
- The next paths each had 7, 10, 12, 20, 22, 27, 30, 37, 40, 42, 52, 55, and 57 days of float.

These kinds of relative values denote a tightly scheduled job. Figure 9.7 illustrates activities from the actual research center CPM planning network. The activities are directly relatable to the construction project elements reported for the research center project in Fig. 5.8, Section 5.6.

As a general rule, an element code item or a project number item listed as a cost code is not necessarily schedulable as a stand-alone activity. What this means is that the element numbers may have to be broken down into schedule activities. Examples of elements broken down into activities are seen in Fig. 9.7.

Figure 5.8 shows a summary project element, 30GA, Interior Finishes. The details of the summary element 30GA may be seen in Figs. 5.15 and 5.16, Section 5.7. Fully coded, the element Interior Finishes comprises the following:

30GA00000	Interior Finishes
30GA09300	Mosaic and Quarry Tile
30GA09650	Resilient Flooring
30GA09680	Carpet and Broadloom
30GA09890	Painting
30GA10270	Computer Access Floor

These code numbers were not utilized in the construction scheduling exercise. As an aside, the five-digit numeric part of these codes is based on the construction industry numbering system, Masterformat.

For construction scheduling by CPM and computer processing these elements became the following schedule activities, as shown in Fig. 9.7:

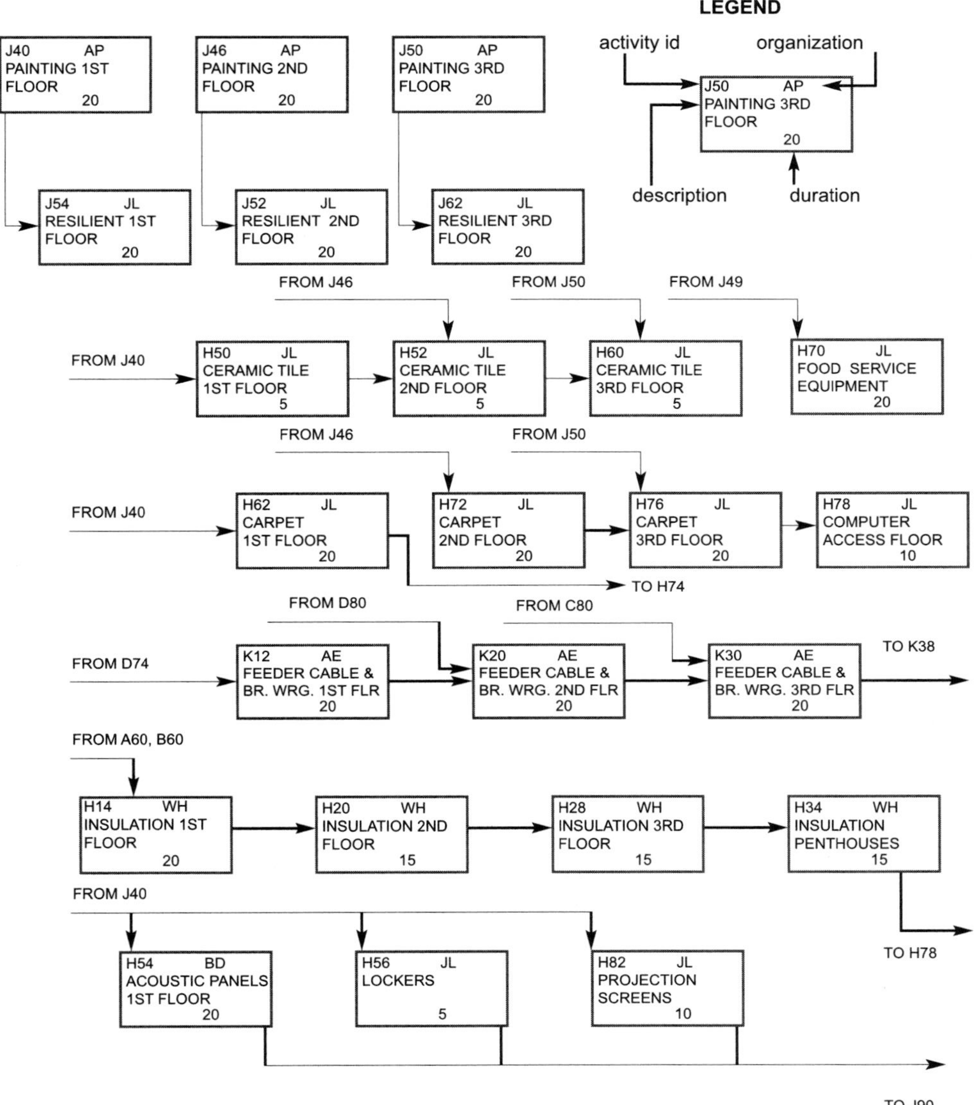

FIGURE 9.7 RESEARCH CENTER, DETAIL CPM ACTIVITIES. These are example activities from the CPM construction network. The features to note are that the activities are based on project elements that exist for project cost control. In other words, they are hard activities. Only some logic connections are shown as an indication that the network is logic driven. The activity IDs are based on a map-finding grid (alpha across, numeric down). Computer processing of logical networks leads to tight schedules.

J40, J46, J50	Painting
J54, J52, J62	Resilient Floor
H50, H52, H60	Ceramic Tile
H62, H72, H76	Carpet and Broadloom
H78	Computer Access Floor

Also shown in Fig. 9.7 are other examples of detail schedule activities broken down from project elements:

30JA00000	Electrical	Activities K12, K20, K30
30HA00000	Fittings and Equipment	Activities H56, H82
30AC00000	Thermal/Moisture Protection	Activities H14, H20, H28, H34

As a matter of interest, the activities J40, H50, and so on, are based on locating activities on a drawing sheet with the alphabetic characters across and the numerical characters down.

9.8 Stage 7, Installation

Traditionally there are no projects in which the owners or users do not have equipment, fixtures, and furnishings that are custom designed to be built in during the construction process, connected during the course of the finishing stages, or plugged in and made part and parcel of the completed project. Indeed, most projects are designed to accommodate specific processes, equipment, and fixtures. In this case provision was made for the installation of fixtures and furnishings, as discussed in Section 5.7.

9.9 Stage 8, Commissioning and Startup

The startup of a complex research facility is at best only time consuming; at worst it could be complex and never ending. In this case the startup was planned as part of a "substantial" completion exercise, with time and budget allocated for it. A project achieves substantial completion when it can accommodate the owner's intended users and their own operating equipment. The budget for commissioning and startup came from the occupancy contingency amount provided.

9.10 Stage 9, Operation

In this case the expectations of the research operating unit, the corporate research group, corporate finance, the chief operating officer, and the chief executive officer were met.

9.11 Summary

The object of this exercise was to show how an industrial project progresses from a want or a need perceived by a research unit to how, through the auspices of professional project management working with the intended users and operators of the finished project, and the timely employment of architects, engineers, and estimators, the concept becomes a C/LAR approved by the corporate hierarchy for a fully funded project. The process involves many life cycle stages. It is described how they inform and depend on each other to generate progress. It was explained how elements were derived, coded, and costed, and how construction elements were broken down for scheduling.

Note: This chapter is based on my experience as project manager for the Xerox Phase II Sheridan Park Research Center (SPRC) project. The project files are the references. These files comprise customer requests, performance specifications, analyses and schematics, architectural and engineering drawings, estimates and budgets, scheduling plans and drawings, computer printouts of budgets and actual costs and schedules, consultant and contractor contracts, letters, memos, minutes of meetings, and all kinds of requests for information and instructions from the customer. The main intent of Chapter 9 is to show the processing of the project through the nine life cycle stages under the auspices of the C/LAR.

QUESTIONS AND EXERCISES

9.1. Form a project team comprising a project manager, an architectural consultant, a mechanical engineering consultant, an electrical engineering consultant, a cost estimator, a scheduler, and a constructor. As no team is complete without a customer, the professor is to fill that role. An alternative approach is for the team to practice consensus building. The team is its own customer.

9.2. Write a capital/lease appropriation request (C/LAR) for the house project developed as PDS, WBS, OBS, cost, and schedule in the previous chapters. There are to be eight C/LAR chapters, a bibliography, and appendixes, as presented in Section 9.4.

9.3. The authority approving the funding is to be your local bank manager, who has agreed to consider the C/LAR for approval. Submit the C/LAR to the bank manager's office for approval. And good luck!

10 HIGH-SPEED RAIL PROJECT CASE EXERCISE

10.1 Introduction

This case study is based on a series of proposals that I made for the purpose of obtaining a consulting contract to develop and implement project management systems for the Ontario/Quebec High-Speed Rail (HSR) project.

The HSR project intends to link the cities of Quebec City, Montreal, Ottawa, Kingston, Toronto, London, and Windsor with a high-speed rail system covering a distance of about 1200 km. The study of the megaproject was under the direction of a government-appointed task force, the Ontario/Quebec Rapid Train Task Force, which reported to the two provincial governments sponsoring the undertaking.

The task force employed consulting groups and professional individuals to design the program of study and develop the conceptual and feasibility phases of the problem or opportunity. The task force and consultants called for input from present providers of rail service, the public as users of transportation systems, and, as the ultimate financiers of the study, public institutions such as municipalities, utilities, consumer interest groups, national and international investors, and high-speed rail system vendors.

I became involved as a proponent for the development and implementation of project management services when public proposal calls were made for consulting services in connection with:

1. Passenger and revenue forecasting
2. Data gathering: travel intercept survey
3. Technology assessment, operating strategy, and costing,
4. Preliminary routing assessment and costing

The intent of these proposal calls was to conclude the task force's final report and to project revenue forecasts.

From a project management systems point of view, the information contained in these kinds of proposal calls is considered to be similar to the kind of information available in corporate or public bodies when considering projects. As a project management consultant, I considered that public calls of this nature are fair game for marketing project management systems, and submitted a number of proposals describing the project management approach that would be developed and implemented as the project management system. These proposals form the basis for this case study.

10.2 Project Definition

The first call for the passenger and revenue forecasting proposals was used as an opportunity to introduce the systems of project management as project driver.

In this exercise the project management role is seen to define the goal or aim of the undertaking. Although the study is to prepare passenger and revenue forecasts, the question is why it is being done. If it is being carried out as a hypothetical exercise to try to ascertain what it would be if it were done, the results cannot be expected to be the same as in an exercise that aims to provide information in respect of set goals. For example:

- How is the exercise being guided?
- What drives the undertaking?
- What is the goal?
- What is the objective of the study?
- Do we see before us a statement to the effect that: "the objective is to operate an HSR system between Windsor and Quebec City at a profit"?
- Or is the goal to: "operate an HSR system between Windsor and Quebec City"?
- Or, to be more challenging, is the study's goal that "the Ontario/Quebec HSR will operate at 300 kph, provide 24-hour a day service, and operate at a profit"?

The foregoing questions are meant only as sample suggestions to set the stage for the kind of mission statement that will serve as the catalyst not only to concentrate the project professional functions, but to put the undertaking into language that is understandable to the ultimate project owners and users, that is, the public and the passengers. Without a project definition, expanded to the extent necessary to prove the project to the target market or to achieve a stated goal, and to give direction to the consultants and their target audience, everything else, including the forecasting and data gathering, becomes only exercises.

The intent of this language is to impress the corporate mind-set, the target owner or user frame of mind, the public's and future passengers' outlook, and the actions of the megaproject functionaries, consultants, and those with a vested interest, such as, the HSR industry. In project management language this kind of terminology represents a hard start at the beginning of project definition.

Project definition, as exemplified by the statement of purpose, thus is system 1 in the systems of project management. Project definition sets the parameters of all subsequent measures of scope, quality, cost, and time, as will be seen by the users of the project—the customers. From a systems coordination and control aspect, project definition takes on a computerized code, which is then used for all scoping, estimating, tasking, and scheduling activities.

The mission statement or objective, as ultimately selected, is thus set as level 1 of the project definition structure (PDS).

Following the agreed, approved mission statement, understood and agreed to by the task force and its steering committee and by all sectors of the public, the PDS takes on the next level of user-oriented, functional breakdown, which in this case, because of the nature of the project, is seen to be a geographic breakdown into major areas.

Because the structured breakdown is intended as a PDS, there must also be made provision for project soft costs, in this case shown as major area H, and for contingencies, seen as major area J.

The level 2 elements of the PDS are thus as follows:

A Quebec–Montreal
B Montreal–Ottawa
C Montreal–Toronto
D Toronto–Ottawa
E Toronto–London
F Toronto–Windsor
G The 300-kph Train
H Management, Engineering, Design, Administration
J Contingencies

The development of a PDS is intended to be an iterative, consensual, cooperative exercise. The most difficult aspect may be the statement of the project objective itself at level 1. The developments are no less difficult at the lower levels of the structure. The major areas and their basic alpha codes as seen at level 2 in the preceding seemed not unreasonable at the beginning.

The next level of definition from the aspect of functional breakdown and coded for project management purposes may be more difficult to develop, and may be even more complex when it comes to concurrence and usage. The first attempt at the level 3 breakdown into major elements is seen in the following format, using major area A, Quebec–Montreal, as the example.

A Quebec–Montreal
- A1 Land
- A2 Quebec City Station
- A3 Montreal Central Station
- A4 Track
- A5 Bridges and Structures
- A6 Electrification

After further study, this level 3 definition of major elements was discarded as being limiting, restrictive, somewhat narrow, and at the same time potentially difficult to comprehend for management and administration purposes. It was replaced with what is considered a more flexible breakdown of major area A, Quebec–Montreal, into major elements as presented next:

A Quebec–Montreal

- A1 Three Rivers–Quebec City
- A2 Three Rivers–Montreal
- A3 Montreal–Drummondville

These major elements are first of all smaller in scope than those selected first. Therefore they are more conducive to management coordination and administration. In addition, the owner and users would be able to identify with them more readily. From the customer or user perspective, however, the project definition development continues to be based on geographic locations.

At level 4 of the PDS, the definition structure would be comprised of completed works, such as structures, facilities, and service points. For example, the A1, Three Rivers–Quebec City, major element might be broken down and coded as follows:

A1 Three Rivers–Quebec City

- A1A Land
- A1B Quebec City Station
- A1C Three Rivers Station
- A1D Track
- A1E Bridges and Structures
- A1F Electrification

It can be seen that down to level 4 of the PDS the system is geared to an identification process aimed at the customers' or users' perception of the completed megaproject. This is intended as the main thrust of the project definition exercise. That is the way to ensure through project management that the owners and users define what the project is to deliver. It is now seen that the definition is not only related to places, such as, Quebec City, but also to project functions, such as track.

As the undertaking must sooner or later take on a life as a construction project, the system must also be able to accommodate management and control measures. That is why, in addition to the permanent facilities and hardware in place upon completion, there are also major areas of "consumables" identified, coded as H, Management/Engineering/Design and Administration, and J, Contingencies.

The project definition is flexible. It is open-ended and accommodating to options and alternatives until decisions are taken and progress is made. Components belong in the system if they are deliverables as seen by the owner, the customer, and the user. That means they take on lives of their own, but always in the context of the language of project management.

To ensure that the flexibility of the PDS will be maintained, codes H and J were eventually switched to X and Y. This made provision for assigning progressive alpha characters in the future for major areas that may arise, and locking in the selected codes for both design and contingencies.

For project control measures, including scope, quality, budget, schedule, tasking, performance criteria, and so on, a code structure is essential. The code needs to be meaningful, simple, flexible, and suitable for computer processing in different environments, such as, stand-alone PCs, local-area networks (LANs), computer-aided design and drawing (CADD) systems, and workstations. As the HSR finally becomes a construction project, the code will need to tie in with construction industry standards such as Masterformat, the master list of titles and numbers for the construction industry.

For example, at level 6 of the PDS the code 0A1B02100 will be representative of the scope and quality definition and the budget for site preparation of the Quebec City station on the Quebec–Montreal leg of the HSR. This example defines the parameters for project coding as follows:

Level 1	Project (Objective)	Code 0
Level 2	Major Area	Code 0A
Level 3	Major Element	Code 0A1
Level 4	Facility and Structure	Code 0A1B
Level 5	Masterformat Division 02	Code 0A1B02
Level 6	Masterformat Element 02100	Code 0A1B02100

The Masterformat code numbers are known, accepted, and used by planners, designers, engineers, builders, manufacturers, and trade contractors throughout the industrialized world. It is thus advantageous in every respect to use these codes. The owner and user side of the code as represented by the characters A1B in the preceding example needs to be adequate enough to define the project for ready user identification, tied to the project objective, and meaningful for project management purposes as practiced by experienced project managers.

10.3 Work Breakdown

The second system of the systems of project management is work breakdown as based on typical project phases. A megaproject like the HSR project would normally require up to ten or more standard control phases per project, subproject, or package.

Even though, for the purposes of this chapter, the current work is only in phases 01 and 02, the problem or opportunity phase and the design criteria, all the other project phases must be recognized and scoped to the degree needed to prove the intent of the current phase. The classic project management phases for this type of undertaking are the following:

01 Problem/Opportunity/Concept Planning
02 Design Criteria/Feasibility
03 Preliminary Design
04 Contract and Procurement Documents
05 Final Design, Drawings, Specifications
06 Procurement, Tender, Award
07 Construction
08 Installation
09 Commissioning and Startup
10 Operation
11 Decommissioning

At the present time this project is considered to be in phases 01 and 02. Generally in project work the phases hardly ever follow each other in lock-step order. Project phases invariably overlap and parallel each other, specially on megaprojects. For example, some late element specifications may not be selected until phase 07, Construction, whereas materials of construction specifications must be selected as early as phase 03, Preliminary Design. Indeed, on megaprojects some major areas are considered megaprojects in their own right. An average megaproject will comprise programs, subprograms, multiprojects, and subprojects. Then within each one of them there will occur phases and stages that are not necessarily the phases named in the systems of project management.

In essence, a megaproject becomes a theater of the absurd, with some actors in the process of planning elements while others are pouring concrete. And it is only systems project management that can track it all, that is, if such a system is in place and viable.

In this case, although the current work is now in phase 01, the successful management of the project requires that all the other phases be defined and provided for now to the extent needed to ensure the stated objective.

To illustrate the concept of phases in the systems of project management, the current phase, Problem/Opportunity/Concept Planning, may be taken to breakdown levels 2 and 3, as shown in the following example:

Level 1 The (Project) Objective
Level 2 01 Problem/Opportunity/Concept Planning
Level 3 011 Task Force Terms of Reference/Final Report

As this is where the action is at the present time, at level 3 of the problem/opportunity/concept planning phase, the exercise is to develop the activities pertaining to code 011, Task Force Final Report. Using the content of the four proposal calls listed initially as the activities themselves, they are inserted into phase 1 of the project WBS as level 4 and 5 activities as follows (with only code 0111 shown at level 4):

Level 4	0111	Analysis of the Market Demand
Level 5	01111	Passenger and Revenue Forecasting
Level 5	01112	Data Gathering
Level 5	01113	Preliminary Routing Assessment and Costing
Level 5	01114	Technology Assessment, Operating Strategy, and Cost

Level 6, the next lower level of the project WBS, provides detail activities which support the packages at level 5. Codes 01111, Passenger and Revenue Forecasting, and 01112, Data Gathering, are broken down to level 6 as follows:

Level 5	01111	Passenger and Revenue Forecasting
Level 6	01111A	Travel Data Analysis
Level 6	01111B	Additional Work Elements
Level 6	01111C	Formulation of a Forecasting Model
Level 6	01111D	Application of Model
Level 6	01111E	Passenger and Revenue Rorecasting Report

Level 5	01112	Data Gathering
Level 6	01112A	Design of the Survey
Level 6	01112B	Organization of Field Surveys
Level 6	01112C	Wave 1 Survey
Level 6	01112D	Wave 2 Survey
Level 6	01112E	Wave 3 Survey
Level 6	01112F	Data Gathering Report

The tasks and activities listed here must meet the test of what comprises an activity in the systems of project management. They must be deliverables. They must exist as hard cost items in the project control system. A hard cost code item is one against which payment is made or withheld.

If an activity meets these criteria, it is lodged in the system and forms an element of cost. It is a part of the project schedule, and it is assignable to a team in the project organization.

Tasks, activities, or packages of tasks or activities arising from early phases in project work thus have the same scope and cost relevance in the life of the project as activities in later project phases, such as the construction phase.

In systems project management every activity belongs in definition, breakdown, and organization, as well as in cost and schedule as a hard, coded invoice item. The activities delineated here are no exception.

To illustrate, the level 6 data gathering activity 01112C, Wave 1 Survey, would be coded in the project definition as seen next (bearing in mind that the change of code H to X, as discussed in Section 10.2, has not yet taken place).

H10A/01112C

H Management/Design/Engineering

H10 Project Management

A Quebec–Montreal

01 Phase 1 Problem / Opportunity / Concept Planning

011 Rapid Train Task Force Final Report

0111 Analysis of Market Demand for HSR

01112 Data Gathering

01112C Data Gathering Wave 1 Survey

The left side codes the project definition area and element that represent scope, quality, and ultimately the budget for this element of the project. The right side codes the activity in the work breakdown, which as a package would have a budget. As the package is awarded, the code item becomes synonymous with the organization hired to deliver the package.

10.4 Functional Organization

System 3 in the systems of project management aims to coordinate and control the project functional organization. While the PDS provides the project aims, targets, and objectives as seen by the users of the completed undertaking, that is, the passengers, and WBS defines and codifies the studies, tasks, and activities, the functional organization is the source of cost to the project.

A simplified bird's-eye view of the triple code measure of any project budget or cost makeup might look like this:

Definition Code: Source of Budget

Breakdown Code: Task or Package Budget

Organization Code: Source of Cost

As the source of costs, the success of the project demands that the organizations be provided clear objectives, precise tasks, and realistic budgets to achieve their targets. Since the HSR project will be managed, conceptualized, designed, engineered, constructed, manufactured, delivered, and operated by a multitude of public- and private-sector companies and individuals, it is essential that their actions and activities be coordinated and managed in a way that allows them to operate interdependently and effectively.

Their effectiveness is a function not only of clear targets and terms of reference, but of their output serving others, and of others' output serving them as input. This is achievable in the first instance through recognition of a project functional organization which incorporates, codifies, and makes known their relationship to the project and to each other in hard terms of scope of work, quality parameters, budgets, and the project schedule. The basis for the HSR project functional organization may be conceptualized as follows:

10 Federal Government

20 Ontario Government

30 Quebec Government

40 Ontario/Quebec Rapid Train Task Force (OQRTTF)/Steering Committee/Project Management

50 VIA Rail/CN/CP

60 Bombardier/ABB/Others

70 Private-Sector Engineers/Architects/Consultants

80 Private-Sector Contractors/Vendors

90 Cities/Towns/Public Utilities

Coded subsets of one of the named organizational groups, the OQRTTF, may be illustrated as follows:

40 OQRTTF/Steering Committee/Project Management

4001 KPMG Peat Marwick Stevenson & Kellog

4002 CIGGT Peat Marwick Stevenson & Kellog

4003 Transportation Management Inc.

4004 Dessau

4005 Alpha Beta Gamma Consultants

4006 Ernst & Young

10.5 Cost Control

System 4 in the systems of project management is the budgeting and cost control system. It is driven initially by project definition, then by work breakdown, and finally by organizations. As the sources of cost to any project are the project functional organizations, the ultimate cost code system is on the basis of organizations delivering services as in-house assignments, under contracts, and through purchase orders.

What this means is project cost control through the development and implementation of a computerized, multibarreled project code system, which incorporates the coded project estimate and budget on the one hand and the packages and organization codes on the other.

For proposal discussion purposes the following assumptions are made:

- The Ontario/Quebec HSR system will operate at 300 kph, provide service 24 hours a day, and operate at a profit.
- The order-of-magnitude capital cost is estimated at $8.5 billion.

The major areas and their order-of-magnitude capital cost estimates as seen by the owners and users (the public and the passengers) of the completed project and by the project sponsors, and committed to by the project team are:

A	Quebec City–Montreal	$1.4 billion
B	Montreal–Ottawa	0.5
C	Montreal–Toronto	2.0
D	Toronto–Ottawa	0.5
E	Toronto–London	0.4
F	Toronto–Windsor	1.1
G	The 300-kph Train	0.6
X	Mgmt./Eng./Design/Admin.	1.0
Y	Contingencies and Inflation	1.0
	Total	$8.5 billion

(It is noted that X for management, etc., and Y for contingencies have been introduced to replace H and J as level 2 codes first introduced in Section 10.2.)

The cost control system is further developed as a continuing breakdown of the project's major areas and the area's major elements, as will be seen by the users of the completed project, that is, the passengers, and by the project managers, designers, and builders.

The project definition system represents only one part of the overall project cost control effort, that is, one barrel of the multibarrel approach. In systems project management cost theory, the estimating and budgeting by functional definition is very important in that it represents the budget on the basis of recognizable completed works, as opposed to the cost of construction elements (even though it is the cost of construction elements that drives the cost of the completed facilities).

The second cost control barrel fires rounds made from packages of design and construction activities emanating from the phases of the WBS. In this case the conversion from definition to breakdown at level 2 of the project structure can be seen in the following list:

01	Problem/Opportunity/Concept Planning	$ 6.0 million
02	Design Criteria/Feasibility	6.0
03	Preliminary Design	100.0
04	Contract and Procurement Documents	40.0
05	Final Design, Drawings, Specifications	840.0
06	Procurement, Tender, Award	20.0
07	Construction	5000.0
08	Installation	1488.0
09	Commissioning and Startup	1000.0
10	Operation (Not in Contract)	—
11	Decommissioning (Not in Contract)	—
Total		$8500.0 million

The description of these definition, packaging, and cost systems at this stage of the project (phase 1) is obviously at a high summary level and is conceptual only. What should be evident is that there are integrated systems being applied, each fulfilling an important and unique purpose, but tied to and dependent on the others.

To demonstrate the tripartite systems application one more time, the following example is taken from the current project phase. Assume that it is wished to code the current activity, Passenger and Revenue Forecasting. It is known to occur in phase 1, the current phase, and it would be paid from major area X, Management, Engineering, etc. (see also Fig. 10.1). Its tripartite code would be:

X10 / 01111 / 7001

/

X10 Definition Code for Source of Funds

/

01111 Package Code for Passenger and Revenue Forecasting

/

7001 Organization Code for Forecasting Consultant

Initially the project is controlled on definition codes. As phase activities and packages are developed and assigned, control is on the basis of both definition and package codes. When the project is 100% awarded, control may be exercised on the basis of the organization code alone.

On all projects, and particularly on megaprojects, as a general rule it should never be expected that the definition will be completed before the project is completed. The breakdown will be finished after the project is finished, and the allocations of payments usually continue long after the completed facility has been started up.

10.6 Computer Systems

If the foregoing paragraphs are considered notes of discussions leading to the development of the project management systems for the HSR project, they are a precursor to the introduction and development of the enabling computer application packages. It is known that in these applications, computer systems are seen as tools, meaning that we do not do things the way we have always done them and then computerize, but that we use the computer program to help us do the thing, with the result that databases of information are formed which are suitable for our intended purposes and which also become information for other project purposes and other project stakeholders, such as, corporate management. Does it need to be recalled that systems not only help us do the job better, faster, and cheaper, but they improve quality and productivity across the entire spectrum of interests?

It is important to keep in mind that we are persistently faced with a technology gap between what we want to do and what we are able do with the tools at hand, and at the same time there is invariably a developmental uncertainty lag between the conceptual idea and its presentation by the PC project management system and its graphic user interface. Once we overcome this uncertainty, the systems can deliver the kind of project definition information that is illustrated in Fig. 10.1, a hierarchical PDS identified as Code Category—OQHSR_DEFINITION.

The structured table is seen to cascade from level 1, Project1, down to the level 6 construction project element, Site Preparation, coded A1B02100, for one branch of the Christmas tree structure, as developed in the preceding discussion. Most of the other branches are taken to level 3, major elements. Major element A3 is broken down into level 4 components. It is seen that X represents the major area for management and design (soft costs), and Y is the code for contingencies. The latter alpha characters are selected to ensure flexibility in the use of early alpha characters for coding purposes.

It is known that the second structure in the systems of project management is the WBS. For this case exercise it is depicted in Fig. 10.2 as Code Category—OQHSR_PHASES_WBS. In this exercise the work breakdown and its developed coding system are taken in detail to level 6 for only one of the four feasibility studies introduced in the opening discourse, namely, the passenger and revenue forecasting study, which falls out of the exercise at level 5 of the structure in Fig. 10.2. The other level 5 studies show only a token level 6 activity each. The important message from these kinds of studies is the realization of how quickly the structure and its related coding develop and take on some complexity.

The project functional organization is the third of the systems of project management. In this case it is seen in Fig. 10.3, Code Category—OQHSR_FUNC._ORG., roughed out at level 2 of the OBS, with a few consulting firms depicted at level 3.

```
CODE CATEGORY - OQHSR_DEFINITION
FORMAT :                                    TABLE LOOKUP - Y

1.... PROJECT1          THE HSR PROJECT
      2.... A                   QUEBEC CITY - MONTREAL
            3.... A1                    THREE RIVERS - QUEBEC CITY
                  4.... A1A                     THREE RIVERS - QUEBEC CITY LAND
                  4.... A1B                     QUEBEC CITY STATION
                        5.... A1B02                     STATION SITE WORKS
                              6.... A1B02100            SITE PREPARATION
                  4.... A1C                     THREE RIVERS STATION
                  4.... A1D                     THREE RIVERS - QUEBEC  TRACK
                  4.... A1E                     THREE RIVERS - QUEBEC  STRUCTURES
                  4.... A1F                     THREE RIVERS - QUEBEC ELECT./SIGNALS.
            3.... A2                    THREE RIVERS - MONTREAL
            3.... A3                    MONTREAL - DRUMMONDVILLE
                  4.... A3A                     MONTREAL - DRUMMONDVILLE LAND
                  4.... A3B                     DRUMMONDVILLE STATION
                  4.... A3C                     MONTREAL CENTRAL STATION
                  4.... A3D                     PARK ALTERNATIVE STATION
                  4.... A3E                     DORVAL ALTERNATIVE STATION
                  4.... A3F                     MIRABEL ALTERNATIVE STATION
      2.... B                   MONTREAL - OTTAWA
            3.... B1                    CN KINGSTON/ALEXANDRIA SUBDIVISION
                  4.... B1A                     MONTREAL - OTTAWA LAND
                  4.... B1B                     OTTAWA STATION HULL ALTERNATIVE
                  4.... B1C                     OTTAWA STATION OTTAWA ALTERNATIVE
            3.... B2                    CP O & M  SUBDIVISION ALTERNATIVE
            3.... B3                    CN TWO MOUNTAINS ALTERNATIVE
            3.... B4                    CP LACHUTE ALTERNATIVE
            3.... B5                    MONTREAL - OTTAWA  NEW DEDICATED TRACK
            3.... B6                    COMBINATIONS OF ABOVE ALTERNATIVES
      2.... C                   MONTREAL - OTTAWA
      2.... D                   OTTAWA - TORONTO
            3.... D1                    CN SMITH FALLS SUB DIVISION
            3.... D2                    CN SMITH FALLS - KINGSTON NEW
            3.... D3                    CN/CP ROW NEW TRACK
      2.... E                   LONDON - TORONTO
            3.... E1                    CN OAKVILLE - BRANTFORD
            3.... E2                    CN WESTON - HALTON - KITCHENER
            3.... E3                    CP GALT SUBDIVISION
            3.... E4                    NEW TRACK
            3.... E5                    COMBINATION ALTERNATIVES
      2.... F                   WINDSOR - TORONTO
            3.... F1                    CN ALTERNATIVE
            3.... F2                    CP ALTERNATIVE
            3.... F3                    CASO SUBDIVISION ALTERNATIVE
      2.... T                   THE 300 KPH TRAIN
      2.... X                   MANAGEMENT/DESIGN/ENGINEERING/ADMINISTRATION
            3.... X10                   PROJECT MANAGEMENT
            3.... X20                   DESIGN/ENGINEERING
            3.... X30                   ADMINISTRATION
      2.... Y                   CONTINGENCIES
            3.... Y10                   INFLATION
            3.... Y20                   PLANNING CONTINGENCY
            3.... Y30                   DESIGN CONTINGENCY
            3.... Y40                   TECHNOLOGY CONTINGENCY
            3.... Y50                   CONSTRUCTION CONTINGENCY
```

FIGURE 10.1 HSR PROJECT COMPUTER REPORT, PDS. This computer-generated report represents the creation of the project definition structure discussed as introductory notes in Section 10.2. The intent is to set up tables which take on code structures as information is input. Levels are important in the development of definition structures. It is seen that four levels of definition are provided for A, Three Rivers–Quebec City, and B, Montreal–Ottawa, and three levels for other major areas.

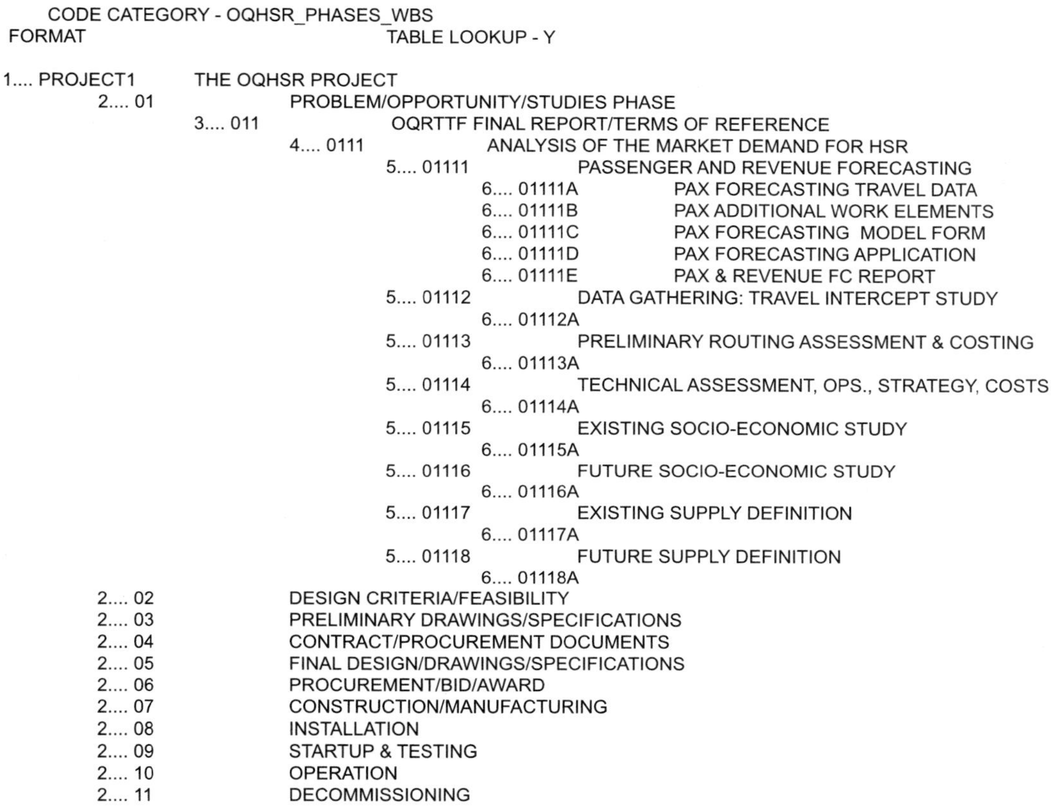

CODE CATEGORY - OQHSR_PHASES_WBS
FORMAT TABLE LOOKUP - Y

Code	Description
1.... PROJECT1	THE OQHSR PROJECT
2.... 01	PROBLEM/OPPORTUNITY/STUDIES PHASE
3.... 011	OQRTTF FINAL REPORT/TERMS OF REFERENCE
4.... 0111	ANALYSIS OF THE MARKET DEMAND FOR HSR
5.... 01111	PASSENGER AND REVENUE FORECASTING
6.... 01111A	PAX FORECASTING TRAVEL DATA
6.... 01111B	PAX ADDITIONAL WORK ELEMENTS
6.... 01111C	PAX FORECASTING MODEL FORM
6.... 01111D	PAX FORECASTING APPLICATION
6.... 01111E	PAX & REVENUE FC REPORT
5.... 01112	DATA GATHERING: TRAVEL INTERCEPT STUDY
6.... 01112A	
5.... 01113	PRELIMINARY ROUTING ASSESSMENT & COSTING
6.... 01113A	
5.... 01114	TECHNICAL ASSESSMENT, OPS., STRATEGY, COSTS
6.... 01114A	
5.... 01115	EXISTING SOCIO-ECONOMIC STUDY
6.... 01115A	
5.... 01116	FUTURE SOCIO-ECONOMIC STUDY
6.... 01116A	
5.... 01117	EXISTING SUPPLY DEFINITION
6.... 01117A	
5.... 01118	FUTURE SUPPLY DEFINITION
6.... 01118A	
2.... 02	DESIGN CRITERIA/FEASIBILITY
2.... 03	PRELIMINARY DRAWINGS/SPECIFICATIONS
2.... 04	CONTRACT/PROCUREMENT DOCUMENTS
2.... 05	FINAL DESIGN/DRAWINGS/SPECIFICATIONS
2.... 06	PROCUREMENT/BID/AWARD
2.... 07	CONSTRUCTION/MANUFACTURING
2.... 08	INSTALLATION
2.... 09	STARTUP & TESTING
2.... 10	OPERATION
2.... 11	DECOMMISSIONING

Figure 10.2 HSR Project Computer Report, WBS. This computer-generated report represents the creation of the work breakdown structure discussed as introductory notes in Section 10.3. The intent is to set up tables which take on activity code structures as information is input. Levels are important in the development of breakdown structures. It is seen that up to 6 levels of breakdown are provided for the problen/opportunity phase, code 01, to create and code detail tasks such as 01111A, Pax Forecasting Travel Data, etc. Project phases 02 through 11 are listed as level 2 code items only.

It should be understood that any project invariably requires inputs and participation from people and firms that specialize in these kinds of projects. In this case the firms named, such as CN and CP, are providers of rail services in the project area and are logical contenders for early participation in the work. To reemphasize, the whole idea of effective project management is not to reinvent the wheel, but to go always with one's strengths. This means recruiting individuals and firms for the broad project team and incorporating their inputs early. This builds management strength, which is reflected in the quality of the project at a very early date.

```
    CODE CATEGORY - OQHSR_FUNC._ORG.
FORMAT                                  TABLE LOOKUP - Y

1.... PROJECT1        THE OQHSR PROJECT
          2.... 10              FEDERAL GOVERNMENT
          2.... 20              ONTARIO GOVERNMENT
          2.... 30              QUEBEC GOVERNMENT
          2.... 40              OQRTTF/STEERING COMMITTEE/PROJECT MANAGEMENT
          2.... 50              VIA/CN/CP
          2.... 60              BOMBARDIER/VIA/OTHERS
          2.... 70              PRIVATE SECTOR CONSULTANTS
                      3.... 7001          PASSENGER & REVENUE FORECASTING CONSULTANTS
                      3.... 7002          DATA GATHERING CONSULTANTS
                      3.... 7003          PRELIMINARY ROUTING & COSTING CONSULTANTS
          2.... 80              PRIVATE SECTOR CONTRACTORS/SUBCONTRACTORS/VENDORS
          2.... 90              CITIES/TOWNS/PUBLIC UTILITIES
```

FIGURE 10.3 HSR PROJECT COMPUTER REPORT, OBS. This computer-generated report represents the creation of the functional organization breakdown structure discussed as introductory notes in Section 10.4. The intent is to set up tables which take on organizational, company, or team code structures as package contracts are awarded and information is input. As this case exercise is being handled in its early problem/opportunity and conceptual phases, only a few project team members, government agencies, and private-sector companies are identified. The OBS shows only three private-sector packages for the tasks identified in Section 10.2. On the other hand, with the flattening of corporate structures and empowerment of small teams and individuals in project work, it should not be expected that OBSs will be deep multilayered structures.

10.7 Cost Estimating and Cost Control

If the project management systems first define the project as major areas, major elements, element groups, and on down to project construction elements at level 6 of the PDS, then that must be the way that the project will be ballpark estimated, detail estimated when the details become available, budgeted, and eventually cost controlled. The code system based on the PDS was shown in discussion and in Fig. 10.1. The ballpark cost figures were introduced in Section 10.5. Now we wish to see the project cost picture as it might look on computer screens run by cost applications.

Figure 10.4 depicts the project cost control numbers as developed earlier in this chapter. The cost information is a summary by major areas. This is obviously a snapshot of the project cost as it might look on a day early in the life of the project. The thing to look for is the consistency in the way in which major areas are defined, coded, and, as we know very little about scope and quality, ballpark estimated against the huge line item amounts in the megaproject.

We know that the PDS scope, quality, and content drive the project cost. We also are aware that the less we know about project details, the more inaccurate and unreliable are the dollar amounts. Professional project managers know that the early numbers are very uncertain, and it is their responsibility to inform the project owners and not to look for approvals before the uncertainty is removed. In real life this is one tough row to hoe. People, including the project manager, want the project to go ahead.

OQHSR PROJECT COST CONTROL: SUMMARY BY MAJOR AREAS

CODE	DESCRIPTION	BUDGET AMOUNT	APPROVED CHANGES	EXP. & CMT. TO DATE	FORECAST FIN. COST	AMT. AUTH. REDISTRIB.	OVER / UNDER
A	QUEBEC-MONTREAL	1,400,000,000	0	0	1,400,000,000	1,400,000,000	0
B	MONTREAL-OTTAWA	500,000,000	0	0	500,000,000	500,000,000	0
C	MONTREAL-TORONTO	2,000,000,000	0	0	2,000,000,000	2,000,000,000	0
D	TORONTO-OTTAWA	500,000,000	0	0	500,000,000	500,000,000	0
E	TORONTO-LONDON	400,000,000	0	0	400,000,000	400,000,000	0
F	TORONTO-WINDSOR	1,100,000,000	0	0	1,100,000,000	1,100,000,000	0
T	THE 300 KPH TRAIN	600,000,000	0	0	600,000,000	600,000,000	0
X	MGMT./DESIGN/ENG./ADMIN.	1,000,000,000	0	0	1,000,000,000	1,000,000,000	0
Y	CONTINGENCIES	1,000,000,000	0	0	1,000,000,000	1,000,000,000	0
	TOTAL	8,500,000,000	0	0	8,500,000,000	8,500,000,000	0

FIGURE 10.4 HSR PROJECT COMPUTER REPORT, COST CONTROL BY MAJOR AREAS. A project definition is incopmplete without a cost estimate. As the project scope and quality are defined, its definition is cost estimated. The estimate eventually becomes the budget. This computer report provides a cost summary of the project at its highest level, i.e., the level 2 project major areas coded A through Y. The aim of this cost exercise is to capture all project costs as allocated budget elements of the finished project. Once so allocated, the amounts become the source of funding for the activities and packages that lead to the delivery of the finished elements. *Note*: The major areas and numbers in these examples are hypothetical only to illustrate the cost control system.

So what happens more often than not are projects being approved on ballpark ±40% accurate, or worse, cost information, with the project eventually costing two or three times more than the budget. (It is a given that projects never cost less.)

The only way project cost can be proved is through the development of structured detail. The development of the detail is depicted in Fig. 10.5, which shows a breakdown of major area A into its major elements. It is important to understand that these types of breakdowns are difficult to achieve, particularly if they are to develop hard project activities as defined in the context of this book. (We know that a hard activity is one that exists as project scope, project cost, and as an organizational task against which the organization invoices the client.)

We also know that cost reports such as those seen in Figs. 10.4 and 10.5 are computer system generated by databases of coded elements, which may go to six or more levels of detail in the PDS.

The second cost look at the project, based on the WBS of phased activities, is taking shape alongside the one based on the deliverables, as depicted by the project functions that are to be delivered to the project owners and users. Based on the discussion of the WBS, this cost report is seen in Fig. 10.6. The activities arising out of the 11 phases would be estimated individually or in packages, and it is these estimates that would form the basis for phase budget amounts, as seen in the third col-

OQHSR PROJECT COST CONTROL: SUMMARY BY MAJOR ELEMENTS

CODE	DESCRIPTION	BUDGET AMOUNT	APPROVED CHANGES	EXP. & CMTS. TO DATE	FORECAST FIN. COST	AMT. AUTH. REDISTRIB.	OVER / UNDER
A1	LAND	40,000,000	0	0	40,000,000	40,000,000	0
A2	SUBGRADE	175,000,000	0	0	175,000,000	175,000,000	0
A3	TRACK	275,000,000	0	0	275,000,000	275,000,000	0
A4	SIGNALS & COMM.	125,000,000	0	0	125,000,000	125,000,000	0
A5	ELECTRIFICATION	150,000,000	0	0	150,000,000	150,000,000	0
A6	BRIDGES & STRUCTS.	250,000,000	0	0	250,000,000	250,000,000	0
A7	CROSSINGS	200,000,000	0	0	200,000,000	200,000,000	0
A8	STATIONS	20,000,000	0	0	20,000,000	20,000,000	0
A9	OTHER ITEMS	165,000,000	0	0	165,000,000	165,000,000	0
	TOTAL	1,400,000,000	0	0	1,400,000,000	1,400,000,000	0

FIGURE 10.5 HSR PROJECT COMPUTER REPORT, COST CONTROL BY MAJOR ELEMENTS. This computer report provides a cost breakdown of major area A, the Quebec–Montreal leg of the HSR project, into major elements A1 through A9. Note the functional nature of the major elements. The aim of this definition breakdown and cost exercise is to capture project costs as allocated budget elements of the finished project at lower and lower levels. Once so allocated, the amounts become the source of funding for the activities and packages that lead to the delivery of the finished elements. It needs to be recognized that cost estimating of lower level project functions may be diffuclt in that it imposes a discipline on the project customer and user, as well as on project management of the finished facility to not only want the project, but to strive to cost it. In other words, the exercise becomes more than the creation of a wish list. *Note:* The major elements and the above codes are not necessarily the same as those presented in the discourse. This simply represents another look at what may constitute major elements. The final look must arise from consensus. If not consensus, then a management decision.

umn of Fig. 10.6. As for the elemental project cost control report, the budget amounts at level 2 as depicted are system generated from databases, depending on the degree of detail available.

The third look at the state of the financial health of your project is provided by the project expenditure report in Fig. 10.7.

As for the PDS-based cost control and the WBS-coded phase control system, the OBS-coded system is dependent on data resident in the system for both its detailed and its high summary level reports. If the PDS-based budget is driven by project functions and elements as they will be delivered to the project operators, and the WBS-linked budget breaks the project down into its design and construction elements, the OBS-dependent expenditure system is the final proof of the project cost based on the contracts, purchase orders, and agreements signed between the project owners and the sources of the project cost.

To be on budget, all three systems must keep coming up with the same bottom lines from beginning to end. So where is the problem? It is in the fact that a megapro-

OQHSR PROJECT COST CONTROL: SUMMARY BY PROJECT PHASES

CODE	DESCRIPTION	BUDGET AMOUNT	APPROVED CHANGES	EXP. & CMTS. TO DATE	FORECAST FIN. COST	AMT. AUTH. REDISTRIB.	OVER/ UNDER
01	PROB./OPPORT./FEASIBILITY	6,000,000	0	0	6,000,000	6,000,000	0
02	DESIGN CRITERIA	6,000,000	0	0	6,000,000	6,000,000	0
03	PRELIMINARY DESIGN	100,000,000	0	0	100,000,000	100,000,000	0
04	CONTRACT DOCUMENTS	40,000,000	0	0	40,000,000	40,000,000	0
05	FINAL DESIGN & DRAWINGS	840,000,000	0	0	840,000,000	840,000,000	0
06	PROCUREMENT/BID/AWARD	20,000,000	0	0	20,000,000	20,000,000	0
07	CONSTRUCTION	5,000,000,000	0	0	5,000,000,000	5,000,000,000	0
08	INSTALLATION	1,488,000,000	0	0	1,488,000,000	1,488,000,000	0
09	STARTUP	1,000,000,000	0	0	1,000,000,000	1,000,000,000	0
	TOTAL	8,500,000,000	0	0	8,500,000,000	8,500,000,000	0

FIGURE 10.6 HSR PROJECT COMPUTER REPORT, COST BY WBS PHASES. Project cost control is a continuous exercise of progressively estimating and budgeting project functions as shown in Fig. 10.4 and 10..5. As project elements are estimated, those same elements are reestimated as activities and as packages of activities. As the project is the sum of its elements, so it is the sum of its activities as developed through the application of phases. Shown above are the 9 phases that comprise the HSR project. The amounts against each phase represent the estimates of the activities that make up the phase. The difficulty in project cost control is that project definitions and project activities are usually ongoing, parallel actions that facilitate and influence each other. Eventually they both finish, usually at about the same time. Both require to be cost controlled. (Phases 10 and 11 are not included in contract.)

ject takes on a life of its own with elements and functions and phases and organizations all jumbled together and going every which way. There is immense difficulty in coding, coordinating, and controlling big projects. And without the concept of the triple-thread code systems as presented, there is no way that cost will ever be under budget. Or the wanted or needed project will not be built.

10.8 Scheduling and Progress Control

In the broad sense of scheduling big happenings or massive events, an initial megaproject schedule can be dictated by an event date, for example: the Salt Lake Olympics shall open on Friday, February 8, 2002. There are no ifs and/or buts. That is the drop dead date. Big-time international show projects such as Expos and Olympic games always open on time. (Whether they are on budget depends on who is telling the story.) Another type of project "must do" schedule may result from an act of nature such as a flood, a hurricane, or an earthquake. In these cases the project invariably

OQHSR PROJECT EXPENDITURE REPORT: SUMMARY BY ORGANIZATIONS (COST SOURCES)

CODE	DESCRIPTION	ORIGINAL COMMITMENT	APP. CMT. CHANGES	CURR. PRD. EXPEND.	EXPEND. TO DATE	CURR. O / S COMMITS.	EXP. & CMTS. TO DATE
10	FEDERAL GOVT. DEPTS	0	0	0	0	0	0
20	QUEBEC GOVERNMENT DEPTS	0	0	0	0	0	0
30	ONTARIO GOVT. DEPTS.	0	0	0	0	0	0
40	STEERING COMMITTEE / PM	6,000,000	0	0	0	6,000,000	6,000,000
50	VIA / CN / CP	0	0	0	0	0	0
60	BOMBARDIER / ABB / OTHER	0	0	0	0	0	0
70	CONSULTANTS / ENGINEERS	0	0	0	0	0	0
80	CONTRACTORS / SUBS.	0	0	0	0	0	0
90	CITIES / TOWNS / P.U.C. s	0	0	0	0	0	0
	TOTAL	6,000,000	0	0	0	6,000,000	6,000,000

FIGURE 10.7 HSR PROJECT COMPUTER REPORT, COST BY ORGANIZATIONS. As a project grows it expands in terms of its information. Initially the project is tightly held by its owner. As the definition expands in terms of functions, elements, activities, and packages, the people involved in the project become more numerous in the owner organization, the project team, consultants, contractors, vendors, manufacturers, etc. As the initial cost control is cast along project definition lines, as seen in Figs. 10.4 and 10.5, and the second cost accounting occurs in relation to project actitvities, as seen in Fig. 10.6, the ultimate cost measures are related to agreements and contracts held by organizations, as seen above. But as definition, activities, and assignments all end at the same time, i.e., when the project is completed, all three cost control systems are current as long as the project is running.

consists of saving lives and property through removals, reconstruction, and reparations. There are no resource-loaded schedules in these cases, except to do the work as fast as humanly possible, to save lives, to prevent additional damage, and to control the disaster with regard to spreading.

Other than world showcase projects like the Olympics or World Fairs, there are schedules to reflect new product launch dates. A new product may be launched to take advantage of a market situation or to capture a market share. In these cases the date may be set by the marketing managers who claim to know the market condition. The date may be set without reference to project management considerations such as functions, phases, scope, quality, cost, and the real time required to do the project. If this happens, the time between "time now" and the hard launch date may not be enough for a commensurate quality project. The front-end approvals may be based on mostly inadequate design and conceptual information, which may result in downstream difficulties involving quality, cost, and ultimate product performance. These kinds of situations lead to reduced assembly and construction times, invariably resulting in monstrous overtime costs and less productive and inefficient use of human resources. But the show must go on.

In this case exercise a proposed undertaking such as the HSR megaproject initially is not schedule driven, except that targets are set for progressive presentations and approvals of front-end tasks. The front end itself is set to a time frame. Succeeding project phases, as listed in Section 10.3 would be scheduled, perhaps as discussed next.

For a megaproject such as the HSR project, an early (optimistic) estimate of a project schedule might be about 10 years. The first 3 years could be for the feasibility studies, environmental assessments, and conceptual design, as well as the associated ballpark (order-of-magnitude) estimating. In the early part of the first 3 years detailed scheduling would be limited to the activities arising out of the four studies cited in the Introduction. The outcome of the studies is expected to be a market strategy.

Using the WBS developed for this exercise as the basis for the planning network, 18 activities were created from the level 5 and level 6 packages highlighted in the WBS in Fig. 10.2. The activities that were cast in the CPM network may be seen in Fig. 10.8 as a typical computer scheduling report after computer processing of the CPM network.

The same activities are then seen in another snapshot in Fig. 10.9. These kinds of logic-driven network-based computer reports are typical and used for detailed

ACTIVITY LISTING REPORT
PROJECT: HSR OVERALL MARKET STRATEGY

ACTIVITY IDENTIFIER	ACTIVITY DESCRIPTION	TYP	ORIG DUR.	REM. DUR.	EARLY START	EARLY FINISH	LATE START	LATE FINISH	TOTAL FLOAT	IMPOSED DATES
0000	FINAL REPORT 31 MAY 91	B	1	1	03JUN91	03JUN91	03JUN91	03JUN91	0	
0001	OVERALL PAX FC STRATEGY		40	40	19MAR92	14MAY92	19MAR92	14MAY92	0	
0003	PAX FC RFP AND SELECTION		35	35	15MAY92	06JUL92	01JUN92	20JUL92	10	
0005	FINAL PAX FC STRATEGY		50	50	07JUL92	16SEP92	21JUL92	30SEP92	10	
0007	PAX FC MODEL FORMULATION		20	20	17SEP92	15OCT92	05JAN93	01FEB93	75	
0009	PRELIM DESIGN DATA GATHER.		40	40	02APR92	29MAY92	02APR92	29MAY92	0	
0010	DATA GATHER. RFP & SELECT.		35	35	01JUN92	20JUL92	01JUN92	20JUL92	0	
0011	EXISTING SOCIO-ECON. COND.		60	60	15JUN92	09SEP92	06NOV92	01FEB93	100	
0012	FINAL DESIGN DATA GATHER.		15	15	21JUL92	11AUG92	21JUL92	11AUG92	0	
0014	DATA GATHER. REVEALED PREF		120	120	12AUG92	01FEB93	12AUG92	01FEB93	0	
0016	DATA GATHER. STATED PREFER		120	120	12AUG92	01FEB93	12AUG92	01FEB93	0	
0018	MODAL USE DATA DEMAND		60	60	12AUG92	05NOV92	06NOV92	01FEB93	60	
0020	EXISTING SUPPLY DEFINITION		60	60	15JUN92	09SEP92	06NOV92	01FEB93	100	
0021	PAX FC MODEL CALIBRATION		20	20	02FEB93	01MAR93	02FEB93	01MAR93	0	
0029	FUTURE SOCIO-ECON. SCENA.		80	80	10SEP92	04JAN93	09FEB93	02JUN93	105	
0030	FUTURE SUPPLY DEFINITION		80	80	10SEP92	04JAN93	09FEB93	02JUN93	105	
0051	PAX FORECASTS		15	15	30MAR93	20APR93	30MAR93	20APR93	0	
1000	REVENUE FORECASTS	E	30	30	21APR93	02JUN93	21APR93	02JUN93	0	

FIGURE 10.8 HSR PROJECT COMPUTER REPORT, SCHEDULE LIST. This is a CPM-based computer report of the detail activities discussed in Section 10.3 and identified as part of the studies to be awarded to consultants in phase 1 of the HSR project. In this report the activities are sorted by activity identifier, in ascending order, and early start date. Activity 0000 is a begin activity (B), and activity 1000 is the end activity (E). Shown are columns for original and remaining durations, early and late start and finish dates, and total float for each activity. *Note*: The activities, their durations, and the CPM logic are hypothetical to illustrate scheduling as part of the project management system.

ACTIVITY LISTING REPORT
PROJECT: HSR OVERALL MARKET STRATEGY

ACTIVITY IDENTIFIER	ACTIVITY DESCRIPTION	TYP	ORIG DUR.	REM. DUR.	EARLY START	EARLY FINISH	LATE START	LATE FINISH	TOTAL FLOAT	IMPOSED DATES
0000	FINAL REPORT 31 MAY	B	1	1	03JUN91	03JUN91	03JUN91	03JUN91	0	03JUN91
0001	OVERALL PAX FC STRATEGY		40	40	19MAR92	14MAY92	19MAR92	14MAY92	0	
0009	PRELIM DESIGN DATA GATHER.		40	40	02APR92	29MAY92	02APR92	29MAY92	0	
0010	DATA GATHER RFP & SELECT.		35	35	01JUN92	20JUL92	01JUN92	20JUL92	0	
0012	FINAL DESIGN DATA GATHER.		15	15	21JUL92	11AUG92	21JUL92	11AUG92	0	
0014	DATA GATHER. REVEALED PREF		120	120	12AUG92	01FEB93	12AUG92	01FEB93	0	
0016	DATA GATHER. STATED PREFER		120	120	12AUG92	01FEB93	12AUG92	01FEB93	0	
0021	PAX FC MODEL CALIBRATION		20	20	02FEB93	01MAR93	02FEB93	01MAR93	0	
0051	PAX FORECASTS		15	15	30MAR93	20APR93	30MAR93	20APR93	0	
1000	REVENUE FORECASTS	E	30	30	21APR93	02JUN93	21APR93	02JUN93	0	
0003	PAX FC RFP AND SELECTION		35	35	15MAY92	06JUL92	01JUN92	20JUL92	10	
0005	FINAL PAX FC STRATEGY		5-	5-	07JUL92	16SEP92	21JUL92	30SEP92	10	
0018	MODAL USE DATA DEMAND		60	60	12AUG92	05NOV92	06NOV92	01FEB93	60	
0007	PAX FC MODEL FORMULATION		20	20	17SEP92	15OCT92	05JAN93	01FEB93	75	
0011	EXISTING SOCIO-ECON. COND.		60	60	15JUN92	09SEP92	06NOV92	01FEB93	100	
0020	EXISTING SUPPLY DEFINITION		60	60	15JUN92	09SEP92	06NOV92	01FEB93	100	
0029	FUTURE SOCIO-ECON. SCENA.		80	80	10SEP92	04JAN93	09FEB93	02JUN93	105	
0030	FUTURE SUPPLY DEFINITION		80	80	10SEP92	04JAN93	09FEB93	02JUN93	105	

FIGURE 10.9 HSR PROJECT COMPUTER REPORT, CRITICAL PATH LIST. This is a CPM-based computer report of the detail activities discussed in Section 10.3 and identified as part of the studies to be awarded to consultants in phase 1 of the HSR project. In this report the activities are sorted by criticality, in ascending order, and early start date. Activity 0000 is a begin activity (B), and activity 1000 is the end activity (E). Shown are columns for orginal and remaining durations, early and late start and finish dates, and total float for each activity. *Note*: The activities, their durations, and the CPM loghic are hypothetical to illustrate scheduling as part of the project management system.

scheduling of activities through the use of imposed dates, the application of human resources, management decisions, or corporate or political agendas. The result of a detailed bar chart scheduling exercise may be seen in Fig. 10.10.

The CPM network that generates the grist for the PC mill which produces the scheduling reports is shown in Fig. 10.11. This CAD drawing is made by a graphics package running from a CPM application. The network logic is reflected in the activity lists and reports in Figs. 10.8 through 10.10. The most striking feature of any CPM type network is the amount of complexity that may be generated with even small networks. In this case there are only 18 activities, but when they are cast as a logic-driven network, including a range of relationships such as FS (finish to start), SF (start to finish), SS (start to start), and FF (finish to finish), and when these relationships are assigned values, the complexity grows exponentially.

When scheduling projects using CPM logic-driven networks it is most important to understand first the kind of complexity that may result, and second that it must be expected that many computer runs are required, sometimes called "massaging," to come up with useful information. Massaging, or the iterative process, is only possible with computer processing. One of the most complex CPM computer reports, but

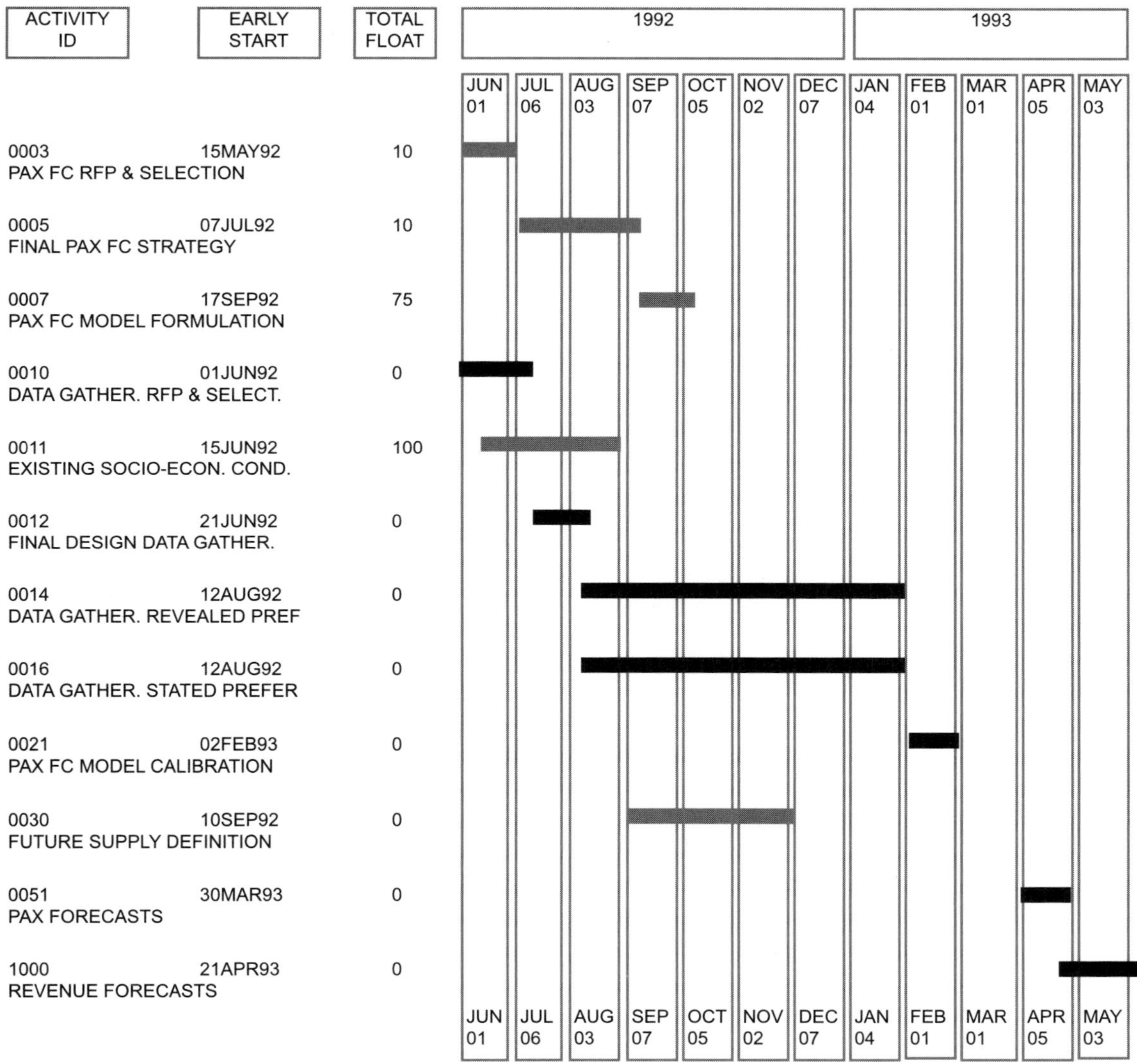

FIGURE 10.10 HSR PROJECT COMPUTER REPORT, BAR CHART. This is a computer bar chart report of some of the activities seen in Fig. 10.8. Some activities are not included so as to simplify the screen. The bars are plotted on early start/finish dates. The dark bars are on the critical path, the light bars have float. Neither the float values nor the late finish dates are plotted.

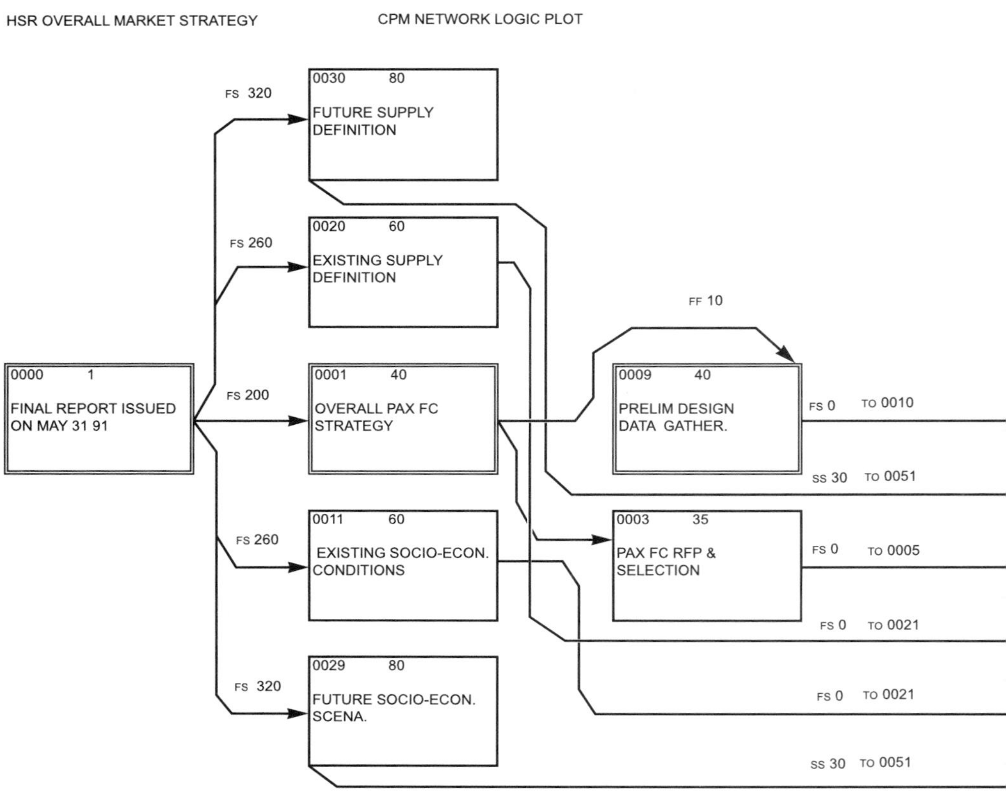

FIGURE 10.11 HSR PROJECT CPM NETWORK, CAD DRAWING. This is the CPM precedence diagram of the project activities developed for the case exercise. This CAD drawing is the result of computer arranging and processing the activities created in Section 10.3. The creation of the drawing is tied to its computer processing of the activity values and logic arrangements as seen in Fig. 10.12. This CPM network is the result of an iterative process of computer arranging, connecting, and massaging preselected activities until an acceptable schedule results.

without which it is difficult to massage a network, is the precedence relationship report seen in Fig. 10.12.

This computer output complements the CAD drawing process. The two go together. They depend on each other for serious CPM network planning as a precursor to logic-based, and resource-loaded project scheduling.

10.9 Summary

Megaprojects often start as a series of more or less unrelated studies, as agenda items of private-sector or public-interest bodies. It is sometimes a matter of "flying it up

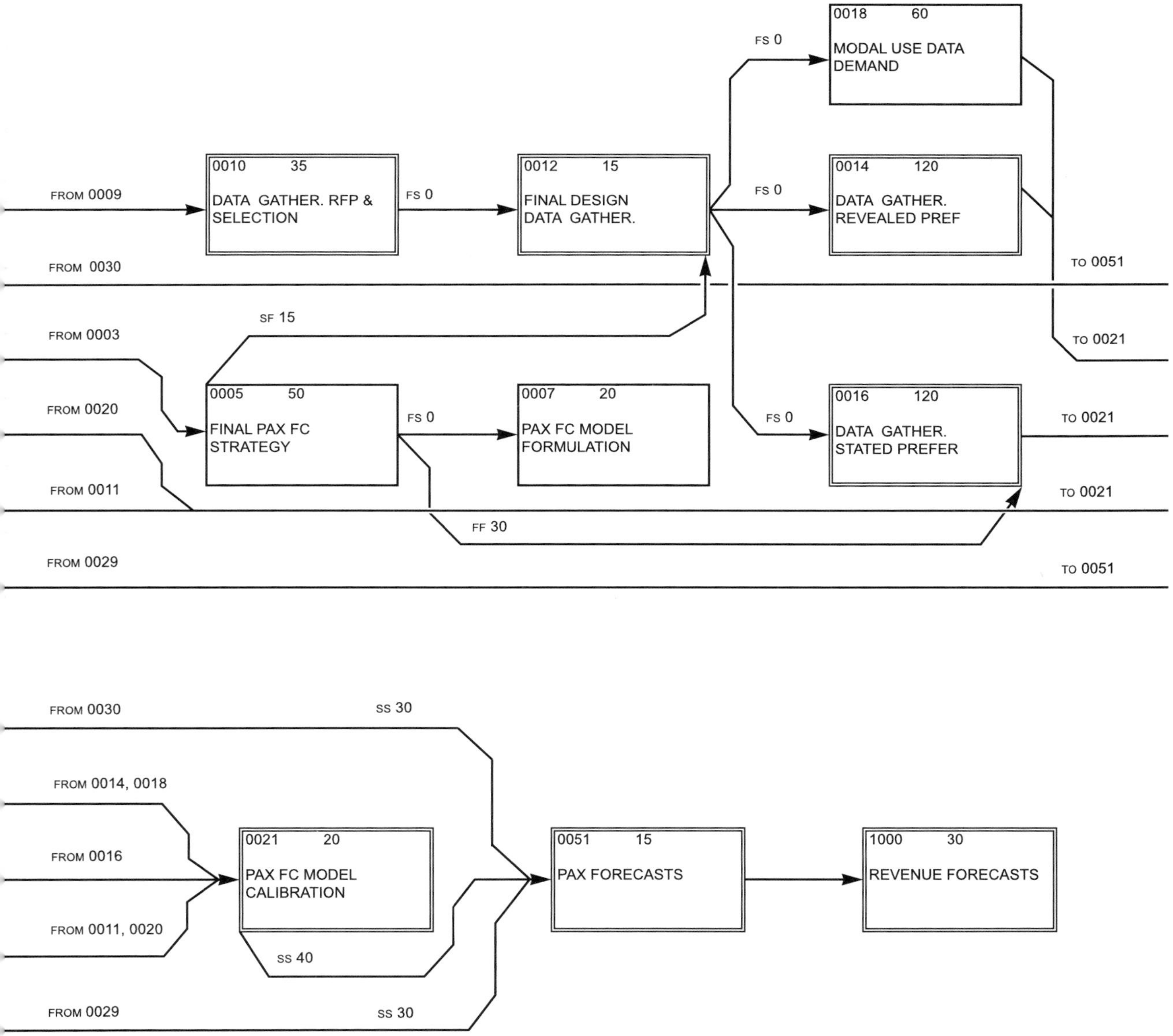

0018 60
MODAL USE DATA DEMAND
FS 0
0010 35
DATA GATHER. RFP & SELECTION
FROM 0009
FS 0
0012 15
FINAL DESIGN DATA GATHER.
FS 0
0014 120
DATA GATHER. REVEALED PREF
FROM 0030
TO 0051
SF 15
FROM 0003
TO 0021
0005 50
FINAL PAX FC STRATEGY
FROM 0020
FS 0
0007 20
PAX FC MODEL FORMULATION
FS 0
0016 120
DATA GATHER. STATED PREFER
TO 0021
FROM 0011
TO 0021
FF 30
FROM 0029
TO 0051
FROM 0030
SS 30
FROM 0014, 0018
FROM 0016
0021 20
PAX FC MODEL CALIBRATION
0051 15
PAX FORECASTS
1000 30
REVENUE FORECASTS
FROM 0011, 0020
SS 40
FROM 0029
SS 30

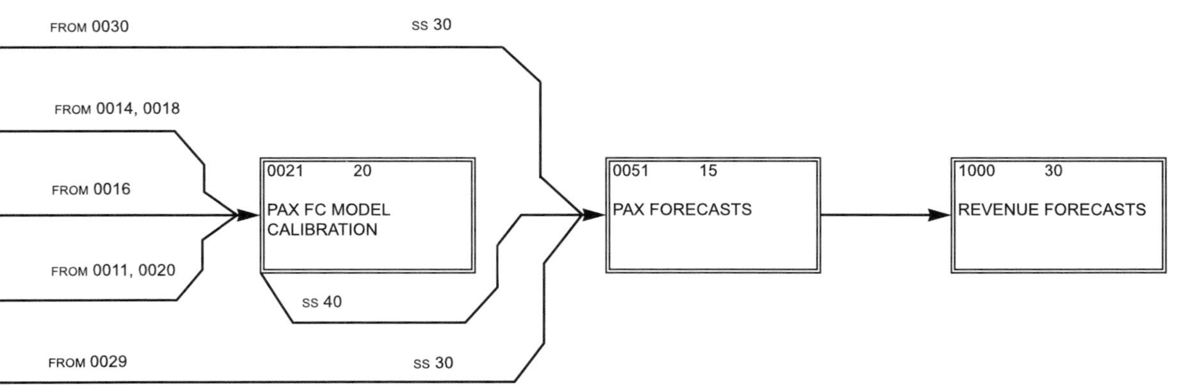

FIGURE 10.11 (CONTINUED).

FIGURE 10.12 HSR PROJECT COMPUTER REPORT, PRECEDENCE RELATIONSHIP. This is the precedence relationship report of the CPM diagram of project activities developed for the case exercise. This report is the result of computer arranging and processing the activities in Fig. 10.11. The creation of the drawing is tied to its computer processing, as seen in this figure. This CPM network is the result of an iterative process of computer arranging, connecting, and massaging preselected activities until an acceptable schedule results.

PRECEDENCE RELATIONSHIP REPORT

PROJECT: HSR OVERALL MARKET STRATEGY

PREDECESSOR	LAG TYPE	LAG ORIG	LAG REM	CAL ID	ACTIVITY DESCRIPTION	FLT	SUCCESSOR	LAG TYPE	LAG ORIG	LAG REM	CAL ID
					0000 FINAL REPORT 31 MAY 91	0	0001	FS	200	200	05
							0020	FS	260	260	05
							0011	FS	260	260	05
							0030	FS	320	320	05
							0029	FS	320	320	05
0000	FS	200	200	05	0001 OVERALL PAX FORECAST STRATEGY	0	0003	FS	0	0	05
							0009	FF	10	10	05
0001	FS	0	0	05	0003 PAX FC RFP & SELECTION	10	0005	FS	0	0	05
0003	FS	0	0	05	0005 FINAL PAX FC STRATEGY	10	0007	FS	0	0	05
							0012	SF	15	15	05
							0016	FF	30	30	05
0005	FS	0	0	05	0007 PAX FC MODEL FORMULATION	75	0021	FS	0	0	05
0001	FS	0	0	05	0009 PRELIM DESIGN DATA GATHER	0	0010	FS	0	0	05
0009	FS	0	0	05	0010 DATA GATHER. RFP & SELECTION	0	0012	FS	0	0	05
0000	FS	0	0	05	0011 EXISTING SOCIO-ECON. COND.	100	0021	FS	0	0	05

the flagpole to see whether anybody will salute it." In the case of the HSR project involving many levels of government and governmental departments, as well as the interest of the private-sector vendors of transportation systems and the construction industry, the initial studies, funded by government, aimed to compare HSR to existing modes of transport with the intention of proving the viability of HSR. This would be done by studying the relationship of revenues to passenger volumes, assessing technology, and considering preliminary routes.

This chapter looked at the HSR project with a view to set up its project management systems so that even in the very early study and analysis stages, the project would be coordinated by the five defined systems of project management. If these systems had been applied, the questions that were asked would not necessarily have been those that were asked.

As the intent of this chapter was to apply the concepts of project management to this kind of project, and to show as simply as possible the use of computer tools in the application, the illustrations worked with a combination of assumptions and assigned tasks.

PRECEDENCE RELATIONSHIP REPORT

PROJECT: HSR OVERALL MARKET STRATEGY

PREDECESSOR	LAG TYPE	LAG ORIG	LAG REM	CAL ID	ACTIVITY DESCRIPTION	FLT	SUCCESSOR	LAG TYPE	LAG ORIG	LAG REM	CAL ID
					0012	0					
					FINAL DESIGN DATA						
					GATHER.		0018	FS	0	0	05
0010	FS	0	0	05			0016	FS	0	0	05
0005	SF	15	15	05			0014	FS	0	0	05
					0014	0					
					DATA GATHER. REVEALED						
0000	FS	200	200	05	PREF		0021	FS	0	0	05
					0016	0					
					DATA GATHER. STATED						
0001	FS	0	0	05	PREFER		0021	FS	0	0	05
					0018	60					
					MODAL USE DATA						
0012	FS	0	0	05	DEMAND		0021	FS	0	0	05
					0020	100					
					EXISTING SUPPLY						
0000	FS	260	260	05	DEFINITION		0021	FS	0	0	05
					0021	0					
					PAX FC MODEL						
0007	FS	0	0	05	CALIBRATION		0051	SS	40	40	05
0016	FS	0	0	05							
0014	FS	0	0	05							
0018	FS	0	0	05							
0020	FS	0	0	05							
0011	FS	0	0	05							
					0029	105					
					FUTURE SOCIO-ECON.						
0000	FS	320	320	05	SCENA..		0051	SS	30	30	05
					0030	105					
					FUTURE SUPPLY						
0000	FS	320	320	05	DEFINITION		0051	SS	30	30	05
					0051	0					
					PAX FORECASTS						
0021	SS	40	40	05			1000	FS	0	0	05
0029	SS	40	40	05							
0030	SS	40	40	05							
					1000	0					
					REVENUE FORECASTS						
0051	FS	0	0	05							

FIGURE 10.12 (CONTINUED).

REFERENCES

Quebec/Ontario HSR Project, Passenger and Revenue Forecasting Terms of Reference, prepared by Transurb/IBI Group/Monenco Consortium, Project Manager, Proposal Call, 1992.

Quebec/Ontario HSR Project, Data Gathering: Travel Intercept Studies Terms of Reference, prepared by Transurb/IBI Group/Monenco Consortium, Project Manager, Proposal Call, 1992.

HSR Quebec–Windsor Corridor, HSR Impacts on the Urban System and Settlement Patterns, Notice to Bidders, prepared by Transurb/IBI Group/Monenco Consortium, Project Manager, Information Meeting re Proposal Call, 1993.

Project Management Systems Proposals for the Quebec/Ontario HSR Project, prepared by GSCON Group Project Management, George Suhanic, President:

1. Passenger and revenue forecasting proposal, June 1, 1992
2. Data gathering: travel intercept studies, June 12, 1992
3. Technology assessment, operating strategy, and costing, June 16, 1992
4. Preliminary routing assessment and costing, June 23, 1992

Information about the current status of the HSR project may be obtained from Government of Ontario, Jan Rush, Deputy Minister, Ministry of Transportation, 77 Wellesley Street West, Toronto, Ontario M7A 1Z8; Web site: www.mto.gov.on.ca.

QUESTIONS AND EXERCISES

Create a project management plan for the Quebec–Ontario HSR Project based on the final report dated August 1995, available as a supplement to this book from the publisher. Use commercially available or educational versions of enterprise and project management software.

This means learning the project scope, quality, and the requirements of the project as stated in the HSR final report; learning the capability of the selected information system and applying this technology to create databases of information suitable for the needs of project management, as represented in this textbook.

The project management systems approach promoted in this textbook is based on project definition as the first among equals of the five systems presented. In real life this may or may not be the way to start a project in terms of project management methodologies. Answers to this question may or may not follow the first-among-equals rule. The intent is that the student or practitioner of project management must work with what is available, which includes the availability of software and systems. This may mean not being able to follow the strictures of this textbook in terms of the development of a project management methodology.

Paying heed to these comments and admonitions, what recourse does the respondent to this question have available (1) on the Internet, (2) on the World Wide Web, and (3) in the marketplace? The answer to this question may be available in the software research and development field, in the academic world, or as current commercial software. Is it possible to answer this question with current software, or does the software have to be invented much as CPM was once invented, or as the PC was invented?

The intent of the question is to test not only the student or practitioner of project management, but also the Internet, the WWW, and the very widely marketed capabilities of enterprise and project management software. Keep in mind that there are many answers to this question.

INTERNATIONAL AIRPORT PROJECT CASE EXERCISE 11

11.1 Introduction

This case exercise is an extension of the theory of project definition and work breakdown structuring based on an airport project example discussed in Chapters 2 and 3 in Part 2 of this text. The intent here is to relate these kinds of megaprojects to real-life scales of project time, scope and magnitude, technical complexity, and political issues that invariably arise.

As an example of an international airport project time frame, its Web site reports that the Kansai International Airport, which opened in September 1993, was the subject of a site search in April 1968. The site was finally approved in 1986. Kansai issued its seventh five-year airport development plan in 1995.

International airports are built for many reasons. Sometimes they are built because there is a real need. A real need is one where there are no space or infrastructure facilities at the existing location to accommodate growth in air passenger or air cargo traffic. Or the available facilities have become obsolete, or too close to an overbuilt and crowded city center. It may be that the land being occupied by an existing airport can now be put to a higher or better use than the now obsolete airport, and a new state-of-the-art facility away from the congested area is planned and constructed.

Denver International Airport, according to its Web site, was the first major U.S. airport to be constructed in the past 25 years when it opened in February 1995.

Whatever the reason for its construction, a major international airport project is a megaproject of the first order. Consider some of the scope parameters that may accompany the delivery of an international airport project.

- *Land.* The requirement may be about 8000 hectares for the ultimate plan, plus controlled usage of up to another 8000 hectares of land exposed to airport operations, and perhaps another 16,000 hectares as a reserve for new or relocated airport-related commercial and industrial infrastructure and facilities. For example, Kansai is built on its own human-made island in Osaka Bay. Denver International Airport was constructed on 53 square miles (13,727.4 ha) of vacant land, one hour's drive from Denver.

- *Runways.* A major world-class international airport may have up to six runways in the final plan. The airport could open initially with two runways or, as a minimum opening-day requirement, one runway. Kansai International Airport opened with one runway in 1993. A second runway is part of the 1996–2000 fiscal year plan. Denver, on the other hand, opened with five runways. According to its Web site, a sixth runway is planned.

• *Terminal Buildings.* About 1000 m of terminal building facilities, complete with associated passenger processing facilities and commercial space, including car parking, able to accommodate up to about 20 aircraft at gate positions, may be adequate as a minimum two-runway airport. Kansai has a four-level passenger terminal in the international passenger gates area. At Denver, passengers travel from the terminal to the gates by shuttle.

• *Roads.* Four-lane access roads, two-lane access roads, and service roads are required to preserve and improve existing traffic and to accommodate the new requirements. Kansai required its own airport bridge as well as a ferry terminal. Denver is connected to the Interstate system through its own access road, Pena Boulevard, which a few years after opening was at capacity, requiring expansion.

• *Utilities.* Electric power, water, sewage, storm drainage, storm sewers, and environmental protection measures are needed. Denver provided an aircraft deicing system that aims to protect the environment by capturing deicing fluids through catch basins, piping, and storage in tanks for reuse.

• *Transportation Systems.* Planned transportation within the airport is essential, as is the mode of transport from the city to the airport for passengers, suppliers, fire and life safety providers, and airport employees. Kansai has its own dedicated railway with a railway station at the airport. Denver is designed for arrival by car.

• *Cargo and Maintenance.* Air cargo is a huge and growing component of air travel. Cargo terminals are usually fixtures of international airports because of the need to integrate with the critical services available for the convenience of air passengers. Airplane maintenance services are best located at the international airport because that is where the planes are most often when on the ground, and short turnaround times are crucial to the economic survival of the airline.

• *Cost.* Within megaproject limits, it is almost a matter of how much the ownership of the project wants to spend and when they want to spend it: $600 million, $1 billion, $2 billion, $6 billion, or $10 billion? Once the basic costs are met to accommodate landings and takeoffs of modern jets, the processing of passengers, safety and rescue, security, and the commercial and third-party facilities that are deemed essential for a minimum operation, the rest is a matter of what is economically feasible.

For example, the Kansai International Airport in Japan, opened in September 1993, was reported to have cost $16.5 billion in 1993, including the cost of the human-made island. The Denver International Airport built on vacant land was reported to have cost between $4.2 and $4.7 billion so far.

International airport project undertakings are planned for the ultimate facility size, say up to six runways. But the initial construction may be only to accommodate a minimum opening-day requirement, say, one runway. To ensure that future programmed growth and expansion from opening day to the ultimate airport capacity can occur without disruption to existing operations, and without demolition of what is there, it is necessary to conceive and plan the ultimate airport in the first instance. And that is where the systems of project management come in, as illustrated by this case exercise.

11.2 Project Definition

For the practice of project management, an airport project must be defined as the sum of its functions, plus full provision for its project consumables as first discussed in Section 2.5 and illustrated in Fig. 2.9. The object of the definition exercise is to scope the opening-day requirements in the form of a strategic coded structure.

As we know, project functions are those that are seen and used by the ultimate users of the finished facility, in this case the passengers and the airport services providers. From that perspective, the airport project can be expressed in the language of project definition presented as a basic tenet of project management in Chapter 2 and illustrated in a number of cases in previous chapters. To apply the systems of project management to an international airport project we would start with its definition, as seen in the preliminary airport project definition chart in Fig. 11.1.

The intent here is to illustrate the process of making such a structure as a key part of the process of project management. The reader may see this as just another hierarchical set of boxes. But to set the process in context, consider the management process and the technological difficulties in the development of such a structured list, including a scope, quality, and cost statement for each.

Simplistically the figure depicts a top-down definition tree of the functions that go into the makeup of the international airport project. This is considered to be defined to level 4, Elements. What makes it a project definition, and not just a laundry list of functions, is the inclusion of elements for design, management, and soft costs.

The other feature of the structure is the level 2 division of the undertaking into what are called "major projects." Some people may call these subprojects, some may say they are subprograms. The important issue is the use that the terminology is put to for project management purposes. The questions to be asked are: are these just words; are they meaningful for quality, scope, and cost control? or will the breakdown lose its validity by virtue of a lack of project management action?

Project management is nothing if not an iterative process. The number and the kind of definition charts required before management locks into the scope and quality picture are a function of executive actions and decision making. The elements seen in Fig. 11.1 may be considered as an early cut at the project. As it is possible that there may be many different elements and many project concepts, the definition elements are not coded.

Assuming that the airport project will consist of the elements shown, with some element name adjustments, as happened in the case history on which this exercise is

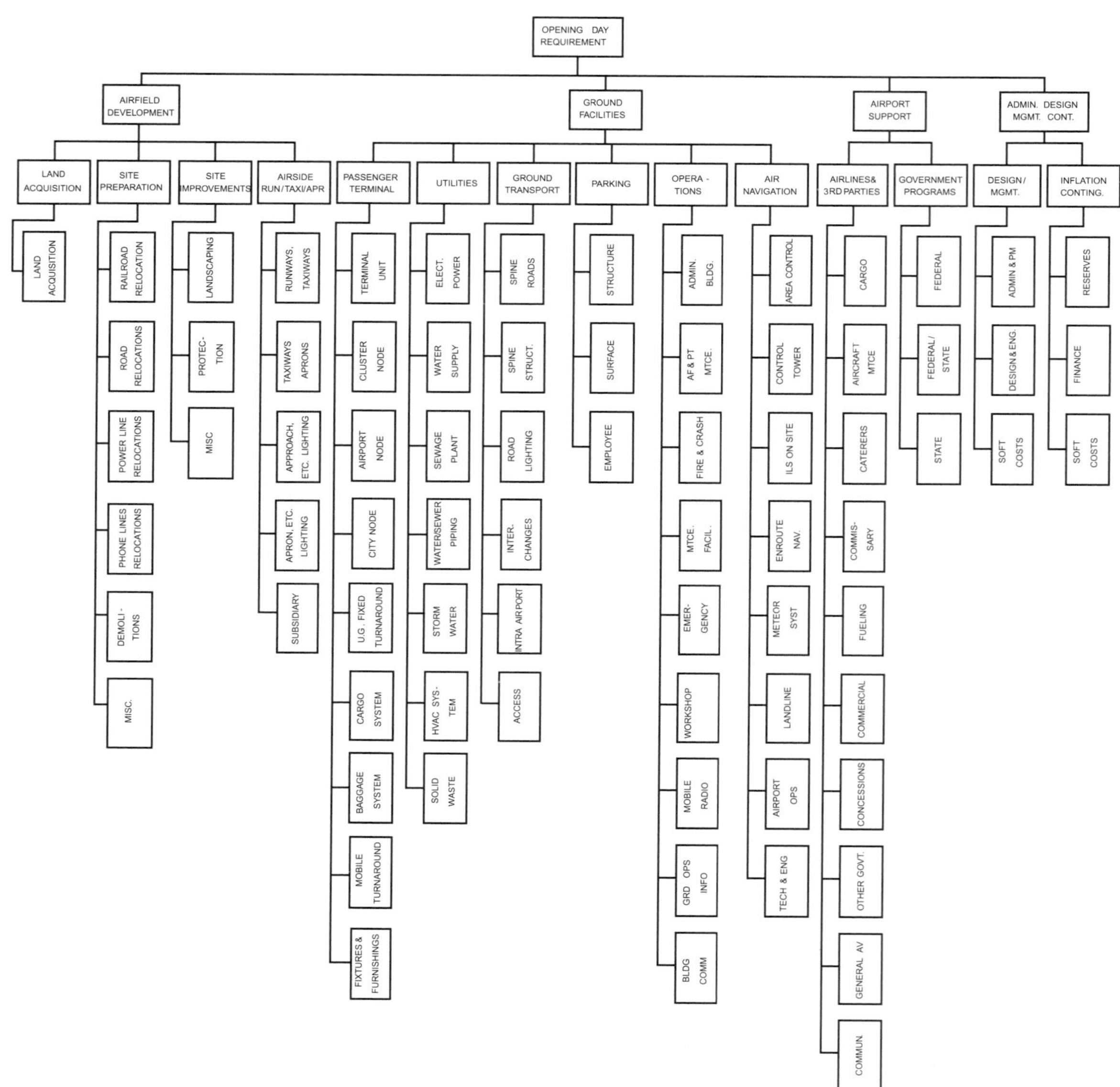

FIGURE 11.1 INTERNATIONAL AIRPORT PRELIMINARY PROJECT DEFINITION. This figure aims to set up the basis for a project management system for an international airport project. As it is an early cut at pulling together the disparate parts of the project, its intent is to grow the structure of deliverables that comprise the opening day requirements at level 1. The structure shows 4 major projects at level 2; 14 major elements a level 3; and 76 elements at level 4. The elements drive the scope of the major elements, and major elements drive the major projects, which are ultimately rendered as the project on its opening day.

based, the definition structure elements approved for processing are coded as seen in Fig. 11.2. (If there are incidental name changes between the two graphics or non-standard abbreviations, it is because of page size and graphic constraints.)

The elements, or the sum of the elements, defined by name and code in Fig. 11.2 represent the functions that will be left in place upon project completion. The elements under code items 9000 and 9900, representing design, management, and other soft costs, are consumed in the process of project delivery.

To understand the concept and complexity of project definition and code structures better, Fig. 11.3 provides proforma codes and capsule definitions for level 2 major projects, level 3 major elements, and the elements at level 4 in Fig. 11.2. These capsule definitions are the precursors to concept design, preliminary engineering, and estimating for budgeting the project and applying for project funding.

11.3 Work Breakdown

The project management team and the ownership should decide very early in the project life cycle, but from experience and according to megaproject track records rarely do, how to define and structure the project for delivery. Will the project be conceptualized, scoped, qualified, measured, and budgeted for and with the input of the users and their representatives, as urged in this book? Or will that exercise be bypassed and replaced by a WBS methodology from the beginning.

An activity-driven WBS approach is often preferred by professional project people in that it tends to remove from the process the difficult and time-consuming exercise of involving the ultimate users (the customers) in the definition process. In a sense, the project professionals say to senior ownership executives: "We know what you want." "Let us get on with it."

What the project professionals do then is convert the now current project into a mould based on a similar project boiler plate. This invariably sees the project cast as architectural and engineering drawings and specifications, quantities of earth, meters of runway, and cubic meters of concrete. This approach is intuitive for architects and engineers. It quickly goes to visual pictures of the project based on the traditional "need/design/build" process.

Corporate chief executive officers prefer that projects go into this mode sooner rather than later because it brings the project out into public view much earlier. It shows progress. It provides photo opportunities. From experience, it does not do much for scope, quality, and cost control. Invariably, because they were not adequately consulted, the project's customers are short-changed.

Every project functional deliverable sooner or later has to go into its tasks phase, or WBS mode. The structural level at which this occurs depends on many factors in the delivery of the project, including the makeup of the elements themselves. In megaproject work it is not likely that we would take the project at level 1, the opening-day requirement, and process it through the WBS, although it is possible to do so. The level 2 major projects are also a possibility for phased WBS treatment. At

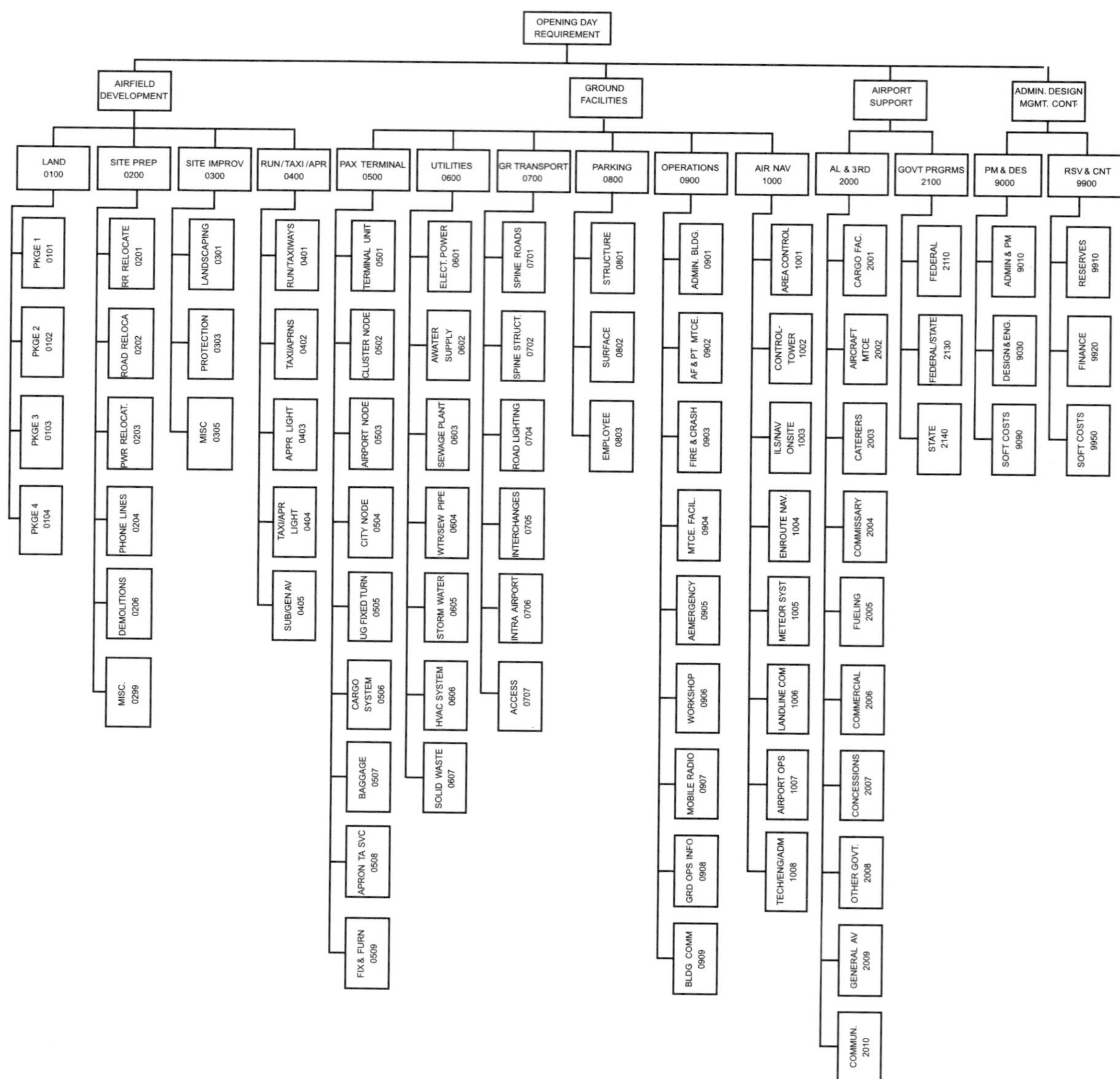

FIGURE 11.2 INTERNATIONAL AIRPORT CODED PROJECT DEFINITION. This figure is the successor to the preliminary definition seen if Fig. 11.1. What makes it the successor is the consensus of the project team and the approval by top management that these elements will make up the project. The approval process leads to progressive scope definition, design, engineering, and budget estimating. The code system is assigned and applied to facilitate project control and coordination.

INTERNATIONAL AIRPORT PROJECT: DEFINITION STATEMENTS

MAJOR PROJECT	ELEMENT CODE	ELEMENT DESCRIPTION	SCOPE/QUALITY SHORT STATEMENT
AD	0101	LAND PKGE 1	RAILROAD LANDS SCOPE PACKAGE ONE
AD	0102	LAND PKGE 2	RAILROAD LANDS SCOPE PACKAGE TWO
AD	0103	LAND PKGE 3	HYDRO POWER LINES LANDS SCOPE PACKAGE
AD	0104	LAND PKGE 4	COUNTY ROADS LANDS SCOPE PACKAGE
AD	0201	RR RELOCATE.	RAILROAD RELOCATIONS AND RECONSTRUCTION PACKAGES
AD	0202	ROAD RELOCAT.	ROAD RELOCATIONS AND CLOSURE PACKAGES
AD	0203	PWR RELOCAT.	POWERLINE RELOCATIONS PACKAGES
AD	0204	PHONE LINES.	TELEPHONE AND COMMUNICATIONS RELOCATIONS PACKAGES
AD	0206	DEMOLITIONS	DEMOLITIONS AND REMOVALS PACKAGES
AD	0299	MISC.	SPECIAL REMOVALS AND RELOCATIONS PACKAGES
AD	0301	LANDSCAPING	REHABILITATIONS, IMPROVEMENTS AND LANDSCAPING
AD	0303	PROTECTION	PERIMETER AND INTERIOR SECURITY FENCING AND LIGHTING
AD	0305	MISC	ENVIRONMENTALLY SENSITIVE AND HISTORICAL SITES
AD	0401	RUN/TAXIWAYS	RUNWAY "A" AND ASSOCIATED TAXIWAYS "AIRSIDE"
AD	0402	TAXI/APRNS	TAXIWAYS AND ASSOCIATED APRONS "LANDSIDE"
AD	0403	APR/LIGHT	APRON LIGHTING AND ITS PRIMARY AND EMERG. POWER SUPPLY
AD	0404	TAXI/APR LIGHT	TAXI/APR LIGHTING AND ITS PRIMARY AND EMERG. POWER SUPPLY
AD	0405	SUB/GEN AV LIGHT	SUBSIDIARY AND GENERAL AVIATION LIGHTING
GF	0501	TERMINAL UNIT	PASSENGER TERMINAL AREA FROM "CURBSIDE" TO "AIRSIDE"
GF	0502	CLUSTER NODE	MODULAR TERMINAL UNITS AT FIXED NODES
GF	0503	AIRPORT NODE	NODES WITH PROCESSING CAPABILITY ADJACENT TO AIRCRAFT
GF	0504	CITY NODE	OFFSITE NODES WITH FULL CAPABILITY TO PROCESS PASSENGERS
GF	0505	UG FIXED TURN	UNDERGROUND FIXED TURNAROUND SERVICES
GF	0506	CARGO SYSTEM	CARGO COMPLEX LOCATED CLOSE TO THE AIRPORT CENTROID
GF	0507	BAGGAGE	PASSENGER BAGGAGE SYSTEMS FROM "AIRSIDE" TO "CURBSIDE"
GF	0508	APRON TA SVC	MOBILE AND FLEXIBLE APRON TURNAROUND SERVICES
GF	0509	FIX & FURN	PASSENGER-RELATED FIXTURES AND FURNISHINGS
GF	0601	ELECT POWER	TOTAL ENERGY PLANT DELIVERING STEAM AND ELECTRIC POWER
GF	0602	WATER SUPPLY	GROUND WATER SOURCE
GF	0603	SEWAGE PLANT	COMPLETE ENVIRONMENTALLY SENSITIVE TREATMENT FACILITY
GF	0604	WTR/SEW PIPE	WATER SUPPLY AND SEWER COLLECTION SYSTEMS
GF	0605	STORM WATER	STORM WATER CONTROL SYSTEM INCLUDING PIPING AND GRADING
GF	0606	HVAC SYSTEM	ALL ASPECTS OF HEATING, VENTILATING AND AIR CONDITIONING
GF	0607	SOLID WASTE	A COMPLETE SOLID WASTE MANAGEMENT SYSTEM
GF	0701	SPINE ROADS	SPINE ROADS AND SPURS FEEDING THE TERMINAL AREA
GF	0702	SPINE STRUCT.	SPINE STRUCTURES FACILITATING GRADE SEPARATIONS
GF	0704	ROAD LIGHTING	THE CONCEPT OF ALL ROAD LIGHTING
GF	0705	INTERCHANGES	INTERSECTIONS OF AIRPORT ROADS WITH FREEWAYS
GF	0706	INTRA AIRPORT	INTRA AIRPORT ROAD SYSTEMS
GF	0707	ACCESS ROADS	ROADS ONSITE OR OFFSITE NECESSITATED BY THE NEW AIRPORT

LEGEND:
AD - AIRFIELD DEVELOPMENT
GF - GROUND FACILITIES
AS - AIRPORT SUPPORT
MA - MANAGEMENT AND ADMINISTRATION

FIGURE 11.3 INTERNATIONAL AIRPORT PROJECT DEFINITION STATEMENTS. The scope and quality definition of a project element is difficult, time-consuming, and expensive because input is required from many skills located in different organizations and working to different agendas. At the same time, few elements are stand alone. They are invariably interconnected and may influence each other. The above are short statements which start the process of definition of the named and coded elements. An element may be defined by specifications, sketches, performance criteria, flow sheets, quantities, and ultimately a cost estimate. If these criteria do not exist, the item is just not defined.

INTERNATIONAL AIRPORT PROJECT: DEFINITION STATEMENTS

MAJOR PROJECT	ELEMENT CODE	ELEMENT DESCRIPTION	SCOPE/QUALITY SHORT STATEMENT
GF	0801	PARKING STRUCT.	STRUCTURE FOR PASSENGER SHORT TERM PARKING
GF	0802	SURFACE PARK.	SURFACE PARKING FOR PASSENGER LONG TERM PARKING
GF	0803	EMPLOYEE PARK.	SURFACE EMPLOYEE PARKING
GF	0901	ADMIN BLDG.	AIRPORT ADMINISTRATION BUILDING
GF	0902	AF & PT MTCE.	AIRFIELD AND PASSENGER TERMINAL MAINTENANCE FACILITIES
GF	0903	FIRE & CRASH	FIRE AND CRASH RESCUE FACILITIES AND ITS EQUIPMENT
GF	0904	MTCE .FACIL.	MAINTENANCE FACILITIES FOR SNOW REMOVAL, FLOODING, ETC.
GF	0905	EMERGENCY	EMERGENCY FACILITIES FOR OTHER THAN FIRES AND CRASHES, E.G., STORM
GF	0906	WORKSHOP	WORKSHOP AND TOOLS FOR REPAIRS OF BUILDINGS, FIXTURES, ETC.
GF	0907	MOBILE RADIO	WIRELESS, PCS, AND CELLULAR SYSTEMS FOR SAFETY AND SECURITY
GF	0908	GRD OPS INFO	GROUND CONTROL TOWER AND ITS INFORMATION SYSTEMS
GF	0909	BLDG COMM	AN ALTERNATE COMMUNICATION SYSTEM AS BACKUP TO TELEPHONE
GF	1001	AREA CONTROL	OVERALL AIRCRAFT MOVEMENT CONTROL AND COORDINATION
GF	1002	CONTROL TOWER	THE ENTIRE CONTROL TOWER AND ITS SYSTEMS
GF	1003	ILS/NAV ONSITE	THE ENTIRE INSTRUMENT LANDING AND NAVIGATION ONSITE SYSTEM
GF	1004	ENROUTE NAV.	THE ENTIRE AIRPORT NAVIGATION OFFSITE SYSTEM
GF	1005	METEOR SYST	WEATHER ANALYSIS AND DELIVERY
GF	1006	LANDLINE COMM	TELEPHONE, AND OTHER HARDWIRE COMMUNICATION SYSTEMS
GF	1007	AIRPORT OPS	AIRPORT OPERATIONS CONCERNS ASPECTS OF ONSITE ACTIVITIES
GF	1008	TECH/ENG/ADMIN	TECHNICAL, ENGINEERING AND ADMINISTRATIVE SPACES AND EQUIPMENT
AS	2001	CARGO FAC.	CARGO BUILDINGS AND SYSTEMS REQUIREMENTS
AS	2002	AIRCRAFT MTCE	DEDICATED AIRCRAFT MAINTENANCE AND TURNAROUND FACILITIES
AS	2003	CATERERS	AIRCRAFT AND GROUND CATERING FACILITIES AND REQUIREMENTS
AS	2004	COMMISSARY	COMMISSARY WAREHOUSING, SECURITY AND DELIVERY SYSTEMS
AS	2005	FUELING	AIRCRAFT AND DEDICATED AIRPORT VEHICLES FUELING SYSTEMS
AS	2006	NON-PT COMM.	NON-PASSENGER TERMINAL COMMERCIAL SUCH AS AIRPORT HOTELS, ETC.
AS	2007	PT CONCESSIONS	PASSENGER TERMINAL CONCESSIONS SUCH AS RESTAURANTS, CAR RENTALS
AS	2008	OTHER GOVT.	OTHER GOVERNMENT SUCH AS MILITARY, CUSTOMS, IMMIGRATION
AS	2009	GENERAL AV	PRIVATE JETS, TRAFFIC REPORTERS, RECREATIONAL
AS	2010	COMMUN.	TRANSMITTER AND RECEIVER STATIONS AND AVIATION-RELATED MOBILES
AS	2110	FEDERAL	ANY FEDERAL GOVERNMENT-RELATED PROGRAM
AS	2130	FEDERAL/STATE	ANY COOPERATIVE FEDERAL/STATE GOVERNMENT-RELATED PROGRAM
AS	2140	STATE	ANY STATE SPONSORED OR RELATED PROGRAM
MA	9010	ADMIN & PM	ADMINISTRATION AND PROJECT MANAGEMENT OF THE AIRPORT PROJECT
MA	9030	DESIGN & ENG	PLANNING, DESIGN AND ENGINEERING OF THE AIRPORT PROJECT
MA	9090	SOFT COSTS	PROJECT RELATED SOFT COSTS SUCH AS COST OF MONEY, INSURANCE, ETC.
MA	9910	RESERVES	CONTINGENCY AMOUNTS FOR INFLATION, RISKS, UNKNOWNS
MA	9920	FINANCE	CONTINGENCY AMOUNTS IN RELATION TO FINANCING THE PROJECT
MA	9950	SOFT COSTS	CONTINGENCY AMOUNTS IN RELATION TO SOFT COSTS
This is a suggested code for level 2 major projects, based on Figure 11.2	This code is based on level 4 element codes in Figure 11.2	These descriptions are based on Figure 11.2	These scope/quality short statements are based on a case history, and are provided as examples of the development of a project scope. The statements would be expanded by words and drawings, as progress is made, and estimated until budgets are established. Project control would aim to manage scope and cost to bring the project in to the expected quality, and on budget.

FIGURE 11.3 (CONTINUED).

level 3 there are 14 functional areas, and they too could be converted into activities and tasks, based on task definitions in this book.

The project management methodology adopted in this case breaks the project down into its deliverable elements at level 4. Experience dictated that these level 4 elements needed to be converted into WBS tasks. To achieve this, each element is assigned to and coded as a standard or typical project phase. The fundamentals of airport project WBSs were introduced in Chapter 3. Section 3.7.1 provides a prototypical airport WBS in Fig. 3.10.

In practice not each element is handled individually as a distinct phase. To accommodate the planning, design, and construction process, some elements can only be designed or constructed in conjunction with other elements. On the other hand, some element or phase items need to be broken down further for scheduling or assignment to resource-driven packages.

To keep the illustration simple, the discussion of elements or phases is limited to the major element 0800, Parking, as seen in Fig. 11.4. The project pyramid (if the entire structure were drawn) would now have five levels, from level 1, the objective, to level 5, the element phases.

To carry the process further, two of the three elements or phases comprising construction are then broken down further to demonstrate a number of construction packages at level 6 of the hierarchy. (As an aside, some project management computer programmers say that the lower level units are the "children" of a higher level "parent." This is not so. In project work the upper functional level cannot exist without the lower elemental level. I do not see this as a parent/child relationship.)

Also shown in Fig. 11.4 are boxed notations of level numbers and short descriptions. Each level is coded as a connected hierarchical set of position-sensitive numerics.

In considering the hierarchical structure that results from this kind of exercise it is to be expected that the PDS rules set out in this text will not apply in the same way to all vertical area pyramids. The way to overcome this is through the judicious and timely application of the definition and breakdown procedures. In other words, a structure has to grow as a management process and not as a system technology. But the rules of both definition and breakdown must be followed to achieve the intended project management objectives.

Second, in Fig. 11.4 we made one combined structure showing both the PDS and the WBS after having said that they are distinct structures serving different needs. Although not differentiated here, the codes in fact show two of the three code systems used for project cost control: (1) the PDS code for the project budget and (2) the WBS code for confirmation of the project budget through packages. The third and final budget check occurs through the assignment of packages to the project functional organization, coded as an OBS, generated through purchase orders, contracts, and the owner's in-house work assignments.

11.4 Functional Organization

There is a general propensity to draw project organizations as military hierarchies with many levels of authority and vertical reporting lines. This approach to the delivery of services is also seen in government agencies, bureaucracies, and large multidepartmental corporations. These kinds of people structures are particularly troubling for megaproject work in which the look of the elements of the project is constantly changing and never in the same stage for very long. If decision making is a multilevel hierarchical exercise, chances are that the process bogs down in its own

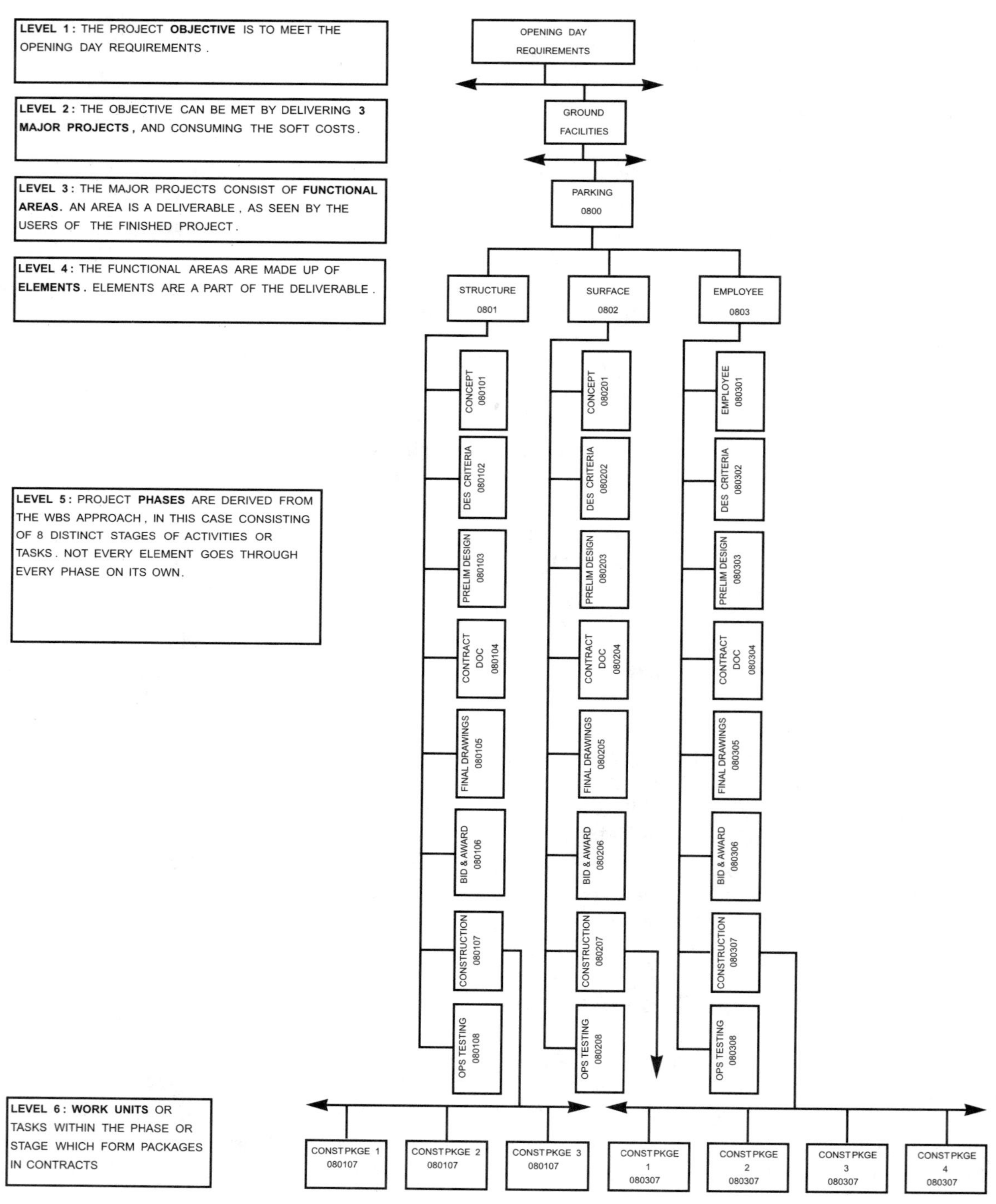
LEVEL 1: THE PROJECT OBJECTIVE IS TO MEET THE OPENING DAY REQUIREMENTS.
LEVEL 2: THE OBJECTIVE CAN BE MET BY DELIVERING 3 MAJOR PROJECTS, AND CONSUMING THE SOFT COSTS.
LEVEL 3: THE MAJOR PROJECTS CONSIST OF FUNCTIONAL AREAS. AN AREA IS A DELIVERABLE, AS SEEN BY THE USERS OF THE FINISHED PROJECT.
LEVEL 4: THE FUNCTIONAL AREAS ARE MADE UP OF ELEMENTS. ELEMENTS ARE A PART OF THE DELIVERABLE.
LEVEL 5: PROJECT PHASES ARE DERIVED FROM THE WBS APPROACH, IN THIS CASE CONSISTING OF 8 DISTINCT STAGES OF ACTIVITIES OR TASKS. NOT EVERY ELEMENT GOES THROUGH EVERY PHASE ON ITS OWN.
LEVEL 6: WORK UNITS OR TASKS WITHIN THE PHASE OR STAGE WHICH FORM PACKAGES IN CONTRACTS
OPENING DAY REQUIREMENTS
GROUND FACILITIES
PARKING 0800
STRUCTURE 0801
SURFACE 0802
EMPLOYEE 0803
CONCEPT 080101
DES CRITERIA 080102
PRELIM DESIGN 080103
CONTRACT DOC 080104
FINAL DRAWINGS 080105
BID & AWARD 080106
CONSTRUCTION 080107
OPS TESTING 080108
CONCEPT 080201
DES CRITERIA 080202
PRELIM DESIGN 080203
CONTRACT DOC 080204
FINAL DRAWINGS 080205
BID & AWARD 080206
CONSTRUCTION 080207
OPS TESTING 080208
EMPLOYEE 080301
DES CRITERIA 080302
PRELIM DESIGN 080303
CONTRACT DOC 080304
FINAL DRAWINGS 080305
BID & AWARD 080306
CONSTRUCTION 080307
OPS TESTING 080308
CONST PKGE 1 080107
CONST PKGE 2 080107
CONST PKGE 3 080107
CONST PKGE 1 080307
CONST PKGE 2 080307
CONST PKGE 3 080307
CONST PKGE 4 080307

red tape, making communication chaotic with people waiting for approval decisions and progress instructions.

An international airport project is achievable only through massive input by a vast array of skills, professions, and private and public cooperation. It is likely that individual organizations will have various internal structures, but as far as their relationship to the project is concerned, the flatter the structure, the easier the communications. An early preliminary version of the organizational structure of the case exercise is presented in Fig. 11.5.

This approach to organization for project work aims to show a participation and communication structure as compared to a command hierarchy. Obviously someone is in command, otherwise there is confusion and chaos. But the structure needs to be a function of the agreement between the project and the service provider. If, for example, electric power for the airport can only be provided by the local power utility, its cooperation and level of service are not coerced by "commands" but by the kind of cooperation and communication set up between a client (the airport project manager's team) and the supplier (the power utility). This would also be the case in relation to local and state governments, federal regulatory agencies, the airlines, and large commercial service groups required to service the airport.

Thus what the project organization consists of, particularly at the professional and working levels, is a massive multidisciplinary communication network of equally powerful groups of people whose common objective is the delivery of the international airport.

11.5 Project Cost

Cost estimating and budgeting follows the coded definition structure outlined in Fig. 11.2. In this case the most meaningful cost information in all likelihood would occur at level 4 of the definition structure, where the elements are identified and coded.

The basis for the cost estimating and cost control system can be set up as seen in Fig. 11.6. Listed are the coded elements for areas 0100, Land, through 2100, Government Programs, and the areas 9000, Project Management and Design, and 9900, Reserves and Contingencies.

FIGURE 11.4 INTERNATIONAL AIRPORT PARKING CONSTRUCTION PACKAGES. There is a fine line in converting a project element, such as a parking garage, from a function into the activities that will lead to its delivery. In this case airport parking is defined as three distinct functions, each of which is then processed through eight phases. Each element/phase would require tasks for its delivery. The tasks would be parts of packages, or their own packages. Shown are only a few construction phase packages for the parking structure, 0801, and for employee parking, 0803.

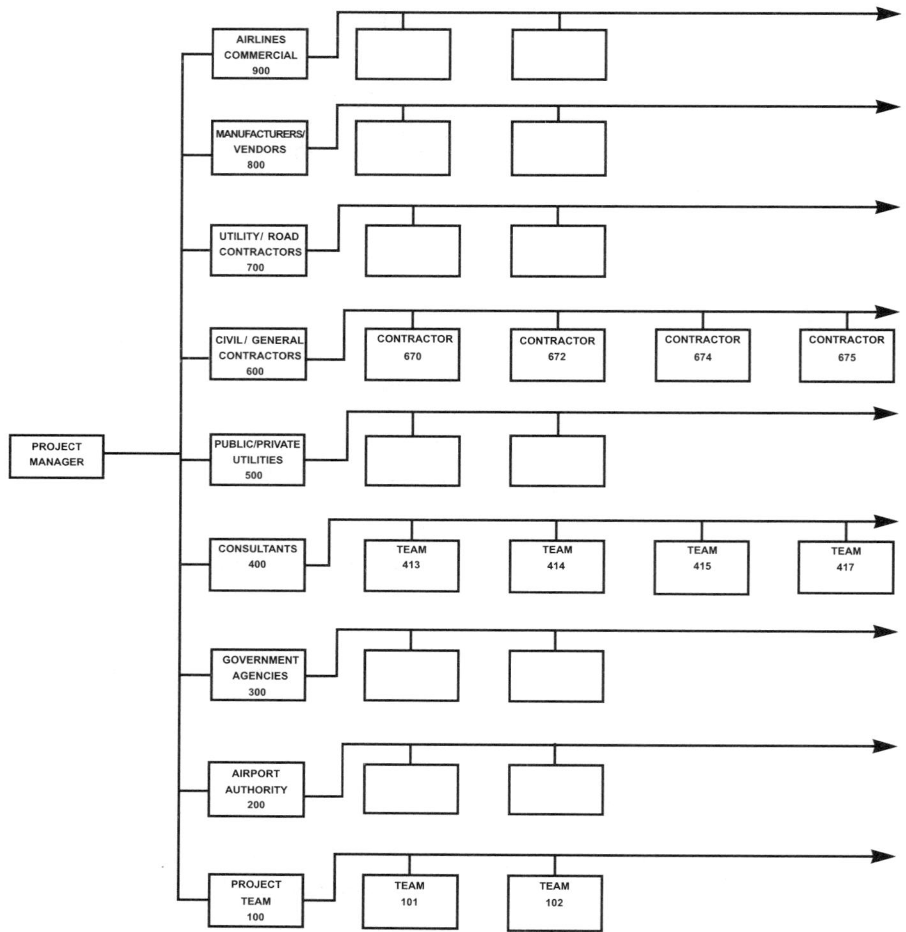

FIGURE 11.5 INTERNATIONAL AIRPORT FUNCTIONAL ORGANIZATION. An airport project is delivered by a range of functional groups who have only one common goal: their role in the project. Their role may be mandated by law, e.g., the FAA, responsible for all aspects of aviation in the United States, would be only one of a number of governmental agencies (300). Another government agency would be GAO, responsible for monitoring the expenditures of federal government funds. Airlines and car rental agencies (900) have a major role in the design and construction of their modules in the passenger terminals. Manufacturers and vendors (800) hold contracts for elements and systems like baggage handling, transportation shuttles, and information systems. Then there are the architects, engineers, consultants, contractors, and subcontractors, all holding agreements not only with the airport authority, but with each other and, with others like utilities and the interstate highway system. For example, in 1995 according to the DIA Web site, there were 324 construction contracts and 3124 subcontracts for the Denver International Airport project.

INTERNATIONAL AIRPORT PROJECT: SUMMARY BY ELEMENTS

ELEMENT CODE	ELEMENT DESCRIPTION	BUDGET AMOUNT	APPROVED CHANGES	EXP & CMT. TO DATE	FORECAST FIN. COST	AMT. AUTH. REDISTRIB.	OVER / UNDER
0101	LAND PKGE 1						
0102	LAND PKGE 2						
0103	LAND PKGE 3						
0104	LAND PKGE 4						
0201	RR RELOCATE						
0202	ROAD RELOCA						
0203	PWR RELOCAT.						
0204	PHONE LINES						
0206	DEMOLITIONS						
0299	MISC.						
0301	LANDSCAPING						
0303	PROTECTION						
0305	MISC						
0401	RUN/TAXIWAYS						
0402	TAXI/APRNS						
0403	APPR/LIGHT						
0404	TAXI/APR LIGHT						
0405	SUB/GEN AV						
0501	TERMINAL UNIT						
0502	CLUSTER NODE						
0503	AIRPORT NODE						
0504	CITY NODE						
0505	UG FIXED TURN						
0506	CARGO SYSTEM						
0507	BAGGAGE						
0508	APRON TA SVC						
0509	FIX & FURN						
0601	ELECT POWER						
0602	WATER SUPPLY						
0603	SEWAGE PLANT						
0604	WTR/SEW PIPE						
0605	STORM WATER						
0606	HVAC SYSTEM						
0607	SOLID WASTE						
0701	SPINE ROADS						
0702	SPINE STRUCT.						
0704	ROAD LIGHTING						

FIGURE 11.6 INTERNATIONAL AIRPORT PROJECT COSTING. This is to show that you must cost that which you define and code. In this case the airport project is shown defined and coded at level 4, Elements. The scope and quality definition of an element is incomplete unless its cost is known. Cost, in the case where funding is being appropriated, requires that the cost estimate be accurate on the order of ±10%. It is this estimate that would go into the budget amount column. The other five columns are the result of project progress. The sum of the budget amounts is the project budget bottom line, that is, the project budget which the project manager guarantees to within 10%.

The six columns in addition to the code and description columns are typical for cost control purposes. As discussed in Chapter 5 and elsewhere in this text, in the project management systems approach action reports, exception reports, and accounting status reports are derived from a database of cost and expenditure information kept by structured code sets derived from the PDS, WBS, and OBS numbers. From this database it is possible to produce cost and expenditure reports for any level of management at any level of the three coded structures.

11.6 Project Schedule

Since the availability of funding is always a difficult problem in megaproject work, the overall project schedule could be most influenced by cash-flow considerations. The schedule may be forced to fit the available cash flow.

INTERNATIONAL AIRPORT PROJECT: SUMMARY BY ELEMENTS

ELEMENT CODE	ELEMENT DESCRIPTION	BUDGET AMOUNT	APPROVED CHANGES	EXP & CMT. TO DATE	FORECAST FIN. COST	AMT. AUTH. REDISTRIB.	OVER / UNDER
0705	INTERCHANGES						
0706	INTRA AIRPORT						
0707	ACCESS						
0801	STRUCTURE						
0802	SURFACE						
0803	EMPLOYEE						
0901	ADMIN BLDG.						
0902	AF& PT MTCE.						
0903	FIRE & CRASH						
0904	MTCE .FACIL.						
0905	EMERGENCY						
0906	WORKSHOP						
0907	MOBILE RADIO						
0908	GRD OPS INFO						
0909	BLDG COMM						
1001	AREA CONTROL						
1002	CONTROL TOWER						
1003	ILS/NAV ONSITE						
1004	ENROUTE NAV.						
1005	METEOR SYST						
1006	LANDLINE COMM						
1007	AIRPORT OPS						
1008	TECH/ENG/ADMIN						
2001	CARGO FAC.						
2002	AIRCRAFT MTCE						
2003	CATERERS						
2004	COMMISSARY						
2005	FUELING						
2006	COMMERCIAL						
2007	CONCESSIONS						
2008	OTHER GOVT.						
2009	GENERAL AV						
2010	COMMUN.						
2110	FEDERAL						
2130	FEDERAL/STATE						
2140	STATE						
9010	ADMIN & PM						
9030	DEIGN & ENG						
9090	SOFT COSTS						
9910	RESERVES						
9920	FINANCE						
9930	SOFT COSTS						

FIGURE 11.6 (CONTINUED).

A cash-flow constraint may only occur after the project has received some form of approval. For a new green-field international airport project the availability of land may be a contentious issue, and therefore considered to be on the critical path. Land use is a function of many considerations, including the ultimate airport size, its location, and the airport configuration itself.

The use of land and its location, the airport configuration, the cost, and therefore the schedule all flow from site planning. Site planning flows from passenger volumes, which are driven by need, growth, and marketing.

We pull these disparate issues together by considering them as project elements, as seen in Figs. 11.1 and 11.2. The elements are expanded as scope definitions in Fig. 11.3. They are then processed as phases, as seen in Fig. 11.4. It is these elements and phases that become the basis for the international airport project schedule.

In the case upon which this exercise is modeled, the project schedule was made as a CPM network, as illustrated in Fig. 6.12 in Chapter 6, which shows only the airport passenger terminal activities.

The CPM network was computer processed and massaged to calculate early and late start and finish dates based on the critical path, and float values for all activities. A sample of the results is presented as a bar chart in Fig. 6.13. Both the network and the bar chart incorporate the element code, the phase code, and the organizational code.

11.7 Summary

This chapter looks to put into perspective the development of a project management system for a megaproject such as an international airport. This is done by sketching out aspects of components of project management such as project definition, work breakdown, and cost and schedule control, and anecdotally relating these issues to two current world-class airport projects, Kansai International Airport in Japan and Denver International Airport in the United States.

The intent is to illustrate big project complexity, which can only be solved and delivered by groups of skilled resources whose only common ground is the project on which they are all working at the time.

The exercise, referring to previous chapters, depicts how the definition codes convert to task codes and functional organization codes, and how they are all merged for computer cost and schedule control.

Note: This chapter is based on my experience as project management consultant for the new Montreal International Airport project and as project management and scheduling consultant for the new Toronto International Airport project. Both consulting assignments occurred at the earliest project definition phases of the respective projects. The Montreal airport was eventually constructed by others and renamed Mirabel. The Toronto airport was never constructed. My involvement on both projects was to create methods to define and scope the projects as deliverables and as activities and packages for planning, costing, and scheduling.

The project files are the references. These files comprise project definition structures, work breakdown structures, project phases and stages lists, coding and classifying systems of the project deliverables, and the functional organizations, scheduling plans, and drawings, and computer printouts of the results of the project management processes.

QUESTIONS AND EXERCISES

11.1. Write a scope and quality definition of the major international airport project, code 0800, Parking, based on the three functional areas 0801, Parking Structure; 0802, Surface Parking, and 0803, Employee Parking, as seen in Fig. 11.4, based on the following assumptions:

Passenger cars, 4000

Passenger parking spaces in structure, 1000

Passenger surface parking spaces, 3000

Employee cars, 400

Employee parking spaces in structure, 100

Employee surface parking spaces, 300

Download or otherwise obtain commercial or educational cost information for the construction in your area of these functions from educational or commercial sources on the Internet, such as R. S. Means at www.rsmeans.com, Richardson Engineering Services, Inc., at www.resi.net, or Timberline at www.timberline.com.

Alternatively, assume the following ballpark cost estimates:

Parking structure costs $20,000 per car

Surface parking costs $5000 per car

Assume that design, engineering, and management adds 20% to these costs. Add an amount of 10% for reserves and contingencies.

Download commercial or educational computer software such as Research Engineers' AutoProject, Microsoft Project, Open Plan Professional, Primavera, or/and others, such as Lotus, Excel, SAP R/3, and so on, capable of supporting and otherwise processing information, as a tool to create project databases in support of the following questions.

11.2. Prepare a work breakdown structure of the three functional areas 0801, 0802, and 0803 from Fig. 11.4 and incorporate all phases from phase 1 to phase 8, Operations Testing. Prepare a database of all project tasks developed through the breakdown.

11.3. Prepare a functional organization diagram for this project based on concepts described in this chapter and in Chapter 2 and using other relevant examples from the text.

11.4. Prepare a budget based on the tasks (activities). Summarize the budget by project phases, including phases 1 through 8. Consider that the project will be bid and awarded for construction using the method of construction management of up to 10 phased packages, way 2, as seen in Fig. 4.5. Develop these packages.

11.5. Design a project database at level 6 of the WBS, including the use of PDS, WBS, and OBS codes developed in this exercise.

11.6. Using project management software prepare a schedule of the project tasks to include all codes, costs, and durations. Base the schedule on only one project start event and only one finish event.

RESEARCH CENTER CPM SCHEDULE EXERCISE 12

12.1 Introduction

This is not the research center referred to in Chapter 9. This exercise is based on a major project consisting of an animal wing and an integrated laboratory and communal wing.

The purpose of this case is to show how to create activities for planning and scheduling a major construction project for owners who are experienced in project management and wish to use the critical path method (CPM) to enhance their participation in the actual planning and scheduling of the construction project. They already have the project functional requirements, the scope and quality definition, the conceptual drawings and performance specifications, and a definitive estimate. The architectural and engineering consultants are in place. The owners now wish the final drawings and specifications to be produced to schedule and the job bid competitively and awarded to the low bidder as a lump sum general contract. The main purpose of this exercise is to create a CPM plan, process it by computer, and schedule the construction activities.

The discussion builds a rationale for the creation of activities using a system of facility functional areas, classical phases, and breakdowns, the elemental cost basis for activity groups, elements, and eventually scheduling activities. The activities, assigned to resource groups, and the durations were cast into logical relationships. They were processed and iterated by computer to establish the critical path and float values for each chain of activities.

Computer processing is tied into milestone events by relating a group of activities or a single activity, with the status of the activity reflecting the status of the milestone event. Features of this particular network are discussed and criticized with a view to improving the design and creation of future networks, based on the lessons in this exercise.

As cost was seen to be under control through the lump sum general contract bidding process, and as project scope and quality were both well defined through the lengthy feasibility and concept planning stages, cost and scope parameters were not seen as issues as long as the lump sum bid came in within budget limitations.

12.2 Using the WBS to Create CPM Activities

The work breakdown structure (WBS) was based on typical project phases as presented in this textbook. For this application, five project phases were considered adequate at level 2 of the WBS, as seen in Fig. 12.1. This allows the project scheduling planner an opportunity to look back to see where the project came from and then plan for the future. As the project was depicted by WBS phases, it became apparent that planning would be aimed at the development of activities within phases.

Referring to Fig. 12.1, phase 1, Planning, was seen to have been completed previously and was left untouched. Phase 2, Design and Drawings, devolved into level 3 traditional drawing tasks, owner and user tasks, and tasks by third parties. The design and drawings phase was not expanded below level 2, as the intent was to develop construction activities.

Phase 3, Bid and Award, was considered to be a conventional exercise and was left untouched. No more planning was deemed necessary in this case.

Phase 5, Startup, was left for future planning.

Phase 4, Construction, is seen in Fig. 12.1 to break down into specific physical project functional areas at level 3 of the structure, namely, Animal Wing, Laboratory & Communal Wing, and Exterior Work & Site Development. Level 4 of the WBS shows standard building systems as developed by the quantity surveyors and cost analysts for the project cost estimate and budget. The use of this terminology starts to tie together the construction cost code and the breakdown being made for CPM scheduling purposes.

Level 5 shows a selection of element groups as breakdowns of level 4.

Level 6 depicts a number of specific elements. It is at about level 6 that the elements would become activities on a CPM network.

The intent was to tie the coded cost elements into CPM activities, because the cost coded elements form the basis for monthly progress billings. Thus the credibility of the activities on the schedule evolves from the fact that the elements exist as themselves for cost and as themselves or as fractions of themselves in the CPM planning network.

In other words they are hard activities in systems of project management language. A hard activity exists as a scope item, a cost item, and a schedule item. It cannot disappear except through a scope change, as caused by a change order.

As seen in Fig. 12.1, both the Animal Wing and the Lab Wing were broken down into level 4 building systems.

It is seen that they are now consistently named and coded from 1 through 13, with 11 left unused. (It is pointed out that if the Masterformat system had been used for the elemental breakdown, there would be 16 divisions of element types at this level for each building. Masterformat was not used in this case.) To keep the exercise simple, the Exterior Work & Site is not broken down into its elements.

At level 5 of the WBS, again for simplicity, only the Lab Wing, 2B, Superstructure; 3, Exterior Walls & Cladding; 4, Weatherproofing; 9, Mechanical (in part);

and 10, Electrical (in part), are broken down into level 6 elements. Again, this is to keep the illustration of the system of WBSs for CPM scheduling as simple as possible, uncluttered, and suitable to fit on a book page.

It is very important to understand that the level 6 elements shown are specific to this project. They exist on working drawings and in the specifications. Many require shop (manufacturers') drawings, which show details of fit to each other and to the building system to which they belong.

Level 6 is about as far as we can go in a WBS exercise aimed at creating activities for a CPM network. Few if any level 6 elements become one-on-one schedule activities. Take element 3.1.1, 4" Face Brick on the Lab Wing, for example. For scheduling purposes the subject building expanse of brick work was broken down by floor number, wall location (N, E, S, W), constraints caused by predecessors, and event milestone dates such as "finish no later than" set by management. Thus the planning not only is an exercise in logic, but also must be based on construction management decisions such as, for example, that the construction of the Lab Wing building will be broken down into two areas; area 1 and area 2.

12.3 CPM Network Schedule

To keep the illustration simple, the CPM network of activities will be based on the Lab Wing, area 1, as seen in Fig. 12.2.

The schedule activities could be developed as a continuation of the WBS with listings at level 7 and lower. But the exercise is thought to be more productive as a listing of activities cast in CPM network form, as seen in Fig. 12.2. The reasons for doing it this way becomes evident when chains of activities are linked based on both logic and management decisions.

For example, in the WBS in Fig. 12.1 it is seen that L.3.1, Masonry, at level 5 is broken down into L.3.1.1, 4" Face Brick; L.3.1.2, 6" Concrete Block, and L.3.3, Expansion Joint in Exterior Walls. It is a matter of fact that an exterior masonry wall is constructed by laying up a number of courses of 6" concrete block, followed by the same height of 4" face brick, and including expansion joints where they exist.

What this means is that a CPM schedule activity for exterior masonry would consist of all three elements listed. This is seen in the CPM network in Fig. 12.2 as activities 3281–3308, 3308–3309, and 3309–3387, lab area 1, 2nd-, 3rd-, and 4th-floor exterior masonry.

On the other hand activities 3278–3306, 3306–3312, and 3312–3393, lab area 1, 2nd-, 3rd-, and 4th-floor shelf angles, are seen as themselves in the WBS (L.2B.4.4) and as a fraction of themselves, that is, area 1 shelf angle, and so on.

In the WBS, L.4.1.1 codes 4-ply roofing on concrete slabs and L.4.1.2 codes 4-ply roofing on steel decks. In the CPM network the group of roofing activities identified as 3450–3466 shows insulation and roofing on four different roof elevations of the lab and is logically combined with cants and curbs, which would be coded as L.4.3.1, roofing and sheet metal, and L.4.3.3 weather proofing carpentry. Other com-

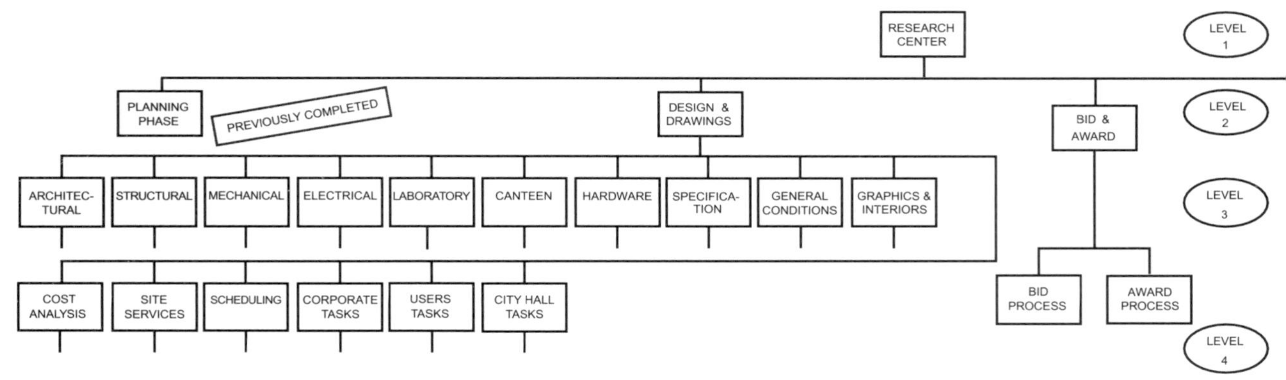

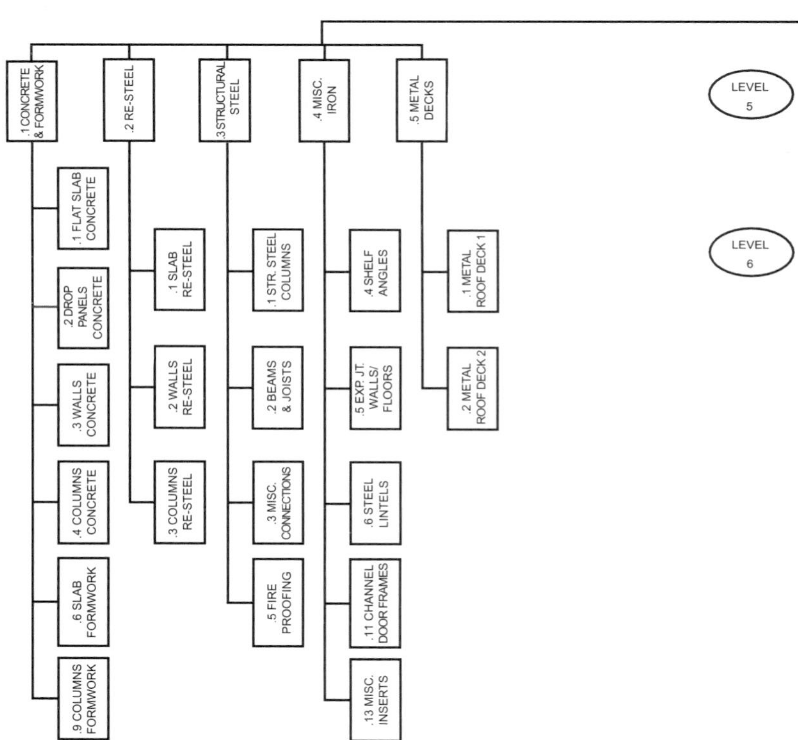

FIGURE 12.1 RESEARCH CENTER CONSTRUCTION WBS FOR CPM. The intent of this WBS is the development of elements that will form the schedule activities. As the project has been planned, scoped, designed, and converted to final drawings, details of those phases are not shown. The bid and award phase has been completed. The intent is to create construction activities for the CPM schedule. At level 4 of the breakdown, the elements are those upon which the monthly progress billings will be based. The schedule activities are based on these elements as illustrated.

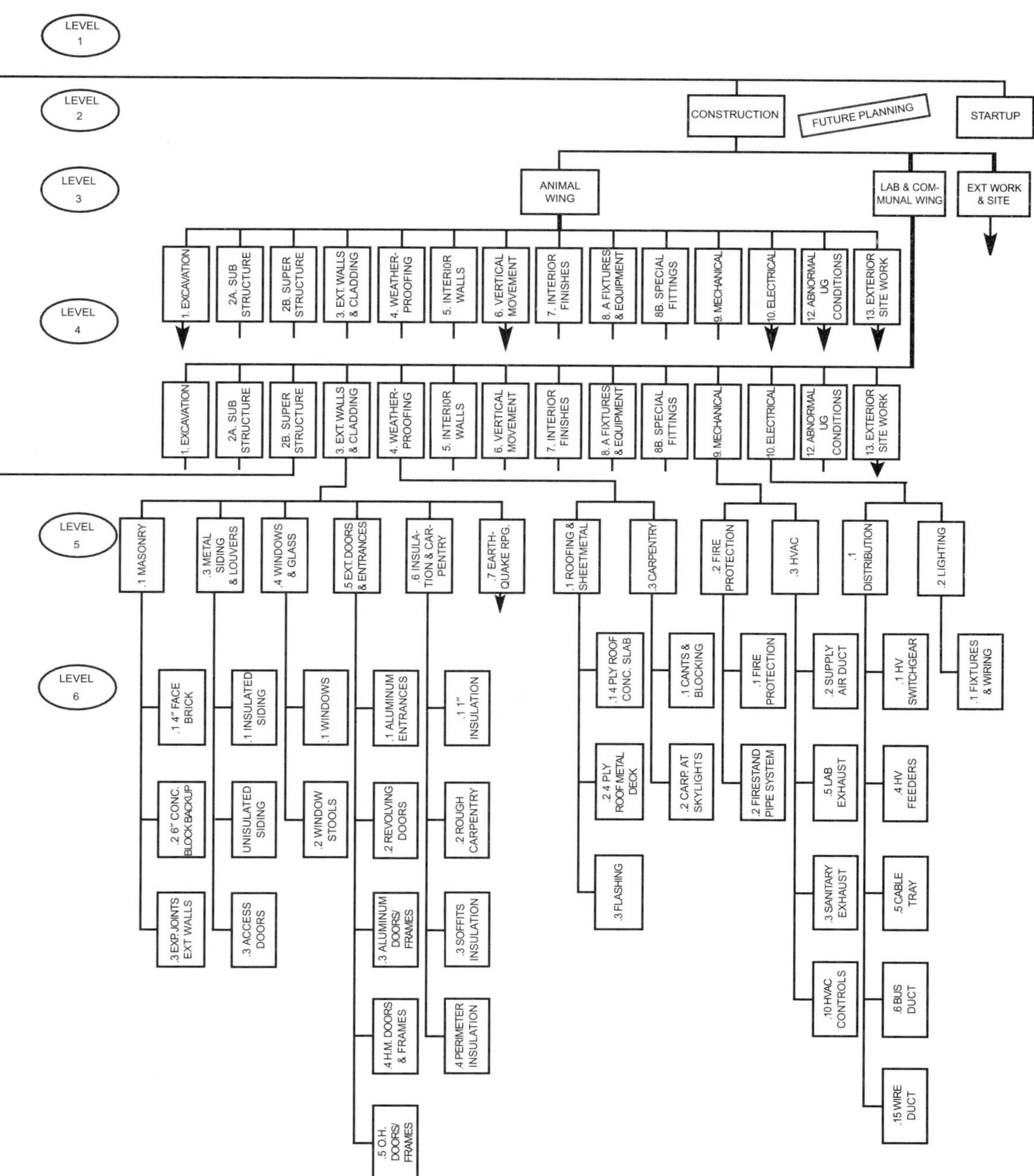

FIGURE 12.1 (CONTINUED).

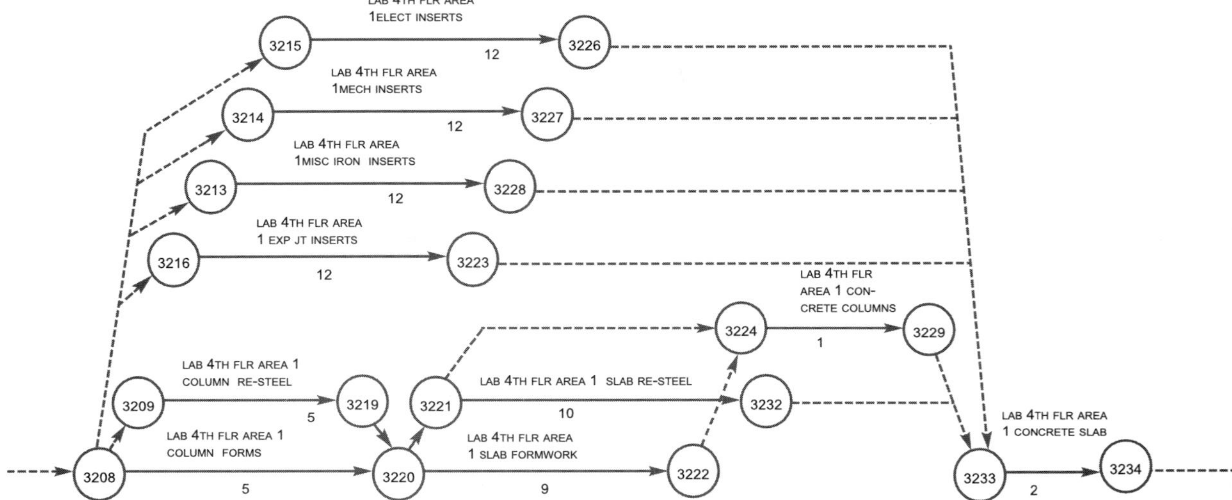

FIGURE 12.2 RESEARCH CENTER CPM NETWORK SCHEDULE. The creation of a CPM network to schedule construction activities requires that the activities be related to and an extension of the elements of the project as developed through a WBS. This sample CAD drawing reflects those properties. As the intent is to produce a computer-generated schedule, the activities shown are each assigned a duration only. Cost and resource codes could also be applied. These three panels making up the CAD drawing are meant to show that an element of project cost is not necessarily a schedule activity. Many elements require further breakdown for scheduling to suit construction pratice and management decisions.

binations are seen in the developments of both the mechanical and the electrical systems.

In this case it is seen that the WBS follows a vertical breakdown pattern tied to the cost estimate, the drawings, and the specifications. In other cases the format for the breakdown may be the 16-division Masterformat. For scheduling purposes the activities either are a combination of a number of elements, or they are further fractions of the elements based on construction trade practice, logical relationships, and management decisions. (Constructing the lab wing as areas 1 and 2 is a construction management decision. On the other hand, the construction of the second floor as a predecessor to the construction of the third floor is a logical relationship.)

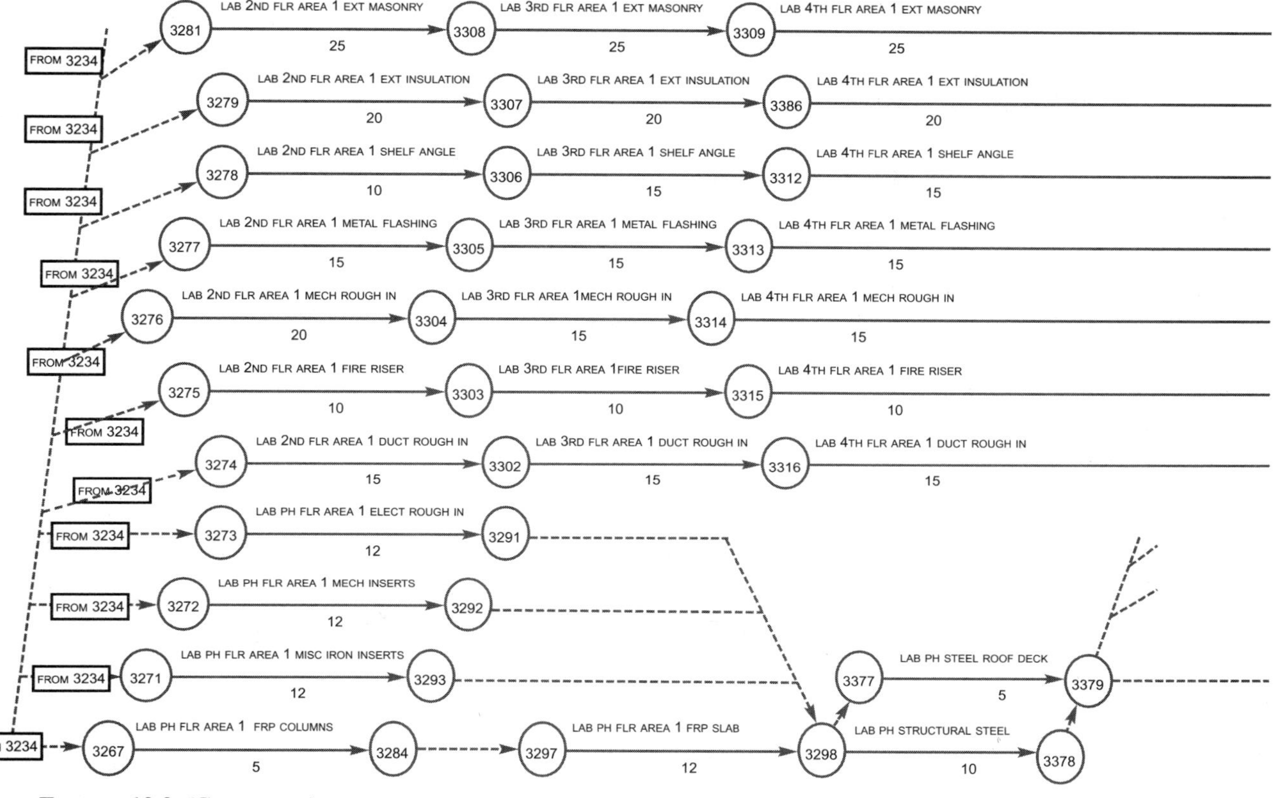

FIGURE 12.2 (CONTINUED)

Using this approach the system delivers a code structure that may or may not be used in cost and schedule management. Even though the WBS was based on the project construction cost estimate, and the elements followed a breakdown pattern based on the contract specifications, which are tied to the general contract divisions of work and to subcontracts by trade contractors, the reporting of cost progress was not connected to schedule progress reporting.

Monthly progress reporting, consisting of the insertion of actual completion dates, updating durations, revising logic connections, inserting change orders, and computer processing, produced a progress status report of all project activities. The computer processing also generated bar charts of activities by trades and subcontractors.

On a monthly basis the computer processing would be summarized into a milestone event report, as seen in Fig. 12.3. To keep it simple, the 20 events were each tied to a representative activity, and the status of the activity represented the status of the schedule of the event.

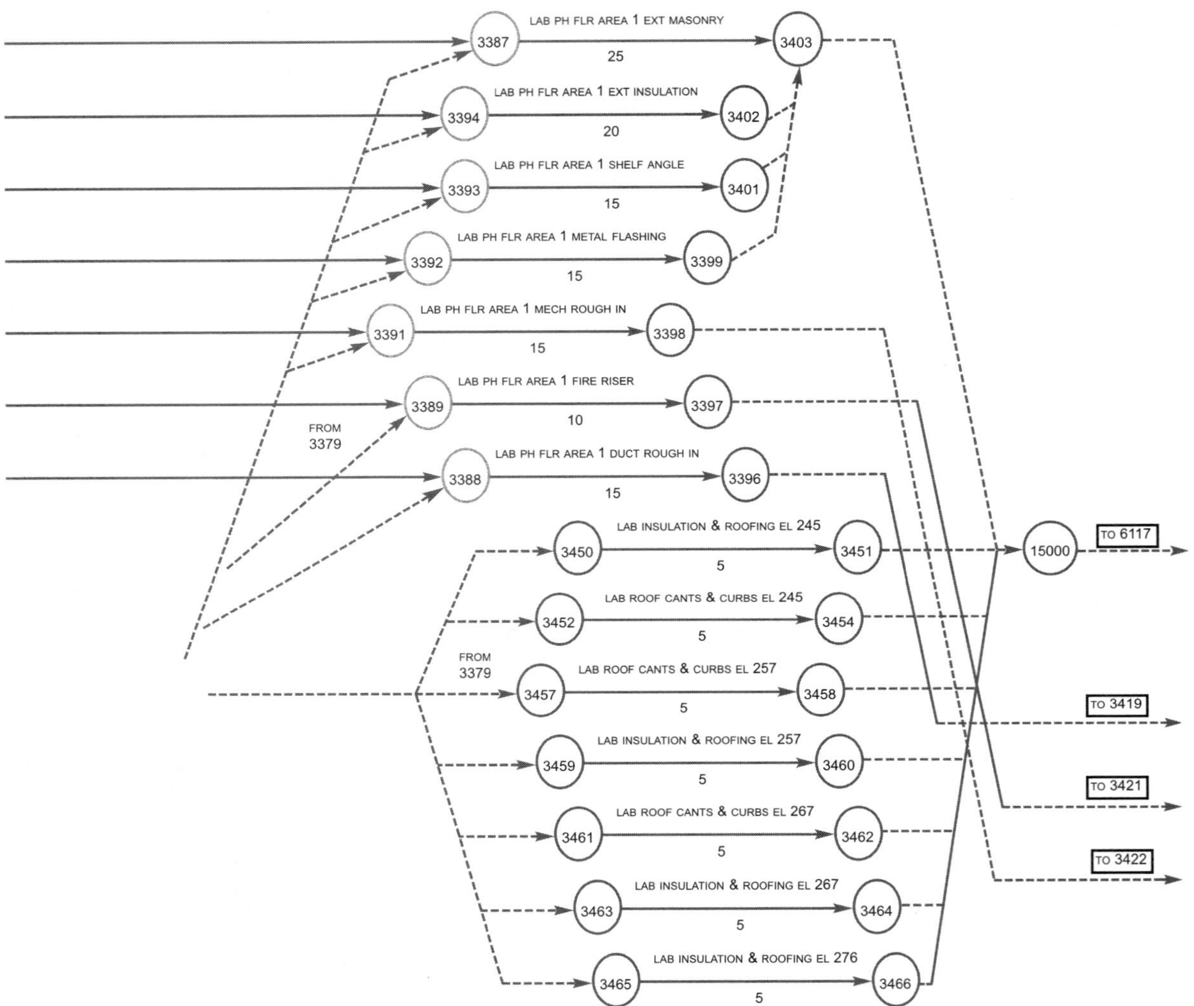

FIGURE 12.2 (CONTINUED)

RESEARCH CENTER CONSTRUCTION PHASE

MILESTONE EVENTS REPORT: NO. 27 - MARCH 9, 1996

EVENT DESCRIPTION	SPECIFIED DATE	PLAN DATE	EXPECTED DATE	EARLY + LATE - (WEEKS)	PREVIOUS REPORT STATUS	ANALYSIS (ACTIVITY LINK)	RESP.	ACTION
1. CONTRACT AWARD	1993 DEC 14	1993 DEC 14	1993 DEC 14*	-	-	0-10	-	-
2. EXCAVATION COMPLETED	1994 MAR 29	1994 JUN 20	1994 OCT 31*	-	-	3009-3019	-	-
3. SUBSTRUCTURE COMPLETED	1994 APR 26	1994 JUL 25	1995 JAN 17*	-	-	3034-3035	-	-
4. SUPERSTRUCTURE COMPLETED	1995 JAN 17	1995 SEP 15	1995 SEP 11*	-	-	3377-3378	-	-
5. BUILDING CLOSED IN	1995 MAR 21	1995 DEC 11	1995 OCT 23*	-	-	9538-9539	-	-
6. SITE SERVICES CONNECTED	1995 MAR 21	1996 JAN 5	1995 NOV 7*	-	-	2527-2528	-	-
7.POWER SYSTEMS ON A WING	1995 MAR 21	1996 MAY 6	1996 JUN 18	6.0-	E - MAR 29 L - MAY 28	4223-4229	FEL	EXPEDITE FINISHES & MECHANICAL
8. PLUMBING COMPLETED A WING	1995 MAY 2	1996 JUN28	1996 JUL 19	3.0-	E - JUN 10 L - JUL 12	4273-4276	CIL	EXPEDITE ALL FINISHES
9. LAB F & F COMPLETED A WING	1995 JUN 6	1996 JUN14	1996 JUN 25	1.2-	E - MAY 27 L - JUN 18	4289-4270	ALF	EXPEDITE ALL FINISHES
10. LIGHTS ON A WING	1995 MAY 2	1996 JUN28	1996 JUL 19	3.0-	E - JUN 10 L - JUL 12	4273-4278	FEL	EXPEDITE ALL FINISHES
11. HVAC COMPLETED A WING	1995 MAY 2	1996 JUL 30	1996 AUG 9	1.6-	E - JUL 9 L - AUG 2	4285-4286	CIL	EXPEDITE FINISHES
12. ENVIRONMENT ON A WING	1995 MAY 2	1996 AUG 13	1996 AUG 23	1.6-	E JUL 23 L - AUG 16	4287-4288	CIL	EXPEDITE FINISHES
13. POWER COMPLETED L/C WING	1995 NOV 7	1996 JUN 21	1996 JUL 25	4.1-	E - JUN 21 L - JUN 25	6273-6278	FBC	ACHIEVE BUILDING COMPLETIONS
14. POWER SYSTEMS ON L/C WING	1995 NOV 7	1996 JUN 28	1996 JUL 19	3.1-	E JUN 28 L - JUL 12	6273-6429	FEL	ACHIEVE BUILDING COMPLETIONS
15. PLUMBING COMPLETE L/C WING	1995 NOV 21	1996 JUN 21	1996 JUL 5	2.0-	E - JUN 21 L JUN 25	6273-6275	CIL	EXPEDITE LAB FURNITURE
16. LAB F & F COMPLETED L/C WING	1996 JAN 23	1996 MAY 24	1996 JUN 18	3.2-	E - MAY 24 L - JUN 11	6264-6268	ALF	EXPEDITE LAB FURNITURE
17. LIGHTS ON L/C WING	1995 NOV 28	1996 JUN 21	1996 JUL 5	2.0-	E - JUN 21 L JUN 25	6273-6278	FEL	EXPEDITE BUILDING AND MECHANICAL
18. HVAC COMPLETED L/C WING	1995 NOV 7	1996 JUL 12	1996 JUL 26	2.0-	E - JUL 13 L - JUL 19	6284-6285	CIL	ACHIEVE ALL EARLY COMPLETIONS
19. INTERIM CERTIFICATE ISSUED	1996 JAN 9	1996 AUG 23	1996 AUG 23	-	E - AUG 16 L - AUG 16	18000-18001	ALL	ACHIEVE ALL EARLY COMPLETIONS
20. FINAL CERTIFICATE ISSUED	1996 FEB 20	1996 SEP 20	1996 SEP 20	-	E - SEP 14 L - SEP 14	20000-20001	ALL	ACHIEVE ALL EARLY COMPLETIONS

NOTE: * DENOTES COMPLETED EVENT.

NOTE: THE EARLY/LATE +/- COLUMN IS BASED ON THE PLAN DATE AND THE EXPECTED DATE

NOTE: NAMES OF SUB-TRADES

FIGURE 12.3 RESEARCH CENTER CPM CONSTRUCTION NETWORK, MILESTONE EVENTS. A large CPM construction network schedule may comprise 3000 to 4000 activities. As many as up to 1000 activities may be under way at one time. To simplify reporting, the schedule status of the project may be monitored by assigning milestone events to key activities in the network. As actual progress is reported, the computer calculates future activity start and finish dates, which are reflected in the status of the milestone events. Thus instead of considering 1000 activities from each computer run, the project status is reflected in 20 milestone events, which are reported as depicted. The milestone events are related to specified dates, plan dates, and expected dates. Shown is also the previous status, as well as the responsible contractor and the action needed to improve status.

12.4 Summary

The intent of this chapter is to show how to create CPM networking to schedule activities using the system of work breakdown structuring promoted as one of the key systems of project management in this book. It is seen that a construction breakdown is relatable to the cost breakdown used for monthly construction progress billings. Although cost and schedule are not integrated in this case, when tied to progress billings, schedule activities have more credibility than otherwise. It is also seen that scheduling activities are different from cost elements. This is to reflect construction trade practice and construction management decisions. Finally, milestone events are important to simplify progress and action reporting to management.

Note: This chapter is based on my experience as the owner's project scheduling consultant for a new Health Protection Research Center Project comprising an animal wing and a communal and laboratory wing. The consulting assignment started at the stage of the final drawings of the project and extended through the bidding and construction stages to the project's substantial completion.

My involvement was: monitoring and reporting progress on the production of the final working drawings for lump sum general contract bidding; creating work breakdown structures for the identification of activities for CPM scheduling; assigning and coordinating activity durations; monitoring and processing construction progress; by computer and reporting the status of the project against a set of milestone events.

The project files are the references. These files comprise CPM arrow diagram network drawings, work breakdown structures, the development of activities and their assignment to the general contractor and subcontractors, monthly computer outputs, and project progress, analysis, and exception reports.

QUESTIONS AND EXERCISES

12.1. Referring to Fig. 12.2, assume that the activities from node 3208 to node 3234 represent a stand-alone network of construction activities for the project Lab 4th floor, area 1.

Assume that the durations shown are in workdays, in a 5-day workweek.

Assume a single start event of 001 as the sole predecessor to node 3208.

Assume the finish event is 3234 with the sole predecessor 3233.

Assume that the resource groups, the contractors and subcontractors responsible for the activities, are as follows:

3208–3220 Column forms KERR1

3209–3219 Column re-steel GILBERT

3213–3228 Misc iron inserts FOUNDATION

3214–3227 Mechanical inserts COMSTOCK

3215–3226 Electrical inserts FEDERAL

3216–3223 Expansion joint inserts FOUNDATION

3220–3222 Slab formwork KERR1

3221–3232 Slab re-steel GILBERT

3224–3229 Pouring concrete columns KERR2

3233–3234 Pouring concrete slab KERR2

Assign the appropriate resource group to each activity.

12.2. Download or procure a commercial or educational copy of a project management software application, which may be similar to CA-SuperProject. Create a PERT (precedence diagram) network or a CPM arrow diagram using the new assumed start and finish events, based on the node numbers provided in Fig. 12.2. The relationships may be FS, SS, or FF, depending on the activity.

12.3. Input, process, massage, and iterate the activities as Gantt and PERT charts and include views and reports of the OBS as resource codes, WBS codes, cost, and schedule. Using the selected software, generate predecessor and succesor reports, functional organization reports, and resources reports. Run all the standard reports and consider their usefulness.

12.4. Assuming a start date of 2000/06/05, calculate the project completion date based on the critical path. Show the early and late start and finish dates for each activity, as well as the critical path and total floats of the activities, based on scheduling with and without resources.

12.5. Pay particular attention to the difficulty and complexity of assigning resources to activities and scheduling with resources.

13 CONSTRUCTION COST AND SCHEDULE INTEGRATION

13.1 Introduction

Chapter 12 showed how to create a CPM network of activities based on a work breakdown structure (WBS) related to the cost estimate. This chapter shows how to create a CPM network based on a contract breakdown for monthly progress billings. The bills are based on the master list of titles and numbers of the 16 divisions of the Masterformat for the construction industry.

The bills in this case are a contractual requirement between the owner and the contractor, with the form of the bill set by the owner. The computerized CPM network is a contractual requirement also, but its form is set by the contractor. It will be seen how the progress bills and computerized CPM activities were integrated, and what dichotomies were encountered. It will become apparent that the way a construction project is planned, drawn, and specified is different from the way it is costed, planned, and constructed. This difference is often the source of conflict between designers and builders.

The lessons to be learned include: how to integrate cost with schedule; the techniques of creating computerized CPM networks; tying activity identifiers to specification-related cost code numbers; schedule progress measurement and reporting; building meaningful logic relationships and showing them diagrammatically; understanding that logic relationships are best devised with computerized networks and not bar charts; understanding that CPM logic networks are not good communication tools; learning the purpose of bar charts as schedule communicators; and how to input progress information to gauge the status of the project in relation to imposed dates and contractual milestones.

13.2 Construction Progress Bills

Figure 13.1 is an illustration of the owner's required project cost breakdown for monthly progress bills. It is seen that there are four bills, based on the North American industry standard 16-division Masterformat specification system. This contract involved only four divisions, as listed. The other activities were under separate contracts.

BILL NO. 1
GENERAL ITEMS

ITEM NO.	SPEC. NO. & DESCRIPTION	LS PRICE $
	00700 - GENERAL CONDITIONS	
01	Permits	0
02	Insurance	4,000
03	Performance Bond	4,000
04	Supervision by GC	25,000
	1045 - CUTTING AND FITTING	
05	Cutting and Fitting	500
	01050 - FIELD ENGINEERING	
06	Surveying	12,000
	1310 - SCHEDULE	
07	Construction Schedule	5,000
	01390 - SUPPORT & RESTORATION	
08	Plant Operations Building	]
09	Administration Building	]
10	Substation Building	500
11	Rail Bending Shed	]
12	Street Car Track Bed	]
	01340 - SHOP DRAWINGS	
13	Shop Drawings	500
	01500 - CONSTRUCTION FACILITIES	
14	Noise Reduction	0
15	Dust Control	500
16	Utilities	0
17	Hoarding	14,000
18	Fire Equipment	500
19	Temporary Buildings	8,000
20	Site Maintenance	2,000
	01570 - TRAFFIC	
21	Traffic	500
	TOTAL BILL NO.1 TO SUMMARY	77,000

BILL NO. 2
SITE WORK

ITEM NO.	SPEC. NO. & DESCRIPTION	LS PRICE $
	0200 - UTILITIES WORK & SERVICES	
22	Temporary Support of Hydro Duct Bank	30,000
	02050 - DEMOLITION	
23	Scrap Bins & Const. Materials Bldg.	3,000
24	Concrete Retaining Walls	2,000
25	Concrete Sidewalk	1,000
	02051 - REMOVAL AND DISPOSAL	
26	Guardrail	400
27	Abandoned Street Car Track	2,000
28	200 mm Combined Sewer	5,000
29	100 mm Track Drain	600
30	100 mm Tile Drain	500
31	50 mm Gas Pipe	1,000
	02220 - EXCAVATION AND BACKFILL	
32	Excavation for Ftgs. & Fdn Walls	100,200
33	Excavation for Storm Sewer*	*
34	Excavation for Sanitary Sewer*	*
35	Excavation for Water Main*	*
36	Removal of water	500
37	Backfill Footings & Foundation Walls	90,000
38	Backfill Storm Sewer*	*
39	Backfill Sanitary Sewer*	*
40	Backfill Water Main*	*
41	Inspection and Testing**	*
	02350 - PILES, SHEATHING, LAGGING, SHORING AND BRACING	
42	Installation	40,000
43	Removal	2,000
	02701 - STORM SEWERS	
44	250 mm Storm Sewer	]
45	300 mm Storm Sewer	]
46	375 mm Storm Sewer	]
47	Manholes	]
48	Connection to Existing Manholes	60,000
49	Connection to Existing Track Drains	]
50	150 mm Weeping Tile, With Fabric	]
51	Inspection and Testing	]
	02702 - SANITARY SEWERS	
52	200 mm Sanitary Sewer	]
53	Connect. Existing Combined Sewers	]
54	TV Inspection of Combined Sewers	20,000
55	Inspection & Testing	]
	02713 - WATER DISTRIBUTION	
56	200 mm PVC Water Main	]
57	Connect. Existing Water Main	]
58	Fire Hydrant and Valve Sets	75,000
59	Gate Valves	]
60	Inspection & Testing	]
	02714 - PIPE JACKING AND BORING	
61	Boring & Jacking 375 mm Storm Sewer	]
62	Boring & Jacking 200 mm Water Main	20,000
	TOTAL BILL NO. 2 TO SUMMARY	453,200

FIGURE 13.1 CONSTRUCTION COST/SCHEDULE INTEGRATION, PROGRESS BILLS. The project owner required that the contractor break down the contract amount according to the Masterformat code items listed. The Masterformat code items represent the way the work is specified, which is not necessarily the way it will be constructed. The contractor, being required to provide the information to facilitate monthly progress billings, submitted the above breakdown, which became acceptable to the owner. It is noted that some items were not broken down to the requested detail. This is not because the contractor would not provide the information. It has more to do with the way the items are bid by subcontractors, or handled between construction trades, in the event these monthly progress bills became the basis for the CPM schedule activities.

BILL NO. 3
CONCRETE

ITEM NO.	SPEC. NO. & DESCRIPTION	LS PRICE $
	03000 - REINFORCING STEEL	
63	Re-Bar for Columns Footings & Piers	]
64	Re-Bar for Fdn Walls & Footings	67,000
64A	Re-Bar for Walls Above Grade	]
	03300 - CONCRETE	
65	Concrete Columns & Piers	80,000
66	Concrete Foundation Walls & Footings	350,000
67	Concrete Walls Above Grade	40,000
68	Inspection & Testing	**
	03345 - SURFACE FINISHES	
69	No. 4 Finish Formed	1,500
	03600 - GROUT	
70	Grout Column Bases	2,000
	TOTAL BILL NO. 3 TO SUMMARY	540,500

Notes: * Cost with 02701
** Cost by owner
] Cost included in line item amount

BILL NO. 4
STEEL ROOF DECK

ITEM NO.	SPEC. NO. & DESCRIPTION	LS PRICE $
	05120 - STRUCTURAL STEEL	
71	Anchor Bolts & Leveling Plates	]
72	Steel Columns	150,000
73	Steel Beams	[
74	Misc. Framing and Bracing	320,000
75	Inspection and Testing	**
	05210 - OPEN WEB STEEL JOISTS	
76	300 mm OWSJ & Bridging	]
77	410 mm OWSJ & Bridging	]
78	460 mm OWSJ & Bridging	160,000
79	560 mm OWSJ & Bridging	]
80	Inspection and Testing	**
	05310 - STEEL ROOF DECK	
81	38 mm Steel Roof Deck	]
82	38 mm Floor Deck	101,000
83	Inspection and Testing	**
	TOTAL BILL NO. 4 TO SUMMARY	731,000

FIGURE 13.1 (CONTINUED).

It is apparent that the owner's managers prepared the bills based on the specifications, and not necessarily on the way construction contractors build. For example, under subdivision 02220, Excavation and Backfill, out of the ten items listed, seven are included in another subdivision, 02701, Storm Sewers. Under 02701, 02702, and 02713 a number of line items are listed, but the contractor provides only a global subdivision amount against each. Global, as opposed to detail, amounts are provided for subdivisions 05210 and 05310.

These kinds of differences are often seen in construction progress billings. The owner invariably wants more or different detail than the contractors can provide. Often the differences arise out of the way consultants specify work as compared to the way builders construct.

Keeping this dichotomy in mind, and allowing that both the owner's managers and the contractors are acting in good faith when requesting and providing cost information, the next step is to prepare a CPM network of activities, based on the itemized and now costed bills, and run the network by computer for progress reporting.

13.3 CPM Construction Network

Although the progress bills are key elements to facilitate the creation of schedule activities, the activities and their relationships and values, such as durations, leads and lags, and so on, are the purview of the construction manager. At the same time there are construction norms and trade practices. All of these factors and issues come into play when creating a schedule.

The resulting CPM network is seen in Fig. 13.2. To provide a link between cost and schedule, the schedule activities are numbered on the basis of the item numbers 01 through 83 in the bills. It is quickly evident that the billing cost details are widely different from the CPM network activities. For example, item 13, Shop Drawings, becomes seven activities, 131, 132, 133, 134, 135, 136, and 137, on the network. Thus an item that shows a value of $500.00 in the billing is converted to seven CPM schedule activities. Shop drawings are very important to the scheduling of a construction project. For scheduling purposes it is absolutely essential that vendor shop drawings be included as CPM activities, as seen in this case. The cost of shop drawings is rarely carried as a separate, stand-alone item. The cost is included by each vendor and subcontractor. In this case a nominal amount of $500.00 is carried in the progress bills.

Item 32 in bill no. 2 provides $100,200.00 for excavation. The construction manager planned the work as three areas, A, B, and C. Activities 321, 322, and 323 are the excavation activities.

Item 37 in bill no. 2 in the amount of $90,000.00 is for backfill. It becomes three backfill activities, 371, 372, and 373, for areas A, B, and C.

Cost amounts for items 33 through 35 and 38 through 41 for excavation and backfill for sewer and water lines are not provided, and they are not separately scheduled as activities. It is not a matter of the contractors resisting a legitimate request by the owner's design managers. It is that these kinds of details are not useful and are not broken out in the process. The construction methodology for underground piping involves a continuous process of excavating, jacking, installing, testing, and backfilling. The costs in this case are included in the global amounts listed for items 44 through 62.

All the other building items, 63 through 83, are then scheduled as areas A, B, and C, and the overhead items 01 through 07 and the indirect construction items 08 through 31 are scheduled to suit the logic of the planned construction, and to be incorporated into the CPM network so that it may be said that the cost and the schedule are truly integrated. This latter point is important in the event that the schedule activities are costed for cash flow or resources loading purposes.

Some comments on the appearance of the CPM network in Fig. 13.2 are in order. First, it is drawn manually. The logic, however, is based on computer processing and provides the schedule answers that were wanted by both the owner and the contractor. Second, when drawing a CPM diagram, the planner wishes to show progress, that is, an activity logically follows another (as in writing and reading in English from left to right and top to bottom), with a higher number preferably fol-

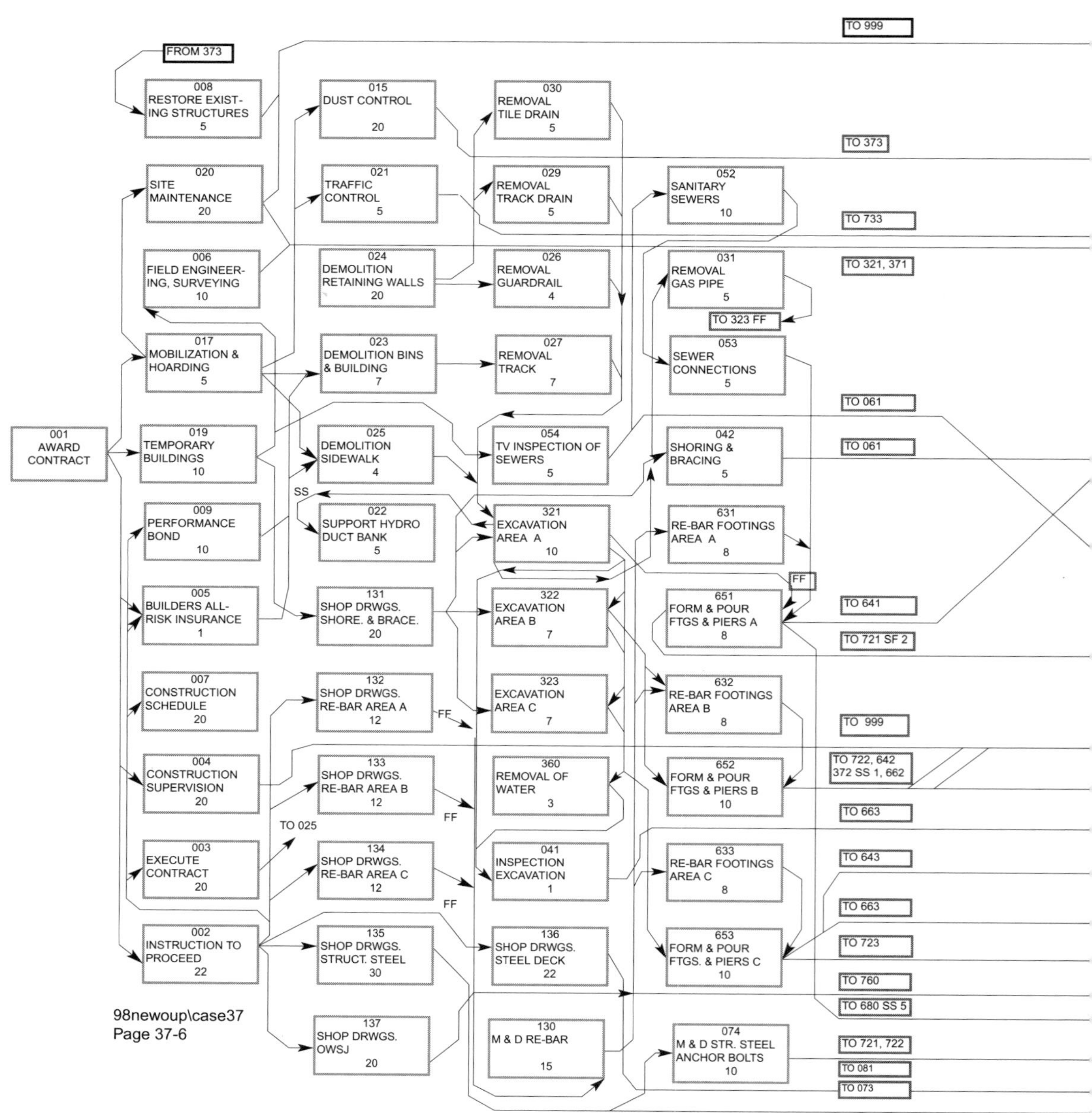

FIGURE 13.2 CPM CONSTRUCTION NETWORK. The activities are based on the cost items listed in Fig. 13.1. Thus project cost and schedule are integrated. The intent is to schedule the work based on this network and computer processing. The activities reflect not only the scope of the project as set by its cost, but management decisions and actions as to how it will be built. The network shows all of the above, as well as the logical relationships. Logic states that excavation precedes form, reinforce, pour (FRP) concrete, and structural steel frame precedes open web steel joists (OWSJ). But that area A precedes area B is a management decision.

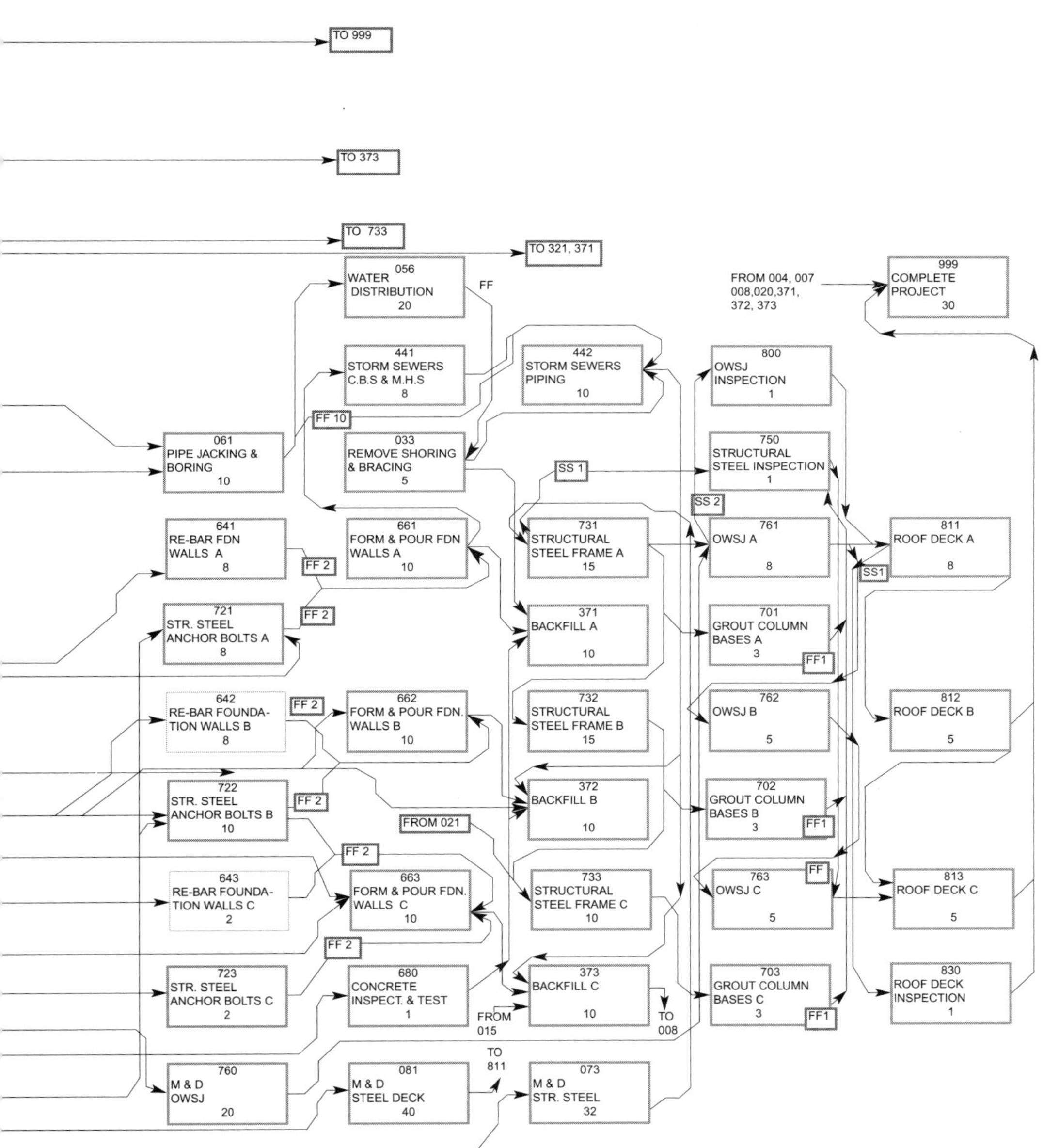

FIGURE 13.2 (CONTINUED).

lowing a lower number. If activity numbers are selected on the basis discussed here, it happens that from time to time a lower number will follow a higher number. In addition, planners wish to make network diagrams as compact as possible, with activities being squeezed in where they can be, rather than where they might logically follow. For example, activity 321 is seen to be a predecessor to activity 022. Although they are drawn in reverse order, the logic is shown correctly.

PRECEDENCE RELATIONSHIP REPORT

PREDE-CESSOR	LAG TYPE	LAG ORIG	LAG REM	ACTIVITY/DESCRIPTION	FLOAT	SUCCES-SOR	LAG TYPE	LAG ORIG	LAG REM	CALEN-DAR
				001	0					
				AWARD CONTRACT						
						002	FS	0	0	
						019	FS	0	0	
						004	FS	0	0	
						005	FS	0	0	
						017	FS	0	0	
*********	*******	*******	******	**************************************	********	************	*********	*********	*********	**********
001	FS	0	0	002	0					
				INSTRUCTION TO PROCEED						
						132	FS	0	0	
						003	FS	0	0	
						007	FS	0	0	
						005	FS	0	0	
						009	FS	0	0	
						133	FS	0	0	
						134	FS	0	0	
						135	FS	0	0	
						136	FS	0	0	
						137	FS	0	0	
*********	*******	*******	******	**************************************	********	************	*********	*********	*********	**********
				003	5					
				EXECUTE CONTRACT						
002	FS	0	0			025	FS	0	0	
						024	FS	0	0	
						023	FS	0	0	
*********	*******	*******	******	**************************************	********	************	*********	*********	*********	**********
				004	5					
				CONSTRUCTION						
				SUPERVISION						
001	FS	0	0			999	FS	0	0	
*********	*******	*******	******	**************************************	********	************	*********	*********	*********	**********
				005	5					
				BUILDERS ALL-RISK						
				INSURANCE						
002	FS	0	0			025	FS	0	0	
001	FS	0	0			023	FS	0	0	
*********	*******	*******	******	**************************************	********	************	*********	*********	*********	**********
				006	22					
				FIELD ENGINEERING						
				SURVEYING						
019	FS	0	0			321	FS	0	0	
						371	FF	0	0	
*********	*******	*******	******	**************************************	********	************	*********	*********	*********	**********
				007	89					
				PREPARE CONSTRUCTION						
				SCHEDULE						
002	FS	0	0			999	FS	0	0	
*********	*******	*******	******	**************************************	********	************	*********	*********	*********	**********
				008	39					
				RESTORE EXISTING						
				STRUCTURES						
373	FS	0	0			999	FS	0	0	
*********	*******	*******	******	**************************************	********	************	*********	*********	*********	**********

FIGURE 13.3 COMPUTER REPORT, PRECEDENCE RELATIONSHIPS. This figure represents the final computer output for the CPM network in Fig. 13.2. The project critical path, the start and finish dates, and the float values are based on the relationships and values seen in this report. The intent is to show the meticulous planning that goes into creating and calculating schedules employing hard cost-based activities and realistic construction management decisions.

PRECEDENCE RELATIONSHIP REPORT

PREDE-CESSOR	LAG TYPE	LAG ORIG	LAG REM	ACTIVITY/DESCRIPTION	FLOAT	SUC-CESSOR	LAG TYPE	LAG ORIG	LAG REM	CALEN-DAR
				009	39					
				PERFORMANCE BOND						
002	FS	0	0			999	FS	0	0	
				015	96					
				DUST CONTROL						
017	FS	0	0			373	FS	0	0	
				017	23					
				MOBILIZATION AND HOARDING						
001	FS	0	0			021	FS	0	0	
						024	FS	0	0	
						025	FS	0	0	
						023	FS	0	0	
						015	SS	0	0	
						020	SS	0	0	
				019	12					
				TEMPORARY BUILDINGS						
001	FS	0	0			131	FS	0	0	
						954	FS	0	0	
						006	FS	0	0	
				020	111					
				SITE MAINTENANCE						
017	FS	0	0			999	FS	0	0	
				021	87					
				TRAFFIC CONTROL						
017	FS	0	0			733	FS	0	0	
				022	74					
				SUPPORT HYDRO DUCT BANK						
321	SS	5	5			371	FS	0	0	
				023	5					
				DEMOLITION BINS & BUILDING						
017	FS	0	0			027	FS	0	0	
003	FS	0	0							
005	FS	0	0							
009	FS	0	0							
				024	8					
				DEMOLITION RETAINING WALLS						
017	FS	0	0			030	FS	0	0	
003	FS	0	0			029	FS	0	0	
						026	FS	0	0	
				025	15					
				DEMOLITION SIDEWALK						
017	FS	0	0			321	FS	0	0	
003	FS	0	0							
005	FS	0	0							
009	FS	0	0							

FIGURE 13.3 (CONTINUED).

13.4 Computer Processing

Although it is possible, and many software packages can do it, a time-scaled CPM diagram is difficult to achieve without either long sheets of drawings or many pages of output. And that is another reason why CPM drawings are not seen as good com-

PRECEDENCE RELATIONSHIP REPORT

PREDE-CESSOR	LAG TYPE	LAG ORIG	LAG REM	ACTIVITY/DESCRIPTION	FLOAT	SUCCES-SOR	LAG TYPE	LAG ORIG	LAG REM	CALEN-DAR
				026 REMOVAL GUARD RAIL	8					
024	FS	0	0			321	FS	0	0	
				027 REMOVAL TRACK	5					
023	FS	0	0			321	FS	0	0	
				029 REMOVAL TRACK DRAIN	8					
024	FS	0	0			321	FS	0	0	
				030 REMOVAL TILE DRAIN	8					
024	FS	0	0			321	FS	0	0	
				031 REMOVAL GAS PIPE	5					
321	FS	0	0			323	FS	0	0	
				033 REMOVE SHORING & BRACING	17					
056	FF	0	0			371	FS	0	0	
						342	FF	0	0	
				041 INSPECTION EXCAVATION	5					
321	FS	0	0			633	FS	0	0	
360	FS	0	0			663	FS	0	0	
				042 SHORING & BRACING	17					
131	FS	0	0			061	FS	0	0	
				052 SANITARY SEWERS	33					
054	FS	0	0			053	FS	0	0	
				053 SEWER CONNECTIONS	33					
052	FS	0	0			651	FF	2	2	
				054 TV INSPECTION OF SEWERS	33					
019	FS	0	0			061	FS	0	0	
						052	FS	0	0	
				056 WATER DISTRIBUTION SYSTEM	17					
061	FS	0	0			033	FF	0	0	

FIGURE 13.3 (CONTINUED).

munication tools. The reason for their existence is to draw logic networks for computer processing. Even in a fairly simple network, say 84 activities as in this case, it becomes very difficult to develop and follow logic without computer processing. The planning process becomes one of creating activities, plotting them on the network, and simultaneously computer processing them for logical relationships, which is best seen through output usually called a "predecessor–successor report" or a "precedence relationship report." In truth, it is most difficult to draw networks without concurrent

PRECEDENCE RELATIONSHIP REPORT

PREDE-CESSOR	LAG TYPE	LAG ORIG	LAG REM	ACTIVITY/DESCRIPTION	FLOAT	SUC-CESSOR	LAG TYPE	LAG ORIG	LAG REM	CALEN DAR
				061	17					
				PIPE JACKING & BORING						
042	FS	0	0			056	FS	0	0	
054	FS	0	0			442	FF	10	10	
				073	0					
				M & D STR. STEEL						
135	FS	0	0			731	FS	0	0	
				074	15					
				M & D ANCHOR BOLTS						
135	FS	0	0			721	FS	0	0	
						722	FS	0	0	
				081	31					
				M & D STEEL DECK						
136	FS	0	0			811	FS	0	0	
				130	18					
				M & D RE-BAR						
132	FS	0	0			631	FS	0	0	
133	FF	0	0			632	FS	0	0	
134	FF	0	0			633	FS	0	0	
				131	12					
				SHOP DRWGS. SHORE. & BRACE.						
019	FS	0	0			321	FS	0	0	
						042	FS	0	0	
						323	FS	0	0	
						322	FS	0	0	
				132	19					
				SHOP DRWGS. RE-BAR AREA A						
002	FS	0	0			130	FF	2	2	
				133	19					
				SHOP DRWGS. RE-BAR AREA B						
002	FS	0	0			130	FF	2	2	
				134	19					
				SHOP DRWGS. RE-BAR AREA C						
002	FS	0	0			130	FF	2	2	
				135	0					
				SHOP DRWGS. STRUCT. STEEL						
						073	FS	0	0	
002	FS	0	0			074	FF	3	3	
				136	31					
				SHOP DRWGS. STEEL DECK						
002	FS	0	0			081	FS	0	0	
				137	43					
				SHOP DRWGS. OWSJ						
002	FS	0	0			760	FS	0	0	0

FIGURE 13.3 (CONTINUED).

computer processing to test for duplications, loops, correct relationships, and scheduling input such as "must finish by" dates, "start not later than" dates, lags, and leads. The reality is that it takes many runs to create the network seen in Fig. 13.2. It would be most difficult to do so without computer processing, as represented by the precedence relationship report illustrated in Fig. 13.3.

PRECEDENCE RELATIONSHIP REPORT

PREDE-CESSOR	LAG TYPE	LAG ORIG	LAG REM	ACTIVITY/DESCRIPTION	FLOAT	SUCCES-SOR	LAG TYPE	LAG ORIG	LAG REM	CALEN-DAR
				321	5					
				EXCAVATION AREA A						
006	FS	0	0			041	FS	0	0	
131	FS	0	0			631	FS	0	0	
027	FS	0	0			022	SS	5	5	
026	FS	0	0			031	SS	10	10	
029	FS	0	0			651	FF	2	2	
030	FS	0	0			360	FF	0	0	
025	FS	0	0							
*********	*******	*******	*****	**************************************	********	************	*********	*********	*********	**********
				322	25					
				EXCAVATION AREA B						
131	0	0	0			652	FS	0	0	
						632	FS	0	0	
						360	FS	0	0	
*********	*******	*******	******	**************************************	********	************	*********	*********	*********	**********
				323	5					
				EXCAVATION AREA C						
031	FF	5	5			633	FS	0	0	
131	FS	0	0			653	FS	0	0	
						360	FF	0	0	
*********	*******	*******	******	**************************************	********	************	*********	*********	*********	**********
				360	5					
				REMOVAL OF WATER						
323	FF	0	0			041	FS	0	0	
322	FS	0	0							
321	FS	0	0							
*********	*******	*******	******	**************************************	********	************	*********	*********	*********	**********
				371	47					
				BACKFILL AREA A						
033	FS	0	0							
680	FS	0	0							
442	FS	0	0							
022	FS	0	0							
006	FF	0	0							
661	FS	0	0			999	FS	0	0	
*********	*******	*******	******	**************************************	********	************	*********	*********	*********	**********
				372	89					
				BACKFILL AREA B						
652	SS	1	1							
442	FS	0	0							
662	FS	0	0			999	FS	0	0	
*********	*******	*******	******	**************************************	********	************	*********	*********	*********	**********
				373	39					
				BACKFILL AREA C		999	FS	0	0	
015	FS	0	0			008	FS	0	0	
442	FS	0	0							
663	FS	0	0							
*********	*******	*******	******	**************************************	********	************	*********	*********	*********	**********

FIGURE 13.3 (CONTINUED).

As predecessor–successor reports are produced, they are accompanied by activity listing reports, as seen in Fig. 13.4. Taking only the first 40 activities of the 84-activity network and listing them on the basis of their numeric activity identifiers in ascending order, conventional CPM information is provided, namely, estimated/remaining duration, early/late start and finish dates, total float, and a column for setting imposed dates.

An important schedule status report is the activity list sorted by criticality in Fig. 13.5. The 40 activities shown are listed by criticality in ascending order from zero total float up to a total float of 9 days.

PRECEDENCE RELATIONSHIP REPORT

PREDE-CESSOR	LAG TYPE	LAG ORIG	LAG REM	ACTIVITY/DESCRIPTION	FLOAT	SUC-CESSOR	LAG TYPE	LAG ORIG	LAG REM	CALEN-DAR
				441	8					
				STORM SEWERS CBS & MHS						
661	FS	0	0			442	FF	0	0	
				442	8					
				STORM SEWERS PIPING						
061	FF	10	10			371	FS	0	0	
441	FF	0	0			372	FS	0	0	
033	FF	0	0			373	FS	0	0	
				631	8					
				RE-BAR FOOTINGS AREA A						
130	FS	0	0			651	FS	0	0	
321	FS	0	0							
				632	26					
				RE-BAR FOOTINGS AREA B						
322	FS	0	0			652	FS	0	0	
130	FS	0	0							
				633	5					
				RE-BAR FOOTINGS AREA C						
323	FS	0	0			653	FF	1	1	
041	FS	0	0							
130	FS	0	0							
				641	8					
				RE-BAR FDN WALLS AREA A						
651	FS	0	0			661	FF	1	1	
				642	26					
				RE-BAR FDN WALLS AREA B						
652	FS	0	0			662	FF	1	1	
				643	5					
				RE-BAR FDN WALLS AREA C						
653	FS	0	0			663	FF	2	2	
				651	8					
				FORM & POUR FTGS. & PIERS A						
321	FF	2	2			641	FS	0	0	
631	FF	2	2			680	SS	5	5	
053	FF	2	2			721	SF	2	2	
				652	25					
				FORM & POUR FTGS. & PIERS B						
322	FS	0	0			662	FS	0	0	
632	FF	1	1			642	FS	0	0	
						372	SS	1	1	
						722	FS	0	0	
				653	5					
				FORM & POUR FTGS. & PIERS C						
323	FS	0	0			663	FS	0	0	
633	FF	1	1			643	FS	0	0	
						723	FS	0	0	

FIGURE 13.3 (CONTINUED).

An important feature worth noting in this report is how tightly the activities are scheduled. The mark of a tightly scheduled job is one where many activities are near the zero critical path as measured by the number of low float values. As can be seen here, 40 activities out of a total of 84 are all within 9 days of the critical path. Within scheduling tolerances, one can assume that they are all critical.

PRECEDENCE RELATIONSHIP REPORT

PREDE-CESSOR	LAG TYPE	LAG ORIG	LAG REM	ACTIVITY/DESCRIPTION	FLOAT	SUCCES-SOR	LAG TYPE	LAG ORIG	LAG REM	CALEN-DAR
				661	8					
				FORM & POUR FDN WALLS A						
641	FF	1	1			441	FS	0	0	
721	FF	2	2			371	FS	0	0	
				662	25					
				FORM & POUR FDN WALLS B						
652	FS	0	0			372	FS	0	0	
642	FF	1	1						0	
722	FF	0	0						0	
				663	5					
				FORM & POUR FDN WALLS C						
041	FS	0	0			373	FS	0	0	
653	FS	0	0							
722	FF	2	2							
643	FF	2	2							
723	FF	0	0							
				680	68					
				CONCRETE INSPECT. & TEST						
651	SS	5	5			371	FS	0	0	
				701	23					
				GROUT COLUMN BASES A						
731	FS	0	0			750	FF	1	1	
				702	10					
				GROUT COLUMN BASES B						
732	FS	0	0			750	FF	1	1	
				703	0					
				GROUT COLUMN BASES C						
733	FS	0	0			750	FF	1	1	
				721	15					
				STR. STEEL ANCHOR BOLTS A						
074	FS	0	0			661	FF	2	2	
651	SF	2	2							
				722	23					
				STR. STEEL ANCHOR BOLTS B						
074	FS	0	0			663	FF	2	2	
652	FS	0	0			662	FF	0	0	
				723	13					
				STR. STEEL ANCHOR BOLTS C						
653	FS	0	0			733	FS	0	0	
						663	FF	0	0	
				731	0					
				STRUCTURAL STEEL FRAME A						
073	FS	0	0			732	FS	0	0	
						701	FS	0	0	
						761	FS	0	0	
						750	SS	1	1	

FIGURE 13.3 (CONTINUED).

13.5 Communicating the Schedule

Not shown on the CPM network, nor in the two activity reports depicted so far, are the responsibility allocations. Each activity belongs to one of the owner, the general contractor, a subcontractor, or a vendor. For networking and computer processing the

PRECEDENCE RELATIONSHIP REPORT

PREDE-CESSOR	LAG TYPE	LAG ORIG	LAG REM	ACTIVITY/DESCRIPTION	FLOAT	SUC-CESSOR	LAG TYPE	LAG ORIG	LAG REM	CALEN-DAR
				732	0					
				STRUCTURAL STEEL FRAME B						
731	FS	0	0			733	FS	0	0	
						702	FS	0	0	
*************	*******	*******	******	**	********	***********	********	*******	********	*********
				733	0					
				STRUCTURAL STEEL FRAME C						
732	FS	0	0			703	FS	0	0	
021	FS	0	0							
723	FS	0	0							
***********	*******	*******	******	**	********	***********	********	*******	********	*********
				750	0					
				STRUCTURAL STEEL						
				INSPECTION						
731	SS	1	1			763	FF	0	0	
701	FF	1	1							
702	FF	1	1							
703	FF	1	1							
*************	******	*******	******	**	********	***********	********	*******	********	*********
				760	43					
				M & D OWSJ						
137	FS	0	0			763	FS	0	0	
*************	*******	*******	******	**	********	***********	********	*******	********	*********
				761	6					
				OWSJ A						
731	FS	0	0			762	FS	0	0	
760	FS	0	0			811	FS	0	0	
						800	SS	1	1	
*************	*******	*******	******	**	********	***********	********	*******	********	*********
				762	9					
				OWSJ B						
761	FS	0	0			763	FS	0	0	
*************	*******	*******	******	**	********	***********	********	*******	********	*********
				763	0					
				OWSJ C						
762	FS	0	0			813	FS	0	0	
750	FF	0	0							
*************	*******	*******	******	**	********	***********	********	******	********	*********
				800	12					
				OWSJ INSPECTION						
761	SS	1	1			811	FS	0	0	
*************	*******	*******	******	**	********	***********	********	*******	********	*********
				811	6					
				ROOF DECK A						
761	FS	0	0			812	FS	0	0	
800	FS	0	0			830	SS	1	1	
081	FS	0	0							
*************	*******	*******	******	**	********	***********	********	*******	********	*********

FIGURE 13.3 (CONTINUED).

responsible organizations were identified with a three-character alphabetic code, which in all cases was simply an abbreviation of the firm's name. The responsibility codes were used to create computerized bar charts and progress report forms.

Examples of resource-allocated or responsibility bar charts are depicted in Fig. 13.6. Figure 13.6*a* depicts the activities that are the project owner's own responsibility. Figure 13.6*b* shows activities for the OWSJ subcontractor, and Fig. 13.6*c* depicts the structural steel construction activities. Other bar charts would show the timing of work for the general contractor, the excavation subcontractor, the formwork and concrete pouring subcontractor, the rebar subcontractor, the sewers subcontractor, and the shoring subcontractor.

PRECEDENCE RELATIONSHIP REPORT

PREDE-CESSOR	LAG TYPE	LAG ORIG	LAG REM	ACTIVITY/DESCRIPTION	FLOAT	SUCCES-SOR	LAG TYPE	LAG ORIG	LAG REM	CALEN-DAR
				812	6					
				ROOF DECK B						
811	FS	0	0			813	FS	0	0	
*********	*******	*******	*****	**************************************	*********	***********	*********	*********	*********	**********
				813	0					
				ROOF DECK C						
812	FS	0	0			999	FS	0	0	
763	FS	0	0							
*********	*******	*******	******	**************************************	********	***********	*********	*********	*********	**********
				830	22					
				ROOF DECK INSPECTION						
811	SS	1	1			999	FS	0	0	
*********	*******	*******	******	**************************************	********	***********	*********	*********	*********	**********
				999	0					
				COMPLETE PROJECT						
830	FS	0	0							
371	FS	0	0							
372	FS	0	0							
373	FS	0	0							
813	FS	0	0							
020	FS	0	0							
004	FS	0	0							
007	FS	0	0							
008	FS	0	0							
*********	*******	*******	******	**************************************	********	***********	*********	*********	*********	**********

FIGURE 13.3 (CONTINUED).

The feature to note here is that although the creation of a CPM network–based schedule is a complex exercise of logic, durations, lags, floats, imposed dates, and so on, the schedule presented to project participants is simplicity itself: bars on a calendar. But the planner should not be lulled into the sense of false security thinking that the bar chart is so simple that just about everybody understands it. There are always people connected with the project who will refuse to understand the schedule, finding it difficult to relate what they do to a bar on a chart.

In this case exercise the discussion and illustrations have been concerned with the creation of the schedule and its setup in the computer. After setup, approval of the completion dates, and dissemination to the project organization, there is the matter of collecting progress information and inputting it for computer processing and progress status reporting.

The progress reporting format used in this case, called "schedule update," is seen in Fig. 13.7. The three parts are related to the owner, OWSJ, and structural steel subcontractor activities depicted as bar charts in Fig. 13.6. In the case history all activities would be treated similarly.

Progress updating is always difficult in that it usually requires concurrence by up to at least three parties that are affected by the completion value assigned to an activity. The subcontractor will hold out for a higher value because it affects the amount that he will be paid. The owner, often represented by a consultant, will hold out for a lower value to hold back money as long as possible. The general contractor wants a higher value to boost his billing, but if too much percentage completion is assigned to an activity, it means that successor activities can go ahead sooner, which may not

ACTIVITY LISTING REPORT

AI	ACTIVITY/DESCRIPTION	DUR EST	DUR REM	EARLY START	EARLY FINISH	LATE START	LATE FINISH	TOTAL FLOAT	IMPOSED DATES
001	AWARD CONTRACT	1	1	19AUG87	19AUG87	19AUG87	19AUG87	0	SE 19AUG87
002	INSTRUCTION TO PROCEED	22	22	20AUG87	21SEP87	20AUG87	21SEP87	0	
003	EXECUTE CONTRACT	1	1	22SEP87	22SEP87	29SEP87	29SEP87	5	
004	CONSTRUCTION SUPERVISION	20	20	20AUG87	17SEP87	29JAN88	25FEB88	111	
005	BUILDERS ALL-RISK INSURANCE	1	1	22SEP87	22SEP87	29SEP87	29SEP87	5	
006	FIELD ENGINEERING SURVEYING	10	10	03SEP87	17SEP87	06OCT87	20OCT87	22	
007	PREPARE CONST. SCHEDULE	20	20	22SEP87	20OCT87	29JAN88	25FEB88	89	
008	RESTORE EXISTING STRUCTURES	5	5	18DEC87	24DEC87	19FEB88	25FEB88	42	
009	PERFORMANCE BOND	1	1	22SEP87	22SEP87	29SEP87	29SEP87	5	
015	DUST CONTROL	20	20	20AUG87	17SEP87	08JAN88	04FEB88	96	
017	MOBILIZATION AND HOARDING	5	5	20AUG87	26AUG87	23SEP87	29SEP87	23	
019	TEMPORARY BUILDINGS	10	10	20AUG87	02SEP87	08SEP87	21SEP87	12	
020	SITE MAINTENANCE	20	20	20AUG87	17SEP87	29JAN88	25FEB88	111	
021	TRAFFIC CONTROL	20	20	27AUG87	24SEP87	04JAN88	29JAN88	87	
022	SUPPORT HYDRO DUCT BANK	5	5	21OCT87	27OCT87	05FEB88	11FEB88	74	
023	DEMOLITION BINS & BUILDING	7	7	23SEP87	01OCT87	30SEP87	08OCT87	5	
024	DEMOLITION RETAINING WALLS	7	7	23SEP87	01OCT87	05OCT87	14OCT87	8	
025	DEMOLITION SIDEWALK	4	4	23SEP87	28SEP87	15OCT87	20OCT87	15	
026	REMOVAL GUARD RAIL	4	4	02OCT87	07OCT87	15OCT87	20OCT87	8	
027	REMOVAL TRACK	7	7	02OCT87	13OCT87	09OCT87	20OCT87	5	
029	REMOVAL TRACK DRAIN	4	4	02OCT87	07OCT87	15OCT87	20OCT87	8	
030	REMOVAL TILE DRAIN	4	4	02OCT87	07OCT87	15OCT87	20OCT87	8	
031	REMOVAL GAS PIPE	5	5	28OCT87	03NOV87	04NOV87	10NOV87	5	
033	REMOVE SHORING & BRACING	5	5	16NOV87	20NOV87	05FEB88	11FEB88	56	
041	INSPECTION EXCAVATION	1	1	11NOV87	11NOV87	18NOV87	18NOV87	5	
042	SHORING & BRACING	5	5	02OCT87	08OCT87	28OCT87	03NOV87	17	
052	SANITARY SEWERS	10	10	11SEP87	24SEP87	29OCT87	11NOV87	33	FL15DEC87
053	SEWER CONNECTIONS	5	5	25SEP87	01OCT87	12NOV87	18NOV87	33	
054	TV INSPECTION OF SEWERS	5	5	03SEP87	10SEP87	22OCT87	28OCT87	33	
056	WATER DISTRIBUTION SYSTEM	20	20	26OCT87	20NOV87	18NOV87	15DEC87	17	FL15DEC87
061	PIPE JACKING & BORING	10	10	09OCT87	23OCT87	04NOV87	17NOV87	17	
073	M & D STR. STEEL	32	32	04NOV87	17DEC87	04NOV87	17DEC87	0	FL27DEC87
074	M & D ANCHOR BOLTS	10	10	26OCT87	06NOV87	16NOV87	27NOV87	15	
081	M & D STEEL DECK	40	40	21OCT87	15DEC87	03DEC87	01FEB88	31	
130	M & D RE-BAR	15	15	22SEP87	14OCT87	19OCT87	06NOV87	18	
131	SHOP DRWGS. SHORE & BRACE	20	20	03SEP87	01DEC87	22SEP87	20OCT87	12	
132	SHOP DRWGS. RE-BAR AREA A	12	12	22SEP87	07OCT87	20OCT87	04NOV87	19	
133	SHOP DRWGS. RE-BAR AREA B	12	12	22SEP87	07OCT87	20OCT87	04NOV87	19	
134	SHOP DRWGS. RE-BAR AREA C	12	12	22SEP87	07OCT87	20OCT87	04NOV87	19	
135	SHOP DRWGS. STRUCT. STEEL	30	30	22SEP87	03NOV87	22SEP87	03NOV87	0	

LEGEND:
AI - ACTIVITY IDENTIFIER
DUR EST - ESTIMATED DURATION
DUR REM - REMAINING DURATION
ES - EARLY START
EF - EARLY FINISH
SE - START NOT EARLIER THAN
FL - FINISH NOT LATER THAN

FIGURE 13.4 COMPUTER REPORT, ACTIVITY LIST SORTED BY AI, ES, EF. This screen shows 40 sample activities from the network in Fig. 13.2, processed by computer as seen in Fig. 13.3, as an example of a classical computer report. The dates are based on the network and a 5-day workweek calendar. This report, as the approved (final) computer run, sets up the schedule for progress reporting. As the work has not started, estimated and remaining duration are the same. The total float is seen to vary from 0 to 111 days. Float values in computer reports sometimes cause consternation. For example, AI 004 Construction Supervision, shows a duration of 20 days and a float of 111 days. The 20-day duration is a nominal value only. The activity needs to be included in the network, and is placed after the project start. But it should not drive the schedule. Similar activities are AI 020 and AI 021. They should not clutter the critical path.

ACTIVITY LIST SORTED BY FLOAT, ES, EF

AI	ACTIVITY/DESCRIPTION	DUR EST	DUR REM	EARLY START	EARLY FINISH	LATE START	LATE FINISH	TOTAL FLOAT	IMPOSED DATES
001	AWARD CONTRACT	1	1	19AUG87	19AUG87	19AUG87	19AUG87	0	SE19AUG87
002	INSTRUCTION TO PROCEED	22	22	20AUG87	21SEP87	20AUG87	21SEP87	0	
135	SHOP DRWGS. STRUCT. STEEL	30	30	22SEP87	03NOV87	22SEP87	03NOV87	0	
073	M & D STR. STEEL	32	32	04NOV87	17DEC87	04NOV87	17DEC87	0	FL27DEC87
731	STRUCTURAL STEEL FRAME A	15	15	18DEC87	12JAN88	18DEC87	12JAN88	0	
732	STRUCTURAL STEEL FRAME B	13	13	13JAN88	29JAN88	13JAN88	29JAN88	0	
733	STRUCTURAL STEEL FRAME C	10	10	01FEB88	12FEB88	01FEB88	12FEB88	0	
763	OWSJ C	5	5	12FEB88	18FEB88	12FEB88	18FEB88	0	
703	GROUT COLUMN BASES C	3	3	15FEB88	17FEB88	15FEB88	17FEB88	0	
750	STRUCTURAL STEEL INSPECTION	1	1	18FEB88	18FEB88	18FEB88	18FEB88	0	
813	ROOF DECK C	5	5	19FEB88	25FEB88	19FEB88	25FEB88	0	
999	COMPLETE PROJECT	3	3	26FEB88	01MAR88	26FEB88	01MAR88	0	
003	EXECUTE CONTRACT	1	1	22SEP87	22SEP87	29SEP87	29SEP87	5	
005	BUILDERS ALL-RISK INSURANCE	1	1	22SEP87	22SEP87	29SEP87	29SEP87	5	
009	PERFORMANCE BOND	1	1	22SEP87	22SEP87	29SEP87	29SEP87	5	
023	DEMOLITION BINS & BUILDING	7	7	23SEP87	01OCT87	30SEP87	08OCT87	5	
027	REMOVAL TRACK	7	7	02OCT87	13OCT87	09OCT87	20OCT87	5	
321	EXCAVATION AREA A	10	10	14OCT87	27OCT87	21OCT87	03NOV87	5	
031	REMOVAL GAS PIPE	5	5	28OCT87	03NOV87	04NOV87	10NOV87	5	
323	EXCAVATION AREA C	7	7	02NOV87	10NOV87	09NOV87	17NOV87	5	
360	REMOVAL OF WATER	3	3	06NOV87	10NOV87	13NOV87	17NOV87	5	
041	INSPECTION EXCAVATION	1	1	11NOV87	11NOV87	18NOV87	18NOV87	5	
652	FORM & POUR FTGS. & PIERS B	10	10	11NOV87	24NOV87	18NOV87	01DEC87	5	
653	FORM & POUR FTGS. & PIERS C	10	10	11NOV87	24NOV87	18NOV87	01DEC87	5	
633	RE-BAR FOOTINGS AREA C	8	8	12NOV87	23NOV87	19NOV87	30NOV87	5	
643	RE-BAR FOUNDATION WALLS C	8	8	25NOV87	04DEC87	02DEC87	11DEC87	5	
663	FORM & POUR FDN. WALLS C	10	10	25NOV87	08DEC87	02DEC87	15DEC87	5	FL 15DEC87
761	OWSJ A	8	8	13JAN88	22JAN88	21JAN88	01FEB88	6	
811	ROOF DECK A	8	8	25JAN88	03FEB88	02FEB88	11FEB88	6	
812	ROOF DECK B	5	5	04FEB88	10FEB88	12FEB88	18FEB88	6	
024	DEMOLITION RETAINING WALLS	7	7	23SEP87	01OCT87	05OCT87	14OCT87	8	
026	REMOVAL GUARD RAIL	4	4	02OCT87	07OCT87	15OCT87	20OCT87	8	
029	REMOVAL TRACK DRAIN	4	4	02OCT87	07OCT87	15OCT87	20OCT87	8	
030	REMOVAL TILE DRAIN	4	4	02OCT87	07OCT87	15OCT87	20OCT87	8	
631	RE-BAR FOOTINGS A	8	8	28OCT87	06NOV87	09NOV87	18NOV87	8	
651	FORM & POUR FTGS. & PIERS A	10	10	28OCT87	10NOV87	09NOV87	20NOV87	8	
641	RE-BAR FOUNDATION WALLS A	8	8	11NOV87	20NOV87	23NOV87	02DEC87	8	
661	FORM & POUR FDN. WALLS A	7	7	13NOV87	23NOV87	25NOV87	03DEC87	8	FL15DEC87
441	STORM SEWERS CBS & MHS	8	8	24NOV87	03DEC87	04DEC87	15DEC87	8	
442	STORM SEWERS PIPING	7	7	25NOV87	03DEC87	07DEC87	15DEC87	8	FL15DEC87
762	OWSJ B	5	5	25JAN88	29JAN88	05FEB88	11FEB88	9	

LEGEND:
SE - START NOT EARLIER THAN
FL - FINISH NOT LATER THAN
ES - EARLY START
EF - EARLY FINISH
AI - ACTIVITY IDENTIFIER

FIGURE 13.5 COMPUTER REPORT, ACTIVITY LIST SORTED BY CRITICALITY, ES, EF. This screen shows all the activities with 0 float, and those with low float values up to 9 days, from the network in Fig. 13.2 and the computer report in Fig. 13.3. The date results are based on the network and a 5-day workweek calendar. This report sets up the schedule for progress reporting. As the estimated and the remaining duration are the same, the work is not yet started. It is evident from the low float values of the many activities near the critical path and the low incremental increases in float that the project is tightly scheduled.

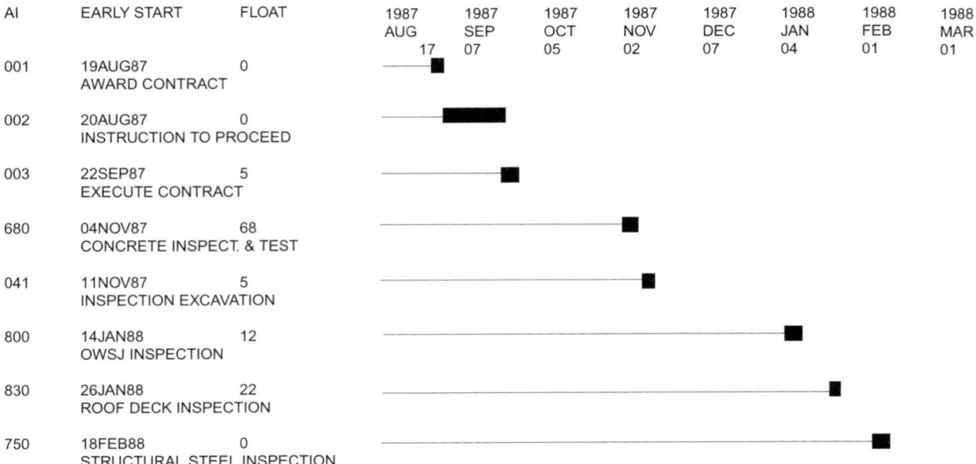

FIGURE 13.6*a* COMPUTER REPORT, OWNER BAR CHART SORTED BY ES, EF. Every activity in the schedule is assigned to a resource, i.e., one of the owner, the contractor, a subcontractor, a vendor, or a consultant. The schedule, created by a computer-processed network of hard activities based on progress billing items agreed between the owner and the general contractor, is communicated by bar charts, as depicted in this graphic, showing the owner's activities and their timelines. The dark bars show the duration and early start date for the activity named.

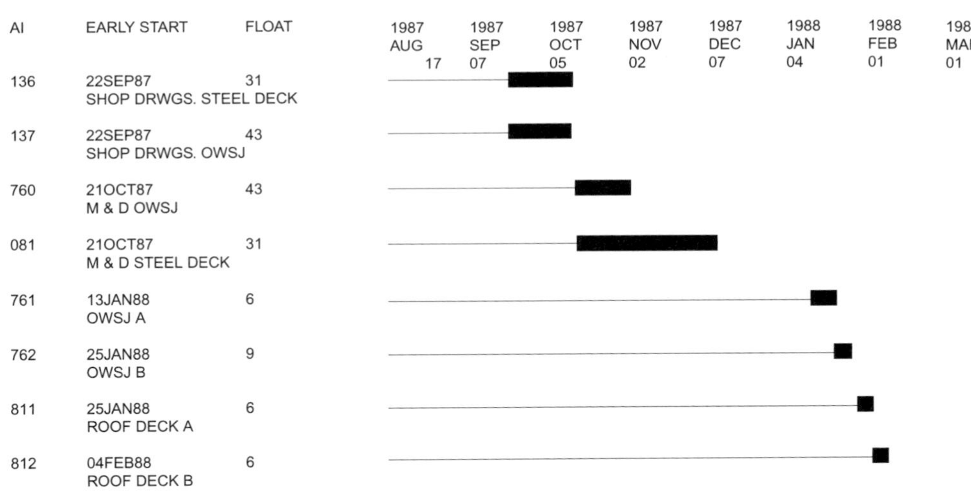

FIGURE 13.6*b* COMPUTER REPORT, OWSJ BAR CHART SORTED BY ES, EF. This graphic shows the OWSJ subcontractor's activities and their timelines. The dark bars shows the duration and early start date for the activity named. If the activities have float, which can be checked from Fig. 13.3, the float is not shown because it does not belong to the OWSJ subcontractor. The float in this kind of a construction schedule belongs to the general contractor. It would be the general contractor's duty to allocate float as required to save the schedule if and when needed.

BAR CHART REPORT FOR STRUCTURAL STEEL SUBCONTRACTOR ORGANIZATION

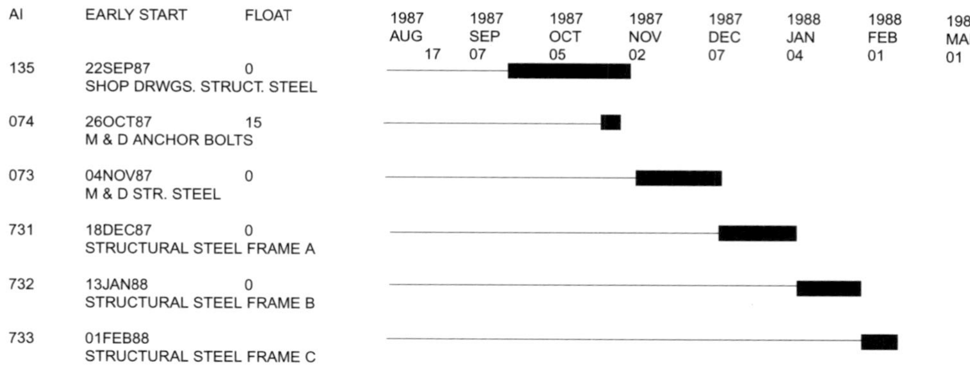

M & D = MANUFACTURE AND DELIVER

FIGURE 13.6*c* COMPUTER REPORT, STRUCTURAL STEEL BAR CHART SORTED BY ES, EF. This graphic shows the structural steel subcontractor's activities and their timelines. The dark bars show the duration and early start date for the activity named. If the activities have float, which can be checked from Fig. 13.3, the float is not shown because it does not belong to this subcontractor.

be the real status. This all depends on activities being hard activities as defined in this book, meaning that they exist in the billing stream, are quantifiable, and are objectively identifiable.

In this particular case history it is seen from a number of printouts that the project start date is 19AUG87. When setting up the CPM network, all activities must be tied to that date. All computer output is geared to a "time now" of 19AUG87.

"Time now" changes only after the project is under way and progress reporting is initiated. To illustrate the system at work, Fig. 13.8 provides the status of every activity in the project as of a time now of 31DEC87. It is seen that the activities are listed in ascending order by activity number. Actual start and actual finish dates are shown under the early column dates for those activities that are finished. Total float is shown for incomplete activities only. Negative total float indicates an activity that is behind schedule. This particular report says that the project is 12 days behind schedule (total float −12), with the projected completion date being 17MAR88 compared with a required completion date of 01MAR88. The project eventually was completed on 10MAR88, compared to the originally required end of 01MAR88.

13.6 Summary

Monthly construction project billings are as regular as clockworks. Most often the billing items are negotiated and agreed before the start of the project. The breakdowns

CURRENT SCHEDULE UPDATE OWNER ORGANIZATION ACTIVITIES

AI	ACTIVITY DESCRIPTION	ORIGINAL DUR.	START ACTUAL	START FORECAST	% COM-PLETE	REMAIN-ING DUR.	FINISH ACTUAL	FINISH FORECAST
001	AWARD CONTRACT	1	START	19AUG87	PC.......... 0 %	RD 1	FINISH	19AUG87
002	INSTRUCTION TO PROCEED	22	START	20AUG87	PC.......... 0 %	RD 22	FINISH	21SEP87
003	EXECUTE CONTRACT	1	START	22SEP87	PC.......... 0 %	RD 1	FINISH	22SEP87
680	CONCRETE INSPECT. & TEST	1	START	04NOV87	PC.......... 0 %	RD 1	FINISH	04NOV87
041	INSPECTION EXCAVATION	1	START	11NOV87	PC.......... 0 %	RD 1	FINISH	11NOV87
800	OWSJ INSPECTION	1	START	14JAN88	PC.......... 0 %	RD 1	FINISH	14JAN88
830	ROOF DECK INSPECTION	1	START	26JAN88	PC.......... 0 %	RD 1	FINISH	26JAN88
750	STRUCTURAL STEEL INSPECTION	1	START	18FEB88	PC.......... 0 %	RD 1	FINISH	18FEB88

LEGEND:
PC - PERCENT
RD - REMAINING DURATION

FIGURE 13.7*a* COMPUTER REPORT, OWNER ACTIVITIES, CURRENT SCHEDULE UPDATE. On lump sum construction contracts the agreement requires that the owner pay the contractor monthly, and that the contractor pay the subcontractors after being paid. This sets up a monthly cost and progress reporting system. This figure shows computer-generated menus suitable for reporting progress. As the above are owner activities, they are not contractor pay items, but they would have an important impact on the schedule and therefore progress billings. The dates shown are computer dates. The actual start and finish dates would be input to reflect progress.

frequently follow an industry standard, like Masterformat, or the Uniform Construction Index. This chapter has shown how to use the billing items to create a CPM network of schedule activities that are credible and reliable because the elements exist as billable items.

To go from cost to schedule it was demonstrated how cost items needed to be broken down to create schedule activities, and the scheduling network designed to reflect both logical relationships and management's strategic decisions. The network must be computer processed, because even a small network of 84 activities, as was the case here, generates complexity.

Computer processing after handling complex calculations, including logic, activity identifiers, descriptions, resource codes, durations, relationships, and a calendar, generates all kinds of communications tools, including schedule bar charts, resources and responsibility assignment reports, and progress report forms, all aimed to schedule the project and monitor its progress.

CURRENT SCHEDULE UPDATE OWSJ SUBCONTRACTOR ACTIVITIES

AI	ACTIVITY DESCRIPTION	ORIGINAL DUR.	START ACTUAL	START FORECAST	% COM-PLETE	REMAIN-ING DUR.	FINISH ACTUAL	FINISH FORECAST
136	SHOP DRWGS. STEEL DECK	20	START	22SEP87	PC.......... 0 %	RD 20	FINISH	20OCT87
137	SHOP DRWGS. OWSJ	20	START	22SEP87	PC.......... 0 %	RD 20	FINISH	20OCT87
760	M & D OWSJ	20	START	21OCT87	PC.......... 0 %	RD 20	FINISH	17NOV87
081	M & D STEEL DECK	40	START	21OCT87	PC.......... 0 %	RD 40	FINISH	15DEC87
761	OWSJ A	8	START	13JAN88	PC.......... 0 %	RD 8	FINISH	22JAN88
762	OWSJ B	5	START	25JAN88	PC.......... 0 %	RD 5	FINISH	29JAN88
811	ROOF DECK A	8	START	25JAN88	PC.......... 0 %	RD 5	FINISH	03FEB88
812	ROOF DECK B	5	START	04FEB88	PC.......... 0 %	RD 5	FINISH	10FEB88
763	OWSJ C	5	START	12FEB88	PC.......... 0 %	RD 5	FINISH	18FEB88
813	ROOF DECK C	5	START	19FEB88	PC.......... 0 %	RD 5	FINISH	25FEB88

FIGURE 13.7*b* COMPUTER REPORT, OWSJ ACTIVITIES, CURRENT SCHEDULE UPDATES. This figure shows a computer-generated menu for reporting progress of activities which are the responsibility of the OWSJ subcontractor. The start and finish forecast dates shown are computer generated. The actual start and finish dates would be input to reflect progress. The percent complete figure and the remaining duration would be negotiated between contractor and subcontractor, and the agreed information input to reflect progress. As these activities are based on billing items, there is a direct linkage created between the reporting of cost and progress.

CURRENT SCHEDULE UPDATE STRUCTURAL STEEL SUBCONTRACTOR

AI	ACTIVITY DESCRIPTION	ORIGINAL DUR.	START ACTUAL	START FORECAST	% COM-PLETE	REMAIN-ING DUR.	FINISH ACTUAL	FINISH FORECAST
135	SHOP DRWGS. STRUCT. STEEL	30	START	22SEP87	PC.......... 0 %	RD 30	FINISH	03NOV87
074	M & D ANCHOR BOLTS	10	START	26OCT87	PC.......... 0 %	RD 10	FINISH	06NOV87
073	M & D STR. STEEL	32	START	04NOV87	PC.......... 0 %	RD 32	FINISH	17DEC87
731	STRUCTURAL STEEL FRAME A	32	START	18DEC87	PC.......... 0 %	RD 15	FINISH	12JAN88
732	STRUCTURAL STEEL FRAME B	13	START	13JAN88	PC.......... 0 %	RD 13	FINISH	29JAN88
733	STRUCTURAL STEEL FRAME C	10	START	01FEB88	PC.......... 0 %	RD 10	FINISH	12FEB88

ACTIVITY LISTING REPORT AS OF 31DEC87

AI	ACTIVITY/DESCRIPTION	DUR EST	DUR REM	EARLY START	EARLY FINISH	LATE START	LATE FINISH	TOTAL FLOAT	IMPOSED DATES
001	AWARD CONTRACT	1	0	19AUG87A	19AUG87A				SE 19AUG87
002	INSTRUCTION TO PROCEED	22	0	09SEP87A	21SEP87A				
003	EXECUTE CONTRACT	1	0	23SEP87A	23SEP87A				
004	CONSTRUCTION SUPERVISION	20	5	14SEP87A	07JAN88		25FEB88	35	
005	BUILDERS ALL-RISK INSURANCE	1	0	22SEP87A	23SEP87A				
006	FIELD ENGINEERING SURVEYING	10	2	22SEP87A	04JAN88		27NOV87	-23	
007	PREPARE CONST. SCHEDULE	20	0	22SEP87A	25SEP87A				
008	RESTORE EXISTING STRUCTURES	5	5	11JAN88	15JAN88	19FEB88	25FEB88	29	
009	PERFORMANCE BOND	1	0	22SEP87A	22SEP87A				
015	DUST CONTROL	20	2	05OCT87A	04JAN88		17FEB88	32	
017	MOBILIZATION AND HOARDING	5	0	14SEP87A	01DEC87A				
019	TEMPORARY BUILDINGS	10	0	14SEP87A	24SEP87A				
020	SITE MAINTENANCE	20	8	05OCT87A	12JAN88		25FEB88	32	
021	TRAFFIC CONTROL	20	4	05OCT87A	06JAN88		29JAN88	17	
022	SUPPORT HYDRO DUCT BANK	5	1	26OCT87A	05JAN88		23FEB88	35	
023	DEMOLITION BINS & BUILDING	7	0	23SEP87A	01OCT87A				
024	DEMOLITION RETAINING WALLS	7	0	05OCT87A	06OCT87A				
025	DEMOLITION SIDEWALK	4	0	05OCT87A	06OCT87A				
026	REMOVAL GUARD RAIL	4	0	02OCT87A	03OCT87A				
027	REMOVAL TRACK	7	0	02OCT87A	03OCT87A				
029	REMOVAL TRACK DRAIN	4	0	02OCT87A	07OCT87A				
030	REMOVAL TILE DRAIN	4	0	02OCT87A	03OCT87A				
031	REMOVAL GAS PIPE	5	0	09OCT87A	09OCT87A				
033	REMOVE SHORING & BRACING	5	5	31DEC87	07JAN88	09DEC87	15DEC87	-14	
041	INSPECTION EXCAVATION	1	0	06OCT87A	27NOV87A				
042	SHORING & BRACING	5	0	22OCT87A	10NOV87A				
052	SANITARY SEWERS	10	0	19NOV87A	23NOV87A				FL15DEC87
053	SEWER CONNECTIONS	5	0	19NOV87A	23NOV87A				
054	TV INSPECTION OF SEWERS	5	0	02NOV87A	21NOV87A				
056	WATER DISTRIBUTION SYSTEM	20	2	09NOV87A	04JAN88		15DEC87	-11	FL15DEC87
061	PIPE JACKING & BORING	10	0	05NOV87A	20NOV87A				
073	M & D STR. STEEL	40	20	01DEC87A	28JAN88		24DEC87	-22	FL27DEC87
074	M & D ANCHOR BOLTS	10	0	26OCT87A	06NOV87A				
081	M & D STEEL DECK	40	40	31DEC87	25FEB88	16DEC87	12FEB88	-9	
130	M & D RE-BAR	15	0	14OCT87A	01DEC87A				
131	SHOP DRWGS. SHORE & BRACE	20	0	25SEP87A	08OCT87A				
132	SHOP DRWGS. RE-BAR AREA A	12	0	24SEP87A	14OCT87A				
133	SHOP DRWGS. RE-BAR AREA B	12	0	24SEP87A	22OCT87A				
134	SHOP DRWGS. RE-BAR AREA C	12	0	13OCT87A	20NOV87A				
135	SHOP DRWGS. STRUCT. STEEL	30	0	08OCT87A	27NOV87A				

LEGEND:
"A" AFTER DATE = ACTUAL DATE
"-" BEFORE FLOAT VALUE=BEHIND SCHEDULE BY VALUE IN DAYS

FIGURE 13.8 COMPUTER REPORT, PROGESS STATUS. This is a list of the status of all the activities in the network in Fig. 13.2 and in the computer report in Fig. 13.3 as of the cut off date of 31 December 1987. It is seen that completed activities have 0 days of remaining duration and 0 float. A number of current activities are seen to have negative float, signifying that they are behind schedule. Activity 999, Complete Project, is forecast to be behind schedule by 12 days.

FIGURE 13.7c COMPUTER REPORT, STRUCTURAL STEEL, CURRENT SCHEDULE UPDATE. This figure shows a computer-generated menu for reporting progress of activities which are the responsibility of the structural steel subcontractor. The start and finish forecast dates shown are computer generated. These forecast dates at the beginning of a project are the early start and finish dates. As progress is made, the forecast dates may be imposed by management. Based on experience, schedule control is more reliable if based on working with actual dates, remaining durations, and percentage completions, and allowing the system to generate the forecast start and finish dates. Other information is as discussed in the two previous parts.

ACTIVITY LISTING REPORT AS OF 31DEC87

AI	ACTIVITY/DESCRIPTION	DUR EST	DUR REM	EARLY START	EARLY FINISH	LATE START	LATE FINISH	TOTAL FLOAT	IMPOSED DATES
136	SHOP DRWGS. STEEL DECK	20	0	25NOV87A	29DEC87A				
137	SHOP DRWGS. OWSJ	20	4	30NOV87A	06JAN88		05JAN88	-1	
321	EXCAVATION AREA A	10	0	05OCT87A	27NOV87A				
322	EXCAVATION AREA B	7	0	09OCT87A	27NOV87A				
323	EXCAVATION AREA C	7	0	16OCT87A	27NOV87A				
360	REMOVAL OF WATER	3	1	08OCT87A	04JAN88		10DEC87	-14	
371	BACKFILL A	10	2	30OCT87A	22JAN88		25FEB88	24	
372	BACKFILL B	10	1	25NOV87A	08JAN88		25FEB88	34	
373	BACKFILL C	10	1	09DEC87A	08JAN88		18FEB88	29	
441	STORM SEWERS C.B.S & M.H.S	8	1	09NOV87A	07JAN88		15DEC87	-14	
442	STORM SEWERS PIPING	7	1	26NOV87A	07JAN88		15DEC87	-14	FL15DEC87
631	RE-BAR FOOTINGS AREA A	8	0	14OCT87A	07DEC87A				
632	RE-BAR FOOTINGS AREA B	8	0	19OCT87A	03DEC87A				
633	RE-BAR FOOTINGS AREA C	8	0	27OCT87A	09DEC87A				
641	RE-BAR FDN. WALLS	8	1	12NOV87A	05JAN88		30NOV87	-23	
642	RE-BAR FOUNDATION WALLS B	8	0	09NOV87A	30DEC87A				
643	RE-BAR FOUNDATION WALLS C	8	1	20NOV87A	05JAN88		11DEC87	-14	
651	FORM & POUR FTGS. & PIERS A	10	0	13OCT87A	26OCT87A				
652	FORM & POUR FTGS. & PIERS B	10	0	14OCT87A	07DEC87A				
653	FORM & POUR FTGS. & PIERS C	10	0	19OCT87A	07DEC87A				
661	FORM & POUR FDN. WALLS A	7	1	13NOV87A	06JAN88		01DEC87	-23	FL15DEC87
662	FORM & POUR FDN. WALLS B	10	1	05NOV87A	05JAN88		15DEC87	-11	FL15DEC87
663	FORM & POUR FDN. WALLS C	10	1	18NOV87A	07JAN88		15DEC87	-14	FL15DEC87
664*	FORM & POUR WALLS ABOVE GR.*	10	10	07JAN88	20JAN88	02DEC87	15DEC87	-23	FL15DEC87
680	CONCRETE INSPECT. & TEST	1	1	08OCT87A	20JAN88		15DEC87	-23	FL15DEC87
701	GROUT COLUMN BASES A	3	3	19FEB88	23FEB88	15FEB88	17FEB88	-4	
702	GROUT COLUMN BASES B	3	3	19FEB88	23FEB88	15FEB88	17FEB88	-4	
703	GROUT COLUMN BASES C	3	3	18FEB88	22FEB88	15FEB88	17FEB88	-3	
721	STR. STEEL ANCHOR BOLTS A	2	0	13NOV87A	07DEC87A				
722	STR. STEEL ANCHOR BOLTS B	2	0	05NOV87A	07DEC87A				
723	STR. STEEL ANCHOR BOLTS C	2	0	18NOV87A	07DEC87A				
731	STRUCTURAL STEEL FRAME A	15	15	29JAN88	18FEB88	13JAN88	02FEB88	-12	
732	STRUCTURAL STEEL FRAME B	13	13	02FEB88	18FEB88	27JAN88	12FEB88	-4	
733	STRUCTURAL STEEL FRAME C	10	10	04FEB88	17FEB88	01FEB88	12FEB88	-3	
750	STRUCTURAL STEEL INSPECTION	1	1	24FEB88	24FEB88	18FEB88	18FEB88	-4	
760	M & D OWSJ	20	20	30DEC87A	03FEB88		02FEB88	-1	
761	OWSJ A	8	8	19FEB88	01MAR88	03FEB88	12FEB88	-12	
762	OWSJ B	5	5	23FEB88	29FEB88	10FEB88	16FEB88	-9	
763	OWSJ C	5	5	25FEB88	02MAR88	12FEB88	18FEB88	-9	
800	OWSJ INSPECTION	1	1	22FEB88	22FEB88	12FEB88	12FEB88	-6	
811	ROOF DECK A	8	8	02MAR88	11MAR88	15FEB88	24FEB88	-12	
812	ROOF DECK B	5	5	04MAR88	10MAR88	17FEB88	23FEB88	-12	
813	ROOF DECK C	5	5	08MAR88	14MAR88	19FEB88	25FEB88	-12	
830	ROOF DECK INSPECTION	1	1	03MAR88	03MAR88	25FEB88	25FEB88	-5	
999	COMPLETE PROJECT	3	3	15MAR88	17MAR88	26FEB88	01MAR88	-12	

LEGEND:
*** ACTIVITY 664 WAS ADDED IN COMPUTER PROCESSING. IT IS NOT SEEN IN FIGURE 13.2**
"A" AFTER DATE = ACTUAL DATE
"-" BEFORE FLOAT VALUE = BEHIND SCHEDULE BY VALUE IN DAYS

FIGURE 13.8 (CONTINUED).

Note: This chapter is based on my experience as the general contractor's project scheduling consultant for the project identified. The consulting assignment started at the award of the contract to the successful or low bidder and extended through the construction stage to the project's substantial completion. My involvement was: creating a work breakdown structure for the identification of activities for CPM scheduling; assigning and coordinating activity durations; monitoring and processing construction progress by computer; and reporting the status of the project against a set of milestone events.

The project files are the references. These files comprise work breakdown structures, the development of activities and their assignment to the general contractor and subcontractors, CPM precedence diagram network drawings, and monthly computer outputs.

QUESTIONS AND EXERCISES

13.1. Create a project team as follows: Assume that the instructor is the customer or owner. The team, including the customer, is to consist of a project manager, a project engineer, an estimator, a scheduler, a construction manager, a cost engineer, and a cost accountant. In a private- or public-sector environment, a CEO or a manager acts as the customer. The roles are as follows:

Customer or owner	Pays the bills. Has a foolproof lump sum general contract.
Project manager	Coordinator, consensus builder, and final authority. The project manager's decision can only be overridden by the customer, with the consent of the project team.
Project engineer	Scribe, writer of record, coordinator of documentation, main communicator of information.
Estimator	Responsible for the assignment and allocation of the amounts available to the coded items and tasks.
Construction manager	Creates packages, and therefore subcontracts, of activities. All construction contractors report to the construction manager.
Cost engineer	Responsible for all project coding, including assigning codes to all items, activities, packages, and contracts. Acts as the liaison between the estimator and the cost accountant.
Cost accountant	Responsible for approving bills for payment by the customer. This involves analysis of work content, development of budgeted cost of work scheduled, budgeted cost of work performed, and analysis of actual cost of work performed.

13.2. Download or obtain a commercial or educational copy of the project management software application Open Plan Professional (OPP), an equal application, or a software package of your choice.

13.3. Using the selected software, its rules and strictures, and the rules in this textbook, recreate some aspects of bills 1, 2, 3, and 4 from Fig. 13.1 as a work breakdown structure.

13.4. Assume that 50% of the costs assigned to the line items in the bills are labor carried out by human resources. Assume that the cost of labor is $50.00 per hour, including all equipment and overheads. Assign the labor costs to the coded work breakdown elements developed in Question 13.3.

13.5. Develop a coded project organizational breakdown structure incorporating the project team from item 13.1 and the construction contractors below. The construction contractors are responsible for the following activities:

Drillco	Shoring and bracing
Gilbert	Rebar
GL	Site service (sewer, water)
Hepburn	Structural steel
Janin	General contractor (all other activities)
London	Excavation
Lorlea	OWSJ and steel deck
Ontario	Form, pour concrete, install anchor bolts
TTC	Owner activities

Create and assign a three-letter alphabetic code to each organization.

13.6. Assign each activity to an organization.

13.7. Using the team's creativity and the processing capability of the software create a schedule using both a bar chart and a network based on the activities from Fig. 13.2. Use the logic and values from Fig. 13.3. Assume a project start date of 2000/06/02. Assuming a five-day workweek and the legal holidays in your state or province, calculate the project completion date.

13.8. Apply the appropriate human resources in hours to the correct activities and computer run a human resources histogram for the whole project. Computer run a resources histogram for each construction organization.

PART 4

PROJECT MANAGEMENT SUPPORT SYSTEMS

PROCUREMENT AND PURCHASING 14

14.1 Introduction

In the North American capital projects industries, the process of project management invariably involves procurement and purchasing. Some form of procurement is necessary in every project, large or small, whether a capital goods undertaking or the purchase of services, such as the development of software. Few if any enterprises are sufficient unto themselves to the extent that purchases are unnecessary. Indeed, the postmodern approach to the delivery of all kinds of goods and services more than ever is dependent on the concept of "just-in-time delivery" making procurement and purchasing more of an integral part of the project management process than ever.

The systems of project management promoted in this textbook recognize procurement as a seamless aspect of the project management process. It is treated in much the same way as engineering, manufacturing, assembling, and constructing. Purchased services, equipment, processes, computers, software, and all kinds of human resources skills purchased for the project are treated as an extension of the makeup of the extended project functional organization. Their roles and responsibilities are set by the terms of the agreement between them and the buyer of their goods and services, that is, the owner, or the agent acting on behalf of the owner.

The Preface first makes mention that most corporations do not employ large numbers of project employees and practice a "buy" policy as opposed to "make" and look for delivery neither earlier nor later than just in time. Issues such as resources leveling are thus downloaded to the selling organizations.

In this textbook procurement as a generic form is assigned its own stage or phase in the life cycle of project stages created by the application of the work breakdown structure. Procurement can be facilitated by a spoken agreement, a verbal order, a handshake, a memo, a journal entry voucher, a requisition, a purchase order, a contract, a request for quotation, a contemplated change notice, a change order, an engineer's order, or a lawful command by an agent or officer of a government body having jurisdiction.

Procurement may be expected to be required at any level of a project definition structure, meaning that a purchaser may buy a complete turnkey project, which signifies that the purchaser only pays the bills for a facility or system that is delivered ready to run by the turning of a key.

At the other end of the spectrum is the project where the purchaser buys every last nut and bolt, hires individual people skills, and acts as the constructor to put it all together. North American automobiles used to be done that way, but no longer. Today entire systems are purchased and assembled as cars. Most projects fall somewhere between these two extremes.

14.2 Procurement Stages

In Chapter 3 the project processes of procurement, bidding, and contract awards are defined as stage 5 in the nine classical project stages identified as concept 1 in Fig. 3.7.

In the same chapter Fig. 3.8, WBS concept 2; Fig. 3.9, WBS concept 3, and Fig. 3.10, airport project WBS example, identify procurement and tendering (or bidding) and awards as the stage 6 processes of the nine programmed phases or stages identified in these work breakdown concepts.

On the other hand, the power generating project WBS, concept 1 in Fig. 3.11, shows procurement, tendering, and award as phase 5 of seven phases.

The discussions on work breakdown processes in Chapter 3 invariably involve procurement and purchasing. Procurement, purchasing, and contracting are integral parts of project management. Project management is not viable without procurement management. On the other hand procurement practices could be "promoted" to become project management.

Section 3.8 expands further the discussion on project procurement phases and provides examples of procurement phase deliverables in Table 3.10. It is seen from this discussion that procurement packages are created for and aimed at all members of the project delivery teams, and not only at vendors and contractors.

Section 4.1 discusses the place of procurement and purchasing in a "non-project- management" environment, where sovereign departments each take turns in being in charge of the project. Figure 4.1 shows procurement, tendering, bidding, and award as stage 7 of the 12 stages of the project life cycle in a non-project-management environment.

14.3 Construction Contracts as Procurement Methods

Section 4.3 illustrates 16 ways to deliver construction projects. Each of these ways may be considered a procurement method, but the ramifications are much broader in that each way affects all aspects of a project, including issues of scope, quality, cost, and schedule. The pros and cons of each way are listed from the perspective of the owner, but the effects would be broadly spread and impact all delivery team members.

The procurement of a project can start with the appointment of a project manager if the person is from outside the owner organization. On the other hand, if the owner appoints (orders, requisitions, seconds) the project manager from within, that too is a form of procurement. The owner or the newly appointed project manager now appoints, orders, or procures designers, planners, experts, programmers, and so on, to carry out the tasks and packages of tasks related to the various project stages to progress the project. The tasks and packages take on identities based on the work breakdown. As the packages are assigned, bid, tendered, and awarded to the project functional organization, they become work orders, purchase orders, contracts, or other enabling documents. At the point in time when all the purchase orders are placed we could say that the project is fully procured or committed. More often than not, this happens after the project is completed.

As reviewed and summarized in Section 4.5, the purchase orders and contracts are the final means for project cost and expenditure control. The tasks within the purchase orders and contracts are the basis for schedule and progress control. And quality control is achieved because of the excellence of the documentation linking project scope to the deliverables resulting from the purchase orders and contracts.

Chapter 5 discusses how project cost flows from project definition and work breakdown to people in functional organizations. As people are ultimately responsible for everything, their relationship with the project is invariably a matter of some form of procurement.

14.4 Purchase Orders as Sources of Cost

Section 5.7 shows project organizations classified into "sources of cost," depending on the service they provide or the type of instrument used to buy their services, such as, purchase order or contract.

Section 5.8 provides a number of project cost and expenditure control reports, while illustrating the important role played by contracts and purchase orders in the financial management of projects.

The case history in Chapter 7 presents project management processes in a corporate engineering department. Section 7.2 includes a discussion on the importance of procurement and purchasing activities in successful management. Figures 7.1, and 7.2 in Section 7.2 show the place and techniques of procurement and purchasing. Procurement in this case is seen to be phase 3 of the five phases used for project management by the subject company. Furthermore purchasing and material management are seen to be linked across a number of aspects of the project delivery process.

Section 7.9, in presenting experienced forms of project cost and expenditure control, shows that the procurement method is a key cost source column in a high-level multiple-project cost summary report, as illustrated by Fig. 7.25. Figure 7.29 depicts an individual project expenditure report where the mode of procurement, the cost source, is the first column.

14.5 Summary

That procurement and purchasing are essential to successful project management is a given. That they are not necessarily considered as project management processes per se is a fact of corporate and bureaucratic life. Even the largest projects are not stand alone in every respect, in that they need to respond to corporate functions of the owner, such as accounting, finance, human resources, legal, operations, and corporate purchasing.

While certain corporate functions such as accounting and finance are project approving bodies, the corporate purchasing function is most often an integral part of the project delivery process. Although the purchasing and procurement people functions may not fall under the direct purview of the project manager, their processes, roles, and responsibilities must be integrated into the systems of project management for successful outcomes.

Note: This chapter is based on my experience as a corporate engineer, systems engineer, project manager, and project management consultant. The 16 ways of procuring projects discussed within Chapter 4 was based on a consulting assignment with a department of public works of the federal government. The public works department was a repeat builder of many different types of projects. As a systems engineer for the engineering department of a large multiplant corporation in the process industry, I identified the many different forms of assignment of tasks and purchasing processes and included them as "sources of cost" in the project control system.

The project files are the references. These files comprise the project management processes, including the development of tasks, packages of work, purchasing requisitions, purchase orders, requests for quotations, bidding documents, bids, contracts, and other documentation normally associated with procurement and purchasing.

QUESTIONS AND EXERCISES

14.1. What are the advantages and disadvantages, from the customer's perspective, of the lump sum general contract way of procuring a new building facility?

14.2. What set of circumstances in the North American business environment gave rise to the invention of new project delivery methods commonly referred to as construction management, including the approaches known as fast tracking, and project management?

14.3. At what stage can procurement occur in project work, considering procurement in the broadest sense?

MATERIALS MANAGEMENT

15

15.1 Introduction

The term "materials management" can have a very narrow or a very broad interpretation. In the narrowest sense it means tracking a package shipped by express from point A to point B. In the broadest interpretation it means conceptualizing the functionality of the gadget and tracking it through its life cycle stages, that is, making a project out of it.

In this book the term is intended to mean the permanent materials, elements, or systems that make up the functionality of the finished project. Discounting overheads and cost of money for the moment, every project is made up of only two components. Labor is one. The other is materials, the subject of this chapter.

15.2 The Origins of Materials

A very important aspect of project control is a materials management, or materials control, system. This is recognized and acknowledged in Section 7.3, where under the heading of materials control, eight aspects of materials takeoff are identified. The need for and the methods of materials control are expanded upon in Section 7.4. In Section 7.5 Fig. 7.4, which depicts 11 project control systems, includes a materials control system.

In project work materials originate with drawings and specifications. They are procured by purchase orders or as packages, alone or in conjunction with labor, by contract. They are identified within startup systems, and after procurement they are expedited by their purchase order and by the startup system to which they belong.

A discussion of the subject of equipment and materials control requires the introduction of the topics of inspection and quality control as well as differentiating materials control methods between the different ways of acquiring projects. For example, from the perspective of the project owner, a materials control system for a lump sum general contract would be different than the materials control system for a construction management contract where the owner is responsible for the purchase of major equipment and strategic materials.

Traditionally, from a corporate multiple-project perspective, corporations buy civil and building facilities by lump sum or cost-plus contracts, making the contractors responsible for materials control. A materials control system is required for those situations where the corporate enterprise is required to buy strategic equipment and associated piping, electrical, instrumentation, and computer control services. Examples of these kinds of projects are health facilities, pharmaceutical plants, process plants, and research and development laboratories.

15.3 Project Materials Control System

Another consideration is that as most drawings are now CAD produced, and as CAD software is designed to produce quantity takeoffs and generate bills of materials, it follows that any materials control system may be based on the CAD system as the first source of materials control information, and progressively computer integrated into the systems of project definition, work breakdown, functional organization, and cost and schedule control systems, as discussed throughout this textbook. Such a project materials control system could be called PROMACO.

PROMACO could be computer integrated up and down the project definition structures, the functional organizational structures, and across all project functions. As project definitions are computer produced, incorporating strategic equipment and their function codes, materials and equipment would be identified and coded from the beginning of design and drawing. As drawings are computer produced by architects and engineers, the drawings would be accompanied by bills of material. And as tasks and packages are assigned to organizations, the packages would include bills of material.

Figure 7.4 shows materials control as one of 11 enterprise systems, including the five systems of dedicated project management presented in this book. Materials control is located on its own, as are other enterprise systems such as procurement and corporate systems. The corporate ownership and location of any information system in an enterprise is often hotly debated. The five dedicated project control systems (plus graphics) are specifically project oriented and belong to the project managers, but as the corporation procures materials for all kinds of other purposes, not only projects, both procurement and materials are depicted outside the project control purview in Fig. 7.4.

The PROMACO computer module as a corporate materials control system, applicable to project control as presented in this textbook, could be developed as a database system capable of warehousing and delivering the following information:

Material code
Material description
Process and instrumentation diagram (P.&I.D.) no.
Project no.
Subproject no.
Area/element code
Quantity required

Drawing no.
Specification no.
Quality control parameters
Requisition no.
Purchase order no.
Contract no.
Work package no.
Startup system no.
Manufacturer's drawing no.
Needed date
Part no.
Vendor name
Commodity type
Quantity delivered
Quantity installed
Shortage or surplus
Current status
Daily material receipt (DMR) no.
Delivered date
Warehouse location
Person responsible for:
- Engineering
- Quantity
- Quality
- Procurement
- Expediting
- Installation
- Startup

As an example of data requirements in the procurement cycle alone, the following schedule information is given:

Requisition schedule date
Requisition issued date
Purchase order schedule date
Purchase order issued date
Required on-site date
Latest promise date

Latest vendor drawing approval date
Inspection requirement (yes/no)

Engineering status may be monitored through the following milestone dates:

No holds on specifications
Specifications completed
Issued for bids
Quotes received
Evaluation completed
Requisition sent to purchasing department
Purchase order placed
Vendor drawing received
Vendor drawing approved
Vendor drawing certified

The preceding pro forma list for a project materials control information database is closely tied to the project management systems discussed in Chapter 7.

For example, the codes referred to as "material code" and "area/element code" are the codes developed in the discussions on project definition fundamentals in Chapter 2, and as a case history in Chapter 7. Other aspects of this list relate to the databases driving the ECCO and PECCO systems presented in Chapter 7. Thus PROMACO is required to receive the following information:

- Creative input as raw data from project people
- Systems input from project cost control systems such as ECCO and PECCO
- Synthesized data from CAD systems creating drawings and bills of material
- Progress information from scheduling systems for milestone dates and schedule data
- Vendors' and contractors' names from procurement and contracting databases
- Enterprise business data from corporate systems such as accounts payable, general ledger, capital cost allowance, and accounting

PROMACO will process these data to be the materials control information system.

15.4 Summary

Materials management is as important an issue as human resources management in the systems of project management. From a project owner's perspective both may be nonissues. The amount and kind of management of both depends on the method used to deliver the project to the owner. In a turnkey project environment, materials management is part of the turnkey contractor's responsibility. The turnkey contractor in turn may make subcontractors and vendors responsible for their own materials, to the same extent as they are responsible for their own labor. In a project management system environment at the owner level, or any contractor or subcontractor level, materials management must be seen from many different perspectives and at different levels, and always handled as a distinct process in its own right, as introduced and discussed in this chapter.

Note: This chapter is based on specific experience as a corporate engineer and systems engineer for the engineering department of a large multiplant corporation in the process industry, as discussed in Chapter 7.

The project files are the references. These files comprise the project management processes, including the development of project functional definition structures, process flow sheets, schematic piping and instrumentation diagrams, equipment requirements, hazard and operability analysis, concept, preliminary, and final drawings and specifications, and a performance specification of a project materials control system (PROMACO).

QUESTIONS AND EXERCISES

15.1. The project life cycle comprises up to 11 stages or phases, as discussed in this textbook. If materials control means identifying and listing of equipment and hardware that forms a functional part of the finished product or facility, at what stage of the life cycle does materials control commence?

15.2. As presented in this textbook, the systems of project management comprise five integrated modules, referred to as PDS, WBS, OBS, cost, and schedule. Which of the systems is most important, and in which way, when identifying the kind, quality, and quantity of equipment and material?

15.3. If the project schedule consists of human activities by the project team, a vendor, or a construction contractor, how does one incorporate the scheduling of equipment and materials?

INDEX